*Progress in*
EXPERIMENTAL PERSONALITY RESEARCH

*VOLUME 1*

# CONTRIBUTORS TO THIS VOLUME

DONN BYRNE

JEAN P. CHAPMAN

LOREN J. CHAPMAN

VICTOR B. CLINE

DOUGLAS T. KENNY

S. H. LOVIBOND

GLENN A. MILLER

ROBERT ROSENTHAL

P. H. VENABLES

# PROGRESS IN
# *Experimental Personality Research*

Edited by Brendan A. Maher

HARVARD UNIVERSITY CENTER
FOR RESEARCH IN PERSONALITY
CAMBRIDGE, MASSACHUSETTS

## VOLUME 1

1964

ACADEMIC PRESS   New York and London

ACADEMIC PRESS, INC.
111 Fifth Avenue, New York, New York 10003


United Kingdom Edition published by
ACADEMIC PRESS, INC. (LONDON) LTD.
Berkeley Square House, London W.1


LIBRARY OF CONGRESS CATALOG CARD NUMBER: 64-8034

Second Printing, 1968

PRINTED IN THE UNITED STATES OF AMERICA

# CONTRIBUTORS

Number in parentheses indicates the page on which the author's contribution begins.

DONN BYRNE (169), *Department of Psychology, The University of Texas, Austin, Texas*

JEAN P. CHAPMAN (49), *Department of Psychology, Southern Illinois University, Carbondale, Illinois*

LOREN J. CHAPMAN (49), *Department of Psychology, Southern Illinois University, Carbondale, Illinois*

VICTOR B. CLINE (221), *University of Utah, Salt Lake City, Utah*

DOUGLAS T. KENNY (285), *Harvard University, Cambridge, Massachusetts*

S. H. LOVIBOND[1] (115), *Department of Psychology, University of Adelaide, Adelaide, South Australia*

GLENN A. MILLER (49), *Department of Psychology, Southern Illinois University, Carbondale, Illinois*

ROBERT ROSENTHAL (79), *Harvard University, Cambridge, Massachusetts*

P. H. VENABLES (1), *Medical Research Council, Social Psychiatry Research Unit, Institute of Psychiatry, Maudsley Hospital, London, England*

---

[1] Present address: The Psychology Department, Dalhousie University, Halifax, Nova Scotia, Canada.

# PREFACE

Personality psychology has changed during the past two or three decades. The change has been marked by a move away from theorizing on the grand scale and toward a greater concern with obtaining empirical answers to questions of manageable and modest proportions. By the same token, research in personality has turned increasingly to the methods and concepts of other areas of behavioral science; the shift from the study of the single case to the use of the controlled experiment is perhaps the most striking instance of this.

With this movement, the lines of demarcation between personality psychology and other areas of psychology have become blurred. The student of personality is faced with considerable extension of his field of interest, and the usual concomitant difficulty in remaining *au fait* with the progress that is made in important technical areas.

In this series, contributors will present both a summary of present knowledge on a specialized topic together with original data from their own investigations of the problem. This book is intended for psychologists and students of psychology, psychopathologists and all whose work requires knowledge of recent developments in the study of personality.

Two original and systematic contributions to the understanding of schizophrenia appear in this first volume. Other papers deal with interpersonal perception, experimenter bias, the personality correlates of repression and sensitization, conditioning and personality, and processes in projective perception.

Much editorial help has been given in the preparation of this volume by Kathleen Sylva.

BRENDAN A. MAHER

*Cambridge, Massachusetts*
*August 1964*

# CONTENTS

ix

## Personality and Conditioning

S. H. LOVIBOND

## Repression-Sensitization as a Dimension of Personality

DONN BYRNE

## Interpersonal Perception

VICTOR B. CLINE

## Stimulus Functions in Projective Techniques

DOUGLAS T. KENNY

# INPUT DYSFUNCTION IN SCHIZOPHRENIA

## P. H. Venables

MEDICAL RESEARCH COUNCIL, SOCIAL PSYCHIATRY RESEARCH UNIT,
INSTITUTE OF PSYCHIATRY, MAUDSLEY HOSPITAL, LONDON, ENGLAND

## I. Introduction

### A. SCOPE OF THE REVIEW

"Input dysfunction," rather than "disorder of perception or sensation," has been chosen as the title of this review because it was felt necessary to avoid the restriction of emphasis which the older terminology connotes. Implicitly, if not explicitly, sensation and perception as elements in cognitive processes have been thought of as confined to the functions of the direct sensory pathways and the receiving and association areas of the cortex. It is necessary at the present stage of our knowledge to bear in mind the many processes which interact before an item of sensory input can arise in consciousness. Not only does sensory input reach the cortex by the classical sensory pathways but it influences mesencephalic and diencephalic structures, via collaterals from the direct pathways to modify states of awareness, attention, arousal, and emotion. In the case of noninformative input such as noise, the main result of this input may in fact be its action upon subcortical structures. In turn the state of the subcortical structures may, by their effects at peripheral re-

1

ceptor organs and at all levels up to the cortex, modify the pattern of sensory input. Neurophysiological studies also suggest that the cortex can have a profound effect on pathways through the brain stem and "indicate the critical role of the cortex, with its highly discriminative properties in the selection and transmission of sensory input" (Samuels, 1959).

On a psychological level, owing possibly to a certain amount of re-thinking which has occurred following the incorporation of information theory and related concepts into everyday psychological currency, the old idea that we cannot consider a sensory impression to be an isolated event has received additional emphasis. An item of sensory input must be considered as one in a set of possible input items having different prob-abilities of occurrence. It must be integrated into a pattern with respect to past events held in memory, it must indeed be *apperceived* to use an old-fashioned but extremely useful term. Thus the relative importance of different items, the degree to which they appear to the subject to form a subset of mutual relevance out of all other items in the sensory field, becomes a matter of necessary consideration. This leads our think-ing back to such a concept as the span of attention, or to the similar but not identical idea, range of cue utilization, defined by Easterbrook (1959) as the "total number of environmental cues in any situation that an organism observes, maintains an orientation towards, responds to or as-sociates with a response." From what has been said earlier, it is apparent that degree of attention is under cortical and subcortical control and is thus subject not only to the temporary phasic emotional states of the organism, but also to the longer-term cortical-subcortical disarrangements that are manifest in mental illness.

Because sensory input must always be thought of as having impor-tance to the organism insofar as it is related to, and may be integrated with, its past experience, the distinction among sensation, perception, and thinking becomes blurred. This means that in dealing with experi-mental studies which are supposed to be concerned with input dysfunc-tion in schizophrenia, the vast literature on thought disorder must always loom large. The boundary between the terms of reference of this review and another covering thought disorder would be vague and difficult to define. Nevertheless the attempt will be made to confine attention to studies which are devoted for the most part to consideration of input into the organism, and only where relevant to the matter of how it is dealt with. The reader's indulgence must, however, be sought in the face of such clearly justifiable statements as the following:

"Norman Cameron has defined overinclusive thinking as the in-ability to preserve conceptual boundaries which results in the incorpora-tion of irrelevant ideas, making thinking more abstract and less lucid.

Payne *et al.* (1959) have extended the definition, regarding it as an attention defect; as some breakdown in a hypothetical filter mechanism which normally screened out those stimuli both internal and external which are irrelevant to a task in hand, to allow the most efficient processing of incoming information" (Payne, 1962).

It is to a large extent with the subject of Payne's extended definition that this review will be concerned.

Work on disturbances of sensation and perception in schizophrenia earlier in the century received limited attention, perhaps because of the findings of Kraepelin, who, using Wundtian techniques, reported little sensory disturbance in schizophrenia. This position was supported by the later pronouncements of Bleuler on the "clear sensorium" of schizophrenics. It is perhaps to the Gestalt and psychoanalytic schools that the present work on input dysfunction in schizophrenia may most clearly be traced; and it is in these historical sources that the origins of the curious patchiness of coverage may be found. As examples we find considerable literature on size-constancy abnormalities, with an extension into work on the perceived size of body parts, and little or no work on other constancy phenomena. There is quite a large amount of work on the effect of social and aversive stimuli on conditioning and performance of schizophrenics and a comparative dearth of studies on the effect of a change in the parameters of simpler sensory stimuli.

Alongside, and perhaps as a consequence of this patchwork coverage of possible dysfunctions in schizophrenia, there is an incompleteness of reporting manifest in many studies that makes difficulties for the later worker who needs more detailed information to compare with his own results. This is particularly the case in reporting the nature of subject groups. This may be due to the bias of the experimenter, who, perhaps testing an idea that all psychotics show a certain abnormality, lumps together schizophrenics and depressives whether chronic or acute.

It is with some relief that a tendency for more complete reporting may be noticed in more recent papers. This, of course, is a cumulative phenomenon and is increasingly reinforced as experimenters report differences between, for instance, paranoid and nonparanoid subjects, between chronic and acute patients, or between process or reactive subgroups. While this is a step in the right direction the warnings of Shakow (1963) should be heeded. Dichotomies themselves lead to oversimplification and frequently overlap. A rating scale to measure withdrawal may possibly measure nearly the same thing as deterioration or elements of process schizophrenia; the label paranoid when based on a scale of nurses' ratings may include a mixture of incoherent and paranoid tendencies.

Equally open to the possibilities of misinterpretation is the acute-chronic dichotomy. A dividing line of more or less than 2 years stay in hospital may be a perfectly reasonable cutting point when based on the probabilities of discharge from hospital (Brown, 1960). However, the transition from the acute to the chronic phase of the illness is part of the process of the disease involving an interaction between the patient and his environment and the determination of the boundary between the two states may be much less easy.

## B. Some Theoretical Viewpoints

The distinction between the acute and chronic phases of the illness is fundamental to the interpretation of much of the literature which will be reviewed. Unfortunately the evidence both on the existence of a clear distinction between these two states and a difference in underlying mechanisms, should such a distinction exist, is incomplete. Two types of theory will be considered. One, typified, for instance, by Mednick (1958) and Fish (1961), suggests a state of high drive or arousal in the acute phase which subsides in the chronic phase. The other type of theory, suggested by, for instance, Hoffer and Osmond (1955) and Weckowicz (1958), is of a parasympathetic imbalance in the acute phase and a late change to sympathetic imbalance as the patient enters the chronic phase. Both types of theory draw much the same sort of distinction between the clinical pictures in each phase, but explain them rather differently.

The point of view of the latter type of theory is stated clearly by Weckowicz (1958). "Early in the illness, function shifts in the direction of parasympathetic activity and through negative feedback mechanisms [see the work of Callaway, Section II,A] size constancy increases. This signifies increased constancy[1] of perception which in its turn may be interpreted as increased awareness of objects in the environment. The patients become sensitive, suspicious, develop ideas of reference, attach important meanings to insignificant events and eventually develop delusions. They react to the environment with increased anxiety, because the low activity of the diencephalic sympathetic centres is accompained by high reactivity. However, as the disease progresses the function of these centres gradually shifts in the opposite direction, namely towards sympathetic activity." This, Weckowicz says, is accompanied by decreased size constancy, which is indicative of a diminished awareness of objects in the environment. Because of the high level of

---

1 Weckowicz is here discussing the results of an experiment on size constancy and the term "increased constancy," or alternatively "overconstancy," implies that the size of a distant object is overestimated.

sympathetic activity, reactivity is low and the patients display "flatness of affect"; they also become withdrawn, "autistic," lose interest in their environment, and sometimes have emotional outbursts which often cannot be related to external events. This suggestion of early parasympathetic and later sympathetic imbalance is in accord with the viewpoint expressed by Hoffer and Osmond (1955), derived on the basis of biochemical theory.

The increased awareness of the environment which is reported here as being characteristic of the acute phase is graphically documented by McGhie and Chapman (1961). Patients are swamped by a flood of sensory input which they are unable to control. They report:

"Everything seems to grip my attention although I am not particularly interested in anything. I am speaking to you just now but I can hear noises going on next door and in the corridor. I find it difficult to shut these out and it makes it more difficult to concentrate on what I am saying to you."

"Things are coming in too fast. I lose my grip of it and get lost. I am attending to everything at once and as a result I do not really attend to anything."

Not only are there these complaints of inability to focus attention, to select between items of sensory input, but there are impressions of abnormalities in the quality of the sensory input.

"Noises seem to be louder to me than they were before . . . . I notice it most with background noises."

"Colours seem to be brighter now almost as if they are luminous."

"The colours of things seem to be much clearer and yet at the same time there is something missing. The things I look at seem to be flatter as if you were looking just at the surface."

Here we have reports of the lack of distinction between relevant and irrelevant background material and of evident changes in distance constancy.

The lack of ability to distinguish "figure" from "ground" is particularly apparent in the perception of speech.

"When people are talking I just get scraps of it. If it is just one person who is speaking that's not so bad but if the others join in then I can't pick it up at all. I just can't get into time with that conversation. It makes me feel open as if things are closing in on me and I have lost control."

"I'm a good listener but often I'm not really taking it in. I nod my head and smile but it's just a lot of jumbled up words to me."

In addition to this disturbance of ability to distinguish relevant from irrelevant items and to place them in their correct order, there also appears to be an inability to absorb items of information if they are presented too quickly. This is particularly the case where an increase in the rate of sensory input is brought about by the patient's own movement.

"When I move quickly it's a strain on me. Things go too quick for my mind. They get blurred and it's like being blind. It's as if you were seeing a picture one moment and another picture the next. I just stop and watch my feet. Everything is all right if I stop, but if I start moving again I lose control."

Heightened awareness of bodily sensations brings about a loss of automatic spontaneity of action; no longer can a sequence of motor acts be carried out without conscious deliberation because the patient is made aware of each stage. Thus, as the authors say, "each action now has to be planned and executed step by step with a great deal of conscious deliberation. The patient finds himself becoming increasingly 'self conscious' in an entirely literal sense."

"People just do things but I have to watch first to see how you do things. I have to think out most things first and know how to do them before I do them."

This clinical material has been quoted in some detail because it presents in a particularly graphic manner the type of dysfunction that is manifest in a large number of patients in the acute phase and which has to be borne in mind when considering experimental studies.

Because such insightful reporting of the nature of sensation in the chronic phase of the illness does not seem to be available, the main evidence for a decreased awareness of the full range of the subject's environment must rely to a large extent on experimental data, which will be presented later (Section II,B).

McGhie and Chapman present suggestions to account for the clinical material which they describe. Their present theoretical position is perhaps all the more interesting because, starting out from an investigation which was psychoanalytic in orientation, they are led by their observations to reject the proposal (Federn, 1953) that early schizophrenic symptoms are defensive activities related to unconscious conflicts and to suggest that the basic pathological breakdown is particularly to be found in the process of perception. From this they say that "if schizophrenia is a disease which has its basic effect in a disruption of the control of attention, then the reticular system may be the main pathological site."

A view which is in many ways similar, but has a somewhat different emphasis, is that of Fish (1961). Starting from a Gestalt analysis of the stages of schizophrenic disorganization advocated by Conrad (1958), which he modifies in terms of Hebb's (1949) theory of perceptual organization, Fish reaches the conclusion that early phases of acute schizophrenia are due to "overactivity of the reticular system producing an undue diversion and disruption of central processes by the sensory input." In the presence of reticular overactivity sensory events thus acquire greater than normal significance, thought processes are disorganized, and anxiety results. When this disruption of the central processes by sensory input occurs frequently a "feeling of some unknown significance is produced by the increased impressiveness of all perceptions." From these processes delusions arise.

As the next stage, Fish proposes that parallel central reverberatory processes develop which are detached from sensory input and are not reorganized by it. This state of affairs may continue to exist in the chronic state after the high reticular activity which engendered it has ceased. It is of interest to note that Fish proposes three types of chronic state: In one the reticular activity does not subside and a paranoid illness remains in which delusions continue to be affect laden. Second and third, reticular activity subsides but the cortical reorganization remains either in the same form as in the acute processes, or in a form different from this but less efficient than the premorbid state. Fish backs up his case for reticular overactivity by several pointers from physiology and pharmacology. For instance, noting that amphetamine overdosage will produce a psychosis which is clinically undistinguishable from paranoid schizophrenia, he points out that amphetamine produces an arousal response in the EEG in animals which is similar to that produced by reticular stimulation. This psychotomimetic effect of amphetamine should be borne in mind when experiments on the effect of alerting agents on the breadth of attention are discussed at a later stage (Section II,A).

In contrast to the previous theories, in that it remains on a behavioral level, is the "learning theory approach" of Mednick (1958). In spite of this difference the picture which results has similarities to many of the foregoing theories and also to that of Rosenzweig (1955). In both these proposals it is the erection of unrealistic defences against anxiety which results in psychotic behavior. In Rosenzweig's theory the anxiety results because of disturbances in central processes which normally integrate ideational and affective processes; in Mednick's theory the anxiety results from a combination of factors due to a high drive state which is said to characterize the acute stage of schizophrenia. This high drive has three results: "(a) schizophrenics more easily acquire a conditioned response; (b) schizophrenics show greater stimulus generalization responsiveness; (c) schizophrenics have great difficulty performing well in complex situations being plagued by irrelevant tangential associative responses competing with adequate modes of response." Mednick goes on to elaborate his theory in terms of a reciprocal augmentation mechanism. An untoward event will, in a person with an already high drive level, raise his anxiety level; consequent upon this, the range of stimulus generalization will increase and further stimuli will acquire anxiety-producing qualities. This process continues until the behavior of the individual becomes noticeably unusual. High drive level keeps thoughts racing in the patient's mind and a rationalizing solution is evoked to reduce anxiety. Lack of discrimination is brought about by high generalization and any associated response, however tangential, may produce anxiety reduction resulting in thought disorder. The anxiety reduction which may be achieved by merely thinking irrelevant thoughts results in the patient displaying less and less emotionality and the chronic stage of the illness is reached.

These theories which have been presented describe rather similar clinical pictures, the acute stage with its excesss of sensory input, and overgeneralization followed by a transition to a chronic stage with diminished awareness of outside stimuli and withdrawal. Although the description of the clinical state roughly corresponds in the various theories, the suggested underlying mechanisms tend to be somewhat opposed. On the one hand Weckowicz, and Hoffer and Osmond, suggest a parasympathetic overactivity in the acute stage followed by a transition to a sympathetically aroused and cortically activated picture in the chronic patient. On the other hand Fish and Mednick propose high reticular activity or high drive in the acute state which later subsides as the patient becomes chronic. The remainder of this chapter will be concerned not so much with theories but with an examination of the experimental justification for them, and an attempt to see how far the rather divergent viewpoints about mechanisms may be either reconciled or verified.

## II. The Span of Attention

### A. Conditions Bringing about Alterations in Span of Attention in Normal Subjects

It was suggested earlier (Section I,A) that perception and attention were influenced by subcortical as well as cortical mechanisms. An examination of relevant experiments on normal subjects under conditions which might be expected to have subcortical effects is valuable insofar as it may enable insight to be gained which will be helpful in the interpretation of experiments with schizophrenic subjects. Perhaps the most relevant of these are a series of studies by Callaway and his associates which are concerned with the effect of certain drugs and procedures on perceptual tasks which are interpretable in terms of extent of attention.

Callaway and Thompson (1953) proposed an hypothetical mechanism which they then proceeded to test, by which the activity of the sympathetic nervous system and the breadth of attention are related. They suggested that a threat to the organism which induces a sympathetic discharge must in turn bring about a rise in the threshold of the input system which will tend to reduce the perception of the threat and hence reduce the sympathetic discharge (i.e., a negative feedback mechanism). Otherwise if increased sympathetic discharge induced a lowering of threshold there would be an increasing rise of sympathetic discharge to an intolerable limit. (This model was later modified because it was found that the common factor in treatments producing narrowing of attention was that they all produced an alert EEG.) The model was tested by the use of a size-constancy experiment. They suggested: "We should expect increased sympathetic activity to decrease that general awareness of gradients by which we correct our shrunken retinal image of distant objects. Objects would then be perceived as smaller than their true size and would seem to approach a size more nearly proportional to their retinal image size."

The size-constancy experiment which was carried out involved the adjustment of the size of a projected rectangular patch of light 200 cm away from the subject to match the size of a rectangular card held in the hand. To induce sympathetic discharge a cold pressor test was employed in which the subject's foot was immersed in a bucket of ice water. This procedure evoked a reduction of size constancy in comparison to that obtained under nonstimulating conditions. Because the cold pressor procedure results in hypertension which would produce increased retinal blood flow in addition to sympathetic discharge, the experiment was repeated with inhalation of amyl nitrite as the sympathetic stimulant. In contrast to the previous procedure amyl nitrite induces hypotension. The previous result was replicated. Various possibilities which might result in the perceptual effect were considered in further experiments; explanations in terms of change of perceived distance to the adjustable stimulus and change of actual size of retinal image akin to atropine micropsia were tested and dismissed. An experimental situation in which there was a reduction in subsidiary cues abolished the effect earlier noticed so that the conclusion was reached that decreased size constancy after induced sympathetic adrenergic discharge resulted from reduced awareness of subsidiary cues which normally act to correct the diminution in retinal size of distant objects. Callaway and Dembo (1958) and Callaway (1959) reported further work on the phenomenon of changes in breadth of attention which tended to confirm the earlier findings. The findings reported with amyl nitrite were replicated with a further group of subjects and other experiments using epinephrine and methamphetamine showed similar changes in size judgment. Size-constancy experiments were eventually abandoned because of the difficulty in showing directly whether the effect was due to decreased awareness of subsidiary cues or had some other explanation. Among others a task which these workers used for further experimentation was that of perceiving the statistical structure of the pattern of onset of lights in a binary guessing game. It has been shown (e.g., Hake and Hyman, 1953) that subjects' guesses on a binary choice game such as this tend to approach very closely the actual frequency with which the two choices are reinforced as correct. Callaway *et al.* argue that this procedure may be used as a measure of narrowed attention. "In the guessing game the central focus of attention will be held alternately by the current guess and the current answer. . . . Since past answers are continually peripheral to current guesses, guess frequency response to answer frequency change reflects the influence of peripheral factors upon behaviour. In other words it can be used to indicate narrowed attention." In specific terms the experimenters predicted that methamphetamine would produce narrowing of attention and hence would result in subjects responding more slowly than control subjects to a change in the imposed statistical pattern.

It should perhaps be noted at this point that although what apparently are on the periphery here are memory traces and not true sensory input, we have a position which is analogous to an information-conveying input situation where the immediately present stimulus should be looked at as one of a set of stimuli, some of which are presently absent.

Two groups were tested on the binary choice guessing task. One group received methamphetamine and the other soda tablets as placebo; on repeat testing 1 week later the groups were reversed. The subjects were started off on a 50:50 ratio of which two lights would appear but were then changed to a 25:75 ratio. The methamphetamine-treated group changed the ratio of their guesses to the imposed ratio more slowly than the sodium bicarbonate treated group. Their behavior was thought to be the result of the restriction of range of attention to immediate clues and away from those which, being in the past, were peripheral.

Another task which Callaway used to show the attention-narrowing effects of methamphetamine is the Stroop test (1935). This test consists of three cards. On the first of these, names of four colors are printed; on the second are dots of the same four colors. On the third card, names of colors are printed in the inks of the four colors used in the first two cards, the name of the color being different from the color used to print it. Using Card I the subject has to read the names of the colors, with Card II he has to name the colors of the dots, and with Card III he has to name the color of the ink used to print the names of conflicting colors. It is assumed that performance on Card III will be facilitated by narrowed attention acting to exclude the printed name of the color. The effect of methamphetamine is in fact to improve performance relatively on Card III.

In summary, Callaway states that the procedures which result in narrowed attention, the cold pressor test, and the use of amyl nitrite and methamphetamine, can all be said to have a sympathetic action; on the other hand, he also reports that an anticholinesterase nerve gas has similar effects. The common factor in all the procedures is that they result in an alert EEG. Whereas, however, the amphetamines produce both behavioral arousal (shown in animals by opening of the eyes, movements of the ears, etc.) and EEG arousal (Bradley and Elkes, 1957), anticholinesterases, such as phystostigmine and nerve gas, produce EEG arousal without behavioral arousal. Callaway's suggestion is that narrowing of attention may be the missing behavioral correlate in this case.

As a corollary of these findings it can be suggested that a drug which produces the opposite of EEG arousal should produce "broadness of attention." This possibility was investigated by Callaway and Band (1958) using atropine and Callaway (1959) using amobarbital. Atropine, while producing high-amplitude slow-wave activity in the EEG indicating drowsiness, is reported not to reduce behavioral alertness. It acts as a reticular formation inhibitor but has minimal sedative effects and is not considered to be a cortical inhibitor. Using the Stroop, the Gottschaldt, and the Luchin's water jar tests, results were obtained with atropine which were consonant with the idea of "broadened attention." Amobarbital was found to have a similar effect in the later study although some reservations in the interpretation of the results must be felt because of skewed distributions due to performance near to task ceilings.

The finding of narrowing of attention in a situation likely to produce sympathetic discharge is shown in a study by Kohn (1954). In this experiment subjects read stories in conditions which could be described as threatening, distracting, or neutral. The threatening situation was a stage managed presentation with high-voltage sparks, and the suggestion of an intense shock across the subject's temples, and thus likely to produce an intense emotional reaction. The distracting condition was similar but with a reassurance that no shock would be delivered. The stories were recalled later in a neutral situation. It was found that both the relevant and irrelevant items of the story studied under threat of shock were less accurately reproduced than those studied under distracting or neutral conditions; however, under threat a greater reduction occurred in irrelevant than relevant items. Thus it was suggested that emotional arousal narrowed the field of attention at the time of the original learning to the relevant points of the story.

Callaway's results with the Stroop test are directly supported by Agnew and Agnew (1963). The state of the subject's drive was manipulated by the use of threat of shock and induction of feelings of failure if above-average performance was not achieved. The effectiveness of this procedure was checked by the finding that heart rate was significantly increased under "high drive" conditions. It was found under these conditions, in contrast to "low drive" conditions, without threat of shock or failure, that performance on the Stroop test was indicative of narrowed attention.

Callaway's studies suggest that narrowing of attention occurs under conditions which increase sympathetic activity or produce an alert EEG. The Agnews' and Kohn's studies lead to very much the same conclusion in that a situation threatening enough to evoke sympathetic discharge produced narrowing of attention.

Bharucha-Reid (1962) suggests that stress of any kind can cut down the intake of stimuli and proposes the term "behavioral anesthetic" for this process. This notion has the same connotation as the "feedback mechanism" of Callaway and suggests that stress produces the means of its own perceptual diminution. While also supporting the notion of narrowing of attention under threat Snygg and Combs (1949) state the rather dissimilar viewpoint that the effect of the threat is to reduce the individual's perceptual field to the area of the perceived threat. It would appear from the experiments described that the effect is best left as an empirical observation whose teleological significance is unclear.

Bharucha-Reid suggests four ways in which the mechanism of the "behavioral anesthetic" might work. First, by an increase in activity in the subcortex the sensory receiving areas may be disorganized selectively, the effect being manifest possibly in a particular area of the cortex representing a single sense modality. Second, even when sensory input is "allowed to be received" it may still not be elaborated for awareness by being received without the presence of adequate secondary reinforcing activity from the subcortex. A third possibility is the suppression of sensory input by the cortex itself, while a fourth is the alteration of cortical activity by the diffuse and specific projection systems acting with a particular time relationship. The trouble with these proposals is the wealth of possible explanations which they offer. We should perhaps make some attempt to delimit more accurately the specific conditions which bring about the attention-restricting behavior before relying on such a general notion as "stress." While stress may not be the correct term to use for sexual excitement it is of interest to note that Kinsey *et al.* (1953) report not only narrowing of attention in the form of inability to visually perceive actions taking place in the surroundings, but also raising of tactual and pain thresholds during orgasm. Unfortunately, apart from changes in the cardiovascular system, physiological changes accompanying sexual excitement are poorly documented and we do not seem to be entitled to say whether narrowing of attention in these conditions is accompanied by increased sympathetic or fast EEG activity.

Drew (1963), discussing work done during World War II (Davis, 1946a,b; Drew, 1940), reported a gradual restriction of the field of attention during a prolonged fatiguing performance on a task resembling flying. Instruments at the extreme periphery ceased to be responded to, or signals were frequently missed, more so than those nearer the center, until eventually even the central flying panel seemed to be responded to one instrument at a time. Drew reports this behavior as occurring in the context of the subject's increased irritability and presumably therefore increased arousal. In discussing this work, Drew makes an important point. He suggests that the term "tunnel vision" which is the label given to this restriction of the attentive field is a misnomer and an artifact of experimental design. It suggests a restriction from the periphery to foveal areas while attention actually "becomes restricted to that part of the field from which stimuli are expected, whether this be central or peripheral. In the usual experimental design, the main task is presented centrally, with less important or less frequent stimuli to the periphery. Under these conditions, restriction is from the periphery to the centre. If the design is changed, however, the restriction will occur to whatever part of the periphery given the most frequent or most important signals."

The finding of restriction of attention to the central task is shown clearly in an experiment by Bahrick, Fitts, and Rankin (1952). The effect of high and low incentives on performance on a central tracking task with a subsidiary task involving response to intermittent peripheral stimuli was studied. Results showed that the high incentive facilitated performance of the central task but in general interfered with the performance of the peripheral task.

The picture arising from this cursory review of some of the relevant literature is that narrowing of attention occurs under conditions which may be loosely classed as arousing, that is, under conditions that might be considered to produce alert EEG or to evoke sympathetic discharge. This is in essence the position which is put forward in an extensive review by Easterbrook (1959), who says, "It is an empirically derived generalization that, when the direction of behaviour is constant, increase in drive is associated with a reduction in the range of cue use. . . . The term drive refers to a dimension of emotional arousal or covert general excitement which underlies or occurs simultaneously with overt action." These phasic conditions which are productive of narrowed attention in normal subjects should be borne in mind when one is considering perceptual dysfunction in the presence of longer-term disorders of activation, or arousal, which may be said to characterize certain stages of the schizophrenic illness.

A possibility which has been glossed over so far is that we should perhaps consider two forms of narrowed attention. In the case of, for instance, size-constancy experiments and those involving awareness of peripheral visual cues we are concerned with spatial narrowing or narrowing concerned with stimuli present at a moment in time. In the binary guessing game used by Callaway, however, the concern is with temporal narrowing. Whether this latter should more correctly be termed a defect of memory is a matter for discussion but it is clearly connected with such terms as "set" in the Rodnick and Shakow (1940) sense of "maintenance of a set to respond."

### B. Experiments on Schizophrenics

#### 1. Spatial

*a. Size Constancy.* It will be remembered that the postulated link between size-constancy experiments and the phenomenon of alterations in the span of attention is the notion that it is by perception of objects and cues in the peripheral field that the reduced retinal image of an object is corrected and appears to maintain its size when viewed from a distance. If, owing to narrowing of attention, peripheral cues are not perceived, this correction will not take place and the distant object will appear smaller.

A study which directly relates the work on normal subjects, particularly that of Callaway (Section II,A), with studies of size constancy in schizophrenia is that of Weckowicz (1958). In this experiment the schizophrenic patient had to adjust the length of a vertical rod, placed near him, so that it had the same apparent size as that of a distant standard. In addition to this measure of size constancy, the patient's blood pressure response to a mecholyl injection (Funkenstein, Greenblatt and Solomon, 1949) was measured. It was found that "schizophrenic patients in whom there is a rise in blood pressure after a mecholyl injection tend to give a higher estimation of the size of distant objects and therefore have a higher and better preserved size constancy, while those schizophrenic patients in whom there is little or no rise of blood pressure tend to underestimate the size of distant objects to a greater degree, thus having decreased size constancy." Using the mecholyl test as a measure of sympathetic reactivity (Gellhorn and Miller, 1961), Weckowicz reasons, no doubt on the principle of "the law of initial value" (e.g., Wilder, 1958), that sympathetic reactivity is greatest in those patients with the lowest sympathetic tonus and vice versa. A high level of sympathetic tonus in a group of schizophrenics therefore tends to be related to a decrease in size constancy, and is in accord with findings on normal subjects. Earlier Weckowicz (1957) carried out an experiment on chronic schizophrenics whose clinical picture, after a mean hospital stay of 7 years 9 months, was that of hebephrenia and schizophrenia simplex, although some initial diagnoses were of paranoid schizophrenia. Nonpsychotic hospitalized patients and normal controls were also tested. Again the task was that of matching the size of a nearby adjustable rod to that of a standard placed at 7.5 or 15 meters from the subject. In comparison with the other groups schizophrenics underestimated the size of the distant object and did this increasingly so at the greater distance.

This finding of decreased size constancy in chronic schizophrenics is replicated in a study by Hamilton (1963). In this experiment a variety of stimulus objects were used. These objects (standards) were placed 1 meter away from the subject; the variable was 3 meters away and under control of the experimenter. The positions of standard and variable are thus the inverse of those of Weckowicz (1957) but similar to those of Callaway and Thompson (1953). An additional feature was the use of two conditions: one, "cueless," in which judgments were carried out with the stimuli exposed in a darkened tunnel, so that peripheral distance cues were reduced; the other, a "cue condition" carried out in full daylight. Thus if the reduced size constancy of the chronic schizophrenic is due to his inability to perceive peripheral cues because of narrowed attention, his performance should not differ significantly from normal when the normal is deprived of distance cues. The study was carried out on chronic nonparanoid and chronic paranoid schizophrenics, a small group of manic depressives, neurotics, and normal controls. In general it was found that there were no differences in performance between normals and neurotics or among the group of psychotics. There was in general, in conditions where cues were present, a significant tendency for the psychotic subjects to display underconstancy in comparison with normals and neurotics, whose scores tended to approach values for perfect constancy. In the absence of distance cues the size judgments even of normal control subjects were liable to considerable error. In the cueless conditions only two of the seven objects used as stimuli gave normal-psychotic constancy differences which were significant. It is important to note that these two objects, a penny and a packet of cigarettes of well-known brand, were familiar and of fixed size, while of the remainder of the stimuli, two diamond-shaped cards, a rod, a playing card, and a medicine bottle, only the playing card had a fixed size. Hamilton employed an index of cue responsiveness in which the size constancy in "cue" and "cueless" conditions was compared. It is of considerable interest to note that, for the total psychotic group, reduced size constancy was significantly correlated with low cue responsiveness, as would be expected from the mechanism suggested at the beginning of this section.

In view of the decrease in test intelligence which has been shown to occur as part of the psychological deficit shown by schizophrenics (Hunt and Cofer, 1944) it is of importance to note that Hamilton confirms the finding of Thouless (1932) of a negative relationship between size constancy and intelligence. The results reported do not therefore appear to be a subsidiary effect of the decrease in tested intelligence shown by schizophrenics.

In some contrast to these findings is an experiment by Raush (1952), who investigated the size constancy of paranoid and nonparanoid schizophrenics and a group of normals. While Raush does not give details of the chronicity of his subjects it is evident from such statements as "the diagnosis was consistent throughout the course of hospitalization" and "cases had been reviewed no more than 6 months prior to the experiments" that it was a relatively chronic population that was used. In Raush's experiment the standard stimulus was a disk of light 20 feet away and in front of the subject; the variable stimulus was a disk of light controlled by the subject and placed on a table 4 feet away from the subject and at right angles to the standard. Trials were given in the dark, i.e., cueless conditions, and with room lights full on, i.e., cue conditions. The results of this experiment were that all subjects showed overconstancy in both conditions. However, the only significant differences were those between the paranoid and nonparanoid schizophrenics, and the paranoid schizophrenics and normals in the cueless, dark conditions, the paranoid patients showing higher constancy than either of the other groups. This very different picture from that obtained by the previous investigations is difficult to explain. The general overconstancy of all subjects was thought by Raush to be due to a space error arising because of the 90-degree angle between standard and variable. This angle was 5 degrees in Hamilton's experiment and was of a similar order in the experiments by Weckowicz and Callaway. Holway and Boring (1941), using a similar orientation of standard and variable to those of Raush's, obtained a larger degree of overconstancy with their normals than did Raush. This finding is in many ways similar to that of Klein (1954), who found that size judgment from memory gave consistent overestimations in comparison with conditions where size judgments were made with the standard in the peripheral field. Clearly the process of comparing stimuli at right angles as in Rausch's experiment involved memory, however immediate. Another puzzling feature is the fact that differences which are shown are found in the cueless condition; however, while the normals and nonparanoids give slightly less constancy in the dark than the light conditions the overconstancy of the paranoids is increased under these conditions. The main contrast between this and the Hamilton experiments, given that the experimental conditions brought about a general bias to overconstancy, is the finding that the paranoid schizophrenics behave differently from the nonparanoids. This finding of exceptional behavior by paranoids will be discussed in Section V.

It is perhaps noteworthy that Raush's schizophrenic population was on the whole younger (about 25 years old) than Hamilton's (40 years) or Weckowicz's (36 years). Not only therefore are they likely to be less chronic, but according to Raush their diagnosis had not changed. Weckowicz noted that although some patients in his experiment had been diagnosed as paranoid on admission this diagnosis no longer applied. The point that is being made here is not that age in itself affects size constancy—indeed Hamilton has shown no differences with age—but that age may reflect differences in chronicity and possible changes in diagnosis. Hamilton showed no changes in size constancy with chronicity when his group of patients was divided at more or less their 5 years stay in hospital. It can be suggested, however, that the change in physiological state which parallels an acute-to-chronic change occurs very early in hospitalization, and by division of his patient group at more or less than five years stay Hamilton would be unlikely to show any differences.

A criticism of Raush's study which is made by Lovinger (1956) is that Raush used patients who were in good contact with reality so as to obtain optimal conditions for size-constancy testing. This selection would tend to bias the results in the direction of not finding reduced size constancy. Lovinger therefore carried out a study in which two groups of schizophrenics in good and in poor contact were selected. The selection of patients was made on the basis of ratings of contact and whether they lived in open or closed wards. Using illuminated disks as targets in line and not a right-angular arrangement of standard and variable, Lovinger found that "under experimental conditions involving minimal distance cues schizophrenics in poor contact manifested less size constancy than either schizophrenics in good contact or normals." It is of importance to note that Lovinger used three cue conditions: (1) maximum, with full lighting, (2) minimal, with reduced lighting, and (3) no cues, darkness. In both the last and the first conditions no differences due to diagnosis were found, probably because even the poor-contact schizophrenics noticed peripheral cues under full lighting, and on the other hand, in darkness the normals were as handicapped as the schizophrenics. The possible intrusion of distance cues even for out-of-contact schizophrenics would seem to be a likely explanation for the finding (Leibowitz and Pishkin, 1961) of fully maintained size constancy in a group of chronic schizophrenics chosen as very withdrawn. The experiment was carried out under fully lit conditions, which might have resulted in extreme prominence of distance cues.

Probably related in a loose fashion to the degree of reality contact used as a factor in Lovinger's experiment is thought disorder. Weckowicz and Blewett (1959) started from the notion that paranoid schizophrenics who show little thought disorder also show a well-maintained size constancy (Raush, 1952), while schizophrenics who show poor size constancy are also likely to be thought disordered. Using 40 chronic schizophrenics as subjects they found that there was a positive correlation between poor size constancy and imparied ability for abstract thinking. Weckowicz and Blewett interpret their result in terms of an inability to "attend selectively" or "to select relevant information" which is responsible for both size constancy and thought disorder. This interpretation of size constancy would seem to be at variance with the ideas of "decreased general awareness of the gradients by which the shrunken retinal image is corrected" which is said (Weckowicz, 1957) to result in decreased size constancy. The relationship of narrowed attention to thought disorder will be discussed later in the context of overinclusion.

A study which has been included in this section because of its very close relationship to size constancy is that of Hartman (1962). This work is on the apparent size of after-images and is a rough converse of size-constancy experiments in that there is a fixed retinal image size which according to Emmerts law changes its phenomenal size with perceived distance. Quoting experiments by Edwards (1953) and Boring (1940), Hartman suggests that if all cues to distance are removed from the viewing situation the size of after-image will depend on its retinal size and will thus remain constant. Two groups of schizophrenics and two normal groups were tested in this experiment; one group of patients was categorized as delusional and the other as nondelusional. In both cases the length of hospital stay was about 4 years. While the scanty reporting of actual details of results makes it difficult to discover actually what happened it was reported that "chronic delusional schizophrenics differed from chronic nondelusional schizophrenics and normals in their perception of size changes of the after-image, i.e., they were less likely to respond as would be predicted on the basis of Emmerts law." No subject, normal or schizophrenic, was able to report after-image changes as distance varied when only monocular cues were available; convergence cues, however, did bring about a difference in after-image size but less in delusional patients than other subjects. These cues were only operative at short distances. While showing that paranoid patients are apparently different from the rest, the light which this single study throws on the size-constancy findings is unfortunately small, apparently because few distance cues were available for even normal subjects to use.

*b. Distance Constancy.* Callaway and Thompson (1953) failed to produce evidence that distance judgment was affected under sympathetic discharge evoked by the cold pressor test, and thus dismissed this as a factor responsible for changes in size constancy under stimulating conditions. Weckowicz, Sommer, and Hall (1958) carried out an out-of-doors distance judgment experiment which showed that chronic schizophrenics underestimate distance. Schizophrenics, when asked to judge successive equidistant intervals, had a steeper perceived gradient and reached zero sooner than normals. The perceptual field of the chronic schizophrenic is apparently lacking in depth, he lives in a "flatter world." Size-constancy scores obtained in a similar way to Weckowicz's other experiments were available for the patients in his experiment. It was found that poor size constancy was significantly correlated with poor distance judgment. This correlation has been criticized by Rump (1961a,b) on the basis of the lack of validity of the "invariance hypothesis" of a reciprocity between perceived size and perceived distance. Hamilton (1963), who asked his subjects to make distance judgments at the end of his size-constancy experiments, agreed with Rump's criticism of Weckowicz *et al.*, insofar as he found almost wholly negative and nonsignificant correlations between distance judgment and size-constancy measurements carried out on the *same* apparatus in contrast to the separate determinations of Weckowicz *et al.* Hamilton's results do, however, show, in agreement with Weckowicz *et al.*, that nonparanoid schizophrenics underestimate distance, but also that paranoid schizophrenics markedly overestimate distance. It was also found that cue conditions benefited the distance judgments of nonpsychotic subjects more than those of the nonparanoid schizophrenics. It might thus appear that distance judgment deficiencies are possibly interpretable in terms of narrowed attention, and hence while full appreciation of peripheral cues is a necessary condition for good size and distance judgments the mechanisms responsible for each are independent. An experiment carried out by Nelson and Caldwell

(1962) gave no indication of an inaccuracy of depth perception in acute schizophrenics. This experiment was, however, carried out in a rather different way from those earlier and involved the positioning of a variable target to have the same apparent distance as a fixed target, an apparently easier task than, for instance, making a judgment of distance in feet (Hamilton) or the doubling or halving of standard distances (Weckowicz et al.). Although it was not significant, there was a tendency for the acute schizophrenics in Nelson and Caldwell's experiment to be more accurate than normals when using a post as a stimulus, possibly indicating some degree of overconstancy in these acute patients. Other objects which might have acted as affective stimuli were used, pictures of a woman, dog, man, or circle, but while there was some tendency for normals to show an order of placement of items this was not shown by schizophrenics.

c. *Perception of Relevant and Irrelevant Material.* Venables (1963a) carried out an experiment concerned with the degree to which schizophrenics perceived irrelevant stimuli with the direct intention of testing the narrowed-attention hypothesis. A card-sorting task was used in which cards had to be sorted on the basis of the presence of one or another of two relevant letters in the context of eight irrelevant letters. Four sortings were made by each subject and then without being informed of any change he was asked to make a fifth sorting on the basis of the same relevant letters but in the context of a different set of irrelevant letters. On the basis of each individual regression line summarizing the trend for the second, third, and fourth sorting, a time for a fifth sorting, had the irrelevant letters not changed, was estimated. This was compared with the observed time for the fifth sorting. It was suggested that the degree to which the subject had paid attention to the irrelevant letters would be reflected in the disturbance shown by the difference between the estimated and observed times for the fifth sorting. Following Callaway (Section II,A) it was thought that narrowed attention would be related to the degree of cortical activation shown by the subject. As an index of cortical activation the subject's threshold of fusion of paired light flashes was measured. Strictly speaking the two-flash threshold should be thought of as a measure not of cortical activity but of cortical responsivity or of temporal resolution. Good temporal resolution, which involves short cortical recovery time, is related to the refractoriness of the cortex. It is evident that a second stimulus may not give rise to a cortical response if it falls into a period of complete refractoriness after an initial stimulus. The shorter this period of refractoriness the better the temporal resolution. The ability of the cortex to resolve pairs of stimuli which are close in time appears from the experiments of Lindsley (1958), Steriade and Demetrescu (1962), and Schwartz and Shagass (1963) to be under the control of the reticular formation whose ascending activating function is usually thought of as increasing cortical activation. Thirty-four chronic schizophrenic patients were tested and their two-flash fusion thresholds correlated with the degree of card-sorting disturbance used as a measure of narrowed attention. It was found that high cortical responsivity was significantly correlated with narrowed attention, thus supporting Callaway's findings. It had been found previously (Venables and Wing, 1962) that there was a relationship between two-flash threshold and a rating scale measure of withdrawal (Venables, 1957) such that high cortical activation was found in the most withdrawn patients, if these were nonparanoid or incoherent paranoid schizophrenics. Narrowed attention could thus be expected to be related to the degree of withdrawal shown by the subject. For the 26 nonparanoid patients in the sample this relation was significant. However, no relationship was evident for the remaining eight coherently paranoid patients. Similar data relating withdrawal and narrowness of attention showed a positive relation between the two measures in another group of nonparanoid patients and no relationship in a larger paranoid group. These results should be compared to those previously reported where for instance Lovinger (1956) found reduced size constancy in a group of patients having reduced contact with their environment and hence most probably comparable to the withdrawn patients in Venables' study. The lack of relation between withdrawal and narrowness of attention in paranoid patients also is in line with the findings previously reported of differences between these patients and other schizophrenics. The need to distinguish those paranoid patients having coherently expressed delusions from those whose delusions are expressed incoherently and who behave in many ways like nonparanoids (Venables and Wing, 1962) may account for the lack of difference between paranoid and nonparanoid schizophrenics in Hamilton's (1963) study.

The idea of stimuli as relevant or irrelevant to the task in hand is at the basis of studies of incidental learning. Greenberg (1953) had a group of 44 chronic schizophrenics and 44 nonpsychiatric patients perform three experimental tasks: (1) "Color-Position" in which the recall of the colors of geometric forms was the directed or intended task and the recall of the position of the form the incidental or undirected task, (2) "Paragraphs," in which the recall of the content of one paragraph from the Wechsler Memory Scale was the intentional task and the recall of the second paragraph the incidental task, when the instructions called only for tallying the frequency of words, (3) "Metal-Nonmetal," in which the recall of familiar metal items was the directed task and the recall of familiar nonmetal items, exposed simultaneousy with the metal items, was the undirected task.

The results showed that the nonpsychiatric group was better than the schizophrenic group on all measures of incidental learning. Even after correction for differences in intentional learning by analysis of covariance, the normal group was superior to the schizophrenic on two of the three incidental learning scores. It is important to note that Greenberg suggests that the conclusion that schizophrenic patients show a greater impairment in incidental than in intentional learning "must be limited to the category of patients tested in this study since there are some indications that it does not apply to other categories such as paranoid and acute schizophrenia."

Further support for the contention that incidental learning in chronic schizophrenics is less than that in normals is given by a study of Topping and O'Connor (1960) in which there is a tendency for nonparanoid subjects to give lower incidental learning scores than normals, with a paranoid group occupying an intermediate position. A study by Winer (1954) showed lower than normal incidental learning in hebephrenic and catatonic schizophrenics, while paranoid schizophrenics had scores indistinguishable from normal. A further study which can be loosely included under the present heading is that of Dunn (1954). The experiment was carried out on 40 chronic schizophrenics and 40 nonpsychiatric hospitalized controls. Four types of scene were exposed briefly to the subject, including three "mother and son" pictures showing "whipping," "scolding," and "feeding." A neutral picture having the same relative sizes of figures showed a house and a tree. There were five versions of each picture, each having differing steps of detail change, such as the position of a branch in the tree-and-house pictures. The subject's task was to report whether there was any difference in a pair of pictures or whether they were the same. It was found that in the whipping and scolding pictures the schizophrenics were significantly worse than normals in the observation of detail; this difference did not reach significance for the feeding and house-and-tree pictures. While this is not Dunn's interpretation these results may be viewed as supporting a view of a narrowing of attention in chronic schizophrenics exaggerated by the emotion evoked by the whipping and scolding pictures. It may be, however, that an emotional reaction is evoked by these pictures in all subjects and it is only the combined effect of this on top of an already aroused schizophrenic "habitus" that is sufficient to produce the narrowing of attention which brought about nonperception of detail in the pictures.

## 2. Temporal

*a. Perception of Statistical Structure.* So far we have discussed experiments interpretable in terms of narrowing of attention that is spatially orientated. In this section we turn to experiments which can be interpreted in terms of temporal narrowing. One of the tasks which Callaway (Section II,A) used to test the hypothesis of narrowing of attention under autonomic stimulation was that of binary choice guessing. He showed that subjects receiving methamphetamine changed the statistical structure of their guesses to that of the reinforced answer pattern more slowly than a group not receiving methamphetamine. The proposed mechanism of this phenomenon is that past answers and guesses, being in the periphery of attention, are not so readily perceived under conditions of narrowed attention and are not responded to. Changes in guess pattern do not then take place so readily.

A somewhat similar experiment was carried out by Ashman (1959) on a group of schizophrenics who were described as first admissions with a median age of 35 years. The length of stay in this first admission was not described, but unless the group contained a large proportion of paranoid patients it might be suggested that at 35 years the group be considered comparatively chronic.

The total group was divided into five subgroups, each having a different pattern of initial, interpolated, and final tasks. The initial and final tasks all consisted of 100% reinforcement for one response, while the interpolated tasks had different patterns of 50:50 reinforcement. Ashman summarized his results as showing that "schizophrenics do not appear to be able to utilize prior probability learning on responding appropriately to later patterns." They tend to perseverate to a reinforced response after the cessation of a reinforcement renders the response inappropriate in terms of a different pattern of events.

Employing a more complicated statistical learning task the present author carried out some preliminary studies on this problem which were eventually abandoned because the task proved too difficult. However, results as far as they went throw light on the problem. The task in this instance was a four-choice sequential probability learning task with probabilities of 0, 17, 33, and 50% of the appearance of any of the four lights following the appearance of any one. The probability pattern was complete on 64 trials and four blocks of 64 trials were used with each subject. Six nonparanoid chronic schizophrenics were tested and as a measure of their activation level, skin potential level was measured (Venables, 1963b). It was found that the three patients with low skin potential levels learned the task reasonably well, whereas the three patients with high skin potential levels, and hence possibly narrowed attention, could not learn the pattern and resorted to position habits. It could be argued that as the three patients with high skin potential levels were also more withdrawn, and hence possibly more sick than the other three patients, their poor performance resulted simply from the fact they were less able to undertake the task. This did not seem to be the case, their performance gave the impression more of consisting of short runs of trials of fresh patterns which, not being reinforced, eventually led to position habits. On the other hand the three patients who learned achieved performances progressively closer to the imposed pattern.

Closely associated with this type of experiment are those on language when the main concern is with its statistical structure. Lewinsohn and Elwood (1961) studied the learning of word lists having different orders of approximation to unconstrained language as in the Miller and Selfridge (1950) experiment. Four groups of subjects were tested, acute and chronic schizophrenics, nonschizophrenic patients, and normals. It was found that the chronic schizophrenic patients stood out from the rest in their inability to make use of the contextual constraints of language. When the vocabulary level was controlled it was found that the difference between chronic patients and the rest disappeared; however, it could be said that vocabulary performance insofar as it is the selection of a verbal description of a word while keeping that word in the forefront of attention might very well be contaminated by the same mechanism of narrowed attention. The confounding effect of vocabulary level is found in experiments by Pearl (1963), who examined the performance of process and reactive schizophrenics on a version of Shannon's (1951) guessing game. Shannon's method assumes that people have an implicit knowledge of language statistics and when required to guess the next letter of a meaningful language sequence, use this information to predict the most likely letter. Pearl found that if the total population of acute schizophrenics which he tested was dichotomized on the basis of vocabulary level, there was no difference in performance of the high-vocabulary process and reactive patients. Low-vocabulary process schizophrenics, however, took significantly more guesses to arrive at the correct content of a sentence than low-vocabulary reactive patients, and both these groups were inferior to normal subjects with similarly low vocabularies.

These language experiments tend to support the general notion that the selection of the immediate response which is in the foreground of attention is not helped in chronic or in process schizophrenics by the pattern or structure of the words or letters normally surrounding it.

b. *Effects of Anchor Stimuli.* Weinstein, Goldstone, and Boardman (1958) carried out an experiment on the time estimation of schizophrenics in which they confirmed the finding of Lhamon and Goldstone (1956) that schizophrenics tend to overestimate the duration of a clock second; their main concern, however, was to determine the effect of anchor stimuli upon performance. They found that both normals and their sample of chronic schizophrenics responded to the "pulling" effect of long- and short-interval anchors. That is, if the series of time intervals used in the determination of "Second Estimate Point" (SEP) started with a short interval the SEP was "pulled" down, whereas if the series started with a long interval the SEP was "pulled" up. However, if a subsequent series was given with the anchors reversed it was found that the judgment of normal control subjects was influenced by the earlier series whereas the schizophrenics tended only to respond to the effect of the immediate series. It appears therefore that the range of attention of these chronic patients was narrowed and did not involve the use of cues presented earlier in time.

Salzinger (1957) studied the effect of a prior experience of lifting a heavy or a light weight on the judgment of the categories of a series of five weights. In this experiment the performance of acute rather than chronic schizophrenics was compared with that of controls. It was found that after the prior experience of the heavy weight the schizophrenics shifted *more* than the controls. Performance did not differ after the light anchor. Thus it would appear that consonant with the idea of increased awareness of objects in the environment or broadness of attention in the acute schizophrenic, the patients were more aware during their subsequent judgments of the impression left by the earlier perceived heavy weight and then judgment was affected.

An experiment carried out by Boardman, Goldstone, Reiner, and Fathauer (1962) on the effect of anchor stimuli on the judgment of a length of one inch provides further evidence to support the earlier studies. Groups of acute and chronic schizophrenics and normals were each divided into three subgroups. The first made size judgments using a modified method of limits technique starting with a neutral 1.0-inch anchor; the second started with a 2.0-inch anchor and after a brief rest followed with a series with a 0.1-inch anchor. The procedure for group 3 was the reverse of group 2. The comparisons of greatest interest are those between the judgments for series with 0.1-inch anchors presented first or second, and with 2.0-inch anchors presented first or second. It was found that neither the normal nor the chronic schizophrenic group showed any significant differences between their initial or final 0.1-inch or 2.0-inch anchor judgments, whereas the effect of the previous anchor situation was marked in the judgment of the acute schizophrenics. The effect of the immediate anchor condition was felt when it was 0.1-inch in all groups but the immediate effect of the 2.0-inch anchor was felt only in the acute group. It is tempting to suggest that owing to "tunnel vision" the extremities of the 2.0-inch anchor were not perceived by the chronic schizophrenics but this explanation seems too facile. We are thus presented with further evidence that the acute schizophrenic still has in his broadened attention the impression left by the previous anchor given while this is excluded from the attention of the chronic schizophrenic. The lack of effect of anchors on normal subjects in this study confirms the results of an earlier study (Boardman, Aldrick, Reiner, and Goldstone, 1959) and suggests that "the concept of an inch is a social standard of magnitude and is stable in a normal population."

### 3. Discussion and Conclusions

It is a pitfall of any review which attempts to gather together a rather disparate set of findings under some blanket hypothesis that some violence is done to the original findings. It is hoped that this has been avoided in the present section and moreover that there has not been unwitting selection of data to fit the thesis.

In summary, what appears to have emerged from the experiments discussed is the finding that on the whole chronic schizophrenic patients behave in a way which suggests that their attention is narrowed. Within this group the extent of the narrowing is related to the patient's withdrawal, or the degree to which he appears to be in contact with his surroundings. There is some evidence that paranoid patients may stand as an isolated group who behave differently from other chronic patients. In addition there is much slighter evidence that patients called either "poor premorbid" or "process" schizophrenics tend to act similarly to chronic patients, and that "reactive" or "good premorbid" patients tend to act with patients classed as acute as though they conformed to the clinical picture of overawareness of their surroundings. This suggestion, however, is much more tenuous than the narrowing of attention in chronic subjects. Following from these results is the collateral proposal resulting from Callaway's findings that narrowed attention is manifest in conditions which produce cortical alertness; that cortical overactivity is to be expected in chronic schizophrenics and the degree of overactivity is related to the patient's mental state.

Another point which has emerged is that the effect of narrowed attention can be felt both in respect to the sensory stimuli incoming at any one time and on items which are not contemporaneous. Thus it is suggested that items which are the more remote members of a set, some of which are presently attended to, may be eliminated from attention by narrowing, thus affecting the "meaning" of the items in the focus of attention. The use of the word "meaning" has evident relevance when one is considering, for instance, the statistical structure of language, but it is just as relevant when we take the view that the meaningfulness of the organism's surroundings is in relation to the degree to which they are perceived as part of a geographic and historic whole.

Close parallels may be drawn between the position reached here and that, for instance, put forward by Osgood (1957). Following the postulates of Hull (1943) Osgood suggests that the effect of drive is to reduce the number of alternative responses in a hierarchy. This comes about because of the multiplicative relationship according to which drive increases the probability of alternative reactions in proportion to their initial habit strengths. Thus, under high drive dominant responses become more dominant and less probable responses in the hierarchy become even less probable. If this is applied (as Osgood does) to language behavior, the number of associates arising from the presentation of a particular word decreases under high drive, and thus meaningfulness in the sense used earlier decreases. This neo-Hullian picture puts narrowing under high drive at the response end of behavior but the parallels between it and perceptual narrowing deserve further attention. In the case of temporal narrowing the division between the two pictures is largely verbal and revolves around the use of terms such as associations, associative responses, and items in the attentive field which are the result of past experience rather than due to present sensory input. It should be noted that this learning theory viewpoint is in contrast to that which is used, for instance, by Mednick (1958) where high drive is said to act impartially upon correct and incorrect responses and therefore tend to push many irrelevant responses above threshold.

This theoretical confusion is possibly resolved by a suggestion of Callaway and Stone (1960) to the effect that "arousal will lead to (1) reduced probabilistic coding (i.e., increased over-all uncertainty with regard to the stimulus ensemble under consideration); (2) increased filtering (as in our previous concept of narrowed attention); and (3) reduced size of stimulus ensemble under consideration." As Callaway and Stone point out, this leads to some ambiguity as it is impossible to tell *a priori* whether a peripheral stimulus will be excluded because of narrowness of attention or included with nearly the probability of the most probable stimulus because of prediction (1). This model does comply with the Hullian prediction used by Mednick in which competing responses are elevated nearer to threshold, but is not very useful as an explanatory concept until the conditions for narrowing of attention and the reduction to equality of the remaining probabilities are examined by experiment.

# III. Relationship to Other Groups of Experimental Studies

## A. OVERINCLUSION

So far, apart from a brief reference in Section I,A, no mention has been made to the extensive work on overinclusion which has obvious relevance to the present review. This has been done deliberately, partly because it would be unnecessary duplication to review the literature on this topic when this has already been done by Payne, Matussek, and George (1959) and Payne (1961), and second because to some extent the findings on overinclusion provide an independent check on the position which has been reached as a result of the present review of an entirely different set of experiments.

Although they do not proceed to test it by other than the more conventional tests of overinclusion, Payne *et al.* (1959) make the suggestion already quoted that overinclusion is an attention defect and is due to the breakdown of a filter mechanism that "cuts out or inhibits the stimuli, both internal and external, that are irrelevant to the task in hand" or, in our terminology, that it results from excessive broadness of attention.

Payne and Friedlander (1962) and Payne (1962) summarize the findings on overinclusion as follows:

Overinclusive thinking may be a relatively specific disorder, independent of general intelligence; it influences performance on a number of different types of tests, yielding a clear factor when intercorrelations between tests are factor analyzed. It is confined to patients diagnosed as schizophrenic and among these is not found in retarded patients. Chronic schizophrenics do not appear to be overinclusive, but the abnormality does appear in patients with delusions. The findings suggest the idea that overinclusive thinking may be a relatively good long-term prognostic indication.

Using the object classification test (Goldstein and Scheerer, 1941), Payne (1962) presented data from five groups of subjects. On this test acute schizophrenics stand out from the other groups of normals, neurotics, depressives, and chronic schizophrenics in showing a greater degree of overinclusive thinking. The chronic schizophrenic group is almost completely within the normal range of scores for numbers of unusual sortings.

The same picture of overinclusive behavior occurring only in acute schizophrenics is found when the scores from three tests are combined (Payne and Friedlander, 1962).

Feinberg and Garman (1961) studying thought disorder in schizophrenics with a modified version of the Progressive Matrices test categorized subjects' responses in terms of their plausibility. Acute schizophrenics made many errors categorized as "implausible" in that their responses showed no geometrical similarity to the stimulus patterns. Chronic schizophrenics, on the other hand, made few errors of this kind and it was suggested that their performance should be interpreted in terms of "underinclusion" rather than "overinclusion."

These studies tend to support the conclusions drawn from the examination of data from experiments not concerned with testing overinclusion (Section II,B) that the perception of the acute schizophrenic is such that there is little selection of relevant and irrelevant material; it is in other words broad, while that of the chronic schizophrenic is narrow. That overinclusion occurs in schizophrenics with good prognosis or those classed as reactive also fits the ideas put forward earlier in this section that overawareness of surroundings is to be found in "good premorbid" patients.

B. STIMULUS GENERALIZATION

Mednick's (1958) learning-theory approach to schizophrenia has as one of its main tenets the notion that acute schizophrenics show an abnormal degree of stimulus generalization. Defined as the condition "when a response, having been trained to a stimulus, is also elicited by similar stimuli," stimulus overgeneralization is a close conceptual counterpart to overinclusion. If we consider that excessive width of attention is a disorder in which many items have equal prominence in the organism's consciousness and may therefore have equal likelihood of eliciting a response, the closeness of this concept to stimulus overgeneralization is apparent.

The work on generalization in schizophrenics does not in fact enable very strong conclusions to be drawn. Mednick (1955) used schizophrenics whose length of hospitalization was over 9 years on a task in which response to a central stimulus light was spatially generalizable to more peripheral lights. He found support for a hypothesis that schizophrenics would show greater generalization than normal. It was not, however, conclusive. On the basis of comparison with work on overinclusion and breadth of attention it should not be expected that the chronic schizophrenics used by Mednick would show generalization; however, the fact that half his sample were diagnosed as paranoid would possibly give rise to the small over-all amount of generalization that was shown. Garmezy (1951), however, using a sample of acute schizophrenics, showed that these patients tended to generalize from a training tone to other stimuli along the pitch dimension.

Knopf and Fager (1959) showed some degree of spatial generalization in schizophrenics, but as the chronicity of the patients was not designated, the value of their results is minimized. Other findings on generalization in schizophrenics tend to be by inference from experiments on verbal learning. Mednick and Devito (1958), for instance, showed that, in a complex learning situation with competing intralist associations where overgeneralization might be expected to worsen performance, acute schizophrenics were more impaired than chronic patients. Carson (1958), also working from the expectation of greater generalization in schizophrenics and hence greater difficulty with rote learning involving increasing intralist similarity, found his schizophrenic group produced results opposite to those predicted. In the light of the present thesis it is interesting to note that Carson's patients were of chronic status.

On the basis of these rather limited results therefore it seems reasonable to conclude that acute schizophrenic patients may show an excess of stimulus generalization, while this is not the case with chronic patients. As these results seem to be parallel and similar to those on broadened attention, it does not seem wise to draw the conclusion that high stimulus generalization in acute patients arises because of high drive in these patients; rather, the reverse seems likely. Generalization on the basis of high drive as suggested by neo-Hullian theories may profitably be distinguished from generalization arising from broadness of attention brought about by decreased arousal. The whole of this conceptual tangle deserves further experimentation.

C. SENSORY DEPRIVATION

The impression gained from experiments reviewed earlier is that acute schizophrenic patients are under constant bombardment from an excess of unrestricted sensory stimulation, whereas the reverse position is the case with chronic patients whose narrowed attention restricts the amount of sensory input consciously perceived. These are changes brought about by the physiological state of the patient; the amount of sensory material available to consciousness can, however, be manipulated externally and by restriction might be expected to produce at least some of the symptoms of chronic schizophrenia in normal subjects. As a corollary, restriction of sensory material might be expected to improve the state of the acute patient.

In a review of anecdotal and experimental material on sensory deprivation in normal subjects, Rosenzweig (1960) says, "One cannot help noting throughout these reports. . . . that there appear again and again Bleuler's cardinal symptoms of schizophrenia; disturbance of associations, disharmony of affect, autism, ambivalence. We see disruption of secondary thought processes, regression to the primary process, impairment of reality testing and in addition such accessory symptoms as distortion of body image, depersonalization, delusions, hallucinations." That these pathological effects arise not merely from diminution of sensory input per se but rather from the diminution in the meaningfulness of sensory input is shown in a study by Davis, McCourt, and Solomon (1960), who restricted the usual patterning of sensation but supplied input in the form of a randomly flashing light. Discussing the pathological disturbances arising from this procedure they state, "It appears that what the brain needs for normal functioning is not quantity or change of sensation per se, but a meaningful contact with the outside world."

Unfortunately experiments to test the other side of the coin are inconclusive. Gibby, Adams, and Carrera (1960) reported an enduring change for the better in a mixed group of patients containing some schizophrenics of unspecified chronicity after exposure to a sensory deprivation situation. Improvement was also reported by Harris (1959), particularly for hebephrenics, but the change did not last beyond the experimental situation. No change was reported by Smith, Thakurdas, and Lawes (1961), who used chronic patients, or by Cleveland, Reitman, and Bentinck (1963). The lack of change in chronic patients might of course be expected as they might be considered to be already in a state of sensory deprivation. More conclusive evidence from this source must await experiments with better attention to diagnostic and chronicity criteria.

### D. "Set" in Reaction Time

One of the largest sections of integrated experimental work on schizophrenia is that on the effect of time uncertainty in RT. This has been discussed by Shakow (1962, 1963). A related set of experiments are those on stimulus uncertainty which have recently been reviewed by Sutton and Zubin (1963). While this work deals with "expectancy" or "set" and is thus not strictly on the topic of the present review, some of the statements which have been made in the course of theoretical discussions make it evident that it should be considered at the present time. As an example, we find in Sutton and Zubin (1963) that "studies strongly suggest that the state of readiness of the patient is disproportionately affected by events which are recent in time"; however, on the other hand, these authors say "it is also clear in the foreperiod experiments, and suggested in recent work on modality experiments that long-range influences operating over the whole series of trials act to 'over influence' and 'over prepare' the schizophrenic subject." There thus seems superficially to be a conflict between these studies, which have mainly been carried out on chronic patients, and those already reviewed, which show temporal narrowing in these patients. In attempting to resolve the conflict it is important to keep in mind the different processes involved in perception and in the development of "sets" or "expectancies." In perception what is always in the forefront is the present stimulus and the narrowness or broadness of attention must be considered in relation to this present anchor point. In the case of expectancy we have a state of the organism built on the basis of past stimuli and experiences and having relevance to response to a future stimulus. The range of relevant items in the attentive field is not anchored to a present stimulus as in the perceptual process. Thus in expectancy we may have the position of the range of attention being narrowed to a particular subset of items in the past so that the subject acts with response to this "minor set" in a manner which is inadequate. For efficient performance attention to a wider range of items is required to develop a "major set" which may bring the range of expectancy up to date. By such an explanation as this the theoretical positions arising from "perceptual" and "expectancy" experiments may be mutually reconciled.

The leading finding of the RT experiments on this subject is that on the effect of regular and irregular foreperiods on speed of reaction. When, in the regular procedure, the foreperiod is kept constant for a block of trials, normal subjects appear to be able to take advantage of this procedure for foreperiods up to 20 sec. Chronic schizophrenics, on the other hand, are only able to benefit from the regularity for foreperiods up to 5 or 6 sec., after which they perform less well than when foreperiods are presented randomly, giving the subject no opportunity to develop a set to respond. This difference in the degree to which subjects were able to utilize the regularity of foreperiod was embodied in an arbitrarily constructed set index (Rodnick and Shakow, 1940), which was found (Rosenthal, Lawlor, Zahn, and Shakow, 1960) to be closely related to a rating of the patient's mental health.

Of particular interest to the present review is a study by Huston and Singer (1945), who examined the effect of sodium amytal on a group of patients whose duration of illness was 9 months and might therefore be considered to be in the early chronic stage. Without drugs these patients showed the same pattern of relationships as those shown by Rodnick and Shakow (1940). The normal subjects had faster reactions with regular foreperiods than with irregular foreperiods up to 20 sec. in length. The schizophrenics, on the other hand, showed that at about 6-sec. foreperiod length the advantage of the regular foreperiod was lost. Under sodium amytal, which it will be remembered (Section II,A) is supposed to induce a broadening of attention and therefore in the

Huston and Singer experiment should enable the subject to benefit from constant foreperiod length, the pattern of schizophrenic results was similar to that of the normals. In a later experiment Huston and Senf (1952) studied the effect of amytal upon the performance on a similar RT task with both early and chronic schizophrenics. Because only three preparatory foreperiods were used results were not strictly comparable to those above. The trend, however, was with the regular procedure under drugs for the chronic schizophrenics to show distinct improvement in comparison with the undrugged condition. The improvement was not marked in the case of the early schizophrenics.

Another study from Shakow's group (Zahn, Rosenthal, and Shakow, 1963) very nicely demonstrates the point under discussion and has particular relevance to the experiments on anchor stimuli (Section II,B,2,b). Using only irregular foreperiods, these experimenters were able to show that when the foreperiod before the one presently involved was longer than the present one the chronic schizophrenic patients were more affected by it than normals. The conclusion is thus reached that, "instead of basing their pattern of preparation on their experience with the series of preparation intervals as a whole, the patients seem to base it, much more than do the normal subjects, on the most recent event in the series."

In the case of stimulus uncertainty experiments (Sutton and Zubin, 1963) the uncertainty is not when the stimulus is going to appear but what stimulus is to appear. In these studies disturbance of performance is shown more by changes of stimulus from light to sound than by the degree to which expectancy for one or another type of stimulus is built up. It is with this sort of influence of the parameters of the stimuli within the total context that the next section will be concerned.

## IV. Stimulus Parameters as Determinants of Input Dysfunction

A further set of factors which are responsible for dysfunctions of input in the schizophrenic patient are those concerned with the simple parameters of stimuli. Other more complex parameters such as their aversive or social content when stimuli act as reinforcing agents have been reviewed recently by Silverman (1963) and will not be considered here. Data are available in any quantity only on the effects of the parameters of modality and intensity and the discussion will be limited to these aspects. It might be expected, however, that the proposals put forward by Kaplan (1960) on the differential sensitization to long and short wavelengths by autonomic arousal would provide a further dimension on which normal-schizophrenic differences might be expected.

A. MODALITY

In Section II,A some proposals by Bharucha-Reid (1962) concerning the way in which subcortical dysfunction may lead to disorganization at the cortex were outlined. One of these was that the subcortex may affect the function of sensory receiving areas selectively and thus possibly affect a single sense modality and thus disturb the normal relationship which exists between the different modalities.

There is some evidence for such a disturbance in schizophrenia. Venables and O'Connor (1959) carried out an experiment on the reaction time to auditory and visual stimulation, using groups of chronic schizophrenic subjects divided on the basis of rating scales measuring withdrawal and paranoid tendency. A control group of normal subjects was also tested. The finding usually reported (cf. Teichner, 1954) that auditory RT's are faster than visual RT's with normal subjects was replicated in the case of the normal subjects in this experiment. It was also shown by those schizophrenics designated as both paranoid and not withdrawn. (This is a group similar to that group labeled coherent paranoids which behaved differently from the remainder of the patients in a study detailed earlier—Section II,B,1,c.) The other schizophrenics had faster reactions to visual stimuli than to auditory stimuli. This result is in conformity with a much earlier study (Wells and Kelley, 1922) in which a group of dementia praecox patients showed a tendency for RT to sound to be relatively longer than to light as compared with normals. The effect of different stimulus modalities was also shown in a study of the effect of background stimulation on the skin potential response of chronic schizophrenics (Venables, 1960). It was found that an auditory background had a greater effect than a visual background in slowing down responses in a nonwithdrawn paranoid subgroup, while in the remainder of schizophrenics the tendency was for the response to be speeded up. The ability of the cortex to resolve pairs of stimuli presented in close temporal proximity has been suggested as a measure of its excitability (Venables, 1963b). The threshold of fusion of paired clicks has been compared to the threshold of fusion of paired flashes in an unpublished experiment. The difference between the two fusion thresholds was used as a measure of the relative dominance of one modality over the other. It was found that in normal subjects all two-click thresholds were lower than two-flash thresholds. Among the chronic schizophrenics who were tested there was in general a smaller difference between the two types of thresholds and among the very deteriorated patients there was a reversal of the normal findings: two-click thresholds were longer than two-flash thresholds. There was found to be a significant correlation between a rating of deterioration and the difference between flash and click thresholds giving an impression as with the earlier studies of a greater disturbance in the auditory than the visual modality. It is an interesting parallel that simple RT to sound is significantly impaired under medication with LSD-25, while simple RT to light is not (Abramson, Jarvik, and Hirsch, 1955), and that under this drug normal subjects often display slowness, proverty of speech, and withdrawal (Rinkel, de Shon, Hyde, and Solomon, 1952), the symptoms that are displayed by the withdrawn deteriorated schizophrenic.

Zahn, Rosenthal, and Lawlor (1962) studied the GSR orienting reactions to visual and auditory stimulation in chronic schizophrenic and normal subjects. The basal log conductance during the series of stimuli was greater with visual than with auditory stimuli in schizophrenics while the reverse was the case with normals. This pattern was shown initially with the numbers of specific GSR's elicited but owing to the faster adaptation displayed by the normal subjects the pattern was not maintained after the first eight trials.

The same sort of alteration of the usual pattern of modality dominance is also shown in a study by Sutton, Hakerem, Zubin, and Portnoy (1961), where in addition to the effect of shifts in sensory modality which was the primary study of the experiment there was a general tendency for RT's to be faster to light than to sound with the chronic schizophrenic patients who were used as abnormal subjects.

This study and others on the same topic reviewed by Sutton and Zubin (1963) all show that with schizophrenics reactions to sound stimuli are impaired if the stimulus in the previous trial was a light, whereas reactions to light stimuli, however preceded, do not yield differences between patients and normals. This could be considered as further evidence for relative impairment of the auditory modality in schizophrenics.

Relative disorganization of the auditory modality in schizophrenics is a possible explanation for the results of the experiment of Fedio, Mirsky, Smith, and Parry (1961). These workers investigated the effect of EEG activation upon RT following the experiment of Lansing, Schwartz, and Lindsley (1959). Fedio et al. used the sound of a bell to evoke alpha blockade and presented a buzzer as a signal for reaction when the EEG alpha was blocked. They compared this condition with others where the EEG alpha was not blocked or was blocked spontaneously. It was found in contrast to the results from normal subjects that the speed of RT of schizophrenics did not increase when alpha was blocked. While not the interpretation put forward by the authors, disorganization of the auditory modality and of the means by which the auditory cortex is aroused is a possible explanation of the results.

To date the studies on the effectiveness of stimuli in the different modalities and their relationship to schizophrenic pathology has not been given much attention. Work on this subject is not easy as other parameters such as intensity may produce swamping effects. However, attempts made, for instance, by Stevens (1955) to produce equivalent intensity scales for the visual and auditory modalities enable experimentation to be carried out.

### B. INTENSITY

A pair of studies which belong partly in this and partly in the preceding section are those which consider the intensity of visual and auditory stimuli on the speed of reaction in schizophrenics (Venables and Tizard, 1956, 1958). In the first study eight intensities of stimulus light were used using a two-log unit range from 16 to 1500 foot-candles. It was found that in contrast to normal subjects, who showed a decrease in RT to an asymptotic value, the RT of chronic nonparanoid schizophrenics tended to increase after a fall to an optimal value at about 200 foot-candles, and became slower with increasing intensity. In contrast this "paradoxical" increase in RT was not shown with a wide range of auditory stimulus intensities up to 115 db with 1000-cps and 200-cps tones and white noise. With relation to the preceding section it is interesting to note that in comparing the effects of visual and auditory stimulus intensities it was evident that whatever the change of intensities the auditory RT tended to be slower than the visual for the nonparanoid chronic schizophrenics used in these studies.

More direct evidence on the effects of intensity of stimuli is given by the work of Shagass and Schwartz (1963a,b). Evoked cortical potentials were examined using averaging techniques to improve signal:noise ratio. Only the results of work on somato-sensory stimuli have been published so far, but in this it can be seen that in relatively acute schizophrenics there is a greater increase in evoked potential amplitude with increase in stimulus intensity than there is in normals. In this characteristic, schizophrenics are similar to other patients with the exception of dysthymic neurotics. This exception is of some theoretical interest as it has been postulated in some theories of schizophrenia that it is because the reactions of early schizophrenics are similar to those of anxiety states that the train of pathological behavior that eventuates in florid schizophrenia begins.

It should be noted that the portion of the evoked response that Shagass and Schwartz are dealing with in their studies is an early component in the evoked complex and there is some evidence (e.g., Allison, 1962) to indicate that it is a thalamo-cortical radiation response. The comparison of this neurophysiological evidence with behavioral evidence is thus somewhat indirect. It will, however, be of direct interest to see whether a nonlinear relationship between visual stimulus intensity and the early component of evoked response appears in schizophrenics; if it does not, the explanation for the paradoxical RT findings must lie in later cortical functioning.

## V. The State of the Patient

At the end of Section I,B two opposing viewpoints were mentioned concerning the relative levels of drive or arousal of acute and chronic schizophrenic states. Increasingly throughout the review of perceptual data the impression has gained ground that, if the findings on normal subjects (Section II,A) concerned with the motivational or arousal correlates of broadened or narrowed attention are applicable to the more long-term physiological disturbances involved in schizophrenic pathology, we shoud expect acute patients to be characterized by low, and chronic patients by high, levels of arousal or drive. There are, furthermore, suggestions that differences in physiological levels of activity may be found within the acute and chronic categories, depending upon the patient's subdiagnosis or state of withdrawal, or whether his past history indicates that he belongs to process or reactive, poor or good premorbid, categories.

The rather glib way in which the terms arousal, drive, and sympathetic or parasympathetic activity have been used so far in discussion may possibly be excused insofar as they are meant to be taken as shorthand summaries for concepts having wider implications. It is not the purpose of this chapter to present a detailed examination of these terms; nevertheless insofar as they have been invoked in explanation a word must be said about their usage. The interrelation between the cortex and such subcortical mechanisms as the hypothalamus and reticular formation is complex, but without doing too great violence to the finer points of detail it may be said that stimulation of both the posterior hypothalamus (which is responsible for sympathetic functions) and the dorsal region of the mesencephalic reticular formation causes cortical arousal signaled by such phenomena as desynchronization of the alpha rhythm. The functions of both these structures are blocked by barbituates and it is this principle which is involved in the sedation threshold test, the results of which are reviewed below. While in general it may be said that the anterior and posterior hypothalamus, as central structures mediating respectively parasympathetic and sympathetic function, operate in a reciprocal fashion so that activity in one tends to promote inhibition of the other, this is not universally the case. Acute emotional disturbance, for instance, is accompanied by signs of both sympathetic and parasympathetic activity. Bearing this in mind in general we may say that conditions which produce activation of the central sympathetic mechanisms tend also to produce cortical arousal. On the other hand, drugs such as tranquilizers which shift the balance between the anterior and posterior hypothalamus to the parasympathetic side decrease the intensity of discharges from the hypothalamus and reticular formation to the cortex and lower the arousal level of the cortex.

The reaction of schizophrenic patients to drugs may allow us to draw conclusions about the patient's physiological state. Thus, if the action of a depressant drug is to improve the patient's condition, it is possible to make the inference that he was formerly in a state of hyperarousal.

One series of studies concerns the reaction of patients to such general depressants as sodium amytal. Lindemann (1932) was one of the first to show a temporary improvement in schizophrenic behavior after medication with sodium amytal. This was shown by increased contact with the environment and warmth of emotion. This work was repeated more recently, for instance, by Fulcher, Gallagher, and Pfeiffer (1957), who found that the number of "lucid intervals" among chronic schizophrenics increased under amobarbital. Stevens and Derbyshire (1958) reported remission of catatonic stupor under amobarbital and by taking EMG, EEG, and EKG recordings were able to show that remission from stupor was accompanied by a decrease in the level of cortical and autonomic activity. These studies all suggest a high degree of arousal in chronic deteriorated or catatonic patients. This idea is supported by the work on sedation threshold summarized by Shagass (1960). Amobarbital is given at a constant rate until the patient's speech is slurred or a point of inflection of the curve relating EEG fast activity to dose is reached. The amount of amobarbital required to reach this point is higher in chronic schizophrenics, other than those diagnosed as simple, than in normals. Patients diagnosed as acute schizophrenic, on the other hand, have the lowest of any sedation threshold reported. This low threshold in acute schizophrenics is confirmed in a study by Herrington and Claridge (1963). Anxiety states are also shown to have a high sedation threshold similar to that of chronic schizophrenics. The outcome of these studies is that there is evidence for high cerebral activity in chronic schizophrenia while the reverse is true of acute schizophrenic patients. This is based on the assumption that a patient in a state of high central activation requires a higher dose of barbiturate to eliminate that activity than one whose level of activity is low. An alternative explanation may, however, be put forward in terms of a differential sensitivity to barbiturates. The study by Fulcher *et al.* (1957) mentioned above also used the drug arecoline and found that like amobarbital it produced "lucid intervals" in chronic schizophrenics. Arecoline is of interest because it has been shown to have pure parasympathetic (muscarinic) activity on the brain in comparison to amobarbital, whose action is more complex. Arecoline is one of the drugs like reserpine, pilocarpine, and physostigmine that inhibit conditioned avoidance in rats. It could be tentatively suggested that withdrawal in schizophrenics is a form of conditioned avoidance. In support of this it has been shown (Venables and Wing, 1962) that withdrawal in a nonparanoid chronic schizophrenic population is positively correlated with the level of skin potential shown by the subject. It has also been shown (Spain, 1963) that in a similar population the degree of eyelid conditioning (a paradigm for conditioned avoidance in humans?) is also positively related to the level of the subject's skin potential. Parasympatheticomimetic drugs may therefore act to produce remissions in deteriorated and withdrawn schizophrenics by decreasing conditioned avoidance and withdrawal. That avoidance conditioning is successful in schizophrenics is shown by the number of studies which give evidence of the greater effectiveness of aversive reinforcers in comparison with rewards in these patients (cf. Silverman, 1963).

Further support for the picture of higher activity in chronic schizophrenics is gained from the study of Williams (1953), who showed that during rest these patients showed higher basal levels of skin conductance, pulse rate, and respiration than normal. Similar results were also reported by Malmo, Shagass, and Smith (1951).

Within the chronic schizophrenic population, as has already been said, withdrawal has been shown to be related to the level of autonomic activity given by skin potential as an index and also to the level of cortical activity exemplified by two-flash fusion threshold (Venables and Wing, 1962). More recent unpublished data support this conclusion by a finding of a relationship between two-click threshold and withdrawal. These results, which show that the greater the degree of autonomic, visual cortical, or auditory cortical activation the greater is the withdrawal, apply only to nonparanoid schizophrenics and paranoid schizophrenics who are markedly incoherent. Standing apart from these are the coherent paranoid schizophrenics in whom there is a tendency (unpublished data) for withdrawal to be related to underarousal. In nonparanoid chronic schizophrenics two-flash threshold and skin potential as measures of cortical and autonomic activation are positively related. This pattern is not found in normal subjects and coherent paranoid patients (Venables, 1963b). The atypical reaction of paranoid schizophrenics has been noted earlier in the review, and is confirmed by these latest results. Support for this view is given by such disparate studies as those of Stevenson, Derrick, Hobbs, and Metcalfe (1957), which suggests that paranoid schizophrenics differ from other schizophrenics in adrenocortical response and phosphate excretion, and by Wertheimer and Wertheimer (1955), who showed that the structure of capillary loops in all but paranoid schizophrenics was different from normals. This viewpoint is in agreement with that put forward by Shakow (1962), who says, "thus of the 58 measurements which we have made of a wide range of psychological functions on groups of normal, paranoid, and hebephrenic subjects, we found the paranoid to be nearer the normal in 31 instances and the hebephrenic nearer in only 7 instances. In 20 instances, however, the paranoid and hebephrenic fell on either side of the normal."

Among studies which are concerned with testing the difference between process and reactive schizophrenics one of the most convincing is that by Gromoll (1961), who, starting with the hypothesis that the process patients would be underaroused and the reactive patients overaroused, using percentage time alpha as his index, in fact found the complete reverse.

In this brief review of the physiological status of different classes of schizophrenic patients there has been the attempt only to consider the *level* of physiological activity. It would appear from perusal of the literature that many false conclusions have been drawn because of failure to distinguish level of ongoing activity from reactivity to stimuli. Attempts to infer one from the other tend to be inconclusive: Although, for instance, Wilder (1958) argues convincingly for the "law of initial value" by which there is an inverse linear relationship between the size of response and the level from which it starts, other workers—for instance, Silverman, Cohen, and Shmavonian (1959)—have argued for a curvilinear relationship between level and responses. It is by invoking the law of initial value, or indeed the initial part of the curvilinear relationship between level and response, that what appears at first sight to be a discrepancy between what is reported in the clinical literature and the state of the patient proposed in this section may be reconciled. Thus it is said that acute schizophrenic patients show large emotional reactions, anxiety, fear, anger, while the affect of the chronic patient tends to be "flat." It is against the proposed low level of activity of the acute schizophrenic that a large emotional response may be seen, while because of the high existing level of activity of the chronic patient only a small response may be evoked.

## VI. Summary

The main thesis which has been put forward in this review is that, for the purpose of considering input dysfunction, schizophrenics cannot be taken as a whole. A distinction must be drawn between acute and chronic patients and, within this subdivision, attention must be paid to the patient's subdiagnosis and whether or not he may be designated as process or reactive. The interrelationships between the subdivisions have not become clear because little attempt has been made to sort them out. It is possible, for instance, that with the slow-onset, process-type schizophrenic we should not expect there to be an acute stage of the illness at all. On the other hand, as has been hinted at in the theory proposed by Fish (Section I,B), we should not perhaps ever think of a chronic stage of paranoid schizophrenia. If, as has become apparent from the experimental work reviewed, there is a marked distinction between the physiological states and hence the perceptual abilities of acute and chronic patients, far more experimental time can be profitably expanded on the analysis of the stage of transition from one to the other stage and the factors—physical, physiological, and social—which accelerate or retard the process. If we bear these points in mind, the experimental work which has been reviewed points to a general statement of the following kind. Chronic schizophrenic patients—and possibly included in this category are process patients—tend to be characterized by a state of restriction of the attentional field resulting from elevated states of sympathetic and cortical activation. Attention is restricted not only to the extent that peripheral sensory items contemporaneously present do not rise into consciousness, but also involved is the nonrecognition of items in memory which form part of the meaningful structure in which the present central item appears. Drugs and procedures which reduce arousal tend to improve the clinical status of these patients alongside (or even because of) an improvement in their perception of the external world and an increase in its meaningfulness resulting from increased breadth of attention.

In contrast to the chronic patient, the acute (and possibly the reactive and paranoid) patient is characterized by an inability to restrict the range of his attention so that he is flooded by sensory impressions from all quarters. Items of all kinds have equal importance, and the meaningfulness of the external world tends to be lost for the opposite reason to that which applies with the chronic patient. The figure-ground relationship which allows a picture to convey information is destroyed equally by making the picture nearly all figure or making it nearly all ground. The acute patient's broadened level of attention would appear to arise from the low level of cortical activation or possibly the para-sympathetic imbalance which he displays. A wide variety of processes and skills seem to be affected by the attentional dysfunctions outlined, but nevertheless the impression should not be gained that what has been described is more than a segment of the total abnormality displayed by the schizophrenic patient.

## References

Abramson, H. A., Jarvik, M. E., & Hirsch, M. W. L.S.D. 25 $\overline{X}$ Effect on RT to auditory and visual stimuli. *J. Psychol.*, 1955, **40**, 39-52.

Agnew, N., & Agnew, M. Drive level effects on tasks of narrow and broad attention. *Quart. J. exp. Psychol.*, 1963, **15**, 58-62.

Allison, T. Recovery functions of somatosensory evoked responses in man. *EEG clin. Neurophysiol.*, 1962, **14**, 331-343.

Ashman, G. R. Binary choice learning strategies in schizophrenics. Paper read at Am. Psychol. Assoc. meeting, Cincinnati, Ohio, 1959.

Bahrick, H. P., Fitts, P. M., & Rankin, R. E. Effect of incentives upon reactions to peripheral stimuli. *J. exp. Psychol.*, 1952, **44**, 400-406.

Bharucha-Reid, R. P. The internal modulating system and stress: a neurophysiological model. *J. Gen. Psychol.*, 1962, **66**, 147-158.

Boardman, W. K., Aldrick, R. C., Reiner, M. L., & Goldstone, S. The effect of anchors upon apparent length. *J. gen. Psychol.*, 1959, **61**, 45-49.

Boardman, W. K., Goldstone, S., Reiner, M. L., & Fathauer, W. F. Anchor effects spatial judgment and schizophrenia. *J. abnorm. soc. Psychol.*, 1962, **65**, 273-276.

Boring, E. G. Size constancy and Emmerts Law. *Amer. J. Psychol.*, 1940, **53**, 293-295.

Bradley, R. B., & Elkes, J. Effect of some drugs on the electrical activity of the brain. *Brain*, 1957, **80**, 77-117.

Brown, G. W. Length of hospital stay and schizophrenia: a review of statistical studies. *Acta psychiat. et neurol. Scand.*, 1960, **35**, 414-430.

Callaway, E. The influence of amobarbital (amylobarbitone) and methamphetamine on the focus of attention. *J. ment. Sci.*, 1959, **105**, 382-392.

Callaway, E., & Band, R. I. Some psychopharmacological effects of atropine. *Arch. Neurol. Psychiat.*, 1958, **79**, 91-102.

Callaway, E., & Dembo, D. Narrowed attention: a psychological phenomenon that accompanies a certain physiological change. *Arch. Neurol. Psychiat.*, 1958, **79**, 74-90.

Callaway, E., & Stone, G. Re-evaluating the focus of attention. In L. Uhr & J. G. Miller (Eds.), *Drugs and behavior.* New York: Wiley, 1960.

Callaway, E., & Thompson, S. V. Sympathetic activity and perception. *Psychosom. Med.*, 1953, **15**, 443-455.

Carson, R. C. Intralist similarity and verbal rote learning performance of schizophrenics and cortically damaged patients. *J. abn. soc. Psychol.*, 1958, **57**, 99-106.

Cleveland, S. E., Reitman, E. E., & Bentinck, C. Therapeutic effectiveness of sensory deprivation. *Arch. Gen. Psychiat.*, 1963, **8**, 455-460.

Conrad, K. *Die beginnende Schizophrenie.* Stuttgart, Germany: Thieme, 1958.

Davis, D. R. The disorganization of behavior in fatigue. *J. Neurol. Psychiat.*, 1946, **9**, 23-29. (a)

Davis, D. R. Neurotic predisposition and disorganization observed in experiments with the Cambridge cockpit. *J. Neurol. Psychiat.*, 1946, **9**, 119-124. (b)

Davis, J. M., McCourt, W. F., & Solomon, P. The effect of visual stimulation on hallucinations and other mental experiences during sensory deprivation. *Amer. J. Psychiat.*, 1959-1960, **116**, 889-892.

Drew, G. C. Mental fatigue. *Flying Personnel Research Committee*, 1940, Rep. No. 227.

Drew, G. C. The study of accidents. (Presidential address to the British Psychological Society), *Bull Brit. Psychol. Soc.*, 1963, **16** (52), 1-10.

Dunn, W. L. Visual discrimination of schizophrenic subjects as a function of stimulus meaning. *J. Pers.*, 1954, **23**, 48-64.

Easterbrook, J. A. The effect of emotion on cue utilization and the organization of behavior. *Psychol. Rev.*, 1959, **66**, 183-200.

Edwards, W. Apparent size of after images under conditions of reduction. *Amer. J. Psychol.*, 1953, **66**, 449-455.

Federn, P. *Ego psychology and the psychoses.* London: Imago, 1953.

Fedio, P., Mirsky, A. F., Smith, W. J., & Parry, D. Reaction time and EEG activation in normal and schizophrenic subjects. *EEG clin. Neurophysiol.*, 1961, **13**, 923-926.

Feinberg, I., & Garman, E. M. Studies of thought disorder in schizophrenia. *Arch. Gen. Psychiat.*, 1961, **4**, 191-201.

Fish, F. A neurophysiological theory of schizophrenia. *J. ment. Sci.*, 1961, **107**, 828-838.

Fulcher, J. H., Gallagher, W. J., & Pfeiffer, C. C. Comparative lucid intervals after amobarbital $CO_2$ and arecoline in chronic schizophrenics. *Arch. Neurol. Psychiat.*, 1957, **78**, 392-395.

Funkenstein, D. H., Greenblatt, M., & Solomon, H. C. Psychophysiological study of mentally ill patients. Part I: the status of the peripheral autonomic nervous system as determined by the reaction to epinephrine and mecholyl. *Amer. J. Psychiat.*, 1949, **106**, 18-28.

Garmezy, N. Stimulus differentiation by schizophrenic and normal subjects under conditions of reward and punishment. *J. Pers.*, 1951, **20**, 253-276.

Gellhorn, E., & Miller, A. D. Methacholine and Noradrenaline tests. *Arch. Gen. Psychiat.*, 1961, **4**, 371-380.

Gibby, R. G., Adams, H. B., & Carrera, R. N. Therapeutic changes in psychiatric patients following partial sensory deprivation. *Arch. Gen. Psychiat.*, 1960, **3**, 33-42.

Goldstein, K., & Scheerer, M. Abstract and concrete behavior: an experimental study with special tests. *Psychol. Monogr.*, 1941, **50**, No. 2.

Greenberg, A. Directed and undirected learning in chronic schizophrenia. Unpublished Ph.D. Thesis, Columbia Univer., New York, 1953.

Gromoll, H. F. The process-reactive dimension of schizophrenia in relation to cortical activation and arousal. Unpublished Ph.D. Thesis, Univer. of Illinois, Urbana, 1961.

Hake, H. H., & Hyman, H. R. Perception of the statistical structure of binary symbols. *J. exp. Psychol.*, 1953, **45**, 64-74.

Hamilton, V. Size constancy and cue responsiveness in psychosis. *Brit. J. Psychol.*, 1963, **54**, 25-39.

Harris, A. Sensory deprivation and schizophrenia. *J. ment. Sci.*, 1959, **105**, 235-236.

Hartman, A. M. The apparent size of after images in delusional and nondelusional schizophrenics. *Amer. J. Psychol.*, 1962, **75**, 587-595.

Hebb, D. O. *The organization of behavior.* London: Chapman & Hall, 1949.

Herrington, R. N., & Claridge, G. S. Personal communication, 1963.

Hoffer, A., & Osmond, H. F. Schizophrenia—an autonomic disease. *J. nerv. ment. Dis.*, 1955, **122**, 448-452.

Holway, A. H., & Boring, E. G. Determinants of apparent visual size with distance variant. *Amer. J. Psychol.*, 1941, **54**, 21-37.

Hull, C. L. *Principles of behavior.* New York: Appleton-Century-Crofts, 1943.

Hunt, J. McV., & Cofer, C. N. Psychological deficit. In J. McV. Hunt (Ed.), *Personality and the behavior disorders.* New York: Ronald Press, 1944, pp. 971-1032.

Huston, P. E., & Senf, R. Psychopathology of schizophrenia and depression. I: Effect of amytal and amphetamine sulphate on level and maintenance of attention. *Amer. J. Psychiat.,* 1952, **109**, 131-138.

Huston, P. E., & Singer, M. M. Effect of sodium amytal and amphetamine sulphate on mental set in schizophrenia. *Arch. Neurol. Psychiat.,* 1945, **53**, 365-369.

Kaplan, S. D. Autonomic visual regulation. *Psychiat. Res. Rep.,* 1960, **12**, 104-114.

Kinsey, A. C., Pomeroy, W. B., Martin, C. E., and Gebbard, P. H. *Sexual behavior of the human female.* Philadelphia, Pennsylvania: Saunders, 1953.

Klein, G. S. Need and regulation. In M. R. Jones (Ed.), *Nebraska Symposium on Motivation.* Lincoln: Univer. of Nebraska Press, 1954, pp. 224-274.

Knopf, I. J., & Fager, R. E. Differences in gradients of stimulus generalization as a function of psychiatric disorder. *J. abn. soc. Psychol.,* 1959, **59**, 73-76.

Kohn, H. Effects of variation of intensity of experimentally induced stress situations upon certain aspects of perception and performance. *J. genet. Psychol.,* 1954, **85**, 289-304.

Lansing, R. W., Schwartz, E., & Lindsley, D. B. Reaction time and EEG activation. *J. exp. Psychol.,* 1959, **58**, 1-10.

Leibowitz, H. W., & Pishkin, V. Perceptual size constancy in schizophrenia. *J. consult. Psychol.,* 1961, **25**, 196-199.

Lewinsohn, P. M., & Elwood, D. L. The role of contextual constraint in the learning of language samples in schizophrenia. *J. nerv. ment. Dis.,* 1961, **133**, 79-81.

Lhamon, W. T., & Goldstone, S. The time sense. Estimation of one second duration by schizophrenic patients. *Arch. Neurol. Psychiat.,* 1956, **76**, 625-629.

Lindemann, E. Psychological changes in normal and abnormal individuals under the influence of sodium amytal. *Amer. J. Psychiat.,* 1932, **11**, 1083-1091.

Lindsley, D. B. The reticular formation and perceptual discrimination. In H. H. Jasper, L. D. Proctor, R. S. Knighton, W. C. Noshay, & R. T. Costello (Eds.), *Reticular formation of the brain.* London: Churchill, 1958.

Lovinger, E. Perceptual contact with reality in schizophrenia. *J. abn. soc. Psychol.,* 1956, **52**, 87-91.

McGhie, A., & Chapman, J. S. Disorders of attention and perception in early schizophrenia. *Brit. J. med. Psychol.,* 1961, **34**, 103-116.

Malmo, R. B., Shagass, C., & Smith, A. A. Responsiveness in chronic schizophrenia. *J. Pers.,* 1951, **19**, 359-375.

Mednick, S. A. Distortions in the gradient of stimulus generalization related to cortical brain damage and schizophrenia. *J. abn. soc. Psychol.,* 1955, **51**, 536-542.

Mednick, S. A. A learning theory approach to research in schizophrenia. *Psychol. Bull.,* 1958, **55**, 316-327.

Mednick, S. A., & DeVito, R. Associative competition and verbal learning in schizophrenia. Paper read at Eastern Psychological Assoc. Meeting, Philadelphia, 1958.

Miller, G. A., & Selfridge, J. Verbal context and recall of meaningful material. *Amer. J. Psychol.,* 1950, **63**, 176-185.

Nelson, S., & Caldwell, W. E. Perception of affective stimuli by normal and schizophrenic subjects in a depth perception task. *J. Gen. Psychol.,* 1962, **67**, 323-335.

Osgood, C. E. Motivational dynamics of language behavior. In M. R. Jones (Ed.), *Nebraska symposium on motivation.* Lincoln: Univer. of Nebraska Press, 1957.

Payne, R. W. Cognitive abnormalities. In H. J. Eysenck (Ed.), *Handbook of abnormal psychology.* New York: Basic Books, 1961.

Payne, R. W. An object classification test as a measure of overinclusive thinking in schizophrenic patients. *Brit. J. soc. clin. Psychol.,* 1962, **1**, 213-221.

Payne, R. W., & Friedlander, D. A short battery of simple tests for measuring overinclusive thinking. *J. ment. Sci.,* 1962, **108**, 362-367.

Payne, R. W., Matussek, P., & George, E. I. An experimental study of schizophrenic thought disorder. *J. ment. Sci.,* 1959, **105**, 627-652.

Pearl, D. Language processing ability of process and reactive schizophrenics. *J. Psychol.,* 1963, **55**, 419-425.

Raush, H. L. Perceptual constancy in schizophrenia. *J. Pers.,* 1952, **21**, 176-187.

Rinkel, M., DeShon, H. J., Hyde, R. W., & Solomon, H. Experimental schizophrenia like symptoms. *Amer. J. Psychiat.,* 1952, **108**, 572-578.

Rodnick, E. H., & Shakow, D. Set in the schizophrenic as measured by a composite reaction time index. *Amer. J. Psychiat.,* 1940, **97**, 214-225.

Rosenthal, D., Lawlor, W. G., Zahn, T. P., & Shakow, D. The relationship of some aspects of mental set to degrees of schizophrenic disorganization. *J. Pers.,* 1960, **28**, 26-38.

Rosenzweig, N. A mechanism in schizophrenia. *Arch. Neurol. Psychiat.,* 1955, **74**, 544-555.

Rosenzweig, N. Sensory deprivation and schizophrenia: some clinical and theoretical similarities. *Amer. J. Psychiat.,* 1959-1960, **116**, 326-329.

Rump, E. E. A note on "Distance constancy in schizophrenic patients." *J. ment. Sci.,* 1961, **107**, 48-51. (a)

Rump, E. E. The relationship between perceived size and perceived distance. *Brit. J. Psychol.,* 1961, **52**, 111-124. (b)

Salzinger, K. Shift on judgment of weights as a function of anchoring stimuli and instructions in early schizophrenics and normals. *J. abn. soc. Psychol.,* 1957, **55**, 43-49.

Samuels, I. Reticular mechanisms and behavior. *Psychol. Bull.,* 1959, **56**, 1-25.

Schwartz, M., & Shagass, C. Reticular modification of somatosensory cortical recovery function. *EEG clin. Neurophysiol.,* 1963, **15**, 265-271.

Shagass, C. Drug thresholds as indicators of personality and affect. In L. Uhr & J. G. Miller (Eds.), *Drugs and behavior.* New York: Wiley, 1960.

Shagass, C., & Schwartz, M. Cerebral responsiveness in psychiatric patients. *Arch. Gen. Psychiat.,* 1963, **8**, 177-189. (a)

Shagass, C., & Schwartz, M. Psychiatric disorder and deviant cerebral responsiveness to sensory stimulation. *Recent advances in biol. Psychiat.,* 1963, **5**, 321-330. (b)

Shakow, D. Segmental set. *Arch. Gen. Psychiat.,* 1962, **6**, 1-17.

Shakow, D. Psychological deficit in schizophrenia. *Behavioral Sci.,* 1963, **8**, 275-305.

Shannon, C. E. Prediction and entropy of printed English. *Bell Syst. Tech. J.,* 1951, **30**, 50-64.

Silverman, A. J., Cohen, S. I., & Shmavonian, B. M. Investigation of psychophysiologic relationships with skin resistance measures. *J. Psychosom. Res.,* 1959, **4**, 65-87.

Silverman, J. Psychological deficit reduction in schizophrenia through response-contingent noxious re-inforcement. *Psychol. Rep.,* 1963, **13**, 187-210.

Smith, S., Thakurdas, H., & Lawes, T. G. G. Perceptual isolation and schizophrenia. *J. ment. Sci.,* 1961, **107**, 839-844.

Snygg, D., & Combs, A. W. *Individual behavior.* New York: Harper, 1949.

Spain, B. Personal communication, 1963.

Steriade, M., & Demetrescu, M. Reticular facilitation of responses to acoustic stimuli. *EEG clin. Neurophysiol.*, 1962, **14**, 21-36.

Stevens, J. M., & Derbyshire, A. J. Shifts along the alert-repose continuum during remission of catatonic stupor with amobarbital. *Psychosom. Med.*, 1958, **20**, 99-107.

Stevens, S. S. Decibels of light and sound. *Physics today*, 1955, **8**, 12-17.

Stevenson, J. A. F., Derrick, J. B., Hobbs, G. E., & Metcalfe, E. V. Adrenocortical response and phosphate excretion in schizophrenia. *Arch. Neurol. Psychiat.*, 1957, **78**, 312-320.

Stroop, J. R. Studies of interference in serial verbal reactions. *J. exp. Psychol.*, 1935, **18**, 643-661.

Sutton, S., & Zubin, J. Effect of sequence on reaction time in schizophrenia. Paper presented to International Colloquium on Biological Bases of Age Changes in the Speed of Behavior. Cambridge, England, 1963.

Sutton, S., Hakarem, G., Zubin, J., & Portnoy, M. The effect of shift of sensory modality on serial reaction time: a comparison of schizophrenics and normals. *Amer. J. Psychol.*, 1961, **74**, 224-232.

Teichner, W., H. Recent studies of simple reaction time. *Psychol. Bull.*, 1954, **51**, 128-149.

Thouless, R. H. Individual differences in phenomenal regression. *Brit. J. Psychol.*, 1932, **22**, 216-241.

Topping, G. G., & O'Connor, N. The response of chronic schizophrenics to incentives. *Brit. J. med. Psychol.*, 1960, **33**, 211-214.

Venables, P. H. A short scale for rating "activity-withdrawal" in schizophrenics. *J. ment. Sci.*, 1957, **103**, 197-199.

Venables, P. H. The effect of auditory and visual stimulation on the skin potential response of schizophrenics. *Brain*, 1960, **83**, 77-92.

Venables, P. H. Selectivity of attention, withdrawal, and cortical activation. *Arch. gen. Psychiat.*, 1963, **9**, 74-78. (a)

Venables, P. H. The relationship between level of skin potential and fusion of paired light flashes in schizophrenic and normal subjects. *J. Psychiat. Res.*, 1963, **1**, 279-287. (b)

Venables, P. H., & O'Connor, N. Reaction times to auditory and visual stimulation in schizophrenic and normal subjects. *Quart. J. exp. Psychol.*, 1959, **11**, 175-179.

Venables, P. H., & Tizard, J. Paradoxical effects in the reaction time of schizophrenics. *J. abn. soc. Psychol.*, 1956, **53**, 220-224.

Venables, P. H., & Tizard, J. The effect of auditory stimulus intensity on the reaction time of schizophrenics. *J. ment. Sci.*, 1958, **104**, 1160-1164.

Venables, P. H., & Wing, J. K. Level of arousal and the subclassification of schizophrenia. *Arch. gen. Psychiat.*, 1962, **7**, 114-119.

Weckowicz, T. E. Size constancy in schizophrenic patients. *J. ment. Sci.*, 1957, **103**, 475-486.

Weckowicz, T. E. Autonomic activity as measured by the mecholyl test and size constancy in schizophrenic patients. *Psychosom. Med.*, 1958, **20**, 66-71.

Weckowicz, T. E., & Blewett, D. B. Size constancy and abstract thinking in schizophrenic patients. *J. ment. Sci.*, 1959, **105**, 909-934.

Weckowicz, T. E., Sommer, R., & Hall, R. Distance constancy in schizophrenic patients. *J. ment. Sci.*, 1958, **104**, 1174-1182.

Weinstein, A. D., Goldstone, S., & Boardman, W. K. The effect of recent and remote frames of reference on temporal judgments of schizophrenic patients. *J. abn. soc. Psychol.*, 1958, **57**, 241-243.

Wells, F. L., & Kelley, C. M. The simple reaction in psychosis. *Amer. J. Psychiat.*, 1922, 2, 53-59.

Wertheimer, N., & Wertheimer, M. Capillary structure: its relation to psychiatric diagnosis and morphology. *J. nerv. ment. Dis.*, 1955, 122, 14-27.

Wilder, J. Modern psychophysiology and the law of the initial value. *Amer. J. Psychother.*, 1958, 12, 199-221.

Williams, M. Psychophysiological responsiveness to psychological stress in early chronic schizophrenic reactions. *Psychosom. Med.*, 1953, 15, 456-461.

Winer, H. R. Incidental learning in schizophrenics. Unpublished Ph.D. Thesis, Purdue Univer., Lafayette, Indiana, 1954.

Zahn, T. P., Rosenthal, D., & Lawlor, W. G. G.S.R. orienting reactions to visual and auditory stimuli in chronic schizophrenic and normal subjects. Paper read to Society for Psychophysiological Research, Denver, Colorado, 1962.

Zahn, T. P., Rosenthal, D., & Shakow, D. Effects of irregular preparatory intervals on reaction time in schizophrenia. *J. abn. soc. Psychol.*, 1963, 67, 44-52.

# A THEORY OF VERBAL BEHAVIOR IN SCHIZOPHRENIA[1]

*Loren J. Chapman, Jean P. Chapman, and Glenn A. Miller*

SOUTHERN ILLINOIS UNIVERSITY, CARBONDALE, ILLINOIS

## I. Theoretical Position

### A. GENERAL PRINCIPLE

Schizophrenics often misinterpret and misuse words in common discourse. Although this observation is commonplace, and despite the fact that several diverse clinical formulations of the phenomenon have gained popularity, very little has been done in the way of systematic exploration of the nature of these errors. The present paper reports three experiments that are directed toward testing predictions from one formulation which may account for many of these errors.

The theory which will be presented here was stimulated in part by earlier findings which indicate a close similarity between schizophrenic disorder of thought and normal error tendencies. There is a large literature which discusses the similarity between schizophrenic thought dis-

---

[1] This study was supported by research grants MH-03481 and MH-07306 from the National Institute of Mental Health, United States Public Health Service.

The authors are indebted to Dorothy Day, Nancy Scott, and Larry Lichenstein for assistance in gathering and analyzing the data. They are also indebted to William Lundin for assistance in obtaining the patients used in Experiments I and III, and to R. R. Knowles for assistance in obtaining those for Experiment II.

49

order and error tendencies of normal subjects under one or another of various special conditions which induce errors. These special conditions include sleep, psychotomimetic drugs, sensory deprivation, fatigue, relaxed attention, emotional excitement, and oxygen deprivation. However, the findings of a number of studies have indicated that a special condition is unnecessary. In a series of studies designed to measure clinically prominent features of the disorder, it was repeatedly found that the kinds of errors that were hypothesized to be features of schizophrenic disorder were also found in normal control subjects, although in reduced number. This was true of (1) associative intrusions into schizophrenic conceptual performance (Chapman, 1958), (2) the interpretation of common concepts in an excessively broad manner so as to include incorrect items which are similar to correct ones (Chapman and Taylor, 1957; Chapman, 1961), (3) the confusion of figurative and literal usages of common words and phrases (Chapman, 1960), and (4) the tendency to solve formal syllogisms by concluding an identity of objects which share a common quality (Chapman and Chapman, 1959; Gottesman and Chapman, 1960).

There are reasons for believing that these findings reflect an accentuated expression, in schizophrenia, of normal response biases. It is as if the response biases are released and expressed more freely. A response bias may be defined as a predisposition toward making a particular one of the various possible kinds of responses that one might make to a given stimulus (Underwood, 1952). It is called a "bias" because psychologists often define it by responses which are incorrect or inappropriate in the context in which they appear, but it may produce correct answers in those situations in which a biased response and the correct response coincide. [Campbell (1959) has catalogued a number of these biases.]

For both normal and schizophrenic persons, response biases act more strongly in situations in which other stimuli are not available as cues which limit the variety of responses that are appropriate. For example, one strong normal response bias is to respond to a word with its associate. (An associate here means that kind of response such as is given on a word association test.) The reader may observe for himself just how strong the associative bias is by trying to think of a list of other words that are *not* associatively related to a single stimulus word—he will probably find that one strong associative response after another comes to mind. In normal discourse the range of appropriate responses to a word is defined by the context in which the word appears. This context supplies a multitude of cues which guide the selection of the overt response to the word. This usually tends to eliminate associative responses. Nevertheless, associates occasionally intrude as inappropriate responses in normal speech. However, they occur far more freely if the contextual cues are reduced. For example, they occur in the word association test itself in which such contextual cues are minimal since the instruction for the test specifies that the S is to say the first word that comes to mind when he hears a single stimulus word. Associates are also abundant in the free association of normal persons, as on the psychoanalytic couch.

It appears clinically that many schizophrenics free-associate much of the time in place of more goal-directed discourse. Similarly, Chapman (1958) found that normal associates intrude as incorrect responses in schizophrenic conceptual performance more than in normal performance. The observation that for normal persons the associative bias is expressed more freely when constraining contextual cues are reduced suggests the possibility that a reason for the schizophrenic's excessive yielding to this normal response bias may be a lesser responsiveness to contextual cues. These are the cues which, for normal persons, guide the selection of appropriate responses in place of biased ones. For example, Bleuler's (1950, p. 26) patient who, in describing a walk with her family began with enumerating the members of her family, listed "Father, son" and then added, "and the Holy Ghost." The context of the sentence would have indicated to a normal person that the response "and the Holy Ghost" was inappropriate even though it would have been an appropriate response to "Father, son" in some other contexts. The utterance then may be seen as reflecting a lesser responsiveness to the contextual cues.

These considerations indicate that many features of the schizophrenic disorder of thought consist of an accentuated expression of those overt responses toward which normal subjects are biased. It seems likely that an elaboration of this principle will explain the schizophrenic misinter- pretation and misuse of the meanings of words. This elaboration was originally suggested by spontaneous comments that some schizophrenic and normal Ss made during testing when presented with items which asked whether two words have the same meaning. One item asked if *bicycle* means the same as *wagon*. The schizophrenics often said things like, "You can ride on a bicycle, and you can ride in a wagon, so they mean the same." Normal Ss would say something like, "You can ride on both a bicycle and in a wagon, but a bicycle has two wheels and a wagon has four, so they don't really mean the same." These responses suggested that schizophrenics do not weigh simultaneously the several different aspects of meaning in order to answer appropriately the question at hand, but instead answer by using a more limited number of aspects of the meaning. Moreover, the aspects of meaning which schizophrenics use to excess appear to be those which are more prominent for normal persons. The tendency to interpret a word in accordance with its most prominent aspect of meaning is a response bias in the same sense that the tendency to respond to a word with associates is a response bias. This may be illustrated most readily with a double-meaning word. If a normal person is asked for the meaning of the word *grain*, he is most likely to define it in terms of various food plants such as wheat or oats. However, if he encounters the word *grain* in the context of a sentence which contains appropriate cues, he will instead interpret it to mean the lines or markings in wood.

As will be seen below (Section I, C) one may infer from schizophrenics' misinterpretation of words a possible explanation of why they fail to respond to the contextual cues which, for normal persons, restrain the expression of response biases. But first we will present further considerations and data on this phenomenon of schizophrenic misinterpretations of the meanings of words.

Actually the phrase, "the meaning of a word," is somewhat inexact, since "meaning" does not reside in the spoken or written word itself, or its physical properties, but instead exists only as a response within the person who uses or encounters the word. It is probably clearer, therefore, in discussing research and theory concerning meaning, to speak of "meaning responses" instead of "aspects of meaning" of a word. A meaning response, according to this usage, is a hypothetical internal event which mediates a person's overt behavioral response to a word.

Several previous writers have used the term "meaning response" and some of them have offered measures designed to define it operationally. Some of these have been concerned with "affective" or "connotative" meaning as measured by the semantic differential (Osgood, Suci, and Tannenbaum, 1957). For example, if one is investigating the meaning of *dog*, the semantic differential would produce measures of how good or bad, how weak or strong, and how quick or slow the concept *dog* is felt to be. Other investigators have been concerned with association as a measure of meaning (Bousfield, Whitmarsh, and Danick, 1958; Deese, 1962). Associative measures of meaning might indicate that the aspects of meaning of *dog* include "cat."

These two approaches may yield valuable information about important varieties of "meaning," and the theory of this paper yields predictions which might be tested in terms of them. However, the present paper is primarily concerned with another variety of "meaning" which is usually called "denotative meaning." Denotative meaning is difficult to define, but it is what the layman usually means by the meaning of a word. It is the representative of the referent of the word, the objects or events to which it refers. When the referent is an object, the denotative meaning is in large part a description of the object. For example, the denotative meaning of *dog* includes "is an animal," "has four legs," etc. Meaning responses are measured by obtaining statements of meaning from judges. The judges are instructed to "tell what the thing named is, or what it is like," or to list "aspects of meaning" for the word. Evidence concerning relative strength of meaning responses is obtained either from the order in which the statements of meaning are listed, or by asking judges to rank order them. In this presentation, we are limiting the term "meaning responses" to internal events which represent the referents of a word, and "statements of meaning" to the overt responses that judges give to questions concerning the aspects of meaning of a word.

Stated in terms of meaning responses, the theory states that schizophrenics' misinterpretations of the meanings of words arise in part from mediation of overt responses to words by their strongest meaning responses with a relative neglect of their weaker meaning responses, while the interpretation of words by normal persons reflects the use of the weaker as well as the stronger meaning responses. It is assumed that meaning responses themselves are similar for schizophrenics and normals. Thus predictions of group tendencies in schizophrenic thinking are made using the average strength of the various statements of meaning offered by a group of normal judges. Variation among schizophrenics in their thinking disorder is predicted using variation in the statements of meaning by normal judges.

## B. Previous Work

Chapman and Chapman (1964) found support for this theory from a study of the characteristics of words which schizophrenics to an excessive extent regard as synonymous. The tendency of schizophrenics to regard some words of only moderate similarity as synonymous is a fairly striking feature of schizophrenic thought disorder, and it is manifested in their tendency to substitute words for one another in ways that normal persons do not. These words often have a similarity that normal persons recognize, but do not regard as sufficient to define the words as synonymous. The present theory states that schizophrenics tend to interpret words in accordance with the strongest meaning responses, neglecting weaker meaning responses. Therefore it predicts that the schizophrenic tendency to treat words of similar meaning as synonymous will occur more often on pairs for which the same meaning response is strongest for both of the two words. For example, 31 of 52 normal judges listed "is an animal" as the strongest statement of meaning for both *pig* and for *dog*. It follows from the theory that schizophrenics, more than normal subjects, should regard *pig* and *dog* as synonymous.

A contrasting word pair is *brassiere–tee shirt*. The five statements of meaning for *brassiere*, listed in order of rated strength, were "supports breasts," "is an undergarment," "clothing," "used by women," and "made of cloth." The five statements of meaning for *tee shirt* were "is clothing," "is an undergarment," "used by fellows (or men)," "made of cloth," and "is white." Although these two words have in common three of their five statements of meaning, only 13 of 52 normal judges ranked the same statement of meaning as first in strength for both of the two words. The prediction from the theory, therefore, was that schizophrenics would less often deviate from normal control Ss by calling pairs like *brassiere* and *tee shirt* synonymous than by calling pairs like *pig* and *dog* synonymous.

In order to test this formulation 38 pairs of words were dichotomized by the measure of the number of judges who ranked the same statement of meaning in first position of strength for both members of a word pair. In addition, ratings of degree of similarity between pairs of words were obtained in separate judgments. It was found that for words of the range of similarity represented in the study, the measure of shared high-strength meaning responses had little relationship to degree of similarity. Similarity may either consist of several low-strength shared meaning responses or of a single high-strength meaning response. For example, *pig–dog* and *brassiere–tee shirt* were close on rated similarity despite their disparity on shared high-strength meaning responses. Two 19-item sets of word pairs were obtained which differed on whether their shared meaning responses were high strength or low strength.

The tendency to respond to word pairs as if they were synonymous was measured by items of the following format:

7. "Pig" means the same as
   A. stocking
   B. dog
   C. neither of the above.

The schizophrenics were found to exceed the normal subjects on the difference between the number of pairs of the two sets which were called the same ($p < .001$). The schizophrenics judged as synonymous more pairs of high-strength shared meaning response than low-strength pairs ($p < .03$), while the normals showed qualitatively the opposite pattern. These differences were found to be independent of the rated similarity between the pairs of words. These findings indicate that schizophrenics are more likely to show an abnormal propensity for regarding two words as synonymous if the words have the same strongest meaning response in common. The findings support the contention that schizophrenics' overt responses are mediated to an excess by the stronger normal meaning responses, with a relative neglect of weaker meaning responses.

## C. PREDICTIONS

We have restricted the definition of meaning responses to internal events which represent the denotative referents of a word. Meaning responses to the specific words which are being interpreted are only one variety of mediating response. As mentioned previously other external stimuli from the context in which the word appears also have an influence on which of the several meaning responses to a word are used to mediate the overt response. The most important of these contextual cues are other words. (However, they also include such stimuli as vocal qualities and gestures.) Presumably, these contextual cues also act through internal mediating responses. As discussed above (Section 1, A), it appears that schizophrenics often fail to respond to the contextual cues which have a restraining influence on the expression of response biases for normal persons. The present findings and theory indicate a possible explanation for this. It seems likely that the schizophrenic excessive use of the strongest meaning responses also holds for other types of mediating responses, such as those aroused by contextual cues, instructions, etc. It was found that schizophrenics tend to mediate their responses to a word only by the strongest normal meaning response, neglecting the weaker. It would then appear reasonable to assume that there is a general propensity to use the strongest normal mediating response with a neglect of the weaker whether the mediating response is a meaning response or is instead another kind of mediating response. The mediating response to each such contextual cue which guides the selection of overt responses may frequently be weak in comparison to the mediating response which evokes the biased overt response. For example, if a person is asked to interpret the meaning of the word *rare* in the statement, "Robert says he likes rare meat," the word *meat* provides a weak contextual cue which for normal persons indicates that the correct meaning is "partially cooked" rather than "uncommon," which is a stronger meaning for rare when contextual cues are absent. The theory predicts that it is in cases such as this, in which the contextual cues are weak, that schizophrenics fail to use these cues. Instead they interpret words in accordance with the meaning responses to the words which are strongest when the words are encountered out of context. The frequent failure of schizophrenics to use contextual cues would then be seen as one manifestation of the tendency to guide behavior by the strongest normal mediating response. It follows that in situations in which the contextual cues are stronger schizophrenics will use them more often and their performance will approach that of normals. (Experiment III, below, will provide some evidence on this.)

Thus restated, the theory postulates that schizophrenics' misinterpretations of the meanings of words arise in part from mediation of behavior by the strongest normal mediating responses with a relative neglect of weaker mediating responses. It should be noted that this theory does not attempt to account for the deviant performance of schizophrenics on verbal tasks by postulating a qualitative difference in the mediating responses. Instead the theory assumes that the mediating responses of schizophrenics show a marked similarity to those of normal persons. The theory states that much schizophrenic misinterpretation of words reflects an excessive reliance on the mediating responses which are strongest for normal persons. Strength, as referred to in this paper, always applies to the degree of relationship between a stimulus and a response, but following the convention of behavior theorists, we will occasionally refer to it in terms of strength of cues or strength of responses. In all cases, however, it is the strength of the "bond" between stimulus and response that is implied.

The assumption of the similarity of schizophrenics and normal persons in the content and relative strength of meaning responses was investigated in a pilot study. Statements of meaning to 20 common words were obtained from a group of 20 chronic schizophrenics and a group of 22 normal control subjects of similar age and education. Of these 20 words, 15 had more than one meaning and 5 had only a single meaning. It was found that for 19 of these 20 words, the statement of meaning which was most frequently given by the normal group was also the statement of meaning most frequently given by the schizophrenics. As a further check on the comparability of the two groups, each subject was given a score, for the 15 multimeaning words, of the number of first position statements of meanings that coincided with the meaning most commonly given by the normal group as a whole. The mean of these scores was 13.5 for the schizophrenics and 13.7 for the normals. The difference was not significant ($t = .46$; $p = .64$). These results lend strong support to the assumption that schizophrenics and normals have a similar hierarchy of meaning responses to common words.

It should also be noted that the theory offers no exact specifications of the nature of the interaction of schizophrenia with mediating responses. The hypothesized excess in schizophrenia of overt responses mediated by the strongest mediating responses could be accounted for by several alternative formulations concerning the corresponding internal events. It could be explained by a strengthening of the strong mediating responses, or by a weakening of the weak mediating responses, or by a multiplication of the strength of both strong and weak mediating responses, or by a selective failure to respond to weak mediating responses, or by some selective inhibitory process. There is no evidence at present for choosing among these alternative explanations. In addition, even if one could arrive at such a specific formulation in terms of mediating responses, one could not assume an isomorphic representation of this pattern in overt behavior.

One of the predictions from the theory in terms of data is that schizophrenics, much more than normals, will interpret words in accordance with the strongest normal mediating responses whether or not these are appropriate. This means that their errors will be more numerous when the correct overt response is mediated by a weak mediating response, as measured by normal group judgments, and these errors will consist of interpreting the word in accordance with a strong normal mediating response. When the correct overt response is mediated by the strongest normal mediating response, schizophrenic accuracy will approach that of normals. Although this differential error propensity will be found for both schizophrenics and normals, it will be greater for schizophrenics. Moreover, these effects will be greater when normal judges show greater agreement as to which is the strongest mediating response.

## II. Experimental Investigations

### A. METHOD AND SUBJECTS

The present paper reports three studies which tested these predictions. All three studies used, as a research tool, words which have more than one meaning in ordinary usage. For example, *a pen* means both "a writing implement" and "a fenced enclosure." The first of these is by far the stronger of the two meanings, as shown by our measures of strength of meaning response. While the theory is intended to apply to the use of all words by schizophrenics, its implications can be conveniently tested with multimeaning words.

These three experiments were not performed in the order in which they are presented, and for all of them the data, except the measures of strength of meaning responses, were gathered prior to the formulation of the theory.

### 1. Schizophrenic Subjects

The patients in all three studies were long-term chronic schizophrenics who were not receiving drug therapy. They were all native-born white male patients whose last admission had been no more recent than 6 months, and most of whom had spent many years in the hospital. No patient was included who showed, either by interview or by examination of the hospital records, indications of brain damage or mental deficiency, or who had received electric shock or insulin shock therapy in the previous 3 months, or "tranquilizing" drugs for the previous 4 weeks. The patients used in Experiments I and III were from a group of patients at Chicago State Hospital who were being maintained without drugs for purposes of other research. The patients in Experiment II were at Kentucky State Hospital in Danville.

For several years now a major obstacle to conducting meaningful research on schizophrenic thinking has been that many hospitalized schizophrenics are kept on maintenance dosages of one or another of the phenothiazines, commonly chlorpromazine. Since the phenothiazines markedly affect clinical symptoms, they might also be expected to affect performance on any research task which reflects psychopathology. A number of studies have tested for drug effects on psychological measures and most have found them. Some of these have found the phenothiazine improves performance on a given measure, while other studies have found that it impairs performance. Chapman and Knowles (1964) have shown recently that phenothiazines produce an increase in some kinds of cognitive errors, and a decrease in others. They found that the drugs exacerbate errors that might be described as unsystematic, careless, or random, but reduce those that reflect a misinterpretation of common concepts in an overly broad manner. The latter kind of error is a striking feature of the disorder of thought in schizophrenia and is probably highly akin to some of the kinds of errors that were studied in the present research. It seems clear from these results that patients receiving the phenothiazines are an unsuitable group for the study of schizophrenic thought disorder.

It is also undesirable to use those patients that the hospital personnel find can be conveniently maintained without drugs without a worsening of the symptoms. Chapman (1963) has shown that selection of such patients can bias the results of research concerned with intellectual functioning in schizophrenia since patients whose symptoms worsen with the withdrawal of phenothiazine tend to be those with the more severe cognitive disorder. The present investigators were fortunate in being able to obtain for all of these studies chronic schizophrenics who were maintained off drugs regardless of their symptoms. Thus a major source of potential bias in the data was avoided.

Another source of possible bias that could not be completely avoided was the exclusion from the study of patients who were unable or unwilling to complete testing. Although this bias is, of course, unavoidable, it was somewhat reduced in the present studies by the use of tests of very simple format, and by extended efforts to develop rapport with the patients over a period of weeks.

## 2. Normal Subjects

The normal control $S$s in Experiments I and III were City of Chicago firemen. Those in Experiment II were hired from among maintenance workers at the University of Kentucky, and from among unemployed workers at the Kentucky Employment Service. Although the $S$s from the Employment Service were currently unemployed, no one

TABLE I

MEAN AND VARIANCE OF AGE, EDUCATION, AND STANFORD–BINET VOCABULARY SCORE
FOR TOTAL GROUPS AND SUBGROUPS MATCHED ON VOCABULARY

|  | $N$ | Age | | Education | | Vocabulary | |
|---|---|---|---|---|---|---|---|
|  |  | $\overline{X}$ | $s^2$ | $\overline{X}$ | $s^2$ | $\overline{X}$ | $s^2$ |
| **Experiment I** | | | | | | | |
| Total groups | | | | | | | |
| Normal | 27 | 43.2 | 36.6 | 10.6 | 5.2 | 21.7 | 29.2 |
| Schizophrenic | 25 | 44.4 | 47.6 | 10.7 | 4.0 | 20.3$a$ | 52.2$a$ |
| **Experiment II** | | | | | | | |
| Total groups | | | | | | | |
| Normal | 22 | 40.4 | 93.3 | 10.7 | 9.8 | 23.2 | 20.6 |
| Schizophrenic | 49 | 47.3 | 67.6 | 9.8 | 11.6 | 16.4$b$ | 35.3$b$ |
| Matched subgroups | | | | | | | |
| Normal | 15 | 39.6 | 100.0 | 10.9 | 11.2 | 22.1 | 21.2 |
| Schizophrenic | 15 | 51.2 | 33.2 | 11.6 | 16.4 | 22.1 | 20.8 |
| **Experiment III** | | | | | | | |
| Total groups | | | | | | | |
| Normal | 25 | 38.7 | 58.4 | 11.0 | 2.5 | 23.9$c$ | 29.6$c$ |
| Schizophrenic | 27 | 45.3 | 16.5 | 10.0 | 5.7 | 19.8$d$ | 58.5$d$ |
| Matched subgroups | | | | | | | |
| Normal | 20 | 38.4 | 48.4 | 11.0 | 2.4 | 22.8 | 20.7 |
| Schizophrenic | 20 | 46.4 | 11.3 | 9.8 | 5.6 | 22.9 | 21.7 |

$a$ Information on only 21 subjects.
$b$ Information on only 44 subjects.
$c$ Information on only 22 subjects.
$d$ Information on only 25 subjects.

was included who had not held a job for at least 6 months during the previous year. A number of them were currently out of work during the winter months, but normally worked steadily in the building trades during warmer weather. The normal control $S$s of Experiment II were paid either $5.00 or $10.00 to participate in a number of experiments including the present ones. The patients for whom they were controls were not paid cash but were given a package of cigarettes or a package of chewing tobacco for each test taken. There were no such payments in Experiments I and III.

Table I shows the mean age, education, and vocabulary score for the schizophrenic and control groups for each of the three studies.

## B. Experiment I.  Misinterpretation in Context

Experiment I was used to test predictions concerning the misinterpretation of double-meaning words which are presented in context.

There are many common English words which have more than one meaning in everyday usage. For example, the word *rare* may mean either "uncommon" or "partially cooked" and a person who receives a communication which includes the word *rare* must decide which meaning is intended on the basis of cues obtained from the context in which the word appears. These cues may be strong or weak or—to state it in terms of mediating responses—they may evoke strong or weak mediating responses. As will be seen below, the present study was concerned with words presented in sentences which contain only weak cues.

When a multimeaning word is encountered alone, i.e., outside the context of other words, the various meanings differ in salience, i.e., the meaning responses which convey the various meanings differ in strength.

If schizophrenics have an inadequate response to weak cues provided by the context in which a multimeaning word appears, their interpretation of multimeaning words in sentences with such weak cues should show an excessive reliance on those meaning responses which are strongest when the words are encountered out of context. Hence, when the correct interpretation of a word in a sentence is consistent with a relatively weak meaning response, schizophrenics should misinterpret the word, and their misinterpretation should be one mediated by a stronger meaning response. This kind of error should exceed the opposite error of making an inappropriate interpretation mediated by a weaker meaning response when a stronger one is appropriate.

*Method.* Items were constructed around two common meanings of multimeaning words in the following format.

21. When the farmer bought a herd of cattle, he needed a new pen.
This means:
    A. He needed a new writing implement.
    B. He needed a new fenced enclosure.
    C. He needed a new pick-up truck.

Here the correct answer is intended to be alternative "B," although the answer in alternative "A" is mediated by the stronger meaning response to *pen*. This item was paralleled by the following item.

40. The professor loaned his pen to Barbara.
This means:
    A. He loaned her a pick-up truck.
    B. He loaned her a writing implement.
    C. He loaned her a fenced enclosure.

Here the correct answer was intended to be alternative "B," and alternative "C" contains a possible misinterpretation mediated by the weaker meaning response. It should be noted in item 21 above that the cues from the context are related somewhat weakly to the meaning responses to *pen*. For example, stronger cues would be given for the weaker meaning of *pen* by the statement, "The farmer put his cattle in the pen." All of the items of the present study were constructed so as to make the cue strength as weak as possible but still of sufficient strength to indicate the correct choice to normal persons.

It is seen that in addition to the alternatives representing the correct and the incorrect meanings of the word there is a third alternative in each item which is unrelated to the word *pen*. This alternative, called here "the unidentified error alternative," was included as a measure of "random" responses, i.e., some Ss might mark either of the other two alternatives for reasons other than their understanding of the statement that they are asked to interpret. For example, schizophrenics might be uncooperative or have difficulty taking the test and so might mark randomly. Such random marking should result as often in the marking of the unidentified error alternative as in marking of the other two alternatives. Therefore, on items measuring misinterpretations mediated by the stronger meaning responses, the number of unidentified error alternatives for each S was subtracted from the number of markings of the alternatives representing the stronger meaning responses, to obtain a corrected measure of the predicted error tendency. A similar correction was used with items measuring misinterpretations mediated by the weaker meaning responses. These corrected scores were used in all analyses of the data.

At test of 38 items was constructed in the format of the above items. It consisted of one item for each of two meanings of 19 double- or multimeaning words. Table II lists the 19 words together with phrases which indicate the two meanings represented in the alternatives.

Evidence concerning the relative strength of the two meanings of each multimeaning word was obtained by presenting a list of the words to a group of normal judges (39 students in introductory psychology), with the instruction: "What is the first aspect of meaning you think of for each of the following words, what is the second, and what is the third?" The resultant statements of meaning were weighted in the following manner. When a statement of meaning was given first, it received a weight of "3"; when it was given second, a "2"; when given third, a "1"; and when not given at all, zero weight. The weights for each statement of meaning of a word were averaged across Ss, which yielded an index of relative strength by which the two meanings in the test could be compared.

TABLE II

THE WORDS USED IN EXPERIMENT I, THE MEAN WEIGHTED SCORES FOR THE TWO
MEANINGS, AND PERCENTAGE OF THE JUDGES WHO AGREED ON WHICH
IS STRONGER

| | Weighted score[a] | Percentage agreement on which is stronger |
|---|---|---|
| **Rare** | | |
| 1. Partially cooked | 1.15 | 76 |
| 30. Uncommon | 2.64 | |
| **Tip** | | |
| 2. Private information | .77 | 73 |
| 34. Money | 1.59 | |
| **Diamonds** | | |
| 3. Red spots on playing cards | .03 | 97 |
| 36. Precious stones | 2.82 | |
| **Cross** | | |
| 5. A religious symbol | 1.49 | 89 |
| 28. An X mark | .28 | |
| **Yard** | | |
| 6. A grassy place | 2.44 | 69 |
| 29. Three feet | 1.54 | |
| **Board** | | |
| 7. Meals | .69 | 89 |
| 32. Flat piece of wood | 2.62 | |
| **Corn** | | |
| 8. A little lump on someone's foot | .13 | 100 |
| 35. Plants in a field | 3.00 | |
| **Pen** | | |
| 21. A fenced enclosure | .72 | 97 |
| 40. Writing implement | 2.90 | |
| **Palms** | | |
| 22. Part of a person's hands | 2.03 | 50 |
| 39. Plants or trees | 2.23 | |
| **Crack** | | |
| 23. Hole or crevice in a wall | 2.46 | 92 |
| 45. A sarcastic remark | .49 | |
| **Pit** | | |
| 24. Hole in the ground | 2.79 | 92 |
| 44. Hard stone of a fruit | .67 | |
| **Toast** | | |
| 27. A drink in honor of someone | 1.85 | 70 |
| 43. Heated and browned bread | 2.54 | |
| **Bats** | | |
| 11. Flying animals | 1.54 | 64 |
| 33. Wooden sticks | 2.28 | |
| **Deck** | | |
| 14. Part of ship | 2.92 | 92 |
| 38. A pack of playing cards | .92 | |

TABLE II (Continued)

|  | Weighted score[a] | Percentage agreement on which is stronger |
|---|---|---|
| **Date** | | |
| 15. Appointment to take a girl out | 1.72 | 92 |
| 37. A piece of fruit from a palm tree | .51 | |
| **Racket** | | |
| 16. Noise | 1.26 | 52 |
| 25. Dishonest business | 1.03 | |
| **Bark** | | |
| 17. Sound made by a dog | 2.23 | 53 |
| 42. Outer covering of a tree | 2.41 | |
| **Bank** | | |
| 19. A financial establishment | 2.85 | 87 |
| 41. Side of a river | 1.56 | |
| **Fall** | | |
| 20. A season of the year | 1.05 | 90 |
| 47. To trip and hurt oneself | 2.82 | |

[a] Higher score means stronger meaning.

Table II shows the mean strength of the two meanings represented by the alternatives in the test items, together with the percentage of judges who concurred in the group decision as to which is strongest. As seen there, the judges showed high agreement for some words, and lower for some others.

The prediction was that schizophrenics, more often than normal Ss, would make misinterpretations mediated by the stronger normal meaning response when the weaker meaning response was appropriate in the context of the sentence in which the word appeared. However, one would also expect schizophrenics sometimes to make misinterpretations mediated by a meaning response which according to the group norms is weaker than the correct one. This should occur because, as seen in Table II, there is not complete uniformity among people as to which is the stronger meaning response. However, misinterpretations in this direction should be fewer than those in the predicted direction, and they should occur more often on the words for which the judges show lower agreement as to which is the stronger meaning.

*Results.* The means of the corrected scores for misinterpretations mediated by the stronger and by the weaker meaning responses are shown in Table III. These data were analyzed using $t$ tests. Double-tailed probability values are reported. The schizophrenics exceeded the normal Ss in the wrong interpretations mediated by stronger meaning responses ($z = 5.13$; $p < .001$) and in wrong interpretations mediated by weaker meaning responses ($z = 2.46$; $p < .02$). However, on a score of the difference between the scores for the two kinds of misinterpretation the schizophrenics again exceeded the normal Ss ($z = 4.22$; $p < .001$), owing to the schizophrenics' differentially greater reliance on the stronger meaning responses.

### TABLE III
#### MEAN NUMBER OF MISINTERPRETATIONS MEDIATED BY STRONGER AND WEAKER MEANING RESPONSES

|  | Total groups | |
| --- | --- | --- |
|  | Schizophrenic | Normal |
| Stronger | 3.80 | .89 |
| Weaker | 1.24 | .44 |
| Strong minus Weak | 2.56 | .45 |

Superficially, the finding that the schizophrenics exceeded the normal Ss in misinterpretations mediated by weaker meaning responses might appear contradictory to the theory. This finding is nevertheless consistent with the theory if the items which contributed to the difference were those on which the judges were less unanimous as to which is the stronger meaning. The logic is that if a meaning response which is weaker by the group judgmental norms is nevertheless the stronger of the two meaning responses to this word for a minority of the judges, it is also stronger for a minority of the schizophrenics. To test this, the 19 items for which the weaker meaning response mediated the correct answer were divided into two sets, 10 for which the judges had relatively high agreement (89% to 100%) on which was stronger, and 9 for which the judges had relatively low agreement (50% to 87%). (The items in these sets may be identified in Table II). As seen in Table IV, the dif-

### TABLE IV
#### MEAN NUMBER OF MISINTERPRETATIONS MEDIATED BY WEAKER MEANINGS FOR 10 ITEMS WITH HIGH AGREEMENT ON RELATIVE STRENGTH AND 9 ITEMS WITH LOW AGREEMENT

|  | Schizophrenic | Normal |
| --- | --- | --- |
| Low Agreement | 1.00 | .22 |
| High Agreement | .24 | .22 |

ference between the normal and schizophrenic Ss on misinterpretations mediated by weaker meaning responses was almost completely accounted for by the nine items on which the judges tended to disagree. The difference between groups was significant ($z = 2.79$; $p < .01$) for these nine items. For the remaining 10 items on which the judges showed high agreement on the relative strength of the two meanings, schizophrenic and normal Ss were almost identical on the score of misinterpretation mediated by weaker meaning responses, as predicted by the theory.

One might wonder whether the finding that schizophrenic misinterpretations are mediated more by stronger meaning responses than by weaker ones might merely reflect a lower intellectual functioning of the schizophrenics. Disturbed chronic schizophrenics show a lowered ability in handling any complex task—even a vocabulary test like the present one. The items were such that when the wrong interpretations were mediated by stronger meaning responses, the correct interpretations were mediated by weaker ones. It may require greater intellectual ability to distinguish the correct answer when it requires mediation by a weaker meaning response than when it requires a stronger one. In order to check on this possibility, it seemed most suitable to use another vocabulary test since the experimental instrument was itself a vocabulary test.

It was possible to obtain Stanford–Binet vocabulary scores for all of the normal Ss and for 21 of the 25 schizophrenics (the remaining four patients being untestable on this instrument). It is most appropriate to test for the relationship in the normal group alone, since the lower vocabulary score of the schizophrenics may reflect inability to take the test in addition to lowered knowledge of words. For normal Ss the score, for the entire test, of the difference between the two kinds of misinterpretation had only a slight nonsignificant relationship to Stanford–Binet vocabulary score ($r = -.13$) in the direction of a high difference score tending to accompany a low vocabulary score. Further evidence against the importance of vocabulary skill in accounting for the results is that the mean Stanford–Binet vocabulary score for the 21 schizophrenics was, as shown in Table I, only slightly lower than that of the normal Ss, and the difference did not approach significance ($z = .75$; $p = .46$). Nevertheless, in order to make certain that the difference between normal and schizophrenic groups on the difference score was independent of vocabulary skill, an analysis of covariance using both normal and schizophrenic Ss was computed in which the effects of Stanford–Binet vocabulary were partialed out. The schizophrenic and normal groups were again found to differ in the predicted direction on the difference score ($F = 22.59$; $df = 1.45$; $p < .001$).

It seems clear, therefore, that we are justified in concluding not only that schizophrenics' excessive misinterpretations of double-meaning words are more often mediated by the stronger than by the weaker meaning responses, but that in addition this error propensity cannot be attributed to lowered vocabulary skill.

## C. Experiment II. Errors of Exclusion from Common Concepts

While schizophrenic thought disorder has many striking features, perhaps the most widely discussed feature of all is the difficulty in assigning objects to common conceptual classes. The better known discussions of this difficulty include those by Cameron (1939), Goldstein and Scheerer (1941), Hanfmann and Kasanin (1942), McGaughran and Moran (1956), and Vigotsky (1934). It may be that some errors of schizophrenics in the assigning of objects to common conceptual classes arise from reliance on the strongest normal meaning responses either to the name of the conceptual classes or to the names of the objects. The present study investigates only the first of these, errors which reflect excessive reliance on a strong meaning response to a class name, with a neglect of weaker ones.

The conceptual class names used were selected from the many common conceptual classes having more than one meaning. For example, the word *head* may mean either the head of an animate thing, such as of a man or a horse, or the head of an inanimate thing, such as of a nail, a match, or a hammer. However, the animate meaning is the stronger of these two meaning responses to *head*. It was hypothesized that when asked to sort the names of objects into such double-meaning conceptual classes, schizophrenics more than normals would interpret the concepts solely in accordance with the stronger normal meaning response to each class name and would exclude examples mediated by the weaker meaning response.

*Method.* The S was required to sort a series of cards, each marked with the name of one object on it, into two piles—those which belonged in a certain named conceptual class, and those which did not.

Two boxes with slots in the top were placed in front of the S. A guide card naming the conceptual class was attached to the top of each box.

For Task A, the guide card on one box said *"Things that have a head"* and on the other box, *"Things that do not have a head."* The sorting cards were of three types, names of living things that have a head (such as *dog* and *horse*), names of inanimate objects that have a head (such as *nail* and *pin*), and irrelevant items.

Task A: The response cards for the concept of *"Things that have a head"* were:

  *animate:*   dog, mouse, horse, pig, cat, sheep, cow, goat.
  *inanimate:* pin, spear, match, nail, spike, hammer, screw, arrow.
  *irrelevant:* sheet, blanket, napkin, tablecloth, quilt, towel, bath mat, dish rag.

Task B: The response cards for the concept of *"Things that have legs"* were:

  *animate:*   cow, mouse, rat, horse, goat, cat, lion, pig.
  *inanimate:* chair, bed, piano stool, table, sofa, foot stool, bench, desk.

*irrelevant:* pear, banana, peach, apple, orange, grape, pineapple, lemon.

Task C: The response cards for the concept of *"Things that have teeth"* were:

*animate:* dog, horse, cow, lion, man, alligator.

*inanimate:* zippers, saw, rake, comb, bear trap, barbers' clippers.

*irrelevant:* hickory, oak, pine, birch, cedar, maple.

Task D: The response cards for the concept of *"Things that have skin"* were:

*animate:* goat, elephant, horse, pig, dog, cow, sheep, cat, man, rat.

*inanimate:* apricot, prune, tomato, potato, apple, cherry, banana, peach, pear, plum.

*irrelevant:* sled, television set, baseball bat, golf clubs, playing cards, ice skates, radio, checkers, marbles, bowling ball.

Evidence concerning differences in strength of meaning responses to each of these four class names was obtained in the same manner as described in Experiment I. Twenty students in an introductory psychology course were used as judges. Each judge was asked to give aspects of meaning for *head, legs, teeth,* and *skin.* The judges almost uniformly interpreted all four concepts primarily in terms of the animate examples, although the other meanings were sometimes given. All 20 students gave as their first response a meaning indicating an interpretation in terms of the animate meaning for *head,* for *legs,* and for *teeth,* while 17 of the 20 did so for *skin.*

The prediction was that schizophrenics, more than normals, would tend to respond to the class names on the experimental instrument in terms of the animate meaning only, and therefore, more than normals would exclude names of inanimate examples from the conceptual classes.

However, random placements would be expected to inflate the number of exclusions of both types by the schizophrenics. For example, schizophrenics would be expected more often than normals to sort carelessly, or to have difficulty reading the cards, or to sort according to box position. Such errors should result in excluding both animate and inanimate representatives from the named conceptual class even though such "random" errors do not truly reflect the patients' interpretation of the conceptual class. The number of "irrelevant" cards placed in the named conceptual class was used as a measure of such random error in the same manner as the number of markings of "unidentified error alternatives" was used in Experiment I as a correction for random marking. Corrected scores of animate exclusions and inanimate exclusions were computed by subtracting the number of the incorrect placements of the irrelevant cards from the number of both the animate and inanimate exclusions.

*Results.* Between-group comparisons were made using a *t* test. Probability values corresponding to double-tailed tests are reported.

The mean corrected scores of animate and inanimate exclusions are shown in Table V. The results were very much as hypothesized. As seen

TABLE V

MEAN CORRECTED SCORE OF EXCLUSIONS OF ANIMATE AND INANIMATE
REPRESENTATIVES FROM THE CONCEPTUAL CLASSES

|  | Schizophrenic | Normal |
|---|---|---|
| Animate | .16 | .19 |
| Inanimate | 11.61 | 3.81 |

in Table V, the schizophrenics exceeded the normal $S$s on the number of exclusions of the inanimate representatives from the named class ($z = 3.07$; $p < .01$) but were about equal to the normal subjects on exclusions of the animate members. The score of the difference between the number of the two kinds of exclusions distinguished the two groups ($z = 4.06$; $p < .001$). This indicates that the schizophrenics tended more than the normal $S$s to narrow their interpretation of the conceptual classes to that one interpretation mediated by the strongest normal meaning response.

As a check on whether these results might reflect lowered vocabulary ability in schizophrenia, the difference score was correlated with Stanford–Binet vocabulary score for the normal $S$s. The correlation was .03, which indicates that no relationship exists and the schizophrenic error pattern was not a reflection of lowered knowledge of vocabulary. Using subgroups matched on vocabulary score, the schizophrenics were again found to exceed the normals on this difference score ($z = 2.82$; $p < .01$).

## D. EXPERIMENT III. THE INFLUENCE OF STRONG CONTEXTUAL CUES

Since in the experiments presented above the patients' performance showed some failure of mediation by the weaker meaning responses, one might wonder whether this reflected an absolute loss, in at least some of the patients, of ability to produce responses mediated by some of the weaker meaning responses regardless of the contextual cues. According to the theory, this is not the case. The theory states that the deficit in performance arises from an excessive reliance on the strongest mediating responses regardless of whether the mediating responses are aroused by the word itself or by a contextual cue. Therefore, it follows that if the contextual cues that indicate the appropriateness of the weaker meaning response are extremely strong, and contextual cues for using the strongest meaning response are absent, the schizophrenics' use of the weaker meaning response will approach that of the normals. If, contrary to the theory, schizophrenia is accompanied by an absolute loss of some weaker meaning responses, then schizophrenics should show a deficit in their use regardless of the context. Experiment III provides a comparison of schizophrenic and normal performance on ability to use weaker meaning responses under these conditions.

*Method.* The task used was a multiple-choice vocabulary test for double-meaning words. The task required $S$ to select the correct meaning from among four alternatives, of which the first two alternatives included both a correct and an incorrect answer, the third stated "neither of the above," and the fourth, "I don't know." There were two items for each multimeaning word, one for each of two meanings. For example, the word *bear* was presented in two items.

28. The word *bear* may mean:
    A. to carry
    B. to command
    C. neither of the above
    D. I don't know.
64. The word *bear* may mean:
    A. a sharp end
    B. an animal
    C. neither of the above
    D. I don't know.

The meanings corresponding to the stronger and weaker meaning responses and their relative strength were identified by the same procedure as used in Experiment I. This measure indicated that the meaning of *bear* corresponding to the stronger meaning response is that of "animal." If some schizophrenics have an absolute loss of some of the weaker meaning responses, the schizophrenic group should show lower accuracy than normal $S$s on items calling for weaker meaning responses to words than on items calling for stronger ones. However, the presentation of the statement of the weaker meaning as one of the alternatives furnishes an extremely strong contextual cue which indicates that the correct response is mediated by that weaker meaning response. The choice of the alternative corresponding to the weaker meaning is actually mediated by a very strong mediating response in this case. Therefore, the theory predicts that schizophrenics would use this strong mediating response to give the correct answer corresponding to the weaker meaning.

The experimental instrument consisted of 130 items of which 74 (the experimental items) were constructed from 37 double- or multimeaning words, i.e., 2 items per multimeaning word. There were also 46 items constructed for single-meaning words and 10 filler items for

TABLE VI

THE WORDS USED IN EXPERIMENT III AND THE MEAN WEIGHTED SCORES
FOR THE TWO MEANINGS

|  | Weighted score[a] |
|---|---|
| **Barrel** | |
| 1. Metal tube on a gun | .36 |
| 31. Large container | 2.85 |
| **Ruler** | |
| 2. Measuring stick | 2.28 |
| 32. A person who governs | 1.59 |
| **Trunk** | |
| 6. Part of an elephant | .56 |
| 42. The main stem of a tree | .59 |
| **Deal** | |
| 7. A bargain | 2.56 |
| 44. To pass out playing cards | 1.62 |
| **Log** | |
| 9. Piece of wood | 2.87 |
| 43. The daily record of a ship's voyage | .67 |
| **Deck** | |
| 70. A pack of playing cards | .92 |
| 90. The floor of a ship | 2.92 |
| **Date** | |
| 88. A sweet fruit from a kind of palm tree | .51 |
| 126. Appointment with a girl | 1.72 |
| **Spring** | |
| 26. A season of the year | 2.15 |
| 52. To leap or jump | .69 |
| **Run** | |
| 27. To move the legs quickly | 2.92 |
| 53. To be a candidate for election | .05 |
| **Bear** | |
| 28. To carry | .36 |
| 64. An animal | 2.72 |
| **Board** | |
| 38. A flat piece of wood | 2.62 |
| 63. Meals provided for pay | .69 |
| **House** | |
| 41. A building in which people live | 2.92 |
| 74. An assembly for making laws | .05 |
| **Note** | |
| 46. A very short letter | 2.49 |
| 73. A musical sign | .38 |
| **Jar** | |
| 48. A container, as of glass | 2.49 |
| 81. To shake or rattle | 1.15 |

TABLE VI (*Continued*)

|  | Weighted score[a] |
|---|---|
| **Seal** | |
| 51. A kind of sea animal with flippers | 1.10 |
| 77. A design stamped on a piece of paper | .28 |
| **Plate** | |
| 57. A dish | 2.85 |
| 85. The home base in baseball | .15 |
| **Mars** | |
| 60. A planet | 2.82 |
| 83. A god of war | .31 |
| **Point** | |
| 61. A sharp end | 1.85 |
| 87. To aim | 1.18 |
| **Pole** | |
| 66. A long slender piece of wood | 2.59 |
| 98. An end of a magnet | .64 |
| **Star** | |
| 67. A heavenly body | 2.92 |
| 97. An outstanding movie actor | .23 |
| **Top** | |
| 71. The highest point or part | 2.82 |
| 124. A toy that spins on a point | .28 |
| **Bolt** | |
| 78. To run away | 1.03 |
| 123. A strong pin of metal or wood | 1.87 |
| **Hail** | |
| 79. A shout of welcome | 1.62 |
| 129. Frozen rain | 1.82 |
| **Count** | |
| 82. A European nobleman | 1.03 |
| 122. To add up | 2.69 |
| **Sign** | |
| 84. To write one's name | 1.62 |
| 125. A billboard | 2.03 |
| **Club** | |
| 89. A heavy stick | 2.08 |
| 110. A social group | 2.44 |
| **Iron** | |
| 92. A metal | 1.90 |
| 108. To press clothing | 1.64 |
| **Bowl** | |
| 93. A hollow rounded dish | 2.18 |
| 109. To play a game with a ball and pins | 1.23 |
| **Box** | |
| 94. A container | 2.87 |
| 116. To fight with the fists | .64 |

TABLE VI (*Continued*)

| | Weighted score[a] |
|---|---|
| **Horn** | |
| 99. A growth on the head of cattle and deer | .36 |
| 115. A kind of musical instrument | 2.82 |
| **Fire** | |
| 100. A flame | 3.00 |
| 114. To discharge from a job | .15 |
| **Lock** | |
| 101. A portion of hair | .08 |
| 117. A means of fastening doors | 2.90 |
| **Saw** | |
| 102. Looked at | .82 |
| 119. A tool for cutting | 2.46 |
| **Fine** | |
| 104. A sum of money paid as a punishment | 1.82 |
| 127. Excellent | 2.15 |
| **Light** | |
| 105. Not heavy | .26 |
| 128. To set fire to | .13 |
| **Racket** | |
| 111. A loud noise | 1.26 |
| 121. A dishonest way of making money | 1.03 |
| **Grain** | |
| 112. Seed of plants, like wheat | 2.62 |
| 120. Little lines and markings in wood | .54 |

[a] Higher score means stronger meaning.

which a correct alternative was not listed among the four alternatives. The latter two kinds of items were included to prevent Ss from discovering the nature of the task and to reduce the set for never marking the last two alternatives. Table VI lists the 37 words used in the experimental items, together with the meanings offered in the alternatives, and the mean strength of the two meanings.

*Results.* For this task, unlike those of Experiments I and II and the earlier study reported in Section I, B, the score measuring differential use of stronger and weaker meanings was related to vocabulary skill in normal Ss. The correlation of Stanford–Binet vocabulary score with the difference between the number of errors on the items requiring use of weaker and stronger meanings for the normal Ss was $-.48$ ($p < .05$), which means that the brighter Ss showed less difference in their error scores on the two kinds of items. As seen in Table I, the schizophrenics scored slightly lower than the normal Ss on Stanford–Binet vocabulary. It seemed inappropriate, therefore, to use the entire normal and schizophrenic groups in testing for the experimental effect since the predicted difference might be found simply as a reflection of the lowered vocabulary skill of the patients. For this reason, the experimental effects were evaluated using subgroups of 20 normal and 20 schizophrenic Ss closely matched on Stanford–Binet vocabulary score, as shown in Table I.

Table VII shows the median number of errors for these matched subgroups on the items calling for answers mediated by stronger and weaker meaning responses. As seen there, the scores were quite similar for the two groups, although qualitatively the pattern of scores was slightly in the direction opposite to that which would result from a schizophrenic loss of weaker meanings. The difference between the groups on the number of weaker meanings failed minus the number of stronger meanings failed did not approach significance ($z = .18$; $p = .95$) as determined by a double-tailed Mann–Whitney test.

TABLE VII

MEDIAN ERROR SCORES ON ITEMS FOR WHICH STRONGER AND WEAKER
MEANING RESPONSES YIELD CORRECT ANSWERS

|  | Schizophrenic | Normal |
|---|---|---|
| Stronger | .79 | .70 |
| Weaker | 2.07 | 2.21 |

These results are in striking contrast to those obtained in Experiments I and II. It appeared possible that this difference in results could be a consequence of differences in the stimulus words instead of the hypothesized differences in strength of contextual cues. For example, if the weaker meanings of the words in Experiment III were not quite as weak as those in Experiment I, the schizophrenics might show less difference between the two kinds of items in Experiment III for that reason alone. This possibility can be evaluated by examining the mean strength of the stronger and weaker meaning responses as listed in Tables II and VI. In Experiment I, the mean strengths of the stronger and weaker meanings were 2.41 and 1.01, respectively; in Experiment III, 2.33 and .77, respectively. Thus, in Experiment III, the weaker meanings are qualitatively weaker (.77 as compared with 1.01) than in Experiment I and the difference in the stronger and weaker meanings is greater for Experiment III (1.56 compared to 1.40). These differences in relative strength are slightly in the direction opposite to that which might account for the differences in the results. Therefore, it seems most likely that the differences in the results obtained with the two tasks are attributable to the differences in the strength of the contextual cues.

These findings are inconsistent with the interpretation that schizophrenics have lost access to weaker meaning responses. However, the findings do support the contention of the present theory that schizophrenics' overt responses, more than those of normal persons, are mediated by the strongest mediating responses, regardless of whether they are aroused by the stimulus words or by contextual cues.

## III. Discussion

Although the theory emerged from other research (Chapman and Chapman, 1964), the primary data of these three studies were gathered prior to the formulation of the theory, and only the measures of meaning responses were gathered with the theory in mind. Therefore, it was not possible to design the experiments so as to maximize the hypothesized effects. It would have been easier to support the theory using only those double-meaning words for which there is a sharp differentiation between the strengths of strong and weak meaning responses. Also, ideally, the same stimulus words should have been used in Experiments I and III. However, the support of the theory by the data is perhaps more convincing since they were not gathered in a manner designed to support it.

The theory generates predictions, enumerated below, concerning the conditions under which a wide range of well-known features of schizophrenic disorder of thought will occur and will not occur. Insofar as these predictions should be confirmed in future research, we will be able to conclude that the theory subsumes these various features of thought disorder under a single explanatory principle.

In the studies reported in the present paper it was found that the theory predicts the ways in which schizophrenics misinterpret double-meaning words presented in context. This kind of misinterpretation is very similar to the confusion of usages of words and phrases which have both a literal and figurative (or metaphoric) usage. This kind of confusion has recently received extensive attention from psychopathologists. Bateson, Jackson, Haley, and Weakland (1956) view the confusion of metaphoric and literal usages as an important feature of schizophrenic thinking. The present theory would predict that schizophrenics will make such misinterpretations under the same conditions as they misinterpret other double-meaning words, i.e., they will choose the interpretation mediated by the strongest normal mediating response regardless of whether it is figurative or literal.

Several investigators have been interested in the observation that schizophrenics seem to have a special difficulty understanding humor. A great many jokes are dependent on double meanings of words, and seeing the point of the joke requires mediation of overt response by both strong and weak meanings of the word. The theory, therefore, yields clear predictions concerning what kinds of jokes schizophrenics should have special difficulty in understanding.

The theory also generates predictions which may resolve a seeming contradiction between clinical observations and experimental evidence concerning errors in syllogistic reasoning. Both von Domarus (1944) and Arieti (1955) have reported that an especially striking feature of schizophrenic disorder of thought is a tendency to conclude, in syllogistic reasoning, that two objects are identical if they share a common quality. However, Gottesman and Chapman (1960) found no differences between schizophrenics and normals on a measure of such errors. The present theory would predict that the von Domarus error is stronger in schizophrenics than in normal subjects only when the quality shared by the two objects corresponds to a strong mediating response to each of them. This was not the case for the syllogisms used in the Gottesman and Chapman study. If further research indicates that the von Domarus phenomena occur only when the shared quality corresponds to a high-strength meaning response, it will appear that such phenomena are better accounted for by the present theory.

The theory also predicts that schizophrenics should show abnormally great semantic generalization or abnormally great transfer in a verbal learning task across some kinds of words and not others. The heightened semantic generalization or transfer should occur across pairs of words which share meaning responses of highest strength but which also have other meaning responses which are not shared. For pairs of words which do not fit this specification, schizophrenics should not show excessive semantic generalization or transfer effects.

The theory also accounts for some of the behaviors, such as schizophrenics show on conceptual sorting tests, which are called "concrete" thinking by various writers, e.g., Goldstein and Scheerer (1941). For example, on one task of the object-sorting test the subject is instructed to sort objects together which "belong together," and on another task he is presented objects already grouped together and is asked, "Why do these objects belong together?" The theory predicts that schizophrenics' sorting on the first task and explanations of belonging-ness in the second will be mediated to an abnormal degree by the strongest meaning responses to the objects. This means that the schizophrenics' grouping of objects and the principle of sorting that they offer in response to a question concerning belongingness should show medi-ation by normal meaning response of highest strength regardless of whether the response would be labeled "abstract" or "concrete." For example, the theory predicts that schizophrenics will show an excessive use of sensory qualities only for sets of objects to which the strongest normal mediating response is that sensory quality.

The data of Experiment II showed that schizophrenics' interpretation of the conceptual class name in accordance with its strongest meaning response may produce errors of overexclusion of objects from the conceptual class. The theory may also account for errors which appear superficially to be an opposite kind of error, that is, errors of overinclusion, and it again predicts the kinds of items on which such errors will occur. Schizophrenics should exceed normal persons in the inappropriate inclusion of names of objects in a conceptual class when the strongest normal meaning response is shared by the incorrect objects and objects that properly belong in the conceptual class.

Another advantage of the present theory is that it might be used to make predictions concerning individual differences among schizophrenics as to the items on which they make various errors. This could be done by obtaining meaning responses from the patients themselves for the words or objects which are used on the tests.

In comparison to other theories of disordered thought in schizophrenia, the present theory is both broad in the range of its predictions and precise in the nature of its predictions. It is precise in that it predicts a certain kind of error for each situation, and predicts the kind of stimuli with which that kind of error will appear and will not appear. A major virtue of the theory is that its predictions are readily amenable to experimental test.

Even if all of these predictions should be confirmed, the present writers would not wish to claim that the theory accounts for *every* deviant verbal production of schizophrenics. It may be that other principles, as well as the present one, are necessary to produce an adequate descriptive system. Also, while the theory and data presented here have been in terms of meaning responses held in common by both schizophrenics and normals, it is possible that in addition schizophrenia produces some increase of deviant meaning responses. Also, this theory does not go beyond description to attempt an explanation of the etiology of the disorder. Nevertheless, the usual first step in understanding a disorder is to describe it, and the chief attraction of the present theory is the promise that it holds for reducing the number of principles necessary for that description.

## References

Arieti, S. *Interpretation of schizophrenia.* New York: Robert Brunner, 1955.

Bateson, G., Jackson, D. D., Haley, J., and Weakland, J. H. Toward a theory of schizophrenia. *Behav. Sci.*, 1956, 1, 251-264.

Bleuler, E. *Dementia praecox or the group of schizophrenias.* Translated by Joseph Zinkin. New York: International Univer. Press, 1950. Originally published 1911.

Bousfield, W. A., Whitmarsh, G. A., and Danick, J. J. Partial response identities in verbal generalization. *Psychol. Rep.*, 1958, 4, 703-713.

Cameron, N. Schizophrenic thinking in a problem-solving situation. *J. ment. Sci.*, 1939, **85**, 1012-1035.

Campbell, D. T. Systematic error on the part of human links in communication systems. *Information and Control*, 1958, **1**, 334-369.

Chapman, L. J. Intrusion of associative responses into schizophrenic conceptual performance. *J. abnorm. soc. Psychol.*, 1958, **56**, 374-379.

Chapman, L. J. Confusion of figurative and literal usages of words by schizophrenics and brain-damaged patients. *J. abnorm. soc. Psychol.*, 1960, **60**, 412-416.

Chapman, L. J. A re-interpretation of some pathological disturbances in conceptual breadth. *J. abnorm. soc. Psychol.*, 1961, **62**, 514-519.

Chapman, L. J. The problem of selecting drug-free schizophrenics for research. *J. consult. Psychol.*, 1963, **27**, 540-542.

Chapman, L. J., and Chapman, Jean P. Atmosphere effect re-examined. *J. exp. Psychol.*, 1959, **58**, 220-226.

Chapman, L. J., and Chapman, Jean P. The interpretation of words in schizophrenia. *J. abnorm. soc. Psychol.*, in press, scheduled for publication in 1964.

Chapman, L. J., and Knowles, R. R. The effects of phenothiazine on disordered thought in schizophrenia. *J. consult. Psychol.*, 1964, **28**, 165-169.

Chapman, L. J., and Taylor, Janet A. Breadth of deviate concepts used by schizophrenics. *J. abnorm. soc. Psychol.*, 1957, **54**, 118-123.

Deese, J. On the structure of associative meaning. *Psychol. Rev.*, 1962, **69**, 161-175.

Goldstein, K., and Scheerer, M. Abstract and concrete behavior: an experimental study with special tests. *Psychol. Monogr.*, 1941, **53**, No. 2, Whole No. 239.

Gottesman, L., and Chapman, L. J. Syllogistic reasoning errors in schizophrenia. *J. consult. Psychol.*, 1960, **24**, 250-255.

Hanfmann, E., and Kasanin, J. Conceptual thinking in schizophrenia. *Nerv. ment. Dis. Monogr.*, 1942, No. 67.

McGaughran, L. S., and Moran, L. J. "Conceptual level" vs. "conceptual area" analysis of object-sorting behavior of schizophrenic and non-psychiatric groups. *J. abnorm. soc. Psychol.*, 1956, **52**, 43-50.

Osgood, C. E., Suci, G. J., and Tannenbaum, P. H. *The measurement of meaning.* Urbana: Univer. Illinois Press, 1957.

Underwood, B. J. An orientation for research on thinking. *Psych. Rev.*, 1952, **59**, 209-220.

Vigotsky, I. S. Thought in schizophrenia. *Arch. Neurol. Psychiat.*, 1934, **31**, 1063-1077.

von Domarus, E. The specific laws of logic in schizophrenia. In J. S. Kasanin (Ed.), *Language and thought in schizophrenia.* Berkeley: Univer. California, 1944, pp. 104-113.

# THE EFFECT OF THE EXPERIMENTER ON THE RESULTS OF PSYCHOLOGICAL RESEARCH[1]

*Robert Rosenthal*

HARVARD UNIVERSITY, CAMBRIDGE, MASSACHUSETTS

The purpose of this paper is to invite consideration of the experimenter himself as a source of variance in the results of psychological experiments. As different as experiments may be from one another with respect to purposes, procedures, and subject sampling, they all have in common that someone must collect the data—the experimenter or his surrogate. To the extent that the experimenter himself may be a significant determinant of the results of his research, it may become necessary to re-evaluate carefully the results of experiments completed and the design of experiments proposed.

---

[1] Most of the studies summarized were supported by research grants (G-17685, G-24826, GS-177) from the National Science Foundation.

We may distinguish two broad types of effects which experimenters may have upon their results: (1) those which operate without directly affecting the subjects of the experiment and (2) those which lead to subjects changing the nature of their responses.

## I. Effects Not Altering Subjects' Responses

### A. OBSERVER EFFECTS

In one way or another the experimenter must observe the subjects' responses. By observer "effects" or "error" we mean over- or underestimation of some criterion value. When two observers disagree in an observation, each may be said to err with respect to the other. Both may be said to err with respect to some third observation which may, for various reasons, be a more or less usefully employed criterion. Given a population of observations, we may choose to define their mean value as the "true" value and regard all observations not falling at the mean as being more or less in error as a direct function of their distance from the mean.

Observer errors or effects may be distinguished from observer "bias" by the fact that observer errors are randomly distributed around a "true" or "criterion" value. Biased observations tend to be consistently too high or too low and may bear some relation to some characteristics of the observer (Roe, 1961), the observation situation (Pearson, 1902), or both.

In considering the act or sequence of acts constituting the observation in the scientific enterprise, we may distinguish conceptually among locations of error or bias. The error of "apprehending" occurs when some sort of misrecording occurs between the event observed and the observer of the event. We may include here such diverse sources of apprehending error as differing angles of observation (George, 1938), imperfections in the sensory apparatus, relay systems, cortical projection areas, and the like. The error of recording may be conceptually distinguished from the apprehending error. We assume an errorless act of apprehending but a transcription of the event to paper, to the ear of another observer, or to another instrument which differs from the event as correctly apprehended. In actual practice, of course, when an event or observation is recorded in error with respect to some criterion, we cannot locate the error as having occurred in apprehending, in transcribing, or in both processes. There is no way we can isolate an apprehending error unconfounded with a recording error. Computational errors are more clearly distinguishable from the foregoing errors since they involve the incorrect manipulation of recorded events. Incorrectness is usually defined here by the formal rules of arithmetic operations.

The magnitude and extent of observer effects are well known in the history of science (Rosenthal, 1963a). In our own discipline, Boring (1950) has made us particularly aware of observer variance by his discussion of the personal equation of the astronomers. Most contemporary discussions of observer effects, however, seem to have become more perfunctory. Reference is made to modern instrumentation which may serve to eliminate observer error. That observer effect may be reduced by mechanical means seems reasonable enough. That instrumentation may not eliminate observer effect must also be considered. If the instrument be a dial, it must be read by a human observer. If the instrument be a computer, the printout must likewise be read by an observer. Observer effect or variability in the reading of scales was well noted by Yule (1927). A general error tendency which he found was the inclination to read scales to quarters of intervals rather than to tenths. Empirical analysis of his own observer effect revealed to Yule his tendency to avoid the number 7 as a final digit and to favor the numbers 8, 9, 0, and 2. Yule, incidentally, was relatively optimistic that proper training could eliminate observer error. The equally reknowned methodologist R. A. Fisher (1936) did not, however, seem to share this optimism.

There have been few investigations of observer effects in the psychological experiment. A notable exception was the work of Sheffield, Kaufman, and Rhine (1952). In an experiment in psychokinesis, they filmed the actual fall of the dice which subjects were trying to influence. They found subjects believing in the phenomenon to make tallying errors in favor of the hypothesis. Subjects who disbelieved made the opposite type of tallying error.

Both recording as well as computational errors of experimenters were systematically and explicitly studied for a person perception task experiment (Rosenthal, Friedman, Johnson, Fode, Schill, White, and Vikan-Kline, in press). In that study, each subject wrote on a pad his rating of the degree of success or failure of persons pictured in photographs. The 30 experimenters of this study transcribed these ratings to a master data sheet during the course of their interaction with their subjects. A comparison of experimenters' transcriptions with subjects' recordings revealed only 20 errors out of 3000 data transcriptions. All errors were made by 12 of the 30 experimenters. Errors were not randomly distributed but tended to fall in the direction of the experimenters' hypotheses.

The computation task for the experimenter in the study under discussion was simply to sum the 20 ratings given him by each of his 5 subjects. Most experimenters erred computationally and nonrandomly so. Not only were more biased experimenters more likely to make computational errors in their favor; they also tended to make larger computational errors. In this same experiment, all subjects rated their experimenters on the variable of "honesty" during the conduct of the experiment. The mean rating was quite high on honesty and the range of ratings quite small. Experimenters could not actually have been "dishonest" even if they had been so inclined. During the experiment, the co-investigators had all experimenters under surveillance (a fact apparent to all experimenters). In spite of the restricted range of the ratings of the experimenters' honesty made by the subjects, these ratings predicted far better than chance whether the experimenter would subsequently favor himself more in the making of a computational error.

In the study under discussion, we found a significant correlation (.48, $p = .01$) between the occurrence of recording errors and the occurrence of computational errors. Thus, experimenters who erred in data transcription tended to err in data processing. However, those experimenters who erred in the direction of their hypothesis in their recording errors were not any more likely to err in the same direction in their computational errors. Numerical errors seemed then to be a consistent characteristic while directionality of error vis-a-vis hypothesis did not.

We should note here that the over-all effects of both recording and computational errors on the grand means of the different treatment conditions of the experiment were negligible. An occasional experimenter did have some real effect on the data he obtained; an effect which could be serious if an entire experiment depended on an experimenter who was prone to err numerically. Only rarely in the psychological literature, however, is attention called to a real or alleged numerical error (Hanley and Rokeach, 1956; Wolins, 1962).

### B. INTENTIONAL EFFECTS

Intentional error production on the part of the experimenter is probably as rare an event in the psychological experiment as it is in the sciences generally (Wilson, 1952; Shapiro, 1959; Turner, 1961). Nevertheless, any serious attempt at understanding the social psychology of psychological research must consider the occurrence, nature, and control of this type of experimenter effect.

In survey research the "cheater problem" is of sufficient importance to have occasioned a panel discussion of the problem in the *International Journal of Attitude and Opinion Research* (1947). Such workers as Blankenship, Connelly, Reed, Platten, and Trescott seem to agree that, though statistically infrequent, the cheating interviewer can affect the results of survey research, especially if the dishonest interviewer is responsible for a large segment of the data collected. Other workers calling attention to the cheating problem in survey research include Crespi (1945–1946), Mahalanobis (1946), and Cahalan, Tamulonis, and Verner (1947). One way in which the problem of intentional error in survey research differs from the problem in the sciences generally is in the status, career aspirations, and identifications of the data collectors. While most data in the sciences are gathered by professional scientists and their professional assistants, the interviewers in survey research are often part-time nonprofessionals with less education and less aspiration, if any, to identification with a scientific career role.

A similar situation exists in the laboratory exercises performed as part of undergraduate courses in experimental psychology. In such laboratory exercises the fabrication of data is commonplace and well known to instructors. Positive sanction is sometimes involved for the fabrication of "real-appearing" data. The same sort of fabrication occurs in undergraduate physics laboratory courses. Students in these undergraduate laboratory courses, like interviewers in survey research, do not generally have the same commitment to "science," however, that professional scientists or research assistants, scientists in the making, have. In two experiments carried out by undergraduate laboratory students, attempts were made to check the incidence of dishonesty. In both situations, the experiments performed were structured not as just "laboratory exercises" but rather as sources of "real data" to be used in the publications of "real scientists." In one of these experiments involving the learning of rats in Skinner boxes, several instances of data fabrication came to light (Rosenthal and Lawson, 1963). In the other experiment, through the use of participant observers, a somewhat more precise estimate of intentional error production was possible (Rosenthal and Fode, 1963a). In that study of discrimination learning in rats, no instances of actual data fabrication were noted, though it is remotely possible that they might have occurred. Rather, error production involved the use of prodding of animals on a number of occasions. These "errors" were randomly enough distributed over treatment conditions that the obtained means, and more importantly, the differences between means, were probably not seriously affected by their occurrence.

Somewhat closer to the situation of the professional, science-oriented, data collector is the situation described by Azrin, Holz, Ulrich, and Goldiamond (1961). They replicated a verbal conditioning study originally conducted by Verplanck (1955) and obtained results similar to his. In both studies, experimenters had been able to control the content of their subjects' verbal productions by verbal reinforcement. It developed, however, that the formal procedure for experimenters was such that, if followed, the experimental effects could not be demonstrated! A number of the experimenters, it was learned, had resorted to the fabrication of the data they believed the investigators to want.

### The Control of Intentional Errors

In discussing the control of intentional errors committed by survey interviewers, Crespi (1945–1946) stated that these errors were more a problem of morale than of morals. After discussing various ways of assessing the data for the likelihood of cheating, he returns to the theme that most of all, we need to know why data collectors cheat. Removal of the conditions motivating intentional error production seems to be the most valuable control of their occurrence. No method of *post hoc* analysis (*International Journal of Attitude and Opinion Research*, 1947) of whether cheating occurred can ever be a satisfactory substitute for eliminating the need to cheat.

Perhaps one long-range improvement in data-collector attitudes would be the revision of the current practice in undergraduate laboratory courses of telling students what data they will obtain. Better put a high reward on data honestly, if unskillfully, obtained than to reward the "correct" data, skillfully but dishonestly manufactured. There seems to be something unresearchman-like in telling students what they will find at the end of a journey whose purpose is really to confront a surprise.

## II. Effects Altering Subjects' Responses

### A. EXPERIMENTER ATTRIBUTES

There are now dozens of studies which show quite clearly that subjects' responses may be in part determined by the characteristics of the experimenter who is interacting with the subjects (Rosenthal, 1963b). The experimenter's sex, race, religion, status, likeability, and warmth all have been shown to affect subjects' responses. Prior acquaintance with subjects, adjustment, hostility, anxiety (Winkel and Sarason, in press), acquiescence, authoritarianism, and intelligence are other experimenter variables found to make a difference (Rosenthal, 1963b). A concrete example of a recent experiment investigating the effect of experimenter attributes follows.

The study employed 40 experimenters (almost all male) and 230 subjects, about half of them male and half of them female (Rosenthal, Persinger, Vikan-Kline, and Mulry, 1963e). Each experimenter requested about six subjects to rate the apparent success or failure of twenty persons pictured in photographs. Thirty-one of the forty experimenters took both the Marlowe-Crowne Social Desirability Scale and the Taylor Manifest Anxiety Scale before running their subjects. A correlation of .48 ($p = .02$)

was obtained between the experimenters' anxiety scores and the degree of success their subjects saw in the photos of faces. For these same experimenters, the correlation between their need for social approval as measured by the Marlowe-Crowne Scale and the ratings of success of the photos obtained from their subjects was —.32 ($p = .10$). Thus, subjects rated persons as more successful when in the presence of experimenters who were more anxious and had a lower need for social approval. (For this sample, the correlation between experimenters' need for social approval and their anxiety was —.14.)

The results reported seemed clear enough and we were quite unprepared for the results of a subsequent experiment (Rosenthal, Kohn, Marks, and Carota, 1963a). With 26 male experimenters running a total of 115 female $S$s in the same photo-rating task we obtained diametrically opposed results. This time *less* anxious experimenters obtained ratings of greater success from their subjects ($\chi^2 = 7.55, p < .01$). Furthermore, experimenters *higher* in need for social approval obtained more ratings of success ($\chi^2 = 3.85, p = .05$). Apparently then, personality variables may interact with replications in partially determining the subjects' responses. The most obvious difference between the two experiments reported was in their locale. The first study had been conducted at a medium-sized state university in the midwest. The second had been conducted at an east coast private university. Exactly how these differences might have served to lead to opposite results remains a question for further study. It does seem, however, that where an experiment is conducted can make a significant difference in its outcome—even when the principal investigator is held constant.

## B. EXPERIMENTER MODELING EFFECTS

Modeling effects are a special case of the effects of experimenter attributes on the data obtained from subjects. The specific attribute involved here is the quality of the experimenter's own performance at the task he subsequently assigns his subjects. The extent to which a subject's task performance is predictable from his experimenter's own performance of the same task is the extent of the modeling effect.

While studies of modeling effects have been conducted for some time in the field and in the clinic, analogous studies in the laboratory have been undertaken only very recently. This may be attributed to a general belief that the greater "rough-and-tumble" of the field and clinic might naturally lead to increased modeling and related effects. Conversely, the greater degree of "control" and "precision" of the laboratory may have led to the view that these extraneous effects are less likely to occur.

The assumptions underlying the development of a program of

research on laboratory experimenters' effects were that (1) there is no discontinuity of control, precision, or operating processes between field studies, clinical studies, and laboratory studies that are a simple function of the site of the research, and (2) that there is no discontinuity between the processes governing the interpersonal experimenter-subject relationship in any sort of social research and the processes governing any other sort of interpersonal relationship.

A total of eight experiments have been conducted which were designed to assess the existence and magnitude of experimenter modeling effects. All of these studies employed the same task. Subjects were asked to rate a series of 10 or 20 photographs on a rating scale of how successful or unsuccessful the persons pictured appeared to be. In all eight studies, experimenters themselves rated the photos before running their subjects. This was accomplished as part of the training procedure, it being most convenient to train experimenters by having them assume the role of subject while the authors acted in the role of experimenter. For each study, modeling effects were defined by the correlation between the mean rating of the photos by the different experimenters themselves and the mean photo rating obtained by each experimenter from all his subjects. The number of experimenters (and therefore the $N$ per correlation coefficient) per study ranged from 10 to 26. The number of subjects per study ranged from 55 to 206. The number of subjects per experimenter ranged from 4 to 20, the mean falling between 5 and 6. In all, 145 experimenters and over 800 subjects were included (Rosenthal, 1963c).

All experimenters were either graduate students or advanced undergraduate students in psychology or guidance. All subjects were drawn from elementary college courses, primarily in psychology but also from education, social sciences, and the humanities. All of the experiments were designed to test at least one hypothesis about experimenter effects other than modeling effects (as, for example, the effects of experimenters' expectancy) on the data obtained by them. All studies, then, had at least two treatment conditions the effects of which would have to be partially transcended by modeling effects.

Table I shows the correlation obtained in each of the eight studies between data produced by experimenters and data later obtained by them from their subjects. In addition to the correlations expressing modeling effects, the number of experimenters on which the correlation is based is shown for each experiment. We see a remarkable inconsistency of obtained correlations, the range of rhos being from —.49 to +.65. Taken individually, only the correlation of .65 ($p = .001$) differed significantly from zero at even the .10 level, two-tailed. (This particular correlation was the only one based on data not available for closer study by the writer.)

However, the hypothesis that this array of correlations could constitute a set of chance fluctuations from some "true" value of rho had to be rejected ($\chi^2 = 20.3$, $df = 7$, $p = .005$). The same analysis omitting data from experiment 2 gave a $\chi^2$ value of 9.80, $df = 6$, $p = .15$. It seems more likely than not that in different experiments utilizing a person perception task there will be significantly different magnitudes of modeling effects, which for any single experiment might often be regarded as a chance fluctuation from a correlation of zero.

TABLE I

MODELING EFFECTS BY SERIAL ORDER OF EXPERIMENT

| Experiment | N | Rho |
|---|---|---|
| 1 | 10 | .52 |
| 2 | 24 | .65 |
| 3 | 12 | .18 |
| 4 | 18 | .31 |
| 5 | 18 | —.07 |
| 6 | 26 | —.32 |
| 7 | 12 | —.49 |
| 8 | 25 | .14 |

Table I shows the obtained correlations in the temporal order in which the experiments were performed. There was a tendency for later studies to show significantly more negative correlations than the earlier studies. The correlation (rho) between the algebraic magnitude of correlation and order of study was .81, one-tailed, $p = .03$. (Omitting experiment 2, rho was .75, two-tailed, $p = .05$.) It therefore appears that in later studies the modeling effect significantly decreased algebraically. This finding is difficult to explain. From the earlier to the later studies there seemed to be no systematic change in the character of the experimenters, subjects, or treatment conditions. Almost a guess is the suggestion that in later studies experimenters were somewhat more likely to suspect that they themselves were the objects of study and that this recognition may have tended to reverse the direction of the effect. Experimenters, perhaps, were on their guard to avoid any possible sort of effect and modeling effects may have been so assiduously guarded against as to reverse their effects. Evidence for this "reversal of experimenter effects" will be summarized later.

## C. EXPERIMENTER EXPECTANCY EFFECTS

All experimenters have some orientation toward the results of their research. Rarely is this orientation one of dispassionate disinterest. Variables are not chosen for inclusion in research by using tables of random numbers. They are, rather, chosen because the experimenter has certain expectations about the relationship or lack of relationship between the selected variables and certain other variables. A superficial exception to this might be seen in so-called heuristic hunts for relationships, which are perhaps more common to the behavioral sciences. Even here, however, the inclusion of variables is not on a random basis, and certain relationships appear more likely to be found than others.

We now raise the question of whether an experimenter's expectations can affect the data actually obtained in his research. We are not so much concerned here with the problem of choice of experimental design and the fact that certain designs may unintentionally be more or less favorable to obtaining expected or unexpected data. Neither are we concerned with the problem of statistical tests of hypotheses and the fact that uniquely most powerful statistics may unintentionally be employed when the expectation is to be able to reject the null hypothesis, while less powerful statistics may be employed when the expectation is to be unable to reject the null hypothesis. These are interesting questions but will not be considered here. Our usage of "results" or "outcome" will be restricted to the raw data obtained by experimenters from their subjects. What we are talking about then is something very much like Merton's (1948) concept of "self-fulfilling prophecy." One prophesies an event (i.e., an experimental result) and the expectation of it then changes the prophet's (experimenter's) behavior in such a way as to make the predicted event more likely.

Evidence for the operation of these expectancy effects has been drawn from everyday life, from the field of education, from clinical practice, and from the field of survey research (Rosenthal, in press a). Until recently, however, there has been little experimental evidence that self-fulfilling prophesies may operate even in a carefully controlled laboratory research setting. Perhaps the earliest laboratory experiment which involved the systematic manipulation of the experimenters' expectancies was that by Stanton and Baker (1942). Twelve nonsense geometric figures were presented to a group of 200 undergraduate subjects. After several days, retention of these figures was measured by five experienced workers. The experimenters were supplied with a key of "correct" responses, some of which were incorrect. Experimenters were explicitly warned to guard against any bias associated with their having the keys before them and therefore influencing their subjects to guess correctly. Results showed that the experimenter obtained outcomes in accordance with his expectations. When the item on the key was correct, the subject's response was more likely to be correct than when the key was incorrect. In a careful replication of this study Lindzey (1951) emphasized to his experimenters the importance of keeping the keys out of the subjects' view. This study failed to confirm the Stanton and Baker findings. Another replication by Friedman (1942) also failed to obtain the significance levels obtained in the original. Still, significant results of this sort, even occurring only in one out of three experiments, cannot be dismissed lightly. Stanton (1942) himself presented further evidence which strengthened his conclusions. He employed a set of nonsense materials, 10 of which had been presented to subjects, and 10 of which had not been. Experimenters were divided into three groups. One group was correctly informed as to which 10 materials had been exposed, another group was incorrectly informed, while the third group was told nothing. The results of this study also indicated that the materials which the experimenters expected to be more often chosen were, in fact, more often chosen.

But the most fascinating and most instructive case of experimenter expectancy effects is no doubt that of Clever Hans (Pfungst, 1911). Hans, it will be remembered, was the horse of Mr. von Osten, a German mathematics teacher. By means of tapping his foot, Hans was able to add, subtract, multiply, and divide both integers and fractions. Hans could spell, read, and solve problems of musical harmony. To be sure, there were other clever animals at the time. There was "Rosa" the mare of Berlin, who performed similar feats in vaudeville, and there was the dog of Utrecht, and the reading pig of Virginia. All these other clever animals were highly trained performers who were, of course, intentionally cued by their trainers.

Mr. von Osten, however, did not profit from his animal's talent, nor did it seem at all likely that he was attempting to perpetrate a fraud. He swore he did not cue the animal and he permitted other people to question and test the horse without his own presence. Pfungst and his colleague, Stumpf, undertook a program of systematic research to discover the secret of Hans' talents. Among the first discoveries made were that if the horse could not see the questioner, Hans was not clever at all. Similarly, if the questioner did not himself know the answer to the question, Hans could not answer it either. Still, Hans was able to answer Pfungst's questions as long as the investigator was present and visible. Pfungst reasoned that the questioner might in some way be signalling to Hans when to begin and when to stop tapping his hoof. A forward inclination of the head of the questioner would start Hans tapping, Pfungst observed. He tried then to incline his head forward without asking a question and discovered that this was sufficient to start Hans' tapping. As the experimenter straightened up, Hans would stop tapping. Pfungst then tried to get Hans to stop tapping by using very slight upward motions of the head. He found that even the raising of the eyebrows was sufficient to stop the tapping. Even the dilation of the questioner's nostrils was a cue for Hans to stop tapping.

When a questioner bent forward more, the horse would tap faster. This added to the reputation of Hans as brilliant. That is, when a large number of taps was the correct response, Hans would tap very, very rapidly until he approached the region of correctness, and then he began to slow down. It was found that questioners typically bent far forward when the answer was a long one, gradually straightening up as Hans got closer to the correct number. For some experiments, Pfungst discovered that auditory cues functioned additively with visual cues. When the experimenter was silent, Hans was able to respond correctly 31% of the time in picking one of many placards with different words written on them, or cloths of different colors. When auditory cues were added, Hans responded correctly 56% of the time.

Pfungst then played the part of Hans, tapping out responses to questions with his hand. Of twenty-five questioners, twenty-three unwittingly cued Pfungst as to when to stop tapping to give a correct response. None of the questioners (males and females of all ages and occupations) knew the intent of the experiment. When errors occurred, they were usually only a single tap from being correct. The subjects of this study, including one experienced psychologist, were unable to discover that they were emitting cues.

Pfungst summarized the difficulties in uncovering the nature of Clever Hans' talents by speaking of "looking for, in the horse, what should have been sought in man." We shall now report the results of a continuing program of research on the effects of experimenters' expectancies on the data they obtain from their subjects. We have then, in a sense, paraphrased and accepted Pfungst's advice. We seek to find in the experimenter a portion of what has most often been sought in the subject.

## III. Demonstration of Expectancy Effects: Human Subjects

The basic paradigm for the study of experimenter expectancy effects has been to create two or more groups of experimenters with different expectancies or hypotheses about the data they would obtain from their subjects. Only the very first experiments carried out will be reported in some detail (Rosenthal and Fode, 1963b). Subsequent experiments will simply be summarized.

### Method

Fifty-seven photographs of faces ranging in size from $2 \times 3$ cm to $5 \times 6$ cm were cut from a weekly news magazine and mounted on $3 \times 5$ inch white cards. These were presented individually to 70 male and 34 female students, enrolled in an introductory psychology class at the University of North Dakota. Ss were instructed to rate each photo on a rating scale of success or failure. The scale ran from —10, extreme failure, to +10, extreme success, with intermediate labeled points. Each S was seen individually by one of the Es (RR) who read to each the instructions given below.

*Instructions to Subjects.* "I am going to read you some instructions. I am not permitted to say anything which is not in the instructions nor can I answer any questions about this experiment. OK?

"We are in the process of developing a test of empathy. This test is designed to show how well a person is able to put himself into someone else's place. I will show you a series of photographs. For each one I want you to judge whether the person pictured has been experiencing success or failure. To help you make more exact judgments you are to use this rating scale. As you can see the scale runs from —10 to +10. A rating of —10 means that you judge the person to have experienced extreme failure. A rating of +10 means that you judge the person to have experienced extreme success. A rating of —1 means that you judge the person to have experienced mild failure while a rating of +1 means that you judge the person to have experienced mild success. You are to rate each photo as accurately as you can. Just tell me the rating you assign to each photo. All ready? Here is the first photo. (No further explanation may be given although all or part of the instructions may be repeated.)"

From the original 57 photos we selected 10 for each sex which met the following requirements: (a) their mean rating was close to zero (between —1 and +1), (b) their distribution of ratings was not significantly skewed, (c) when the mean ratings for each of the ten cards was summed, they summed to zero exactly. Thus we obtained a set of "neutral" stimulus-value photos which were rated on the average as neither successes nor failures.

*Experimenters.* Ten of the eleven students in a class in undergraduate experimental psychology served in this capacity. All were psychology majors and three of them were first-year graduate students in psychology. All but two of the Es were males.

*Subjects.* Ss were 206 students enrolled in a course in introductory psychology (92 males and 114 females). Because Ss were given class credit for participating in the experiment, most of the class volunteered, thus reducing the selective effect of using "volunteer" Ss (Rosenthal, in press b). Each E ran from 18 to 24 subjects.

*Procedure.* The E's task was structured as a laboratory exercise to see whether they could replicate "well-established" experimental findings as "students in physics labs are expected to do." Es were told to discuss their project with no one and to say nothing to their Ss other than what was in the Instructions to Subjects. All Es were paid a dollar an hour except that if they did a "good job" they would be paid double; $2.00 an hour. All 10 Es received identical instructions except that five Es were told that their Ss would average a +5 rating on the ten neutral photos. The other Es were told that their Ss would average a —5 rating. Thus the only difference between the two groups of Es was that one group had a plus mark written in the front of the "5" while the other group had a minus mark written in front of the "5." As a warm-up for the Es, each of them also rated the standardized set of 10 photos. The exact instructions to Es were as follows:

*Instructions to Experimenters.* "You have been asked to participate in a research project developing a test of empathy. You may have seen this project written up in the campus newspaper. There is another reason for your participation in this project—namely, to give you practice in duplicating experimental results. In physics labs, for example, you are asked to repeat experiments to see if your findings agree with those already well established. You will now be asked to run a series of Ss and obtain from each ratings of photographs. The experimental procedure has been typed out for you and is self-explanatory. DO NOT DISCUSS THIS PROJECT WITH ANYONE until your instructor tells you that you may.

"You will be paid at the rate of $1.00 per hour for your time. If your results come out properly—as expected—you will be paid $2.00 instead of $1.00. The Ss you are running should average about a —5 rating.

"Just read the instructions to the Ss. Say *nothing* else to them except hello and goodbye. If for any reason you should say anything to an S other than what is written in your instructions, please write down the exact words you used and the situation which forced you to say them.

"GOOD LUCK!"

*Results*

The results of this experiment are shown in Table II. The difference between the mean photo ratings obtained by Es expecting higher ratings and those expecting lower ratings was significant at the .007 level (one-tailed $p$, $t = 3.20$, $df = 8$). Data obtained by the two female Es, one in each treatment condition, did not differ from the mean ratings obtained by the male Es of their respective experimental conditions. The grades earned by all Es in their experimental psychology course were not related to either the mean photo ratings obtained from subjects, or the magnitude of the biasing phenomenon.

Because of the striking nature of the results obtained, we decided to undertake another demonstrational experiment (Rosenthal and Fode, 1963b).

TABLE II
EXPERIMENTAL RESULTS UNDER TWO EXPECTANCIES

| Expectancy | |
|---|---|
| +5 | —5 |
| +.66 | +.18 |
| +.45 | +.17 |
| +.35 | +.04 |
| +.31 | —.37 |
| +.25 | —.42 |
| Means: | |
| +.40 | —.08 |

## Method

*Experimenters.* Twelve of the 26 male students enrolled in an advanced undergraduate course in industrial psychology were randomly assigned to serve as Es. In this sample of Es, few were psychology majors; most were majoring in engineering sciences.

*Subjects.* Ss were 86 students enrolled in a course in introductory psychology (50 males and 36 females). These Ss were also given class credit for participating in the experiment. Each E ran from 4 to 14 Ss.

*Procedure.* The procedure of this experiment was just as before with the exception that Es did not handle the photos. Instead, each set of 10 photos was mounted on cardboard and labeled so that Ss could call out their ratings of each photo to their E. It seemed reasonable that less handling of the photos might serve to reduce the effects of Es' expectancies on the data obtained from Ss. As before, half the Es were led to expect ratings of +5, and half were led to expect ratings of —5.

## Results

The results of this second demonstration are shown in Table III. Once again, all Es expecting higher ratings obtained higher ratings than did any E expecting lower ratings ($p = .0005$, one-tailed, $t = 4.99$).

In this replication Ss tended to rate photos as more successful than did the Ss of the first experiment. This difference was greater for the "+5" groups of Es ($p = .004$, two-tailed) than for the "—5" groups ($p = .08$, two-tailed). The second experiment also showed a significantly greater difference than the first between the means of the two treatment conditions ($p = .0005$, two-tailed, $t = 12.25$, $df = 9$). Why the Ss of the replication rated photos as more successful and why they were significantly more biased by their $E$s is difficult to interpret. Any one or more of four fairly obvious reasons may have contributed to these differences:

1. Different samples of $E$s were involved, engineering rather than psychology majors.

2. Different samples of $S$s were involved; but these should not have differed particularly.

3. $E$s did not handle the photos in the second study, as they had in the first.

4. $E$s were instructed by a faculty member in the first experiment and by a graduate student in the replication.

TABLE III

EXPERIMENTAL RESULTS UNDER TWO EXPECTANCIES: REPLICATION

| Expectancy | |
| --- | --- |
| +5 | —5 |
| +3.03 | +1.00 |
| +2.76 | +0.91 |
| +2.59 | +0.75 |
| +2.09 | +0.46 |
| +2.06 | +0.26 |
| +1.10 | —0.49 |
| *Means:* | |
| +2.27 | +0.48 |

*Conclusions*

What can we conclude from the two experiments described? It seems clear from the data that $E$s' expectancies or hypotheses can be partial determinants of the results of their experiments. Since $E$s were not permitted to say anything to their $S$s other than the standard instructions, the communication of $E$'s biases must have been by some subtle paralinguistic (e.g., tone) or kinesic (e.g., facial expressions, gestures) signals.

The $E$s engaged in our studies were not, of course, Ph.D. psychologists. How safe is it therefore to generalize from these student $E$s to "real life" $E$s? Two factors are relevant to the answer. One factor is the increasing amount of data collected in *real life* by other than Ph.D. psychologists. More and more data appear to be collected by research assistants. This trend will likely continue as psychological researchers continue to obtain increasing financial support for their research. Looking now at the pattern for a given psychological researcher, it appears that the better established he has become, the more likely that he has greater financial support for his research. He is therefore able to hire more research assistants. For many of the more productive behavioral researchers, therefore, the actual data collection is often primarily carried out by research assistants. Most of these assistants are graduate students but there is an increasing number of undergraduate research assistants. This trend is properly endorsed and encouraged by various government programs including the Undergraduate Research Participation Program of the National Science Foundation. It is for these reasons that we feel it to be fairly safe to generalize from our student $E$s to the real life data collector.

The other factor relevant to the problem of the generalizability of our findings assumes for the moment that "*real*" researchers *are* Ph.D. behavioral scientists. Our position then is that generalizing from advanced students in undergraduate or graduate psychology programs to "real" researchers is somewhat risky business. Risk of this sort, however, is a relative matter and we deem the risk less than the risk of generalizing from the behavior of college freshmen or sophomores to "human behavior" in general, and much less risky than generalizing from infrahuman to human behavior.

## IV. Demonstration of Expectancy Effects: Animal Subjects

Pavlov was aware of the fact that experimenters could influence their animal subjects. In speaking of experiments on the inheritance of acquired characteristics, he suggested that the noted increase in learning ability of successive generations of mice was really more an increase in teaching ability on the part of the experimenter (Gruenberg, 1929, p. 327).

Two studies in experimenter expectancy effects have been conducted using animal subjects (Rosenthal and Fode, 1963a; Rosenthal and Lawson, 1963). In the first experiment, a total of 12 experimenters each ran five albino rats on a simple discrimination problem daily for a 5-day period. On the basis of ratings of how well they thought they would like working with rats, six matched pairs were formed. For each pair, one member was assigned to a group of experimenters who were told that the subjects they were running were maze-bright, while the other member was assigned to a group who were told that their subjects were maze-dull. Subjects for the two treatment groups were from a homogeneous colony and matched for age and sex.

Results indicated that on 3 of the 5 days and for the experiment as a whole, experimenters believing their subjects to be bright obtained performance from them significantly superior to that obtained by experimenters believing their subjects to be dull ($p = .01$). The subjects believed to be bright appeared to be learning the problem while those believed to be dull did not. These results occurred in spite of the fact that on the level of verbal report both groups of experimenters wanted their subjects to perform well. In addition, a research assistant following the identical experimental procedure was able to obtain without "cheating" performance from her animals superior even to that obtained by experimenters believing their subjects were bright. Comparing the degree of correlation between what each experimenter specifically expected to obtain from his animals and what he actually did obtain from them for the "bright" and "dull" groups suggested that these groups were about equally biased, although, of course, in opposite directions.

In the second experiment a total of 38 experimenters were divided into 14 research teams each of which had one rat assigned to it. Eight of the teams were told that the subjects they would be working with had been bred for brightness while the remaining six teams were told that their subjects had been bred for dullness. All subjects were drawn from the same animal colony, all were female, and all were 80 days old. Animals were assigned at random to one of the two treatment conditions, which were experimenters' beliefs or expectations about subjects' ability.

Seven subexperiments including (a) magazine training, (b) operant acquisition, (c) extinction and spontaneous recovery, (d) secondary reinforcement, (e) stimulus discrimination, (f) stimulus generalization, and (g) chaining of responses were performed. Differences in performance favored the groups of experimenters believing their subjects to be bright in seven out of the the eight comparisons and these differences could not often have occurred by chance ($p = .02$). There was no trend over the course of the experiments for the treatment effects to either increase or decrease nor were the performances of subjects in any experiment save one correlated significantly with their performances in the subsequent experiment. It appeared then, that the several experiments were, to a great extent, independent. Comparisons of the treatment effects among each of the five laboratory sections to which experimenters had been assigned showed no real difference, all sections showing the mean differences in the predicted direction and at similar levels of significance.

These differences were obtained in spite of the fact that laboratory instructors gave more help to experimenters whose subjects were performing poorly and that all experimenters were motivated to have their animals perform well in order to complete the sequence of experiments. In addition, a laboratory instructor was present in each laboratory so that gross recording errors and differences in experimenters' treatment of their subjects would have been observed and corrected.

On the basis of questionnaire data obtained in both experiments, it appeared that experimenters believing their subjects to have been bred for brightness were more satisfied with their participation in the experiments, liked their subjects more, watched them more intently, and found them to be more pleasant. They tended also to be more enthusiastic, friendly, encouraging, and pleasant; but were less talkative and less loud when working with their subject. Perhaps the most crucial difference was these experimenters' handling their animals more. The potentially facilitating effect of handling on learning seems well established (Bernstein, 1957).

## V. Effects of Excessive Reward on Expectancy Effects

We have seen that experimenters can obtain from their human or animal subjects the data they expect to obtain. The studies described which have employed human subjects offered mild incentives for the operation of the experimenter expectancy effect. Experimenters were offered $2.00 instead of $1.00 "if their data came out as expected." The studies which employed animal subjects offered no incentive for the operation of experimenter biasing of their experimental findings. On the contrary, these experimenters were motivated by the nature of the situation to obtain uniformly good performance from their rat subjects. In these studies then, it appeared that an experimenter's expectancy was a more powerful determinant of the results of his experiment than his desires regarding the results.

In order for any scientist to do any research, he must be motivated to do so, and probably more than casually so. It is, after all, a lot of trouble planning and executing an experiment. The motivation to conduct research is usually related to certain motivations associated with the results of the research. Rarely is the investigator truly disinterested in the results he obtains from his research. William James put it thus: ". . . science would be far less advanced than she is if the passionate desires of individuals to get their own faiths confirmed had been kept out of the game . . . if you want an absolute duffer in an investigation, you must, after all, take the man who has no interest whatever in its results: he is the warranted incapable, the positive fool" (1948, p. 102).

Two experiments were conducted to investigate the effects of "unusual" motivation on the operation of experimenter expectancy effects (Rosenthal, Fode and Vikan-Kline, 1960b; Rosenthal, Friedman, Johnson, Fode, Schill, White, and Vikan-Kline, in press. In the first of these studies, 12 graduate student experimenters ran a total of 58 undergraduate subjects in the photo-rating task described earlier. All experimenters were given an expectancy about the data they would obtain from their subjects. Half the experimenters were moderately motivated to obtain this data by the promise of $2.00 for "obtaining good data." The remaining experimenters were more extremely motivated by the promise of $5.00 for "obtaining good data." Results indicated that the more moderately motivated experimenters obtained data more in accord with their expectancies than did more extremely motivated experimenters ($p = .01$). There was, in fact, a tendency for the more extremely motivated experimenters to obtain data opposite to that which they had been led to expect.

In the second study 30 advanced undergraduate experimenters ran a total of 150 subjects in the same photo-rating task. Again, all experimenters were given an expectancy about the data they would obtain from their subjects. Half the experimenters were "excessively" motivated by telling them that if the data they obtained was "better" than that of an unknown partner they would be paid not only their own $1.00 but their partner's as well. If, on the other hand, their "partner" did a "better job" he would get their reward as well as his own. Results again suggested that more moderately motivated experimenters obtained data more consistent with their expectancy. Again, more extremely motivated experimenters tended to obtain data opposite to what they had been led to expect. The results of this second study were not so statistically significant, but the two studies taken together yielded a $p$ of .05.

Why might the effect of excessive incentive to bias the subjects' data be to reduce or even to reverse the biasing effect of the experimenters? In a postexperiment group discussion with the experimenters of the second reported study, many of them seemed somewhat upset by the experimental goings-on. Several of them used the term "payola," suggesting that they felt that the investigators were bribing them to get "good" data which was, in a sense, true. Since money had been mentioned and dispensed to only the more motivated experimenters of this study, it seems likely that they were the ones perceiving the situation in this way. Kelman (1953) found that subjects under higher motivation to conform to an experimenter showed less such conformity than did subjects under lower conditions of motivation. One of several of Kelman's interpretations was that the subjects who were rewarded more may have felt more as though they were being bribed to conform for the experimenter's own benefit, thus making subjects suspicious and resentful, and therefore less susceptible to experimenter influence. This interpretation fits the present situation quite well.

## VI. Subjects' View of Biased Experimenters

Riecken has discussed the social nature of the experimenter-subject interaction in some detail (1962). An important aspect of this interaction is the subject's perception of the experimenter. What sort of person is the experimenter seen to be in his relationship to the subject? The answer to this question has general relevance to an increased understanding of the social psychology of the psychological experiment. More particularly, is a more biased experimenter seen as a somewhat different person than a less biased experimenter? The answer to this question might increase our understanding of the mediation of experimenter expectancy effects.

### Subjects' Perceptions of Experimenters' Behavior

At the conclusion of one of the experiments involving the photo-rating task each of 56 subjects completed a questionnaire describing the behavior of his experimenter during the conduct of the experiment. Twelve experimenters completed the same forms describing their own behavior during the experiment. Neither experimenters nor subjects knew beforehand that they would be asked to complete these questionnaires, and no one save the investigators saw the completed forms (Rosenthal, Fode, Friedman, and Vikan-Kline, 1960a). These forms consisted of 27 20-point rating scales ranging from —10 (e.g., extremely discourteous) to +10 (e.g., extremely courteous).

Mean ratings of the experimenters by their subjects and by themselves reflected very favorably on the experimenters. The profile of the experimenters as they were viewed by subjects showed remarkable similarity to the profile of the experimenters as viewed by themselves (rho = .89). To summarize and facilitate interpretation of the obtained ratings, all variables were intercorrelated and cluster analyzed (see Table IV). Four clusters emerged for which the associated $B$ coefficients were all considerably larger than generally deemed necessary to establish the significance of a cluster. For mnemonic purposes we may label Cluster I as "Casual-Pleasant," Cluster II as "Expressive-Friendly," Cluster III as the "Kinesic Cluster," and Cluster IV as "Enthusiastic-Professional."

Experimenters differ in the degree to which their expectancy is predictive of the data they obtain from their subjects. We could therefore ask the question of whether those experimenters whose expectancies determined their results more were perceived by subjects as behaving differently during the course of the experiment. Magnitude of expectancy effect or bias was therefore correlated with all the ratings subjects had made of their experimenters' behavior.

The median correlations with degree of experimenter bias of the variables in Clusters I and IV were .26 and .21, respectively; neither was significantly greater than a correlation having a $p = .50$. The median correlations with degree of experimenter bias of the variables in Clusters II and III were .47 and .43, respectively. Both of these median correlations were significantly greater than a correlation to be often expected by chance; two-tailed $p$'s were .04 and .01, respectively. More biased experimenters, then, were characterized by higher loadings on the "Expressive-Friendly" and the "Kinesic" clusters. These findings suggest that kinesic

TABLE IV

CLUSTER ANALYSIS OF SUBJECTS' PERCEPTION OF EXPERIMENTERS

| Cluster I: $B = 6.48$ | Cluster II: $B = 3.97$ |
|---|---|
| Honest | Liking |
| Casual | Friendly |
| Relaxed | Personal |
| Pleasant | Interested |
| Courteous | Encouraging |
| Business-like | Expressive face |
| Slow-speaking | Expressive-voiced |
| Pleasant-voiced | Use of hand gestures |
| Behaved consistently | Satisfied with experiment |
| *Mean rating* = 5.91 | *Mean rating* = 2.57 |
| Cluster III: $B = 9.10$ | Cluster IV: $B = 3.55$ |
| Use of head gestures | Enthusiastic |
| Use of arm gestures | Professional |
| Use of trunk | Quiet (nontalkative) |
| Use of body | |
| Use of legs | |
| *Mean rating* = —1.96 | *Mean rating* = 3.01 |

and possibly paralinguistic aspects of the experimenter's interaction with his subjects serve to communicate the experimenter's bias to his subjects.

*Subjects' Predictions of Experimenters' Computational Errors*

All experimenters are rated as very honest by their subjects, but some are rated more so than others. In one of our studies, 11 out of 24 experimenters made computational errors in their data processing in the direction of their expectancy. These experimenters were rated as significantly less honest ($p = .02$) by their subjects during the course of data collection. Just how subjects were able to predict their experimenters' computational errors from their judgments of experimenters' behavior during the experiment is a fascinating question for which we presently have no answer. It seems clear, however, that subjects learn a good deal about their experimenter in the brief interaction of the person-perception experiment conducted. Furthermore, when a subject rates the behavior of an experimenter, we may do well to take his rating seriously. It may prove to be a valuable predictive, postdictive, or paridictive variable (Rosenthal *et al.*, in press).

## VII. Interaction of Subjects' and Experimenters' Expectancies

In the experiments described so far, and those to be reported here, experimenters' expectancies have been experimentally manipulated. In this section we shall describe the additional effects of the simultaneous experimental manipulation of subjects' expectancies.

Riecken (1962) has discussed the subjects' "deutero-problem" in the psychological experiment, which exists beyond the problems of simply performing the formal task required of him by the experimenter. The most favorable solution to the deutero-problem would involve the maximal satisfaction of the subject's three aims in the experiment: (1) the attainment of some sort of reward, (2) the divination of the experimenter's true purposes, and (3) the favorable presentation of self for the experimenter's scrutiny. Those stimuli in the experimental situation which provide cues to the subject as to how he may best solve his deutero-problem have been called "demand characteristics" (Orne, 1962). One of the major purposes of the two studies to be reported here was to investigate the role of subtle and of blatant demand characteristics in determining the results of psychological research (Rosenthal, Persinger, Vikan-Kline, and Fode, 1963d; White, 1962).

In the first of these studies, 18 experimenters positively reinforced a total of 65 subjects for high positive ratings of the success of persons pictured on photographs. Half the experimenters were led to expect high rates of awareness from their subjects, while the remaining experimenters were led to expect low rates of awareness. Each of these two groups was further divided into a group of experimenters whose subjects' instructions favored their "seeing through" the experimental situation and a group whose subjects received standard instructions. An additional group of four experimenters running a total of 26 standard-instruction subjects was used as a control group. These experimenters were biased to expect high photo ratings but did not reinforce any subject's response.

Experimenters biased to expect higher rates of awareness obtained higher rates of awareness ($p = .07$) and subjects who had been given a set to "see through" the experiment tended to be more often aware, though this effect was not as reliable as the effect of experimenter's bias. The obtained effects were most powerful and most significant statistically ($p = .05$) when they were operating conjointly. Subject set was, however, significantly related to magnitude of conditioning with subjects set to "see through" conditioning less. Sets favoring "seeing through" an experiment may carry an implied set to not conform to more superficial demand characteristics of the experimental situation.

In the second experiment, 18 experimenters ran a total of 108 subjects in the photo-rating task described earlier. Six different expectancies (ranging from −6 to +6) were induced among both experimenters and subjects. The expectancies created in subjects were far less subtle than was the case in the preceding study. Results suggested the operation of contrast effects wherein subjects confronted with experimenters of radically different expectancies seemed to make more entrenched responses. In addition to this contrast effect and regardless of the direction of the expectancies involved, subjects tended to rate the photos as more successful when their expectancy and that of their experimenter were in greater accord.

These studies served to increase the generality of the findings bearing on the effects of experimenters' and subjects' expectancies. In addition, however, they indicated that more subtle demand characteristics had more predictable effects on the responses made by subjects. As with unusually motivated experimenters, unusually "expectant" or cued subjects provided data less directly predictable from a knowledge of experimenters' hypotheses.

## VIII. Effects of Experimenter Expectancy: Negative Instances

The title of this section may prove misleading. It may imply that until the work reported here was accomplished, there was only unequivocal and highly predictable and predicted evidence bearing on the question of the effects of experimenters' expectancies on the results of their research. Nothing could be further from the truth. The results of the first experiment described in the section on the effects of excessive reward were at least in part quite unpredicted. *Post hoc,* these results made sense but it was, after all, *post hoc.* With the results of the second experiment reported in that section we gained confidence that our initially "negative" instances were negative only with respect to our initial predictions. They made sense after further data collection and seemed consistent with each other.

White's (1962) experimental data, summarized in the last section, similarly did not conform to our expectation. There was no neat regression line ascending from congruent experimenter-subject expectations for negative data to those expectations congruent for positive data. In one sense, that study also provided a negative instance. More data are needed to make conceptual good sense of a hopefully orderly phenomenon. As we turn then to a consideration of "negative" instances, we must bear in mind that they are neither the first nor the last such instances. Nor does their "negative" nature imply that we cannot learn from them something useful about the phenomenon under discussion.

In the first of the two studies to be summarized here, eight experimenters administered an intelligence test (Block design of the WAIS) to to a total of 32 subjects (Wartenberg-Ekren, 1962). Experimenters were to be led to expect that half their subjects would perform well and half would perform poorly.

Results of this study showed no effect of experimenters' expectancies on the data obtained from subjects. Wartenberg-Ekren's analysis of experimenters' questionnaires revealed that all experimenters expected the "brighter" subjects to perform better. In addition, none of the experimenters felt that they had treated their subjects differentially as a function of their perceived group membership. The over-all negative findings may have been due in part to the fact that one of the eight experimenters intentionally instituted a double blind procedure to avoid bias! He simply did not look at the code identifying the treatment condition of his next subject. Another experimenter was "blind" for half his subjects, although not intentionally so.

Subjects' ratings of their experimenters in the Wartenberg-Ekren study were not directly comparable to those of our earlier studies because she used a three-point scale rather than our 20-point scale. We were able, however, to group many of her scales into two of our four earlier derived clusters: Cluster I (Casual-Pleasant) and Cluster II (Expressive-Friendly). Subjects labeled as brighter did not rate their experimenters any differently on the scales included in Cluster I. These subjects, however, rated their experimenters as significantly higher on Cluster II variables than did subjects labeled as less bright ($p = .03$). This suggests that although all experimenters believed they treated all subjects alike, they made some distinction in their treatment of subjects as a function of their perceived group membership. We should emphasize that not only were subjects unaware of which group they belonged to, indeed, they were unaware that they belonged to *any* group. It seems safe to accept their ratings of their experimenter as reflecting real differences in experimenters' treatment of subjects. The Cluster II variables included in the Wartenberg-Ekren study, and on which "brighter" subjects rated their experiments as higher, were friendly, likeable, interested, encouraging, expressive-faced, and use of hand gestures. Apparently even the most careful conscious safeguards against differential treatment of subjects in different treatment conditions may prove ineffective.

The second study to be summarized in this section is one conducted by Pflugrath (1962). He had three sets of three graduate student counselors administer the Taylor Manifest Anxiety Scale to a total of 142 subjects. One set of experimenters was led to believe their groups of subjects were very anxious, another set was led to believe their groups of subjects were nonanxious, and the third set was told nothing about their groups of subjects.

The over-all analysis of the results showed no significant differences in anxiety scores earned by the subjects of the three groups of experimenters. Among the subjects run under the condition of their experimenter believing them to be highly anxious, a significantly greater proportion scored as relatively less anxious than the subjects of the control group ($p = .02$). This finding was unpredicted. Nevertheless, the phenomenology of the situation must be considered. Here we have a group of counselors-in-training told nothing about their subjects—the control group. Another group of counselors is told their subjects are not anxious—so much the better for the subjects! But when counselors are told they will be testing very anxious subjects who even have had contact with the counseling center, might not all their counseling skills be subtly brought to bear upon the task of reducing their subjects' anxiety? This interpretation seems so plausible, at least on a *post hoc* basis, that we wonder why we did not predict it in the first place.

The simplest conclusions to draw from the results of the experiments discussed in this section might be that experimenters' expectancies do not affect subjects' intelligence test or anxiety scale performance. Indeed, there may be a large array of tasks which will prove relatively resistant to the effects of experimenter expectancies. What sorts of tasks are more or less resistant is a question deserving further research. Some questions remain, however, about the particular two experiments summarized. To what extent was the absence of an expectancy effect in the intelligence test study due to the intentional and unintentional instituting of a double-blind procedure, which if it remains truly blind, must eliminate expectancy effects?

Less in the nature of a question and more as an illustration of the potential power of expectancy effects, we have the subjects' word for it that experimenters treated them differentially as a function of the experimenters' expectancies, the existence of which were unknown to the subjects, and this in a context of tremendous emphasis on experimenters' need for objectivity, standardization, and nondifferential treatment of subjects.

Whether therapeutically oriented experimenters in the social sciences generally try to reduce the anxiety of those subjects perceived to be anxious is a question deserving of further research. Not only in administering anxiety scales, but in a great deal of contemporary social research, subjects are exposed to conditions believed to make them anxious. What might be the effect on the outcome of experiments of this sort of the covert therapeutic zeal and/or skill of various investigators carrying out this research? Might certain investigators typically conclude "no difference" because they tend to dilute the effects of treatment conditions? And conversely, might others be led to conclude "significant difference" by their increasing the anxiety of subjects known to belong to the "more anxious condition" of an experiment? Clearly, these are not necessarily effects of experimenters' expectancies, but they are effects of experimenter attributes which may have equally serious implications for how we do research in the social sciences.

## IX. The Effect of Early Data Returns

We have been discussing the effects of experimenters' expectancies on the data they obtain from their subjects. We shall discuss here the effect of the data experimenters obtain upon their expectancies. Except in the most exploratory or heuristic experimental enterprise, the experimenter's expectancies are likely to be based upon some sort of data. It need not be formal, experimental data. It may be based upon a nearly casual observation of behavior. The observation need not even be the experimenter's own. If data are in any case the most likely determinant of experimenter expectancies, then we may fairly ask: What about the data obtained early in an experiment? What are their effects upon data subsequently obtained within the same experiment?

That the "early returns" of psychological research studies can have an effect on experimenters' expectancies was noted and well discussed by Ebbinghaus (1885). After saying that investigators notice the results of their studies as they progress he stated, "Consequently it it unavoidable that, after the observation of the numerical results, suppositions should arise as to general principles which are concealed in them and which occasionally give hints as to their presence. As the investigations are carried further, these suppositions, as well as those present at the beginning, constitute a complicating factor which probably has a definite influence upon the subsequent results" (p. 28). He went on to speak of the pleasure of finding expected data and surprise at obtaining unexpected data and continued by stating the hypothesis of the present studies: Where "average values" were obtained initially, subsequent data would tend to be less extreme and where "especially large or small numbers are expected it would tend to further increase or decrease the values" (p. 29).

Ebbinghaus was, of course, speaking of himself as both experimenter and subject. Nevertheless, on the basis of his thinking and of the reasoning described earlier, it was decided to test Ebbinghaus's hypothesis of the effect of early data returns on data subsequently obtained by experimenters.

Two experiments were conducted. In the first of these studies (Rosenthal *et al.*, 1963c) 12 biased experimenters, each running six subjects on the photo-rating task, were equally and randomly divided into three treatment conditions. One group of experimenters obtained "good" or expected data from their first two subjects (who were actually accomplices), another group of experimenters obtained "bad" or unexpected data from their first two subjects (who were also accomplices), while the third group, utilizing only naïve subjects, served as a control. Comparisons were made of the mean data obtained by experimenters from the last four naïve subjects run.

Results indicated that experimenters obtaining "good" initial data also obtained good subsequent data. Experimenters obtaining "bad" initial data obtained bad subsequent data.

In the second study (Rosenthal, Kohn, Marks, and Carota, 1963a), 26 experimenters each running about six subjects were given one of two opposite experimental expectancies. By the same method employed in the earlier study, half the experimenters had their expectancies confirmed by their first two subjects and half had their expectancies disconfirmed. Within each of the conditions described, half the experimenters were praised for their experimental technique and half were reproved. Results of this study were more complex than those of the first experiment, but showed that experimenter expectancies were most clearly determinants of experimental results when they were confirmd by the early data returns. This effect depended, however, on the personality of the investigator who administered the praise or reproof to the experimenter.

## X. The Mediation of Experimenter Expectancy Effects

Granting the occurrence and some generality of experimenter expectancy effects, how do they operate? Cheating cannot reasonably account for the observed effects since at least those instances of cheating of which we have become aware tended on the whole to diminish the biasing effect, as when experimenters who believed their rat subjects to be dull prodded them, and, in a very few cases, presented fraudulent data. Experimenters' data recording and computations were checked and were found to be so accurate that, in general, written recording and computational errors could not be reasonably implicated as agents of expectancy effects. If neither cheating nor honest errors could account for our findings, what might?

### A. Verbal Conditioning

The most obvious hypothesis seemed to be some form of verbal conditioning. If an experimenter expects to obtain high ratings of photographs, might he not subtly reinforce this type of response? Conversely, if he expects low ratings of photos, might he not reinforce subtly those responses which are low? He might be capable of this system of subtle reinforcement even without any implication of dishonesty, for it might be an unintended response on his part. Fortunately, we were able to test this hypothesis. If indeed verbal conditioning were mediating the phenomenon, we might expect to find that expectancy effects increase as a function of the number of photos rated. Certainly, we would not expect to find any biasing on the very first photos rated by subjects run by different groups of experimenters. There had, after all, been no reinforcement possible prior to the very first response. In a test of this hypothesis (Rosenthal *et al.*, 1964) we found, if anything, that biasing decreased over the course of the photo ratings. Furthermore, there was a significant biasing effect in evidence on the first photo alone, thus ruling out verbal conditioning as a necessary mediator or even as an augmentor of the phenomenon. An important implication of this finding is our need to pay special attention in our search for the mediators of the expectancy bias phenomenon to the brief pre-data-gathering interaction during which the experimenter greets, seats, "sets," and instructs the subject.

A subsequent study (Fode, Rosenthal, Vikan-Kline, and Persinger, 1961) was conducted to learn whether operant conditioning *could* drive the ratings of photos up or down according to the will of the experimenter. Results showed clearly that this was possible, and that it worked best with certain types of subjects. We may therefore conclude that, while verbal conditioning is neither a necessary nor necessarily frequent antecedent of biasing, it nevertheless could be.

### B. Modality of Cue Communication

Are visual or verbal cues, such as tone, more important for the mediation of bias? Fode (1960) studied this question by using a group of experimenters behind screens to eliminate visual cues, and a group of experimenters who remained silent throughout the experiment to eliminate verbal cues. He found that verbal cues of tone are probably sufficient to mediate expectancy effects but that they can be greatly augmented by visual cues. Restriction of visual cues accounted for about 80% of the variance of bias magnitude.

### C. Personal Characteristics of Experimenters and Subjects

It seems reasonable to suppose that it is the behavior of the experimenter in the experimental situation that determines the occurrence and magnitude of expectancy effects. Without knowing exactly what occurs in the experimenter-subject interaction we can only posit that certain personal characteristics of experimenters are likely to be associated with different behavior vis-à-vis the subject in the experimental situation. As a first step, therefore, we have tried to find some more enduring personal characteristics associated with greater or lesser experimenter expectancy effects.

Experimenter's need for approval as measured primarily by the Marlow-Crowne Social Desirability Scale (M-C SD) appears to predict expectancy effects in a fairly reliable way. In seven samples (Persinger, 1962; Rosenthal, 1963d; Rosenthal *et al.*, 1963b), experimenters' need for approval was correlated with the magnitude of their expectancy effects. For a total of 57 experimenters of medium anxiety level (or unselected for anxiety) and previously not acquainted with their subjects, the obtained correlations averaged .64 ($p < .001$). A recently completed study, however, yielded contradictory data (Rosenthal *et al.*, 1963a). In that study experimenters with higher need for approval scores showed *less* expectancy effects ($p=.04$). Disregarding that finding for the moment, it appears that experimenters who may have a greater need to please the principal investigators obtain more of the sort of data they are led by him to expect; at least when their anxiety level is average. For a total of 50 experimenters scoring either very high or very low on the Taylor Manifest Anxiety Scale (MAS) the correlations between need for approval and expectancy effects tended to be negative though not significantly so. In none of our studies have we obtained a significant relationship between subjects' need for approval and their susceptibility to experimenter expectancy effects.

Experimenter's anxiety level (MAS) has been found related to expectancy effect in a remarkably inconsistent manner. In three experiments, experimenters with medium levels of anxiety showed the greatest expectancy bias (Fode, 1963; Rosenthal *et al.*, 1963a; Rosenthal *et al.*, 1963b). In two experiments, experimenters with high levels of anxiety showed the greatest expectancy bias (Rosenthal *et al.*, 1962; Rosenthal *et al.*, 1963e). Finally one experiment showed experimenters scoring low in anxiety to have the greatest expectancy bias (Persinger, 1962). This confusion of findings is matched by the irregularity of the correlation between subjects' level of anxiety and their susceptibility to experimenter expectancy effects. In two experiments medium anxious subjects were most susceptible (Fode, 1963; Vikan-Kline, 1962). In two other studies highly anxious subjects were most susceptible (Rosenthal *et al.*, 1963e; Rosenthal *et al.*, 1963b). In a single study, least anxious subjects were found most susceptible (Persinger, 1962) and in another, medium anxious subjects were found *least* susceptible (Rosenthal *et al.*, 1963a). We can only conclude that experimenters' and subjects' anxiety level are related significantly to expectancy effects in an as yet indeterminate manner.

In most of our studies we have employed primarily male experimenters. In three experiments enough female experimenters were included to allow us to compare the magnitude of expectancy effects for male and female data collectors. In all three cases male experimenters showed the greater expectancy effects (Marcia, 1961; Persinger, 1962; Rosenthal et al., 1963b). It may be that the culturally prescribed relative assertiveness of males may make them more successful sources of unintended social influence. Again on the basis of role prescription we might expect female subjects to be more susceptible to the unintended social influence process implied by expectancy effects in the experimental situation. In several studies we found no difference between male and female subjects in this regard. In three experiments where significant differences were obtained, however, we did find female subjects more susceptible to expectancy effects (Persinger, 1962; Rosenthal et al., 1963b; Rosenthal et al., 1963c). These findings were heartening in their consistency within themselves and with the general, analogous findings in the more usual literature on susceptibility to interpersonal influence processes.

Prior acquaintanceship between male experimenters and their subjects seemed to facilitate the expectancy biasing phenomenon. In one experiment this appeared to be true for both male and female subjects (Rosenthal et al., 1963e), but in a second study (Persinger, 1962) it appeared true only for female subjects. The perceived status of the experimenter was also found to be related to his degree of biasing. Vikan-Kline (1962) found higher-status experimenters better able to bias their subjects' responses.

If, on the basis of the data available to date, we were forced to describe the paradigm fostering maximal experimenter expectancy effects, we would postulate an experimenter with a high need for social approval and with an anxiety level neither very high nor very low. The experimenter would have high status, be gesturally inclined, and behave in a friendly, interested manner vis-à-vis his subjects. Subjects might best be acquainted with their experimenter and be female rather than male.

The pattern described might be understood best by considering the experimental dyad as a signal exchange system. The signals under discussion are, of course, unintentional. Experimenters high in need for social approval may typically be more precise in their signaling behavior. The business of impression management (Goffman, 1956), or signal editing, is more important to them in their everyday life. Their motivation for biasing may also be greater because of their need to please the source of the hypothesis. The high status and friendly manner may serve to focus subjects' attention onto the signal source and increase the likelihood of the experimenter's unintentional message being understood.

## XI. Methodological Implications of Studies of Expectancy Effects

It seemed reasonable to conclude from our findings that systematic expectancy effects might be eliminated by employing as data collectors, research assistants who did not know the experimenters' hypothesis or expectancy. Not only did this technique seem logically implied by our data, but it would be practical as well. More and more data collection is actually carried out by research assistants. We decided, however, to test the soundness of this methodological suggestion (Rosenthal et al., 1963e).

We began by conducting a by now fairly standard experiment in experimenter expectancy effects. Fourteen experimenters ran a total of 76 subjects in the photo-rating task with half the experimenters led to expect +5, and half led to expect −5 mean ratings of the success of persons pictured in photos. At the conclusion of this experiment, each experimenter was awarded a "research grant" from which he could draw a small salary and also hire two research assistants. Assistants were randomly assigned to experimenters who then trained and supervised their two assistants. Each of these then ran 5 or 6 randomly assigned subjects of his own. Unlike the original instructions to experimenters, instructions to their assistants did not inform them as to what perceptions to expect from their subjects. Experimenters, however, were subtly led, by their printed instructions, to expect their assistants to obtain data of the same sort they had themselves obtained from their own subjects.

Experimenters biased their subjects, and assistants in turn biased *their* subjects. The correlation between magnitude of experimenters' bias and their respective pair of assistants' bias was .67 ($p = .01$). Apparently, the experimenters' hypothesis or expectancy may be communicated to his research assistants without the assistants being told the nature of the hypothesis or expectancy.

What methodological suggestions remain then which might serve to reduce or eliminate experimenter expectancy effects? For those studies in which it is possible to do so, the experimenter might eliminate himself and his surrogates from the interaction with subjects. Automated setups make this feasible for some kinds of behavioral research, but not for others. Any technique of instruction of data collectors by the principal investigator which would eliminate the possibility of the subtle communication of his expectancies would be a methodological improvement. This would be no easy matter and no perfect solution. The too frequent failure of the double-blind method in medical research attests to this. It is a failure not of "double-blindness" but of maintenance of "blindness." During the experimenter-subject interaction each may learn too much about the other to insure "blindness-maintenance."

Not only because of the danger of bias, but also because of the general nature of experimenter differences, it would be desirable to employ samples of experimenters drawn as randomly as possible from a relevant population of relevantly uninformed experimenters. Following Brunswik (1956), this would greatly increase the generality of all our research findings and thus be' of benefit even if *no* bias were ever operating. Alternatively, there may be value in employing samples of experimenters with known distributions of bias as Mosteller (1944) has suggested in the case of interviewers. The particular biases, however, need not be pre-existing ones and it may be useful to *purposefully* induce different biases in our sample of experimenters, giving us better control over the nature and degree of experimenters' biases. That this is a practical technique has been demonstrated recently by Rosenhan (personal communication), who had his own research repeated by an experimenter in whom the opposite hypothesis had been ingeniously induced.

One fairly concrete implication for the design of experiments may emerge from our research, the addition of "expectancy control groups." In any study employing an experimental (treatment) and a control (no treatment) condition, a group would be added for whom the experimenter(s) is reasonably led to expect the same sort of data as is expected from the treatment group but in which the treatment is not administered. Differences between the treatment group and the expectancy control group might then be attributable to the treatment truly or to a treatment and expectancy interaction rather than to expectancy alone.

## XII. Some Substantive Implications of Studies of Expectancy Effects

Perhaps the most compelling and the most general conclusion to be drawn is that human beings can engage in highly effective and influential unprogrammed and unintended communication with one another. The subtlety of this communication is such that casual observation of human dyads is unlikely to reveal the nature of this communication process. Sound motion pictures may provide the necessary opportunity for more leisurely, intensive, and repeated study of subtle influential communication processes. We have obtained sound motion picture records of 29 experimenters each interacting with several subjects. Preliminary analyses have given us cause to hope that we may be able to learn something of consequence about the mediation of expectancy effects in particular, and about subtle communication processes in general. In these films, all experimenters read identical words to their subjects so that the burden of communication falls on the gestures, expressions, and intonations which accompany the highly programmed aspects of experimenters' inputs into the experimenter-subject interaction.

Some interesting practical questions arise from these considerations. When an experienced physician or psychotherapist tells the neophyte therapist that the neophyte's patient has a poor or good prognosis, is the experienced clinician only assessing or is he actually "causing" the poor or good prognosis? When the master teacher tells his apprentice that a pupil appears to be a slow learner, is this prophecy then self-fulfilled? When the employer tells the employee that a task cannot be accomplished, has the likelihood of its accomplishment thereby been reduced? More subtly, might these phenomena occur even if the supervisors never verbalized their beliefs? The data cited suggest that they may.

## References

Azrin, N. H., Holz, W., Ulrich, R., and Goldiamond, I. The control of the content of conversation through reinforcement. *J. exp. anal. Behav.*, 1961, 4, 25-30.

Bernstein, L. The effects of variations in handling upon learning and retention. *J. comp. physiol. Psychol.*, 1957, **50**, 162-167.

Boring, E. G. *A history of experimental psychology.* (2nd ed.) New York: Appleton-Century-Crofts, 1950.

Brunswik, E. *Perception and the representative design of psychological experiments.* Berkeley: Univer. of California Press, 1956.

Cahalan, D., Tamulonis, Valerie, and Verner, Helen W. Interviewer bias involved in certain types of opinion survey questions. *Int. J. opin. attit. Res.*, 1947, 1, 63-67.

Crespi, L. P. The cheater problem in polling. *Publ. Opin. Quart.*, 1945-1946, 9, 431-435.

Ebbinghaus, H. *Memory: a contribution to experimental psychology.* (1885) Translated by Ruger, H. A., and Bussenius, Clara E. New York: Teachers College, Columbia Univer., 1913.

Fisher, R. A. Has Mendel's work been rediscovered? *Ann. Sci.*, 1936, 1, 115-137.

Fode, K. L. The effect of non-visual and non-verbal interaction on experimenter bias. Unpublished master's thesis, Univer. of North Dakota, Grand Forks, 1960.

Fode, K. L. The effect of experimenters' and subjects' level of anxiety and need for approval on experimenter outcome-bias. Unpublished doctoral dissertation, Univer. of North Dakota, Grand Forks, 1963.

Fode, K. L., Rosenthal, R., Vikan-Kline, Linda L., and Persinger, G. W. Susceptibility to influence in a verbal conditioning situation. Unpublished data, Univer. of North Dakota, Grand Forks, 1961.

Friedman, Pearl. A second experiment on interviewer bias. *Sociometry*, 1942, 5, 378-379.

George, W. H. *The scientist in action: a scientific study of his methods.* New York: Emerson Books, 1938.

Goffman, E. *The presentation of self in everyday life.* Univer. Edinburgh Soc. Sci. Res. Centre, Monogr. 2, 1956.

Gruenberg, B. C. *The story of evolution.* Princeton, New Jersey: Van Nostrand, 1929.

Hanley, C., and Rokeach, M. Care and carelessness in psychology. *Psychol. Bull.*, 1956, **53**, 183-186.

James, W. *Essays in pragmatism.* New York: Hafner, 1948.

Kelman, H. Attitude change as a function of response restriction. *Hum. Relat.*, 1953, **6**, 185-214.

Lindzey, G. A note on interviewer bias. *J. appl. Psychol.*, 1951, **35**, 182-184.

Mahalanobis, P. C. Recent experiments in statistical sampling in the Indian Statistical Institute. *J. Roy. statist. Soc.*, 1946, **109**, 325-370.

Marcia, J. Hypothesis-making, need for social approval, and their effects on unconscious experimenter bias. Unpublished master's thesis, Ohio State Univer., Columbus, Ohio, 1961.

Merton, R. K. The self-fulfilling prophecy. *Antioch Rev.*, 1948, **8**, 193-210.

Mosteller, F. Correcting for interviewer bias. In H. Cantril, (Ed.), *Gauging public opinion.* Princeton, New Jersey: Princeton Univ. Press, 1944, pp. 286-288.

Orne, M. T. On the social psychology of the psychological experiment: with particular reference to demand characteristics and their implications. *Amer. Psychologist,* 1962, **17**, 776-783.

Pearson, K. On the mathematical theory of errors of judgment wtih special reference to the personal equation. *Phil. Trans. Roy. Soc. Lond.,* 1902, **198**, 235-299.

Persinger, G. W. The effect of acquaintanceship on the mediation of experimenter bias. Unpublished master's thesis, Univer. of North Dakota, Grand Forks, 1962.

Pflugrath, J. Examiner influence in a group testing situation with particular reference to examiner bias. Unpublished master's thesis, Univer. of North Dakota, Grand Forks, 1962.

Pfungst, O. *Clever Hans (the horse of Mr. von Osten); a contribution to experimental, animal, and human psychology.* Translated by Rahn, C. L. New York: Holt, 1911.

Riecken, H. A program for research on experiments in social psychology. In N. F. Washburne, (Ed.), *Decisions, values and groups.* New York: Pergamon Press, 1962, Vol. II, pp. 25-41.

Roe, Anne. The psychology of the scientist. *Science,* 1961, **134**, 456-459.

Rosenthal, R. The effects of the experimenter as observer on the results of the psychological experiment. Unpublished manuscript, Harvard Univer., Cambridge, Massachusetts, 1963. (a)

Rosenthal, R. Experimenter attributes as determinants of subjects' responses. *J. proj. Tech. Pers. Assess.,* 1963, **27**, 324-331. (b)

Rosenthal, R. Experimenter modeling effects as determinants of subjects' responses. *J. proj. Tech. Pers. Assess.,* 1963, **27**, 467-471. (c)

Rosenthal, R. On the social psychology of the psychological experiment: the experimenter's hypothesis as unintended determinant of experimental results. *Amer. Scient.,* 1963, **51**, 268-283. (d)

Rosenthal, R. Experimenter outcome-orientation and the results of the psychological experiment. *Psychol. Bull.,* in press. (a)

Rosenthal, R. The volunteer subject. *Hum. Relat.,* in press. (b)

Rosenthal, R., and Fode, K. L. The effect of experimenter bias on the performance of the albino rat. *Behav. Sci.,* 1963, **8**, 183-189. (a)

Rosenthal, R., and Fode, K. L. (Psychology of the scientist: V.) Three experiments in experimenter bias. *Psychol. Rep. Monogr.,* 3, V12, 1963. (b)

Rosenthal, R., and Lawson, R. A longitudinal study of the effects of experimenter bias on the operant learning of laboratory rats. *Amer. Psychologist,* 1963, **18**, 345. (Abstr.)

Rosenthal, R., Fode, K. L., Friedman, C. J., and Vikan-Kline, Linda L. Subjects' perception of their experimenter under conditions of experimenter bias. *Percept. mot. Skills,* 1960, **11**, 325-331. (a)

Rosenthal, R., Fode, K. L.. and Vikan-Kline, Linda. The effect on experimenter bias of varying levels of motivation of *Es* and *Ss.* Unpublished manuscript, Harvard Univer., Cambridge, Massachusetts, 1960. (b)

Rosenthal, R., Persinger, G. W., and Fode, K. L. Experimenter bias, anxiety, and social desirability. *Percept. mot. Skills*, 1962, **15**, 73-74.

Rosenthal, R., Kohn, P., Marks, Patricia, and Carota, N. Experimenters' hypothesis-confirmation and mood as determinants of experimental results. Unpublished manuscript, Harvard Univer., Cambridge, Massachusetts, 1963. (a)

Rosenthal, R., Persinger, G. W., Mulry, R. C., Vikan-Kline, Linda, and Grothe, M. A motion picture study of 25 biased experimenters. Unpublished manuscript, Harvard Univer., Cambridge, Massachusetts, 1963. (b)

Rosenthal, R., Persinger, G. W., Vikan-Kline, Linda, and Fode, K. L. The effect of early data returns on data subsequently obtained by outcome-biased experimenters. *Sociometry*, 1963, **26**, 487-498. (c)

Rosenthal, R., Persinger, G. W., Vikan-Kline, Linda, and Fode, K. L. The effect of experimenter outcome-bias and subject set on awareness in verbal conditioning experiments. *J. verb. Learn. verb. Behav.*, 1963, **2**, 275-283. (d)

Rosenthal, R., Persinger, G. W., Vikan-Kline, Linda, and Mulry, R. C. The role of the research assistant in the mediation of experimenter bias. *J. Pers.*, 1963, **31**, 313-335. (e)

Rosenthal, R., Fode, K. L., Vikan-Kline, Linda, and Persinger, G. W. Verbal conditioning: mediator of experimenter expectancy effects? *Psychol. Rep.*, 1964, **14**, 71-74.

Rosenthal, R., Friedman, C. J., Johnson, C. A., Fode, K. L., Schill, T. R., White, C. R., and Vikan-Kline, Linda. Variables affecting experimenter bias in a group situation. *Genet. Psychol. Monogr.*, in press.

Shapiro, A. P. The investigator himself. In S. O. Waife and A. P. Shapiro (Eds.), *The clinical evaluation of new drugs*. New York: Hoeber-Harper, 1959.

Sheffield, F. D., Kaufman, R. S., and Rhine, J. B. A PK experiment at Yale starts a controversy. *J. Amer. Soc. Psychical Res.*, 1952, **46**, 111-117.

Stanton, F. Further contributions at the twentieth anniversary of the psychological corporation and to honor its founder, James McKeen Cattel. *J. appl. Psychol.*, 1942, **26**, 16-17.

Stanton, F., and Baker, K. H. Interviewer bias and the recall of incompletely learned materials. *Sociometry*, 1942, **5**, 123-134.

Symposium: Survey on problems of interviewer cheating. *Int. J. opin. attit. Res.*, 1947, **1**, 93-106.

Turner, J. What laymen can ask of scientists. *Science*, 1961, **133**, 1195.

Verplanck, W. S. The control of the content of conversation: reinforcement of statements of opinion. *J. abnorm. soc. Psychol.*, 1955, **51**, 668-676.

Vikan-Kline, Linda. The effect of an experimenter's perceived status on the mediation of experimenter bias. Unpublished master's thesis, Univer. of North Dakota, Grand Forks, 1962.

Wartenberg-Ekren, Ursula. The effect of experimenter knowledge of a subject's scholastic standing on the performance of a reasoning task. Unpublished master's thesis, Marquette Univer., 1962.

White, C. R. The effect of induced subject expectations on the experimenter bias situation. Unpublished doctoral dissertation, Univer. of North Dakota, Grand Forks, 1962.

Wilson, E. B. *An introduction to scientific research*. New York: McGraw-Hill, 1952.

Winkel, G. H., and Sarason, I. G. Subject, experimenter, and situational variables in research on anxiety. *J. abnorm. soc. Psychol.*, in press.

Wolins, L. Responsibility for raw data. *Amer. Psychologist*, 1962, **17**, 657-658.

Yule, G. U. On reading a scale. *J. Roy. statist. Soc.*, 1927, **90**, 570-587.

# PERSONALITY AND CONDITIONING

## S. H. Lovibond

UNIVERSITY OF ADELAIDE, ADELAIDE, SOUTH AUSTRALIA[1]

## I. Introduction

Since the publication of the early work of Pavlov (1927), which described marked individual differences in the conditioning performance of animals, the method of conditioning has held promise of elucidating basic parameters of human personality functioning. Early attempts to apply the method to human subjects encountered serious methodological difficulties. Apart from such technical problems as the measurement of the output of saliva in salivary conditioning of human subjects, it became apparent that the central factors of "attitude," "set," or "expectancy" are important sources of variability in human conditioning. The conditioning of other responses, such as the GSR, brought new problems of measurement. It is probably true, however, that the most significant barriers to progress were conceptual, rather than methodological. In the Soviet Union there was apparently a long period in which little advance

---

[1] Present address: Dalhousie University, Halifax, Nova Scotia, Canada.

was made on Pavlov's thinking in relation to the problems of individual differences in conditioning. In the Western world this aspect of Pavlov's theorizing had little impact, and there were no alternative theories which might have systematized the findings of existing research, and pointed the way to significant areas of future study.

The resurgence of Western interest in problems of conditioning and personality over the past decade or so seems to have resulted chiefly from the development of two psychological theories of relevance to problems of personality. These are the theories of Hull (1943, 1952) and Eysenck (1957). Between them these two theories have inspired the majority of Western studies of conditioning in relation to personality functioning over the past decade. Most of the remaining Western investigations have been largely empirical in character. In the USSR, interest continues in the problem of developing Pavlov's typological conceptions.

A review of recent research suggests that studies of personality dynamics through conditioning may most conveniently be grouped under two main headings. First, there are the studies which begin with groups differentiated on the basis of personality characteristics, and proceed to examine the relationship between these personality characteristics and parameters of conditioning performance. Possibly the most important subgroupings within this class of investigation may be defined in terms of the theoretical bases from which the studies derive. Thus the study may be designed to test predictions from a theory of personality of wide generality, it may be concerned with predictions derived from a theory of limited aspects of personality functioning, or it may be unrelated to systematic theory of any sort.

In the second group of studies, techniques of conditioning are used in the process of defining major personality variables. Virtually all investigations of personality and conditioning in Western countries fall into the first major class, whereas the most significant studies in the USSR belong to the second major grouping.

A further development leading to renewed interest in personality–conditioning relations has been the application of direct conditioning methods in the therapy of behavior disturbances. This work received a good deal of its impetus from the application of conditioning methods in the study of experimental neuroses. Whereas the studies previously considered are concerned with understanding personality dynamics, investigations of experimental neuroses and behavior therapy are concerned with changing certain aspects of personality functioning.

An examination of the literature on personality and conditioning quickly reveals the extent to which further advance is dependent as much on the solution of basic issues in conditioning as on conceptual development in relation to personality functioning. For this reason it has been found necessary to devote a good deal of attention in the following pages to problems of methodology, and to such fundamental issues as the criteria of conditioning.

Although the procedures of classical conditioning of involuntary responses are often referred to as "simple conditioning," it is becoming increasingly clear that, at this level of behavioral modification, we are confronted with sufficient complexity to make interpretation far from straightforward. Since the study of the instrumental conditioning of voluntary responses in human beings (e.g., verbal conditioning) introduces further complexity, it has been considered wisest to place exclusive emphasis on classical procedures at this stage. In any case, classical conditioning studies account for the great majority of the investigations of personality and conditioning which have been carried out to date.

Recently Diamond, Balvin, and Diamond (1963) have declared in favor of a return to the use of the terms "conditional" and "unconditional" in place of "conditioned" and "unconditioned" reflexes. These authors point out that "the context of Pavlov's discussion never leaves any doubt that the meaning he wished to convey is that of the words conditional and unconditional. He spoke of the conditional reflexes as 'temporary connections,' and he emphasized that they lack the certainty and regularity of occurrence of innate reflexes which can, by contrast, be called unconditional; that is, the reaction is sure to occur in response to the adequate stimulus despite other circumstances and conditions" (Diamond *et al.*, 1963, p. 183). Following the lead of these writers, the terms conditional and unconditional will be used in the present paper in place of the more conventional conditioned and unconditioned.

## II. Investigations of Personality Dynamics

A. STUDIES OF RELATIONS BETWEEN INDEPENDENTLY DEFINED PERSONALITY VARIABLES AND PARAMETERS OF CONDITIONING PERFORMANCE

*1. Tests of Predictions from Personality Theories of Wide Generality*

The only comprehensive theory of personality which has given rise to explicit predictions concerning the differential conditioning performance of groups distinguished on the basis of personality is that of Eysenck. Conditioning is allotted a crucial role in Eysenck's theory. In the development of his theory, Eysenck began with a study of the problems of taxonomy or classification. At this stage the question asked was, "What are the major dimensions of personality with respect to which persons vary?" The answer, proposed on the basis of previous findings and original research, was that most of the variance in personality functioning can be accounted for in terms of the three orthogonal dimensions of psychoticism, neuroticism, and introversion-extraversion. Psychoticism is defined as a predisposition to develop such symptoms of mental disorder as delusions, hallucinations, mood disturbances, motor retardation, and the like. Neuroticism is identified with emotionality or lability of the autonomic nervous system, which is considered to act as a predisposition to neurotic disorders. The introversion-extraversion dimension is defined in terms of a wide range of behaviors. The behavior of introverts is characterized by a relative lack of sociability, high persistence, high level of aspiration, an emphasis on accuracy rather than speed, reliance on inner standards of conduct, and a stress on moral scruples. Extraverts, on the other hand, are sociable, impulsive, dependent on the social valuations of others, low in level of aspiration, and tough minded in their attitudes. Following Jung, Eysenck proposes that hysteria is the syndrome to be found in the extraverted neurotic, whilst dysthymia (syndrome characterized by anxiety, reactive depression, and/or obsessive-compulsive features) is typically found in the introverted neurotic.

In seeking likely neurophysiological mechanisms of the personality differences between extraverts and introverts, Eysenck formulated his individual difference and typological postulates in terms of excitation-inhibition balance. The essence of these postulates is that individuals in whom excitatory potentials are generated quickly and strongly, and in whom inhibitory potentials are generated slowly and weakly, will tend to be introverted in personality, and to develop dysthymic disorders in the case of neurotic breakdown. Conversely, individuals who generate weak excitatory potentials slowly, and who generate strong inhibitory potentials quickly, tend to be extraverted in personality, and to develop hysterical-psychopathic disorders in case of neurotic breakdown.

A link between excitation-inhibition balance and (a) the personality patterns of introversion *versus* extraversion, and (b) hysterical-psychopathic disturbances *versus* dysthymia, is provided by conditioning.

In brief, a key difference between extraverts and introverts is the degree of socialization which is typical of each. Socialization, or the establishment of social controls over egoistic impulses, is mediated by conditioning. Because of their rapid and strong development of excitation and their weak tendency toward the development of reactive inhibition, introverts condition well, and hence tend to become oversocialized. Conversely, the slow development of weak excitatory potentials, and the rapid and strong development of inhibitory potentials, makes extraverts condition poorly. As a consequence extraverts tend to be undersocialized.

Strong autonomic-emotional lability and reactivity produce excessive fear reactions to painful stimuli in all persons high on neuroticism, but in the introverted neurotic, the strong capacity for conditioning causes these fear reactions to become attached to a multitude of fortuitous stimuli, thus producing the excessive anxiety reactions of the dysthymic. The dysthymic, then, is characterized by oversocialization and excessive anxiety, whilst the hysteric is characterized by undersocialization and autonomic lability without excessive conditional anxiety.

It is clear that Eysenck's theory postulates a general factor of conditionability or acquisition of CR's. It also leads to the prediction that introverted normals will condition more rapidly than extraverted normals with any reliable conditioning procedure. Furthermore the theory predicts that neurotic introverts (dysthymics) will condition better than unselected normals, and that neurotic extraverts (hysterics and psychopaths) will condition less well than unselected normals. There is no suggestion, however, that neuroticism, anxiety, or emotionality as such will be related to conditioning performance.

The first experiment designed to test these hypotheses was carried out by Franks (1956), who used the eyeblink conditioning method with 20 hysterics, 20 normals, and 20 dysthymics. In accordance with prediction, the groups were ordered dysthymics, normals, and hysterics in terms of rate of conditioning and resistance to extinction. In a later experiment, Franks (1957) used 55 normal undergraduate Ss who had been given the Maudsley Personality Inventory (MPI). This inventory included an extraversion (E) scale. Eyeblink conditioning was again used, and the correlation between conditioning and extraversion was −.46 for acquisition, and −.34 for extinction.

More recent studies of eyeblink conditioning in relation to scores on the E scale of the MPI have mostly produced relationships in the direction predicted by Eysenck, but few of the correlations have reached statistical significance. Willet (1960) used the Fisher Z transformation to obtain an estimate of the true correlation between eyeblink acquisition score and the E scale. The estimate, which was based on the studies of Franks (1957), Das (1957), O'Connor (1959), and Willet (1960), was −.188. Since Willet's publication, further investigations of the relation between the E scale and eyeblink conditioning have included those by Barendregt (1961), Field and Brengelmann (1961), and Sweetbaum (1963). Barendregt reported a correlation of −.29 but Sweetbaum obtained a correlation of near zero. Field and Brengelmann found that their introverted Ss conditioned insignificantly faster than their extraverted Ss. It would appear that the results of the later investigations agree with those cited by Willet (1960) in suggesting that the relationship between the E scale and eyeblink conditioning is best represented by a correlation of −.2.

Several investigators have studied the relationship between extra-version questionnaire measures and GSR conditioning. Becker (1960) and Becker and Matteson (1961) twice presented a list of 104 words spaced at 5-sec intervals. The word "repeat" occurred 20 times followed by a .1-sec shock on 12 trials. Using two different measures of conditioning, Ss with introverted scores on Guilford's R scale were not differentiated from Ss with low scores on the scale, in either experiment, despite the fact that in the second experiment extreme scoring groups were selected.

Vogel (1960, 1962), however, using a very similar GSR method, obtained highly significant differences in conditioning performance between extraverts and introverts. Lovibond (1963a) also used the GSR in a study of conditioning in 63 university students for whom E-scale scores were available. There were two conditioning sessions. In one session the US was electric shock and in the other the US was provided by pictures of nude females. The correlation between E score and a measure of rate of aversive conditioning was −.05. The correlation for positive reinforcement was −.10.

A change of conditioning technique appears to leave the correlation between the E scale and conditioning performance essentially unchanged, and it is clear that the amount of common variance between the two types of measures is small. Possible reasons for the failure to demonstrate a stronger relationship, other than invalidity of the theory, include unreliability of the conditioning measures, and inadequacy of the E scale as a measure of extraversion. By and large it is clear that the reliability of both eyeblink and GSR conditioning measures is reasonably satisfactory (Becker, 1960; Franks, 1957; Lovibond, 1963b; Welch and Kubis, 1947).

It will be suggested in Section III, D,2 that the validity of GSR conditioning measures can often be questioned, but the arguments advanced there do not apply to the Becker (1960) experiment, nor to Lovibond's (1963a) positive reinforcement measure, both of which failed to produce an appreciable correlation with E scores. Willet (1960) has argued that the E scale is a very poor measure of extraversion, and cites a study of Claridge which showed that careful behavioral ratings produced predicted relationships whereas questionnaire scores did not. Eysenck (Eysenck and Claridge, 1962) has recently recognized that the E scale is not unidimensional, and in fact measures a "behavioral" extraversion factor as well as a "constitutional" extraversion factor, the former being irrelevant to predictions from the original theory. Whilst a purified E scale may improve the position, it is likely that questionnaire studies of personality-conditioning relationships have reached the limit of their fruitfulness. It would now seem advisable to concentrate research effort on the development of a set of rating scales along the lines of those developed by Olson (1930) for the study of behavior disorders in children, and to use these scales in conjunction with objective tests of excitation-inhibition balance (Eysenck and Claridge, 1962).

2. *Tests of Predictions from Theories of Limited Aspects of Personality Functioning.*

*a. Anxiety and Conditioning.* The personality variable which has been most studied in relation to conditioning performance is anxiety. Since the majority of personality theories had their origins in the field of abnormal psychology, where anxiety is a pervasive problem, it is understandable that anxiety has become a central personality concept. As Jensen (1958, p. 313) has put it, "Few, if any, other concepts sustain as much of the superstructure of personality theory."

The early studies of anxiety and conditioning were largely empirical, but since developments of Hull's general behavior theory gave rise to testable predictions concerning the relation between anxiety and conditioning, interest in this area of investigation has increased markedly. Much of the recent work has been carried out by the group at Iowa (Spence, 1954; Spence and Taylor, 1951, 1953; Spence and Farber, 1953; Taylor, 1951, 1956).

The aspects of Hullian theory which are of relevance to the relation between conditioning and anxiety have been stated by Taylor (1956) as follows:

"According to Hull, all habits (*H*) activated in a given situation, combine multiplicatively with the total effective drive state (*D*) operating at the moment to form excitatory potential or $E$ $[E = f\ (H \times D)]$. Total effective drive in the Hullian system is determined by the summation of all extant need states, primary and secondary, irrespective of their relevancy to the type of reinforcement employed. Since response strength is determined in part by $E$, the implication of varying drive level in any situation in which a single habit is evoked is clear; the higher the drive, the greater the value of $E$ and hence of response strength. Thus in simple, noncompetitional experimental arrangements involving only a single habit tendency, the performance level of high drive Ss should be greater than that for low drive groups."

In a series of experiments designed to test this prediction from Hull's theory, the Iowa group chose classical conditioning of the eyeblink as "a simple, noncompetitional experimental arrangement involving only a single habit tendency." In the search for a drive which could readily be varied in strength, Spence and his associates made the assumption that anxiety possesses the energizing and reinforcing properties attributed to drive in Hullian theory.

The next step was to provide a means of manipulating the strength of the anxiety drive. There are three principal procedures which experimenters have used for this purpose. The first selects Ss who manifest symptoms of anxiety in different degrees by means of clinical observation or responses to questionnaires. The second induces anxiety experimentally by means of ego threat (e.g., failure in a competitive situation) or threat of painful stimulation (e.g., electric shock). The third method makes use of real life situations considered to be productive of anxiety (imminence of examinations or surgical operations).

The most favored procedure has been the first named, and most experiments have made use of a specially devised questionnaire, the Manifest Anxiety Scale (MAS). The MAS was constructed by asking clinicians to select from a pool of personality questionnaires those items, the endorsement of which would be indicative of manifest anxiety. Although the rationale of this procedure has not been discussed in any detail, it is clear that when the MAS was constructed, it was assumed that high scorers on the scale were in a chronic state of high anxiety drive.

A sufficient number of studies has now been carried out to indicate that MAS scores are positively related to eyeblink conditioning performance (Baron and Connor, 1960; Spence and Farber, 1953; Spence, Farber and Taylor, 1954; Spence and Taylor, 1951, 1953; Taylor, 1951). The strength of this relationship is represented by a correlation of about +.25. In other words, differences in MAS score account for about 6% of the variance in eyeblink conditioning performance.

Bitterman and Holtzman (1952), Gilberstadt and Davenport (1960), and Lacey, Smith, and Green (1955), were unable to demonstrate a significant relationship between MAS scores and GSR conditioning. More recently, however, Becker and Matteson (1961), using extreme scores on the MAS, found that the rate of acquisition of a conditional GSR was substantially greater in anxious Ss than in nonanxious Ss. The relatively low correlations obtained between the MAS and conditioning, as well as the not infrequent failure of scores on the scale to correlate as predicted with complex learning performance, has led to a more critical attitude toward the MAS, and a tendency to use other methods of manipulating the anxiety variable. At the same time the conception of anxiety itself has undergone some change. It is now fairly generally agreed that the MAS does not measure present defensive arousal, proneness to defensive arousal, or chronic, persisting tension, but rather S's tendency to react to anxiety in a way "characteristic of the psychasthenic neurotic" (Jenkins and Lykken, 1957). There seems to have been a definite shift toward the conception of anxiety as sensitivity to defensive arousal or reactivity to threat. Anxiety thus becomes a disposition rather than a state, but it is still considered to have drive properties when activated by threat or stress. This shift in emphasis in the definition of anxiety has resulted in part from the greater frequency of significant findings in tests of drive theory when threat has been experimentally induced. For example, Beam (1955) made use of the real life stress produced by impending doctoral examinations in a study of GSR conditioning. Under stress, conditioning was significantly faster. Sweetbaum (1963), in a similar type of study, relied on impending surgical operation to induce anxiety. In this case the response conditioned was the eye blink. Subjects under stress conditioned very much more rapidly than did control Ss who had made a successful recovery from surgery. Willet (1963) compared the eyeblink conditioning performance of youths taking part in a stressful selection procedure with that of controls who had already been selected. The acquisition of the CR was significantly faster in the experimental group.

Experiments which have made use of clinical ratings of anxiety have also tended to produce more significant results than studies using the MAS. Some of the earlier experiments of this type were not prompted by the theory of anxiety as a drive, but because of their relevance for an evaluation of this theory, they are mentioned here. Welch and Kubis (1947) investigated the effects of pathological anxiety on the rate of GSR conditioning. A group of 51 mixed psychiatric patients was rated for anxiety by psychiatrists. The CS was one of 54 nonsense syllables presented at a rate of one per 6 sec. The US was the sound of a buzzer. The conditioning score was number of trials required for 3 successive GSR's to the CS greater than the GSR's to control syllables. All but 4 of 36 normals scored from 14 to 58, whilst, with one exception, all patients diagnosed as having anxiety had a score of 14 or less. The retest correlation on 36 normals was +.88. Other investigators who have found clinically assessed anxiety to be positively related to GSR conditioning performance are Bitterman and Holtzman (1952), Gilberstadt and Davenport (1960), and Schiff, Dougan, and Welch (1949). No failures to find such a relationship appear to have been reported.

Altogether there is a considerable body of evidence that psychiatric patients suffering from anxiety, and normal individuals subjected to stress, condition more rapidly in experiments using aversive reinforcement than do persons not suffering from anxiety. The theory of Spence and Taylor, however, predicts similar findings from nonaversive conditioning experiments. According to the theory, anxiety as an irrelevant drive should summate with relevant drive to increase performance in this sort of situation also. In order to test this prediction, Bindra, Paterson, and Strzelecki (1955) undertook a salivary conditioning experiment with high and low scorers on the MAS. The performance of the anxious and nonanxious Ss was virtually identical. Bindra *et al.* interpreted their results as favorable to the view of anxiety as a response to threatening situations. The findings of Bindra *et al.* have been accepted uncritically into the literature as indicating that anxious and nonanxious Ss perform equally well in classical conditioning experiments involving no threat (Eysenck, 1957; Franks, 1960; Jenkins and Lykken, 1957; Kimble, 1961; Stewart, Winokur, Stern, Guze, Pfeiffer and Hornung, 1959). The Bindra experiment, however, is open to such serious methodological criticism (see Section III, D, 3) that its results cannot be accepted as evidence for or against any theory. Hence the issue of whether or not anxiety increases performance in nonaversive conditioning must be regarded as still open.

An alternative to the general drive theory of the relation between anxiety and conditioning can be derived from recent work in the field of electrophysiology and Pavlovian theory. As Malmo (1958) has argued, the concept of general drive or $D$ may be regarded as identical with the neurophysiological concept of "nonspecific arousal." Since the pioneering work of Moruzzi and Magoun (1949), nonspecific arousal has been seen as the chief function of the brain stem reticular formation. It is now recognized, however, that the reticular formation can no longer be regarded simply as a nonspecific arousal system, the function of which is merely that of an excitatory amplifier. The work of such investigators as Kaada and Johannsen (1960) has made it abundantly clear that the reticular formation selectively activates some areas of the brain whilst it inhibits others. As Diamond *et al.* (1963, p. 228) put it, the work on the reticular formation assumes "its full significance only with the recognition that multiple inhibitory effects, exerted both upwards and downwards, are essential to all behavior."

Microelectrode and intracranial chemical stimulation techniques have demonstrated the existence of "centers," or functional systems associated with unconditional reactions of various types, and have confirmed Pavlov's view of reciprocal inhibitory relationships between these centers. The experiments of Wyrwicka and Dobrzecka (1960) on goats confirmed the hypothesis of Anand and Brobeck (1951) that the lateral hypothalamus contains a "feeding center" and the ventromedial nucleus a "satiation center." Considering this and related experiments, Diamond *et al.* (1963, p. 368) comment that "feeding, as an element of the behavioral repertoire, is embedded in several different behavior pairs or polar opposites. First, we have the contrast between feeding and satiation as originally postulated. Second, there is a conflict between feeding and fear, . . . third, in the feeding center itself, there is the differentiation between eating and drinking. When an animal chooses not to eat, there may be at least three kinds of motivational influence: satiation, fear, or felt need for liquid. It is an established fact that any one of these inhibits the feeding mechanism." Wolpe (1958), on the other hand, has developed a system of psychotherapy based on animal experiments in which reciprocal inhibition of anxiety responses is effected by the activation of positive responses such as feeding.

Anokhin (1961) has elaborated a conception of the selective action on the cerebral cortex of reticular and other subcortical nuclei in relation to the formation and elicitation of conditional reflexes. Summarizing the results of electrophysiological experiments which made "a comparative evaluation of the activating effect on the cerebral cortex in two biologically opposed states: defensive and alimentary," Anokhin (1961) says, "It may be assumed that all forms of desynchronization of slow cortical activity that arise during the orienting-investigatory, defensive, and alimentary reactions, although outwardly remaining to some extent similar, are actually physiologically entirely specific, ensuring entirely different biological activities . . . the activating influence on the cortex is always of a functionally specific character . . . only the imperfection of the electroencephalographic index fostered the emergence of the ideas of a 'generalized,' 'nonspecific,' and 'diffuse' activating effect of the subcortex on the cerebral cortex."

In the light of these considerations, it would seem reasonable to postulate that individuals in a state of strong anxiety, whether chronic or acute, will manifest a decreased capacity for forming positive reward conditional reflexes. This prediction is based on the assumption that defensive arousal will inhibit the functionally specific arousals considered necessary for the formation of positive reward, or appetitive, conditional reflexes. No clear-cut evidence relevant to this prediction is available. The results of Bindra et al. (1955) are equivocal, and, although Finesinger, Sutherland, and McGuire (1942) have shown that neurotic Ss are able to form salivary conditional reflexes, no control data were obtained. Lovibond (1963a) compared the positive reward GSR conditioning performance of high and low scorers on Eysenck's Neuroticism (N) scale, which had previously been shown to correlate highly with the MAS (Eysenck, 1957). There was an insignificant tendency for Ss with low N scores to perform at a higher level than Ss with high N scores.

With the redefinition of anxiety in terms of emotional sensitivity to threatening situations, it is now clear that experiments using questionnaire scores as anxiety criteria are of little relevance in the study of the relationship between anxiety and appetitive conditioning. What is required is a study of the effects of real life stress, such as impending surgical operation (Sweetbaum, 1963), on appetitive conditioning performance using either the GSR technique of Lovibond, or a methodologically acceptable technique of salivary conditioning (see Section III, D, 3).

We have seen that the two theories which have generated most of the research into personality conditioning relations emphasize different personality variables as being related to differences in conditionability. For Eysenck, the personality dimension which is related to conditionability is introversion-extraversion whilst for Spence and Taylor it is anxiety. We have seen also that both variables in fact appear to some degree to be related to aversive conditioning performance. Hence the question of the relation between these two variables naturally arises. It will be remembered that Eysenck's theory of personality postulates three orthogonal dimensions, introversion-extraversion, neuroticism, and psychoticism. Neuroticism has been defined tentatively in terms of emotionality, or autonomic nervous system lability, and since Eysenck has in mind defensive emotionality and autonomic lability, it would appear that neuroticism and anxiety may reasonably be equated. The essence of Eysenck's thinking on the subject appears to be conveyed if we think of anxiety-neuroticism in terms of "defense arousability," i.e., sensitivity to arousal by aversive stimulation and threatening situations.

Eysenck has postulated that introverts generate excitatory potentials rapidly and strongly. His findings that, in contrast to extraverts, introverts have high levels of aspiration, persistence, perceptual rigidity, and sedation threshold, support this assumption, although Eysenck has emphasized the differences in inhibitory potential between introverts and extraverts rather than differences in excitatory potential.

A reconcilation between the views of Eysenck and Spence and the accumulated evidence may be effected by acceptance of the following propositions.

1. The level of cortical excitation, which determines the speed of formation of conditional linkages, is dependent on
   (a) the degree of subcortical arousal and
   (b) the general excitability of the cortex, i.e., the capacity of the cortex for developing excitation from a given level of subcortical arousal.

2. Individuals differ with respect to three dimensions of nervous activity which are at least partially independent:
   (a) general excitability of the cortex,

(b) defensive arousability, and

(c) appetitive arousability.

3. The personality dimension which is related to general excitability of the cortex, and hence to a general factor of conditionability, is introversion-extraversion, and the relationship is such that introverts will manifest higher levels of general cortical excitability, and conditionability, than will extraverts.

4. The personality variable of anxiety is related to level of defensive arousability, and a group factor of aversive conditionability.

5. The relationship between different arousal systems is a mutually inhibitory one, so that, e.g., a high level of defensive arousal at a particular time will reduce the capacity for appetitive arousal, and hence appetitive conditioning performance.

6. The relationship of reciprocal inhibition between different types of arousal will be to some degree asymmetrical. Because of the generally greater strength of defensive arousal, the inhibitory effects of this type of arousal are likely to be more readily observable than the inhibitory effects of nondefensive arousal.

Table I sets out the predicted differences in the aversive and appetitive conditioning performance of anxious introverts, anxious extraverts,

TABLE I

CONDITIONING PERFORMANCE OF VARIOUS GROUPS EXPECTED ON THE HYPOTHESIS OF A
RELATION OF RECIPROCAL INHIBITION BETWEEN
DIFFERENT AROUSAL SYSTEMS

| | Anxious (stress situation) | | | | Nonanxious (nonstress situation) | | | |
|---|---|---|---|---|---|---|---|---|
| | Aversive conditioning | | Appetitive conditioning | | Aversive conditioning | | Appetitive conditioning | |
| | General | Specific | General | Specific | General | Specific | General | Specific |
| Introvert | + | + | + | — | + | 0 | + | 0 |
| Extravert | — | + | — | — | — | 0 | — | 0 |

nonanxious introverts, and nonanxious extraverts. It is important to note that "anxious" refers here to a presently high level of defensive arousal, whether this is achieved through a high degree of defensive arousability and moderate stress, or a moderate degree of defensive arousability and a high level of stress.

Considering the anxiety dimension alone, the predictions are quite clear cut and readily tested. It is predicted that an unselected group under real life stress will condition better than nonstress controls with aversive reinforcement, but less well with appetitive reinforcement. We have seen that the evidence of Beam (1955), Sweetbaum (1963), and

Willet (1963) is favorable to the prediction relating to aversive conditioning, but evidence relevant to appetitive conditioning is entirely lacking.

Considering the introversion-extraversion dimension separately, it is
predicted that introverts will condition more readily than extraverts with
both aversive and appetitive reinforcement. The only unambiguous
studies bearing on these predictions are those which have used questionnaires to select Ss. In all cases except one (Lovibond, 1963a), aversive
conditioning procedures have been used, and the evidence, on balance,
favors the prediction of superior performance by introverts. In Lovibond's
(1963a) appetitive GSR conditioning experiment, there was a tendency
for introverts to perform at a higher level than extraverts. This performance difference, although in the required direction was not significant.

It was suggested in Section II, A, 1 that the selection of extraverts and
introverts by means of personality questionnaires alone is an unsatisfac-
tory procedure. Efforts to obtain behavioral ratings which emphasize the
temperamental disposition factor of extraversion might well prove
fruitful, particularly if combined with objective indicators such as level
of aspiration, persistence, and so forth. Extraverts and introverts selected
by these means could be equated on the anxiety dimension by means of
questionnaires and measures of autonomic reaction to stress.

Turning now to the predictions derived from the interaction of the
two dimensions, it will be seen that, in Table I, pluses, zeroes, and
minuses are allotted under the various headings. A plus signifies better-
than-average conditioning expected, a zero indicates average conditioning, and a minus below-average conditioning. The heading "general"
refers to the expected influence of the assumed general factor, and the
heading "specific" refers to the expected influence of defensive arousal.

Assuming equal weight for each positive and negative tendency, the
algebraic sums of general and group factor influences give the expected
order of the groups in terms of each type of conditioning performance.
The decreasing order of predicted aversive conditioning performance for
the groups is anxious introvert, nonanxious introvert, anxious extravert,
nonanxious extravert. The corresponding order for appetitive conditioning is nonanxious introvert, anxious introvert, nonanxious extravert,
anxious extravert.

*b. Conceptual Thinking Disturbances and Conditioning.* From
studies of the responses of schizophrenics and normals to various tests of
concept formation, Lovibond (1954) concluded that the characteristic
feature of schizophrenic thought disorder is a failure to inhibit linkages
or associations which the context makes irrelevant. According to this
hypothesis, in normal thinking, the context, including the experimenter's

instructions, the nature of the test materials, or the theme of a discussion, permits the activation of only a limited number of "relevant" linkages in the S's conceptual structures. The majority of the manifold linkages that are potentially available are selectively inhibited by a process akin to the active, differential inhibition manifest in conditioning experiments. On the basis of these assumptions, a method was developed to permit analysis of responses to the Object Sorting Test in terms of the in-essentiality of the definitions offered (Lovibond, 1954, 1964a). Further work with this test indicated that something like 20% of normals obtained high, or schizophreniclike, scores. It was concluded that certain aspects of schizophrenic-type thinking could conveniently be studied in these high-scoring normals whose thinking was free from the complications of mental disorder.

In an extension of the original theorizing, it was hypothesized that the differential inhibition of irrelevant linkages in normal thinking takes place through a process of negative induction, which necessitates a relatively strong process of excitation. On the basis of this analysis, a number of predictions was made concerning the differential conditioning performance of normals with high and low scores on the Object Sorting Test. In particular, it was predicted that high scorers would show lower reactivity (including weaker initial orienting reactions, and a slower rate of conditioning) and a lower capacity for differentiation. With use of positive, or appetitive, reinforcement of the GSR, the main predictions were confirmed. When the GSR was reinforced by electric shock in another session, however, the differences between the two groups largely disappeared. It was concluded that the stronger activation from the aversive US was sufficient to mask the differences in conditioning performance between the two groups.

This study raises the question of the relationship between the personality dimension tapped by the Sorting Test, and other dimensions known to be related to conditioning performance. The Sorting Test dimension would seem to be closely akin to the "cortical excitability" assumed by Eysenck to be one of the properties of nervous activity which differentiates introverts and extraverts. The finding of stronger differential inhibition in Ss with strong excitatory processes introduces a contradiction, however, since Eysenck's work suggests a negative correlation between strength of excitation and strength of inhibition. Nevertheless, it is possible that this contradiction is more apparent than real. Eysenck has been concerned primarily with the "work decrement" type of inhibition, which may be not at all the same process as the active inhibitory process assumed by Pavlov to underlie differentiation. In this connection it is of interest to note that, in differential delayed conditioning, when inhibition with reinforcement occurs, the response to the differential stimulus usually shows little further decrease, and may actually increase. This suggests the possibility that response decrement inhibition may be inimical to differential inhibition. No consistent correlations have been obtained between Sorting Test scores and scores on the MPI, but in view of the criticisms of this and related questionnaires, it would be unwise to conclude that the tests are measuring different dimensions.

The correlation of Sorting Test scores and measures of extraversion based on ratings and objective tests might well produce a different result.

### 3. Empirical Studies of Personality and Conditioning

In a number of purely empirical studies, comparisons have been made of the conditioning performance of groups known to differ in terms of certain personality characteristics. Usually the groups have been distinguished on the basis of psychiatric diagnosis or symptomatology.

The earliest reported studies of conditioning in psychiatric patients were carried out by Russian investigators, including Ivanov-Smolensky (1925), Guk (1934), and Landkof (1938). Usually very small numbers of subjects were used, but the invariable finding was that, with psychotic subjects, conditional reflexes were difficult to establish, and, when finally established, the reflexes were quite unstable. The reflexes conditioned in these studies included defensive, motor, and avoidance reactions.

Bender and Schilder, (1930) in agreement with the Russian findings, reported difficulty in establishing conditional avoidance reactions in a small group of schizophrenics. Mays (1934), however, found that conditional GSR's were more resistant to extinction in a group of 20 schizophrenics than in 16 normal controls. Shipley (1934) studied the acquisition and resistance to extinction of conditional GSR's in psychiatric patients. The Ss were 17 schizophrenics, 10 manic depressives, 9 mixed neurotics, and 6 normals. The schizophrenics were found to condition at the fastest rate, with normals next, followed by the manic depressives and neurotics. The neurotic Ss were the most resistant to extinction, with the other groups undifferentiated on this measure.

Pfaffman and Schlosberg (1936) used a knee jerk conditioning procedure with schizophrenics, manic depressives, and normals. The schizophrenics tended to be the least responsive group, but the over-all level of conditioning was too low to permit definite conclusions.

Peters and Murphree (1954) investigated differential GSR conditioning to shock in schizophrenics and normals. The difference in response to the conditional stimulus and the differential stimulus after training was markedly less in the schizophrenics.

Taylor and Spence (1954) compared the rate of eyeblink conditioning of 74 Ss suffering from neurosis or personality disorder, and a group of 42 psychotics, including 31 schizophrenics. The difference in performance favoring the psychotics just failed to reach the 5% level of significance.

In a large-scale study of GSR conditioning, Howe (1958) used 60 hospitalized Ss with anxiety states, 60 hospitalized chronic schizophrenics, and 60 normal Ss. Taking magnitude of response during extinction as the measure of strength of conditioning, Ss with anxiety states showed stronger conditioning than schizophrenics or normals. The difference between the latter groups was not significant.

In a further study of GSR conditioning in psychiatric patients, Stewart et al. (1959) used 70 Ss, comprising 27 manic depressives in the depressed phase, 18 schizophrenics, 15 Ss with personality disorders, and 10 with anxiety neurosis. The US was shock, and a delayed conditioning procedure was used with a 4-sec CS–US interval. GSR's were classed as orienting responses, responses to shock, or anticipatory CR's. It was found that Ss with personality disorders conditioned more rapidly than either schizophrenic or manic depressive Ss, and that Ss with anxiety neuroses tended to condition more rapidly than those with schizophrenia. The resistance to extinction of personality-disordered Ss was significantly greater than that of the schizophrenics, but no other group differences were significant. The frequency of orienting responses to the CS during training was significantly greater in the anxiety neurotics than in either of the psychotic groups.

Another finding of interest was that the rate of adaptation to the CS before pairing with the US began was significantly slower in the anxiety neurotics than in either schizophrenics or manic depressives.

The contradictions in the reported findings which have been reviewed, and the marked differences in the procedures used in the various studies, make interpretation somewhat hazardous. Nevertheless, the evidence points to a number of conclusions which perhaps need not be too tentative. In the first place those studies which have used neurotic Ss suffering from symptoms of anxiety have added further weight to the already established fact that anxious persons tend to acquire aversive CR's more rapidly, and to extinguish them more slowly than other groups. Apart from one or two inexplicable discrepancies, it appears that schizophrenics tend to be less generally responsive to either mild or strong stimuli, and also to condition rather less readily than normals. The conclusion concerning the lack of responsiveness of schizophrenics is in accord with a considerable amount of evidence of a nonconditioning nature. There is quite a strong suggestion that schizophrenics tend to be deficient in "arousal" or "drive," and that this manifests itself in a somewhat retarded rate of conditioning (Lovibond, 1963a). In view of Meehl's (1962) suggestion that schizophrenics may show a deficiency of functioning of the positive reinforcement centers, it is interesting to speculate whether schizophrenics would not show a more marked deficiency in positive reward conditioning than in aversive conditioning. Lovibond's (1963a) findings with normals who gave schizophreniclike responses to the Object Sorting Test (see Section II, A, 2, b) suggest that this may well be the case.

The finding that psychiatric patients, other than schizophrenics and anxiety neurotics, usually condition less well than normals, possibly reflects a somewhat lowered cortical efficiency which is common to all patients, but which sometimes does not manifest itself if the patient has heightened drive relevant to the response being conditioned.

### B. Studies in the Definition of Personality Variables through Conditioning

Very recently, some noteworthy advances appear to have been made by Soviet investigators in the development of Pavlov's conceptions of types of higher nervous activity. Of particular interest is the work of Teplov and his associates (Nebylitsyn, 1961, 1963; Nebylitsyn, Rozhdestvenskaya and Teplov, 1960; Rozhdestvenskaia, Nebylitsyn, Borisova and Ermolaeva-Tomina, 1963; Teplov, 1961).

The essential difference between the approaches of Soviet and Western workers to problems of personality and conditioning can be illustrated by a comparison with the work of Eysenck (see Section II, A, 1). Eysenck's initial investigations were made at the level of personality functioning. The first task was to determine the major dimensions of personality. The next step was to seek, at the neurophysiological level, for likely mechanisms of the differences observed at the personality level. Predictions derived from the theory of neurophysiological mechanisms were then tested by the procedures of experimental psychology, including conditioning.

The method of the Soviet workers is quite different. For them the starting point is at the level of hypothetical neurophysiological mechanisms suggested by Pavlov's theory of brain functioning and general behavior. Laboratory procedures, with an emphasis on conditioning, are used in an attempt to define the major dimensions with respect to which people vary at this level. The next step in the program is to move to the level of personality, and there to seek correlates of differences at the neurophysiological level. Teplov's position with respect to the relation between personality theory and general behavior theory has been very clearly stated: "The problems of the psychology of personality are first and foremost problems of general psychology" (Teplov, 1961, p. 21).

Teplov believes that, before proceeding to questions of typology, it is necessary to carry out a much more thorough investigation than hitherto of the basic properties of the nervous system—the dimensions of higher nervous activity. The starting point of a series of investigations was Pavlov's conception of the fundamental properties of nervous activity: strength, balance, and mobility. Instead of taking these properties as given, Teplov raised the question: In the higher nervous activity of human beings, is each of these properties a single, unidimensional property, or a group of similar properties?

Strength was the first property investigated. For this purpose it was necessary to develop a number of laboratory test methods, including conditioning procedures. Most of these techniques are based on the assumption that the physiological essence of the strength property is maximum nerve cell capacity. The "method of reinforced extinction of the photochemical reflex, with and without caffein" is fundamental. The essence of this method (Rozhdestvenskaia *et al.*, 1963) is as follows. A conditional reflex reduction in absolute visual sensitivity of the dark-adapted eye is elaborated to a visual or auditory CS, using a very strong light as US. After consolidation of the CR, its magnitude is measured in one "experiment." (In Soviet literature it is often necessary, as in this case, to read for "experiment" the word "trial.") The measure of CR magnitude is percentage diminution of sensitivity to the CS relative to the background level of sensitivity. Ten reinforcements or CS–US combinations are then given with 2-min intervals, followed by a further measure of CR magnitude. In another session the procedure is repeated after the administration of 0.2 gm caffein. The measure of strength derived from this method is the percentage change in magnitude of the CR from the first to the second test trial, i.e., following "reinforced extinction." A diminution of the CR on retest is an indicator of weakness, or in other words the indicator of strength is the amount of resistance to "inhibition of reinforcement." The administration of caffein is designed to increase the excitability of the nerve cells, and hence to reduce their capacity to withstand prolonged stimulation.

Other techniques are based on the assumption that strength will manifest itself in concentration of excitation and positive induction effects under circumstances where weakness will lead to irradiation, and diminished, rather than increased, response.

The research of Rozhdestvenskaia *et al.* (1963) may be taken as illustrative of work in this area. In this study, 17 techniques were employed with each of 40 Ss to determine nervous system strength. Each of these methods had been individually studied and the theoretical validation (construct validity) of each was generally accepted. In addition, four measures of magnitude and rate of extinction of vascular orientation responses were included. The 17 strength measures included four measures of reinforced extinction of the photochemical CR (visual and auditory CS, with and without caffein) and four variants of the "induction method" (measures of effects of a punctuate extraneous stimulus on sensitivity to a second punctuate stimulus). Four other measures were derived from ergographic recordings under conditions of diminished nerve cell capacity, achieved by the administration of caffein, and muscular fatigue.

Centroid factor analysis of rho rank order correlations revealed a clear strength factor. Thirteen of the 17 strength measures showed high loadings with respect to this factor. A second factor was tentatively identified as "nervous system stability." The only measures showing high loadings with respect to Factor II were the four vascular orientation reflex indices. A third factor, loading only "photochemical reflex to acoustic stimuli with and without caffein," was interpreted as a special intensity effect of the auditory CS.

Nebylitsyn (1961) has published an account of a similar factor analytic study in which the principal strength measure was inhibition with reinforcement of the conditioned alpha blocking response of the EEG.

The results of studies such as these have led Teplov and his associates to conclude that strength is a unidimensional property of the nervous system. The position is not nearly as clear with respect to the properties of mobility and balance. According to Teplov (1961, p. 36), theoretical considerations and factual evidence suggest that the property of mobility "includes all the time characteristics of the work of the nervous system, and all aspects of this work in which classification by speed can be applied." Possible indices of mobility suggested by Teplov include (a) the speed of development and arrest of nervous processes, and (b) the speed of replacement of excitation by inhibition, and of inhibition by excitation. According to Nebylitsyn (1962), indices of mobility have not been found to correlate highly, and the conviction is growing that it is not a unidimensional property.

Teplov (1961) takes the view that balance is a secondary, derivative property of the nervous system, "for the simple reason that here it is a question of balance in strength or mobility . . . . It is now hardly a matter of doubt that there can be disequilibrium in the mobility of the nervous processes" (p. 35). Nevertheless, Nebylitsyn (1963) has carried out an investigation based on the hypothesis that balance is a unitary property. In this study, seven indicators of balance were used with 22 student subjects. On the assumption that "one must give preference to the 'conditional reflex (involuntary)' indicators of the relationship among nervous processes," two reference indicators were defined. These were (a) the rate of extinction of the conditional-reflex depression of the alpha rhythm elaborated in the course of "activating" reinforcement (see Section III, D, 4) and (b) the rate of elaboration of differentiation to an acoustic stimulus in alpha depression conditioning. The other indicators were a strength of CR measure, a measure of response to the "unconditional" light stimulus, and measures of strength and rate of extinction of the initial orienting response (alpha depression) to the acoustic CS.

The results revealed that all of the intercorrelations between measures, except two, were significant at the 5% level or better. It was concluded that the results supported the hypothesis that a common property of the nervous system, that of equilibrium, underlay the various response measures. Dominance of excitation over inhibition "causes greater resistance to extinction of alpha rhythm depression, orientation, and conditional reactions, retardation of differentiation, and longer depression of the alpha rhythm upon application of orienting, conditional and reinforcing stimuli" (Nebylitsyn, 1963, p. 27). When excitation and inhibition are in equilibrium, or inverse relationship, the opposite picture is sometimes observed.

Presumably, as indicators of equilibrium become more firmly based, it will be possible to begin to answer the question of the extent to which strength and equilibrium, or balance, are independent dimensions of nervous activity. Certainly the orienting reflex activity measures used by Rozhdestvenskaia et al. (1963), which were similar to those of Nebylitsyn (1963), were virtually independent of the main strength measures.

The mobility concept is likely to continue to be recalcitrant as there seems to be considerable overlap between Teplov's suggested mobility indicators, which were referred to earlier, and the present measures of equilibrium.

A further question may be raised at this point. What is the relationship between "strength," measured in terms of capacity to withstand intense and prolonged stimulation, and what would ordinarily be thought of as "strength of excitation" and which would be measured in terms of amplitude of response? Since it has been shown in a number of studies that strength and sensitivity (in terms of thresholds) are inversely related, it might be expected that strength in these two senses would be inversely related also. In the study of Rozhdestvenskaia et al. (1963) there were two amplitude measures: the mean levels of the vascular orienting reactions to the auditory stimulus and to the visual stimulus. Neither of these measures correlated at all highly with any of the measures of capacity to withstand adverse conditions of stimulation. However, the auditory and visual vascular amplitude measures correlated only .29 with each other. This low correlation suggests low reliability in one or both of these measures.

It is not surprising, nevertheless, that the two vascular magnitude measures correlated reasonably well with their respective extinction measures, since the two types of measures were not really independent. That is to say, if, as in this case, the measure of extinction is the level of response after a given number of applications of the stimulus, or the number of stimulus presentations necessary to reach zero response, the extinction measures of Ss with initially high levels of response will be relatively low, unless they show a very rapid decrease in response with continued stimulus presentations. Usually this will not occur to any marked degree, and the result will be an inverse relationship between initial response level and "rate of extinction." In Nebylitsyn's case, such a result makes possible an interpretation in terms of predominance of excitation. If, however, the slope of the extinction curve is used as a measure of rate of extinction, a positive relationship may be obtained between initial magnitude of the orienting reaction and its rate of extinction (Lovibond, 1963a). Clearly in this case one can no longer talk in terms of predominance of excitation or inhibition. It should be noted that Nebylitsyn is not alone in using the type of extinction measure he favors, since this measure is conventional in the Western literature.

Despite contradictions and queries such as those mentioned above, one cannot but be impressed by the work of Teplov and his associates. The character of this work has been stated modestly by Teplov: "We are striving to obtain such information about the individual differences in people as will form some system. We are attempting to put forward hypotheses which can be verified experimentally. We have chosen the path from the physiology of higher nervous activity to psychology. We do not consider that this is the only possible path, but we are firmly convinced that it is one of the possible paths." To this might be added the observation that the path being followed is potentially a very rewarding one, and one hopes that as more details of the work become available, Western psychologists will be induced to join in its exploration.

## III. Problems in the Investigation of Personality Dynamics by Conditioning Procedures

### A. Nonassociative Factors and the Measurement of Conditioning

It has long been known that not all changes in the response measures which occur during conditioning represent "true conditioning," or "experimental extinction," in the sense of being a direct function of CS–US pairing and unpairing. It is customary to describe as "nonassociative factors" any influences on response measures which do not result from the association (or subsequent dissociation) of CS and US. Nonassociative factors giving rise to response increment have been referred to as pseudoconditioning and reflex sensitization. Nonassociative factors producing response decrement have been termed habituation and adaptation. All of these factors, but particularly those leading to response increment, tend to confound measures of CR acquisition.

It has become conventional to refer to the control procedure of presenting the US only during the conditioning phase as pseudoconditioning control, whereas presentation of the CS and US separately is termed sensitization control. It is unlikely, however, that different mechanisms are responsible for pseudoconditioning and sensitization, and it is convenient to use the term pseudoconditioning to refer to non-associative response increment in general. The precise nature of pseudoconditioning effects is still a matter of controversy (Martin, 1962).

One view is that pseudoconditioning results from a reduction of peripheral response thresholds (Davis, Buchwald, and Frankmann, 1955). Wickens and Wickens (1942) have argued that pseudoconditioning is a process essentially the same as that of conditioning proper. These authors emphasize the associative elements which must necessarily be present in any pseudoconditioning experiment, e.g., the similarity of the situation in which the CS and US are presented. Recent electrophysiological studies (Voronin and Sokolov, 1960) suggest that nonassociative response increment is often a manifestation of the return of the generalized orienting reflex when reinforcement is introduced. Autonomic responses, such as GSR, heart rate change, and vasomotor responses, tend to occur as part of a generalized orienting response to any sudden stimulus change. Consequently, when the CS is presented alone during habituation or adaptation trials, the GSR, for example, occurs as an "unconditional" reaction. Repeated presentation of the CS usually results in a marked diminution in the amplitude of the response to the CS. Voronin and Sokolov (1960) have produced evidence that this adaptation of the orienting reflex results from the development of a process of inhibition, and not merely from a decrease in arousal. Presentation of any new stimulus after adaptation disinhibits the orienting reflex, and produces a marked increase in response to the CS. If, however, the new stimulus is an aversive US, such as shock, the increased response to the CS is of greater amplitude, and is more prolonged, indicating an increase in arousal as well as disinhibition of the orienting reflex. As conditioning proceeds with further CS–US pairings, the generalized orienting reflex gives way to more specific arousal (Voronin and Sokolov, 1960). If the response being conditioned is an indicator of generalized arousal, there will be a resultant tendency toward response decrement during this stage. Presentation of isolated test stimuli, in a context of repeated CS–US pairings, will again tend to disinhibit the generalized orienting response, as will the change from 100% reinforcement to an extinction series.

It has often been assumed that pseudoconditioning, or nonassociative response increment, is limited to conditioning involving aversive stimulation (Kimble, 1961). Recent work has suggested that this type of response increment may also occur with "neutral" reinforcement, as in conditioning of the alpha blocking response, and with positive reinforcement, as in salivary conditioning (see Section III, D).

The investigation of personality dynamics by conditioning methods would benefit greatly from detailed investigations of the mechanism of nonassociative factors in conditioning. It is unlikely, however, that the operation of these factors can be elucidated fully within the confines of the typical "acute," or very short-term conditioning experiment. Meanwhile, on the reasonable assumption that pseudoconditioning follows laws which differ from those of conditioning proper, investigators of personality and conditioning must seek ways of eliminating nonassociative influences from their response measures. Possible ways of achieving this aim are considered in the discussion of specific conditioning procedures in Section III, D, where it is suggested that the methods of delayed and differential conditioning offer partial solutions to the problem of obtaining uncontaminated conditioning measures.

## B. The Influence of Central "Set" Factors

Although classical conditioning is concerned with the modification of involuntary responses, performance during conditioning experiments may be markedly influenced by complex central factors which are usually described in terms of "set," "expectancy," or "attitude." The influence of such factors is perhaps most striking when the response to be conditioned may be performed both voluntarily and involuntarily. In eyeblink conditioning, for example, sets induced by instructions to "let your reactions take care of themselves" or "be sure not to wink before you

feel a puff," can produce very clear-cut facilitatory or inhibitory effects.
In an experiment on the effect of instructions on differential eye-blink conditioning, Hilgard and Humphreys (1938) used both supporting and antagonistic instructions. They found that responses increased in frequency and amplitude and decreased in latency—when they were ordered—from voluntary restraint, through uninstructed, to voluntary facilitation. It should be emphasized that these effects occur in relation to involuntary responses, i.e., responses outside the range of latencies appropriate to voluntary self-induced responses. Furthermore, voluntary restraint does not eliminate conditional responding.

When eyeblink conditioning is used in personality study, it is usual to give facilitatory instructions, but it is not a simple matter to determine the extent to which the instructional set is counteracted by self-induced sets. Razran (1936) suggests that, in salivary conditioning, attitudinal factors are responsible for greatly increased variability of response. Stability of performance is enhanced if Ss have no knowledge of conditioning, or if they can be kept unaware of the nature of the experiment by engaging them in some extraneous task.

Al-Issa (1963) has assumed that "if the inconsistency and variability of adult human conditioning is due to the influence of the subject's verbal and attitudinal activities, then by the mere absorption of the subject in performing some task, these interferences may be ruled out and conditioning may become regular and reliable. These attitudinal interferences are reduced because the absorbing activity takes the subject's attention from the CS and the US and thus he will have less voluntary control over the activities related to conditioning." Accordingly, in an eyeblink conditioning experiment conducted by Al-Issa (1963), one group had the task presented to them as a reaction-time study. Subjects in this group were required to respond to the CS as rapidly as possible by pressing a Morse key. Key pressing was found to result in significantly higher levels of responding.

In an early study of the effect of instructions on the GSR, Cook and Harris (1937) gave their Ss a series of adaptation trials with the stimulus to be conditioned (light). No mention was made of the fact that an electric shock was to be used in the experiment. One group of Ss was then told that electric shock would follow the light on subsequent trials. A further test with the CS alone showed a greatly increased level of response in this group. The subsequent magnitude of response did not increase further with 30 CS–US pairings. Cook and Harris further investigated the effect of instructions on extinction. They found that when Ss were told that the light would no longer be followed by shock, the GSR to the light was very rapidly eliminated in comparison with controls.

The effect of $S$'s expectations on his reactivity is illustrated in a study by Lovibond (1963a). Negative reinforcement of the GSR (shock) was used in one session, and positive reinforcement (nude pictures) was used in another. The test sessions were approximately 1 week apart, and order of sessions was counterbalanced. Before the beginning of each session $S$s knew whether shock was to be used or not. The response to the first adaptation trial of the CS was approximately 50% higher in the shock session than in the nonshock sessions.

In a recent study of the effect of instructions on GSR conditioning, Silverman (1960) showed that the CS–US interval interacts with the effects of instructions. Wickens, Allen, and Hill (1963) found that instructions to the effect that no more shocks are to be presented do not immediately eliminate GSR's to the CS, but rather result in a faster rate of extinction.

It is clear that the course of conditioning, differentiation, and extinction can be influenced by central processes arising partly out of contextual stimuli, including instructions, and partly out of the varied attitudes and expectations which $S$s bring to the laboratory. It seems probable that most of these influences are mediated by language, and hence it is likely that their laws of operation differ from those governing conditioning of simple responses. If this is the case, it follows that these factors must serve to increase the error variance in conditioning measures. Further, since these central factors undoubtedly play a more important role in some conditioning procedures than in others, the instrusion of these influences will tend to vitiate cross-technique comparisons of conditioning. Nevertheless, it is easy to exaggerate the influence of complex central factors. Most of the dramatic effects obtained with GSR conditioning (such as rapid extinction when no shock instructions are given, and increased response to the CS when $S$s are merely told of impending shock after the CS) act on nonassociative components in the response measures. As we gain more understanding and control of nonassociative factors in conditioning, our understanding and control of central set factors should likewise increase.

## C. General Factor of Conditionability

A problem which is frequently raised in relation to studies of conditioning and personality is the extent to which a general factor of conditionability, or ease of conditional reflex acquisition, underlies performance in the various types of conditioning situations commonly employed. It is argued that theories of personality, such as that of Eysenck, assume the existence of a strong general factor, but such a factor has not been shown to exist. In fact, measures of conditioning have seldom been found to correlate at all highly. At first sight it would appear to be a simple matter to undertake a factor analytic study of conditioning, with a variety of techniques, to decide the issue of the existence and strength of a general factor. There are, however, many diffculties in the way of a definitive general factor study, and some of the more important ones will shortly be taken up. Before turning to these problems, the possible existence of group and specific factors of conditionability will be considered.

### 1. Functionally Specific Arousal Systems and the Possibility of Group and Specific Factors

In a preceding section (II, A, 2, a), the probable existence of functionally specific arousal systems, in addition to a general arousal system, has been discussed. Whilst a degree of intraindividual consistency in the reactivity of these systems is to be expected, such consistency is likely to be far from perfect. To the exent that functionally specific arousal systems are of importance in the establishment of conditional linkages, intraindividual variability in the reactivity of these systems will reduce the strength of any general factor of conditionability.

It seems then that it is reasonable to expect a general factor of conditionability, and, in addition, specific and/or group factors. It is possible, if not probable, that there exists group factors associated with the broad defense-arousal and positive reward systems, in other words, factors related to aversive and appetitive conditioning. It is clear, however, that differentiations exist within these broad systems (attention has already been drawn to the division within the feeding center). The work of Olds (1956) is of interest here. Using the technique of self-stimulation through implanted electrodes, Olds mapped out areas centering on the hypothalamus within which mild electrical stimulation has either positive or negative reward value. In later experiments, Olds (1958) investigated the possibility of differentiation within the positive reward areas. Response rates with given electrode placements were determined under conditions of high and low hunger and sex drive. The results pointed to the existence of a localized hunger-reward system differentiated from a local sexual reward system with a reciprocally inhibitory relationship between the two. It is possible that each arousal-reward system will be found to be associated with a specific factor of conditionability.

There are many reasons that the low intercorrelations which have been found between different types of conditioning measures do not constitute decisive evidence against the existence of an important general factor of conditionability (Eysenck, 1962). Among the many influences which, in addition to specific conditionability factors, will tend to attenuate observed correlations, may be listed the following.

a. *Variability in Peripheral Response Mechanism Sensitivity.* Since the development of a central conditional linkage can be measured only through the medium of some peripheral response mechanism, such as blinking of the eyes or activity of the sweat glands, it follows that any intraindividual variability in the sensitivity of the peripheral mechanisms, which is not highly correlated with variability in conditionability, will reduce the correlations between conditioning measures.

b. *Nonassociative Contamination of Conditioning Measures.* To the extent that nonassociative factors not highly correlated with conditionability enter differentially into various types of conditioning measures, the observed relationship between the measures will be spuriously low. For example, different degrees of such confounding in negatively reinforced and positively reinforced GSR's almost certainly reduced the correlation obtained by Lovibond (1963b) between these two types of conditioning.

c. *Central Set Influences in Conditioning Measures.* In the discussion of central "set" and "attitude" factors in relation to conditioning, it was pointed out that different types of conditioning are susceptible to these influences to different degrees. Since set and attitude are unlikely to covary consistently with conditionability, these factors represent another possible source of attentuation of correlations between different types of conditioning measures.

d. *Procedural Variations.* Among the many possible procedural dimensions with respect to which conditioning experiments can and do vary, the following appear to be some of the most important: (i) Strength of US; (ii) CS–US interval; (iii) length of intertrial interval; (iv) nature of the intertrial interval (silent, filled, or partially filled (see Section III, D, 2); (v) percentage of reinforcement.

The influence of variations in the above aspects of procedure are far from being fully determined for any one type of conditioning. Sufficient is known of their operation, however, to suggest that, at least to some degree, optimal conditions are likely to vary with the type of conditioning. For example, intertrial intervals of around 20 sec, which appear not to be detrimental to eyeblink conditioning, are too short for optimal GSR conditioning (Prokasy, Hall, and Fawcett, 1962). Furthermore, the interactions between procedural variations are, as might be expected, far from simple. For example, although a CS–US interval of about 450 msec has been shown to produce maximum performance in the conditioning of finger withdrawal (Fitzwater and Thrush, 1956; Spooner and Kellog, 1947), eyeblink conditioning (Kimble, 1947; Kimble, Mann and Dufort, 1955; McAllister, 1953), and GSR conditioning (Moeller, 1954; White and Schlosberg, 1952), a recent study by Kimmel and Penny-packer (1963) has shown that differential conditioning of the GSR in-creases as a function of CS–US interval up to the maximum value studied (2 sec). Caution is in order, however, in interpreting GSR studies such as those of White and Schlosberg (1952), and Moeller (1954), because of the probability that conditional and orienting GSR's were confounded in the response measures.

Pavlov (1927) apparently found no significant differences in ease of salivary conditioning between CS–US intervals up to 5 sec, as CR's formed with these intervals were all termed "simultaneous" CR's. No relevant data on human salivary conditioning is avaliable, and the issue of whether or not the optimal CS–US interval is the same for all types of condition-ing remains open.

For the purposes of investigating a general factor of condition-ability, it would appear desirable to seek optimal procedures for each technique, rather than to attempt a purely mechanical standardization of procedures. Until such optima are firmly established, the procedures adopted with different techniques are likely to fall short of optimal conditions by different degrees. Since this is unlikely to affect all indi-viduals equally, intercorrelations between measures will be correspond-ingly reduced.

### 2. Other Parameters of Conditioning Performance

The concept of "conditionability" refers to the ease of acquisition of conditional reflexes, i.e., the development of excitatory linkages. There are, however, other aspects of conditioning performance which are of relevance for personality functioning. Diamond et al. (1963) have argued cogently for their view that inhibitory processes enter into every be-havioral act, and must be given equal consideration with excitatory processes if we are to understand any aspect of psychological function-ing. The conditional reflex was developed by Pavlov as a methodological technique for studying the interaction of excitation and inhibition in higher nervous activity. Manifestations of inhibitory processes in condi-tioning were considered to occur in the phenomena of differentiation, the acquired capacity of a stimulus to suppress or delay a response to a long-acting stimulus, and extinction of conditional reflexes, both with and without reinforcement. These aspects of conditional reflex activity have received attention only occasionally in studies of conditioning and personality. An exception is to be found in the work of Solymon and Beach (1961), who, in their studies of memory defect in the aged, have investigated the conditioning parameters of rate of extinction, differentiation, inhibition of delay, and rate of extinction of the orienting reflex, in addition to rate of acquisition of a conditional reflex.

It would seem that a concept of conditionability that deals only with excitatory processes ignores aspects of conditioning performance which, in the long run, could possibly account for more of the variance in personality functioning than excitatory measures such as rate of CR acquisition.

### D. Problems and Possibilities of Specific Conditioning Techniques

#### 1. Eyeblink

Conditioning of the eyeblink to a puff of air is a technique which has been widely used in personality study, and it is the most standardized method. It is standard practice to use of CS–US interval of 450–500 msec, and an air puff of approximately 1 psi. Also a pure tone is commonly used as the CS, mainly because light CS's have been shown to elicit UR's under some conditions. The transducer may be mechanical (microtorque potentiometer) or photoelectric. Both systems are highly developed and generally satisfactory. The different types of response which occur in eyeblink conditioning have been studied in detail. The most important criterion for distinguishing various types of response is latency, but form is also useful as a secondary criterion. The usually accepted categories of response and their latency ranges, with a 500-msec CS–US interval, are reflex blink to light (alpha response), 50–110 msec; beta response (reflex blink to light in dark-adapted eye), 120–240 msec; conditional response, 250–500 msec; voluntary response, 200–500 msec; unconditional response to puff, 50–100 msec after US.

Whilst UR's to the CS can readily be distinguished from CR's in terms of latency, the differentiation of voluntary responses from CR's poses a problem. The accepted criterion of a voluntary response is that of possessing characteristics similar to responses given by Ss who are instructed to blink to the CS in order to avoid the puff, or who report that they responded voluntarily in order to avoid the puff. Since the majority of these voluntary responses have latencies from 200 to 300 msec, Spence and Ross (1959) have proposed that only responses occurring in the interval 300–500 msec after CS onset should be termed CR's.

The form of a voluntary response is often characteristically different from that of a CR, but in many cases the criterion of form is difficult to apply, and there has been a tendency to rely on the criterion of latency.

Random blinking poses another problem for eyeblink conditioning, and some experimenters reject Ss whose natural blink rate is above a predetermined level. Since a high blinking rate has often been considered a sign of anxiety, it is clear that the investigator of relations between personality and conditioning faces something of a dilemma in reaching a decision concerning whether or not to reject Ss. A similar problem arises in connection with Ss who respond voluntarily to the CS before training. It may happen that such voluntary responses are related to the personality parameter under study. For example, Willet (1963), in his study of the effect of high and low drive on eyeblink conditioning, rejected any S whose natural blink rate was faster than one blink every 500 msec. He reports that he rejected 7 of 62 Ss in the high drive group "through apparatus failure or because they responded to the CS signals during the control trials." Of the 60 low-drive Ss, on the other hand, "five were rejected through apparatus failure."

The personality psychologist's dilemma will be solved only by more fundamental work on the differentiation of associative and nonassociative factors in conditioning, and the relation of these factors to dimensions of personality. It will probably be necessary to recognize, however, that there are some Ss from whom adequate measures of eyeblink conditioning cannot be obtained, just as some Ss have an insufficiently defined alpha blocking response to permit EEG conditioning, and some Ss produce insufficient GSR's to make GSR conditioning possible.

## 2. Galvanic Skin Response

The galvanic skin response (GSR) rivals the eyeblink in popularity as a conditioning procedure with human Ss. The usual finding is that the GSR can readily be conditioned with an electric shock as the US, and it can also be conditioned with a loud auditory stimulus in place of the shock. An advantage of the GSR is that it varies continuously over a wide magnitude range, and hence lends itself to quantification. Nevertheless, there have been endless debates concerning the appropriate unit of measurement of the GSR. Investigators have laid down criteria for suitable measures, such as independence of basal resistance and normality of distribution. Units commonly employed have included percentage change in resistance, change in conductance, the square root of conductance change, and log conductance change. Various ratio measures have also been proposed. A large-scale study by Eysenck (1956) showed that the extent to which various measures met the usual criteria varied with the experimental conditions, and that none had any marked advantage over the others.

In the author's view, the problem of the most appropriate unit of measurement cannot be decided in the absence of an external criterion. Personality study offers the possibility of providing such a criterion. If, for example, it were possible, on the basis of personality theory, to define groups with widely differing conditioning performance, these groups could be used as external criteria. That is to say, the GSR measure which most effectively and consistently separated samples from the groups in terms of conditioning would be the unit of choice. Until some such basis for a rational choice exists, it would seem reasonable to use the unit of measurement most convenient for one's purpose.

GSR conditioning is the least standardized of all the conditioning procedures. Whereas, in the case of eyeblink conditioning, the favored CS–US interval is almost always around 450–500 msec, this interval may vary from 450 msec to 20 sec in GSR conditioning. The characteristics of the US also vary considerably from experiment to experiment. Thus the electric shock US may differ in current type (for example, alternating or direct current, condenser discharge), electrode type, electrode placement, intensity, and duration. If the current type conforms to a standard pattern, for example 60 cycles ac, it can be specified adequately in terms of amperage if the electrode size and position are known. In many cases, however, the electric shock used to condition the GSR is unspecifiable.

The range of intertrial intervals commonly used in GSR conditioning is not great. The average is about 45–60 sec, but the interval may be as short as 15–25 sec (Prokasy, Hall, and Fawcett, 1962). The importance of the intertrial interval is emphasized by the failure of Prokasy et al. (1962) to find a difference between conditioning and pseudoconditioning groups with the very short interval of 15–25 sec, whereas separation of conditioning and pseudoconditioning groups was achieved with longer intertrial intervals in a later experiment (Wickens, Allen, and Hill, 1963).

What happens during the intertrial interval is another important source of difference between GSR experiments. The interval may be either "silent" or "filled." The term "silent" simply refers to the procedure, usual in other forms of conditioning, in which no other stimuli are presented between punctuate trials of CS, CS–US, or US. "Filled" (or "partially filled") intertrial intervals, on the other hand, are those in which a series of stimuli similar to the CS is presented between trials of CS, CS–US, or US. In the most common experiment of this type, the CS is a word, and other words are used to fill the intertrial interval (Becker, 1960; Becker and Matteson, 1961; Vogel, 1960, 1962). It can be seen that the "filled interval" experiment is simply one in which multiple differential stimuli are presented.

The question of filled *versus* unfilled intervals assumes some importance in the light of recent concern over the separation of associative from nonassociative factors in GSR conditioning. It has long been known that the GSR may be elicited by any novel stimulus, but electrophysiological studies of the mechanisms of arousal and the orientation reflex have given this fact a new significance. The usual practice in GSR conditioning is to present the stimulus to be conditioned a number of times prior to conditioning in order to adapt or habituate the GSR to this stimulus. After the adaptation trials, the conditioning phase is begun with several CS–US pairings, followed by the first test stimulus (CS presented alone). Any increase in the GSR to the test stimulus, beyond the level of response to that stimulus after adaptation, is attributed to conditioning. However, recent work by Sokolov (1960) and others has emphasized the extent to which the habituated orienting reflex, of which the GSR is a manifestation, is re-evoked by any relatively sudden change in the stimulus input. Evidence that the components of the orienting reflex can be habituated in different patterns, depending on the sensory input, suggests the operation of selective inhibitory mechanisms. To account for these and other findings, Sokolov (1960) has proposed the concept of "neuronal model." The neuronal model is a cortical representation, by a pattern of excitation, of recent past experience, against which incoming stimulation is compared. As long as the incoming stimulation corresponds to the model, it is checked by inhibition at the level of the brain stem collaterals, but in the case of a lack of concordance, afferent impulses are fed into the arousal system, which then discharges into cortical centers, increasing capacity for discrimination and causing the formation of a new model more consonant with the new stimulus input.

Grings (1960) has proposed a related concept which he terms the perceptual disparity reaction. Applied to the GSR conditioning situation, these concepts suggest, first, that the first reinforcement following an adaptation series will release the orienting reflex from inhibition, and this release will be reflected in subsequent response measures. In addition, moreover, any change in the pattern of stimulation, including the omission of a stimulus, will tend to disinhibit the orienting reflex. This means that occasional test trials of CS alone, in a series of CS–US pairings, will evoke an orientation reflex which will be confounded with any CR which occurs. If test trials ʻre massed at the end of a conditioning sequence in the form of an extinction series, the initial trial will tend to evoke a strong orientation reflex, followed by the development of habituation on subsequent trials. Any conditional GSR's, and their subsequent experimental extinction, will be confounded with the orientation GSR's and their habituation.

It would be expected that the strength of the re-establishment of the orienting reflex by a change in the stimulus conditions will depend on the extent of the disparity between the original and the new stimulus conditions, and the suddenness of the change. Consider, for example, the experiment of Prokasy *et al.* (1962) which compared the GSR's, in an extinction series, of groups given

(a) tone-shock pairings (regular conditioning),
(b) shock-tone pairings (backward conditioning),
(c) random shocks and random tones (sensitization),
(d) shocks only (pseudoconditioning), and
(e) tones only.

The ordering of the groups from highest to lowest GSR on the first extinction trial was shock only; backward conditioning; regular conditioning; random shocks and random tones; and tones only. This is precisely the ordering that judges give if they are asked to rank the groups in terms of decreasing perceptual disparity between training and extinction test trials. In the experiment of Prokasy *et al.*, the response levels of the shock-only and backward-conditioning groups decreased rapidly compared with those of the true conditioning group. The response level of the random group tended to remain relatively high, possibly as a result of trace conditioning with the very short intervals used.

Stewart, Stern, Winokur, and Fredman (1961) have argued recently that "so far work on GSR conditioning has dealt with the adaptation and recovery of unconditioned responses rather than conditioning of responses." The argument that *no* unequivocal evidence of GSR conditioning had previously been produced could be sustained only by ignoring the results of long-delay GSR conditioning experiments (Rodnick, 1937, Switzer, 1934), which measured anticipatory responses similar to those advocated by Stern *et al.*, and also the results of differential GSR conditioning experiments. The latter include experiments using a single differential stimulus (Kimmel and Pennypacker, 1963; Lovibond, 1963a), and those using multiple differential stimuli ("filled" intertrial intervals) (Becker, 1960; Becker and Matteson, 1961; Vogel, 1960, 1962).

Further unequivocal evidence of GSR conditioning has been obtained by experiments in which an extended extinction test series has demonstrated a significantly higher level of response in a forward conditioning group by comparison with a backward conditioning group (Prokasy *et al.*, 1962). The backward conditioning procedure provides an acceptable control, since the perceptual disparity between training and extinction is greater with this procedure than with forward conditioning.

From the foregoing analysis it would appear that incontrovertible evidence of GSR conditioning (other than differential conditioning) can most readily be obtained if the stimulus relations remain constant throughout the experiment, or if the changes in stimulus pattern are below the level of discriminability of the "neuronal model" or orienting reflex comparator mechanism.

In practice, experiments of the first type are limited to those employing the delayed conditioning method in which anticipatory CR's are distinguished in terms of latency. It is necessary, of course, to employ a sufficiently long CS–US interval to avoid masking of anticipatory CR's by orienting GSR's. Conditioning with delays of 10 sec or longer presents no great difficulty, and contradicts the belief that GSR conditioning can be obtained only with a CS–US interval of 450–500 msec.

It seems likely that the function relating CS–US interval and strength of conditioning rises to a new peak beyond intervals of 4–5 sec, but curiously enough nobody has investigated this possibility. In considering the problem of CS–US interval, however, it should be borne in mind that measures of conditioning derived from short intervals will necessarily be confounded with orienting GSR's if silent intertrial intervals are used. This suggests that examination of the CS–US interval function can best be carried out with experiments which reduce the suddenness of changes in the stimulus pattern below the point where orienting GSR's will be evoked. This implies filling the intertrial interval with multiple differential stimuli to produce a "constancy in change." Current work in the Adelaide laboratories suggests that under these circumstances orienting GSR's will be almost entirely suppressed in many Ss. The fact that CR's appear to form readily enough against this background suggests that generalized arousal may not be necessary for the establishment of conditional linkages, and that the inhibition which suppresses the orienting reflex may have little or no effect on the elicitation of the GSR by specific arousal mechanisms. It must be stressed, however, that there is as yet insufficient evidence to permit firm conclusions concerning these possibilities.

From the point of view of personality study, the advantage of long-delay and filled-interval GSR conditioning procedures is that they give relatively pure measures of conditioning, and make possible a measure of rate of acquisition of the CR. Although the strength of orienting CR's is likely to be positively correlated with rate of conditioning (Lovibond, 1963a; Martin, 1963), confounding of the two measures is clearly undesirable if one wants to test theories relating personality and conditioning, or to investigate the generality of conditionability.

Positive reward conditioning of the GSR has been investigated by Lovibond (1963a,b) using still pictures of nude females as the US. Using a delayed differential conditioning procedure with silent intervals, it was found that the intrusion of orienting GSR's was much less pronounced than in the case of shock conditioning. Without distingushing the latencies of responses, a rising curve of response to the CS was obtained, together with a falling curve of response to the differential stimulus (DS). This technique promises to be a useful supplement to salivary conditioning in the investigation of positive reward conditioning. A "filled interval" moving film version is at present being investigated. In this form of the technique, short sequences of moving pictures of nudes are separated by intervals of neutral shots of outdoor scenery. Both visual and auditory long-delay conditional and differential stimuli are being used. Substitution of a shock US in this procedure should make possible a more satisfactory comparison of positive and negative conditioning of the GSR, since the usual confounding of orienting and conditional GSR's with aversive reinforcement should be markedly reduced.

A further response measure which might be used with this form of reinforcement is change in penis volume. Freund (1963) has reported on the use of a penile plethysmograph in the differentiation of homosexual from heterosexual interests. According to Freund (1962), change in penis volume is a more sensitive index of arousal by pictures of nudes than is the GSR. Since this response should be relatively independent of the generalized arousal or orienting response, its comparison with the GSR offers interesting possibilities in the investigation of generalized *versus* specific arousal in the formation of conditional reflexes.

### 3. Salivary Response

Since the principles of conditional reflex activity were derived by Pavlov from studies of salivary conditioning in animals, there would appear to be obvious advantages to be gained from the adoption of this method in the study of human conditioning. However, the salivary conditioning of human Ss poses some difficult methodological problems.

In early attempts to study salivary conditioning in man (Finesinger and Sutherland, 1939; Lentz, 1935; Richter and Wada, 1924), salivary secretion was measured by means of the suction cup method originally devised by Krasnogorski (1931). In the modified version of this method published by Finesinger and Finesinger (1937), capsules, held by suction over Stenson's ducts, collect the secretion of the parotid glands. The saliva collected is transmitted by rubber tubes to a bottle filled with saline solution. The displaced saline passes through a tube with a capillary tip into a burette. The passage of each drop of saline closes an electric circuit between two platinum wires in the wall of the burette, and sends a pulse to a kymograph pen. A measure of rate of salivary secretion is thus given by the number of pen movements per unit time. Lemon, or other fruit juice, which serves as the US, is conveyed to the patient's mouth via a third tube positioned by the suction cup.

In an experimental application of the technique, Finesinger *et al.* (1942) used a CS (metronome) presented for 3–10 sec in a delayed conditioning procedure, with a 1-sec CS–US overlap. The magnitude of the CR was measured by presenting the CS for 25 sec on test trials. The amount of saliva secreted during this period was corrected by subtraction of the average quarter-minute rate of secretion during the minute preceding the presentation of the test CS.

Razran (1935) published an account of a new technique for measuring salivary secretion in conditioning experiments with human Ss. Salivation was measured by means of a standard dental roll inserted under S's tongue. The roll was weighed before insertion and after removal, the difference in weight being taken as a measure of secretion during the intervening period. Razran noted considerable variation in the magnitude of the salivary CR, and believed that a good deal of this variation could be attributed to the influence of central "attitude" or "set" factors. When the attention of S was directed elsewhere, so that there was minimal awareness of the stimulus relations of the experiment, the stability of the CR improved (Razran, 1936).

The most recent studies of human salivary conditioning (Bindra *et al.*, 1955; Willet, 1960) have used the cotton roll method. Willet's carefully controlled study showed that increased salivation occurred in the presence of the CS when no reinforcement was used. The experiment of Bindra *et al.* was replicated in the Adelaide laboratories with the addition of a control group. The Ss in the control group were presented with the CS and US separated by random intervals rather than in conjunction. The curves of both experimental and control groups ($N = 20$ in each group) were virtually identical in form to those obtained by Bindra *et al.* On the first test trial, after 8 reinforcements, the amount of salivation had reached a maximum which was sustained through the next 32 CS–US pairings. The difference between the experimental and control groups was not significant, but the response level of the control group was consistently higher than that of the experimental group. In a comparable experiment, with a test trial after each reinforcement, most of the increase in salivation to the CS occurred after the first reinforcement, and no further increase occurred beyond three reinforcements. This pattern conforms closely to that observed in the responses of "sensitization" control groups used in GSR conditioning.

In a further unpublished study, John (1962) used a similar procedure with 80 experimental Ss and 80 control Ss. During the conditioning phase, salivation to the CS increased over 12 reinforced trials, but the rate of increase was significantly greater in the control group. A possible explanation of this result can be derived from Pavlov's (1927) observation that if a CS of relatively long duration overlaps rather than precedes a relatively long US, the CS becomes inhibitory. John's Ss were instructed to start sucking a lollipop (US) on a given signal, and the CS and US were presented simultaneously for 2 min. Under these circumstances it is likely that the development of inhibitory potential by the CS offset the development of excitatory potential by this stimulus, by way of either sensitization or CS–US pairing.

The foregoing studies demonstrate quite unequivocally the occurrence of nonassociative contamination in the response measures of salivary conditioning experiments such as that of Bindra, but they do not elucidate the sources of this contamination. There are at least three possible explanations of the increased response to the CS during the conditioning phase observed in the control group Ss of the Adelaide and John experiments. The first two emphasize the possibility of measurement artefact, and the other suggests the occurrence of some form of pseudoconditioning.

First, when the intertrial interval is short, there may be a carryover of unconditional salivation into the period of CS test presentation. The intertrial interval in the experiments in question, as in the Bindra study, was only about 1 min. In this connection, Finesinger et al. (1942), using a suction cup method, have observed that sometimes salivation persists for "a considerable time" after presentation of the US. Second, presentation of the US (such as a lollipop) to a hungry person may sensitize the salivary reflex to the point where it will be elicited by any object (such as a cotton roll) placed in the mouth. Third, reinforcement may sensitize the salivary reflex to the previously indifferent CS, thus producing a form of nonassociative response increment similar to the sensitization that has been observed in aversive conditioning.

The possible contribution of each of these factors to response contamination in cotton roll salivary conditioning could readily be subjected to experimental analysis. If it is found important, the factor of carryover of salivation could be controlled by longer intertrial intervals. Sensitization would need to be controlled by such measures as the use of long-delay conditioning. As it is a reasonable inference from accounts of Pavlov's work that sensitization could scarcely have been a problem in work with dogs, it might seem a priori that it should not be a problem with human beings. There is, however, other evidence to suggest that the salivary reflex may be significantly more sensitive in human beings than in animals. For example, Finesinger et al. (1942) found that not a few Ss secrete saliva continuously irrespective of the external situation. Some degree of "interval" or intertrial secretion was so common that it was necessary to correct for its effect on response measures. As Finesinger *et al.* point out, Pavlov makes no mention of interval secretion, and it is a reasonable inference that it was not a problem.

If, as seems likely, it is found that measurement artefact results from the use of cotton rolls themselves, there will be no choice but to return to the direct measurement of salivary secretion. This would appear highly desirable in any case, since direct measurement has a number of important advantages over the cotton roll technique. In the first place, continuous monitoring of salivary flow enables selection of the intertrial interval necessary to avoid carryover of unconditional salivation. Second, it gives a precise measure of interval secretion, and thus makes possible correction for background level of salivation. Third, the method of direct presentation of the US, which is a natural corollary of direct recording, permits far more precise control over the timing and amount of reinforcement than can be achieved with the cotton roll method. Fourth, the whole procedure can be carried out without any movement whatever on the part of *S*. Once *S* has adapted to the tubes and suction cups in his mouth, the course of conditioning is uninterrupted by any extraneous stimuli. In other words, we have a situation similar to that which Pavlov found essential for the salivary conditioning of dogs. By contrast, the cotton roll method , as it is commonly used, requires *S* to insert some solid reinforcing agent (lollipop or tablet) into his mouth, and to begin sucking on a given signal. In addition, *S* not infrequently has the US in view and is required to engage in some task. It seems not unlikely that these varied patterns of stimulus input will either facilitate or inhibit salivary flow, and account for at least some of the variability of response which is commonly noted. The results obtained with the suction cup method make it clear, nevertheless, that there is a good deal of inherent variability in the human salivary response. A direct experimental comparison of the suction cup and cotton roll methods would be most instructive.

It is of interest to consider possible modifications to the Finesinger and Finesinger suction cup method in the light of recent developments in instrumentation. Possibilities which suggest themselves include (a) substitution of an inkwriting rate recorder for the kymograph; (b) presentation of the liquid US by a small, fixed-delivery pump, automatically timed; (c) substitution of a plastic cannula for the suction cup. It is not immediately obvious what improvement could be made on the original method of transducing salivary flow into electrical impulses, but it is quite likely that a superior method exists or could be developed. It is clear that, modern developments notwithstanding, direct salivary recording methods are technically demanding. Nevertheless, the available evidence suggests that serious application of salivary conditioning procedures in the study of personality can scarcely be undertaken without them.

### 4. Alpha-Blocking Response

The early work of Durup and Fessard (1935) and Loomis, Harvey, and Hobart (1936) suggested the possibility of conditioning the blocking or desynchronization of the alpha rhythm, for which a strong light is an adequate stimulus.

In most experiments a tone has been used as the conditional stimulus. An extensive exploratory study was undertaken by Jasper and Shagass (1941) to (a) investigate "the depression (blocking) of the alpha rhythm in man as a conditional response, and (b) appraise the value of the electroencephalograph as an instrument for the study of conditioning problems, especially in man." Jasper and Shagass claimed to have demonstrated practically all of the Pavlovian conditioning phenomena, including temporal, trace, delayed, differential, and backward conditioning. In their view, the advtantages of EEG conditioning lie in the facility and rapidity with which conditioning of alpha blocking may be achieved, and its relative independence of voluntary influence. The main disadvantages are the instability of the CR and the fact that S must exhibit "an almost continuous alpha rhythm which is free from 'spontaneous' variations, and which responds clearly to visual stimuli" before unequivocal conditional responses can be obtained.

Most investigators who have studied EEG conditioning in man have found the CR to be "poorly sustained" (Wells and Wolff, 1960a) or "unstable" (Knott and Henry, 1941). Knott and Henry (1941), in a very careful study, drew attention to the possibility of sensitization of the response to the tone in EEG conditioning. They noted that alpha blocking can be produced by a wide variety of stimuli. In fact, the tones ordinarily used as conditional stimuli are by no means "indifferent" stimuli; they are only relatively ineffective in comparison with strong light stimuli. In order to differentiate between sensitization of the previously adapted response to the conditional stimulus, and conditioning proper, Knott and Henry used the method of delayed conditioning with a 4-sec CS–US interval. This interval permitted full recovery of the alpha rhythm after its response to the CS and before the US occurred. The results gave rather clear-cut evidence of both sensitization of the initial response to the CS and the development of a conditional anticipatory response in the 1-sec interval prior to US onset.

The curve of the sensitized response to CS onset showed an abrupt rise to approach its maximum during the first five trials, although the peak did not occur until trials 21–30. From this point there was a slow decline in the response. The anticipatory response showed a negatively accelerated increase to reach its peak in trials 21–30, followed by a fairly rapid decline.

Despite this early demonstration that nonassociative factors such as sensitization must be controlled in EEG conditioning, not all subsequent investigators have heeded the warning. Thus the Wells and Wolff (1960a) study of EEG conditioning in brain-damaged patients employed a CS– US interval of only .8 to 1 sec, and did not include a control group. A temporary cerebral connection was considered to have occurred "if the alpha rhythm was obliterated or strikingly depressed after the presentation of the tone and before the appearance of the light." The "conditioning" curve obtained showed a decline from an initial peak value similar to the usual adaptation curve. Stern, Das, Anderson, Biddy, and Surphlis (1961) questioned whether Wells and Wolff had demonstrated the development of a conditional cerebral response, and undertook a replication of the Wells and Wolff experiment. Their results showed a decline in the desynchronization response to tone over the 20 adaptation trials, followed by a rise to above the preadaption level in the first five trials of tone-light pairing, and a subsequent rather regular decline over the next 40 trials. Since the curve of the response to the tone almost exactly paralleled that of the response, to the light, Stern et al. interpret the rise in tone response, during the early stage of tone-light pairing, to a return of the adapted "orienting response" analogous to that observed in GSR conditioning.

The implication of these results is that Wells and Wolff did not provide unequivocal evidence of EEG conditioning, and hence, did not provide evidence concerning the differential susceptibility to this type of conditioning of brain-damaged patients and normal controls. Since Wells and Wolff (1960b) used an identical procedure in their study of anxiety and EEG conditioning, it follows that this study too failed to produce evidence of differential rates of conditioning in anxious patients and normals.

It should be obvious that Wells and Wolff have simply failed to disprove the null hypothesis of no difference between their clinical groups and normals. It is probable, however, that there is a positive correlation between disinhibition of adaptation and rate of conditioning [as Lovibond (1963a) has demonstrated for positive reward conditioning of the GSR] and that results similar to those of Wells and Wolff would be obtained with unequivocal measures of EEG conditioning.

It is clear from the foregoing that conditioning of alpha desynchronization is susceptible to masking by nonassociative factors in much the same way as the conditioning of other components of the orienting reflex and also the defensive reflex. When it is considered that only about 60% of normals produce EEG records with alpha rhythm present 50% of the time (Davis, 1938; Henry and Knott, 1941), it is clear that conditioning of alpha blocking leaves much to be desired as a method of personality study.

Nebylitsyn (1963) describes a method which he claims improves the stability of the conditional reflex connection in EEG conditioning. He notes that the reaction of depression or complete disappearance of the alpha rhythm always occurs upon the presentation of a light stimulus, and, under conditions of "novelty," when a stimulus of any modality appears. "In the former instance this reaction possesses virtually all the properties of an unconditional reflex, while in the second case it possesses those of an orientation reflex" (Nebylitsyn, 1963, p. 23). In subsequent discussion, however, Nebylitsyn points out that "rapid and significant diminution" of the "unconditional" depression of the alpha rhythm usually occurs with repeated presentation of the light stimulus. Consequently, he uses what he terms "activating reinforcement" in the elaboration of conditional blocking of the alpha rhythm. Activating reinforcement refers to a reinforcement that "supports the orientation-investigatory reaction of the individual and thereby makes for stable retention of the conditional reflex." A series of slide pictures displayed on a screen is employed for the purpose of activating reinforcement, and Nebylitsyn (1962) claims that more than 90% of Ss with a reasonably clear-cut alpha rhythm develop stable CR's using this method.

## IV. Changing Personality Functioning by Conditioning Methods

### A. Experimental Neuroses

One of the earliest applications of conditioning procedures to problems of personality was the study of experimental neuroses.

This line of research began with some observations made in Pavlov's laboratory while training a dog in a difficult differentiation (Pavlov, 1927). After a CR of salivation to a circle was formed, a series of ellipses with different semiaxis ratios was presented as differential stimuli. Following the usual practice, simple differentiation was first established by reinforcing the circle and omitting reinforcement to an ellipse with a ratio of 2:1 between the semiaxes.

In following trials the shape of the ellipse was changed by steps until it approximated that of the circle. When an ellipse with a ratio between the semiaxes of 9:8 was presented the dog's behavior suddenly changed markedly. Its capacity for differentiation deteriorated, and its general behavior changed from quiet cooperation to violent resistance. Pavlov used the term "experimental neurosis" to characterize the sudden disturbance in behavior which developed under the given experimental conditions.

In another experiment, a salivary CR to a strong electric shock was established, but when an attempt was made to generalize the CR by applying the shock to other parts of the skin, a breakdown of behavior occurred. The salivary CR disappeared and was replaced by a violent defensive reaction even in response to weak stimuli. Pavlov interpreted these observations as demonstrating that the clash of excitation with inhibition led to a profound disturbance of the usual balance between these two processes "and finally gave way to an undisputed predominance of one of them, producing a pathological state."

A comprehensive and detailed review of later work on experimental neuroses (Liddell, 1947, 1956; Gantt, 1942, 1944; Masserman, 1943; Wolpe, 1952, 1958) has been published recently by Broadhurst (1960). Consequently the present treatment will be confined to a brief discussion of some of the issues of general importance which have arisen in relation to this work.

Broadhurst very laudably sets out to establish criteria for determining whether or not experimentally induced behavioral disturbances in animals may properly be termed neuroses. In this endeavor he is guided by Hebb (1947), who lists the following six criteria of human neuroses: The behavior must be (a) undesirable, or evaluatively abnormal, (b) emotional, (c) generalized, i.e., not solely a response to a specific excitant, (d) persistent following cessation of the specific excitant, (e) statistically abnormal, i.e., occurring in a minority of the population, (f) without origin in a gross neural lesion. Broadhurst, with Hebb, rejects the following three common criteria: (i) neurosis has no known physiological base, (ii) neurosis produces a marked change of behavior from early base line, (iii) neurosis follows from some "traumatic" experience like conflict or frustration.

Broadhurst very properly concludes that a great deal of the work in the field has lacked rigor and sophistication in experimental design, and has been inadequately reported. Furthermore, many of the behavior disturbances produced fall far short of warranting the description experimental neurosis. However, Broadhurst meets certain difficulties in the application of Hebb's criteria. Because of lack of data concerning the behavior of experimentally neurotic dogs external to the experimental situation, he is forced to conclude that there is insufficient proof that the breakdowns of behavior produced in Pavlov's laboratories can properly be described as neuroses. This difficulty arises, of course, from the fact that Pavlov himself emphasized criteria not included in Hebb's list, particularly the criterion of disorders in conditional reflex activity other than that activity through which the disturbance was produced. An example was the failure of the dog in the original experiment to perform even the simplest differentiation which had previously been performed with ease. Other examples were the disappearance of all recently trained reflexes, either inhibitory or excitatory, and performing a negative response to a positive stimulus, and vice versa. For Pavlov these were the essential criteria, and it is of interest that nothing like them occurs in Hebb's list. The closest approach to this sort of criterion would be one of those rejected by Hebb, namely, "neurosis produces a marked change in behavior from an earlier baseline." Certainly, as it is formulated by Hebb, this criterion would fail to distinguish the behavior under consideration from a number of nonneurotic behavioral changes, but it would seem to do so if reformulated along the following lines: "inability to perform tasks which were performed with ease prior to breakdown, or which are performed with ease by individuals of similar behavioral capacity." This would seem to be a not unimportant criterion of human neurosis. If a patient with an hysterical paralysis is unable to lace his shoes, a practiced accountant is unable to add a few simple figures, or a dweller in a large city is unable to enter and operate an automatic elevator, we have examples of this sort of behavioral deficiency.

Broadhurst rejects the various theoretical interpretations of experimental neuroses which have been made previously, and seeks to account for the phenomena in terms of conditional emotional responses. Both Hebb (1947) and Wolpe (1952) earlier offered a similar interpretation. Hebb was forced to make an exception in the case of breakdown occasioned by training in very difficult differentiation as originally reported by Pavlov. Wolpe, however, in support of his thesis that all experimental neuroses, and all human neuroses, can be regarded as maladaptive learned behavior patterns, attempts to bring the difficult differentiation case within his general framework. Wolpe classifies situations which precipitate experimental neuroses into those which use strong shock, those which use mild shock, and those which present ambiguous stimuli. Experiments of the first type produce conditional fear or anxiety, i.e., stimuli associated with the strongly aversive shock come to elicit intense anxiety by virtue of this association. (It is of interest to note that the Pavlovians draw a sharp distinction between experimental neuroses in which there is evidence of generally disordered nervous activity as previously discussed, and manifestations of "defense reflex" activity unaccompanied by signs of general disorder.)

In order to explain how the repeated application of mild shock can eventually give rise to a severe anxiety reaction, Wolpe postulates that "when emotional conditioning first begins to be established, the conditioned stimulus evokes a small amount of anxiety. Let us call this $x$, and let it be half the amount evoked by the shock $(2x)$. At this time, when the shock follows shortly on the conditioned stimulus, the anxiety from the two sources will add together, giving a total of $3x$. As the result of conditioning, the next presentation of the conditioned stimulus will evoke, say, $1\frac{1}{2}x$, and the shock that follows will bring the total to $3\frac{1}{2}x$. It may then be found that the next presentation of the conditioned stimulus evokes $2\frac{1}{4}x$, that is, more than the shock itself. By repetition, the amount of anxiety evocable by the conditioned stimulus will gradually rise to a magnitude many times $2x$. At some stage the anxiety will be great enough to produce obvious signs, and as experimenting continues these will be intensified."

Wolpe's interpretation of the third precipitating situation, that of "ambiguous stimulation," is as follows. However slight and transient the anxiety produced by this conflict of tendencies may be at first, the drive reduction associated with its cessation results in the anxiety responses becoming reinforced to whatever stimuli are contiguous, and among these is the ambivalent stimulation itself. In the same way as suggested above for the case of mild noxious stimuli, the strength of the anxiety response is conceived to be gradually stepped up at each presentation of the ambivalent stimulus situation while the drive-reduction potential correspondly grows. Eventually very powerful anxiety responses are evoked, and strong avoidance behavior entirely replaces the approach responses to the experimental situation which were previously established by repeated feeding (Wolpe, 1952, p. 266).

Broadhurst does not regard Wolpe's interpretation as wholly satisfactory, and he suggests an alternative way of bringing the behavior disturbance resulting from ambiguous stimulation into the general category of conditional emotional reactions. Broadhurst's hypothesis involves the application of a reformulation of the Yerkes–Dodson law. According to this law, there is a curvilinear relationship between motivation and performance. Performance improves with increased motivation up to an optimum, beyond which further increase in motivation results in poorer performance. Second, the more difficult the task the lower the optimum level of motivation. In Hullian terms, "increasing drive level may increase the functional difficulty of a discrimination, so that objective increases in difficulty are in fact rendered more severe than the circumstances otherwise warrant. Once the optimum motivation is reached, then the decrease in task performance may be viewed as an energization of incorrect responses which are lower in the habit family hierarchy than the correct ones" (Broadhurst, 1960, p. 754).

Broadhurst's application of these principles to the difficult differentiation situation is as follows. Initially S's fear reactions to the restraint and to the experimental situation generally are gradually inhibited and replaced by food-seeking responses. In training the discrimination, the difficulty of the task progressively increases. Optimum performance would thus require a progressive lowering of motivation, but as S is likely in the past to have encountered mainly simple situations requiring high drive for optimum performance, he is likely to have learned to respond to failure by increased motivation. Failure to receive reinforcement for wrong response to the negative stimulus thus results in increased drive, resulting in further failure and so on. Broadhurst suggests that at a certain stage "the increased drive level energizes incorrect responses in competition with the correct ones—responses, especially fear ones, which were suppressed early on in the training. So it is that struggling, howling, and agitated behavior in general, which were previously characteristic of the subject's initial reactions to the sitaution are reinstated anew" (Broadhurst, 1960, p. 755).

Finally, in relation to the finding that after the behavior disturbance occurs S is unable to make even simple differentiations, Broadhurst says, "It seems probable that this characteristic failure of a simple discrimination can be accounted for if it is recalled that even relatively simple tasks have an optimum motivation, which may well be surpassed if anxiety is added to the motivational complex."

The attempts of Wolpe and Broadhurst to account for the phenomena of difficult differentiation neuroses in terms of learned emotional reactions, although ingenious, are scarcely convincing. Wolpe's assumption of an additive relationship between conditional and unconditional fear is somewhat implausible, especially in relation to breakdown in the difficult differentiation experiment. Equally implausible is Broadhurst's hypothesis that increased drive level energizes initial fear reactions to produce the "struggling, howling and agitated behavior" observed when breakdown occurs. In the first place, it would appear from the descriptions available that animals in whom breakdown occurred did not necessarily show initial fear or resistance to the restraining harness. Broadhurst's hypothesis that increasing drive results from continued failure, and increases the probability of further failure, is, in all probability, correct, but it is unlikely that the increased drive is dependent on prior learning. It is far more likely that the increase is an unconditional effect of failure of stimulus input to match the "neuronal model" or "expected" input (Sokolov, 1960). Broadhurst's increasing-drive hypothesis thus gives a plausible account of why discrimination fails, but not of the resultant breakdown of behavior. One aspect of behavior disturbance in discrimination experiments which creates difficulties for both theories is the relative suddenness with which the behavior disturbance typically occurs. The term "breakdown" appears to give an apt description of what happens. The theories of both Wolpe and Broadhurst, however, would lead one to expect a gradual development of behavioral disturbance. As it is also difficult to see how either theory could account for the many phenomena of disturbance of "phasic activity" which Pavlov (1927) describes, there would seem to be reason to question whether the phenomena of experimental neuroses in animals can adequately be described purely in terms of maladaptive responses. This question has important implications for the therapy of human neuroses, which will be taken up briefly in section IV, B.

## B. Therapy of Behavior Disturbances by Direct Conditioning Methods

During the past decade there has been an increasing interest in the possibility of treating behavior disorders by direct conditioning methods. The procedures used are direct in the sense that they are aimed at the elimination of undesirable behavior patterns, or the development of desirable patterns, by the presentation of specific and precise stimulus relationships. By contrast, the conventional therapeutic methods based on Freudian theory, or one of its derivatives, may be termed indirect because attention is directed primarily toward the "complex" which is assumed to give rise to the symptoms.

The method of direct conditioning in the treatment of behavior disorders has been termed "behavior therapy" by Eysenck (1960), but not all psychologists who use direct conditioning techniques find the implications of this term acceptable. Eysenck (1960) has brought together virtually all of the papers dealing with behavior therapy which were published prior to 1960. The disorders which have been treated by this method with apparent success include phobias, obsessions, stuttering, fetishes, writer's cramp, alcoholism, hysterical paralyses, frequency of micturition, and enuresis.

Criticisms of direct conditioning methods of treatment have centered mainly around the charge that the treatment deals only with symptoms, and since the underlying conflict is left unresolved, symptom substitution or exacerbated anxiety is to be expected. No clear case of symptom substitution appears to have been recorded, however, and the general personality changes accompanying the relief of specific symptoms appear to be beneficial in the great majority of cases (Eysenck, 1960; Lovibond, 1964b).

Studies of direct conditioning treatment have usually dealt with single cases, or at best very small numbers of *Ss*, and hence are open to the criticism that, as in the case of verbal psychotherapy (Eysenck, 1960), improvement over spontaneous recovery rates has not been demonstrated. In a few cases, predictions of the outcome of changes in therapeutic technique (e.g., Yates, 1958) have provided strong evidence of internal consistency, but only controlled group studies can establish the efficacy of direct conditioning treatment beyond any doubt. Eysenck (1960) has discussed the problems involved in providing unequivocal evidence of the effectiveness of any form of treatment of neurotic disorders. In the case of enuresis, the problems are far less formidable, and there is now sufficient evidence to warrant making direct conditioning therapy the treatment of choice for this disorder (Jones, 1960; Lovibond, 1964b). Initial arrest of wetting is achieved in 90% of cases, but as in direct conditioning treatment generally, the problem of preventing relapse or extinction of conditioning is a pressing one. Recent experimental work has been directed to the application of laboratory techniques, including partial reinforcement schedules, to this problem (Lovibond, 1963c). By and large the demonstrational phase of direct conditioning treatment has passed, and it can be expected that the future will see more research into the precise mechanisms of particular behavioral disturbances, and a consequent increase in the precision of application of conditioning principles.

The limits of applicability of direct conditioning methods is a moot question. We have seen that theorists such as Wolpe (1952, 1958) regard all neurotic disorders as learned maladaptive behavior patterns, and hence susceptible to direct conditioning or behavior therapy. According to this approach, which has been discussed in detail by Eysenck (1960) and Yates (1958), a neurosis is symptoms and nothing else. It follows that treatment can only be symptomatic, i.e., aimed directly at the maladaptive behavior patterns. This conception of neurotic disorders is usually contrasted with the Freudian or "dynamic" view that the neurosis is an unconscious conflict of which the symptoms are merely surface indicators.

There is, however, a third view which has been associated in particular with the work of Pavlov (1927) and Hebb (1947). According to this view, it is necessary to make a sharp distinction between behavior arising from a central state or event and that central state itself, in the present case between neurotic behavior and an hypothesized disturbance of nervous activity which constitutes the neurosis. This, of course, is a distinction which those who take the "maladaptive habit" view of neurosis do not recognize.

If the distinction is accepted, a satisfactory explanation of neuroses must be sought in the neurophysiological mechanisms of behavior rather than the behavior itself. The implication of this point of view is that neurosis may be manifest primarily in a set of maladaptive behavior patterns, or it may be manifest primarily in an inability to cope with previously simple tasks and problems, and difficulty in acquiring new, adaptive learning. To the extent that the latter features predominate, there will be an emphasis in therapy on procedures designed to affect the central state as such, including rest and sleep therapy, and the use of drugs, but conditioning procedures may be used in the development of new adaptive behavior patterns. To the extent that maladaptive behavior patterns predominate, the therapeutic emphasis may well be placed on such methods as reciprocal inhibition, desensitization, and aversive therapy. Those maladaptive behavior patterns which have been acquired under conditions of trauma or extremes of excitation are likely to have the character of S-R linkages, which, it is reasonable to hypothesize, will be outside the range of possible central integration and modification. It follows that the behavior patterns in question will be beyond the scope of verbal psychotherapy, and direct conditioning procedures will be the only methods with a reasonable chance of success. It will be recognized, however, that neurosis will often involve disturbances of central processes as manifest in attitudes and beliefs, for the modification of which verbal psychotherapeutic procedures will be appropriate. The form of such psychotherapy will not necessarily bear a very close resemblance to conventional Freudian procedures.

## References

Al-Issa, I. The effect of attitudinal factors on conditioning. In H. J. Eysenck (Ed.), *Experiments in motivation*. New York: Pergamon Press, 1963.

Anand, B. K., and Brobeck, J. R. Hypothalamic control of food intake in rats and cats. *Yale J. Biol. & Med.*, 1951, 24, 123-140.

Anokhin, P. K. Electroencephalographic analysis of corticosubcortical relations in positive and negative conditioned reactions. *N. Y. Acad. Sci.*, 1961, 92, Art. 3, 899-938.

Barendregt, J. P. *Research in psychodiagnostics*. The Hague, Netherlands: Mouton, 1961.

Baron, M. R., and Connor, J. P. Eyelid conditioned responses with various levels of anxiety. *J. exp. Psychol.*, 1960, 60, 310-313.

Beam, J. C. Serial learning and conditioning under real-life stress. *J. abnorm. soc. Psychol.*, 1955, 51, 543-551.

Becker, W. C. Cortical inhibition and extraversion-introversion. *J. abnorm. soc. Psychol.*, 1960, 61, 52-66.

Becker, W. C., and Matteson, H. H. GSR conditioning, anxiety, and extraversion. *J. abnorm. soc. Psychol.*, 1961, 62, 427-430.

Bender, L., and Schilder, P. Unconditioned and conditioned reactions to pain in schizophrenia. *Amer. J. Psychiat.*, 1930, 10, 365-384.

Bindra, D., Paterson, A. L., and Strzelecki, J. On the relation between anxiety and conditioning. *Canad. J. Psychol.*, 1955, 9, 1-9.

Bitterman, M. E., and Holtzman, W. H. Conditioning and extinction of the galvanic skin response as a function of anxiety. *J. abnorm. soc. Psychol.*, 1952, **47**, 615-623.

Broadhurst, P. Abnormal animal behavior. In H. J. Eysenck (Ed.), *Handbook of abnormal psychology.* London: Pitman, 1960, pp. 726-763.

Cook, S. W., and Harris, R. E. The verbal conditioning of the Galvanic Skin Reflex. *J. exp. Psychol.*, 1937, **21**, 202-210.

Das, J. P. An experimental study of the relation between hypnosis, conditioning and reactive inhibition. Thesis submitted for Ph.D. Univer. of London, 1957.

Davis, H. The electroencephalogram. *Tabulae Biologicae*, 1938, **16**, 116-131.

Davis, R. C., Buchwald, A. M., and Frankmann, R. W. Autonomic and muscular responses, and their relation to simple stimuli. *Psychol. Monogr.*, 1955, No. 405, **69** (20).

Diamond, S., Balvin, R. S., and Diamond, F. R. *Inhibition and choice: A nuerobehavioral approach to problems of plasticity in behavior.* New York: Harper, 1963.

Durup, G., and Fessard, A. L'éctrencéphelogramme de l'homme. *L'annee Psychol.*, 1935, **36**, 1-32.

Eysenck, H. J. *The dynamics of anxiety and hysteria.* London: Routledge & Kegan Paul, 1957.

Eysenck, H. J. *Handbook of abnormal psychology.* London: Pitman, 1960.

Eysenck, H. J. Conditioning and personality. *Brit. J. Psychol.*, 1962, **53**, 299-305.

Eysenck, H. J., and Claridge, G. The position of hysterics and dysthymics in a two-dimensional framework of personality description. *J. abnorm. soc. Psychol.*, 1962, **64**, 46-55.

Eysenck, S. B. G. An experimental study of psychogalvanic reflex responses of normal neurotic, and psychotic subjects. *J. Psychosom. Res.*, 1956, **1**, 258-272.

Field, I. G., and Brengelmann, J. C. Eyelid conditioning and three personality parameters. *J. abnor. soc. Psychol.*, 1961, **63**, 517-523.

Finesinger, J. E., and Finesinger, G. L. A modification of the Krasnogorski method for stimulating and measuring the secretions from the parotid glands in human beings. *J. lab. clin. Med.* 1937, **23**, 267-273.

Finesinger, J. E., and Sutherland, G. F. The salivary conditional reflex in man. *Trans. am. neurol. assn.*, 1939, p. 50.

Finesinger, J. E., Sutherland, G. F., and McGuire, F. F. The positive conditional salivary reflex in psychoneurotic patients. *Amer. J. Psychiat.*, 1942, **99**, 61-74.

Fitzwater, M. E., and Thrush, R. S. Acquisition of a conditioned response as a function of forward temporal contiguity. *J. exp. Psychol.*, 1956, **51**, 59-61.

Franks, C. M. Conditioning and personality: A study of normal and neurotic subjects. *J. abnorm. soc. Psychol.*, 1956, **52**, 143-150.

Franks, C. M. Personality factors and the rate of conditioning. *Brit. J. Psychol.*, 1957, **48**, 119-126.

Franks, C. M. Conditioning and abnormal behavior. In H. J. Eysenck (Ed.), *Handbook of abnormal psychology.* London: Pitman, 1960.

Freund, K. Personal communication, 1962.

Freund, K. A laboratory method for diagnosing predominance of homo- or heterosexual interest in the male. *Behav. Res. Ther.*, 1963, **1**, 85-93.

Gantt, W. H. The origin and development of nervous disturbances experimentally produced. *Amer. J. Psychiat.*, 1942, **98**, 475-481.

Gantt, W. H. *Experimental basis for neurotic behavior: Origin and development of artificially produced disturbances of behavior in dogs.* New York: Hoeber-Harper, 1944.

Gilberstadt, H., and Davenport, G. Some relationships between GSR conditioning and judgments of anxiety. *J. abnorm. soc. Psychol.*, 1960, **60**, 441-443.

Grings, W. W. Preparatory set variables related to classical conditioning of autonomic responses. *Psychol. Rev.*, 1960, **67**, 243-252.

Guk, E. D. The conditioned reflex activity in schizophrenics. *Sovetsk. Nevropatol.*, 1934, pp. 76-84.

Hebb, D. O. Spontaneous neurosis in chimpanzees. Theoretical relations with clinical and experimental phenomena. *Psychosom. Med.*, 1947, **9**, 3-16.

Henry, W. E., and Knott, J. R. A note on the relationship between personality and the alpha rhythm of the electroencephalogram. *J. exp. Psychol.*, 1941, **28**, 362-366.

Hilgard, E. R., and Humphreys, L. G. The effect of supporting and antagonistic voluntary instructions on conditioned discrimination. *J. exp. Psychol.*, 1938, **22**, 291-304.

Howe, E. S. GSR conditioning in anxiety states, normals, and chronic functional schizophrenic subjects. *J. abnorm. soc. Psychol.*, 1958, **56**, 183-189.

Hull, C. L. *Principles of behavior.* New York: Appleton-Century-Crofts, 1943.

Hull, C. L. *A behavior system.* New Haven, Connecticut: Yale Univ. Press, 1952.

Ivanov-Smolensky, A. G. Uber die bedingten Reflexe in der depressiven Phase das manisch-depressiven Irreseins. *Mschr. Psychiat. Neurol.*, 1925, **58**, 376-388.

Jasper, H., and Shagass, C. Conditioning the occipital alpha rhythm in man. *J. exp. Psychol.*, 1941, **28**, 373-388.

Jenkins, J. J., and Lykken, D. Individual differences. *Ann. Rev. Psychol.*, 1957, **8**, 79-112.

Jensen, A. Personality. *Ann. Rev. Psychol.*, 1958, **9**, 295-322.

John, I. D. Personal communication. Univer. of Melbourne, Australia, 1962.

Jones, H. G. The behavioral treatment of enuresis nocturna. In H. J. Eysenck (Ed.), *Behavior therapy and the neuroses.* New York: Pergamon Press, 1960.

Kaada, B. R., and Johannsen, N. B. Generalized electrocortical activation by cortical stimulation in the cat. *EEG clin. Neurophysiol.*, 1960, **12**, 567-573.

Kimble, G. A. Conditioning as a function of the time between conditioned and unconditioned stimuli. *J. exp. Psychol.*, 1947, **37**, 1-15.

Kimble, G. A. *Hilgard and Marquis' Conditioning and learning.* (2nd ed.) New York: Appleton-Century-Crofts, 1961.

Kimble, G. A., Mann, L., and Dufort, R. H. Classical and instrumental eyelid conditioning. *J. exp. Psychol.*, 1955, **49**, 407-417.

Kimmel, H. D., and Pennypacker, H. S. Differential GSR conditioning as a function of the CS-UCS interval. *J. exp. Psychol.*, 1963, **65**, 559-563.

Knott, J. R., and Henry, W. E. The conditioning of the blocking of the alpha rhythm of the human electroencephalogram. *J. exp. Psychol.*, 1941, **28**, 134-144.

Krasnogorski, N. I. Bedingte und unbedingte Reflexe im Kindersalter und ihre Bedeutung für die Klinik. *Ergebn. d. inn. Med. u. Kinderh.*, 1931, **36**, 613.

Lacey, J. I., Smith, R. L., and Green, A. Use of conditioned autonomic responses in the study of anxiety. *Psychosom. Med.*, 1955, **17**, 208-217.

Landkof, B. L. Unconditioned and conditioned vascular reflexes in schizophrenics. *Trud. Tsentral. Psikhonevrol. Inst.*, 1938, **10**, 37-63.

Lentz, A. K. Les reflexes conditionnels salivaires chez l'homme sain et aliéné et leur rapprochement avec les donnes de la conscience. *L'encephale*, 1935, **11**, 394.

Liddell, H. S. The experimental neurosis. *Ann. Rev. Physiol.* 1947, **9**, 569-580.

Liddell, H. S. *Emotional hazards in animals and man.* Springfield, Illinois: Charles C Thomas, 1956.

Loomis, A. L., Harvey, E. N., and Hobart, G. A. Brain potentials during hypnosis. *Science*, 1936, **83**, 239-241.

Lovibond, S. H. The Object Sorting Test and conceptual thinking in schizophrenia. *Austral. J. Psychol.*, 1954, **6**, 52-70.

Lovibond, S. H. Conceptual thinking, personality, and conditioning. *Brit. J. soc. clin. Psychol.*, 1963a, **2**, 100-111.

Lovibond, S. H. Positive and negative conditioning of the GSR. *Acta Psychologica*, 1963b, **21**, 100-107.

Lovibond, S. H. Intermittent reinforcement in behavior therapy. *Behav. Res. Ther.*, 1963c, **1**, 127-132.

Lovibond, S. H. Manual for the Object Sorting Test. Unpublished manuscript, Univer. of Adelaide, Australia, 1964. (a)

Lovibond, S. H. *Conditioning and enuresis*. New York: Pergamon Press, 1964. (b)

McAllister, W. R. Eyelid conditioning as a function of the CS-US interval. *J. exp. Psychol.*, 1953, **45**, 417-422.

Malmo, R. B. Measurement of drive: an unsolved problem in psychology. In M. R. Jones (Ed.), *Nebraska Symposium on Motivation*. Lincoln: Univer. of Nebraska Press, 1958.

Martin, I. GSR conditioning and pseudoconditioning. *Brit. J. Psychol.*, 1962, **53**, 365-371.

Martin, I. Delayed GSR conditioning and the effect of electrode placement on measures of skin resistance. *J. Psychosom. Res.*, 1963, **7**, 15-22.

Masserman, J. H. *Behavior and neurosis: an experimental psychoanalytic approach to psychobiologic principles*. Chicago, Illinois: Univer. of Chicago Press, 1943.

Mays, L. L. Studies of catatonia. V. Perseverational tendencies in catatonic patients. *Psychiat. Quart.*, 1934, **8**, 728-735.

Meehl, P. E. Schizotaxia, schizotypy, and schizophrenia. *Amer. Psychologist*, 1962, **17**, 827-838.

Moeller, G. The CS-UCS interval in GSR conditioning. *J. exp. Psychol.*, 1954, **48**, 162-166.

Moruzzi, G., and Magoun, H. W. Brainstem reticular formation and activation of the EEG. *EEG clin. Neurophysiol.*, 1949, **1**, 455-473.

Nebylitsyn, V. D. Die Anwendung der Faktorenanalyse bei der Erforschung der Struktur der höheren Nerventätigkeit. *Probleme und Ergebnisse der Psychologie*, 1961, **3-4**, 119-126.

Nebylitsyn, V. D. Personal communication, 1962.

Nebylitsyn, V. D. Certain electroencephalographic indicators of equilibrium in nervous processes. *Soviet Psychol. & Psychiat.*, 1963, **1**, 22-27.

Nebylitsyn, V. D., Rozhdestvenskaya, V. I., and Teplov, B. M. Concerning the interrelation between absolute sensitivity and strength of the nervous system. *Quart. J. exp. Psychol.*, 1960, **12**, 17-25.

O'Connor, N. 1959. Ref. in Willet, R. A. Measures of learning and conditioning. In H. J. Eysenck (Ed.), *Experiments in personality*. London: Routledge & Kegan Paul, 1960, Vol. II.

Olds, J. A preliminary mapping of electrical reinforcing effects in the rat brain. *J. comp. physiol. Psychol.*, 1956, **49**, 281-285.

Olds, J. Effects of hunger and male sex hormone on self-stimulation of the brain. *J. comp. physiol. Psychol.*, 1958, **51**, 320-324.

Olson, W. C. *Problem tendencies in children*. Minneapolis: Univer. of Minnesota Press, 1930.

Pavlov, I. P. *Conditioned reflexes.* (Transl. by C. V. Anrep.) London and New York: Oxford Univer. Press, 1927.

Peters, H. N., & Murphree, O. D. The conditioned reflex activity in the chronic schizophrenic. *J. clin. Psychol.,* 1954, **10,** 126-130.

Pfaffman, C., and Schlosberg, H. The conditioned knee-jerk in psychotic and normal individuals. *J. Psychol.,* 1936, **1,** 201-205.

Prokasy, W. F., Hall, J. F., and Fawcett, J. T. Adaptation, sensitization, forward and backward conditioning, and pseudo-conditioning of the GSR. *Psychol. Rep.,* 1962, **10,** 103-106.

Razran, G. H. S. Conditioned responses: an experimental study and a theoretical analysis. *Arch. Psychol.,* 1935, No. 191.

Razran, G. H. S. Attitudinal control of human conditioning. *J. Psychol.,* 1936, **2,** 327-337.

Richter, C. P., and Wada, T. Method of measuring salivary secretion in human beings. *J. lab. & clin. Med.,* 1924, **9,** 271.

Rodnick, E. H. Characteristics of delayed and trace conditioned responses. *J. exp. Psychol.,* 1937, **20,** 409-425.

Rozhdestvenskaia, V. I., Nebylitsyn, V. D., Borisova, M. N., and Ermolaeva-Tomina, L. B. A comparative study of various indicators of the strength of the human nervous system. *Soviet Psychol. & Psychiat.,* 1963, **1,** 10-22.

Schiff, E., Dougan, C., and Welch, L. The conditioned PGR and the EEG as indicators of anxiety. *J. abnorm. soc. Psychol.,* 1949, **44,** 549-552.

Shipley, W. C. Studies of catatonia: VI. Further investigation of the perseverational tendency. *Psychiat. Quart.,* 1934, **8,** 736-744.

Silverman, R. E. Eliminating a conditioned GSR by reduction of experimental anxiety. *J. exp. Psychol.,* 1960, **59,** 122-125.

Sokolov, E. N. Neuronal models and the orienting reflex. In Mary A. B. Brazier (Ed.), *The central nervous system and behavior.* Madison, New Jersey: Madison Printing Co., 1960.

Solyom, L., and Beach, L. Further studies upon the effects of the administration of ribonucleic acid in aged patients suffering from memory (retention) failure. *Neuropsychopharmacol.,* 1961, **2,** 351-355.

Spence, K. W. The relation of anxiety to differential eyelid conditioning. *J. exp. Psychol.,* 1954, **47,** 127-134.

Spence, K. W., and Farber, I. E. Conditioning and extinction as a function of anxiety. *J. exp. Psychol.,* 1953, **45,** 116-119.

Spence, K. W., and Ross, L. E. A methodological study of the form and latency of eyelid responses in conditioning. *J. exp. Psychol.,* 1959, **58,** 376-385.

Spence, K. W., and Taylor, J. A. Anxiety and strength of the UCS as determiners of the amount of eyelid conditioning. *J. exp. Psychol.,* 1951, **42,** 183-188.

Spence, K. W., and Taylor, J. A. The relation of conditioned response strength to anxiety in normal, neurotic, and psychotic subjects. *J. exp. Psychol.,* 1953, **45,** 265-272.

Spence, K. W., Farber, I. E., and Taylor, E. The relation of electric shock and anxiety to level of performance in eyelid conditioning. *J. exp. Psychol.,* 1954, **48,** 404-408.

Spooner, A., and Kellogg, W. N. The backward-conditioning curve. *Amer. J. Psychol.,* 1947, **60,** 321-334.

Stern, J. A., Das, K. C., Anderson, J. M., Biddy, R. L., and Surphlis, W. Conditioned alpha desynchronization. *Science,* 1961, **134,** 388-389.

Stewart, M. A., Winokur, G., Stern, J. A., Guze, S. B., Pfeiffer, E., and Hornung, F. Adaptation and conditioning of the galvanic skin response in psychiatric patients. *J. ment. Sci.,* 1959, **105**, 1102-1111.

Stewart, M. A., Stern, J. A., Winokur, G., and Fredman, S. An analysis of GSR conditioning. *Psychol. Rev.,* 1961, **68**, 60-67.

Sweetbaum, H. A. Comparison of the effects of introversion-extraversion and anxiety on conditioning. *J. abnorm. soc. Psychol.,* 1963, **66**, 249-254.

Switzer, S. A. Anticipatory and inhibitory characteristics of delayed conditioned reactions. *J. exp. Psychol.,* 1934, **17**, 603-620.

Taylor, J. A. The relationship of anxiety to the conditioned eyelid response. *J. exp. Psychol.,* 1951, **41**, 81-92.

Taylor, J. A. Drive theory and manifest anxiety. *Psychol. Bull.,* 1956, **53**, 303-320.

Taylor, J. A., and Spence, K. W. Conditioning level in the behavior disorders. *J. abnorm. soc. Psychol.,* 1954, **49**, 497-502.

Teplov, B. M. Typological properties of the nervous system and their psychological manifestations. In N. O'Connor (Ed.), *Recent Soviet psychology.* New York: Pergamon Press, 1961.

Vogel, M. D. The relation of personality factors to GSR conditioning of alcoholics. An exploratory study. *Canad. J. Psychol.,* 1960, **14**, 275-280.

Vogel, M. D. GSR conditioning and personality factors in alcoholics and normals. *J. abnorm. soc. Psychol.,* 1962, **63**, 417-421.

Voronin, L. G., and Sokolov, E. N. Cortical mechanisms of the orienting reflex and its relation to the conditioned reflex. In H. H. Jasper & G. D. Smirnov (Eds.), *Moscow Colloquium on Electroencephalography of Higher Nervous Activity. EEG clin. Neurophysiol.,* 1960, Suppl. No. 13.

Welch, L., and Kubis, J. Conditioned PGR (psychogalvanic response) in states of pathological anxiety. *J. nerv. ment. Dis.,* 1947, **105**, 372-381.

Wells, C. E., and Wolff, H. G. Formation of temporary cerebral connections in normal and brain-damaged subjects. *Neurology,* 1960a, **10**, 335-340.

Wells, C. E., and Wolff, H. G. Electrographic evidence of impaired brain-function in chronically anxious patients. *Science,* 1960b, **131**, 1671-1672.

White, C. T., and Schlosberg, H. Degree of conditioning of the GSR as a function of the period of delay. *J. exp. Psychol.,* 1952, **43**, 357-362.

Wickens, D. D., and Wickens, C. D. Some factors related to pseudoconditioning. *J. exp. Psychol.,* 1942, **31**, 518-526.

Wickens, D. D., Allen, C. K., and Hill, F. A. Effect of instructions and UCS strength on extinction of the conditioned GSR. *J. exp. Psychol.,* 1963, **66**, 235-240.

Willett, R. A. Measures of learning and conditioning. In H. J. Eysenck (Ed.), *Experiments in personality.* London: Routledge & Kegan Paul, 1960, Vol. II.

Willet, R. A. Eyeblink conditioning and situation induced anxiety drive. In H. J. Eysenck (Ed.), *Experiments in motivation.* New York: Pergamon Press, 1963.

Wolpe, J. Experimental neuroses as learned behaviour. *Brit. J. Psychol.,* 1952, **43**, 243-268.

Wolpe, J. *Psychotherapy by reciprocal inhibition.* Stanford, California: Stanford Univer. Press, 1958.

Wyrwicka, W., and Dobrzecka, C. Relationship between feeding and satiation centers of the hypothalamus. *Science,* 1960, **132**, 805-806.

Yates, A. J. The application of learning theory to the treatment of tics. *J. abnorm. soc. Psychol.,* 1958, **56**, 175-182.

# REPRESSION-SENSITIZATION AS A DIMENSION OF PERSONALITY

*Donn Byrne*

THE UNIVERSITY OF TEXAS, AUSTIN, TEXAS

Psychologists in the field of personality have evidenced a consistent and long-continued interest in unconsciously motivated behavior. It may be observed that some individuals fail to verbalize feelings of anxiety when confronted by stimuli judged by outside observers to be anxiety evoking. Further, these same individuals are seen subsequently to engage in activities which may be hypothesized to control or reduce anxiety. Observations and speculations of this variety have stimulated a considerable amount of research, especially during the past two decades.

Anxiety-reducing activities which are unconsciously motivated are given the label of defense mechanisms. Various descriptions of these mechanisms, originating almost exclusively in psychoanalytic theory, have been proposed over the years. A unidimensional categorization which encompasses many diverse mechanisms grew out of the research of the new look in perception in the 1940's: repression-sensitization. At one end of this continuum of defensive behaviors are those responses which involve avoidance of the anxiety-arousing stimulus and its consequents. Included here are repression, denial, and many types of rationalization. At the sensitizing extreme of the continuum are behaviors which involve an attempt to reduce anxiety by approaching or controlling the stimulus and its consequents. The latter mechanisms include intellectualization, obsessive behaviors, and ruminative worrying.

Beginning with his 1950 doctoral dissertation at Stanford, Charles Eriksen was one of the first investigators to make and to pursue this distinction of types of defense mechanisms while Jesse Gordon (1957) introduced the terms "repressor" and "sensitizer." The specific research which formed the background for much of the current work on the repression-sensitization dimension will be reviewed briefly.

## I. Approach versus Avoidance Responses to Threatening Stimuli

### A. PERCEPTUAL DEFENSE

#### 1. Initial Investigations

An early and extremely influential article in the postwar perceptual studies was co-authored by Jerome Bruner and Leo Postman (1947a). The basic assumption underlying most of the new-look approach was stated at the outset of that article (p. 300):

"Perception is a form of adaptive behavior. Its operation reflects not only the characteristics of sensorineural processes, but also the dominant needs, attitudes, and values of the organism. For perception involves a *selection* by the organism of a relatively small fraction of the multiplicity of potential stimuli to which it is exposed at any moment in time. In perception, moreover, certain stimuli are *accentuated* and vivified at the expense of others. Finally, what is "habitually seen" in any given perceptual situation is a function of the *fixation* of past perceptual responses in similar situations. Through these three processes—selection, accentuation, and fixation—the adaptive needs of the organism find expression in perception."

Individual differences in perceptual adaptation to threat soon became evident in investigations emerging from the Laboratory of Social Relations at Harvard. With 19 undergraduates as subjects, Bruner and Postman (1947b) obtained associative reaction times for each of 99 words including a large proportion of potentially threatening ones such as "raped," "death," "penis," "agony," and "blush." Two weeks later, each subject was presented with 18 stimulus words (those yielding the individual's six fastest, midmost, and slowest reaction times) on a tachistoscope. Each word was presented at increasingly slower exposure speeds until correct recognition was obtained. A significant relationship between reaction time and recognition exposure speeds was found. Of primary interest here was the finding of two different patterns of response among the subjects. In attempting to achieve an explanation of the two patterns, the authors suggested that some individuals revealed a defense process in which recognition threshold was a monotonic increasing function of associative reaction time. The greater the anxiety, the greater the "perceptual defense." The responses of other subjects suggested a sensitizing process in which recognition time was actually faster for the most anxiety-provoking words than for the six midmost words. Rather than avoiding the perception of threat, the latter individuals were characterized as vigilant in perceiving it. Perceptual vigilance had been found previously in response to goal-relevant stimuli congruent with need reduction (Bruner and Goodman, 1947) and value systems (Postman, Bruner, and McGinnies, 1948), but the notion of sensitization to threat created a new wave of research interest.

## 2. Individual Differences in Perceptual Defense

The bulk of the perceptual defense literature which followed the Harvard studies dealt with demonstrations, explanations, and criticisms of findings reporting threshold differences for threat *versus* nonthreat stimuli. In addition, however, individual differences in characteristic defensive reactions along a repressing-sensitizing dimension were also under investigation. In general, research was conducted in which subjects were categorized as to defensive mode by one means or another and then tested for perceptual threshold differences for threat *versus* nonthreat stimuli (Carpenter, Wiener, and Carpenter, 1956; Eriksen, 1951, 1952a; Kissin, Gottesfeld, and Dickes, 1957; Kogan, 1956; Kurland, 1954; Lazarus, Eriksen, and Fonda, 1951; Nelson, 1955; Perloe, 1960; Shannon, 1962).

The subjects in these studies consisted of the usual groups of college undergraduates, hospitalized neuropsychiatric patients, and ambulatory clinic patients. Differential recognition thresholds or differential accuracy scores were obtained for a variety of neutral and conflictful (primarily sex and hostility) stimuli which included words, drawings, Blacky pictures, and sentences recorded on tape. Recognition was made difficult by variations in speed of exposure, intensity of illumination, legibility of successive carbon copies, loudness of recordings, and intelligibility of auditory presentations partially masked by white noise. Independent indicators of defensive mode included readiness to verbalize conflictful material on sentence completion tests and in TAT stories, ability to recall failure versus success words in an experiment using scrambled sentences, ability to recall Blacky pictures, scores on the California *F* Scale, scores on the Defense Preference Inquiry for the Blacky pictures, clinical ratings of Rorschach and Machover Figure-Drawing protocols, and classification as to characteristic defensive mode on the basis of interviews and case history material.

Although these studies utilized a variety of subject populations, perceptual tasks, and measures of defenses, significant relationships were consistently reported between perceptual behavior and defenses with few exceptions (e.g., Kurland, 1954). Those individuals who have difficulty in perceiving threatening material accurately also give evidence of blocking, repression, and avoiding when responding to conflictful stimuli in other contexts. Conversely, those who perceive threatening stimuli as accurately as or more accurately than neutral stimuli respond in other situations with intellectualization, sensitization, and general approach behavior.

It should be noted that the explanation for these findings is far from clear. As with other perceptual defense data, some investigators prefer to explain the findings in terms of variables other than defense mechanisms and unconscious motives. For example, after reviewing the literature on individual differences, Brown (1961, p. 323) suggests:

"The individual-difference method does not, however, preclude the possibility that the reactions to all tests are due to differential experiences with the materials of the tests rather than to percepual defense. When individuals who are "expressive" with respect to sexual matters are selected out of a group, we may simply be selecting those who, in addition to being expressive, or perhaps because of their expressiveness, have had more extensive experiences with sexual words, symbols, and ideas. On the other hand, the test-defined 'sexual inhibitor' might well have had fewer exposures to, and experiences with materials of a sexual nature. If such groups differ in their ability to identify sexual words, it might be more sensible to explain these results by referring to individual differences in associative strength rather than to traits of defensiveness or to value systems with vague motivational overtones."

Given such an explanation, the mysterious quality of perceptual defense vanishes in the clear air of the known relationship between word familiarity and perceptual accuracy (e.g., Solomon and Postman, 1952). Thus, theoretical speculations about the perceptual data have tended to move away from some of the more colorful earlier notions such as unconscious perception. We are nevertheless, as Lazarus et al. (1951) point out, left with individual differences in expressiveness, experiences with conflictful material, defenses, or whatever label one chooses to apply. For personality psychologists, the questions still remain as to the antecedents, correlates, and consequents of these individual differences.

## 3. Repression-Sensitization in Other Response Measures

At approximately the same period in time as the differential threshold studies, many other investigations utilizing repressing-sensitizing variables were conducted. It was found, for example, that subjects who tend to recall their failures in an experimental task tend to recall material associated with a painful shock, while those who forget one forget the other (Lazarus and Longo, 1953). Individuals who recall incomplete tasks in a threatening situation learn affective words as easily as neutral ones, while those who forget the incompleted tasks experience relative difficulty in learning affective words (Eriksen, 1952b). Those subjects who are able to verbalize a pattern of electric shock applied during a learning task are able deliberately to avoid giving the punished responses (Eriksen and Kuethe, 1956). Relatively shorter latency for aggressive and succorant words on a word-association test is associated with the acceptance of such concepts on the Rorschach, while relatively longer latency is associated with failure to accept the concepts on the Rorschach (Eriksen and Lazarus, 1952). Giving emotional words in response to appropriate TAT cards is positively related to the number of Rorschach responses given (Ullman, 1958). Patients identified as facilitators according to their case histories prefer sexual and aggressive humor while patients identified as inhibitors prefer nonsense humor (Ullman and Lim, 1962).

An examination of the perceptual studies and the subsequent work suggests rather strongly the presence of an approach-avoidance sort of dimension with respect to response to threatening stimuli. It should also be noted that these behavior tendencies appear to be fairly pervasive ones in that they are identifiable in perceptual responses, responses given to projective tests, behavior in learning and memory tasks, and in symptoms of maladjustment. Such relational fertility is a convincing argument for the value of pursuing this variable in further research.

### B. MEASUREMENT OF REPRESSION-SENSITIZATION

A familiar problem which arises, though, is that of agreeing upon a suitable defining operation for repression-sensitization. In the work outlined above, almost every investigator utilized a different measure of the defense dimension. And, while significant correlations were generally reported between the various approach-avoidance indices, the magnitude of the relationships is hardly sufficient to conceptualize them as interchangeable measures of a single construct. An additional difficulty with the measures used in the various experiments is the problem of low or even unknown reliability (Byrne and Holcomb, 1962). As a first step in establishing the presence of a relationship between variables, relatively low reliability of measurement only acts to increase the probability of making Type II errors. It is essential, however, in order for research in an area to progress beyond these first crude findings that $Y$ is related to $X$, to obtain reliable measures of the variables involved and to utilize operations consistently across experiments.

If the preceding assumption is accepted, what would be the next logical step in measurement? One possibility would be to investigate the reliabilities of each reported defining operation (differential thresholds, memory scores, TAT responses, etc.) and select the most reliable as the measure of repression-sensitization in all future work. If satisfactory reliabilities were not found, the best measure could be used as a starting point for further test construction. The decision is a somewhat arbitrary one, but the goal in any event would be a consistent measuring instrument which yields scores that correlate with behaviors already defined as repressing-sensitizing. Consistency here means that the device has homogeneous response variations across items, stability of scores over time, and an objective scoring system on which any two independent judges can obtain close agreement. A measurement approach meeting those criteria is one based on a combination of repression-sensitization indices which have not yet been discussed.

### 1. Use of the MMPI to Measure Defensive Behavior

While the Minnesota Multiphasic Personality Inventory (MMPI) (Hathaway and McKinley, 1951) was originally devised as a diagnostic aid, it has subsequently been used in both research and clinical work for a wide variety of additional purposes. Since the individuals classified into the various psychiatric syndromes identified by the test tend to differ in characteristic defensive modes and since some of the validity scales have been considered as reflecting defenses, it was perhaps inevitable that MMPI scales would be utilized in work on repression-sensitization.

A summary of the scales and combinations of scales used by various investigators is shown in Table I. There was relatively good agreement among investigators as to the type of MMPI items most indicative of repressing and sensitizing defenses.

In the work cited in Table I, the MMPI measures of repression-sensitization were found to be related to such variables as differential recall of completed and incompleted tasks, frequency of dream recall, defense mechanisms in hospitalized neurotics, differential perceptual recognition thresholds, and interpersonal perception. With these findings as a promising start, two independent efforts were made at approximately the same time to devise a single, comprehensive MMPI scale to measure the repression-sensitization dimension.

TABLE I
MMPI SCALES USED AS DEFENSE MEASURES

| Scales | Represser score | Sensitizer score | Reference |
|---|---|---|---|
| K | High | Low | Page and Markowitz (1955) |
| L | High | Low | Page and Markowitz (1955); Tart (1962) |
| F minus K | Low | High | Ullmann (1958) |
| Hy | High | Low | Eriksen (1954); Mathews and Wertheimer (1958) |
| Hy denial | High | Low | Carlson (1954); Gordon (1957); Gordon (1959) |
| Hy admission | Low | High | Gordon (1959) |
| Hy minus Pt | High | Low | Eriksen and Davids (1955); Truax (1957) |
| Pt | Low | High | Carlson (1954); Eriksen (1954); Eriksen and Browne (1956); Eriksen and Davids (1955); Eriksen, Keuthe and Sullivan (1958) |
| MAS | Low | High | Eriksen and Davids (1955); Gordon (1959) |
| Welsh A | Low | High | Tart (1962) |
| Welsh R | High | Low | Tart (1962) |

## 2. A Repression-Sensitization Scale

At the Behavioral Research Laboratory of the Veterans Administration Hospital at Palo Alto, a number of investigations were undertaken to follow up and extend Shannon's (1955, 1962) work with facilitators and inhibitors. Ullmann (1958) devised a scoring system for case history material which was used in several projects. As a primary measure, however, the case history scoring approach was limited by problems of interjudge reliability, the use of discrete categories of individuals rather than a continuum, and its inapplicability to nonpatient populations. To overcome these difficulties, Ullmann (1962) undertook the construction of an empirically derived MMPI scale to measure facilitation-inhibition (or repression-sensitization). Using an item-analysis approach, he compared the responses of 38 facilitators and 24 inhibitors (identified by the case history method) on each of the 566 MMPI items. A cross-validation sample consisted of 48 facilitators and 22 inhibitors. A total of 21 items met the criterion of differentiation at the .05 level in both samples. An additional 23 items differentiated at the .10 level *and* were related to the total facilitation-inhibition score in a third sample of 61 subjects. The final scale consisted of 44 items. On a new sample of subjects, a corrected split-half reliability of .96 and test-retest reliabilities of .88 (1 to 18 months), .71 (19 to 36 months), and .54 (37 to 85 months) were obtained. Studies utilizing Ullmann's scale will be reported in a following section.

At about the same time that Ullmann's work was under way, Altrocchi, Parsons, and Dickoff (1960) at Duke University approached the measurement of repression-sensitization via the MMPI in a somewhat different way. On the basis of the work of Eriksen and Gordon, three MMPI scales were selected as likely measures of sensitization (*D, Pt,* and Welsh Anxiety) and three others as measures of repression (*L, K,* and *Hy* denial). A repression-sensitization index was determined by subtracting each subject's total score on the latter three scales from his total score on the three former ones. In neither this paper nor a subsequent report (Altrocchi, 1961) were reliability data presented.

In work at the University of Texas, the author (Byrne, 1961, p. 337) attempted to refine Altrocchi's scale because "Several potential measurement difficulties arise with this measure because of item overlap among the six MMPI scales which are combined in it. For example, item 32 contributes to *D, Pt,* and Welsh Anxiety scores, thereby giving it an arbitrary weight of three. More confusing possibilities also arise. For example, item 30 contributes to *D and* to *L, K,* and *Hy* denial; thus, it is included in opposing halves of the index with a net weight of two for repression. While such differential item weights could conceivably prove to be the optimum ones, their accidental nature in this instance is clear."

To get around such difficulties, the author substituted a scoring system in which each item on the six scales was scored only once and all inconsistently scored items eliminated. The result was a 156-item Repression-Sensitization (R-S) Scale in which high scores indicated sensitizing responses. Both the corrected coefficient of internal consistency and the coefficient of stability (six weeks) were found to be .88. In subsequent work (Byrne, Barry, and Nelson, 1963), an internal-consistency item analysis was undertaken with two independent samples of 370 students each. Those 127 items which yielded correlations with the total R-S score significant at the .001 level or better in *both* samples were retained as scorable items in the revised R-S scale. This revised scale was found to have a corrected split-half reliability of .94 and a test-retest reliability (3 months) of .82.

The following section surveys the published and unpublished research in which these MMPI repression-sensitization measures have been used. Approximately 97% of Altrocchi's items were retained in the original and about 70% in the revised R-S scale. The Facilitation-Inhibition Scale has been found to correlate .76 with the R-S scale in one student population (Byrne, 1961), .88 in another (Liberty, Lunneborg, and Atkinson, in press), and .94 in a neuropsychiatric patient population (Ullmann, 1962). Almost half of the items in the F-I scale also are contained in both the original and revised R-S scales. Therefore, it seems defensible to consider the instruments as interchangeable measuring devices.

## II. A Review of Research on the R-S Scale

### A. REPRESSION

Basic to the construct validity of the R-S scale is evidence relating scores on the test to repressive *versus* sensitizing behavior. As with most variables in the field of personality, the conceptualizations regarding defensive modes range from nonoperational theoretical formulations based on clinical observations to quite specific operations devised for research purposes. Since no single variable of the latter variety can encompass all of the surplus meaning contained in the clinical theories of repression, the construct validity of the R-S scale must rest on a series of correlational and experimental findings. Seven different types of evidence have been reported.

### 1. Judgments Concerning Defense Mechanisms

Dr. Vincent Tempone compared the R-S scale with judgments by clinicians of the meaning of this variable. He had nine staff members at the Massachusetts Mental Health Center fill out the test as they thought a repressing individual would. He defined agreement as concurrence by at least seven of the nine judges. On the original R-S scale, judges corresponded with the key on 72% of the items, and on the revised scale there was correspondence on 90%. On none of the items did the judges agree on a response opposite to the key (Byrne et al., 1963).

A second investigation by Tempone (1963) utilized ratings of 18 therapy patients by six first-year psychiatric residents. Patients' scores on the R-S scale and clinical ratings of their repression-sensitization were found to correlate .38, which falls short of statistical significance in this small sample.

Davison (1963) administered several measures of coping mechanisms, including the R-S scale, to 48 male students. A cluster analysis of the 32 variables led to the identification of three clusters. The first was essentially defined by the R-S scale, and it included (in addition to the MMPI scales used in constructing the R-S scale) the *F, Pd,* and *Ma* scales from the MMPI, intellectualization as judged in an interview situation, and Identification on the Heath Phrase Association Test.

## 2. Selective Forgetting

At the University of Arkansas, Gossett (1964) attempted to elicit repressive mechanisms by combining threatening conditions with a memory task. The subjects consisted of 48 repressers and 48 sensitizers drawn from a pool of 296 introductory psychology students. Each subject learned a list of 12 nonsense syllables. Their performance on the fifth trial constituted the first recall test. Following this, they were given an "Intelligence and Personality Test" made up of 12 subtests, each titled with one of the nonsense syllables. In the experimental group, failure was induced via false norms, and the failures were attributed to certain intellectual and/or personality problems. The control group took the test as a "standardization sample" without false norms or induced failure. After a filler task, all subjects were asked to recall the 12 syllables. As a control for suppression, half of the subjects were offered rewards for remembering correctly ($10 and the chance to avoid several hours of tedious tasks) while half were given standard instructions to attempt to remember the syllables. After an explanation of the purpose of the experiment to the subjects, a third recall test was given. Gossett found significant differences between repressers and sensitizers in their recall of the syllables when the effects of suppression were controlled. He interpreted this finding to mean that those with low scores on the R-S scale repress threatening material while those with high scores do not.

McReynolds and Ullmann (1964) with 40 students in an advanced psychology class obtained recall data for 36 words projected briefly on a screen immediately after the last word had been presented. Of the 30 nonpractice words, 12 were pleasant, 12 were unpleasant, and 6 were neutral. The recall score consisted of the difference between the number of unpleasant and pleasant words recalled. With anxiety, number of neutral words recalled, and general tendency to use pleasant or unpleasant words held constant, the correlation between scores on the F-I scale and the recall score was not significant.

## 3. Perceptual Defense

Considering the origin of the conceptualizations of repression-sensitization, it is obvious that scores on the R-S scale would be expected to be related to differential perceptual recognition thresholds for threatening versus nonthreatening stimuli. Tempone (1962) tested this proposition, utilizing an induced failure manipulation as the source of threat. From a pool of 244 University of Texas undergraduates, he selected 40 repressers (below 25th percentile) and 40 sensitizers (above 75th percentile) on the basis of scores on the R-S scale. On an eight-item anagrams task taken with a group of stooges, half of the subjects were given a failure experience (two or less anagrams correct) and half a success experience (six or more anagrams correct). The correct solution to each anagram was given to the subjects after each trial. Following this phase of the experiment, a perceptual test was given in which 19 words were presented at gradually increasing exposure speeds tachistoscopically; the stimuli consisted of three practice words, the eight correct anagram solu-

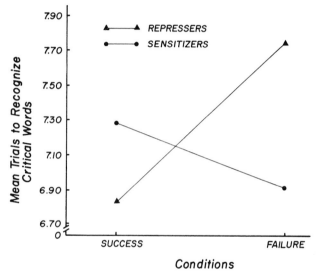

Fig. 1. Perceptual recognition thresholds for critical words under success and failure conditions. [After Tempone (1962).]

tions, and eight neutral words. The order of the latter 16 words was counterbalanced, and the critical and neutral words were matched for word length and frequency based on the Thorndike-Lorge word count. Word thresholds were measured as number of trials required for correct recognition. Analysis of variance indicated a significant interaction effect for repression-sensitization times success-failure. Repressers and sensitizers did not differ significantly in the success condition, but repressers obtained significantly higher thresholds for the threat words in the failure condition than did sensitizers. For the neutral words, thresholds were not related to defensive mode or experimental conditions. The relationship is shown graphically in Fig. 1.

Ullmann, Weiss, and Krasner (1963) were able to change the perceptual performance of repressers by means of a process of verbal conditioning for use of emotional words just prior to responding to a perceptual defense task. The task was the recognition of matched neutral and threatening words on a series of successively better carbon copies. Compared to the control group, inhibitors in the experimental group showed significantly less difference in their recognition thresholds for threatening and neutral words; facilitators in the two groups did not show a significant difference. The change evidenced by those with repressive defenses could be interpreted as a function of increased familiarity with the threatening words, desensitization to the threat represented by such words, or as learning that the use of such words was socially acceptable in the context of the experiment.

### 4. Awareness of Anxiety

In his dissertation research at the University of Rochester, Pomeranz (1963) investigated the relationship between verbalized response to threat and repression-sensitization. Three types of movies (control, stressor, and alleviation of emotional arousal) were shown, and the subjects' affective states during each were obtained on an Adjective Check List and an Anxiety Differential measure. The subjects were 63 male undergraduates selected from a larger group on the basis of R-S scale scores. It was found that sensitizers indicated significantly more emotional arousal in response to the stressor (movie of unpleasant surgical operation) than did repressers.

Byrne and Sheffield (in press) created a potential threat situation by exposing subjects to 11 vividly descriptive sexual passages from various novels. Subjects were all males with 22 sensitizers and 22 repressers serving in the sex arousal condition. In the control group 22 sensitizers and 22 repressers read neutral descriptive passages from the same 11 novels. Immediately after the reading task, all of the subjects were asked to fill out six five-point rating scales dealing with their feelings while reading the literary material. On the "Sexually Aroused" scale, ratings were significantly higher in the experimental than in the control group for both repressers and sensitizers. On the "Anxious" scale, however, there was a significant interaction in that repressers and sensitizers did not differ in the neutral condition, but sensitizers rated themselves as significantly more anxious in the experimental condition. The relationship is shown in Fig. 2. A possible interpretation of this finding is that repressers were unaware of or were denying any feelings of anxiety as a concomitant of sexual excitement. It would be important, therefore, to be able to find some other evidence of disturbance accompanying the denial of anxiety. With experimental and control groups combined, self-ratings of sex arousal correlated with self-ratings of disgust ($r = .34$, $p < .05$) and anger ($r = .36$, $p < .05$) for repressers. For sensitizers, sex arousal was significantly related to anxiety ($r = .67$, $p < .01$), lack of boredom ($r = -.57$, $p < .01$), and feeling entertained ($r = .33$, $p < .05$).

Relevant data are also presented by Lomont (1964) in an investigation utilizing 35 hospitalized psychotic and nonpsychotic patients. During their first month of hospitalization, the subjects were given the R-S scale, a 66-item word association test containing both threatening and nonthreatening words, and the IPAT Self Analysis Form. The word association test was scored for 31 signs of disturbance including reaction

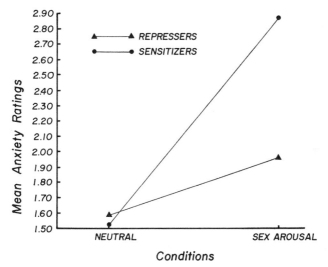

FIG. 2. Self-ratings of anxiety after reading neutral and sexually arousing literary material. [From Byrne and Sheffield (in press).]

time over 2.5 seconds, blocking, and reproduction failures. A significant positive correlation was found between R-S scale scores and IPAT scores ($r = .76$) and a significant negative correlation between the R-S scale and disturbance scores on the word association test ($r = -.45$). Thus, sensitizers responded with greater verbalized anxiety than repressers on a self-report measure while the repressers indicated greater disturbance than sensitizers on the indirect measure.

### 5. Physiological Response to Threat

Lazarus and Alfert (in press) report an investigation in which cognitive appraisal of a stress situation and physiological response to that stress were compared. In previous research (Lazarus, Speisman, Mordkoff, and Davison, in press; Speisman, Lazarus, Mordkoff, and Davison, in press), a silent movie of a primitive subincision ritual was used to produce stress reactions. In the Lazarus and Alfert study, three experimental conditions were employed: the silent film without introduction or commentary, the film with both an introduction and a movie sound track that emphasized denial and reaction formation, and the silent film with the denial and reaction formation introduction. The latter two conditions were conceptualized as possibly alternate ways to reduce the threat of the film; there was denial of the painful aspects of the operation and of its possible physical harm and an emphasis on the joy of the native boys in participating in the ceremony. The subjects were 69 male students at the University of California. During the movie, measurements of skin conductance and heart rate were made continuously. Immediately after the film, several psychological measures were obtained including the Nowlis Adjective Check List of Mood (Nowlis and Nowlis, 1956). In a separate research session, the subjects were given the MMPI which was scored for $K$, $Hy$ denial, Welsh Repression, and Repression-Sensitization. In general they found on both the physiological measures and mood ratings that the silent film condition was the most stressful and the silent film plus denial introduction the least stressful. Scores on the four personality variables were divided at the median. In the various comparisons which were made, the $K$ and $Hy$ denial scales were the most effective predictors of individual differences. The R-S scale did not yield as many significant findings (possibly because of a median split rather than the use of extreme groups), but it followed the same general pattern as the other variables. The over-all tendency was for those individuals with denying and repressing defenses to show higher levels of skin conductance and lower levels of discomfort on the verbal measures when compared with subjects with sensitizing defenses. The skin conductance data for the R-S scale are shown in Fig. 3. Even though Lazarus and Alfert found that those with low scores on the R-S scale indicated less anxiety and depression on the Nowlis Mood Scale than did those with high scores, the reverse pattern was found for skin conductance. The authors conclude:

"Judging from these Nowlis patterns, verbally derived measures of stress response in the form of disphoric affect interacts with personality variables in a direction opposite from what is found with autonomic indicators. High deniers refuse to admit disturbance verbally but reveal it autonomically, while low deniers are apt to say they are more disturbed while showing less autonomic reactivity."

In his doctoral research at the University of California, Davison (1963) also utilized the subincision ritual movie as a stressor. A group of 48 male undergraduates viewed the film weekly for a total of three exposures. On each occasion, recordings of several physiological responses were obtained. Scores on the repression-sensitization dimension predicted reaction to the film in terms of skin conductance, heart rate, and bodily movement. Dividing the subjects into high, medium, and low groups, he found that the medium group was the most physiologically responsive to the film while the sensitizer group was the least responsive. A possible implication is that the development of strong consistent defenses of either type protects the individual from physiological stress, but that sensitization is more effective in this respect than repression. The

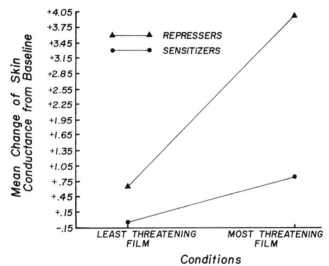

FIG. 3. Changes in skin conductance from baseline to least threatening and most threatening film conditions. [From Lazarus and Alfert (in press).]

greatest differences were between the sensitizer group and the other two; Davison (1963, p. 123) suggests,

"We have some support for the construct validity of the Byrne scale as a measure of sensitization in two facts: (1) the high sensitizers show least movement during the film and our previous findings associate immobility in this situation with attention; (2) the high sensitizers obtain the largest first-session mean on Nowlis "Activation," which on its content would seem to reflect self-reported mental alertness and interest, and they demonstrate a progressive decline in this dimension. In other words, they appear to be reacting to the first exposure to the film, a threatening situation, with mobilization of their preferred coping mechanisms, and this response diminishes as the film loses its threatening capability."

## 6. Responding to Ambiguous Stimuli

Responses to relatively ambiguous or unstructured stimuli have been found to be in part a function of the subjects' characteristic defense mechanisms. Those who repress tend to respond to ambiguous material with neutral or nonthreatening interpretations, while individuals employing intellectualizing or obsessional defenses respond to such material with conflict-laden and emotional content. Are scores on the R-S scale related to these differences? If repression-sensitization scores indicate a general tendency to avoid or approach threatening stimuli and if sexual and aggressive cues represent some degree of threat to almost everyone in our culture, interpretation of projective material as sexual or aggressive should be a function of R-S scale scores.

From a group of 213 undergraduates, 29 sensitizers and 24 repressers were asked to respond to nine TAT cards (Byrne, 1961). Each protocol was scored for sexual content, aggressive content, and percentage of emotional words. Neither the aggression score nor the percentage of emotional words was related to repression-sensitization. For both sexes, sensitizers had higher sexual scores than repressers. The difference for males was significant at beyond the .01 level. The females had a larger mean difference than the males, but with a smaller $N$ and a larger variance the difference did not reach statistical significance.

A TAT investigation by Tempone (1963) yielded quite different results. With 46 male undergraduates at the University of New Hampshire as subjects, stories given in response to five TAT cards were scored for aggressive and sexual content. In this study, sensitizers gave significantly ($p < .05$) more aggressive content than repressers, but the differences in sexual responses were not significant.

In a word association study, Blaylock (1963) utilized a 100-item list made up chiefly of homonyms with aggressive and neutral meanings. A group of 37 Texas undergraduates was given this test and the R-S scale. Repression-sensitization was found to correlate .37 ($p < .05$) with number of stimulus words perceived as aggressive. When this investigation was repeated with a similar word association test administered individually, no relationship to R-S scale scores was found in a group of 54 undergraduates.

## 7. Response to Humor

On the basis of Freudian theory, O'Connell and Peterson (1964) hypothesized differential response to humorous material as a function of repressing *versus* sensitizing defenses. Specifically, they predicted that individuals with low appreciation for humor are rigid repressers, those with high appreciation for humor are normals (middle part of the R-S scale), and that sensitizers should fall in between the other two groups in humor appreciation. The humor test was composed of 17 jokes and anecdotes which had been unanimously classified by six clinical psychologists as falling in the category of humor (rather than aggressive or hostile wit or nonsense wit). In defining these categories for the judges, the authors indicated that ". . . humor is characterized by an *objectively* stressful situation in which the principal reacts with a jest which is relatively free of hostility directed toward others." For example, one of the humor items was, "A condemned prisoner was being led to the gallows early one Monday morning. As he left his cell, he waved to the other prisoners and said, 'Well, this is a good beginning to the week.' " In its final form, the humor test required the subjects to respond to each item on a five-point scale ranging from "dislike very much" to "like very much"; its corrected split-half reliability was found to be .96.

TABLE II

REPRESSION-SENSITIZATION AND HUMOR APPRECIATION[a]

| Humor appreciation | N | R-S scale | |
| | | M | SD |
|---|---|---|---|
| High | 54 | 39.20 | 17.82 |
| Medium | 70 | 42.20 | 18.36 |
| Low | 54 | 36.10 | 17.42 |

[a] After O'Connell and Peterson (1964).

Both the humor test and the R-S scale were administered to 178 students at Baylor University. The sample was divided approximately into thirds on the basis of their humor appreciation scores. As shown in Table II, the mean repression-sensitization scores for these three groups fell in the predicted order. A simple analysis of variance did not yield a significant $F$, but group comparisons by means of $t$ tests indicated the low-appreciation group was significantly more repressing than either the middle- or high-appreciation groups.

*8. Conclusions*

Predictions based on the assumption that scores on the R-S scale indicate individual differences in the tendency to repress or deny or avoid threatening stimuli have been relatively well supported. There is evidence that behavior which clinicians define as repressive is related to the behavior measured by the test. When confronted by threatening or anxiety-provoking situations, individuals on the two ends of the scale differ in the predicted direction in terms of memory, perception, and reported anxiety; further, these differences are not manifest in neutral situations. It has not yet been conclusively demonstrated that repressers give physiological evidence of anxiety while verbally denying such feelings, but the work of Lazarus and others offers some encouragement along this line. Response to projective material with emotionally disturbing content is not consistently related to repression-sensitization. It is possible that the inconsistent results in the latter work may be a function of the degree of threat provided by the stimuli. It would be hypothesized, therefore, that if the content of the stimulus material and/or the accompanying instructions and experimental setting were sufficiently threatening, differences in repression-sensitization would lead to differences in response. Finally, the relative dislike of humor by repressers as compared with other individuals is consonant with Freudian humor theory. In their excellent review of the general concept of repression, MacKinnon and Dukes (1962) describe three experimental approaches to the study of this behavior. Within that categorization system, the R-S scale has been found relevant in predicting (1) inhibition of perception, (2) inhibition of memory, and (3) inhibition of response. The construct validity of the scale as a measure of differences in defenses seems moderately well established.

B. MEASURES OF SELF-DESCRIPTION

On several bases it has been hypothesized that repression-sensitization is related to measures of the self concept. Individuals on the repressing end of the continuum would be expected to be unaware of those aspects of themselves which involve anxiety-arousing cues. Thus, in response to the typical assessment devices utilized in research on self theory, repressers should be less likely than sensitizers to indicate negative self attributes or to indicate discrepancies between their actual and ideal attributes. Sensitizers, in contrast, would be expected not only to be aware of negative attributes and self-ideal discrepancies but also to dwell on them and even to exaggerate them.

1. Self-Ideal Discrepancy

A number of earlier investigations reported that repressing individuals tend to describe themselves more positively on Q-sort tasks than do sensitizing individuals (e.g., Block and Thomas, 1955; Chodorkoff, 1954). With the R-S scale, the self-ideal discrepency of repressers on Leary's Interpersonal Check List was found to be significantly less than that of sensitizers in two different samples of student nurses (Altrocchi et al., 1960). The magnitude of the relationship is a relatively substantial one; on Worchel's (1957) Self-Activity Inventory (SAI) the R-S scale has been found to correlate with self-ideal discrepancy scores .62 ($p < .01$) and

.55 ($p < .01$) in two groups of undergraduates (Byrne, 1961) and .63 ($p < .01$) in a third sample (Byrne *et al.*, 1963). The self-ideal discrepancy scores on Bill's Index of Adjustment and Values and the R-S scale were found to correlate .61 ($p < .01$) in a group of 227 nursing students in New Jersey (Hanson, 1963).

### 2. Self Concept

Presumably, self-ideal discrepancy can come about as a function of variations in either self concept or ideal concept. It is reasonable to inquire, then, whether represser-sensitizer differences in discrepancy are a function of differences in descriptions of self, ideal, or both. Altrocchi *et al.* (1960) reported that repressers and sensitizers did not differ in ideal self, only in self concept. Sensitizers were found to have a more negative self concept and hence a greater discrepancy between self and ideal. Sensitizers described themselves as more rebellious, aggressive, and self-effacing, and as less dominant than repressers.

These findings were verified in subsequent research using the SAI. Each item on the latter was rated in terms of whether or not the behavior represented a negatively valued characteristic. On this basis, both self-descriptions and ideal-self descriptions could be scored in terms of negativeness. In two different investigations (Byrne, 1961; Byrne *et al.*, 1963), repression-sensitization was found not to be significantly related to negative ideal-self descriptions ($r = .25$; $r = .16$) but substantially related to negative self-descriptions ($r = .66$, $p < .01$; $r = .68$, $p < .01$). It seems clear that the findings regarding repression-sensitization and self-ideal discrepancy are a function of differences in self-descriptions. Repressers and sensitizers do not differ systematically in their ideals. Rather, it is their self-pictures which differ markedly, with repressers presenting themselves positively and sensitizers negatively.

### 3. Incongruency

A somewhat different sort of self-descriptive measure is that of incongruency or inconsistency of percepts. As has been discussed elsewhere (Byrne *et al.*, 1963, p. 330),

"McReynolds (1956) has proposed that anxiety is a function of the quantity of perceptual material not assimilated into perceptual systems. He uses the term "incongruency" to describe unassimilated material. Incongruent percepts are those which are difficult to harmonize because they are contradictory, inconsistent, or dissonant (McReynolds, 1958), and the existence of such percepts motivates individuals to reduce incongruencies. In a slightly different terminology, a stimulus is incongruent for an individual if it elicits incompatible responses. The concept of incongruency is quite similar to Festinger's (1957) formulation of cognitive dissonance."

Incongruency has been operationally defined as inconsistency in self-report between values (good-bad) and feelings (like-dislike) with respect to various types of behavior, events, or objects. In order to measure incongruency, several researchers have constructed tests consisting of a series of items which take the form "Hunting for game with a gun" and "Insisting on my rights." Ss respond to the items in terms of values by rating each activity as good or bad. Later, they respond to the same items in terms of feelings by rating each as something that they like or dislike. Each item is then scored for congruency-incongruency across the two sets of ratings. A congruent response (Good-Like or Bad-Dislike) receives no points. An incongruent response (Good-Dislike or Bad-Like) receives one point. The total incongruency score is the number of items to which S has responded in an incongruent way. Among other findings, incongruency has been found to be positively related to scores on the Manifest Anxiety Scale (McReynolds, 1958). Also, incongruency with respect to hostility was found to be inversely related to the accuracy of perception of hostile cartoons while sexual incongruency was found to be inversely related to the accuracy with which sexual cartoons are identified (Byrne, Terrill, and McReynolds, 1961).

Since incongruency is conceptualized as anxiety arousing, it would follow that repressers should be less aware of their incongruent percepts than are sensitizers. In extending the incongruency concept, three types of incongruency were investigated. A series of 50 hostility items were used, and subjects rated each on the basis of their feelings of like-dislike, their values of good-bad, and their estimation of environmental consequences as pleasant-unpleasant. Thus, three types of incongruency were possible: feelings *versus* values (like-bad, dislike-good), values *versus* consequences (good-unpleasant, bad-pleasant), and feelings *versus* consequences (like-unpleasant, dislike-pleasant). A group of 114 undergraduates was given the R-S scale and the Hostility Incongruency Test. Each type of incongruency was significantly related to repression-sensitization: .38 ($p < .01$) for feelings *versus* values, .33 ($p < .01$) for feelings *versus* consequences, and .19 ($p < .05$) for values *versus* consequences. Further, in each of the former two instances, one of the two possible types of incongruency entirely accounted for the relationships. R-S scale scores correlated with number of items checked like-bad ($r = .40$, $p < .01$) but not with items checked dislike-good ($r = .00$), and repression-sensitization correlated with number of items checked like-unpleasant ($r = .45$, $p < .01$) but not with items checked dislike-pleasant ($r = -.03$). Sensitizers, then, are more likely to indicate that they enjoy behavior which they believe to be morally wrong and which they believe is likely to have unpleasant environmental consequences.

### 4. Hostility

Using the Rosenzweig P-F test and a 14-item rating scale as hostility measures, Altrocchi, Shrauger, and McLeod (1964) found that repressers attributed less hostility to themselves than did sensitizers or expressors. In research which is as yet unpublished, Lomont (1963) investigated the relationships among the R-S scale, a self-report measure of hostility (the Buss–Durkee Inventory), and hostility as measured by the Holtzman Ink Blot Test. With 27 college students, repression-sensitization correlated .74 ($p < .01$) with scores on the Buss–Durkee scale but only negligibly with hostility as measured by the ink blots. A more unusual finding, however, had to do with the fact that repression-sensitization acts to obscure the relationship between the two hostility variables. The latter do not correlate significantly ($r = .28$) unless scores on the R-S scale are partialled out; in the latter case, the two hostility measures correlated .49 ($p < .05$). Lomont concludes:

"These results, I think, are nicely consonant with the clinical assumption that an ink blot test can tap unacknowledged hostility. In keeping with the implications of the clinical belief, repression appears to be an intervening variable which affects the correspondence between self-reports of aggression and aggression measures on an ink blot test. This picture of repression as an intervening variable implies that, given a certain degree of self-reported aggression, the degree of hostility which shows up on an ink blot test is positively related to the degree of repression operating on the self-reported aggression. . . . The results fit the clinical belief regarding the relation of repression to self-reported and ink blot aggression particularly well since R-S is highly related to self-reported aggression but not at all with ink blot aggression. This finding is in keeping with the clinical hypothesis that repression censors an individual's self-report of aggression but that the ink blot measure of aggression largely circumvents censorship."

### 5. Conclusions

In the research conducted to date, the relationship between R-S scale scores and measures of self-description is clearly and firmly established. The higher an individual's score on the R-S scale, the more likely he is on other instruments to indicate a discrepancy between his self concept and his self ideal, to describe himself in negative and self-depreciating terms, to report incongruencies among feelings, values, and environmental consequences, and more specifically to say that he enjoys behavior which he believes to be morally wrong and which is likely to have unpleasant consequences. Further, as R-S scale scores increase, the more likely an individual is to describe his own behavior and feelings as hostile. These findings may represent differences in the tendency to present oneself in the most favorable or most unfavorable possible light.

## C. Maladjustment

If each end of the repression-sensitization continuum represents an extreme of the respective defensive modes, scores on the R-S scale would be expected to have a curvilinear relationship with various indices of psychological adjustment. Neither overintellectualization of conflicts nor denial of them should result in optimal adjustment.

### 1. Population Comparisons

Because of the multitude of differences involved besides that of maladjustment, comparison of hospitalized neuropsychiatric patients with college students provides equivocal evidence at best. Nevertheless, the

TABLE III

REPRESSION-SENSITIZATION IN ALCOHOLICS AND NORMALS[a]

|  | Normals | | | Alcoholics | | | Mean difference | CR |
|---|---|---|---|---|---|---|---|---|
|  | N | M | SD | N | M | SD | | |
| Males | 394 | 63.08 | 17.71 | 69 | 75.58 | 16.77 | 12.50 | 6.19[b] |
| Females | 230 | 61.80 | 16.20 | 11 | 77.82 | 17.69 | 16.22 | 2.99[c] |

[a] Data from Gynther (1963).
[b] $p < .001$.
[c] $p < .01$.

curvilinear hypothesis leads to the prediction that neuropsychiatric patients should have more extreme scores on the repression-sensitization measure and hence a larger standard deviation than normal subjects. Ullmann (1962) compared scores on the F-I scale for 47 male Texas students ($M = 29.38$, $SD = 6.50$) with those of two samples ($N = 90$ and 64) of male neuropsychiatric patients at the Veterans Administration Hospital at Palo Alto ($M = 25.74$ and 25.39, $SD = 11.22$ and 11.44). The patients had a significantly higher standard deviation than the students, as predicted. In addition, mean differences were also significant; the patients were further toward the facilitating or sensitizing end of the continuum.

In a group of 35 undergraduates, Joy (1963b) found a correlation of .91 between scores on the R-S scale and scores on an MMPI scale which measures Alcoholic Tendency. Because of item overlap on the two instruments, the meaning of this finding is open to question. Confirmation of the relationship between sensitizing defenses and alcoholism has been provided, however, by Gynther (1963) at the Malcolm Bliss Mental Health Center in St. Louis. As part of an investigation of married and unmarried alcoholics which is now in progress, Dr. Gynther obtained R-S scale scores on 69 male and 11 female alcoholics. As shown in Table III, for both sexes the alcoholics are significantly more sensitizing on the original R-S scoring system than the college students in the normative sample.

## 2. Deviation from the Norm

In his work on the Deviation Hypothesis, Berg (1959) has presented evidence to suggest that responses to test items which differ from those of the total group are indicative of abnormality. He has stated the Deviation Hypothesis (Berg, 1957, p. 159) as follows:

"Deviant response patterns tend to be general; hence those deviant behavior patterns which are significant for abnormality (atypicalness) and thus regarded as symptoms (earmarks or signs) are associated with other deviant response patterns which are in noncritical areas of behavior and which are not regarded as symptoms of personality aberration (nor as indicators, signs, earmarks)."

The tendency to respond deviantly, then, should be more characteristic of repressers and sensitizers than of those falling in the middle of this dimension. An adjective check list to measure deviancy was devised by Grigg and Thorpe (1960) by determining the 33 most commonly and 39 least commonly checked adjectives on Gough's Adjective Check List. Deviant scores consist of the number of adjectives of the first type *not* checked and the number of the latter that *are* checked. With two independent samples of undergraduates who had taken the R-S scale, deviant response scores on the Grigg–Thorpe list were obtained (Byrne, 1961). For one group the correlation was .42 ($p < .01$) and for the other .33 ($p < .01$) with no evidence of curvilinearity. Sensitizers tended to make deviant responses while repressers tended to make modal responses. It may be observed, though, that the commonly checked adjectives are primarily positive attributes and the least commonly checked adjectives negative attributes. If the adjective check list were viewed as simply a self-description measure, an alternative interpretation of the findings is that they represent an additional instance of sensitizers and repressers differing in the extent to which they describe themselves in positive or negative terms.

Further evidence on this point has been reported by Lucky and

Grigg (1964). Two measures of deviant response tendency were utilized, one which involved self-description (the Grigg–Thorpe adjective check list) and one which did not. The latter consisted of an "ESP" task in which subjects indicated for each of 72 items whether they believed that the experimenter wanted them to mark it; deviancy scores were defined as the number of items that deviated 1.5 $SD$'s from the mean number of items circled by the group. Again, a positive linear relationship was found between R-S scale scores and deviant response scores on the adjective check list ($r = .40$, $p < .01$). With the ESP task, however, no relationship to deviancy was found ($r = .07$). It would appear that existing data simply support the relationship between repression-sensitization and self description with no evidence of a relationship with deviant response tendency per se.

### 3. Anxiety

Since anxiety is given a prominent position in the dynamics of most psychological malfunctioning, a relationship between repression-sensitization and anxiety measures would be hypothesized. Extreme sensitizers might be expected to verbalize feelings of anxiety readily while controlling the emotional experience itself while extreme repressers should avoid both the verbalization and the subjective experience. Presumably, only the verbal expressions of anxiety are amenable to investigation.

Ullmann and McReynolds (1963) reported a significant correlation of −.50 between scores on the F-I scale and ward ratings of anxiety on 53 neuropsychiatric patients. As predicted, anxiety is more characteristic of those on the facilitating or sensitizing end of the scale. As noted earlier, the R-S scale and the IPAT Self Analysis Form were found to correlate .76 in a group of 35 hospital patients (Lomont, 1964).

Instruments such as Taylor's Manifest Anxiety Scale and the Welsh Anxiety Scale are built from MMPI items just as the R-S and F-I scales are; further, there is even item overlap. Given these circumstances, a substantial relationship between repression-sensitization and anxiety could hardly be avoided. Ullmann and McReynolds (1963) reported correlations between the F-I scale and Welsh Anxiety of −.95 for psychiatric patients and −.85 for college students. Similarly, Joy (1963b) found a .91 correlation between the R-S scale and the MAS with undergraduates. Not only are sensitizers found to be more anxious, but scores on the repression-sensitization measure are about as highly correlated with these two anxiety scales as is possible with the instruments' reliabilities. A few of the implications of this somewhat disturbing finding are discussed in the final section of this chapter.

## 4. Emotional Stability and Social Approach-Withdrawal

Weinberg (1963) carried out a factor analytic investigation of 37 variables in which the R-S scale was included along with word association scores, field dependency measures, and several personality scales. The subjects were 62 outpatients at the UCLA Medical Center Clinics. Ten factors were obtained; the first four (accounting for 70% of the variance) were labeled Emotional Stability *versus* Instability, Word Association Style, Field Dependence, and Social Approach-Withdrawal. The R-S scale loaded substantially on the first and fourth of these factors. Also loading on Factor I with the R-S scale were Impulsivity, Cyclothymia, Thinking Introversion, *Ma, Pd,* and two depression scales, while the opposite pole was represented by Achievement via Conformance and Responsibility. On Factor IV at the same pole as the R-S scale were Social Introversion, Depression, and sleeplessness while extraversion and rhathymia loaded in the opposite direction.

## 5. MMPI Variables

As with the anxiety measures, relationships between the R-S scale and other MMPI scales are complicated by overlapping items, identical test format, and so forth. In spite of these confounding factors, the findings reported by Joy (1963b) are of interest. With a group of 35 Texas undergraduates, he obtained significant correlations with a number of MMPI scales as shown in Table IV. Also shown are significant correlations found by Endler (1963) with a group of 42 undergraduate males

TABLE IV

CORRELATIONS BETWEEN R-S SCALE AND MMPI SCALES

| | r | |
|---|---|---|
| | Joy (1963b) | Endler (1963) |
| MMPI Diagnostic Scales | | |
| Depression | .72 | .66 |
| Hysteria | —.53 | .01 |
| Masculinity-Femininity | .50 | — |
| Psychasthenia | .60 | .92 |
| Social Introversion | .84 | — |
| Hypochondriasis | —.25 | .52 |
| MMPI Validity Scales | | |
| Lie | —.61 | —.38 |
| F | .62 | — |
| K | —.91 | —.76 |
| MMPI Special Scales | | |
| Neuroticism | .75 | — |
| Ego Strength | —.66 | — |

at York University. As a brief and tentative summary, the two investigations suggest that sensitizers, compared with repressers, tend to respond to
the test as do members of the opposite sex, to give unusual or uncon-
ventional responses, to be depressed and discouraged, to be anxious and
agitated, to be socially introverted, and neurotic. In addition, compared
with repressers, sensitizers tend to be more cynical and self-debasing and
to have less ego strength. Rather than a curvilinear relationship with
adjustment, sensitizers tend to present a less emotionally healthy picture
than repressers.

### 6. CPI Variables

The California Psychological Inventory (CPI) (Gough, 1957) was
designed to measure 18 personality variables. In contrast to the psycho-
diagnostic orientation of the MMPI, the CPI centers on areas of behavior
relevant to a normal population in four areas: Poise, Ascendancy, and
Self-Assurance; Socialization, Maturity, and Responsibility; Achievement
Potential and Intellectual Efficiency; and Intellectual and Interest Modes.
On each variable, high scores indicate better adjustment than low scores.

TABLE V
REPRESSION-SENSITIZATION AND CPI VARIABLES

| | *r* | | |
|---|---|---|---|
| | Joy (1963b) 35 Undergraduates | Byrne, Golightly, and Sheffield (in press) | |
| | | 43 Males | 48 Females |
| Dominance | —.52*a* | —.21 | —.16 |
| Capacity for Status | —.65*a* | —.29 | —.22 |
| Sociability | —.66*a* | —.32*b* | —.29*b* |
| Social Presence | —.47*a* | —.24 | —.43*a* |
| Self-Acceptance | —.33 | —.08 | —.15 |
| Sense of Well-Being | —.80*a* | —.43*a* | —.61*a* |
| Responsibility | —.37*b* | —.14 | —.24 |
| Socialization | —.38*b* | —.22 | —.32*b* |
| Self-Control | —.60*a* | —.38*b* | —.53*a* |
| Tolerance | —.78*a* | —.45*a* | —.39*a* |
| Good Impression | —.67*a* | —.39*a* | —.52*a* |
| Communality | —.03 | —.11 | —.23 |
| Achievement via Conformance | —.72*a* | —.46*a* | —.46*a* |
| Achievement via Independence | —.55*a* | —.33*b* | —.07 |
| Intellectual Efficiency | —.55*a* | —.32*b* | —.52*a* |
| Psychological-Mindedness | —.41*b* | —.21 | —.16 |
| Flexibility | —.17 | —.24 | —.07 |
| Femininity | .38*b* | .18 | .10 |

*a* $p < .01$.
*b* $p < .05$.

Two investigations have included the correlation of each CPI scale with the R-S scale in groups of undergraduates. Joy (1963b) utilized 35 undergraduates of both sexes while Byrne, Golightly, and Sheffield (in press) obtained samples of 43 male and 48 female undergraduates. The coefficients are shown in Table V. As may be seen, all three samples yielded significant correlations between repression-sensitization and seven of the 18 CPI scales: Sociability, Sense of Well-Being, Self-Control, Tolerance, Good Impression, Achievement via Conformance, and Intellectual Efficiency. On the basis of the CPI manual, repressers and sensitizers would tend to be differentially described by others as in Table VI.

TABLE VI

| Repressers | Sensitizers |
|---|---|
| 1. Active, alert, ambitious, competitive, energetic, enterprising, forward, industrious, ingenious, productive, progressive, quick, resourceful, strict and thorough in their own work and in expectations for others, and valuing work and effort for its own sake | 1. Apathetic, excitable, lacking in self-direction, leisurely, overly judgmental in attitude, passive, pessimistic about their occupational futures, quiet, submissive, unambitious, and unassuming |
| 2. Broad and varied interests, capable, clear-thinking, high value on cognitive and intellectual matters, intellectually able, intelligent, original and fluent in thought, valuing intellectual activity and intellectual achievement, verbally fluent, versatile, and well-informed | 2. Coarse, constricted in thought and action, conventional and stereotyped in thinking, narrow, opinionated, shallow, and shrewd |
| 3. Calm, conscientious, deliberate, diligent, efficient, honest, inhibited, organized, patient, persistent, planful, practical, responsible, self-denying, sincere, slow, stable, thorough, and thoughtful | 3. Awkward, cautious, confused, easily disorganized under stress or pressures to conform, easygoing, impulsive, insecure, lacking in self-discipline, stubborn, and uninhibited |
| 4. Concerned with making a good impression, cooperative, helpful, informal, outgoing, sociable, and tolerant | 4. Aggressive, aloof, apologetic, assertive, cool and distant in their relationships with others, defensive, detached, disbelieving and distrustful in personal and social outlook, irritable, overemphasizing personal pleasure and self-gain, overly influenced by others' reactions and opinions, retiring, self-centered, self-defensive, suggestible, suspicious, too little concerned with the needs and wants of others, and wary |

Though these data are not entirely consistent with all of the findings with the R-S scale reported in this chapter, they present a relatively convincing picture of repressers as appearing better adjusted than sensitizers. This characterization is even more striking in Fig. 4, in which Byrne, Golightly, and Sheffield's (in press) subjects were divided roughly into thirds on the basis of their R-S scale scores (29 repressers, 29 sensitizers, and 33 neutrals) and their mean standard scores on the CPI plotted. The

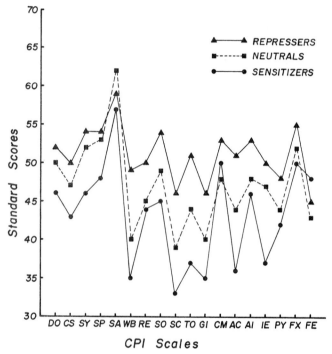

Fig. 4. California Psychological Inventory profiles of repressers, neutrals, and sensitizers. [From Byrne, Golightly, and Sheffield (in press).]

repressers may be seen to fall at or above the mean of Gough's standardization sample with the neutrals and sensitizers falling progressively lower on most of the scales.

## 7. Overcontrol

Megargee (1964) has presented evidence supporting the hypothesis that extremely assaultive criminals (e.g., murderers, those who commit assault with a deadly weapon) appear less aggressive in their everyday behavior and in test responses than do other criminals or normals. The picture is one of a chronically overcontrolled individual who suddenly breaks forth with extreme violence, often to the surprise of those who know him.

In subsequent work, Megargee and Mendelsohn (1964) developed and cross-validated an MMPI scale which discriminates extremely assaultive offenders from other criminals and from normals. Since repression and denial are among the mechanisms utilized by the overcontrolled individual, they hypothesized a negative relationship between this new scale and the R-S scale. With a sample of 14 extremely assaultive, 28 moderately assaultive, and 44 nonviolent criminals plus 50 male undergraduates, the two scales were found to correlate $-.41$ ($p < .01$) as predicted. Thus, extreme repressers are seen to fit into the pattern of chronic overcontrol which includes rigidity, conventionality, moralistic views, and (at least in the criminal group) a greater probability of psychosis (Megargee and Mendelsohn, 1964).

### 8. Conclusions

The proposition that the two extremes of the repression-sensitization dimension represent different but equally maladjusted ways of responding to anxiety and conflict is not consistent with the majority of evidence now available. The only supportive data are the findings which indicate greater variance on the defensive measure in a neuropsychiatric than in a college population and the correlation with the Megargee and Mendelsohn measure of overcontrol. All other findings strongly suggest a linear relationship between sensitizing defenses and maladjustment. Scores on the R-S scale are positively related to tendencies toward alcoholism, the number of deviant responses given on an adjective check list, anxiety, emotional instability, social withdrawal, and a number of MMPI and CPI scales which indicate various types of psychological maladjustment. Those on the repression end of the continuum were found to be higher on the hysteria dimension in one investigation but not in another. Repressers also receive higher scores on a measure of ego strength. The weakness of the majority of this evidence is that paper-and-pencil tests are utilized as indicators of maladjustment, and repressers by definition are those who respond to such instruments by denying that anything is wrong with them. Whether they are presenting an accurate picture of their emotional health will ultimately have to be determined by means other than asking them again on a different paper-and-pencil test.

### D. ADDITIONAL ANTECEDENTS, CORRELATES, AND CONSEQUENTS

#### 1. Tendency to Give Socially Desirable Responses

In 1953, Allen Edwards published an article which was to prove the precursor of a body of fruitful and at times disturbing research dealing with the effect of the social desirability of the content of test items. When he obtained social desirability scale values for a series of questionnaire items, the correlation between this value and the proportion of subjects agreeing with the item content was .87. This substantial relationship has been confirmed by subsequent investigations.

A related, but somewhat different concept, is Edwards' (1957) social desirability hypothesis, which simply proposes the existence of individual differences in the tendency to give socially desirable responses to questionnaire items. He has built a 39-item Social Desirability (SD) scale to measure this tendency. In a number of investigations, scores on the SD scale have been found to correlate highly with scores on many personality measures, including most of the MMPI scales (Edwards, 1959).

It would seem reasonable to expect that the R-S scale would also show a relationship because it is made up of MMPI items. In addition, individuals who utilize repressive mechanisms should stress socially desirable characteristics while sensitizing individuals should emphasize socially undesirable characteristics. With a group of 35 undergraduates, Joy (1963b) found a correlation of —.91 between the Edwards SD scale and the R-S scale.

Liberty, Lunneborg, and Atkinson (in press) conducted a factor analytic investigation in which several personality measures were given to 150 male students. The MMPI was scored for 62 scales including the R-S and F-I scales. Factor analysis of the intercorrelation matrix yielded 10 factors. Most of the variance was accounted for by the first three factors: social desirability, acquiescent set, and lie. Both repression-sensitization measures primarily loaded on the first of these factors. Factor I was labeled social desirability because loadings of scales on that factor correlated .93 with proportion of keyed SD items in the scales and because the Edwards SD scale was a relatively pure measure of that factor.

In a similar investigation, Wiggins (in press) factor-analyzed 30 scales from eight tests, including the F-I scale, with a group of 137 University of Illinois students. Of the six factors identified, the F-I scale had its highest loading on the first or social desirability factor.

Another approach to social desirability has been that of Crowne and Marlowe (1960), who point out that the Edwards SD scale is characterized by items containing primarily pathological implications. In a normal population, a high score, then, may mean that the subject is attempting to give the most socially desirable responses or that he is actually free of pathological symptoms. To remedy this problem, they built a scale consisting of items dealing with culturally sanctioned behaviors that are not likely to occur. The resulting Crowne–Marlowe SD scale was found to correlate .35 ($p < .01$) with the Edwards SD scale.

In both of the factor analytic studies indicated above (Liberty *et al.,* in press; Wiggins, in press), the Crowne–Marlowe SD scale loaded high in a different factor from the Edwards SD scale and from the repression-sensitization measures. In unpublished research at the University of Texas, however, a significant negative correlation ($r = -.37$, $p < .01$) between the Crowne–Marlowe SD scale and the R-S scale was found in a group of 115 students.

### 2. Authoritarianism and Dogmatism

In characterizing the personality dynamics of authoritarians, Adorno, Frenkel-Brunswik, Levinson, and Sanford (1950) stressed the mechanism of repression as one of the basic components. A correlation of $-.40$ ($p < .01$) between the R-S and $F$ scales has been reported (Byrne, 1961). The authoritarian measure was a 10-item scale composed of five of the original $F$-scale items and the five reversed items of Couch and Keniston (1960). Subsequent research at Texas (Byrne and Bounds, 1964) has found that there is no relationship between response to the Couch and Keniston items and scores on the original $F$ scale. Therefore, the meaning of the reported correlation is ambiguous at best.

An unpublished study by Friedman (1963) used a 32-item $F$ scale (27 original items and 5 successfully reversed ones). This scale correlated .28 with the R-S scale; with 33 subjects this coefficient was not significant. In another unpublished study, Byrne and Goldberg (1962) used the original $F$ scale and found a nonsignificant correlation of .13 between authoritarianism and repression-sensitization in a group of 76 students.

Rokeach (1960) in his work on open and closed mindedness has developed a Dogmatism scale designed to tap rigidities of both the political left and right. In addition, his Opinionation scales directly tap extreme political attitudes. In the Byrne and Goldberg investigation, in addition to the $F$ scale and the R-S scale, Rokeach's Dogmatism, Left Opinionation, and Right Opinionation scales were administered to the 76 subjects. Significant positive correlations were found between the R-S scale and dogmatism ($r = .36$, $p < .01$) and left opinionation ($r = .33$, $p < .01$), while repression-sensitization was not related to right opinionation ($r = .05$). Joy (1963b) reported a correlation of .55 ($p < .01$) between R-S scale scores and scores on the MMPI Prejudice Scale.

In unpublished research at York University, Sermat (1962) sought a relationship between repression-sensitization and belief in the likelihood of atomic war. Scores on this item correlated .38 ($p < .05$) with the R-S scale for 30 male students but only .02 for 30 female students.

### 3. Other Personality Variables

In the Weinberg (1963) factor analytic study cited earlier, 62 out-patients were given a series of measures including the R-S scale, the

Myers–Briggs Type Indicator, and Guilford's Inventory of Factors STDCR. As shown in Table VII, seven of the nine variables measured by these tests were significantly related to repression-sensitization. On the basis of these relationships, sensitizers would tentatively be described as more introverted, neurotic, emotionally maladjusted, and as responding

TABLE VII

Correlations of the R-S Scale with the Myers-Briggs and Guilford Tests[a]

|  | r |
|---|---|
| Myers-Briggs Type Indicator | |
| Extraversion | —.42[b] |
| Sensation | —.21 |
| Thinking | .16 |
| Judgment | .28[c] |
| Guilford Inventory of Factors STDCR | |
| Social Introversion; Seclusiveness | .58[b] |
| Thinking Introversion; Reflectiveness | .44[b] |
| Depression; Unhappiness; Pessimism | .81[b] |
| Cycloid Disposition; Emotional Instability | .77[b] |
| Rhathymia; Carefreeness; Happy-Go-Lucky Disposition | —.28[c] |

[a] After Weinberg (1963).
[b] $p < .01$.
[c] $p < .05$.

on the basis of perception rather than judgment. Repressers, on the other hand, appear to be extraverted and well adjusted, to have self-control, and to utilize judgment in preference to perception.

*4. Intellectual Ability*

In delineating the meaning of test variables, the absence of certain relationships may be as meaningful as the presence of other relationships. Four investigations have included the repression-sensitization variable and an intellectual measure. Nonsignificant correlations have been found between the R-S scale and the Shipley–Hartford Scale with 132 undergraduates ($r = -.15$) (Byrne, 1961) and with 35 hospital patients ($r = .07$) (Lomont, 1964), standard scores on a college entrance test with 26 male undergraduates ($r = .25$) (Byrne, 1961), and college ability as measured by the SCAT with 30 male students ($r = .26$) and 30 female students ($r = .03$) (Sermat, 1962), and with 42 male students ($r = .24$) (Endler, 1963). In addition, Endler (1963) failed to find a relationship between R-S scale scores and High School Grade Point Average ($r = .09$) or College Final Grade Average ($r = -.02$) with 42 first-year men at York University.

The only suggestion of a relationship here is that of a small positive correlation between repression-sensitization and intelligence for males.

Following up this possibility, the author divided the 132 students in the Shipley–Hartford study into subgroups of 60 males and 72 females and computed the correlations separately. The $r$'s of $-.18$ and $-.11$ were not significantly different from zero. On the basis of existing data, then, the R-S scale and measures of intellectual ability appear to be independent.

### 5. Parental Antecedents

In an experiment reported in 1957, Dulany successfully "taught" patterns of repression and sensitization to subjects. With geometrical figures as the stimuli, perceptual repression was induced by punishing subjects' responses to a threatening stimulus, thus allowing competing responses to be reinforced via anxiety reduction. Perceptual sensitization was induced by punishing competing responses while allowing perceptual responses to the threatening stimulus to occur and hence receive reinforcement.

Generalizing from these findings, Byrne (in press) hypothesized that parental influences on the development of repressive and sensitizing defenses should be similar to Dulany's laboratory procedures. That is, in childhood repressers experienced punishment in their attempts to express conflictful impulses while sensitizers were permitted to express such material, at least at a verbal level. Thus, child-rearing attitudes falling along a permissive-restrictive dimension should be related to the development of sensitizing *versus* repressive mechanisms in the offspring. In three investigations, R-S scale scores were correlated with responses of mothers on the Parent Attitude Research Instrument (Schaefer and Bell, 1958), subjects' responses on the Hereford Parent Attitude Survey (Hereford, 1963), and subjects' perceptions of their mother's responses to the Stanford Parent Attitude Questionnaire (Winder and Rau, 1962). The findings were that a relatively small but consistent group of the parental variables were related to repression-sensitization, as summarized in Table VIII. Though the findings must be cross-validated, the repressers indicate a home atmosphere characterized by permissiveness, acceptance, and confidence. Their mothers were consistent and high in self-esteem while the two parents had a positive affective relationship with one another. The sensitizers, on the other hand, report a restrictive and rejecting home, and a lack of confidence in assuming the role of parent. Their mothers were inconsistent, low in self-esteem, and had a negative affective relationship with the father. It is obvious that the findings are quite different from those which were hypothesized.

Another investigation of represser-sensitizer differences in their descriptions of their parents was carried out by McDonald (in press). The subjects were 177 unmarried pregnant women, ranging in age from

14 to 39. Most of them were from lower middle class homes. On the R-S scale, the group's mean and standard deviation were comparable to those of female college students (Byrne, 1961). McDonald also identified subjects as expressors on the basis of MMPI scores: 2 *Pd*–(Welsh repression + *Hy* denial). Subjects were classified into four extreme groups consist-

TABLE VIII

REPRESSION-SENSITIZATION AND CHILD-REARING ATTITUDES[a]

| Repressers | Sensitizers |
|---|---|
| *Males* | |
| 1. Mother permissive about sexual behavior | 1. Mother suppressive about sexual behavior |
| 2. Mother perceived as having high self-esteem | 2. Mother perceived as having low self-esteem |
| 3. Mother perceived as having high expectations of son achieving masculine role | 3. Mother perceived as *not* having high expectations of son achieving masculine role |
| *Females* | |
| 1. Mother strict | 1. Mother permissive |
| 2. Mother does not expect deification of parents | 2. Mother expects deification of parents |
| 3. Feels confident in parental role | 3. Does not feel confident in parental role |
| 4. Mother perceived as accepting | 4. Mother peceived as rejecting |
| 5. Mother perceived as nonpunitive and not using physical punishment | 5. Mother perceived as punitive and as using physical punishment |
| 6. Mother perceived as having high self-esteem | 6. Mother perceived as having low self-esteem |
| 7. Father-Mother relationship perceived as positive | 7. Father-Mother relationship perceived as negative |
| 8. Mother perceived as consistent | 8. Mother perceived as inconsistent |

[a] After Byrne (in press).

ing of 34 repressers, 14 sensitizers, 23 expressors, and 34 expressor-sensitizers. Each subject filled out the Interpersonal Check List for self, mother, and father. The major emphasis of the investigation was on the hostility items. As would be expected, repressers indicated significantly fewer of the hostility items in the self-ratings than each of the other three groups. With respect to ratings of parents, repressers attributed significantly less hostility to their fathers than did any of the other groups. On the mother ratings, repressers and sensitizers were not significantly different, but repressers did attribute significantly less hostility to their mothers than either the expressors or the expressor-sensitizers. When the data were analyzed on the basis of self-parent discrepancies, the repressers consistently indicated the least discrepancy (especially with their mothers) while the expressor-sensitizers indicated the greatest discrepancy.

### 6. Interpersonal Behavior

Any pervasive personality variable, such as repression-sensitization, is potentially an important determiner of some aspects of interpersonal behavior. An individual's socially relevant motives, his perception of others, his response to the demands of group situations, and his effect on others are likely to be in part a function of his characteristic defense modes.

Altrocchi (1961) asked each member of a group of student nurses (46 repressers and 46 sensitizers selected from a much larger group) to describe herself and three randomly selected classmates in terms of the items on Leary's Interpersonal Check List. He found that the assumed dissimilarity between self and others was significantly higher for sensitizers than for repressers, regardless of the degree of actual similarity-dissimilarity. Further analysis of the data indicated that the findings could be explained on the basis of the familiar represser-sensitizer differences in self concept rather than differences in the perception of others.

Altrocchi's Expressor Index [2 $Pd$–(Welsh $R + Hy$ denial)] has proven to be a useful means of differentiating two types of sensitizing individuals. Altrocchi and Perlitsh (1963) hypothesized differences in attribution of hostility to self and others by sensitizers, repressers, expressors, and expressor-sensitizers. The 101 subjects were selected from a group of 296 senior nursing students at Duke University. Attribution of hostility was measured by the Love scores of Leary's Interpersonal Check List. It was found that expressor-sensitizers attributed more hostility to themselves than did repressers or expressors, expressors attributed more hostility to others than did repressers, and more hostility was attributed by others to expressors than to sensitizers. Altrocchi and Perlitsh (1963, p. 817) suggest,

"As in previous studies, the present results demonstrate no difference between repressors and sensitizers in attribution of hostility to others, but add the expected finding that neither of these two groups is seen by others as particularly hostile. Repressors do not seem to think that feelings of anger or hostile behavior are salient aspects of their functioning . . . , and their associates in this study seem to agree; clinicians, however, do not. It remains to be demonstrated experimentally whether clinicians are correct in believing that hostile impulses are aroused as readily in repressors as in other people, but are simply repressed."

A subsequent investigation (Altrocchi et al., 1964) suggests that there are sex differences in the attribution of hostility to others in addition to differences based on defenses.

In correlating the R-S scale with various MMPI scales, Joy (1963b) found repression-sensitization to correlate −.87 with leadership. Partly on the basis of this finding, he instituted an investigation (Joy, 1963a) with 30 three-man groups, each composed of one represser, one sensitizer, and one neutral (a subject scoring in the middle quarter of the scale). The groups discussed a standard human relations problem, and then each subject rated himself and the other two group members on a series of variables. Half of the groups were given a task orientation and half an ego threat orientation. The only significant finding based on ratings by others was that sensitizers were chosen less often as desirable work partners than either repressers or neutrals. He also found that repressers rated themselves as showing more concern for maintaining friendly relations than did the sensitizers; neutrals rated themselves as showing more leadership ability than did the two extreme groups.

Turk (1963) investigated several aspects of dyadic relationships in teams composed of a student nurse and a student physician. The nurses were classified as sensitizers or repressers, but Turk preferred to label the former as having low presentational conformity and the latter high presentational conformity. The physicians were not measured on this variable but were assumed to vary randomly in assignment to the two types of nurses. Each team provided three weeks of professional health care in the outpatient clinic of a university hospital. After the work period, each subject completed a questionnaire, including questions concerning their enjoyment in working on the task and the amount of enjoyment attributed by teammates to each other. It was found that the correlation between the enjoyment which the physician attributed to the nurse and that which she herself expressed was significant only in the groups with sensitizing nurses: nurse's self-rating and physician's rating of nurse correlated .69 ($p < .001$) in the sensitizer groups and −.17 in the represser groups. While the physicians were accurate only in the sensitizer groups, assumed similarity in enjoyment was significant only in the groups with repressing nurses. Physician's self-rating and his rating of the nurse correlated .80 ($p < .001$) while nurse's self-rating and her rating of the physician correlated .62 ($p < .01$) in the repressing groups. In the sensitizing groups, these two correlations were .35 and .30. One interpretation of these findings is that accuracy of interpersonal perception is most likely to occur when the perceptual target is a sensitizer who exhibits consistency in expressions of affect in overt behavior and in self-ratings. With repressers, the overt communication of feeling and the self-ratings were apparently inconsistent, thus making possible distortion via assumed similarity.

Silber and Baxter (1963) have supplied preliminary data from an investigation in which repressers and sensitizers were compared on several aspects of a verbal conditioning task. It seems possible to interpret their findings as reflecting differential responses to an interpersonal situation. They attempted to condition 52 undergraduates at the University of Kentucky to respond with either thought or motor-action verbs. On the basis of R-S scale scores, each subject was classified as a sensitizer or a represser. On index cards, the pronoun "he" appeared at the top with three alternative words (thinking, motor-action, and verbal activity) at the bottom. The subjects were instructed to make a two-word sentence, using the pronoun and one of the verbs. There was an operant level phase of 20 trials, an acquisition phase of 100 trials ("Mmm-hmm" for a thought verb for half the group and for a motor-action verb for the other half), and an extinction phase of 40 trials. A postconditioning interview was conducted to determine the subjects' awareness of the experimental conditions and their estimate of the frequncy of verbal reinforcements by the experimenter. Among the results relevant to repression-sensitization, Silber and Baxter found no differences between the groups in operant levels for the verbs, a significant interaction between repression-sensitization and awareness (aware repressers gave the greatest number of responses and aware sensitizers the smallest number) during acquisition, and greater extinction effects for repressers than sensitizers. Finally, compared with sensitizers, repressers overestimated the number of reinforcements emitted by the experimenter. It might be concluded that in this type of social situation repressers differ from sensitizers in that they respond more to the implicit demands of the other person when they realize what those demands are. They more readily respond with a given class of words when the experimenter offers approval for this and more readily cease this type of response when the experimenter withdraws his approval. In addition, they misperceive the situation such that they remember receiving a greater number of social reinforcements than was actually the case. Sensitizers, in contrast, appear to reject or resist the demands of the situation. If this interpretation of the findings is an accurate one, repressers and sensitizers should not differ in response to an operant conditioning task which does not involve an interpersonal context.

Shrader (1963) at the University of Massachusetts selected a group of 72 male subjects from a pool of 194 who had taken a self-ideal discrepancy questionnaire and the R-S scale. The experimental task was a modified Ames Thereness-Thatness apparatus in which subjects made size and distance judgments of three full-face, life-sized photographs of college males. Each was described as a superior achiever in intellectual, social, or physical activities. Shrader's findings with respect to the defense groups were that repressers perceived the stimuli as larger and closer than the sensitizers and that they were more variable in their responses. The difference between repressers and sensitizers decreased as the stimulus distance increased. Shrader interpreted these results as meaning that the repressing individuals were more suggestible in responding to the experimenter's instructions and that they were more labile in responding. The differences decreased when the stimulus was farther away because of the reduced threat qualities at the greater distance.

### 7. Obstetric Complications

The effects of emotional stress and of personality differences in dealing with stress have been studied in connection with various obstetrical complications. Several research projects are under way to determine the part played by psychological variables in abortion, fetal mortality, labor time, and mental retardation. Recent findings suggest that differences along the repression-sensitization dimension are related to the probability of occurrence of some of these abnormalities.

McDonald, Gynther, and Christakos (1963) obtained data on 86 patients from the Obstetrical Clinic at the Medical College of South Carolina. Each patient was given the IPAT Anxiety Scale, the Kent EGY, and the MMPI, which was scored for repression-sensitization. On the basis of pregnancy, delivery-room, and postpartum records, the patients were classified as normal ($N = 42$) or abnormal ($N = 44$). The latter consisted of disorders of the gestation period, developmental abnormalities observed at birth, and delivery irregularities. The two groups of patients did not differ significantly in infant birth weight, labor time, Kent EGY scores, or age. They were, however, different at beyond the .01 level of significance in anxiety and repression-sensitization. The abnormal birth group was more anxious and more sensitizing. In the normal group, R-S scale scores were comparable to those of university coeds (Byrne, 1961) while patients in the abnormal group had a mean score higher than 85% of the women in the university sample.

One of the questions which arises from that finding is whether the high sensitization scores represent the characteristic functioning of these women in the abnormal group or whether they represent a special condition induced in part by the stress of pregnancy. McDonald and Parham (in press) investigated 160 unmarried women before and after the birth of their first child. The MMPI and Kent EGY were administered at the beginning of the seventh month of gestation; shortly after delivery (7–10 days) the

MMPI was readministered. As in the previous investigation, patients were divided into groups of 79 with normal and 81 with abnormal births. Comparison of test scores before and after delivery revealed that patients had significantly lower R-S scale scores (about 8 points) after the the baby was delivered. Comparison of the normal and abnormal groups indicated that they did not differ in IQ or age. Both groups were significantly less sensitizing after delivery, but at both periods the abnormal group was significantly more sensitizing than the normal group. They differed by 5.50 points before delivery and by 1.65 points after delivery. As the authors indicate, the reasons for the differences in ego defenses in the normal and abnormal groups and the shift toward more repressiveness after delivery are not clear.

### 8. Conclusions

To date, a number of relationships have been established between repression-sensitization and other personality variables. That the Social Desirability variable is negatively related to the repression-sensitization dimension is well established, but the meaning of this relationship is open to more than one interpretation. The R-S scale appears to be unrelated to authoritarianism, right opinionation, or intelligence, but positively related to dogmatism, left opinionation, and prejudice. A theoretical explanation for the latter three unexpected findings has not been offered. There are, on the contrary, quite reasonable grounds for expecting that individuals who utilize repressive defenses would be prejudiced, dogmatic, and opinionated. To find that it is those with sensitizing defenses who tend to be high on those three dimensions will require reevaluation of existing formulations. The substantial relationships between repression-sensitization and various measures of introversion-extraversion raise the possibility of interconnections between the type of work described in this chapter and that of Eysenck.

The attempts to extend knowledge about the repression-sensitization dimension by investigating its antecedents in child-rearing attitudes and its consequents in interpersonal behavior and somatic functioning represent a potentially important type of research with personality variables.

The area of personality shows increasing maturity as the antecedents and consequents of individual differences become known. With respect to repression-sensitization, it may be fair to state that *nothing* is yet known about its antecedents. The reported investigations can be interpreted most parsimoniously as relationships between the R-S scale and particular types of self-report measures. The fact that repressers and sensitizers report different things about their parents is informative, but it quite probably provides no evidence about actual parental differences in attitudes or behavior. Some of the findings concerning consequents in interpersonal behavior are subject to the same comments. However, the results indicating that sensitzers were not chosen as work partners, that perception by outsiders of the feelings of sensitizers was more accurate and less distorted than the perception of the feelings of repressers, that repressers and sensitizers differ in their responses in an operant conditioning task, and that they differ in judgments of size and distance of photographs, give promise of fruitful research possibilities in this area. Similarly, when sensitizing women are found to have greater difficulty in giving birth to their infants, it is clear that more is involved in represser-sensitizer differences than simply verbal response sets on paper-and-pencil tests. A variable is "good" to the extent that it is related to other variables; repression-sensitization appears to qualify for that designation.

## III.  Repression-Sensitization: What Are the Next Research Steps?

The research findings with the repression-sensitization dimension lead to two major questions about subsequent developments in this area. First, is the present conceptualization of this variable as involving individual differences in approach and avoidance defenses a reasonable one or does some other concept better fit the data? Second, what are the next steps in theory and research to be taken with this variable?

### A.  WHAT IS BEING MEASURED BY THE R-S SCALE?

It seems prudent to view any investigation which uses a personality test as constituting, at least in part, a construct validity study. In the traditional psychometric sense, there is literally no way of validating or invalidating a personality test. Instead, the instrument may be evaluated with respect to its measurement consistency or reliability, its relationships with other personality variables may be determined, and its antecedents and consequents may be specified. It may then be discarded as an unreliable measure or shelved by researchers because it lacks relational fertility. The nearest thing to invalidation that can occur is a change in the name of the test. As the author (Byrne, 1964, p. 51) has suggested elsewhere:

"Another way of asking the validational question is, 'What is the best name to apply to the responses measured by this instrument?' As simple (or simple-minded) as this question appears, much of the controversy centering around many tests resolves itself to the naming problem. Hopefully, the name designated for any measured behavior may be thought of as tentative. Perhaps the following qualifying statement should be assumed wherever the name of a test appears: 'in view of the item content of this test and its relationships with other variables, at this time the instrument appears to be conceptualized as a measure of ——'."

If one is able to tolerate a certain amount of confusion and ambiguity, the characteristics of the variable being measured may be made more clear after a sufficient period of research activity. In the research reviewed in the previous section, for example, the dimension which we have discussed as repression-sensitization has been designated by others as facilitation-inhibition, affector-effector, and presentational conformity. In addition, evidence has been presented which suggests that the labels self concept, anxiety, neuroticism, or social desirability would be reasonable alternates. To assert that the R-S scale is *only* measuring response set or *really* measuring anxiety, as if these new labels somehow brought about conceptual clarity or as if existing data were no longer meaningful, is a sort of word magic.

Do the labels or the test names matter then? Would it not be wise to use nonsense syllables or zip codes as the names of personality variables and thus side-step the problem? This approach seems unwise because the name of the variable and the surplus meaning attached to that name are likely to have a great influence on the type of research that is conducted and on the theoretical structure into which the findings are placed. Differences in labels and theory mean that data may be sought which would otherwise seem irrelevant. Farber (1964, p. 36), for example, points out that the fruitfulness of the MAS is its supposed relevance as a measure of drive in Hull–Spence theory. Even though the MAS and Edwards Social Desirability Scale correlate —.84, he suggests that it is doubtful whether investigators using the latter variable would have conducted studies "of eyelid conditioning, or psychophysical functions, or the steepness of stimulus generalization gradients, or paired-associate learning."

As with the R-S scale, users of the MAS point to the very high relationships reported among the MAS, the *Pt* and *K* scales of the MMPI, and the Social Desirability Scale of Edwards. Farber (1964, p. 30) asks,

"What, then, does the test measure?

"In one sense, this is a trivial question, and requires but a trivial answer, though, unfortunately, one that constructors and users of tests sometimes fail to see, namely, that giving tests different names does not guarantee that they reflect different characteristics, and giving them the same names does not necessarily mean they reflect the same determinants. If all these highly interrelated measures are related to all other kinds of behaviors in the same way, they measure the same thing, regardless of their labels.

"Occasionally, however, this confusion among the characteristics inferred from behavior is not merely nominal. For instance, height and weight are highly correlated in the general population, yet no one supposes they are merely different names for the same thing. What if defensiveness and desire to make a favorable impression are independent, but nevertheless empirically related in a given population? How, then, could we decide whether they reflect different organismic states or processes? Or better, if the one measure is related to some other mode of behavior, which hypothetical variable is responsible for the relation?

"These are not trivial questions, and their answers are not easily come by. One kind of answer is simply the observation that there is never any guarantee in science against the inaccurate identification of determinants."

Farber (1964, p. 31) goes on to suggest:

"It is usually possible, given skill and patience, to tease out ever finer specifications of the variables entering into behavioral laws. If we consider response-defined variables, by careful selection of cases, statistical correction, or the elimination of errors of measurement, we can frequently decide which of several variables, even though they be highly correlated, determine the form of the relation under consideration. If it turns out, as it frequently does, that a given behavior is a joint function of several response variables, the circumstance is one quite familiar to experimentalists. For instance, no one is unduly disturbed by the finding that the probability of drinking is a function of both dryness of the mucous membranes and general water deficit. The additional fact that these two variables are themselves frequently related, under many conditions, is a complication, to be sure, but not an insuperable one.

"All we can reasonably ask in regard to either experimental or differential variables is that they be specified as precisely as possible. We should then be prepared to discover, soon enough, that more precise and detailed specifications are necessary."

With the repression-sensitization measures, the evidence would appear to be rather clear-cut that the defense scales and the Edwards SD scale are essentially interchangeable, two different names for the same variable. Even though this interpretation seems obvious, Ullmann and McReynolds (1963) have presented data which indicate otherwise. As reported earlier, they found a —.50 correlation between the F-I scale and ward ratings of anxiety in a group of neuropsychiatric patients. This relationship was also computed with scores on the Edwards SD scale held constant by means of partial correlation. The resulting coefficient was still a significant one ($r = -.38$, $p < .01$), which suggests clearly that something is being measured by the defense test in addition to social desirability.

Given such a finding plus the many studies which contribute to the construct validity of the instrument, at the present time the label "repression-sensitization" does not appear inconsistent with what is known about the R-S scale. There is as yet no compelling reason to rename the test.

### B. CONSIDERATIONS IN BUILDING A THEORY OF REPRESSION-SENSITIZATION

The history of the field of personality may be seen as containing the discarded remains of a vast number of variables investigated over the years—each measured more or less adequately, each the object of a flurry of research interest, and each passing out of favor. Except at the methodological level, it is difficult for even the most hardened optimist to view all of this activity as representing the forward motion of behavioral science with each generation more enlightened than the previous one. If this characterization can be accepted, it may be helpful to consider the nature of research and theory building at a more general level than is represented by the specific problem of repression-sensitization. What is involved in pursuing an area of research such as that described in the present chapter and what would it mean to proceed with the building of a theory of repression-sensitization?

#### 1. General Considerations

The goal of that branch of science which is psychology is the building of theories which permit the accurate prediction of behavior. Beyond a general acceptance of "the scientific method," however, there are a diversity of positions taken by psychologists with respect to the strategy and tactics best suited to attaining that goal. One of the differences among psychologists is in their conception of the role of theory in research. This question includes the assumptions which underlie a theory and guide its general framework (e.g., self theory with a phenomenological base *versus* S-R theory with a mechanistic determinism), the point at which theory assumes importance in research (e.g., prior to the design of *the* first experiment *versus* only after a long period of data gathering), the type of theory which is constructed (e.g., artistic description *versus* mathematical relationships among operationalized variables), and the breadth of the theory (e.g., a global framework which encompasses all of behavior *versus* relatively narrow theories tied to a specific series of behaviors). Each of these issues will be considered briefly.

#### 2. Pretheoretical Assumptions

Behavioral science seems to mean quite different things to different individuals. One of the best descriptions of the kinds of assumptions held by psychologists in the experimental, behavioristic, operational tradition has been presented by Farber (1964). The basic assumption is that behavior is a function of its antecedents (i.e., determinism). Farber (1964, p. 32) says,

"What they come to, in a word, is an emphasis on the formulation of empirical laws and the analysis of the variables comprising them. As we have noted, the assumption that it is the business of behavioral science to explicate the relations between objectively defined environmental and behavioral events is in itself no theory, but rather a metatheoretical or pretheoretical preference. Those who adopt this approach, especially if they have an interest in the phenomena of learning, are likely to use the terms 'S' and 'R' to refer, respectively, to the environmental and behavioral events, and the familiar formula 'S-R' to indicate a relation between these two classes of variables."

From this frame of reference, then, the repression-sensitization variable should be placed within a framework of empirical laws. It will be possible to predict individual differences along this dimension when its antecedents are known and to predict the effects of these differences on other behavior when its correlates and consequents are known. Our goal is not the *Verstehen* of the Romantic movement which would purport to provide an understanding of repression-sensitization, but rather the goal is to place this variable in a predictive framework as Holt (1962) has cogently argued. The end point will be the specification of lawful relationships among variables rather than a colorful literary description of repressers and sensitizers.

### 3. Time for Theory Building

In a sense, it is virtually impossible to design any piece of research and execute it without the operation of at least an implicit theory. Variables are seldom selected through the use of tables of random numbers. Beyond one's pretheoretical assumptions, there are expectations or hypotheses or hunches or general notions about relationships between $X$ and $Y$. With the R-S scale, the author's initial expectations may be summarized briefly:

(1) Individuals may be placed along a continuum with respect to their characteristic learned response to threatening stimuli; avoiding mechanisms define one end of this continuum and approaching mechanisms the other.

(2) A curvilinear relationship should be found between an individual's position on this continuum and various indices of his maladjustment.

All of the research on repression-sensitization which has been conducted by the author and much of the research conducted by others follow from these two propositions. There is a great deal of support for the first and only modest support for the second. In addition to these findings, there are a number of other relationships which have been investigated and reported. Is it now time to tie all of these findings together into a more inclusive theory of repression-sensitization? It would certainly be the "socially acceptable" thing to do in terms of the mores of the field of personality. Perhaps, however, it is time to offer a dissenting opinion. It is instructive to compare work in personality with that of other scientists, including some of our psychological colleagues. Among the basic differences between the work of astronomers, biologists, physicists, chemists, and even learning theorists and the work of personality psychologists is a superficially simple one. In the other fields, the number of different variables is relatively small and there is relatively general agreement within the field as to what those variables are. Individual scientists may differ in what they do with the variables and certainly in how they interpret the findings, but there is a great deal of agreement otherwise. In personality research, the mode is an unenviable creativity with respect to both stimulus and response variables. It is difficult to find as many as half a dozen studies in our journals which utilize the same independent or dependent variables. It would be a disheartening exercise to survey and list the number and variety of different defining operations for hostility, anxiety, threat, or any other variables widely studied in personality.

At some point in the development of our field, this way of proceeding must change. Personality psychologists must find their equivalents of planetary motion, speed of a falling body, running speed in a straight alley runway, and frequency of the lever-pressing response. The next step will be the establishment of empirical laws which indicate the relationships between and among these variables. A law relating repression-sensitization to amount of anxiety aroused in response to threat, for example, will not arise from a series of investigations each of which involves the use of different operations to define anxiety and threat, each significant at least at the .05 level, and each conducted only a single time. When a series of such laws are in fact established, it will be the appropriate time to devise theories in an attempt to organize these laws into more inclusive units.

In the meantime, it is possible to formulate simple predictions and hypotheses based on generalizations from observation, deductions from other theories, and inductions from previous research. Any attempt to get more elaborate in our preliminary theorizing would seem to be an unfruitful endeavor on the basis of past experience. Many possibilities for research have been raised by those working with repression-sensitization and interpersonal behavior, obstetric complications, and maladjustment, for example. There would seem to be little advantage in jumping from these interesting possibilities to a formal theory without pausing first to obtain much more extensive data.

### 4. Type of Theory

For many psychologists, the field of personality has been synonymous with broad descriptive formulations employing anecdote, allusion, metaphor, and analogy while eschewing operational definitions and mathematical formulas. Obviously, the typical investigator in personality research does not match that characterization. It seems equally clear that the individual research efforts, the emerging laws, and the future theories of personality will bear considerably more resemblance to physics than to psychoanalysis.

For most behavioral scientists, these points are either too absurd to consider seriously or too obvious to bear further elaboration.

### 5. Breadth of Theories

Again, existing personality "theories" are characterized by their breadth. Typically, an attempt is made to explain all of man's behavior in terms of a given series of descriptive formulations. Moreover, the crowning achievements of other fields tend to be theories which are extremely broad and hence able to unify a multitude of established findings: Geocentrism, evolution, and $e = mc^2$ are familiar examples.

Perhaps it would be prudent for personality psychologists to attempt somewhat less ambitious theory building at this point in the development of knowledge about human behavior. The necessary combination of individual genius and a suitable body of data apparently has a fairly low base rate. Instances of the former without the latter have been characteristic of personality psychology, and Sigmund Freud is the outstanding example. Instances of the latter without the former are met daily in most sciences. One of the reasons for the rarity of the successful broadly encompassing theory is that error is increasingly easy as one moves from the data on which the laws were built. As Rogers (1959, p. 191) puts it,

"A slight error in a theory may make little difference in providing an explanation of the observed facts out of which the theory grew. But when the theory is projected to explain more remote phenomena, the error may be magnified, and the inference from the theory may be completely false . . . . Thus, every theory deserves the greatest respect in the area from which it was drawn from the facts and a decreasing degree of respect as it makes predictions in areas more and more remote from its origin."

What, then, might our theoretical goals be? Elsewhere the author suggests (Byrne, in preparation),

"It would seem that a potentially fruitful approach to theory building in the science of personality is the construction of small theories dealing with specific and limited behavioral events rather than a general theory of personality. Personality theories should be limited in scope but predictively powerful. As tight and accurate theories are built in areas such as achievment, authoritarianism, and self-consistency, the finding of still more general relationships will tie them together into increasingly inclusive overall theories. This, however, is an end-point rather than a starting point. First, we need to devise psychological laws analogous to those of the pendulum, of gases, of the lever, of the effect of gravity on momentum, etc. As satisfying and useful as it would be to have a complete theory of behavior immediately available, a more limited and more attainable goal should be sought for the present."

Hopefully, the comments in this concluding section will be viewed as a blueprint for future progress in work on repression-sensitization and not as a criticism of any of the work which has been reported. On the contrary, it seems that a great many investigators in a wide variety of locations are engaged in worthwhile and exciting research on this dimension. It is clearly possible to continue these research efforts in such a way as to extend our knowledge about one aspect of personality. And, oddly enough, if we do our work well, it is inevitable that the knowledge will have relevance to all aspects of personality.

#### ACKNOWLEDGMENTS

A great many individuals were extremely helpful in providing suggestions, reprints, unpublished data, reports on research in progress, and doctoral dissertations. In addition, a number of individuals were kind enough to offer suggestions and criticisms of the original manuscript. The contributions of the following investigators to this chapter are gratefully acknowledged: John Altrocchi, James C. Baxter, Barbara Blaylock, Leslie Davison, Norman S. Endler, Tom Friedman, John T. Gossett, Austin Grigg, Malcolm D. Gynther, Judith E. Hanson, Vernon Joy, Richard Lazarus, Paul Liberty, James F. Lomont, Arthur W. Lucky, Robert L. McDonald, Louis J. Moran, Walter O'Connell, Vello Sermat, William K. Shrader, Vincent J. Tempone, Herman Turk, Leonard P. Ullmann, Norris H. Weinberg, and Jerry S. Wiggins.

## References

Adorno, T. W., Frenkel-Brunswik, Else, Levinson, D. J., and Sanford, R. N. *The authoritarian personality*. New York: Harper, 1950.

Altrocchi, J. Interpersonal perceptions of repressers and sensitizers and component analysis of assumed dissimilarity scores. *J. abnorm. soc. Psychol.*, 1961, **62**, 528-534.

Altrocchi, J., and Perlitsch, Hilda D. Ego control patterns and attribution of hostility. *Psychol. Rep.*, 1963, **12**, 811-818.

Altrocchi, J., Parsons, O. A., and Dickoff, Hilda. Changes in self-ideal discrepancy in repressors and sensitizers. *J. abnorm. soc. Psychol.*, 1960, **61**, 67-72.

Altrocchi, J., Shrauger, S., and McLeod, Mary A. Attribution of hostility to self and others by expressors, sensitizers, and repressors. *J. clin. Psychol.*, 1964, **20**, 233.

Berg, I. A. Deviant responses and deviant people: the formulation of the Deviation Hypothesis. *J. counsel. Psychol.*, 1957, **4**, 154-161.

Berg, I. A. The unimportance of test item content. In B. M. Bass and I. A. Berg (Eds.), *Objective approaches to personality assessment*. Princeton, New Jersey: Van Nostrand, 1959. Pp. 83-99.

Blaylock, Barbara A. H. Repression-sensitization, word association responses, and incidental recall. Unpublished master's thesis, Univer. of Texas, Austin, Texas, 1963.

Block, J., and Thomas, H. Is satisfaction with self a measure of adjustment? *J. abnorm. soc. Psychol.*, 1955, **51**, 254-259.

Brown, J. S. *The motivation of behavior*. New York: McGraw-Hill, 1961.

Bruner, J. S., and Goodman, C. C. Value and need as organizing factors in perception. *J. abnorm. soc. Psychol.*, 1947, **42**, 33-44.

Bruner, J. S., and Postman, L. Tension and tension release as organizing factors in perception. *J. Pers.*, 1947, **15**, 300-308. (a)

Bruner, J. S., and Postman, L. Emotional selectivity in perception and reaction. *J. Pers.*, 1947, **16**, 69-77. (b)

Byrne, D. The Repression-Sensitization Scale: Rationale, reliability, and validity. *J. Pers.*, 1961, **29**, 334-349.

Byrne, D. Assessing personality variables and their alteration. In P. Worchel and D. Byrne (Eds.), *Personality change*. New York: Wiley, 1964. Pp. 38-68.

Byrne, D. Child-rearing antecedents of repression-sensitization. *Child Develpm.*, in press.

Byrne, D. *Personality: An approach to the science of human behavior*. Englewood Cliffs, New Jersey: Prentice-Hall, in preparation.

Byrne, D., and Bounds, C. The reversal of F Scale items. *Psychol. Rep.*, 1964, **14**, 216.

Byrne, D., and Goldberg, June. Repression-sensitization, authoritarianism, dogmatism, and political attitudes. Unpublished manuscript, 1962.

Byrne, D., and Holcomb, Joan. The reliability of a response measure: Differential recognition-threshold scores. *Psychol. Bull.*, 1962, **59**, 70-73.

Byrne, D., and Sheffield, J. Response to sexually arousing stimuli as a function of repressing and sensitizing defenses. *J. abnorm. Psychol.*, in press.

Byrne, D., Terrill, J., and McReynolds, P. Incongruency as a predictor of response to humor. *J. abnorm. soc. Psychol.*, 1961, **62**, 435-438.

Byrne, D., Barry, J., and Nelson, D. Relation of the revised Repression-Sensitization Scale to measures of self-description. *Psychol. Rep.*, 1963, **13**, 323-334.

Byrne, D., Golightly, Carole, and Sheffield, J. The Repression-Sensitization Scale as a measure of adjustment: Relationship with the CPI. *J. consult. Psychol.*, in press.

Carlson, V. R. Individual differences in the recall of word-association-test words. *J. Pers.*, 1954, **23**, 77-87.

Carpenter, B., Wiener, M., and Carpenter, Janeth T. Predictability of perceptual defense behavior. *J. abnorm. soc. Psychol.*, 1956, **52**, 380-383.

Chodorkoff, B. Self-perception, perceptual defense, and adjustment. *J. abnorm. soc. Psychol.*, 1954, **49**, 508-512.

Couch, A., and Keniston, K. Yeasayers and naysayers: Agreeing response set as a personality variable. *J. abnorm. soc. Psychol.*, 1960, **60**, 151-174.

Crowne, D. P., and Marlowe, D. A. A new scale of social desirability independent of psychopathology. *J. consult. Psychol.*, 1960, **24**, 349-354.

Davison, L. A. Adaptation to a threatening stimulus. Unpublished doctoral dissertation, Univer. of California, Berkeley, California, 1963.

Dulany, D. E., Jr. Avoidance learning of perceptual defense and vigilance. *J. abnorm. soc. Psychol.*, 1957, **55**, 333-338.

Edwards, A. L. The relationship between the judged desirability of a trait and the probability that the trait will be endorsed. *J. appl. Psychol.*, 1953, **37**, 90-93.

Edwards, A. L. *The social desirability variable in personality assessment and research.* New York: Dryden, 1957.

Edwards, A. L. Social desirability and personality test construction. In B. M. Bass and I. A. Berg (Eds.), *Objective approaches to personality assessment.* Princeton, New Jersey: Van Nostrand, 1959. Pp. 100-118.

Endler, N. S. Personal communication, 1963.

Eriksen, C. W. Perceptual defense as a function of unacceptable needs. Unpublished doctoral dissertation, Stanford Univer., Stanford, California, 1950.

Eriksen, C. W. Some implications for TAT interpretation arising from need and perception experiments. *J. Pers.*, 1951, **19**, 282-288.

Eriksen, C. W. Defense against ego-threat in memory and perception. *J. abnorm. soc. Psychol.*, 1952, **47**, 230-235. (a)

Eriksen, C. W. Individual differences in defensive forgetting. *J. exp. Psychol.*, 1952, **44**, 442-446. (b)

Eriksen, C. W. Psychological defenses and "ego-strength" in the recall of completed and incompleted tasks. *J. abnorm. soc. Psychol.*, 1954, **49**, 45-50.

Eriksen, C. W., and Browne, C. T. An experimental and theoretical analysis of perceptual defense. *J. abnorm. soc. Psychol.*, 1956, **52**, 224-230.

Eriksen, C. W., and Davids, A. The meaning and clinical validity of the Taylor anxiety scale and the hysteria-psychasthenia scales from the MMPI. *J. abnorm. soc. Psychol.*, 1955, **50**, 135-137.

Eriksen, C. W., and Kuethe, J. L. Avoidance conditioning of verbal behavior without awareness: A paradigm of repression. *J. abnorm. soc. Psychol.*, 1956, **53**, 203-209.

Eriksen, C. W., and Lazarus, R. S. Perceptual defense and projective tests. *J. abnorm. soc. Psychol.*, 1952, **47**, 302-308.

Eriksen, C. W., Kuethe, J. L., and Sullivan, D. F. Some personality correlates of learning without awareness. *J. Pers.*, 1958, **26**, 216-228.

Farber, I. E. A framework for the study of personality as a behavioral science. In P. Worchel and D. Byrne (Eds.), *Personality change.* New York: Wiley, 1964. Pp. 3-37.

Festinger, L. *A theory of cognitive dissonance.* Stanford: Stanford Univer. Press, 1957.

Friedman, S. T. The relationship between attitudes toward children and authoritarianism. Unpublished manuscript, 1963.

Gordon, J. E. Interpersonal predictions of repressors and sensitizers. *J. Pers.*, 1957, **25**, 686-698.

Gordon, J. E. The stability of the assumed similarity response set in repressors and sensitizers. *J. Pers.*, 1959, **27**, 362-373.

Gossett, J. T. An experimental demonstration of Freudian repression proper. Unpublished doctoral dissertation, Univer. of Arkansas, Fayetteville, Arkansas, 1964.

Gough, H. G. *California Psychological Inventory manual.* Palo Alto: Consulting Psychologists Press, 1957.

Grigg, A. E., and Thorpe, J. S. Deviant responses in college adjustment clients: A test of Berg's Deviation Hypothesis. *J. consult. Psychol.*, 1960, **24**, 92-94.

Gynther, M. D. Personal communication, 1963.

Hanson, Judith E. Personal communication, 1963.

Hathaway, S. R., and McKinley, J. C. *Manual for the Minnesota Multiphasic Personality Inventory.* (Rev. ed.) New York: Psychological Corporation, 1951.

Hereford, C. F. *Changing parental attitudes through group discussion.* Austin: Univer. of Texas Press, 1963.

Holt, R. R. Individuality and generalization in the psychology of personality. *J. Pers.,* 1962, **30**, 377-404.

Joy, V. L. Repression-sensitization, personality, and interpersonal behavior. Unpublished doctoral dissertation, Univer. of Texas, Austin, Texas, 1963. (a)

Joy, V. L. Repression-sensitization and interpersonal behavior. Paper read at Amer. Psychol. Ass., Philadelphia, August, 1963. (b)

Kissin, B., Gottesfeld, H., and Dickes, R. Inhibition and tachistoscopic thresholds for sexually charged words. *J. Psychol.,* 1957, **43**, 333-339.

Kogan, N. Authoritarianism and repression. *J. abnorm. soc. Psychol.,* 1956, **53**, 34-37.

Kurland, S. H. The lack of generality in defense mechanisms as indicated in auditory perception. *J. abnorm. soc. Psychol.,* 1954, **49**, 173-177.

Lazarus, R. S., and Alfert, Elizabeth. The short circuiting of threat by experimentally altering cognitive appraisal. *J. abnorm. soc. Psychol.,* in press.

Lazarus, R. S., and Longo, N. The consistency of psychological defense against threat. *J. abnorm. soc. Psychol.,* 1953, **48**, 495-499.

Lazarus, R. S., Eriksen, C. W., and Fonda, C. P. Personality dynamics and auditory perceptual recognition. *J. Pers.,* 1951, **19**, 471-482.

Lazarus, R. S., Speisman, J. C., Mordkoff, A. M., and Davison, L. A. A laboratory study of psychological stress produced by a motion picture film. *Psychol. Monogr.,* in press.

Liberty, P. G., Jr., Lunneborg, C. E., and Atkinson, G. C. Perceptual defense, dissimulation, and response styles. *J. consult. Psychol.,* in press.

Lomont, J. F. Personal communication, 1963.

Lomont, J. F. The repression-sensitization dimension in relation to anxiety responses. Unpublished manuscript, 1964.

Lucky, A. W., and Grigg, A. E. Repression-sensitization as a variable in deviant responding. *J. clin. Psychol.,* 1964, **20**, 92-93.

McDonald, R. L. Ego control patterns and attribution of hostility to self and others. *J. abnorm. soc. Psychol.,* in press.

McDonald, R. L., and Parham, K. J. Relation of emotional changes during pregnancy to obstetric complications in unmarried primigravidae. *Amer. J. Obst. Gynec.,* in press.

McDonald, R. L., Gyther, M. D., and Christakos, A. C. Relations between maternal anxiety and obstetric complications. *Psychosom. Med.,* 1963, **25**, 357-363.

MacKinnon, D. W., and Dukes, W. F. Repression. In L. Postman (Ed.), *Psychology in the making.* New York: Knopf, 1962. Pp. 662-744.

McReynolds, P. A restricted conceptualization of human anxiety and motivation. *Psychol. Rep.,* 1956, **2**, 293-312.

McReynolds, P. Anxiety as related to incongruencies between values and feelings. *Psychol. Rec.,* 1958, **8**, 57-66.

McReynolds, P., and Ullmann, L. P. Differential recall of pleasant and unpleasant words as a function of anxiety. *J. clin. Psychol.,* 1964, **20**, 79-80.

Mathews, Anne, and Wertheimer, M. A "pure" measure of perceptual defense uncontaminated by response suppression. *J. abnorm. soc. Psychol.,* 1958, **57**, 373-376.

Megargee, E. I. Undercontrol and overcontrol in assaultive and homicidal adolescents. Unpublished doctoral dissertation, Univer. of California, Berkeley, California, 1964.

Megargee, E. I., and Mendelsohn, G. A. The assessment of the chronically overcontrolled assaultive person. Unpublished manuscript, 1964.

Nelson, S. E. Psychosexual conflicts and defenses in visual perception. *J. abnorm. soc. Psychol.*, 1955, **51**, 427-433.

Nowlis, V., and Nowlis, Helen H. The description and analysis of mood. *Ann. N. Y. Acad. Sci.*, 1956, **65**, 345-355.

O'Connell, W., and Peterson, Penny. Humor and repression. *J. existential Psychiat.*, 1964, **4**, 309-316.

Page, H. A., and Markowitz, Gloria. The relationship of defensiveness to rating scale bias. *J. Psychol.*, 1955, **40**, 431-435.

Perloe, S. I. Inhibition as a determinant of perceptual defense. *Percept. mot. Skills*, 1960, **11**, 59-66.

Pomeranz, D. M. The repression-sensitization dimension and reactions to stress. Unpublished doctoral dissertation, Univer. of Rochester, New York, 1963.

Postman, L., Bruner, J. S., and McGinnies, E. Personal values as selective factors in perception. *J. abnorm. soc. Psychol.*, 1948, **43**, 142-154.

Rogers, C. R. A theory of therapy, personality, and interpersonal relationships as developed in the client-centered framework. In S. Koch (Ed.), *Psychology: A study of a science*, Vol. III: *Formulations of the person and the social context*. New York: McGraw-Hill, 1959. Pp. 184-256.

Rokeach, M. *The open and closed mind.* New York: Basic Books, 1960.

Schaefer, E. S., and Bell, R. Q. Development of a parental attitude research instrument. *Child Develpm.*, 1958, **29**, 339-361.

Sermat, V. Personal communication, 1962.

Shannon, D. T. The effects of ego-defensive reactions on reported perceptual recognition. Unpublished doctoral dissertation, Stanford Univer., Stanford, California, 1955.

Shannon, D. T. Clinical patterns of defense as revealed in visual recognition thresholds. *J. abnorm. soc. Psychol.*, 1962, **64**, 370-377.

Shrader, W. K. Size-distance perception of human images as a function of self-ideal discrepancy and defensive mode. Unpublished doctoral dissertation, Univer. of Massachusetts, Amherst, Massachusetts, 1963.

Silber, L. D., and Baxter, J. C. Personal communication, 1963.

Solomon, R. L., and Postman, L. Frequency of usage as a determinant of recognition thresholds for words. *J. exp. Psychol.*, 1952, **43**, 195-202.

Speisman, J. C., Lazarus, R. S., Mordkoff, A. M., and Davison, L. A. The experimental reduction of stress based on ego defense theory. *J. abnorm. soc. Psychol.*, in press.

Tart, C. T. Frequency of dream recall and some personality measures. *J. consult. Psychol.*, 1962, **26**, 467-470.

Tempone, V. J. Differential thresholds of repressers and sensitizers as a function of a success and failure experience. Unpublished doctoral dissertation, Univer. of Texas, Austin, Texas, 1962.

Tempone, V. J. Construct validity studies of Byrne's Repression-Sensitization Scale. Paper read at Amer. Psychol. Ass., Philadelphia, August, 1963.

Truax, C. B. The repression response to implied failure as a function of the hysteria-psychasthenia index. *J. abnorm. soc. Psychol.*, 1957, **55**, 188-193.

Turk, H. Norms, persons, and sentiments. *Sociometry*, 1963, **26**, 163-177.

Ullmann, L. P. Clinical correlates of facilitation and inhibition of response to emotional stimuli. *J. proj. Tech.*, 1958, **22**, 341-347.

Ullmann, L. P. An empirically derived MMPI scale which measures facilitation-inhibition of recognition of threatening stimuli. *J. clin. Psychol.*, 1962, **18**, 127-132.

Ullmann, L. P., and Lim, D. T. Case history material as a source of the identification of patterns of response to emotional stimuli in a study of humor. *J. consult. Psychol.*, 1962, **26**, 221-225.

Ullmann, L. P., and McReynolds, P. Differential perceptual recognition in psychiatric patients: Empirical findings and theoretical formulation. Paper read at Amer. Psychol. Ass., Philadelphia, August, 1963.

Ullmann, L. P., Weiss, R. L., and Krasner, L. The effect of verbal conditioning of emotional words on recognition of threatening stimuli. *J. clin. Psychol.*, 1963, **19**, 182-183.

Weinberg, N. H. Word association style, field dependence, and related personality variables. Unpublished manuscript, 1963.

Wiggins, J. S. Convergences among stylistic response measures. *Educ. psychol. Measmt.*, in press.

Winder, C. L., and Rau, Lucy R. Parental attitudes associated with social deviance in preadolescent boys. *J. abnorm. soc. Psychol.*, 1962, **64**, 418-424.

Worchel, P. Adaptability screening of flying personnel: Development of a self-concept inventory for predicting maladjustment. SAM, USAF, Randolph AFB, Texas, No. 56-62, 1957.

# INTERPERSONAL PERCEPTION

*Victor B. Cline*

UNIVERSITY OF UTAH, SALT LAKE CITY, UTAH

## I. Introduction

Appraising, understanding, and judging others underlies nearly all human intercourse. Most kinds of mental and emotional illness involve fairly serious distortions or breakdowns in communication as well as in interpreting and evaluating social and interactional cues. The evaluation and assessment of others by all men is such a consistent and on-going process that it operates almost automatically at times, commonly at non-verbal and sometimes at almost unconscious levels. It can be a highly rational or even formal process. As Asch has put it, "To take our place with others we must perceive each other's existence and reach a measure of comprehension of one another's needs, emotions, and thoughts."

In a great variety of formal occupations, positions of leadership, and marital, parental, and psychotherapeutic relationships, as well as in informal social units, effective functioning would appear to be critically related to and dependent upon our ability to perceive subtleties and nuances in the behavior of others. We must anticipate their reactions to different decisions and discern those inner states and convictions which, as Gough (1955) has put it, ". . . although determining choice and behavior are often concealed and/or denied in overt expression."

The judging process has been referred to by many names including empathy, insight, clinical intuition, identification, diagnostic competence, understanding, social sensitivity, social acuity, social perception, interpersonal perception (or perceptiveness), person perception, and person cognition. All have slightly varying meanings. For example, "person perception" implies that the judge or perceiver exists apart and outside the world of the person being judged. Such is the case when one uses still photographs of an "other" as the primary source of cues from which judgments are made. If, however, the judging situation involves a double interaction between judge and "other," as usually occurs in real life, it might be more accurately referred to as "interpersonal perception." Tagiuri and Petrullo (1958) have commented, "Through his own presence and behavior in the perceptual situation of the 'other,' the perceiver (judge) may alter the perceptual characteristics of the person whose state he is trying to judge. This is, of course, eminently different from the way in which a rock is a source of cues for a perceiver." Despite differences such as these in the conditions and nature of the judging task, this general area of investigation continues to receive increasing attention from many investigators despite a plethora of methodological complexities.

## II. Standardized Judging Tests

When one surveys the literature and such references as "Buros Mental Measurements Year Book" for signs of carefully validated published social sensitivity, empathy, or judging tests, the cupboard is bare. The only tests of note reported in Buros (1959) are Kerr and Speroff's Empathy Test (1951) and Kerr's Primary Empathic Abilities procedure (1957). These, however, tend to be somewhat misnamed in that they attempt to measure sensitivity to the "generalized other"[1] by requiring such things as ranking the circulation of 15 magazines, the popularity

---

[1] "Sensitivity to the generalized other" is a term introduced by Bronfenbrenner et al. (1958) and is defined as an awareness of the social norm or of the typical response of a large class or group. Example: predicting the results of a public opinion poll, or a typical response of a special class of people—say, college students. This is also sometimes called "stereotype accuracy."

of 15 types of music, and so forth. The evidence for validity for these tests is so slight as to eliminate them from serious consideration as genuine measures of empathy.

Gough (1953) developed an Opinion Prediction Scale which seems to measure accuracy of knowledge or stereotype about people in general, or, in other words, sensitivity to the "generalized other." Judges are required to predict the percentage of "true" responses to a number of MMPI-like items for "people in general" and for male prison inmates using a multiple choice response format. The options are 0–25%, 26–50%, 51–75%, and 76–100%. While this is not a measure of judging ability for specific individual persons (often referred to in the literature as "social objects" or "others"), Gough (1955) has found it a useful instrument in some studies of "social acuity."

In addition there are some procedures such as Chapin's Social Insight Test (1942) which have not been published but which have been used in occasional studies with the author's consent on an experimental basis. Knowledge of their existence has been circulated informally as well as through occasional references in the psychological literature. Frequently, as in the case of Chapin's test, the results have been equivocal. With Chapin's test several paragraphs of a true-to-life situation are presented and the judge is asked to choose the correct outcome from several alternatives. In some cases this involves predicting what an individual feels or will do. Other situations require predicting what a group will say, or do. In one study (Gough, 1955) correlations of .47, .47, and .39 were found between Chapin's test and the Terman Concept Mastery Test of Intelligence, the Crutchfield Battery of Insight Puzzles, and the Bennett Mechanical Comprehension Test.

The sound films and judging instruments of Cline (1955a) and Cline and Richards (1958, 1963) are further examples of judging procedures which are still "experimental" and available for research purposes only. These include three entirely separate sets of films developed over a decade, with up to 12 separate judging tests per film and up to 30 films to a set.

From Flanagan's Aptitude Classification Test the "Judgment and Comprehension" subtest has some items that might be regarded as tapping judging ability or social sensitivity though Flanagan makes no claims that this subtest measures other than the "ability to understand a situation and determine the proper action to take." The "How Supervise," (Remmers and File, 1948) sometimes used as an executive or foreman selection test, could conceivably be regarded as an interpersonal perception test. However, its validity data limits it to being a "crude device for screening first level supervisory personnel of low educational level."

The Moss *et al.* (1944) "Social Intelligence Test" might be classed as a measure of empathy. However, existing research suggests that it is a somewhat disguised measure of verbal intelligence and not much more.

TABLE I

VARIETIES OF STIMULUS INFORMATION USED IN MAKING JUDGMENTS

1. Photographs
2. Motion pictures (sound or silent)
3. Unobserved or hidden observation of live behavior (such as through one-way mirror)
4. Face-to-face interactions (from brief interviews through long-term associations such as in work, social, neighborhood groups, or marriage)
5. Tape recordings (using only auditory cues)
6. Test materials and scores (IQ, MMPI, Rorschach protocols, etc.)
7. Written material (biography, autobiography, interview typescripts, descriptive paragraphs, etc.)
8. Personal productions (handwriting, drawings, etc.)
9. Past experience with people in a culture (where the judge is predicting local, regional, or national group norms, such as estimating percentage of population responding "yes" to a particular personality test item)
10. Any combination of the above

TABLE II

TYPES OF JUDGING INSTRUMENTS

1. Trait-rating procedures (adjective checklists, Likert-type rating scales, etc.)
2. Postdicting real life behavior (usually using a true-false or multiple choice format)
3. Postdicting responses to specific test items (such as an MMPI, Strong Vocational Interest Blank, etc.)
4. Postdicting scores on achievement, intelligence, and personality tests (MMPI, IQ, etc.)
5. Postdicting theoretical constructs (such as a psychiatric diagnosis)
6. Writing free global descriptions of social object being judged
7. Using matching techniques (where 2 to x stimulus persons are matched on 2 to x sets of data). Thus one might read personality descriptions of 10 people and try to match up 10 Rorschach protocols to these)
8. Ranking procedures (2 to x stimulus persons are rank ordered on degree of possession of trait or variable)
9. Forced-choice procedures. These are infinite in variety, but for example, might involve choosing which of two statements a pair of "others" agrees or disagrees with
10. Q sort (Here a group of persons can be Q sorted with regard to one personality trait or one person may have 50 variables Q sorted from "most like" to "least like" him)
11. Any combination of above

Most researchers have tended in the past to develop their own judging tests in the absence of any valid procedures available through test publishers. These are usually simple in nature and tailor-made to the needs of the study. They involve such things as predicting ratings on traits, responses to personality test items, or the like.

*Why the conflicting findings in the literature?* Analysis of the hundreds of interpersonal perception studies published in the past two decades reveals that the kinds of stimulus information given to judges vary very greatly in type, quality, and quantity. Table I lists a few examples of these. In addition, the choice of judging instrument or procedure can vary from simple rating instruments to elaborate $Q$ sorts, as demonstrated in Table II. When we observe the varieties of sources of criterion information (Table III), and the different possible scoring procedures

TABLE III
SOURCES OF CRITERION INFORMATION

1.  (a) Self-provided information. This is where one uses the self-ratings, self-$Q$ sorts, test scores, or other information coming from the person one is judging, as the criterion.
    (b) Group responses to ratings, variables, personality test items, etc. are predicted by judge. This becomes a measure of stereotype accuracy.
2.  Associates (peers, subordinates, spouse, teacher, boss, acquaintances, etc.) provide criteria in form of ratings, evaluations, $Q$ sorts, or other types of information about the person being judged
3.  Experts (where psychologists, social scientists, therapists, personnel managers, or other "experts" provide ratings, diagnoses, $Q$ sorts, etc.)
4.  Combinations of above

available (Table IV), it is easy to understand why searches of the "judging literature" reveal so many apparently contradictory findings. We are dealing with an area of such extreme complexity that experimental methods to determine judging accuracy are seldom identical, and generally varied. There does not exist as yet a single, adequate, demonstrated test of judging accuracy for either global- or component-type measures, though some valiant efforts have been made to produce such an instrument or instruments.

Writers who have argued that there is no general ability to judge others for empathy, intuition, or a general trait, etc. have invariably cited the fact that the findings of judging studies show considerable inconsistency. While this is a legitimate argument, it could be applied to many other areas of psychological research. The reasons for conflicting findings are complex, and cannot be referred to single simple factors.

## III. Cronbach's Components and the End of Naïve Empiricism

In 1955, Ronald Taft reviewed the psychological literature in the area of interpersonal perception. He appraised and evaluated several score of the most significant studies to that date. This was, at the time, a definitive and major assessment of the literature. However, later in the

TABLE IV

SCORING PROCEDURES

1. Number of correct predictions (where multiple-choice, accuracy of diagnosis, rank order, true-false, forced-choice, matching, or paired-comparison-type formats are used)

2. Difference score or "$D^2$ statistic," where rating scales are used; in its simplest form the predicted rating is subtracted from the criterion rating on a "1 to 5 scale" to give a $D$ or difference score. These can be summed over all traits or they can be first squared and then summed. This can also be broken down mathematically into a number of components (see Cronbach, 1955; Cline and Richards, 1960, 1961b, 1962)

3. Correlation statistic (where one correlates a number of predictions made by one judge against criteria or correlates one variable for a number of judges against criteria. Partial correlation technique would be one form of this

4. Quantified evaluations of "free global written description or responses," usually done by experts

5. Special scoring procedures. These can be infinite in variety but two examples from the literature will be cited

   (a) Crow (1954) has developed a "Random-Comparison" method for determining Differential Accuracy which differs from Cronbach's method also discussed in that it is distribution-free, or nonparametric. Whenever the judges make estimations about several "others," a distribution of comparisons is generated by comparing every estimation with every "other's" score, ignoring signs. Thus if eight judges each made an estimation for each of ten "others," the comparison procedure would yield 800 difference scores. The difference score obtained by comparison of the judge's estimation with the score of the "other" for whom the estimation was intended can be compared with the median of the random comparison distribution. If this difference score is more accurate (lower) than the median of the random comparisons, then the judge has obtained Differential Accuracy with that "other." The final score is the percentage of "others" upon which the judge was more accurate than the median of the random comparison distribution

   (b) Bronfenbrenner et al. (1958) developed the "Method of Differential Comparison" as a measure of judging accuracy. They believed this to be independent of the judge's similarity to the person judged and sensitivity to the generalized "other" (Stereotype Accuracy). Any tendency to "assume similarity" could not affect this score. It was obtained by computing the correlation on a within-item basis; that is, by expressing each particular judging estimate as a deviation ($x_i$) from the mean of the estimates made by the judge for all "others" on that item. Each criterion rating was expressed as a deviation ($y_i$) from the mean rating given by all "others" for that item. Computation of the simple correlation ($r_{x_i y_i}$) between $x_i$ and $y_i$ over all items and "others" for the particular judge provides an index of the judge's ability to recognize individual differences among subjects in their response to each item. It is also an index of the judge's ability to estimate correctly the *relative position* of self-ratings made by the various "others" on a particular item

6. Nonaccuracy measures. These include such things as Elevation, Differential Elevation, variance of ratings, etc. which do not measure accuracy of judgment per se but may be quite important in interpreting and understanding the accuracy scores obtained

year several papers were published (Cronbach, 1955; Gage and Cronbach, 1955; Campbell, 1955; Hastorf, Bender, and Weintraub, 1955) that seriously challenged nearly all previous research in the area of judging accuracy. Using logic, mathematics, and analyses of studies, it was demonstrated that most judging experiments in the literature had serious flaws which rendered them largely uninterpretable. There had been earlier critical studies (Cohen, 1953; Cronbach and Gleser, 1953; Hastorf and Bender, 1952; Leytham, 1951), and others have appeared since (Crow, 1957; Crow and Hammond, 1957; Gage, Leavitt and Stone, 1956). However, Cronbach's (1955) paper provided a major methodological critique. Using the simple $D^2$ statistic (i.e., the arithmetical difference between judgment and criterion ratings, squared), he found that this apparently straightforward measure of judging accuracy contained a Pandora's box of "components, artifacts, and methodological problems" which would vitiate many previous research results. Cronbach demonstrated that "difference scores" on trait ratings could be analyzed mathematically into four component parts some of which could be reduced further into variance and correlation parts.

### A.  Cronbach's Components

#### 1.  Elevation (E)

This component measures the difference between the (a) grand mean of an *individual judge's* predictions for all "others" judged on all items and (b) the grand criterion mean. This tells us primarily something about the way in which a judge uses the rating scale and does not deal with accuracy per se.

#### 2.  Differential Elevation (DE)

This measures the variance of the individual judge's ratings. It measures the extent to which the judge can predict the deviation from the grand mean of the mean of individual "others" taken over all traits. This score can be broken down into a correlation term (which represents the judge's ability to judge *which* "other" rates highest on the elevation scale) and a variance term which measures the extent to which judged differences between "others" are large or small.

#### 3.  Stereotype Accuracy (SA)

This is a measure of what Bronfenbrenner has called "Sensitivity to the Generalized Other," or the degree to which a judge can predict how the whole $N$ of "others" responded to a set of items. The predicted item means averaged across persons are compared with the actual criterion item means across persons. This provides a correlation term which gives the relationship between a given set of predicted item means and the actual criterion means (of all "others" judged) and a variance term which is an index of the variability and/or complexity of the judges' stereotype.

### 4. Differential Accuracy (DA)

This measures the ability of the judges to predict the differences between "others" on each trait or item considered separately. To put it another way, this measures the difference between the scores for "others" on individual items in the judging matrix *versus* the criterion matrix where in each case the "other's" score is the deviation from both his own mean and the item mean. Thus this can be derived mathematically by subtracting $E$, $DE$, and $SA$ from the trait rating total score. It also has a correlation and variance term. This is considered a "pure" accuracy measure by some, even though under some circumstances it also has flaws.

Cronbach (1955) concluded that, "Social perception research has been dominated by simple operationally defined measures (of judging accuracy). Analysis has shown that any such measure may combine and thereby conceal important variables or may depend heavily on unwanted components. Only by a careful subdivision of global measures can an investigator hope to know what he is dealing with." Later (1958) he commented, "Investigators have been attracted to this area by their interest in such constructs as transference, identification, projection, empathy, and insight. We must question whether these terms should be employed in future interpretations of social perception experiments. If a behavior which looks like 'projection' can arise out of many different processes, there is little point in trying to formulate hypotheses using the concept 'projection.' Instead, theories of perceptual response should take into account the traits being perceived, the constant tendencies in this perceiver (judge) with respect to those traits, and finally the effect of the particular 'other' as a social stimulus to this perceiver. Worthwhile hypotheses of this order cannot be formulated until data from exploratory studies have been treated *analytically* (i.e., mathematically broken down into component scores) . . . a single global index (of judging accuracy) can now be replaced with a series of components of the perceptual relation and a separate analysis can be made for each. Even the simplest examples make it evident that insight, assumed similarity, and the other global phenomena are the shadow not the substance of social perception."

In recent research by Cline and Richards (1960, 1962), and Richards and Cline (1963) it was demonstrated that the system used in assigning numerical scores to the characteristics (traits) included in the judging matrices could produce artifacts tending to reduce or, in extreme cases, to eliminate Stereotype Accuracy and Differential Elevation correlation terms. Cronbach's Differential Accuracy in certain circumstances is thus made difficult or impossible to interpret. These artifacts were seen as particularly objectionable in the case of Differential Elevation and Differential Accuracy. To overcome these difficulties, Cline and Richards (1962) and Richards and Cline (1963) proposed a new measure, Interpersonal Accuracy (IA), which appears to be the linear combination of Differential Elevation and Differential Accuracy but is free of the aforementioned artifactual effects of the scoring system. This new component is discussed in detail later in this paper.

Other investigators have become increasingly chary of naïve empiricism in interpersonal perception research with the omnipresent danger of misinterpretation of results. A good example of this is Leytham's (1951) review of Taft's (1950) study of the personality correlates of judging ability. In Taft's research, using 40 graduate students, he studied judging ability by requiring each subject to rate a number of his fellow assessees, with whom he was familiar. Six personality variables were rated on a conventional five-point scale. Each judge also predicted how his peers would rate him. The criterion was the consensus of experts (research staff) and peer ratings. The more accurately the judge rated others and predicted self ratings, the better judge of personality he was assumed to be. The next step was to find test and rating correlates of judging ability as thus defined. Leytham later pointed out a statistical artifact, i.e., that cautious judges (who made many "three" or average ratings) were given a major advantage over those who tended to use the more extreme ratings. If judging accuracy were computed by the sum of the differences from the criteria consensus ratings then the rater who gave *nothing but* "three" or average rating would be easily the "most accurate" judge, because he could never obtain a discrepancy or error score greater than two (i.e., $5 - 3 = 2$ or $3 - 1 = 2$). Since the criteria consensus ratings (a summary mean score) tended to regress toward the mean of three, this amplified the spurious advantage already given to the cautious judges. Thus when Taft correlated his judging accuracy scores with other outside measures, he found a relationship between them and a "response set" to judge cautiously, but not necessarily "accurately."

Cronbach (1955) has commented on this point: "If two diagnosticians can each judge some trait with the correlational validity of .40, the one who differentiates strongly (i.e., makes extreme statements) will make far more serious absolute errors than the one who differentiates moderately. Indeed, the person who makes extreme differentiations based on a validity of .40 may have larger errors than a judge who has zero correlational validity but gives the same estimate for everyone."

In another example, Dymond, Hughes, and Raabe (1952) had sixth grade pupils rank each other sociometrically and also predict what sort of ratings they (the raters) received from the others. They found that accuracy of judgment or estimation correlated .50 with sociometric acceptance. However, the students generally tended to predict that they would be highly accepted. This meant that those students who, in fact, were highly accepted automatically obtained higher accuracy scores. This fact alone is sufficient to account for the apparent relationship between judging accuracy and sociometric acceptance.

In a study by Nagle (1954) 14 supervisors were each asked to predict the number of their own subordinates responding in a favorable direction to some morale items having to do with their attitudes toward the supervisor. Accuracy of prediction was obtained for each supervisor by summing, over the items, the *differences* between the supervisors' predictions and the in-fact responses of the subordinates. For each one of the supervisors' groups a summary morale score (based on subordinate attitudes toward the supervisor) was obtained from this same instrument. A correlation of .90 was found between supervisors' empathic accuracy and the morale index. Nagle thus concluded that empathy, or judging accuracy, was related to "morale," as defined in this study, and his data apparently supported this conclusion. However, a more parsimonious explanation would be that most supervisors predicted highly favorable attitudes toward themselves by the men in their group. Thus the supervisor whose group morale (as indicated by the favorable attitudes shown toward him by his subordinates) was highest would have to receive the highest empathy or judging score. Spuriously high scores on empathy measures will be made by the truly popular subject when his empathy is tested by ability to assess his own popularity; a common human response set toward rating oneself as popular will guarantee this even in the most imperceptive of popular people.

### B. THE RS-AS-ACC PROBLEM

Various investigators have been concerned with the RS-AS-ACC problem. In this case,

$a$ = the judge's self-description on a trait variable,
$b$ = the "other's" (person being judged) self-description,
$c$ = the judge's prediction of b.

*Real Similarity* (RS) is where $a = b$, *Assumed Similarity* (AS) is where $a = c$, and *Accuracy* (ACC) is where $b = c$. Many social perception studies have gone awry because of the lack of understanding that while any two of these relationships are independent, the third remaining relationship is directly and mathematically linked to and a resultant of the other two. Hatch (1962) has commented that, "Where each of a number of judges possesses high RS with their others (persons being judged) their accuracies will correlate perfectly with the degree to which the judges assume similarity with their others. A typical situation is one in which each of the judges predicts with a high degree of assumed similarity. The accuracy score then varies directly with the amount of real similarity existing between the judges and their respective others. This latter relationship, real similarity, may best be viewed as a fixed constant which exists between a judge and a specified other, as a function of the sampling. With the high degree of assumed similarity often found in empathy studies (especially where judges predict for some variable allowing self-flattering predictions), the resulting accuracy scores bear a highly significant relationship to this original constant, RS. Such accuracy scores certainly do not represent novel emergents reflecting on empathic sensitivity of some kind. They are simply the logical consequences of RS-AS-ACC linkages and are impossible to interpret."

An example of an "RS-AS-ACC study" is Smith's (1957) study of rapport and social perception in mother-adolescent relationships. Some 15 different judging scores were derived from the four types of data listed below.

(a)  Daughters took Kuder Preference Record for themselves;
(b)  Mothers predicted their daughter's responses on this Kuder test;
(c)  Mothers predicted typical adolescent responses to the Kuder test;
(d)  Mothers took Kuder for themselves.

The following 15 scores were derived from this information.

(1) *Accuracy* (ACC): Number of items on daughter's Kuder which coincide with mother's predictions for her.

(2) *Real Similarity* (RS): Number of items on which mother's self-Kuder and daughter's self-Kuder coincide.

(3) *Real Dissimilarity* (RD): Number of items on which mother's and daughter's self-Kuders differ.

(4) *Assumed Similarity* (AS): Number of items on which mother's self-Kuder and mother's prediction of her daughter's Kuder coincide.

(5) *Assumed Dissimilarity* (AD): Number of items on which mother's self-Kuder and mother's prediction for her daughter differ.

(6) *Warranted Assumed Similarity* (WAS): Number of items on which mother's self-Kuder, daughter's self-Kuder, and mother's prediction for her daughter all coincide.

(7) *Warranted Assumed Dissimilarity* (WAD): Number of items on which mother's self-Kuder does not agree with daughter's self-Kuder, but does agree with mother's prediction for her daughter.

(8) *Unwarranted Assumed Similarity* (UAS): Number of items on which mother's self-Kuder agrees with her predictions for her daughter but not with the daughter's actual self-Kuder responses.

(9) *Unwarranted Assumed Dissimilarity* (UAD): Number of items on which the mother's self-Kuder coincided with her daughter's self-Kuder but not with the mother's predictions of her daughter's Kuder responses.

(10) *Stereotype Accuracy* (SA): Number of items on which mother's prediction of a typical adolescent response on Kuder coincide with her daughter's self-description, or responses, on the Kuder.

(11) *Stereotype Inaccuracy* (SI): Number of items on which mother's prediction of the typical adolescent response differs from her daughter's self-description or responses on the Kuder.

(12) *Assumed Conventionality* (AC): Number of items on which mother's prediction of a typical adolescent response and her prediction of her daughter's Kuder responses coincide.

(13) *Assumed Unconventionality* (AU): Number of items on which mother's predictions of a typical adolescent response and a prediction of her daughter's Kuder response differs.

(14) *Warranted Assumed Conventionality* (WAC): Number of items where mother's prediction of typical adolescent responses, her daughter's self-description, and the mother's prediction of the daughter's Kuder responses all coincide.

(15) *Warranted Assumed Unconventionality* (WAU): Number of items where mother's prediction of typical adolescent responses agrees with the mother's prediction of her daughter's responses, but does not agree with her daughter's actual self-description on the Kuder.

Smith found low positive correlations between mother-adolescent offspring rapport and judging accuracy scores. However, the evidence suggested that this accuracy was due in part to the tendency of high-rapport judges (mothers) to assume similarity and also possibly to assume conventionality. But because of the methodology of the study no evidence could be presented showing how much of the accuracy variance could be attributed to these artifactual processes.

Cronbach's (1955) previous analysis of the components of judging scores emphasized the "difference score" already described. An alternative is the correlation between predicted scores and criterion scores. These methods may be compared for their respective freedom from artifacts.

Crow (1954) commented that, "The use of the correlation scoring method defines predictive accuracy as the ability to vary one's predictions as the actual situation varies. The 'difference score' method defines predictive accuracy as the ability to approximate the actual situation. By the 'difference score' method a subject (judge) is penalized for a systematic error in estimation of the magnitude of the actual situation. By the correlation method the subject (judge) is not so penalized. Conversely, a subject (judge) is penalized by the correlation method, if although he has approximated the actual situation, his predictions do not vary concomitantly with the actual scores."

Thus, in the correlation method such response sets as Cronbach's Elevation or those associated with the variability of prediction and response are removed, though the RS-AS-ACC linkages remain. It should be noted that a correlation approach can require a judge to predict for many "others" on a single variable, IQ for example, or it may require him to make predictions for a single "other" on a large number of separate trait variables. In either case methodological complexities remain which can render judging accuracy scores suspect. For example, special problems in interpretation arise in the case where a correlation is calculated between criterion and a judge's predictions of the self-score of each of a number of "others" on a single variable. Here, as Hatch (1962) has pointed out, there is a tendency for the judge to assume similarity (defined as perceiving others as similar to oneself). This must be considered as a response set and this will differ from "other" to "other" apparently as a function of the judge's generalized attitude toward the "other."

The tendency to assume similarity is fairly constant over preferred "others." However, knowledge of the degree of assumed similarity between a judge and a liked "other" provides no basis for predicting the degree of assumed similarity which will be exhibited by the judge for a disliked "other."

Gage and Cronbach (1955) have noted that assumed similarity is highly general over items, and people tend to assume similarity to the same degree throughout a questionnaire despite marked variety in the item content with this tendency being somewhat general for preferred "others." Thus, a judge's attitude and set toward an "other" will influence the AS score.

Hastorf and Bender have tried to clarify and solve the problems associated with ACC, or accuracy, which they call "raw empathy," by subtracting AS from it to give a "refined empathy" score. The major problem here is that they lose important data when they do this because some of the subtracted AS data represent true accuracy of judgment. Gage and Cronbach (1955) in an excellent discussion of this note that spurious relationships can occur wherever the "other's" self-score correlates with the "outside" variable, which is to be paired in a correlation with the judge's accuracy scores. They suggest that researchers test for the presence of spurious or artifactual relationships between the accuracy and empathy scores on the criterion variables by checking the relationship between the "response to be judged" and these same criterion measures. An example is given to further illustrate this point. Employees are asked to rate their department supervisor and he in turn predicts their ratings on a 1-to-5 point scale. If every supervisor predicts that his group will rate him 5 (very good), as might be expected, then there will be an automatic perfect correlation, 1.00, between the supervisors' "empathic ability" and receiving high ratings as a supervisor.

### C. Other Sources of Error in Judging-Accuracy Scores

To give the reader an even more detailed and clearer idea of the kinds of biases and response sets, etc., which can add error variance as well as "chance success" to judging-accuracy scores, a few will be listed below.

(1) *Social desirability bias:* This refers to the tendency for judges usually to predict the most socially desirable response in making judgments and predictions about "others."

(2) *Similarity of the judge to the "other":* This may be in sex, age, personality, religion, occupation, class level, ethnic, social, and cultural background. This in turn may lead the judge to believe that "the other" is like himself, and respond to the items as if this were so. This is very similar to (9) below.

(3) *Acquiescence set:* This refers to a tendency to agree with or predict "Yes" to items rather than to choose the negative or "No" responses.

(4) *Use of stereotype:* Wherein the judge uses an undifferentiated stereotype of "fraternity men," "Jewish women," etc. to predict for specific "others," and only if his "other" fits the stereotype will he achieve accuracy.

(5) *Personal reactions:* Liking or disliking the individual being judged can produce a "halo" effect in rating or judging.

(6) *Making use of an implicit personality theory:* Wherein the judge assumes there is an invariant relationship between trait *a* (observed in the "other") and traits *b, c,* and *d* (not observed but assumed correlated).

(7) *Tendency to make extreme ratings or judgments:* This is a response set wherein the judge overdifferentiates in his ratings of "others."

(8) *The central tendency response set:* Wherein the judge sees most "others" as being very similar or alike and gives mostly middle range or average scores with very little differentiation from "other" to "other."

(9) *To assume similarity or project:* In this case, the judge sees "others" as being very similar to himself (as defined by his self-ratings).

(10) *To assume dissimilarity or project "in reverse":* Wherein one perceives most "others" as being different from oneself.

(11) *Semantic ambiguities in trait terms:* Here the judge interprets the trait name in the judging instrument assuming a meaning other than that intended in its criterion development and use.

Mathematical linkages between predictor and criterion variables (as already discussed), and the use of "global scores" which contain numerous components sometimes working in opposite directions, can also be a further source of error. Several investigators (Cline and Richards, 1960; Hatch, 1962; Crow, 1954; Bronfenbrenner, Harding, and Gallwey, 1958; Grossman, 1963) have attempted to design studies that would meet these objections. However, their researches have met with only partial success.

Grossman (1963) used 5-min movies of adult subjects being interviewed. Three films were of males and three of females. These sound-color movies had been developed previously by Cline and Richards. By showing three sets of film at a time and using a matching method, it was possible for Grossman to control or eliminate the Elevation and Differential Elevation components as discussed in Cronbach's 1955 paper. Grossman then attempted to eliminate Stereotype Accuracy, the third of Cronbach's four components, by the following technique.

Starting with 240 judging items for the six films, two item analyses were undertaken. The first was an internal consistency analysis to choose the most highly discriminating "interpersonal sensitivity" items. The second involved giving a four-part test on *group* sensitivity to the same subjects (judges). This test was believed to be a measure of Stereotype Accuracy. Items retained in the final judging test were highly discriminating for interpersonal sensitivity, but nondiscriminating for group sensitivity or Stereotype Accuracy. The final correlation between the interpersonal sensitivity index and the group sensitivity index was .12, or nonsignificant. The final judging test thus derived was believed to be a relatively pure measure of Differential Accuracy. This index was correlated with 38 personality, demographic, and other types of variables. Grossman found some evidence for generality of judging ability. His cross-sexes correlation when corrected for attenuation was .48. His cross-persons correlation when corrected for attenuation was .60. He also found that the more observant a judge was, the higher his judging score. He obtained a measure of observant accuracy by testing how much the judge could remember about the appearance, actions, and behaviors of the people in the film. He also found that the better judges tended to be more "open-minded" as measured by three subscales, Religious Skepticism, Nonconformity, and Liberalism. He also found low positive correlations between judging ability and intelligence, using ACE Total, Quantitative, and Language scores.

### D. HATCH'S FORCED-CHOICE DIFFERENTIAL ACCURACY APPROACH

Hatch (1962) tackled the methodological problems of interpersonal perception research with great care, going to considerable lengths to control bias, response set, and other artifacts. He identified three primary difficulties to be overcome in any research of this kind: (1) solving the RS-AS-ACC problem; (2) controlling for miscellaneous response sets; and (3) developing an adequate "better than chance" test for one's judging-accuracy results. He first proceeded to develop a Forced Choice Differential Accuracy Test which gave a score corresponding to Cronbach's Differential Accuracy correlation term. The judges (30 branch managers of Minnesota Mining and Manufacturing Co.) were required to predict which *one* of two statements, both of a pair of their subordinates *disagreed* on. *Example* (slightly modified):

|          Mr. Brown          |          Mr. Jones          |
| --------------------------- | --------------------------- |

Check One

1. My sales manager assigns first priority to problems brought to him
   by a salesman.                                                   □
2. My sales manager should consult me more often for my opinion or
   advice.                                                          □

A large number of subordinates (318) previously responded either Strongly Agree, Agree, Disagree, or Strongly Disagree to items in a sales attitude questionnaire from which the pairs of men and their responses to items had been taken in developing this empathy test. Hatch found that any two subordinates might have identical responses (IR) or non-identical responses (NIR) to an item. There were three kinds of NIR response subcategories: (A) Maximally Dissimilar Responses (MDR) where one subordinate says "Strongly Agree" *versus* "Strongly Disagree" for the other; (B) Dissimilar Responses (DR) of Agree *versus* Disagree; and (C) Similar Responses (SR) of Agree *versus* Strongly Agree, or Disagree *versus* Strongly Disagree. All three of these were classified as "disagreed on" (or NIR) responses of the supervisor's subordinate pair in the empathy test.

Using this Forced Choice Differential Accuracy technique, Hatch demonstrated empirically that the structure of the forced-choice items did not permit a confounding statistical linkage to exist between RS, AS, and ACC. Thus, the judge might obtain accuracy under any combination of RS and AS conditions. "Accuracy depends only upon the correct identification of the NIR statement and is uninfluenced by the real similarity and high-low assumed similarity conditions; thus, judges with any combination of RS-AS relationship may be scored as accurate or inaccurate." Hatch arranged to control for four specific types of response sets and set up his experimental design so as to control "unidentified response sets." These four response sets were identified as "response variability," "response intensity," "atypical response pattern of judge," and "atypical response pattern of others." The first ("response variability") will be discussed briefly for illustration purposes. From the responses of salesmen to the original sales attitude questionnaire, it was found that some items were controversial, with much disagreement among respondents. With other items there was very little response variance. If most of the NIR statements had high response variance, it would be possible for a judge knowing only this to obtain a high accuracy score by always picking the most controversial item, as the empathy test required predicting which of two statements the subordinates disagreed on. To control this, statements were matched so that the IR statement variance exceeded the NIR statement variance in exactly one half of the forced-choice items prepared for each judge. Elaborate experimental controls in item selection were also established for the other three response sets mentioned previously.

In an effort to assess the practical validity of his empathy test, Hatch correlated it with (a) a measure of human relations skill (by having company executives nominate branch managers who were most and least successful in interpersonal relations with subordinates), (b) degree of acquaintance (between branch manager and subordinate), and (c) degree of extrapolation or inference required between information input and outtake (prediction). The latter item was assessed by comparing judges' accuracy on each of the three NIR items (SR, DR, and MDR) matched with the IR item. Thus, the greatest extrapolation or inference required of a judge (and also theoretically the most difficult judgment) would be on an IR *versus* SR item, whereas the easiest would be an IR *versus* MDR item. Each manager made predictions on 12 SR items, 12 DR items, and 12 MDR items. In this way the degree of measured discordance in the attitudes of a subordinate pair was varied for each manager, though held constant from manager to manager. The subordinates under each branch manager were also classified into three groups: (a) AP (attitude predictable); these were the subordinates that a branch manager felt most confident in making predictions about and with whom he was most acquainted; (b) AU (attitude unpredictable); these were the subordinates that a branch manager felt least confident in making predictions about and was least acquainted with; and (c) AD (attitude divergent); these were salesmen at either extreme on a "dissatisfaction index" taken from the sales attitude questionnaire. Each judge predicted on 12 items for each of the three pairs of subordinates, AP, AD, and AU.

Each judge (branch manager) received a different 36-item pair inventory devised individually for him. Because of the highly restrictive conditions set in controlling the four response sets in addition to AP, AU, AD and SR, DR, and MDR conditions, it was necessary to program a "look up and comparison" table using the Univac 1103 computer. Over 14,000 IBM cards and 20 hours of computer time were necessary to list the eligible items in order of priority. Following this, some 40 additional hours were involved in selecting the 10,080 forced-choice items from the computer printout. Hatch concluded that the costs were excessive and that the Forced Choice Differential Accuracy approach, "Is probably not a practical solution to the empathic measurement problem." It was also indicated that if the same computer data were used by another investigator, precisely the same inventories would *not* result and, in fact, Hatch would not be able to repeat the process if he were, himself, to do it again.

The final results indicated that empathy as measured here was not related to human relations skills but was somewhat related to degree of acquaintance between manager (judge) and subordinate as well as degree of inference or extrapolation required. While his good judges as a group were able to predict at better than chance ($P < .05$), Hatch noted that "much but not all of the prediction of the study could be accounted for by chance alone."

Because this study represents a major effort to eliminate the methodological gremlins which plague interpersonal perception research, it is a significant contribution to the literature. Yet the lack of any relationship with human relations skills, as well as the only slightly above chance accuracy scores obtained by judges, is of considerable concern to this reviewer. Serious questions arise about the potential future of an approach where such costly and careful controls yield such modest results.

E. ACCURACY VERSUS PROCESS APPROACHES IN RESEARCH

In the person perception literature a sharp cleavage is apparent between research which emphasizes accuracy of judgment and that which focuses on process (i.e., how we judge).

A growing number of researchers have abandoned work on the assessment of judging ability as a trait in favor of the view that this exists only in a specific instance with a particular person using a certain instrument.

Tagiuri and Petrullo (1958) have tried to turn the tide in favor of research emphasizing process by the publication of a major collection of papers contributed predominantly by workers in this group. Tagiuri, in the same volume, has stated the case with considerable vigor: "For a number of reasons, attempts at studying correlates of accuracy have with very few exceptions produced negligible correlations and yielded very little insight into processes. First there is no single satisfactory criterion against which to match the judgments. The criteria used—objective behavior, self ratings by the object person, ratings by the experts, consensual ratings by peers—do not always agree and have very different psychological implications. Second, the disparity of tasks and abilities subsumed under the various operations called measures of accuracy have been glossed over. It is also probable that different judgmental skills may be involved in different situations. In addition, most accuracy scores contain some seven different and not necessarily correlated components. There is furthermore the extreme dependence of results upon judgmental sets and upon the distributions of the variables that are to be judged. Finally, most of the studies are inconclusive because of the lack of representativeness in the design employed. In sum, investigations yield data that are difficult to interpret and impossible to compare. It is the process rather than its achievement that one must investigate if a broad understanding of the phenomenon is to be reached. This point cannot be stressed sufficiently. It is also important to realize that the difficulties encountered in quantitative studies of *accuracy* cannot be eliminated by resorting to careful qualitative approaches. Such phenomena as real and assumed similarity, stereotype and differential accuracy, favorability sets, and artifactual relations, to mention but a few, apply to any kind of inquiry into person perception."

Fiedler (1960) stated that he is not interested in accuracy of judgment per se, but only in what kinds of perceptions, regardless of accuracy, are related to such behavioral outcomes as winning basketball games, accuracy of bomber crews, etc.

However, Crow (1960) has responded to this position by commenting, "Only in recent decades has physical perception been freed from the preoccupation with mediational detail and the stimulus bias that has characterized its history. In person perception research, we must examine cautiously any call to focus on process that turns its back on accuracy. My point is not that we should ignore process nor should we fail to eliminate from our scores those components which invalidate our conclusions. The danger lies in the possibility that we will ignore accuracy and that the components once eliminated will not receive the attention they require. We should study process but we should not become bogged down in the technological details of the machinery by which the organism arrives at interpersonal perceptions. We must keep in mind that the process we are studying is a process of functional achievement. If we fail to do this in person perception research we may engage in a tedious reinactment of the history of physical perception."

## IV. Analysis of Judgments from Motion-Picture Samples

The present author has been conducting a series of research studies in the area of interpersonal perception since 1951. Many have been in the nature of large-scale pilot studies which have frequently yielded negative results and have not been published. However, negative results are frequently as important and necessary to progress as positive findings and both kinds will be reviewed in the following section.

In preliminary consideration of the literature the writer noticed the frequent use of still photographs as stimuli for judgments. While this kind of "limited cue" study has its place, the writer is in agreement with Bruner and Tagiuri (1954), who commented that "A vast literature arose based on judgments of emotions from still pictures and drawings of human faces, when we know that it is rarely that one makes a judgment based upon a frozen millisecond of exposure to a face expressing emotion with all other forms of information lacking—it seems unlikely that conventional analysis of expression carried out with callipers will yield much value and understanding of stimulus properties of faces in a state of emotion. . . ."

The writer and his collaborators were of the opinion that a more dynamic true-to-life type of stimulus was needed. A sound film of an interview (following the work of Estes, 1938; Gage, 1952; Giedt, 1951; Luft, 1949; and others) appeared to be a possible alternative to immobile photographs or drawings of faces. This permits the recording of a variety of verbal and visual cues in situations allowing for repeated observation. Interview behavior appears also to be more typical of the kind of phenomenon upon which judgments are made in real life. In early research conducted at the University of California by the writer, a dilemma presented itself. It was found on an experimental basis that 2 hours proved to be the maximum period for which most judges could tolerate looking at films and fill out judging instruments, at least at one sitting. Thus, one might make a film of an interview lasting 45 minutes to an hour and present one or two of these to a group of judges for evaluation, but the number of "others," (social objects or persons judged) was extremely small and limited. Or as another alternative the experimenter could present a fairly large number of 1-minute filmed interviews, but so limit his judges in the amount of information presented to them that it almost approached the still photographs as a source of data. Thus, in time, it became apparent that the filmed interview could not be a typical, unstructured, loose, clinical type of interview, but must in as short a time possible compress, capture, and present a wide range of information both objective and factual in content as well as emotional and reactional in nature.

## A. Construction of Films

After some 6 months of experimentation, the following procedure was developed. Sound motion pictures in black and white were taken of nine male college students using a hidden camera and microphone. Interviewees initially knew only that they were to report for job interviews in their particular fields of study. The interviews were very highly structured and were held relatively constant for all those participating. Each interview had three phases: (1) A standard opening session in which stock employment questions were asked by a mature and skilled actor posing as a prospective employer; (2) a stress session in which the "employer" became critical and mildly stressful in his questioning; and (3) an abreaction session in which the inteviewer stopped playing the role of the employer, revealed the true experimental intent of the interview, and became quite humble and deferential. He invited comments about how the interviewee had felt in such a situation and what had bothered him the most. It was at this point that the interviewee relaxed greatly and usually became quite verbal and very frank, indicating points of tension, blocking, embarrassment, and his degree of insight into the total situation. This was all recorded by the hidden camera and microphone. Permission was then secured to use the films for research. The four best films of the nine, representing the most diverse personalities, were presented to large populations of judges.

This employment interview which was in part a stress interview, had been suggested by one of the OSS (1948) situational procedures used during World War II. In developing this technique for the present research everything possible was done to compress in 11 minutes a great range of information about the individual being interviewed, both objective and emotional.

Three judging tests were constructed.

### 1. Behavior Postdiction Test

Here the judge was required to describe or postdict how the interviewee behaved in everyday life. A series of questions was set up with a multiple-choice format. Example:

> 14. When the interviewee (in the film) is in a violent argument usually he:
>   (a) Becomes very sarcastic,
>   (b) Uses profanity and obscene words,

(c)  Leaves the room or area,
(d)  Strikes his opponent with his fists.

There was only one correct response. The other alternatives were were carefully constructed so as not to include even partially correct statements. A separate and individually tailored Behavior Postdiction Test was constructed for each interviewee. Other items tapped such areas as relations with women, behavior at social gatherings, handling money, etc. The experimenter knew how each interviewee characteristically behaved, and was able to write items tailored specifically to his personality because intensive interviews had been held with him, and his family, close friends, fraternity brothers, and/or fiancee, or wife, where available. Only those behaviors which all agreed upon as being characteristic were used, and the incorrect alternatives were chosen with equal care so as to eliminate even partial or occasional kinds of behaviors. The judging score was the total number of correct predictions made for all four filmed interviews.

### 2. Personality Word Card

Next the judges were required to predict the interviewees' "verbal behavior." This was done in the following manner. The interviewees had on three previous occasions, about a month apart, filled out the Personality Word Card, checking those adjectives which they felt best described themselves. This card was merely a group of 200 descriptive adjectives such as, "frank," "bossy," "sexy," "persistent," "anxious," "aggressive," and so forth. It was found that certain adjectives were "marginal," that is, the S checked them on only one of the three occasions he filled it out for himself. Other adjectives proved to be more central and important in nature, being checked as self descriptive two and/or three times out of three. These were retained in a final key. Thus, each interviewee had a unique pattern of adjectives which represented an important and consistent part of his self perception. Each judge then was required, after seeing the film, to predict which adjectives had been checked by the interviewee in describing himself. Each judge was told to check only about one third of the adjectives in making his predictions on each interviewee because the interviewee keys average one third the total number of adjectives. The judging accuracy score for each judge was based upon the percentage of correct predictions averaged for all four of the test films.

### 3. Multiple Choice Sentence Completion Test

This technique was also used but abandoned because of low reliability. Here the judge attempted to predict the sentence completion responses, using a multiple-choice format, for each of the interviewees in the films.

## B. PRELIMINARY RELIABILITY AND VALIDITY

Reliability coefficients for each of the three techniques were computed by employing the Spearman–Brown formula to the correlation between odd and even halves. The Postdiction test yielded a reliability of .56. The Personality Word Card yielded a reliability of .83. The reliability of the Multiple Choice Sentence Completion Test was only .35, and for this reason was discarded as an index of judging ability. None of these were corrected for attenuation, which would have given them higher reliabilities. An equally weighted composite of scores on the first two judging tests (Postdiction Test and Personality Word Card) was obtained for each judge. These two measures intercorrelated .43 ± .10. In the initial experiment five groups of judges viewed these four films and made judgments. After each filmed interview had been shown the projector was stopped and they were asked to make their judgments on the instruments discussed. These Ss were (a) 109 undergraduate college students, (b) 106 professionals (clinical psychologists, psychiatrists, and graduate clinical trainees), (c) 47 adult members of a Protestant church congregation, (d) 43 nursing trainees, and (e) 11 advanced engineering students.

The results may be briefly summarized as follows: All groups of judges performed at very much better than chance success (.001 level of confidence) on both the Behavior Postdiction Test and the Personality Word Card. The question arose, however, "To what extent would the judges have done just as well without seeing the films but merely filling in the tests according to their stereotype of a typical college male?" To answer this question a special control group of 57 undergraduates filled out the forms without seeing any of the films whatsoever, merely using hunches or social stereotypes about college males, in responding to the various questions. Their level of accuracy was termed "psychological chance." When the control and experimental groups of judges were compared in their performance the test indicated significant differences, better than the .001 level of confidence, on both judging instruments, favoring those people who had *seen* the films. The evidence seemed to be fairly conclusive that the judges who saw the films were making fairly accurate predictions or judgments on the basis of a differential analysis and a real evaluation of the personalities of the films rather than from some crude internalized stereotypes of what college males were like.

This study was conducted in 1952 prior to the publication of most of the articles suggesting components, RS-AS-ACC problems, and the like. However, it should be noted that the $D^2$ statistic, which later proved so fallible, was not used in this study, even though the possibility of other "error" or artifacts remains.

When the judges of the five subgroups were compared for accuracy a three-level hierarchy was found. Most accurate and proficient were the professionals, that is, the psychiatrists, psychologists, and clinical trainees. At level two were the nursing trainees, and at level three the college students and members of the church congregation as well as the advanced engineering trainees. The differences in accuracy between levels one and three on both the Postdiction Test and Personality Word Card were significant at the .05 level of confidence. The differences between levels one and two, and two and three, however, did not quite reach significance. It was also found that women consistently obtained slightly higher judging scores than men. While these differences never quite reached significance they were consistent in this study as well as most other studies conducted by the author. It was also found that some of the interviewees or "others" in the films appeared generally easier to judge than others. Length of professional psychological or psychiatric experience was related to (a) greater accuracy in using the Personality Word Card, that is, predicting "verbal" behavior, and (b) decreased accuracy in predicting real life social behavior on the Behavior Postdiction Test. This finding was based upon a comparison of the accuracy of predictions made by psychiatrists and psychologists having more than ten years experience with the accuracy of predictions made by those having less than three years experience. The relatively new and less experienced clinicians were a little less accurate in predicting verbal behavior ($P = .10$), but were considerably more accurate in predicting real life behavior ($P = .02$) than were their much more experienced and "older" colleagues. This suggested that there may be danger with increasing experience in becoming more sensitive and aware of verbal behavior but less aware and less in contact with reality with real life social behavior. The top and bottom quartiles in judging ability of the college sample filled out Gough's Adjective Check List describing themselves. The better judges significantly more often characterized themselves on this check list as "sympathetic" and "affectionate." The adjective self checks characterizing the poorest judges included "dissatisfied," "irritable," "awkward," "praising," and "hurried."

With regards to the personality correlates of judging ability, as here defined, results were available for the sample of 109 college undergraduates. They were given a battery of tests which included the MMPI scored for 22 scales, the California Public Opinion Scales (including E, F, and PEC), the Henmon–Nelson Intelligence Test, the Gough Adjective

Check List, the Brunswik Faces Test (wherein one estimates the intelligence, likeability, and so forth of 46 males on the basis of small still photographs of their faces); the Barron–Welch Art Scale, the Group Opinion Estimate (where one attempts to predict what percentage of the general population responds true to each of 30 MMPI items, such as "I pray several times a week"), and the Klein Social Prediction Technique, wherein one is given a transcript of a patient's remarks in a clinical interview that is interrupted at a crucial point, and five possible endings are presented, only one of which is correct (the task here being to predict the correct alternative).

In summary it was found in this study that the most significant correlates of judging ability were (a) absence of ethnocentric-authoritarian attitudes (Fascism and Ethnocentrism correlated −.46 and −.32), (b) superior intellectual ability, (c) lower scores on MMPI scales for Hypochondriasis, Dissimulation, Paranoia, Schizophrenia, Psychopathic Deviate, Prejudice, and F (validation), and (d) higher scores on the MMPI Social Status and Intellectual Efficiency measures. When correlations were run between judging ability and these various tests, for the sexes separately, some male-female differences emerged, which are discussed in greater detail elsewhere (Cline, 1955a). Sex differences in interpersonal perception have been found in nearly all studies conducted by this investigator, indicating the necessity of separate analyses of data for male and female judges, and probably for "others" when they include both sexes.

## C. The Generality of Judging Ability

Cline and Richards in 1957 began a new series of studies at the University of Utah in the area of interpersonal perception. The initial focus was on the problem of generality and its relation to a component type of analysis of global accuracy scores. A new set of filmed interviews in sound and color as well as much larger and varied group of judging instruments was developed. These instruments included

(1) *Behavior Postdiction* test. The development and format of this were similar to the same test cited in the previous study.

(2) *Sentence Completion* test. This is very similar to the previously discarded Multiple Choice Sentence Completion test described previously.

(3) *Adjective Check* (ACL). This evolved from the older previously mentioned Personality Word Card. In this case the judges were required to predict which of 20 adjectives the interviewee (or "other") had previously checked as being self descriptive. Only those adjectives which the interviewee had consistently checked on three different occasions as applying to himself were used as the "correct" items, and only those

adjectives never checked as self descriptive were used as the incorrect alternatives. Ten of the 20 adjectives were "correct" and the other ten "incorrect." In choosing the "correct" and "incorrect" adjective items for this judging test from the original 300 adjective pool, an attempt was made to choose socially desirable items as well as undesirable items in about equal numbers as correct and incorrect on the scoring key.

(4) *Opinion Prediction* test. Here the judge was required to predict how the interviewee (in the film) answered 20 MMPI items such as, " 'I fall in love easily,' True or False?" Only those MMPI items which the interviewee on three different occasions answered consistently the same way were used. It will be noted that each of the 25 interviewees had previously filled out answers to a selected group of 80 MMPI items on three occasions (several weeks apart). It was from this 80-item pool that the 20 consistently answered items were selected. An attempt was made to obtain ten of these items scored in the True direction and ten in the False direction and, additionally, that ten should have "favorable" type responses correct and ten "unfavorable" correct to prevent the judges from obtaining high accuracy scores merely by going through and check- ing only the "socially desirable" (or favorable) responses. Since this scale was constructed on the basis of each interviewee's responses, the particular items included in the scale differed from one interviewee to another.

(5) *Trait Rating* test. Here the judge was required to rate the interviewee on 50 traits (later reduced to 25) such as "cooperative," "impulsive," "efficient," "a leader," etc., on a six-point scale ranging from "very like" to "very unlike." The criterion was obtained from the mean of the ratings (on each of the items) of the interviewee by his friends and associates. Two other secondary types of criterion scores were also obtained: (1) the researcher's final summary ratings of the interviewee after evaluation of all of the test and interview data; and (2) the mean of the interviewee's own self ratings, done three times. This Trait Rating procedure was amenable to a Cronbach-type analysis into components.

Various revisions in scoring systems and format occurred with all of these instruments over time and a number of other instruments were developed, some of which are mentioned later in this paper.

While the problems in interpreting global scores of any kind were recognized, the different judging instruments were intercorrelated with results indicated in Tables V through XIII.[2] In addition, correlations

---

2 The author wishes to express appreciation to the following journals for per- mission to extract or reprint in full the following tables: *Journal of Abnormal and Social Psychology*, Tables V–IX, XIII, XIV; *Journal of Applied Psychology*, Tables XX–XXII; *Psychological Record*, Table XIX; and *Psychological Reports*, Tables XVI– XVIII.

were obtained between single instruments and Total Judging scores. In this case, Total Judging scores were obtained by converting scores on each judging instrument to standard scores and adding across instruments. All correlations between individual instruments and Total Judg-

TABLE V

INTERCORRELATIONS AMONG JUDGING MEASURES FOR UNIVERSITY OF UTAH STUDENTS
USING THE SIX- AND TEN-FILM FORMS
$(N = 295)$

| | Ten-film form[a] | | | Six-film form[a] | | |
|---|---|---|---|---|---|---|
| | Trait Rating | Adjective Check | Total Judging[b] | Trait Rating | Adjective Check | Total Judging[b] |
| Behavior Postdiction | .24 | .04 | .31 | .36 | .28 | .39 |
| Trait Rating | | .31 | .44 | | .41 | .50 |
| Adjective | | | .31 | | | .44 |
| | | $r .05 = .11$ | | | $r .01 = .15$ | |

[a] Note: Through procedures resembling item analysis, the number of films used during a judging test was eventually reduced to the "best six." And unless otherwise specified in the tables, it is this group of films which was used. Where the "10-film form," "20-film form," etc. are referred to it means that the particular research was performed before the final "best six" films had been selected.

[b] Part-whole correlations corrected for the contribution of the part.

TABLE VI

INTERCORRELATIONS BETWEEN ACCURACY SCORES ON DIFFERENT JUDGING MEASURES FOR
UNIVERSITY OF UTAH STUDENTS
$(N = 51)$

| | Trait Rating | Opinion Prediction | Adjective Check | Total Judging[a] |
|---|---|---|---|---|
| Behavior Postdiction | .16 | .20 | .37 | .37 |
| Trait Rating | | .31 | .13 | .28 |
| Opinion Prediction | | | .25 | .32 |
| Adjective Check | | | | .36 |
| $r .05 = .27$ | | | $r .01 = .35$ | |

[a] Part-whole correlation corrected for contribution of the part.

TABLE VII

INTERCORRELATIONS AMONG JUDGING MEASURES FOR
IDAHO STATE (MENTAL) HOSPITAL PATIENTS
$(N = 32)$

| | Trait Rating | Adjective Check | Total Judging[a] |
|---|---|---|---|
| Behavior Postdiction | .41 | .61 | .67 |
| Trait Rating | | .31 | .37 |
| Adjective Check | | | .57 |
| $r .05 = .35$ | | $r .01 = .45$ | |

[a] Part-whole correlation corrected for contribution of the part.

ing scores were part-whole correlations corrected for contribution of the part. In Table XV are given some of the reliabilities of the judging instruments. In Table XIV are listed the correlations between Trait

TABLE VIII

INTERCORRELATIONS AMONG JUDGING MEASURES FOR $T$ GROUP MEMBERS

($N = 118$)

|  | Trait Rating | Opinion Prediction | Adjective Check | Total Judging[a] |
|---|---|---|---|---|
| Behavior Postdiction | .28 | .36 | .36 | .52 |
| Trait Rating |  | .27 | .03 | .26 |
| Opinion Prediction |  |  | .07 | .47 |
| Adjective Check |  |  |  | .35 |
| $r\ .05 = .17$ |  |  | $r\ .01 = .23$ |  |

[a] Part-whole correlation corrected for contribution of the part.

TABLE IX

INTERCORRELATIONS AMONG JUDGING MEASURES FOR UNIVERSITY OF UTAH STUDENTS

($N = 50$)

| Measure | Trait Rating Total | Behavior Post- diction | Sentence Com- pletion | Opinion Pre- diction | Adjective Check | Total Judging[a] |
|---|---|---|---|---|---|---|
| Trait Rating Total | — |  |  |  |  |  |
| Behavior Postdiction | .30 | — |  |  |  |  |
| Sentence Completion | .48 | .47 | — |  |  |  |
| Opinion Prediction | .52 | .50 | .47 | — |  |  |
| Adjective Check | .65 | .24 | .58 | .54 | — |  |
| Total Judging[a] | .63 | .44 | .63 | .65 | .66 | — |
| $r\ .05 = .27$ |  |  |  | $r\ .01 = .35$ |  |  |

[a] Part-whole correlations corrected for the contribution of the part.

TABLE X

INTERCORRELATIONS AMONG JUDGING MEASURES FOR UTAH STATE (MENTAL) HOSPITAL STAFF

($N = 62$)

|  | Behavior Postdiction | Trait Rating | Adjective Check | Total Judging[a] |
|---|---|---|---|---|
| Behavior Postdiction | — | .50 | .22 | .42 |
| Trait Rating |  | — | .36 | .48 |
| Adjective Check |  |  | — | .31 |
| Total Judging Score |  |  |  | — |
| $r\ .05 = .25$ |  |  | $r\ .01 = .33$ |  |

[a] Part-whole correlations corrected for the contribution of the part.

Rating Total score (where Trait Rating is a difference score judging instrument susceptible to a Cronbach-type component analysis, and the Trait Rating Total score is the global unanalyzed measure), its various components, and four other entirely different types of judging instruments (Behavior Postdiction, Sentence Completion, Opinion Prediction, and Adjective Check—none of which were susceptible to a component analysis), plus a final Total Judging score, combining scores on all five instruments (through conversion to standard scores).

The conclusions drawn from these studies and data were that the evidence indicated that a general, global ability to judge others accurately could be meaningfully measured. However, the data in Table XIV suggested that this global ability involved a complicated dynamic process, or, more precisely, a factorially complex process that helped to clarify what was general in the global measure. Stereotype Accuracy appeared to

TABLE XI

INTERCORRELATIONS AMONG JUDGING MEASURES FOR UTAH STATE (MENTAL) HOSPITAL PATIENTS

$(N = 56)$

|  | Behavior Postdiction | Trait Rating | Adjective Check | Total Judging[a] |
|---|---|---|---|---|
| Behavior Postdiction | — | .41 | .32 | .42 |
| Trait Rating |  | — | .30 | .44 |
| Adjective Check |  |  | — | .31 |
| Total Judging |  |  |  | — |
| $r \ .05 = .26$ |  |  | $r \ .01 = .31$ |  |

[a] Part-whole correlation corrected for the contribution of the part.

TABLE XII

INTERCORRELATIONS AMONG JUDGING MEASURES FOR UNIVERSITY OF UTAH STUDENTS USING 20-FILM FORM

$(N = 23)$

|  | Behavior Postdiction | Trait Rating | Adjective Check |
|---|---|---|---|
| Behavior Postdiction | — | .36 | .09 |
| Trait Rating |  | — | .06 |
| Adjective Check |  |  | — |
| $r \ .05 = .40$ |  | $r \ .01 = .51$ |  |

account for a large portion of this generality. However, after this component was eliminated, considerable generality remained, which appeared to be related mainly to the Differential Accuracy component. Thus these two components were to some degree independent. It appeared that one might be an accurate judge because one has an accurate stereotype or because one is able to predict specific differences between individuals or both. Bronfenbrenner et al. (1958) came to a nearly identical conclusion using quite different research procedures. They referred to the two components as "Sensitivity to the Generalized Other" and "Interpersonal Sensitivity" (or Stereotype Accuracy and Differential Accuracy in Cronbach's terminology).

It would appear paradoxical (or inappropriate) to conclude both that judging ability is general and that at the same time it consists of two relatively independent components. However it is probable that these seemingly conflicting conclusions mean that the ability to judge others

TABLE XIII

INTERCORRELATIONS AMONG JUDGING MEASURES FOR UNIVERSITY OF UTAH STUDENTS USING NINE-FILM FORM

$(N = 26)$

| | Behavior Post-diction | Sentence Com-pletion | Opinion Pre-diction | Adjec-tive Check I | Adjec-tive Check II | Trait Rating I | Trait Rating II |
|---|---|---|---|---|---|---|---|
| Behavior Postdiction | — | .12 | —.20 | .04 | .01 | —.20 | .06 |
| Sentence Completion | | — | .20 | .13 | .44 | .32 | .08 |
| Opinion Prediction | | | — | .26 | .42 | .26 | .16 |
| Adjective Check I (no. of adjectives correctly predicted) | | | | — | .41 | .00 | .19 |
| Adjective Check II (% adjectives correctly predicted) | | | | | — | .29 | .18 |
| Trait Rating I[a] (sum of difference scores where criterion is 5 friends' ratings of "other") | | | | | | — | .50 |
| Trait Rating[a] (sum of difference scores where criterion is the "other's" self ratings) | | | | | | | — |
| $r\ .05 = .38$ | | | | | $r\ .01 = .49$ | | |

[a] Signs of correlations have been changed so that they are consistent with other judging instruments.

accurately is factorially complex and that the independent components reflect this complexity. It is, therefore, still meaningful to talk about a general trait. There are numerous precedents for this in the history of psychology. For example, intelligence, which has been demonstrated to consist of several independent components, is still treated as a meaningful general trait. In investigations of intelligence, even those studies indicating a $G$ factor have typically also shown several independent group factors.

One possible criticism of the above research would relate to the

TABLE XIV

CORRELATIONS BETWEEN TRAIT RATING COMPONENTS AND OTHER JUDGING MEASURES

$(N = 50)$

| Measures | Elevation | Differential Elevation | Stereotype Accuracy | Differential Accuracy | Trait Rating Total Score[a] |
|---|---|---|---|---|---|
| Elevation | — | | | | |
| Differential Elevation | .12 | — | | | |
| Stereotype Accuracy | .04 | .01 | — | | |
| Differential Accuracy | .29 | .29 | .16 | — | |
| Trait Rating Total Score[a] | .25 | .24 | .16 | .25 | — |
| Behavior Postdiction | —.05 | —.23 | .66 | .01 | .30 |
| Sentence Completion | —.20 | .08 | .60 | .25 | .48 |
| Opinion Prediction | .20 | .00 | .59 | .28 | .52 |
| Adjective Check | .05 | .23 | .44 | .56 | .65 |
| Total Judging (All Instrument) | .16 | .10 | .76 | .53 | .63 |
| M | .1015 | .1162 | .7704 | 1.4392 | 2.4273 |
| σ | .1154 | .0589 | .3911 | .5759 | .8139 |
| $r\ .05 = .27$ | | | $r\ .01 = .35$ | | |

[a] The correlations between the various components and the *Trait Rating* Total Score involve the total score with the contribution of the particular component under consideration eliminated. In computing the correlations between these component scores and the *(all instrument)* Total Judging score, however, it proved to be impossible to eliminate the contribution of the particular component under consideration, since the components represent the relative contribution of these components to the variance accuracy.

TABLE XV

RELIABILITIES OF JUDGING INSTRUMENTS

| | 5 Films vs. 5 films $N = 50$ | 10 Films vs. 10 films $N = 20$ | 6 Films only, $N = 149$[a] |
|---|---|---|---|
| Trait Rating | .72 | .81 | .60 |
| Behavior Postdiction | .66 | | .37 |
| Sentence Completion | .67 | | — |
| Opinion Prediction | .67 | | .59 |
| Adjective Check | .79 | | .61 |
| Total Judging | .71 | | .54 |

[a] Reliabilities for Behavior Postdiction, Opinion Prediction, and Adjective Check are computed by Kuder Richardson Formula 21. Trait Rating Reliability is a Spearman–Brown Coefficient based on the first three films—second three films split. Total Judging reliability was estimated using the formula presented by Mosier (1943).

possibility that the generality obtained was due to real similarity between persons judged. This view would suggest that the selection of the films on the basis of their discrimination of good judges from poor, as was done in this research, would result in a selection of films in which the "others" or interviewers were more similar to one another than they were to the "others" in the eliminated films.

In order to check this possibility, a special key was prepared for the Trait Rating, based on the mean rating on each trait of the criterion scores of the 10 films included in the study. Then an "Index of Similarity" was computed for each of the 10 best films included and for each of the 10 films eliminated on the basis of the earlier pilot study by scoring the *criterion* ratings for each film against this special key. The two groups of films were then compared with regard to this Index. The results of this comparison ($t = 1.694$, $df = 18$) fail to support a significant difference between the groups of films in this respect. The small "chance" difference that does occur, however, is in the expected direction. Generality of judging ability to the extent found in this study cannot, therefore, be explained on the basis of real similarity to one another of the persons judged.

### D. RELATIONSHIP BETWEEN THE SCORING SYSTEM AND COMPONENTS

In Cline and Richard's early research it appeared that Cronbach's Stereotype Accuracy and Differential Accuracy components were going to provide a way out of the methodological morass in which most research had bogged down. However, additional work with Stereotype Accuracy and Differential Elevation demonstrated empirically that differences in the scoring system could spuriously increase, reduce, or even eliminate them, making Differential Accuracy difficult or impossible to interpret and generating misleading conclusions. Therefore a new measure termed "Interpersonal Accuracy" was developed (Richards and Cline, 1963) in the following manner.

Preliminary consideration of the components problem led to the development of a Belief-Values Inventory which required the judge to predict "other's" responses to 12 Likert-type items dealing with religious beliefs and values. The following is a sample item:

When in doubt, I have found it best to stop and ask God for guidance.

> A. Strongly agree
> B. Agree
> C. Neither agree nor disagree
> D. Disagree
> E. Strongly disagree

In the filmed interview the "other" had been asked direct questions about his attitudes toward religion.

Subsequent research with this instrument indicated that the scoring system had a differential effect upon the components involved in a Cronbach-type analysis. With items of the type included in the Belief-Values Inventory, there are two possible scoring methods. The first of these is to score "Strongly Agree" as 1, "Agree" as 2, etc., without regard to whether or not on that particular item, "Strongly Agree" is a pro-religious answer. The second possible scoring system is to score the most conventional proreligious response as 1, regardless of whether that answer is "Strongly Agree" or "Strongly Disagree." If the first of these scoring systems is used, the Stereotype Accuracy variance is large, but the Differential Elevation variance is made artificially small. On the other hand, if the second of these scoring systems is used, the Stereotype Accuracy variance is artificially reduced, while the Differential Elevation variance is maximized. These effects are illustrated by Table XVI, which presents the responses of three hypothetical persons to items of this type, with each item score presented in both of the two scoring systems. In Table XVI, the first hypothetical person always answered with the most conventional religious answer; the second hypothetical person always answered with the second most conventional religious answer, and the third hypothetical person always gave the middle or neutral response. In this table the consistency of responding by each person is, of course, somewhat exaggerated to make the point clear.

In addition to the effects of the scoring system on the variance of Stereotype Accuracy and Differential Elevation, several other things are apparent from Table XVI. If these three hypothetical persons were used as "others" in the films and the first scoring system were used (i.e., where "Strongly Agree" is always scored as 1, regardless of religious direction), no matter what degree of accuracy a judge attained in predicting their responses, the Differential Elevation correlation component could take no other value than .00. The Differential Elevation correlation term could have no relationship to other measures of judgment and might compel the erroneous conclusion that there is no generality of judging ability. Use of the second scoring system (i.e., where the most proreligious response is always scored 1 regardless of whether it is "Strongly Agree" or "Strongly Disagree") has a similar effect on the Stereotype Accuracy correlation and again could lead to an invalid conclusion that there is no generality of judging ability. It will also be seen from Table XVI that, if the first scoring system were used in a study of judging ability, Differential Elevation and also Elevation would reflect primarily the extent to which judges interpreted items in the same way as the "others," but

TABLE XVI

COMPARISONS OF RESPONSES OF THREE HYPOTHETICAL PERSONS TO BELIEF-VALUES-INVENTORY-TYPE ITEMS USING TWO DIFFERENT SCORING SYSTEMS[a]

| Inventory item | A | B | C | Stereotype Accuracy $M$ |
|---|---|---|---|---|
| | | Scores of three hypothetical people (A, B, C) when Strongly Agree is always scored 1 | | |
| I believe in God. | 1 (Strongly Agree) | 2 (Agree) | 3 (Neither | 2 |
| Religion is nonsense. | 5 (Strongly Disagree) | 4 (Disagree) | 3 Agree | 4 |
| Prayers are answered | 1 (Strongly Agree) | 2 (Agree) | 3 nor | 2 |
| All churches should be closed. | 5 (Strongly Disagree) | 4 (Disagree) | 3 Disagree) | 4 |
| Differential Elevation $M$ | 3 | 3 | 3 | |

| Inventory item | A | B | C | Stereotype Accuracy $M$ |
|---|---|---|---|---|
| | | Scores of three hypothetical people (A, B, C) when the most proreligious answer is always scored 1 | | |
| I believe in God. | 1 (Strongly Agree) | 2 (Agree) | 3 (Neither | 2 |
| Religion is nonsense. | 1 (Strongly Disagree) | 2 (Disagree) | 3 Agree | 2 |
| Prayers are answered. | 1 (Strongly Agree) | 2 (Agree) | 3 nor | 2 |
| All churches should be closed. | 1 (Strongly Disagree) | 2 (Disagree) | 3 Disagree) | 2 |
| Differential Elevation $M$ | 1 | 2 | 3 | |

[a] Note: Person A always responds in the most conventional proreligious fashion. Person B responds in the second most proreligious manner (i.e., "Agree" instead of "Strongly Agree," and "Disagree" instead of "Strongly Disagree" where appropriate). Person C always chooses the neutral middle category, "Neither Agree nor Disagree."

that, if the second scoring system were used, Differential Elevation would be a measure of the judges' "sensitivity to individual differences" in over-all religiosity, and Elevation would be a measure of the judged average religiosity of the group of "others." Thus, the apparent paradox in Cronbach's formulation is resolved. All of this, taken together, strongly suggests that in investigations of accuracy of person perception, and particularly of its generality, neither of these scoring systems is by itself satisfactory, but rather that the first scoring system should be used in computing Stereotype Accuracy and its components and the second scoring system should be used in computing Differential Elevation and its components. It should be emphasized that, in the hypothetical example, the items differed greatly in their over-all degree of religiosity. In studies of accuracy of interpersonal perception, both of these would be important and yet either one or the other would inevitably be artificially eliminated if either scoring system alone were used.

These two scoring systems also have another effect which is not readily apparent in the hypothetical example since it eliminates all the persons-by-items interaction that would occur in a real problem. This effect is that the Differential Accuracy component and its correlation and variance constituents will all take on different values depending on which scoring system is used, and there is apparently no criterion which would indicate in a real problem which of these values are the most appropriate measures of judging ability. This indicated that under certain circumstances none of the values of Differential Accuracy and its constituents are particularly good measures of judging ability. Thus it was replaced with the new index of judging ability called Interpersonal Accuracy.

There is no difference score form of this measure; it consists only of a correlation term and a variance term. The correlation term is computed by determining the correlation between each judge's predicted values and the corresponding actual responses by "others" on individual items and then averaging across items (without converting these scores in terms of their discrepancy from item and person means as is the case with Differential Accuracy). Similarly, the Interpersonal Accuracy variance term involves the computation of the variance of each judge's predictions on individual items, averaged across items. In terms of Cronbach's scheme, it appears to be a linear combination of Differential Elevation and Differential Accuracy. It offers the strong advantage over other measures that it is invariant under changes of scoring system.

There are several additional considerations in the interpretation of the hypothetical example mentioned above. The first of these is that there is a strong general "religiosity" factor underlying the questions.

In Cronbach's scheme, this general factor should be tapped by the Differential Elevation component, and this does occur under the scoring system in which the conventional religious answer is always scored 1. It might be objected, therefore, that the scoring system in which "Strongly Agree" is always scored 1 "randomizes" this general factor. This effect of this scoring system is, however, exactly the point of the hypothetical example; and it should be emphasized again that the scoring system in which "Strongly Agree" is always scored 1 is the only scoring system which permits the real differences in the average degree of endorsement of the items (Stereotype Accuracy) to appear. It should also be noted that the nature of the questions presented in the hypothetical example was intentionally made such as to emphasize the inappropriateness of this scoring system for the Differential Elevation component. It is a more usual procedure in studies of person perception to use rather heterogeneous groups of personality traits as items, and, as Cronbach points out, the assignment of scores to such items is frequently arbitrary. As a result, if such items are used, the scoring system will still have the effects outlined above, but in such complex and confusing patterns as to make the various component scores almost wholly uninterpretable (with the possible exception of the Total score). The fact that there is a strong general factor in the hypothetical example would contribute greatly to the clarity of interpretation of the Interpersonal Accuracy component, and the author is in agreement with Cronbach's position that several factorially pure sets of items analyzed separately are preferable to one factorially complex set of items treated in a global fashion.

If the argument is accepted to this point, it is still an open question whether the considerations outlined have any practical effect on investigations of accuracy of person perception. A study providing some information with regard to this point has been conducted. In this research 46 undergraduates, both male and female, at the University of Utah, predicted the responses of six standard "others," presented through the filmed interview procedure, on the Belief-Values Inventory. Details of the experimental procedure of using these filmed interviews are presented elsewhere (Cline and Richards, 1960). The predictions of these judges were scored twice against the criterion, once with each of the two scoring systems discussed above, and the various judgment scores intercorrelated. When this program is used all correlation terms are expressed in terms of Fisher's z. Results of both of these analyses are presented in Table XVII. In this table, correlations above the diagonal were obtained when "Strongly Agree" was always scored 1 regardless of whether or not it represented a proreligious answer, and correlations below the diagonal were obtained when the most conventional proreligious answer was

TABLE XVII

INTERCORRELATIONS OF BELIEF-VALUES INVENTORY COMPONENTS FOR EACH OF TWO SCORING SYSTEMS[a]

| | Total | Elevation | Differential Elevation | Stereotype Accuracy | Differential Elevation z[b] | Stereotype Accuracy z | Interpersonal Accuracy z | Differential Elevation σ² | Stereotype Accuracy σ² | Interpersonal Accuracy σ² |
|---|---|---|---|---|---|---|---|---|---|---|
| Total[c] | | .00 | .24 | .37 | .21 | .72 | .84 | −.40 | .46 | .07 |
| Elevation | .55 | | .03 | −.11 | −.06 | −.07 | .11 | .03 | −.16 | .18 |
| Differential Elevation | .38 | .36 | | .13 | .80 | .06 | .30 | −.41 | .08 | −.20 |
| Stereotype Accuracy | .01 | .11 | −.17 | | .06 | .95 | .56 | −.15 | .58 | .35 |
| Differential Elevation z | .67 | .46 | .80 | .01 | | .05 | .25 | .06 | .08 | −.03 |
| Stereotype Accuracy z | .19 | .02 | .05 | .53 | .18 | | .51 | .10 | .45 | .32 |
| Interpersonal Accuracy z | .84 | .62 | .72 | .08 | .86 | .23 | | −.16 | .37 | .33 |
| Differential Elevation σ² | .28 | .42 | −.07 | .21 | .33 | .26 | .25 | | .06 | .47 |
| Stereotype Accuracy σ² | −.11 | −.17 | .22 | −.71 | .10 | .17 | .05 | −.10 | | .40 |
| Interpersonal Accuracy σ² | .07 | .33 | −.21 | .20 | .22 | .22 | .33 | .96 | −.13 | |

[a] Note: Correlations above the diagonal were obtained when Strongly Agree was always scored 1, and correlations below the diagonal were obtained when the most conventional religious answer was always scored 1. r .05 = .29; r .01 = .37.

[b] All z components are Fisher's z transformations of Pearson correlations.

[c] All correlations between Total and difference score components are corrected part-whole correlations.

always scored 1. On the basis of either of these two groups of correlations alone, one would have to conclude that there is no consistent pattern of generality in judging ability, particularly as reflected in the three correlation measures, but rather that there appear to be two relatively independent factors measured respectively by the Differential Elevation correlation term and the Stereotype Accuracy correlation term, thus confirming the previous results of Bronfenbrenner and his associates (1958) and Cline and Richards (1960).

A further analysis of these data was made, however, in which judgment scores were intercorrelated across scoring systems in such a way that each component was scored most appropriately. More specifically, Stereotype Accuracy and its correlation and variance terms were computed using the scoring system where "Strongly Agree" was always scored 1, and Differential Elevation and its components and Elevation were computed using the scoring system where the most proreligious answer was always scored 1. Results are presented in Table XVIII. In this table, there is a consistent pattern of a significant degree of generality across the correlation terms of all components, thus suggesting that judging ability is, to some degree, a general trait.

These results indicate that the scoring system may be an important artifact in investigations of the generality question when components of accuracy scores are used, and therefore strongly support the argument advanced in the hypothetical example discussed earlier, though it is still most important to avoid overgeneralization from these results.

### E. Effect of Varied Stimulus Information on Judging-Accuracy Scores

The next focus was on the fate of the various components when the amount of information about the stimulus person or "other" is systematically increased.

Using the Belief-Values Inventory (judging instrument) and the standard set of six filmed interviews, one group of 95 judges made their judgments on the basis of seeing and hearing the filmed interviews and were termed the full information group. A second group consisted of 50 persons who filled out the Belief-Values Inventory without seeing the films at all, only knowing the age, sex, marital status, and number of children of the six stimulus persons. The third group consisted of 58 judges who filled out the same inventory only twice, once as they thought it would apply to a typical American adult male and once for a typical adult American female. Thus, in these last two groups the judges were required to make judgments solely on the basis of stereotypes, though these stereotypes differed in the amount of information on which they

TABLE XVIII

INTERCORRELATIONS OF BELIEF-VALUES INVENTORY COMPONENTS WHEN EACH COMPONENT IS SCORED APPROPRIATELY[a]

| | Total | Elevation | Differential Elevation | Stereotype Accuracy | Differential Elevation z | Stereotype Accuracy z | Interpersonal Accuracy z | Differential Elevation $\sigma^2$ | Stereotype Accuracy $\sigma^2$ | Interpersonal Accuracy $\sigma^2$ |
|---|---|---|---|---|---|---|---|---|---|---|
| Total[b] | | | | | | | | | | |
| Elevation | .55 | | | | | | | | | |
| Differential Elevation | .38 | .36 | | | | | | | | |
| Stereotype Accuracy | .37 | .93 | .25 | | | | | | | |
| Differential Elevation z | .67 | .46 | .80 | .40 | | | | | | |
| Stereotype Accuracy z | .72 | .82 | .22 | .95 | .38 | | | | | |
| Interpersonal Accuracy z | .84 | .62 | .72 | .56 | .86 | .51 | | | | |
| Differential Elevation $\sigma^2$ | .28 | .42 | −.07 | .48 | .33 | .43 | .25 | | | |
| Stereotype Accuracy $\sigma^2$ | .46 | .70 | .18 | .58 | .26 | .45 | .37 | .48 | | |
| Interpersonal Accuracy $\sigma^2$ | .07 | .33 | −.21 | .35 | .22 | .32 | .33 | .96 | .40 | |

[a] Note: All z components are Fisher's z transformations of Pearson correlations.  $r$ .05 = .29; $r$ .01 = .37.

[b] All correlations between Total and difference score components are corrected part-whole correlations.

were based. The results (see Richards, Cline, and Rardin, 1962) for the Interpersonal Accuracy z and Total Error score indicated that the judges in the "full information" group were significantly superior both at rank ordering the stimulus persons in terms of conventional religious values *and* at predicting exactly the responses of these same stimulus persons. Results for Interpersonal Accuracy variance indicated that differentiation among stimulus persons increased as the amount of information provided about them increased. Contrary to what would be expected, Stereotype Accuracy z varied significantly among the three groups while Stereotype Accuracy variance decreased as the amount of information increased. This probably indicates that Stereotype Accuracy is a measure of considerable complexity and contrary to previous opinion probably involves some degree of sensitivity to individual persons. Additional research is needed on this point.

### F. Components of Judging-Accuracy Scores Applied to the Clinical *versus* Statistical Prediction Controversy

A controversy relevant to some of the basic issues in interpersonal perception relates to clinical *versus* statistical prediction. Meehl (1955) in surveying all studies extant in which the relative predictive accuracies of clinical and actuarial techniques were compared concluded that no published study indicated a clear superiority for clinical procedures. More recently, Holt (1958) has suggested that these conclusions resulted from the fact that the studies on which they were based involved kinds of predictions to which actuarial procedures are better suited than are clinical procedures. Richards (1963) has suggested a conceptual scheme to clarify this issue using a modification (Cline and Richards, 1960) of the analytic model for person perception scores developed by Cronbach (1955).

Cline and Richards (1962) conducted an empirical study to compare the clinician and the actuary, using a component analysis of the judging accuracy scores. They argued that in investigations of predictive accuracy using the component method of analysis, Interpersonal Accuracy, and particularly its correlation subscores, is the most appropriate measure of sensitivity to individual differences. Cronbach states that Stereotype Accuracy is not a measure of this type of sensitivity, but rather of the accuracy of prediction of the norm for the group of persons about whom the predictions are made (and, in some circumstances, for people in general). It may be argued that while all components are important, the central goal of "real life" clinical prediction is to achieve accuracy on components measuring sensitivity to individual differences. On the other hand, as Richards (1963) points out, the accuracy of actuarial prediction can only be due to the fact that actuarial tables have an accurate stereotype. Since this is the case, studies which indicate that actuarial prediction is superior to clinical prediction must indicate that actuarial tables have a more accurate stereotype than clinicians do; in other words, a higher score on the Stereotype Accuracy correlation term. This has been demonstrated in research (Halbrower, 1955) cited by Meehl (1956) to support his position.

On those components measuring "sensitivity to individual differences," however, actuarial prediction is at an inherent disadvantage in that it must predict all members of a given class of persons to have obtained the same score. On those components, therefore, any accuracy achieved by actuarial procedures must be due to differences between classes. The clinician has no such restriction on his predictions: he can easily predict differences within classes, thus increasing the range and thereby his possible accuracy on components measuring sensitivity to individual differences. It is obvious that if he does predict differences within classes, it may either increase or decrease his accuracy. However, the author knows of no reason to suppose that it would always result in a decrease, and concludes that in any given case it is an empirical question whether accuracy is increased or decreased.

Much of the above was, of course, recognized explicitly by Meehl in his original book, but he could find no evidence that the clinician's greater freedom resulted in greater accuracy. Probably two factors account for this. The first of these is that no studies of clinical *versus* statistical prediction have made either an explicit or implicit comparison of the various components of accuracy scores. This is not a criticism, since no such analytic scheme was available at the time most of these studies were conducted. The second major reason for Meehl's findings was, in the opinion of Cline and Richards, that many, or most, studies comparing clinical and statistical prediction have used measures which reflect mainly Stereotype Accuracy, which would favor the actuarial procedures. This is particularly clear in the case of the "$Q$ correlation," which is commonly used in studies of clinical prediction. $Q$ correlation is a within-persons correlation and is therefore based on differences between items. Differences between items, however, are defined as Stereotype Accuracy both in Cronbach's model and in the author's modified model.

On the basis of the rationale outlined above, Cline and Richards developed two hypotheses for the application of this scheme of analysis into component scores to the clinical *versus* statistical prediction studies. These hypotheses were that (1) in all studies using an acceptable actuarial prediction procedure, actuarial prediction will be superior to clinical on the Stereotype Accuracy correlation component; and (2) in some such studies clinical prediction will be superior to actuarial on the Interpersonal Accuracy correlation subscore. The purpose of the present study was to obtain data illustrating the use of component scores in a study of clinical *versus* statistical prediction, and to demonstrate that it is possible to obtain results favoring actuarial prediction on many of the commonly used measures of accuracy, but favoring clinical prediction on Interpersonal Accuracy.

It is true, of course, that the accuracy of actuarial prediction on Interpersonal Accuracy can always be increased by more and more accurate division into classes of persons. This, however, does not invalidate the basic argument, since it would still be an open question whether or not the accuracy of actuarial prediction on this component could be increased with reasonable economy to a level equal to or higher than the accuracy of clinical prediction. Most actuarial prediction procedures have used relatively crude classifications, achieved with considerable effort.

In this study the Ss were 56 students, male and female, from undergraduate psychology classes at the University of Utah. While it is hazardous to generalize from such a population of naïve untrained students to a population of highly trained clinical psychologists, this is a conservative error, likely to penalize clinical prediction. If this is the case, then any superiority over actuarial prediction found for these judges can be generalized to trained clinicians.

In this research, the "clinical predictions" were made after the Ss had seen sound color movies of brief interviews of six different persons. These films were selected from a large group of 25 films on the basis of procedures resembling item analysis which are reported in detail elsewhere (Cline and Richards, 1960). The six films used presented the interviews of three males and three females, and the persons interviewed were selected so that they were diverse in age and background. With particular regard to the present research, they were selected so that they were heterogeneous in their self-reported acceptance of conventional religious beliefs and practices. The filmed interviews included direct questions about views on religion.

The task for Ss in this experiment was to fill out one judging instrument, the Belief-Values Inventory, as they thought the persons who were interviewed in the films had filled it out. The Belief-Values Inventory consisted, as previously mentioned, of Likert-type items dealing with personal values in the religion area. There were 12 items for each of the six films, and the same 12 were used for every film.

Six scores for each S were computed on the basis of this instrument. Five of these were Total Error Score, Stereotype Accuracy z, Stereotype Accuracy variance, Interpersonal Accuracy z, and Interpersonal Accuracy variance. In the present study, the Interpersonal Accuracy $z$ score measured primarily the success with which these six persons were rank ordered in terms of their over-all "religiosity."

The sixth score calculated on the basis of the Belief-Values Inventory is called $Q$-$Z$, still another expression of correlation in terms of Fisher's $z$. In determining the value of this score for a given judge, the responses to the items predicted by the judge for each of the six persons in the films were correlated with corresponding actual responses for the six persons individually. In other words, it is a "within persons" correlation, highly similar to correlations based on $Q$ sorts. These correlations were then converted to Fisher's $z$ and averaged across the six persons. This score was used in this study because it corresponds closely to a common measure of accuracy of clinical prediction, and therefore makes possible comparisons between the present research and earlier studies of the clinical and statistical prediction problem.

At the start of each judging session, the $S$s filled out forms, dealing with necessary background information, after which the film of the first interview was shown. The projector was stopped, and the $S$s made their predictions or judgments about the first film. As soon as all $S$s completed their judgments, the film of the second interview was shown. This procedure was repeated until all six films had been shown and all judgments completed.

In previous studies comparing clinical and statistical prediction a variety of methods had been used. What these methods appear to have in common is the establishment of norms for some group or set of subgroups and then the derivation of predictions about members of an independent group. Meehl (1955) has suggested a further requirement, that both prediction procedures use exactly the same information, but Estes (1961) has pointed out that none of the studies cited by Meehl actually met this requirement. This "defect" did not prevent Meehl from deriving important and legitimate conclusions, and therefore should not prevent other investigators from deriving important and legitimate conclusions from similar studies.

This implies that the most appropriate procedure to use for statistical prediction in this study would be to establish norms for the Values-Belief Inventory on the basis of an independent group and use these norms in predicting the responses of the smaller set of persons appearing in these filmed interviews. Accordingly, the following procedure was used. The group used in defining the norms consisted of 56 persons who were interviewed and filmed at two different periods during the course of the author's on-going research project on interpersonal perception. The 56 films did not, of course, include the six used in the present research. On the basis of a "total religiosity" score on the Belief-Values Inventory, these films were divided into two groups on the basis of a median split, one "high" on religiosity (i.e., above the median) and one "low." The "total religiosity" score is defined as the sum of the scores on the 12 Belief-Values Inventory items when the scoring is adjusted so that a high score on each item represents acceptance of conventional religion. Norms were then computed for each of these two groups by averaging the responses of persons falling into each group to the 12 Belief-Values Inventory items.

The next step was to compute the "total religiosity" score for the six films used in the present research. The responses of the six persons appearing in the films were then "predicted" from the norm groups by determining if their individual "total religiosity" score would have placed them above or below the median of the norm group, and predicting that they had responded with the appropriate 12 average responses. Two of the persons used in this research fell above the median, and four fell below the median. It would appear that the information used by the actuarial prediction procedure is equivalent to that used by the clinical prediction procedure, although it is not identical.

There is one important thing that should be noted about this procedure: this is, if a group of similar studies were conducted, the scores for statistical prediction would be subject to sampling variation. Unfortunately, it is impossible to estimate what this variation would be and use it in statistical tests of significance of difference between clinical prediction and statistical prediction. This makes it necessary that the statistical test used be the $t$ test for significance of deviation from a point of value (McNemar, 1955), with the error estimate involving only variation in clinical predictions (i.e., variation among judges). It should be emphasized that this is not a conservative error, since it would result in rejecting a true null hypothesis too often. Accordingly, it was decided to require the .01 level of significance before rejecting the null hypothesis rather than the conventional .05 level. All $t$ tests reported in this study are two-tail tests.

The comparisons between clinical prediction and the actuarial prediction procedure on the six scores used in this study are presented in Table XIX. The results of these comparisons indicate that clinical prediction was significantly poorer on the Total Error Score, the $Q$-$Z$ score, and the Stereotype Accuracy correlation term, but was significantly superior to statistical prediction on the Interpersonal Accuracy correlation score. The results of these comparisons can be summarized as indicating that the statistical prediction procedure had a more accurate "stereotype" than did the $S$s who made the "clinical" judgments, but that the "clinician" $S$s were more successful than the statistical prediction procedure in judging differences among persons. The comparison of the procedures on the variance components as expected indicates that the clinicians differentiated much more among persons than did the actuarial procedure. These results, taken together, reveal a complex pattern not reflected in the global Total Error Score, and thus strongly support the usefulness of component scores analysis in studies of clinical and statistical prediction. This suggests that the present research may be generalized to other such studies.

TABLE XIX

COMPARISON OF CLINICAL AND STATISTICAL PREDICTION ON COMPONENTS OF ACCURACY SCORES[a]

| Score | Clinical prediction mean ($N = 56$) | Standard error of mean | Statistical prediction score | $t$ | $p$ |
|---|---|---|---|---|---|
| Total error score | 1.22 | .0334 | .61 | 18.26 | .001 |
| Stereotype Accuracy $Z$ | 1.09 | .0494 | 2.09 | 20.24 | .001 |
| Stereotype Accuracy variance | .45 | .0267 | .39 | 2.25 | NS |
| Interpersonal Accuracy $Z$ | .89 | .0227 | .73 | 7.05 | .001 |
| Interpersonal Accuracy variance | 1.20 | .0601 | .45 | 12.48 | .001 |
| $Q$-$Z$ | .82 | .0251 | .89 | 2.79 | .01 |

[a] Note: Owing to the fact that no estimate of the sampling variation in statistical prediction is available, the statistical tests would reject a true null hypothesis too often. Therefore, a $p > .01$ rather than $> .05$ in the significance tests is required.

One purpose of this research was to demonstrate that it is possible to obtain results favoring actuarial prediction on many of the commonly used measures of accuracy, but also favoring clinical prediction on Interpersonal Accuracy, and this goal has clearly been achieved. While the results of the present study should not be overgeneralized, they should not be undergeneralized either. In particular, this statistical prediction procedure, while limited, is comparable to those used in many, or most, previous studies of clinical and statistical prediction.

In addition, the present research clearly suggests that, contrary to common opinion among clinicians, the activity at which clinicians are most likely to exceed the actuary is not making predictions about a "unique individual." This does not mean that there are no dramatic instances in which a clinician makes successful predictions about a single individual by deviating markedly from actuarial expectancy, but rather that if the average clinician's major activity is making predictions within individual persons, his average accuracy will at best be equal to and at worst considerably less than the accuracy of statistical prediction since his stereotype tends to be less accurate. On the other hand, the present research does suggest that the most appropriate activity for clinicians is predicting differences among persons who are grouped into the same class by statistical prediction, and it is easy to suggest many ordinary activities of clinicians that are of this type. An example of this might be a mental hospital in which 10 patients had roughly the same statistically derived "predicted benefit from psychotherapy" scores, but which had such a limited staff that only three of these patients could actually be given psychotherapy. The results of this study suggest that the clinician might be quite successful in picking the three "best bets" although all 10 had been given an "equal" rating by the statistical prediction procedure.

### G. Comparisons of Groups versus Individuals in Making Judgments about Others

A question with a somewhat different direction—whether a group of people can collectively make more accurate judgments than a single individual—was asked. The rationale of this experiment (Cline and Richards, 1961) grew out of the recent survey of studies comparing group performance and individual performance made by Lorge, Fox, Davitz, and Brenner (1958). The general conclusion of this survey was that a group, on almost any task, will perform better than a typical individual, but not necessarily better than a superior individual on the task in question. This finding is true whether the "group performance" is made by a genuine group or is merely a statistical combination of several independent individual performances. An unresolved question is the degree to which these findings can be attributed to a reduction in the variability of the group performance.

The trend of the studies cited in this survey suggested the hypothesis to be tested in this experiment. This hypothesis was the following:

The accuracy of predictions (about the behavior of other persons) made by a group of persons arriving at a consensus prediction through group discussion will be significantly greater than the average accuracy of the predictions made by the individuals composing the group. The average accuracy of the prediction made by the individuals composing the group will also be significantly less than the accuracy of an "artificial group" (composed of pooled independent judgments for each item) and also less than the accuracy of prediction of the best individual among the individuals composing the group.

A secondary question relates to the presence or absence of a consistent pattern of superiority in accuracy among predictions made by the best individual judges, consensus groups, and artificial groups composed of pooled independent judgments for each item.

The subjects were 186 students, both male and female, in the introductory psychology classes at the University of Utah. The procedure involved the presentation of six filmed interviews or "standard others."

In this study, two prediction instruments were used. The first of these was the Adjective Check (ACL), which required the subject to determine which of a pair of adjectives the interviewee had checked as being descriptive of himself. There were 20 such pairs for each of the six films, making a total of 120. The score on the ACL was the number correct. Thus the ACL is similar to a forced-choice rating procedure. The second instrument used was the Belief-Values Inventory (BVI), already discussed.

There were 12 BVI items for each film or interview. Several different scores were computed from judges' responses to this instrument using a program developed for the IBM 650 computer. The first of these was a total score, which was based on the average of the squared discrepancies (using the one-to-five point scale) between predicted responses by each judge for each interviewee, and actual responses of each interviewee. This is an error score and in order to make these scores comparable with other scores used in this study, the scores were converted to accuracy scores through a standard score transformation, setting the mean equal to 50 and standard deviation equal to 10.

The second two BVI scores are components of what Cronbach (1955) has called "Stereotype Accuracy": (a) correlation between each judge's predicted item means and obtained item means, converted to a Fisher's $z$, and (b) the variance of each judge's predicted means. Cronbach has demonstrated these two scores to be the two parameters in Stereotype Accuracy when the criterion is held constant, and they permit independent evaluation of the effect of grouping on accuracy and on variability of prediction in this study. The last two scores on the BVI are measures of Interpersonal Accuracy.

The 186 subjects in this experiment were divided into 62 three-person groups. The division was made at the time the experiment was conducted, and most groups consisted of three persons seated next to each other in the experimental room. Group composition in terms of sex of group members was roughly random. The Ss saw each film and then completed the judging instruments independently. Next, they joined together in a group discussion fashion and proceeded to arrive at a consensus judgment for the items on the judging instruments without referring back to their earlier independent judgments.

The "artificial group" judgment (pooled independent judgments for each item) was derived from the individual judgments of the group members. Thus, on the ACL, the artificial group judgment was determined on the basis of a "majority vote" of the judges on each item (by inspecting their individual judging protocols). On the BVI, it was calculated by determining the average of the values predicted by the three judges for each interviewee on each item. It is important to emphasize that this artificial group is only a statistical combination of the original independent judgments for each item.

The average accuracy of individuals composing the group was obtained by computing the mean of the total accuracy scores of the three individuals who made up each group. This is not the same as the artificial group procedure where the actual item-by-item predictions of the three group members were averaged rather than their total accuracy scores.

The best judge in each group was selected on the basis of his accuracy scores. In interpreting the results of this study, therefore, it is important to note that this selection was done on an after-the-fact basis, thus maximizing accuracy scores for this condition by capitalizing on chance. It would, therefore, be impossible for a best judge selected in advance to obtain a higher score than this, and such a best judge would, in fact, probably score somewhat lower, since some error would be involved in any advance selection. The best judges were selected independently for the ACL and the BVI and therefore were not necessarily the same person on the two different instruments. On the BVI, however, the best judges, selected on the basis of total score, were also used as best judges in making the comparisons involving the other scores derived from this instrument.

The mean and standard deviations for each judgment procedure on each judgment score are presented in Table XX. In Table XX, all scores are accuracy scores. Since total score on BVI is based on error score, in Table XX this judgment score is transformed to a standard score distribution with mean $= 50$ and standard deviation $= 10$.

As a first step in the statistical analysis of these data, over-all $F$ tests were calculated for each of the judgment scores separately. The results of this analysis are presented in Table XXI. No test for homogeneity of variance was made before calculation of these $F$ tests. This procedure was followed because the recent work of Boneau (1960) strongly suggests that $F$ is not significantly affected by heterogeneity of variance if the sample

## TABLE XX
### MEANS AND STANDARD DEVIATIONS OF JUDGMENT SCORES

|  | Average of individuals composing the group | Best judge | Three-person group consensus | Artificial group derived by pooling three independent judgments |
|---|---|---|---|---|
| Adjective Check List |  |  |  |  |
| $\overline{X}$ | 97.27 | 101.66 | 102.52 | 103.32 |
| $\sigma$ | 3.51 | 3.91 | 3.95 | 4.55 |
| Belief-Values Inventory Total |  |  |  |  |
| $\overline{X}$ | 43.29 | 53.92 | 49.47 | 52.87 |
| $\sigma$ | 8.61 | 8.31 | 11.16 | 8.02 |
| Stereotype Accuracy $z$ |  |  |  |  |
| $\overline{X}$ | 1.19 | 1.44 | 1.28 | 1.41 |
| $\sigma$ | .28 | .37 | .45 | .37 |
| Stereotype Accuracy variance |  |  |  |  |
| $\overline{X}$ | .35 | .40 | .31 | .30 |
| $\sigma$ | .14 | .22 | .15 | .13 |
| Interpersonal Accuracy $z$ |  |  |  |  |
| $\overline{X}$ | .90 | 1.01 | 1.00 | .98 |
| $\sigma$ | .12 | .14 | .16 | .15 |
| Interpersonal Accuracy variance |  |  |  |  |
| $\overline{X}$ | 1.09 | 1.06 | 1.06 | .91 |
| $\sigma$ | .23 | .28 | .31 | .25 |

## TABLE XXI
### RESULTS OF OVER-ALL $F$ TESTS FOR JUDGMENT SCORES

| Judgment score | Between-variance $(df = 3)$ | Within-variance $(df = 244)$ | $F$ |
|---|---|---|---|
| Adjective Check List Total | 451.82 | 13.82 | 32.62[a] |
| Belief-Values Inventory |  |  |  |
| Inventory total | 1423.02 | 84.33 | 16.87[a] |
| Stereotype Accuracy $z$ | .8633 | .1432 | 6.03[a] |
| Stereotype Accuracy variance | .1333 | .0282 | 4.72[b] |
| Interpersonal Accuracy $z$ | .1633 | .0213 | 7.67[a] |
| Interpersonal Accuracy variance | .3900 | .0754 | 5.17[b] |

[a] $p > .01$.
[b] $p > .05$.

TABLE XXII

Tests for Significance of Difference Between Individual Means for Each Judgment Score[a]

| Judgment score | Average of individual vs. best judge | Average of individual vs. group consensus | Average of individual vs. artificial group | Best judge vs. group consensus | Best judge vs. artificial group | Group consensus vs. artificial group |
|---|---|---|---|---|---|---|
| Adjective Check List | | | | | | |
| Total | 4.39[b] | 5.25[b] | 6.05[b] | .86 | 1.66[c] | .80 |
| Belief-Values Inventory | | | | | | |
| Total | 10.63[b] | 6.18[b] | 9.58[b] | 4.45[b] | 1.05 | 3.40[c] |
| Stereotype Accuracy $z$ | .25[b] | .09 | .22[b] | .16[c] | .03 | .13[c] |
| Stereotype Accuracy variance | .05 | .04 | .05 | .09[b] | .10[b] | .01 |
| Interpersonal Accuracy $z$ | .11[b] | .10[b] | .08[b] | .01 | .03 | .02 |
| Interpersonal Accuracy variance | .03 | .03 | .18[b] | .00 | .15[b] | .15[b] |

[a] Note: Entries in this table represent the absolute difference between groups without regard to the direction of the difference.
[b] $p < .01$.
[c] $p < .05$.

sizes are identical and relatively large, i.e., 20. Both of these conditions hold in the present study. It is also known that available tests for homogeneity of variance are affected too much by other variables than that involved in the null hypothesis to justify their use prior to an analysis of variance (Box, 1953).

Since all of the $F$ tests in Table XXI are significant at or beyond the .01 level of confidence, a test for significance of difference between individual means was made. This test was made using the multiple range test (Li, 1957, p. 238), which is an appropriate procedure for making "post-mortem" type comparisons between individual means after an over-all $F$ test has been made. Briefly, the multiple range test involves computing a value which represents how large the difference between two means must be in order to be significant at a stated level, and then comparing the obtained difference to this value. Results of this analysis are summarized in Table XXII.

On each of the four accuracy measures, the best judge and both group judgments are significantly superior to the average of the individuals composing the group. Thus the major hypothesis of this experiment was confirmed. There is no consistent pattern of significant differences among the first three procedures mentioned above. As would be expected, on the two scores representing the amount of variability in predictions, the artificial group mean tends to be lower than the means of the other three procedures. This tendency is significant, however, only for the Interpersonal Accuracy variance score. It is somewhat surprising to find that the artificial group (or pooled independent judgments of items) is superior to the best judge on the ACL. The interpretation of this finding seems to be that if both other judges disagree with the best judge, they are more likely to be right than is the best judge. If, on the other hand, only one of the other judges disagrees with the best judge, he is more likely to be wrong than is the best judge.

This study clearly implies that satisfactory ratings are least likely to be obtained from a single unselected individual. In exploring further implications of these results for an operational rating setup, several other considerations enter. The first of these is that typically the best judge would be difficult to select on an *a priori* basis, and (because of selection error) best judges selected *a priori* would probably score lower than the best judges used in this study. Since each of the group procedures produces results roughly equivalent to those for the best judge selected on an after-the-fact basis, an extensive (and expensive) effort to identify best judges and use them as raters would appear to be unnecessary.

The second consideration involved in applying these results is that by far the most time in this experiment was consumed in arriving at consensus judgments through group discussion, a finding which one would certainly expect to generalize to other situations. Since the artificial group (or pooled independent judgments of items) procedure produced results as good as or better than the results produced by the consensus judgment, and required much less time, it would appear to be most appropriate when accuracy and time are both considered. Thus, the best procedure for using ratings in many applied situations would be to obtain several independent ratings from different raters for each ratee, and then combine these ratings statistically into a single rating. It should be noted, however, that the superiority of the artificial group in terms of time required (and therefore expense) might disappear if only a single summary rating were required rather than the many relatively specific judgments required by the experimental procedure used in this study.

A limitation to these conclusions is the fact that each rater in this experiment was basing his ratings on the same or identical information (i.e., seeing the same movies of the interviews). If different raters are basing their ratings on different information, some other procedure involving the sharing of this information might be superior.

In addition to the practical implications outlined above, these results present at least two more additions to previous psychological research. The first of these is the demonstration through both the Stereotype Accuracy correlation term and the Interpersonal Accuracy correlation term of the BVI that accuracy is increased through grouping independent of a reduction in variability (see Table XX). Unlike the other results of this experiment, this would not necessarily be expected on the basis of previous studies comparing group and individual performance, although it certainly is consistent with previous studies. The second major addition is related to the current controversy in the interpersonal perception literature over the relative merits of various different types of accuracy scores (Cronbach, 1955). In the current study the total score on the ACL, the total score on the BVI, and the Stereotype Accuracy and Interpersonal Accuracy correlation terms all gave consistent results and, more important, results which make sense in terms of previous research comparing group and individual performance.

## H. A Factor Analytic Study of the Interpersonal Accuracy Component

The Interpersonal Accuracy judging score component has been discussed previously and used in a variety of settings. As already mentioned the correlation term of this component is regarded as most closely related to what is ordinarily meant by accuracy of interpersonal perception. This term is computed by determining the correlation between predicted, or judged, scores on individual items, and then averaging across items after transforming the item correlations to Fisher's z values. Where a strong general factor underlies the items, such as religiosity, this component measures the extent to which the persons judged are rank ordered accurately on that factor. Review of the results of Cline and Richard's various studies of this component has proven them complex and at times confusing. While it has responded at the *group* differences level to experimental manipulation in meaningful ways, it has tended to show little generality at the *individual* differences level across different measures (i.e., different sets of items or persons judged).

One possible interpretation of this pattern of results is that this component has validity but not reliability. Such a paradoxical result would be possible if the component were factorially complex, and this possibility suggested the hypothesis for the present study. This hypothesis is that when the individual item z's are treated as scores, intercorrelated, and rotated to an analytic solution, there will be several group factors rather than a strong general factor.

In order to determine whether this might be the case, the following study was undertaken in which 129 University undergraduate students participated as Ss. They were shown the standard six filmed interviews and given the judging tests (for each film), each of which was susceptible to an analysis in terms of components. The titles of the judging instruments and the characteristics underlying their item content are given below:

(1) Personal Practice Questionnaire (participation in religious activities),

(2) Activities Preference Inventory (femininity of interests),

(3) Interpersonal Relations Inventory (socialization).

All of the items from these scales were put into a Likert format. On the Activities Preference Inventory and the Interpersonal Relations Inventory, five responses were provided for each item, ranging from "Strongly Agree" to "Strongly Disagree." Scores from 1 to 5 were assigned to these responses so that "Strongly Disagree" always received a score of 5. On the Personal Practices Questionnaire four responses were provided for each item varying from "Frequently" to "Never." Scores from 1 to 4 were assigned to these responses so that "Never" always received a score of 4. There were ten Likert items per measure.

For each S, his scores on a given instrument were his 10 individual item Interpersonal Accuracy correlation values. In other words, on each item his score was the Z conversion of the correlation between his predicted scores for the six stimulus persons on that item and their corresponding "true" scores. It was thus a measure of his success in rank ordering the stimulus persons on that item.

These scores were intercorrelated and factor analyzed for each instrument separately using a principal components solution and varimax orthogonal rotation. Unity was placed in the diagonal and all components

TABLE XXIII

ROTATED LOADINGS FOR FACTOR ANALYSIS OF INDIVIDUAL ITEM ACCURACY SCORES ON THE PERSONAL PRACTICES QUESTIONNAIRE[a]

| | Factors | | | |
|---|---|---|---|---|
| Item | A | B | C | $h^2$ |
| 1. Within the past few years I have attended religious services. | .80 | —.26 | —.04 | .71 |
| 2. I have taught "Sunday School" or given another religious class or group within the last two years. | .00 | .53 | .18 | .31 |
| 3. Within the last two years I have invited someone not of my faith to attend religious services with me. | .69 | —.05 | .18 | .51 |
| 4. Within the last few years I have discussed religious topics with my friends. | .34 | —.33 | .21 | .27 |
| 5. Within the past two years I have prayed. | .22 | .79 | —.04 | .67 |
| 6. In my family we have the practice of having family prayer. | .53 | .05 | .32 | .39 |
| 7. Within the past two years I have spent periods of time in private religious thought and meditation. | —.25 | .65 | —.10 | .50 |
| 8. Within the past two years I have read the Holy Scriptures. | .15 | —.17 | .76 | .63 |
| 9. Within the past two years I have read books, magazine articles, etc. with religious themes or "inspirational messages." | .04 | .23 | .79 | .68 |
| 10. Within the past two years I have given money (or donations) to a church or religious group. | .64 | .20 | —.06 | .45 |

[a] Note. For each item four choices were provided ranging from "Frequently" to "Never."

with an eigenvalue greater than 1.00 extracted. Kaiser (1960) presents in detail the rationale for this factoring procedure.

The rotated factor loadings and communalities for the Personal Practices Questionnaire are presented in Table XXIII, for the Activities Preference Inventory in Table XXIV, and for the Interpersonal Relations Inventory in Table XXV.

The implications of these results are clear. Interpersonal Accuracy is a complex measure, involving several orthogonal factors rather than a large general factor and the factorial complexity is a much more important finding than the details of the individual factors. This indicates that accuracy probably should not be interpreted as a single unidimensional trait, but rather as a group of relatively independent traits. It should be emphasized that even though this is true one can still talk

TABLE XXIV

ROTATED LOADINGS FOR FACTOR ANALYSIS OF INDIVIDUAL ITEM ACCURACY SCORES ON THE ACTIVITIES PREFERENCE INVENTORY[a]

| Item | Factors | | | | |
|---|---|---|---|---|---|
| | A | B | C | D | $h^2$ |
| 1. I would like the work of a clerk in a large department store. | .54 | —.37 | —.23 | —.16 | .51 |
| 2. I like adventure stories better than romantic stories. | —.11 | .58 | —.24 | .29 | .49 |
| 3. I would like to be a soldier or a WAC. | —.09 | .08 | —.56 | .05 | .33 |
| 4. I very much like hunting. | —.02 | .03 | —.19 | —.76 | .62 |
| 5. I think I would like the work of a librarian. | —.04 | —.03 | —.22 | .67 | .50 |
| 6. I think I would like to be a professional golfer. | —.12 | —.10 | .66 | .04 | .46 |
| 7. I think I would like the work of a professional musician. | —.74 | —.42 | —.12 | .09 | .75 |
| 8. I think I could do better than most of the present politicians if I were in office. | .02 | —.68 | .07 | .23 | .52 |
| 9. I get excited very easily. | .04 | .43 | .54 | —.04 | .48 |
| 10. The average person is not able to appreciate art and music very well. | —.75 | .17 | —.06 | —.14 | .61 |

[a] Note: Five choices were provided for each item varying from "Strongly Agree" to "Strongly Disagree."

meaningfully about differences in over-all ability to judge others accurately. In order to do this, however, one must interpret variations in over-all accuracy as variations in the elevation of a profile (Cronbach and Gleser, 1953). This is a very different conception from variation along a single dimension, and one with important implications for future research on accuracy of interpersonal perception. At the very least, it implies that one cannot expect to adequately describe a person's accuracy of judging others with a single score. For example, if variations in over-all accuracy are conceived of as variations in profile elevations, one must also consider other characteristics of profiles such as scatter and shape.

Finally it should be noted that the scores for each item in the factor analysis were *accuracy* measures. These factors are not necessarily the same as the factors that would be obtained by analyzing the responses of the persons judged to these items. In other words, the dimensions of

TABLE XXV

ROTATED LOADINGS FOR FACTOR ANALYSIS OF INDIVIDUAL ITEM ACCURACY SCORES ON THE
INTERPERSONAL RELATIONS INVENTORY

| Item | Factors | | | | |
|---|---|---|---|---|---|
| | A | B | C | D | $h^2$ |
| 1. When I get bored I like to stir up some excitement. | .09 | .06 | —.80 | —.11 | .66 |
| 2. I would do almost anything on a dare. | .62 | —.14 | —.31 | .24 | .56 |
| 3. I think I am stricter about right and wrong than most people. | —.32 | —.51 | .38 | —.19 | .54 |
| 4. It is all right to get around the law if you don't actually break it. | —.16 | .19 | .30 | .60 | .51 |
| 5. I often act on the spur of the moment without stopping to think. | .19 | —.31 | —.21 | .69 | .65 |
| 6. I have often gone against my parents' wishes. | .71 | —.12 | —.08 | .06 | .53 |
| 7. My home life was always happy. | —.05 | .56 | —.03 | .15 | .34 |
| 8. Before I do something, I try to consider how my friends will react to it. | .17 | —.62 | —.09 | .17 | .45 |
| 9. I seem to do things I regret more often than most people. | —.27 | —.28 | —.02 | —.48 | .38 |
| 10. Every family owes it to the city to keep their sidewalks cleared in the winter and their lawns mowed in the summer. | .67 | .21 | .45 | —.18 | .73 |

*a* Note: Five choices were provided for each item varying from "Strongly Agree" to "Strongly Disagree."

accuracy of judged religiosity are not necessarily the same as the dimensions of religiosity itself.

## I. EFFECT OF SOCIAL DESIRABILITY RESPONSE SET ON JUDGING ACCURACY

A study was conducted by Cline and Richards (1964 Annual Report) on the effects of different kinds of motivation on judging accuracy where three motive strengths or incentive conditions were used with 65 Ss.

(a) *Low incentives:* The Ss were urged to do their best but no reward was provided. (b) *Medium incentive:* Subjects were told that the most accurate judge would receive a $15 prize to be mailed out in several weeks. (c) *High incentive:* Here the subjects were told that the best judge would receive a prize of $25; the second best, $15; the third, fourth, and fifth, $10; and the sixth through tenth best judges would each receive $5. They were told that they would receive these prizes a few minutes after the experiment was completed and the money was displayed in full view at the front of the room while the experiment was taking place.

When the results yielded negligible differences in judging accuracy between the experimental groups, the researchers speculated that this might be accounted for by some uncontrolled response set affecting the judging instruments. However, in the construction of these instruments attempts had been made to control for the two most obvious response sets, namely always choosing "True" (or "False"), and always choosing the socially desirable or (undesirable) response. However, no evidence had been available to indicate whether this had been successfully accomplished or not. That this should be checked is suggested by the experience of Edwards with his Personal Preference Schedule: he thought that he had controlled for social desirability, but in fact had not (Corah *et al.,* 1958).

Accordingly, special keys were developed to give evidence about these matters.

The first step in constructing these keys was to obtain ratings of the socially desirable answer to each item of each judging instrument. These ratings were made by four persons, one Ph.D. psychologist and three advanced graduate students in psychology. The criterion for determining the socially desirable answer to an item was that at least three out of the four raters agree that the answer in question was the socially desirable one. If there was a two-two split among the raters as to the socially desirable answer, it was concluded that social desirability had been controlled on that item.

Keys were then constructed to make it possible to analyze separately all possible combinations of correct response and socially desirable response. In other words, for the Behavior Postdiction and the Opinion Prediction tests, the keys were: (a) socially desirable answer true, correct answer true; (b) socially desirable answer true, correct answer false; (c) socially desirable answer false, correct answer true; and (d) socially desirable answer false, correct answer false. For the Adjective Check, the keys were (a) socially desirable alternative correct, and (b) socially desirable alternative wrong. On each of these keys, the score is the total number correct. Another key for each of the three instruments consisted of those items where social desirability was controlled (regardless of whether the correct answers were "true" or "false"). Again the score was the total number correct. Finally, another special key, the Popular Responses key, was constructed on the basis of the sample reported in the author's 1962 Annual Report (Cline, Richards, and Abe, 1962), who took this same judging test. A "popular response" was defined as an answer chosen by 80% of the sample regardless of whether that response was correct or not.

TABLE XXVI

CORRELATIONS AMONG VARIOUS KEYS WITHIN JUDGING INSTRUMENTS

| Instrument | Key | 1 | 2 | 3 | 4 |
|---|---|---|---|---|---|
| Behavior Postdiction | 1. Socially desirable answer True, correct answer True | — | | | |
| | 2. Socially desirable answer True, correct answer False | —24 | — | | |
| | 3. Socially desirable answer False, correct answer True | —27 | 27 | — | |
| | 4. Socially desirable answer False, correct answer False | 39 | —35 | —03 | — |
| Opinion Prediction | 1. Socially desirable answer True, correct answer True | — | | | |
| | 2. Socially desirable answer True, correct answer False | —38 | — | | |
| | 3. Socially desirable answer False, correct answer True | —12 | 21 | — | |
| | 4. Socially desirable answer False, correct answer False | 13 | —58 | 01 | — |
| Adjective Check | 1. Socially desirable answer Correct | — | | | |
| | 2. Socially desirable answer Wrong | —39 | — | | |
| $r \ .05 = .24$ | | | | | |

TABLE XXVII

CORRELATIONS AMONG TOTAL CORRECT KEYS FOR THE THREE JUDGING INSTRUMENTS

| | 1 | 2 | 3 |
|---|---|---|---|
| 1. Behavior Postdiction | — | | |
| 2. Opinion Prediction | —03 | — | |
| 3. Adjective Check | 14 | 00 | — |
| $r \ .05 = .24$ | | | |

The score on this key was the total number of popular responses chosen. The hypothesis emerged that the Ss in making their judgments differed more in the extent to which they chose socially desirable answers than they did in accuracy. This was determined by computing correlations among the various keys within forms. If social desirability were a more important factor than accuracy, the correlation between keys where the socially desirable answer is the same and the correct answer different would be negative. For example, there would be a negative correlation between the "socially desirable answer True, correct answer True" key and the "socially desirable answer True, correct answer False" key. If accuracy were more important than social desirability, these correlations would be positive.

The correlations among the various keys within instruments are presented in Table XXVI. In order to permit a further comparison of social desirability with accuracy, correlations were also computed among the Total Correct keys for the three judging instruments. These correlations are presented in Table XXVII. The results indicate quite clearly that variation with respect to tendency to choose the socially desirable response is more important in these judging instruments than variation in accuracy—at least for this study. This is true in spite of the fact that, as previously indicated, efforts had been made to control this response set. And while this is just one study, it does demonstrate the problems one encounters in attempting to develop judging instruments tailored to individual "others."

While it cannot be proved, the "social desirability" variable might also account, in part, for some of the generality found across judging instruments and "others" reported earlier in this paper.

One possible solution to this problem would be to use a paired comparison method. Use of this technique with filmed interviews stimulus material would mean that $S$s would be shown separate movies of interviews of, say, two persons and then asked which of these two persons were, say, more intelligent, dominant, neurotic, etc. This would also make sense in terms of the findings of clinical *versus* statistical predictions study where the clinician-judge can best beat the actuary by ranking, ordering, or comparing several others at one time.

## V. Summary

In the middle 1950's Cronbach, Gage, and several other researchers criticized naïve empiricism in interpersonal perception research. They pointed out serious weaknesses and flaws in most published studies as well as in traditional methodology common to much research in this area. The possibility of fractionating or "breaking down" global judging scores was suggested as a possible solution or way out of this problem. This would allow experimenters to obtain "pure" accuracy scores uncontaminated by other components ofttimes working at cross purposes and in contradictory ways when combined into a global index or measure. In a series of researches by Cline and Richards, the power and utility of this component approach was demonstrated and helped clarify some of the issues in the clinical *versus* statistical prediction controversy, problems with the generality of empathic ability, the judging accuracy of groups *versus* individuals, and so forth. Despite this, these components still revealed some weaknesses and under certain conditions produced conflicting and contradictory results. It was demonstrated that the nature of the scoring system could affect these components in undesirable ways and in certain situations lead to unjustified conclusions. Because of this, a new Interpersonal Accuracy (IA) measure (component) was developed which was believed free of the methodological shortcomings of the older Differential Accuracy and other components. Factor studies of this new IA component revealed that (as a "pure" measure of judging ability) it was factorially complex and not unidimensional. It involved several orthogonal factors rather than a large general factor. However, even though this was true, it was believed that one could still talk meaningfully about differences in over-all ability to judge others accurately. In order to do this, however, one must interpret variations in over-all judging accuracy as variations in elevation of a profile where scatter and shape must be considered.

It was also demonstrated that the social desirability factor exerts an extremely powerful influence in the use of all judging instruments and must be considered or reckoned with in the actual judging process as well as on the criterion development side of the problem.

The use of stereotypes in judging was found, also, to be an extremely important variable in judging. Much evidence suggested that having an accurate stereotype of a certain class or subclass of social objects or "others" being judged could, apart from any other variable, contribute significantly to accuracy.

However, it was noted at the date of writing this review that there still does not exist a fully satisfactory and validated test or procedure for measuring judging accuracy. And certainly one of the major unsolved problems is the lack of a good external criterion with which we might validate the new experimental judging tests which are occasionally developed. This is a situation not unlike that which Binet faced when the first tests of intelligence were constructed.

Because of the many methodological problems encountered where single persons or "others" are judged individually, the suggestion was made that the judging task could be greatly simplified by having one compare pairs or rank-order triads of "others" on a variety of personality variables. Thus the only discrimination required would be to indicate which of two "others" was the most dominant, intelligent, etc. Or one might rank-order three "others" on these same traits after first seeing all three films of them or observing them in interviews etc. This would solve the problem of projection, social desirability, and idiosyncracies of the judges in their approach to standard rating instruments.

Experience has suggested that filmed interviews of "others" have to be considered as something akin to unselected items in a test. Some will prove confusing, too difficult, or too easy and will have to be discarded. And the same is true for the material in the individual judging instruments. In the author's experience a considerable amount of time and energy must be spent in refining and developing these for even a minimum payoff.

Since the author's bias is in the direction of studying "ultimate achievement" in judging, he would be of the opinion that the "best" judging measure ultimately will prove to be a sophisticated global index which will combine all the crucial elements contributing to accuracy in a measurable and meaningful way. This might involve developing five or six factorially pure tests, or a procedure similar to that used by Guilford to measure dimensions of intellect, or the much cruder Wechsler Adult Intelligence Scale where various subtest scores are combined to give a Full Scale IQ, or it might possibly even make use of a composite of a profile.

In any event, the current status of interpersonal perception research is not yet in sharp focus. A fully satisfactory measure of judging accuracy still eludes us.

ACKNOWLEDGMENTS

From 1957 to 1963, James M. Richards, Jr. was an associate with the author in all of his interpersonal perception research. The author wishes to acknowledge the outstanding contribution made and the many ideas contributed by Dr. Richards to this research effort. Mr. Clifford Abe and Mr. Max Rardin, research assistants, were especially valuable in many phases of the data analysis. Grateful appreciation is also expressed to Stanford University Press, Prentice-Hall, *Psychological Record, Journal of Abnormal and Social Psychology, Psychological Bulletin,* and *Journal of Consulting Psychology,* as well as Dr. L. J. Cronbach, Dr. N. L. Gage, Dr. Richard Hatch, and Dr. Renato Tagiuri, for permission to quote from their published works and make use of some of the material contained therein.

# References

Boneau, C. A. The effect of violations of assumptions underlying the *t* test. *Psychol. Bull.,* 1960, **57,** 49-64.

Box, G. E. P. Non-normality and tests on variances. *Biometrika,* 1953, **40,** 318-335.

Bronfenbrenner, V., Harding, J., and Gallwey, M. The measurement of skill in social perception. In D. C. McClelland (Ed.), *Talent and Society.* New York: Van Nostrand, 1958, pp. 29-111.

Bruner, J. S., and Tagiuri, R. The perception of people. In G. Lindzey (Ed.), *Handbook of social psychology.* Cambridge, Massachusetts: Addison-Wesley, 1954.

Brunswik, E. Social perception of traits from photographs. *Psychol. Bull.,* 1945, **10,** 535. (Abstr.)

Buros, O. K. *Fifth mental measurements yearbook.* New Jersey: Gryphon Press, 1959.

Campbell, D. T. An error in some demonstrations of the superior social perceptiveness of leaders. *J. abnorm. soc. Psychol.,* 1955, **51,** 694-695.

Chapin, F. S. Preliminary standardization of a social insight scale. *Amer. social. Rev.,* 1942, **7,** 214-225.

Chowdhry, K., and Newcomb, T. M. The relative abilities of leaders and non-leaders to estimate opinions of their own groups. *J. abnorm. soc. Psychol.,* 1952, **47,** 51-57.

Cline, V. B. *The assessment of good and poor judges of personality using a stress interview and sound film technique.* Unpublished doctoral dissertation, University of California, Berkeley, 1953.

Cline, V. B. Ability to judge personality assessed with a stress interview and sound film technique. *J. abnorm. soc. Psychol.,* 1955, **50,** 183-187. (a)

Cline, V. B. *An analysis of the performance of 100 Air Force officers on the social acuity test.* USAF Pers. Train. Res. Center Tech. Memos, 1955, Project No. 7730, No. AF 18 (600)-8, Maxwell AFB. (b)

Cline, V. B., and Richards, J. M., Jr. *Variables related to accuracy of interpersonal perception.* Ann. Repts. 1958, 1959, 1960, and 1961. Group Psychology Branch, Office of Naval Research; Dept. of Psychology, Univ. of Utah, Salt Lake City.

Cline, V. B., and Richards, J. M., Jr. Accuracy of interpersonal perception—A general trait? *J. abnorm. soc. Psychol.,* 1960, **60,** 1-7.

Cline, V. B., and Richards, J. M., Jr. A comparison of individuals versus groups in judging personality. *J. appl. Psychol.,* 1961, **45,** 150-155. (a)

Cline, V. B., and Richards, J. M., Jr. The generality of accuracy of interpersonal perception. *J. abnorm. soc. Psychol.,* 1961, **62,** 446-449. (b)

Cline, V. B., and Richards, J. M., Jr. Components of accuracy of interpersonal perception scores and the clinical and statistical prediction controversy. *Psychol. Rec.,* 1962, **12,** No. 4, 373-379.

Cline, V. B., and Richards, J. M., Jr. A methodological note on Cline and Richard's studies of accuracy of interpersonal perception: A reply. *J. abnorm. soc. Psychol.,* 1963, **66,** No. 2, 195-196.

Cline, V. B., Richards, J. M., Jr., and Abe, C. *Variables related to accuracy of interpersonal perception.* Ann. Repts. 1962 and 1964. Group Psychology Branch, Office of Naval Research; Dept. of Psychology, Univer. of Utah, Salt Lake City.

Cohen, E. The methodology of Notcutt and Silva's "Knowledge of Other People": A critique. *J. abnorm. soc. Psychol.,* 1953, **48,** 155.

Corah, N. L., Feldman, M. J., Cohen, I. S., Gruen, W., Meadow, A., and Ringwall, E. A. Social desirability as a variable in the Edwards personal preference schedule. *J. consult. Psychol.,* 1958, **22,** 70-72.

Cronbach, L. J. Processes affecting scores on "understanding of others" and "assumed similarity." *Psychol. Bull.* 1955, **52,** 177-193.

Cronbach, L. J. Proposals leading to analytic treatment of social perception scores. In R. Tagiuri and L. Petrullo (Eds.), *Person perception and interpersonal behavior.* Stanford, California: Stanford Univer. Press, 1958, pp. 359-379.

Cronbach, L. J., and Gleser, G. C. Assessing similarity between profiles. *Psychol. Bull.,* 1953, **50,** 456-473.

Crow, W. J. *A methodological study of social perceptiveness.* Unpublished doctoral dissertation, Univer. of Colorado, Boulder, 1954.

Crow, W. J. The effect of training upon accuracy and variability in interpersonal perception. *J. abnorm. soc. Psychol.,* 1957, **55,** 355-359.

Crow, W. J. *Process vs. achievement and generality over objects and judging tasks.* Presented as part of 1960 APA Symposium on New Frontiers in Person Perception Research. (Privately mimeographed) 1960.

Crow, W. J., and Hammond, K. R. The generality of accuracy and response sets in interpersonal perception. *J. abnorm. soc. Psychol.,* 1957, **54,** 384-390.

Dymond, R. F., Hughes, A. S., and Raabe, V. L. Measurable changes in empathy with age. *J. consult. Psychol.,* 1952, **16,** 202-206.

Estes, S. G. Judging personality from expressive behavior. *J. abnorm. soc. Psychol.,* 1938, **33,** 217-236.

Estes, W. K. *The human observer and the clinician as diagnostic instruments.* Western Psychological Association Invitational Address, Seattle, Washington, 1961.

Fiedler, F. Unpublished address. American Psychological Association. Ann. Meeting, Chicago, 1960.

Flanagan, J. C. *Flanagan Aptitude Classification Test.* Chicago: Science Research Associates, 1958.

Gage, N. L. Judging interests from expressive behavior. *Psychol. Monogr.,* 1952, **66** (18), No. 350.

Gage, N. L. Accuracy of social perception and effectiveness in interpersonal relationships. *J. Personality,* 1953, **22,** 128-141.

Gage, N. L., and Cronbach, L. J. Conceptual and methodological problems in interpersonal perception. *Psychol. Rev.,* 1955, **62,** 411-422.

Gage, N. L., and Suci, G. Social perception and teacher-pupil relationships. *J. educ. Psychol.,* 1951, **42,** 144-152.

Gage, N. L., Leavitt, G. S., and Stone, G. C. The intermediary key in the analysis of interpersonal perception. *Psychol. Bull.,* 1956, **53,** 258-266.

Giedt, F. H. *Judgment of personality characteristics from brief interviews.* Unpublished Ph.D. dissertation, Univer. of California, Los Angeles, 1951.

Gough, H. G. *The opinion prediction scale.* Berkeley: Univer. of California Institute of Personality Assessment and Research, 1953.

Gough, H. G. *The assessment of social acuity.* Research Report. Berkeley: Univer. of California, 1955.

Grossman, B. A. *The measurement and determinants of interpersonal sensitivity.* Unpublished Master's thesis, Michigan State Univer., East Lansing, 1963.

Gulliksen, H. *Theory of mental tests.* New York: Wiley, 1950.

Halbrower, C. C. A comparison of actuarial vs. clinical predictions to classes discriminated by the MMPI. Unpublished doctoral dissertation, Univer. of Minnesota, Minneapolis, 1955.

Hastorf, A. H., and Bender, I. E. A caution respecting the measurement of empathic ability. *J. abnorm. soc. Psychol.,* 1952, **47,** 574-576.

Hastorf, A. H., Bender, I. E., and Weintraub, D. J. The influence of response patterns on the "refined empathy score." *J. abnorm. soc. Psychol.,* 1955, **51,** 341-343.

Hatch, R. S. *An evaluation of a forced choice differential accuracy approach to the measurement of supervisory empathy.* Englewood Cliffs, New Jersey: Prentice-Hall, 1962.

Holt, R. R. Clinical and statistical prediction: A reformulation and some new data. *J. abnorm. soc. Psychol.,* 1958, **56,** 1-12.

Kaiser, H. F. The application of electronic computers to factor analysis. *Educ. psychol. Measmt.,* 1960, **20,** 141-151.

Kerr, W. A. *Primary empathic abilities.* Chicago: Psychometric Affiliates, 1957.

VICTOR B. CLINE

Kerr, W. A., and Speroff, B. J. *Measurement of empathy* (manual). Chicago: Psychometric Affiliates, 1951.

Kerr, W. A., and Speroff, B. J. Validation and evaluation of the empathy test. *J. gen. Psychol.*, 1954, 50, 269-276.

Leytham, G. *Some factors influencing the ratings on self and others.* Unpublished Master's thesis, Univer. of California, Berkeley, 1951.

Li, J. C. R. *Introduction to statistical inference.* Ann Arbor, Michigan: Edwards, 1957.

Lorge, I., Fox., D., Davitz, J., and Brenner, M. A survey of studies contrasting the quality of group performance and individual performance, 1920-1957. *Psychol. Bull.*, 1958, 55, 337-372.

Luft, J. *Some relationships between clinical specialization and the understanding and prediction of an individual's behavior.* Unpublished doctoral dissertation, Univer. of California, Los Angeles, 1949.

McNemar, Q. *Psychological statistics.* New York: Wiley, 1955.

Meehl, P. E. *Clinical versus statistical prediction.* Minneapolis: Univer. of Minnesota Press, 1955.

Meehl, P. E. Wanted—A good cookbook. *Amer. Psychologist,* 1956, 11, 263-272.

Mosier, C. I. On the reliability of a weighted composite. *Psychometrika,* 1943, 8, 161-168.

Moss, F. A., Hunt, T., and Omwake, K. T. *Social intelligence test.* Washington, D. C.: Center for Psychological Service, George Washington Univer., 1944.

Nagle, B. F. Productivity, employee attitudes and supervisory sensitivity. *Personnel Psychol.,* 1954, 18, 53-58.

OSS Assessment Staff. *Assessment of men.* New York: Rinehart, 1948.

Remmers, H. H., and File, Q. W. *How Supervise?* New York: Psychological Corp., 1943-1948.

Richards, J. M., Jr. Reconceptualization of the clinical and statistical prediction controversy in terms of components of accuracy of interpersonal perception scores. *Psychol. Repts.,* 1963, 12, 443-448.

Richards, J. M., Jr., and Cline, V. B. Accuracy components in person perception scores and the scoring system as an artifact in investigations of the generality of judging ability. *Psychol. Repts.,* 1963, 12, 363-373.

Richards, J. M., Jr., Cline, V. B., and Rardin, M. W. Stereotypes and components of accuracy of person perception scores. *J. Personality,* 1962, 30, No. 4, 601-612.

Richey, M. H. *Ability to predict responses of acquaintances: A comparison of institutional and community adolescents.* Unpublished doctoral dissertation, Univer. of Illinois, 1952.

Smith, A. E. *Rapport and social perception in mother adolescent relationships.* Unpublished doctoral dissertation, Univer. of Illinois, Chicago, 1957.

Stone, G. C., and Leavitt, G. S. *Generality of accuracy in perceiving standard persons.* Univer. of Illinois, Chicago, 1954. (Mimeo.)

Taft, R. *Some correlates of the ability to make accurate social judgments.* Unpublished doctoral dissertation, Univer. of California, Berkeley, 1950.

Taft, R. The ability to judge people. *Psych. Bull.,* 1955, 52, 1-23.

Tagiuri, R., and Petrullo, L. (Eds.) *Person perception and interpersonal behavior.* Stanford, California: Stanford Univer. Press, 1958.

Talland, G. A. The assessment of group opinions by leaders and their influence on its formation. *J. abnorm. soc. Psychol.,* 1954, 49, 431-434.

# STIMULUS FUNCTIONS IN PROJECTIVE TECHNIQUES

*Douglas T. Kenny*[1]

HARVARD UNIVERSITY, CAMBRIDGE, MASSACHUSETTS

## I. Introduction: Stimulus Factors in Projective Measures

### A. VARIANCE-INVARIANCE IN PERCEPTION

The fact that stimuli facilitate and inhibit behavior is not without prior attention in the field of psychology. Ever since the early beginnings of behaviorism at the turn of this century, it has been generally assumed that behavior involves some interaction with stimulus situations. In fact, some psychologists have been so bold as to propose that such interactions constitute the empirical data of psychology. Doubtlessly here lies the basis for the protopostulate of many researchers that an intensive analysis

---

[1] On leave of absence from the Department of Psychology, University of British Columbia, for the period 1963–1965.

of the role of stimulus functions in behavior will yield findings of considerable theoretical and practical import for the discipline of psychology. Underlying most conceptions of stimulus functions is the broad proposition that the stimulus is the entering wedge into a behavior setting. The central problem or puzzle for psychology emerges when we attempt to find out what happens after an individual is stimulated.

A significant finding to emerge from early studies on the interaction between stimulation and perceiving was the clear-cut evidence that perception is not completely tied to stimulation at the sensory surface. Perhaps the classic experimental demonstrations of this lack of invariance between sensory input and perception are the phi phenomenon and reversible figures. The data on ambiguous figures immediately face us with the problem and the possibility that percepts may change without any alteration in stimulation, proximal or distal. From a historical perspective, such phenomena paved the way for the acceptance of the belief that input stimulation is only one of the many possible variables determining perception and behavior.

Such data and other interlocking findings show that we do not perceive directly either the distal stimulus or the proximal stimulus (cf. Brunswik, 1944, 1952, 1955). The former term may simply be defined as the physical object in the objective environment. The energy changes impinging on receptors refer to proximal stimulation, and they constitute the initial starting point or occasion for perception. However, if we perceive neither the distal object nor the proximal stimuli, then what do we perceive? It is at this juncture in the sequence of perceptual events that theory starts to take over. As Woodworth (1958) formulated in his characteristically middle-of-the-road fashion, it seems necessary to postulate that the individual decodes the raw proximal stimulation into objective or distal terms and then encodes the consummatory response before translating it into peripheral action. Hence, perception is the utilization of proximal stimuli as indicators of physical or social objects in the objective environment; in short, perception is a translation or decoding of proximal stimulation into distal objects.

Since the decoding of stimulation is an inferential process, veridical perception depends upon assigning the stimulation to the appropriate categories which bear correspondence to distal objects. If the inferential process decodes the proximal stimuli into an inappropriate category or code, then perception will be nonveridical, and behavior may be inappropriate. The two challenging problems in perception are to discover the empirical laws as to how proximal stimuli are decoded and how the codes are initially developed. To the extent that the formation and utilization of codes may possess individual consistencies, then these two problems are of interest to both the perceptual theorist and the person-ologist.

B. STIMULUS FUNCTIONS IN EARLY PROJECTIVE MODELS

The foregoing oversimplified and sketchy comments on the decoding or processing of stimuli lead us to the launching platform of projective techniques. They had their origins in empirical findings dealing with the relative lack of correspondence between sensory stimulation and perception, and in individual consistencies in perceiving. The effective application of these findings to the construction of projective techniques, however, depended critically upon the early theorizing of Freud and the Gestalt psychologists concerning the role of organismic variables in deter-mining what was perceived at the sensory surface.

By and large, the early projective test constructors and interpreters were influenced profoundly by the psychoanalytic concepts of primary and secondary processes and the role they played in coping and adapting to focal and incidental stimulation. Freud's notions on cathexes and hypercathexes of stimuli (cf. Holt, 1962) also provided a point of contact between projective test constructors and psychoanalysis. The unstructured stimuli of projective techniques were thought of as devices for reducing the reality base of stimulation, thereby permitting and encouraging primary process material to become dominant. The unclear stimuli of projective measures presumably interfere with the process of hyper-cathexis. What is equally important, the permissive test instructions and the general context of the test situation add further difficulty for the material being hypercathected. Or, putting these statements at the other end of the primary process–secondary process continuum, it was believed by early constructors of projective techniques that ambiguous stimuli, in a context of permissive instructions and test situations, weakened or impaired reality-oriented secondary process thought. Veridical percep-tions would fail as a consequence of difficulties in the hypercathexis of unstructured stimuli.

However, the veridicality of perception also had to be dealt with by projective personologists. While Rorschach provided the penetrating insight that the manner of perceiving was a function of intrapsychic functions, he did not attempt to develop any systematic theory to explicate his perceptual findings. This conceptual task was left to others. Unfortunately, as Lindzey (1961) has shown, this assignment is still far from completed.

Endeavors to explain the stability of perceptions in projective tests have most frequently invoked structural or autochthonous principles of perceptual determination. Extrapolation of gestalt principles of perceptual organization has been primarily limited to the Rorschach test (Arnheim, 1951, 1954; Beck, 1933; Belden and Baughman, 1954; Berliner, 1955; Brosin and Fromm, 1942; Klein and Arnheim, 1953; Rickers-Ovsiankina, 1960; Stein, 1951; and Wertheimer, 1957). Despite the fact that many authors have proposed that projective techniques have affinities to gestalt principles, the application of these principles to such tests is by no means clear. The main shortcoming of the theorizing relating principles of perceptual organization to projective techniques is that it has been very casual and has not led to much fruitful experimentation.

The essentials of a gestalt explanation of projective percepts, based in large part upon Wertheimer's (1957) discussion of the relations between the Rorschach and gestalt laws of organization, starts with the notion that a projective stimulus is a multiple reversible figure, with the autochthonous factors setting limits on the influence of intrapsychic factors. If the autochthonous variables are excessively strong, then personality parameters will play only a negligible part in the formation of percepts and cognitions. On the other hand, stimuli that are weak in structural determinants (ambiguous stimuli) will maximize personality processes in perception and cognition. In spite of ambiguous test material, however, the principles of perceptual organization would still have their effects on projective responses. The specific consequences would vary within a particular projective technique, especially for any test with test items varying in degree of stimulus ambiguity.

Within these two boundary conditions, the gestalt principles of perceptual stabilization have been assumed to operate as follows:

1. *Law of good continuation.* Perceptual structuring of projective stimuli will eliminate the irregularities in the stimulus material. For example, an irregular round object on the Rorschach may be perceived as a bowling ball, just as small parts may be perceptually omitted to provide a good gestalt.

2. *Law of similarity.* Similar stimuli will arouse perceptual processes leading them to be perceptually united or grouped. It is probable that similar forms and similar colors are the two most important similarity factors which lead to perceptual separation of the Rorschach cards into major and minor details.

3. *Law of closure.* Incomplete stimuli will create perceptual processes that will induce complete figures. For example, contour gaps on the Rorschach should elicit absolute or partial completion, thereby creating unitary percepts. Difficulties in closure may also appear on the Rorschach, e.g., the incomplete closure at the top of Card VII.

4. *Law of proximity.* Percepts will be formed between structural parts of a projective stimulus that are near one another. This principle,

in conjunction with that of symmetry, helps to divide the inkblots into their major details. The interaction of these two principles is seen most clearly at work on Card X of the Rorschach, where whole responses are difficult to form.

5. *Law of symmetry.* Symmetrical aspects of the projective stimulus will facilitate perceptual grouping. Symmetry of shape undoubtedly plays a critical role in form accuracy on the Rorschach.

While these structural laws of perception are assumed to apply to all individuals and to all stimuli, it may be hypothesized that their relative influence will vary with the structuredness of the stimulus material. From this assumption, it follows that inkblot stimuli weak in autochthonous factors would increase the frequency of color-form percepts and vague whole responses and decrease form plus percepts and popular responses. These predictions rest on the implicit assumption that form dominant *prägnant* percepts reflect autochthonous grouping principles. The testing of these predictions would necessitate the construction of inkblots that systematically vary in structure. This formulation bears close affinity to the recent analysis of Rorschach protocols, based on Werner's (1957) developmental stage theory of cognition, first applied by Friedman (1953) and summarized by Hemmendinger (1953, 1960).

It is to be noted that the gestalt and psychoanalytic models of stimulus functions have in common the conjecture that ambiguous stimuli heighten the influence of intrapersonal variables in perception.

Given the empirical findings on ambiguous stimuli and the theoretical formulations of psychoanalysis, it is not at all surprising that Rorschach (1921) and Christiana Morgan and Henry Murray (1935) chose unclear visual stimuli to maximize the variance between the physical stimulus and response output. Almost inevitably, the Rorschach and the Thematic Apperception Test (TAT) became viewed as open-end functions which tapped the major motivational, cognitive, and defensive systems of individuals. They are open-end stimulus functions in the sense that any particular ambiguous stimulus is open to multiple perceptions and interpretations. Of course, such tests could equally well have been called open-end or free-response assessment techniques to the extent that the subject has to produce his own responses.

From the working assumption that ambiguous situations facilitated the operation of drive-oriented thinking, it was further assumed by projective theorists that the greater the ambiguity, the greater the personality revelation. That is, the somewhat cavalier assumption was made of a monotonic relationship between stimulus ambiguity and personality revelation. With respect to fantasy productions, McClelland (1958, p. 31) has put this assumption rather succinctly in his statement that fantasy "capitalizes on the generalization, repeatedly confirmed in studies of the effects of motivation on behavior, that the more ambiguous the situation, the greater the effect of motivation." This hypothesis is consonant with gestalt predictions, for Wertheimer (1957, p. 212) also posits, "With more ambiguous material, a greater influence of the personality factors can be expected." We shall cite evidence later on to show that this assumption may have a questionable empirical base.

The foregoing discussion presents the stimulus model guiding early theorists and interpreters of projective techniques. Naturally the question arises as to whether this stimulus model is still adhered to in contemporary times. Indirect evidence of the continued acceptance of this model is shown by the results of a recent study by Seeman and Marks (1962). Thirty-six experienced Ph.D. clinical psychologists were asked to rank order tests on the dimensions of stimulus ambiguity, response freedom (degree of restriction of the response), and "depth" (availability to consciousness). The tests were the Bender-Gestalt, Rorschach, Sentence Completion, Strong, Szondi, TAT, and Word Association. The rank order correlation between stimulus ambiguity and depth was .86, reflecting the continued adherence to the proposition that the greater the stimulus ambiguity, the greater the depth or revealingness. The correlation between response freedom and stimulus ambiguity was .91. Thus the concept of stimulus ambiguity seems to imply the conception of many degrees of freedom in response production. Interestingly enough, response freedom and depth evidently reflect the same dimensions in the thinking of clinical psychologists since the rank order correlation between the two variables was 1.00.

With a projective model of this type, based largely on gestalt and analytic principles, it is not surprising that the specific role of the stimulus in evoking responses was largely overlooked by early theorists. Content and formal analysis of projective protocol data became *personality centered*, with the role of how the stimulus articulates with inner psychological systems ignored. In a singularly lucid and picturesque manner Rosenzweig (1951, p. 215) summed up this position when he said "The stimulus was dethroned. . . ." The stimulus remained in limbo until approximately 1950. An analysis of the historical reasons for the stimulus remaining in neglected confinement has been presented elsewhere (Kenny, 1961).

C. Recent Developments Focusing Attention on Stimulus Functions

The past decade or so has witnessed a gradual renaissance of theoretical and empirical interest in the role that stimuli play in prompting responses to projective techniques, especially for thematic apperceptive methods. What factors contributed to the restoration of the stimulus to grace?

Certain developments within psychology as a whole undoubtedly provided the strongest impetus to a fresh interest in the stimulus. Two, somewhat correlated, developments should be singled out for special mention. In the first instance, the examination of the behavioral determinants in perception, in contrast to the autochthonous factors, helped to rekindle an interest in the perceptual aspects of projective techniques. Bartlett's (1932) and Sherif's (1935) studies on autism set the stage for this research trend, as did the pioneering studies of Sanford (1936, 1937) and Levine, Chein, and Murphy (1942) on the influence of the hunger drive upon the interpretation of ambiguous figures. The broad assumption that needs influence perception was given close attention by the studies of Bruner and Postman and their colleagues (e.g., Bruner, 1951; Bruner and Postman, 1947; Bruner and Postman, 1949; Postman, Bruner, and McGinnies, 1948; Postman and Solomon, 1949) and a legion of other investigators.

The studies on perceptual defense and vigilance soon came under a bombardment of criticism, especially for failing to control adequately the nature of the stimulus material. Two of these attacks centered around the necessity of controlling the relative frequency of word usage (Solomon and Howes, 1951) and of ensuring the emotional relevance of the stimuli to the subjects (Chodorkoff, 1955).

That the stimulus properties in such experiments are intimately associated with the resulting perceptual reactions was hinted at by one of the earliest studies in this broad area of investigation. The results of Levine, Chein, and Murphy (1942) suggested that the more ambiguous stimuli favored reality processes, whereas the less ambiguous figures facilitated the operation of autistic processes. Not only did this experiment demonstrate the need for careful manipulation of stimulus material, but it also questioned the validity of the assumption that the influence of need increases with increasing stimulus ambiguity.

The relevancy of these experiments to projective techniques was obvious, in that they helped to make clear the fact that any interpretation of projective material in terms of personality dynamics alone would be grossly deficient. The data showed unequivocally that the findings were partly dependent upon the stimulus.

Further developments within psychology also helped personologists to look again to the stimulus, namely, the new theorizing on perception (e.g., Bruner, 1948, 1957) and the advances in psychoanalytic ego psychology (e.g., Hartmann, 1950, 1958). This new theorizing indicated that a "new" look had to be given to the role that stimulus variables might play in perception and in projective methods.

Thus developments within psychology as a whole contributed to a renewed appreciation of the importance of stimulus functions in behavior determination. The convergence of this trend with two developments within projective techniques themselves helped to forge a sharpened interest in the stimuli of these instruments. On the one hand, the research journals in the early 1950's were honeycombed with evidence of the failures of the Rorschach and the TAT in personality assessment. Kelly (1954), reflecting the growing belief that these techniques lacked validity, suggested that social psychologists might wish to study the adherence to tests in the face of so much negative validity. (For the clinical psychologist, projective techniques are like theories to many experimental psychologists; they will not be given up until supplanted by more valid techniques.) The problems encountered in attempting to establish the validity of the two standard projective instruments led many investigators to attempt construction of their own custom-built projective tests. The latter instruments immediately caused the researcher to look at the stimulus, and, as a consequence, much new evidence was produced about stimulus functions in projective test material. Some of this provocative research will be examined in a later section. On the other hand, a small number of investigators had always been interested in determining the role that the stimulus played in projective instruments. Some investigators, for example, were examining the problem of whether or not "color shock" on the Rorschach is attributable to the effects of color by removing the color from the chromatic cards. Other investigators were concerned with the issue of stimulus ambiguity and personality revelation in that TAT.

The coalescence of these trends within psychology as a whole with those in the projective area has recently prompted many investigators to look more closely at the stimulus aspect or input of projective techniques. The results of these studies will ultimately be useful in the construction of better personality assessment techniqus and will also help clinical psychologists and others to understand more fully how projective instruments function psychologically.

## II. A Set of Stimulus Postulates for Projective Methods

As the preceding discussion has shown, early attempts to specify the stimulus model of projective techniques usually involved weak analogizing from psychoanalytic and gestalt theory. Many assumptions about the stimulus were implied, but not explicitly stated. We shall now try to make these assumptions more explicit. A set of stimulus postulates will be developed, from which it is hoped that specific predictions may be derived, and tested. The postulate set requires verification.

The first systematic endeavor to specify clearly the interpretative assumptions, including those relating to the stimulus, was made by Lindzey (1952) for the TAT. Similar, but more modest, attempts have been provided by Henry (1956), Kagan (1960), and Murstein (1963b). These beginnings were expanded upon by Lindzey (1961) for all projective techniques in his book *Projective Techniques and Cross-Cultural Research*. However, since these endeavors have glossed over stimulus assumptions somewhat, our purpose is to bring into sharper focus the stimulus postulates that seem to be reasonable in terms of theory and empirical evidence.

As a starting point, the protopostulate for the entire set is: *Responses produced to projective techniques are controlled, to varying degrees, by by the projective stimulus.*

Researchers and practicing clinical psychologists have pretty well abandoned the earlier notion that projective techniques stand majestically above the influence of stimulus variables, revealing in pristine purity true personality variance. Three major kinds of empirical data have helped to fashion the proposition that responses to projective techniques are deeply dependent upon the stimulus. Since most of the important research will be discussed in later sections of this paper, no attempt is made to provide a detailed discussion of it at this point. The diverse kinds of data indicating that the stimulus, in part, controls the response to projective stimuli are as follows:

*1. Normative Data*

Popular responses on the Rorschach indicate that specific areas of this test are well structured, at least for certain age, sex, and cultural groups. Moreover, the fact that only 10% of the percepts to the Rorschach are "man-made" objects may be attributed to the inkblot stimuli (Edmonston and Griffith, 1958). The general shape and form of the inkblots restrict the type of response that may be made to the Rorschach. Similarly, common themes to particular TAT cards (Cox and Sargent, 1950; Eron, 1948, 1950; Lindzey and Goldberg, 1953; Rosenzweig and Fleming, 1949; Wittenborn, 1949) support the proposition that responses to thematic apperception techniques are influenced significantly by the stimulus. No useful purpose would be served by reviewing normative data in this paper. We shall indicate briefly some of their implications.

One of the most important implications of normative data is that clinical psychologists must eliminate from the total test variance that part due to the stimulus properties of their instruments. Research is required on how best to do this. At the moment, clinicians must perform this delicate task in a highly subjective manner. A related implication of normative data is that an individual's level of psychological functioning will vary within an instrument as a consequence of the varying stimulus pull of the projective test material. That is to say, it would be unwise to interpret all data from a single test as if it were originating from a single level of personality functioning.

The last item deserves more attention than in has received in either research or the clinical application of projective tests. Projective personologists have frequently made the assumption that similar responses represent similar intraindividual dynamics. However, the data on common themes and popular responses suggest that such an assumption is very questionable. A more reasonable assumption is that intraindividual consistency in the same class of behavior due to functionally similar test stimuli reflects a different kind of psychological functioning than does intraindividual consistency in the same class of behavior to dissimilar test stimuli. This supposition immediately leads one to the representativeness and type of stimuli that should be used within a projective test. This topic is discussed under the first postulate.

### 2. Connotative Meanings of the Stimuli

The connotative meaning of the Rorschach inkblots has received a great deal of attention recently, with the result that it is now clear that there is a great deal of communality in the meanings assigned to specific inkblots. Findings from this research show that the percepts to inkblots are, in part, anchored to the stimulus properties of the inkblots.

Historically speaking, the recent rash of studies on the connotative meanings of inkblots stems from the hypothesis that specific Rorschach inkblots have special symbolic meanings. Card IV, for example, is the so-called "father" card, Card VI is the "sex" card, and Card VII indicates "mother." In early research (e.g., Meer and Singer, 1950; Taniguchi, De Vos and Murakami, 1958) on the mother-father cards, subjects (Ss) were asked to indicate the card that reminded them of father and the card that reminded them of mother. Today, however, Osgood's semantic differential (Osgood, Suci, Tannenbaum, 1957) has become the popular device to investigate not only the father-mother hypothesis but also other stimulus values of the Rorschach (Little, 1959; Loiselle and Kleinschmidt, 1963; Rabin, 1959; Rosen, 1960; Zax and Benham, 1961; Zax and Loiselle, 1960a,b; Zax, Loiselle, and Karras, 1960). The semantic differential has also been used to assess the stimulus properties of the Blacky Picture Test (Stricker, 1963) and of the Bender-Gestalt (Tolar, 1960).

The most striking contribution that the semantic differential studies have made is the general finding that each Rorschach inkblot has a somewhat unique meaning. A consensus of the findings on the semantic differential research and the specific studies (Levy, 1958; Mayer and Binz, 1961; Meer and Singer, 1950; Rosen, 1951; Sappenfield, 1961; Schleifer and Hire, 1960; Taniguchi et al., 1958) testing the mother and father notions permits the following characterizations of the Rorschach inkblots:

Card I: ugly, dirty, cruel, large, strong, rugged, active, ferocious
Card II: happy, strong, active, fast
Card III: good, clean, happy, light, active, fast
Card IV: bad, dirty, cruel, strong, heavy, slow, ferocious, masculine
Card V: light, active
Card VI: large
Card VII: good, beautiful, clean, happy, light, delicate, peaceful, feminine
Card VIII: clean, active
Card IX: strong, active, hot
Card X: good, beautiful, clean, happy, light, active, fast

While the foregoing data show that individual inkblots tend to instigate somewhat specific connotative reactions, they do not, however, indicate what specific properties of the inkblots determine the reactions.

## 3. Experimental Manipulations

Much attention has been given to the general problem of how projective responses change as a function of experimental manipulation of the projective stimulus. Researchers (e.g., Framo, 1952; Horiuchi, 1961; Stein, 1949) have impoverished Rorschach inkblots physically by tachistoscopic techniques. They have shown generally that the form quality of whole responses ($W$) and percentages of usual detail responses ($D$) increase with longer exposure times. Another kind of stimulus manipulation of the Rorschach has involved alteration of some assumed critical property of the inkblots, such as color. Since this type of study will be reviewed in depth later, it suffices to say at this point that such stimulus changes do produce some shifts in the response.

Similarly, manipulation of the stimulus properties of thematic apperception pictures has received a great deal of attention. Several workers have examined fantasy production as a function of similarity between the central figure in a picture and the subject. Investigators have also tested the hypothesis of a monotonic relationship between stimulus ambiguity and personality revelation. Several recent studies have focused on the problem of what kind of picture is most likely to reveal drive manifestations. These and other tantalizing questions will be examined in later sections. Accordingly, it need only be stated that the research evidence shows that there are important interactions between projective test performance and stimulus properties of the pictures.

At this juncture in the development of projective techniques, what is required is a more precise delineation of these interactions. An attempt will be made in this paper to present a framework within which the interactions between stimulus properties of projective materials and response performance can be intensively explored. In essence, then, the following set of postulates attempts to provide this framework.

### A. POSTULATE ONE: PSYCHOLOGICAL PROCESSES AS A FUNCTION OF TEST STIMULUS MODEL

*Similar responses to a projective test will increasingly reflect analogous dynamics as a test approximates a cumulative homogeneity test stimulus model.*

Following the views expressed by Fiske (1963), three test stimuli models may be distinguished in current projective methods. The commonest model today is the *pure relative frequency* one and is best exemplified by the Rorschach and the TAT. Other perceptual tests based on this model are the Behn–Rorschach (Zulliger, 1946), the Holtzman-Inkblot Technique (Holtzman, Thorpe, Swartz, and Herron, 1961), and the Z-test (Zulliger, 1948). The Picture Story Test (Symonds, 1949), the Michigan Picture Test (Andrew, Walton, Hartwell, and Hutt, 1951; Andrew, Hartwell, Hutt, and Walton, 1953), the Make-A-Picture Story Test (Shneidman, 1948), the Four Picture Test (Lennep, 1948), the Children's Apperception Test (CAT) (Bellak, 1954), and the Object Relations Test (Phillipson, 1955) may serve as additional examples for constructive projective techniques which employ the pure relative frequency model.

In this model, many different stimuli are used to assess numerous personality characteristics and an inference about a particular personality characteristic is formed by counting similar response productions from relatively different test stimuli. For example, on the Rorschach one counts the number of whole responses, major detail responses, minor detail responses, and the like. On the TAT, we count the number of aggressive themes, succorance themes, achievement themes, and so on. It is to be noticed that the same stimuli are used to assess different personality variables and, as a consequence, the counting operation is performed independent of the stimuli.

A second and increasingly popular approach with projective methods is to custom-build tests based on the specific relative frequency model. With this model the investigator selects stimuli for the measurement of a specific personality characteristic, and simply counts the number of times that the characteristic manifests itself in the response productions. Unlike the next model to be described, no attempt is made to order the stimuli in terms of their evoking strength for the particular personality variable under consideration. In principle, any stimulus which seems relevant to the personality dimension under investigation will do. The general usefulness of this model was highlighted by McClelland (McClelland, Atkinson, Clark and Lowell, 1953) and his colleagues, who constructed TAT-type pictures specifically designed to engage the achievement motive. Kagan (1956) made use of this test model when he constructed a special set of TAT pictures to measure aggression toward peers. The Levy Movement cards (Rust, 1948) is a perceptual test employing the relative frequency model. The use of doll play with structured questions around sibling rivalry also employs this model (Levy, 1937).

A third, but still relatively uncommon, approach with projective techniques is the cumulative homogeneity model. The two distinguishing features of this model are that the stimuli are ordered by scalogram analysis along a continuum of decreasing ambiguity with which they measure a single personality characteristic. Since this model assumes that the stimuli have exactly the same order for all subjects, any two subjects with the same total score should have identical answer patterns. For projective techniques, the stimuli would be ordered in terms of increasing percentage of individuals manifesting a given variable, such that once an individual gives a response reflective of the variable, he should continue to give similar responses to the remaining stimuli. Thus the stimuli are arranged in order of increasing stimulus demand for a variable. A subject with a weak tendency for a variable would have to continue up the scale of decreasing ambiguity much further than would a person with either a moderate or strong tendency. Preferably, a rectangular distribution of stimulus demand frequencies should obtain for such a test, with a minimum of stimulus items of demand frequencies near .5 since such items are unstable (Fiske, 1963).

Guttman's (1950) scalogram analysis was successfully applied by Lesser (1958) in the construction of 10 pictures to measure fantasy aggression. This study provides convincing evidence that the cumulative homogeneity model may be applied to projective techniques, providing that the test constructor designs his materials to ensure the elimination of stimulus elements that may evoke unwanted response systems. Auld, Eron, and Laffal (1955) were only partially successful in their application of Guttman's scaling method to the TAT because the pictures were not purified of unwanted stimulus elements. A method basically similar to scalogram analysis, but dealing more directly with the concept of a threshold, has been employed by Barron (1955) to inkblots. In fact, Barron's achromatic inkblots, constructed specifically to provide a threshold measure of human movement (M), would lend themselves quite readily to a scalogram analysis. A study of Spivak, Levine, and Sprigle (1958) with Barron's series of blots show that the percentage of subjects giving M to the blots ranged from .00 to .72, with an average increment of .03 between adjacent inkblots. Moreover, their data indicate that a good approximation to a rectangular distribution could be obtained with only 13 of the original 26 inkblots, with an average step interval of .05.

After this brief examination of models underlying various kinds of projective methods, we may now return to the original proposition that similar responses to a projective test will increasingly reflect analogous dynamics as the test approximates a cumulative homogeneity model. This postulate explicitly asserts that the pure relative frequency and the cumulative homogeneity models represent polar opposites on a continuum of internal consistency, with the specific relative frequency model in the middle.

The published data on projective techniques based on the pure relative frequency model indicate that prudence must be shown before superficially similar responses are combined to reflect similar dynamics [see Jensen (1959) for a comprehensive review of the literature on the internal consistency of standard projective methods]. The vital importance of cautiousness is indicated by the results of a rarely cited study by Wittenborn (1950). He examined the hypothesis that responses to the TAT which are similar to each other should be more frequently related to each other than should dissimilar responses. Three separate tests of this hypothesis were made. In the first analysis, he tested for the interrelationships between the "good woman" response role assigned to the woman in cards 4, 6GF, and 13MF. As none of these relationships were significant, the "good woman" role must reflect different dynamics in the three cards. The second analysis tested for significant interrelationships between "conflict evidence" frequently ascribed to the heroes for cards 2, 4, 7BM, and 13MF. Again, the conflict response categories were not significantly interrelated. The third analysis tested for the interrelations among "hostile" responses given to cards 7BM, 7GF, 4, 6BM, 6GF, and 13MF. The data also failed to support the assumption that hostile feelings reported to different TAT cards will be significantly related to each other.

Confirmation of Wittenborn's early finding that similar responses to different TAT cards reflect dissimilar dynamics is contained in the studies by Child, Frank, and Storm (1956), Lindzey and Goldberg (1953), and Epstein (1964). Employing a group-administered TAT, Child, Frank, and Storm (1956) found that internal consistency estimates for 10 need variables ranged from −.07 to .34, with a mean of only .13. Similarly, Lindzey and Herman (1955) obtained split-half reliability figures ranging from .12 to .45, with 8 TAT cards on six different personality variables. In a recent study (Epstein, 1964), conducted under the author's guidance, a rank order method was first used to order nine TAT pictures in terms of hostility. The initial nine cards (1, 2, 3BM, 4, 6BM, 11, 14, 18BM, 18GF) were selected on the basis of experience to represent a range of aggression in terms of card pull. Cards 2, 4, and 6BM were eliminated from further study because there was considerable variation between subjects in the ranks assigned to them. Cards 1 and 14 were designated the low-aggressive, cards 3BM and 11 as moderately aggressive, and cards 18BM and 18GF as highly aggressive. Previous research and clinical experience would seem to support the classification of these six TAT cards. Forty volunteers from an introductory course in psychology told TAT stories to these cards. The stories were scored on Stone's (1956) aggressive content scale, Purcell's (1956) internally based punishment score, and his externally based punishment score. Internal consistency was assessed by intercorrelating the data on each of the three sets of aggressive cards for the three aggressive measures. Of the nine correlations, only one was significantly different from zero. The correlation between the low and the medium aggressive cards on internal punishment was .48 ($p < .05$). The results of this study provide further support for the proposition that superficially homogeneous responses to projective tests based on the pure relative frequency model may not be assessing similar psychological dynamics.

While the first postulate leads to the prediction that, in general, a projective test composed of homogeneous stimuli will be more sensitive to analogous psychological processes, direct empirical evidence is lacking on this prediction for projective tests based on either the specific relative frequency model or the cumulative frequency model. However, this assumption has received some highly indirect empirical support from a study by Carr (1956) on intraindividual consistency in response to projective tests of varying degrees of ambiguity. The major finding of this research was that there was greatest consistency in level of inference about affect between the TAT and Rorschach and between the TAT and Sentence Completion Test. If the Rorschach and Sentence Completion test stimuli are thought of as extremes on a continuum of stimulus homogeneity, then the finding of greatest consistency between each of these projective techniques and the TAT lends indirect support for our assumption. This study also gives no support for the hypothesis of an inverse relationship between psychological processes as a function of test stimulus dimensions. In other words, irrespective of the kind of stimuli employed, test indices of apparently similar psychological processes will either produce positive relationships or no appreciable correlations. The correlations will not be negative, as some individuals have hypothesized.

*Summary*. Despite the lack of direct evidence bearing on the first postulate, there is reason to believe that it will hold up because of the test construction procedures implied by the specific relative frequency model and the cumulative frequency model. Furthermore, theory and research in the fields of aptitude and attitude measurement point to the reasonableness of the postulate.

### B. POSTULATE TWO: FUNCTIONAL STIMULUS

*Valid interindividual and group comparisons necessitate the assumption of constancy of the functional stimulus on a projective technique for all individuals.*

Projective personologists have been slow in their acceptance of this postulate, perhaps because such a proposition severely complicates no-end clinical inferences and research. Research evidence in many different areas of psychology has gradually taught investigators at least one important lesson about the stimulus in psychological experiments. It is that a subject may not be responding to the stimuli that the experimenter thinks he is. Hull (1943) was aware of this problem when he distinguished between the potential stimuli of a situation and the actual stimuli received by a subject. In a somewhat similar fashion, Underwood (1963), in a lucid discussion of stimulus selection in verbal learning, has distinguished between the apparent or *nominal* stimulus and the actual or *functional* stimulus. The nominal stimulus is what the experimenter presents to the subject, whereas, the functional stimulus refers, in part, to the properties of the nominal stimulus which the subject employs to cue his behavior. In many psychological experiments, there may be serious discrepancies between the nominal and functional stimulus, rendering any isomorphic assumption between the nominal and functional stimulus suspect.

With respect to projective techniques, the nominal stimulus is what the psychologist presents to the individual. For example, the item stem "My mother . . . ," the scene portrayed in picture 6BM of the TAT, and Card VII of the Rorschach are nominal stimuli. For these materials the term *functional stimuli* refers to how an individual perceives the meaning of the item stem; how he perceives what is portrayed in picture 6BM; and what meaning he attributes to card VII of the Rorschach. Do each of these three projective items signify "mother" as a functional stimulus for most *Ss*? The information necessary to answer this query would be shown by the degree of consistency of perceptual reactions to these projective stimuli. That is, a functional stimulus is specified by the perceptual decoding of the nominal stimulus by the individual. A simple physical specification of the nominal stimulus will not enable the investigator to discover the functional stimulus. The notion of a functional stimulus is expressed by the following proposition:

$$FS = f(Dimensions \ of \ nominal \ stimulus \leftrightarrow decoding \ schemes)$$

where the double arrow indicates that the stimulus dimensions of the nominal stimulus and the decoding systems of an individual interact continuously with one another.

The assumption that the FS must be the same for all individuals, if valid individual or group comparisons are to be made, may be brought into initial focus by dealing first with the problem of cross-cultural comparisons with projective techniques. Suppose we wish to compare n-Achievement between the Wisconsin Menomini and Algerian Arabs by means of a TAT-type test. Before constructing his test pictures, the projective personologist would obtain ethnographic data on the kinds of cues in each society which arouse achievement-oriented dispositions. Successful construction of one set of pictures, suitable for both groups, depends upon discovering trans-cultural cues for achievement arousal. If the nominal picture stimuli do not possess trans-cultural equivalence or functional stimulus equivalence for both groups, then group differences between the Arabs and Monomini could not be attributed to differences in achievement drive. That is, differential group perceptions of what is portrayed in the pictures would vitiate any valid cross-cultural comparisons. On the other hand, the investigator may construct different sets of pictures for the separate groups. In principle, such a procedure is entirely suitable, providing his ethnographic data permit him to match the cue strength for achievement in the two sets of pictures. Of course, the practical problems involved in such an approach are almost insurmountable, largely because of the absence of good ethnographic data which would enable the investigator to equate different nominal stimuli for functional stimulus equivalence.

Most, if not all, projective personologists would readily grant the need for functional stimulus equivalence in a comparison of two widely different cultural groups. However, the whole thrust of the principle at issue has not been so widely accepted in the comparison of various subgroups within the North American culture. It would be most unfortunate if the general principle of functional equivalence of stimulus meaning were disregarded when group comparisons were performed between groups within the same society, whether the comparisons be between males and females, young and old subjects, lower and middle class groups, or other similar group comparisons.

Consider, for example, the following problem: Suppose we wished to compare the achievement drive of Radcliffe students and home economics, students from a state university. It probably would be inappropriate to use a picture which presents a scene of a young lady baking a cake as a means of assessing the achievement drive differences between the two groups. It is most unlikely that such a scene would possess equal cue strength for achievement or similarity in perceptual meaning for the two groups. Likewise, Card 1 of the TAT probably would not be suitable in any valid comparisons of differences in the achievement drive for young and old persons, largely because older persons usually do not perceive this card as an achievement-arousing scene (Atkinson, 1950).

What is equally important, the second postulate applies not only to group comparisons but also to comparisons between individuals. It is not possible to assert that one individual has more of one personality variable than another person, unless one can reasonably assume that both individuals decoded the nominal stimulus into the same functional stimulus. That is, valid individual comparisons require the assumption that the individuals concerned agree on what they perceive in the projective stimulus. If one says it is an aggressive stimulus and the other says it is an achievement stimulus, then one is not in a position to say on the basis of TAT stories that one individual has more achievement or aggression than the other person.

Until recent times, very little attention has been given to the problem of ensuring that the projective stimuli have equivalent functional properties before two or more individuals or groups are compared. Moreover, research aimed at the construction of projective stimuli which have similar functional stimulus properties for different groups should make a significant contribution to the personality measurement field.

Numerous studies (Lindzey, 1961) have utilized projective techniques in cross-cultural research. While it is not surprising that these studies show many group discriminations, the exact meaning of the differences remains a puzzling issue. Within the context of this paper, a basic factor producing the obtained differences may be attributable to differential perceptions of the meaning of the test materials. For example, the failure of a group on the Rorschach to perceive the central detail on Card I as human, the figures in Card III as human, and the whole blot of Card V as a winged animal may only reflect cross-cultural differences in perception. The form, shading, figure-ground relationships, color, and textural aspects of the inkblots readily lend themselves to "perceptual biases" for divergent cultural groups. Cross-cultural differences may merely indicate "perceptual biases" and not genuine differences in personality. As far as this author is aware, no attention has been given in cross-cultural research to the problem of determining if individuals from different societies can actually perceive certain percepts within specifically designated areas of the Rorschach. Until such data are obtained, there is no need to assume that cross-cultural differences on the Rorschach originate in personality differences.

Similarly, social class and age differences on the Rorschach for North American samples may only reflect differential "perceptual biases" and not differential personality functioning. While research (Auld, 1952; Haase, 1956; Riessman and Miller, 1958; Stone and Fiedler, 1956) indicates that there are social class differences on the Rorschach, it remains to be shown that these discriminations can be ascribed to personality variables. Similarly, studies (Douvan, 1958; McArthur, 1955; Veroff, Atkinson, Feld and Guria, 1960) with the TAT indicate that there are differences in need-Achievement between the middle and lower classes. The differences may be class-oriented "perceptual biases" transcending personality factors. We are again faced with the need for research to determine if members of different social classes can perceive percepts in specifically marked-out areas of the Rorschach. Moreover, the same matters are at issue in age and sex comparisons on the Rorschach and TAT.

As part of a comprehensive research program on stimulus factors in thematic apperceptive techniques, this author and his associates have conducted a series of studies to determine if TAT cards have functional stimulus meaning for different groups. Underlying the methodology of these studies is the premise that when a projective stimulus is presented to a subject he will attempt to identify, categorize, or otherwise decode the nominal physical dimensions of the stimulus. Such decoding systems are the operational specifications of what we mean by functional stimuli. If a person is asked to describe what he sees in card 3BM of the TAT, he may say, "This is a person who is broken up over something," or "The person is thinking of or has tried to take his own life." Such reactions are attempts to assign the nominal stimuli of a TAT card to decoding systems. They represent what Bartlett calls "an effort after meaning" (1932, p. 44). While stimulus oriented, most individuals clearly go beyond the nominal physical stimulus properties of TAT cards when they are asked to describe what they see in each card. By decoding the nominal stimulus, the perceiver adds something to the nominal stimulus, thereby making the functional stimulus (decoding system) somewhat different from the nominal stimulus.

The first phase of this research required Ss to examine each TAT card for a 20-second period and to "describe what is in each picture." The next step was similar to a critical incident study in that the card descriptions were assigned to decoding categories that seemed best to reflect the codes used by the subjects in assigning functional stimulus properties to the TAT pictures. That is, the decoding systems were not formed *a priori*, but were empirically derived from a detailed analysis of the perceptual reactions. In the first studies (Kenny, Harvey, and Wilson, 1961), a total of 40 hospitalized psychiatric patients and 40 normal control Ss were used to obtain the initial decoding reactions to 26 TAT cards—1, 2, 3BM, 3GF, 4, 5, 6BM, 7BM, 8BM, 9GF, 10, 11, 12M, 12BG, 13MF, 14, 15, 17BM, 17GF, 18BM, 18GF, 19, and 20. The Ss were told that the experimenter was interested in having people tell her what they see in pictures and that during a 20-second exposure of each card they were to describe what they saw in each picture. The patients (23 male and 17 female) were severely disturbed psychoneurotics who were institutionalized in a provincial mental hospital, in which the maximum allowable period of hospitalization is 4 months. The controls or normals were matched with the patients for level of education. The modal number of perceptual codes, required to categorize the reactions of the Ss per card, was 8, with a range of 6 to 12. Scorer reliability, based on two independent judges assigning the perceptual reactions to the codes, was 91.2% agreement.

Do severely disturbed neurotics and normals employ different decoding mechanisms in assigning functional stimulus meaning to TAT cards? Out of a total of 216 decoding categories, only 19 showed significant chi square tests at the .01 or .05 level between the groups. Accordingly, it may be concluded that the functional stimulus meaning of TAT cards for normal and neurotic adults manifests high communality.

The propitious finding of a striking congruence between normals and neurotics in their decoding systems should not be generalized to other group comparisons. In order to determine whether extreme cultural differences make for dissimilar decoding reactions to the TAT, another study (Moriya, 1962) compared the decoding mechanisms of Japanese and Canadian samples. On the basis of data obtained from previous studies in this series, the five most common perceptual coding reactions for each TAT card were prepared and the Ss were asked to check the perceptual reaction which they thought best described what they saw in each TAT card. The Japanese sample consisted of 40 male and 60 female students of the Gakushuin University in Tokyo. The Canadian group consisted of 30 female and 54 male students from the University of British Columbia. In general, the results indicated that Japanese Ss decode the nominal stimulus of TAT pictures in significantly different ways from Canadian Ss. Examination of these differences does not support the proposition that Japanese Ss decode the world in socially stereotyped ways. For example, the Japanese proportions for the "suicide" code was greater on Card 3BM, but smaller on Card 17GF than for the Canadian sample. The Canadian proportion for the "spying" code was greater on Card 9GF but smaller on Card 5 when compared with those of the Japanese. On the other hand, some of the results do seem to reflect the strong cultural pressures within the Japanese culture upon perceptual codes. Without exception, the Japanese sample has larger proportions in the "sadness," "aggressive," and "disphoric" codes than does the Canadian group.

It would seem, then, that culture is a significant determinant of the functional stimulus in a thematic apperceptive technique. Although the data on differences in perceptual codes between subgroups within one culture are scant, Veroff's (1961) data imply that blue-collar workers and white-collar workers may have differential perceptions of the stimulus meaning of achievement oriented pictures. Although problems of interpretation are posed by his study because no data were collected on the specific decoding categories used by his two groups, the finding that $n$ Achievement scores based on pictures of blue-collar workers, in comparison with pictures of white-collar workers, elicit more productive relationships to other variables for white-collar workers than for blue-collar workers suggests indirectly that the coding reactions of the two groups are probably different to the blue-collar pictures. In the same study, Veroff also showed college-educated women may interpret the functional stimulus of a picture of a career work setting differently from grade school–educated women. While the high school– and grade school–educated females appeared to interpret a career picture in terms of achievement, college-educated women viewed this picture as a cue for achievement-conflict. This general finding is in accordance with the notion that the functional stimulus of a career picture is not the same for the two groups.

In the light of the foregoing findings and considerations, any valid comparison of two different groups must ensure that the functional stimulus of thematic apperception pictures is the same for both groups. That is, the decoding systems to pictures must be the same for different groups, if the results are to be attributed to personality factors.

For some obscure reason, cross-cultural research and studies comparing groups within a society continue to be marred by the failure to provide methodological control over the functional stimulus. While it is invidious to single out any one research from a host of studies as an illustration of the confounding effects of the functional stimulus, a recent contribution (Bradburn, 1963) will be used to provide final clarification of the conceptual and methodological questions posed by our second postulate. On the basis of previous research, Bradburn hypothesized that father dominance is associated with low achievement in men. Since interview data indicated that Turkish fathers are more dominant than American fathers, he predicted that Turkish junior executives, as compared with American junior executives, would have significantly lower achievement. Both groups told TAT stories to six pictures described in Atkinson (1958) and the data show that the American sample had significantly higher achievement scores. While it was Bradburn's conclusion that the data supported his hypothesis, such a motivational explanation of the results only follows if the investigator can rule out the possibility that the six pictures possess trans-cultural equivalence for achievement cues. It is entirely possible in this study that the average differences between American and Turkish males are due to the differential functional stimulus strengths that the six American-constructed pictures had for the two groups. That is, the obtained differences might be due to the fact that the nominal picture stimuli could be more readily decoded as reflecting achieving cues by American than Turkish subjects.

*Summary.* Research aimed at between-group comparisons must establish that projective stimuli evoke the same decoding systems for the groups. Unless the investigator controls for trans-group equivalence of stimulus meaning, his results must be viewed with reservations.

C. POSTULATE THREE: PROJECTION AS A FUNCTION OF PERCEIVED SIMILARITY

*Attribution of tension-producing affects in awareness will increase as a function of increasing perceived similarity between the individual and the projective stimulus; attribution of tension-producing affects not in consciousness will increase as a function of decreasing perceived similarity between the individual and the projective stimulus.*

Most recently, the empirical evidence and theorizing of a trio of investigators (Feshbach and Feshbach, 1963; Feshbach and Singer, 1957) have indicated that affective attribution is dependent not only upon the affective state of the perceiver but also upon the nature of the perceived stimulus. The following discussion takes as its frame of reference a recent theoretical article by Singer (1963).

In a pioneering and ingenious experiment on projection, Murray (1933) showed that frightened female children perceive pictures of adults as malicious. Murray called this type of affective attribution "complementary projection." The attribution to a stimulus figure or object of affect present in the perceiver may be called "supplementary projection." Unfortunately, Murray did not assess for the possibility of supplementary projection effects in his experiment, nor did he attempt to determine how projection is critically dependent upon stimulus variables.

In the first of their studies, Feshbach and Singer (1957) used three groups, a control, a fear-expression group (who were encouraged to become conscious of their anxiety feelings), and a fear-suppression group (who were encouraged to suppress their affect). In support of their predictions, both fear groups projected fear onto a male graduate student appearing in a film, with the fear-suppression group ascribing more anxiety to the stimulus figure than the fear-expression group. The two most interesting features of these findings are that supplementary projection was demonstrated and that suppression of affect facilitates projection. In another follow-up study on the projection of anxiety, Singer and Feshbach (1962) showed that anxiety-aroused normals and psychotics attributed more anxiety to a series of human pictures than did control groups. More importantly, the specific prediction that psychotics would attribute more fear to a set of pictures labeled as "mentally ill" persons than to "never mentally ill" stimuli was supported.

Since these two experiments and Murray's left partially unanswered the question of what conditions generate supplementary or complementary projection, Feshbach and Feshbach (1963) hypothesized that the type of projection manifested will be contingent upon the relationship between the perceiver and the stimulus figure being perceived. Specifically, they predicted that supplementary projection will occur to stimulus figures viewed as similar to the perceiver, but that complementary projection will occur to stimulus figures perceived as dissimilar. In the study, young boys judged 16 pictorial stimuli, equally divided among men, women, boys, and girls, for the personality characteristics of maliciousness and fearfulness. In accordance with their predictions, the fear-aroused children, as compared with the controls, manifested complementary projection to the adult male stimuli and supplementary projection to young boy pictures. Such results strongly suggest that if the stimulus figure is perceived as similar to the perceiver, then direct attribution of affect is to be expected; on the other hand, dissimilar stimuli will instigate complementary projection.

The findings from the foregoing experiments indicate that anxiety affects will be projected in accord with the third postulate. Will the assumption apply to other affects? In an unpublished study discussed by Singer (1963), it was shown that college males and females who were made hostile attributed more hostility to college-age male stimuli than to a 12-year-old boy pictorial stimulus. In another study examining the interactions between the similarity of the perceiver and the projective stimulus, Feshbach, Singer, and Feshbach (1963) had college students describe 26 stick figures and 28 TAT-like two-person interaction scenes. Both classes of stimuli conveyed the impression of hostility. In the TAT-type pictures, one person could be seen as frustrating another. In one series of the TAT pictures, five of the situations portrayed the receiver of the frustration as a college-age male, and in the other four situations he was a 12-year-old boy. In the other series of the TAT pictures, the ages of the stimulus figures were reversed, with the object of frustration and its source similar to those in the first series. While there was no difference between experimentally aroused hostile Ss and controls in attribution of hostile affect to the stick figures, both male and female angered Ss showed a heightened increment in the ascription of hostility to same-age college male stimuli on the TAT pictures. The experimentally aroused Ss showed no significant increment in hostility attribution to the younger stimulus individuals on the TAT pictures. Thus, the major findings of this study warrant the conclusion that hostile attribution only occurs to same-age figures and not to stick figures or to younger boys. The conclusion provides evidence in support of the proposition that supplementary projection is contingent upon the perceived similarity between the stimulus and the perceiver.

In another study in this series, Kiesler and Singer (1963) reported that college female Ss, who are made hostile but remain relatively unaware of their affects, attribute hostile feelings more to dissimilar persons than to similar individuals. This finding is consistent with the notion that affects not in awareness will be attributed to dissimilar stimulus figures.

In the most recent of this provocative series of investigations, Feshbach (1963) showed clearly that supplementary projection takes place for a socially acceptable and positive affect, namely, that of "happiness." Twenty-nine female Ss were made to feel happy by the joint interaction of a monetary reward and successful performance on a jigsaw puzzle designed to measure spatial ability. Twelve of the 29 Ss were assigned to an affective restraint group by instructing them not to reveal their feelings to other Ss. The experimental subjects, plus an additional 27 females in a control group, then evaluated for happiness 14 photographs of male and female pictures which had been previously scaled by a modified Thurstone technique on a continuum of happiness-sadness. At least one male and female photograph appeared at each point on the scale. The results of the ratings supported the hypothesis that a positive affect may be projected in that the affectively restrained Ss attributed more happiness to the happy-appearing female photographs than the controls. That supplementary projection depends upon similarity between stimulus figure and perceiver was also upheld, as shown by the finding that there was more attribution of happiness to female faces than to male faces.

The results of all these studies are, in general, congruent with what would be expected in terms of the third postulate. It should be emphasized that this assumption should hold even when socially unacceptable affects are at issue. A particularly striking example of the independence of this assumption from the social acceptability of affects is provided by the research of Bramel (1962). In his experiment, Ss were made to feel that they were homosexually aroused by male photographs. This procedure caused the Ss to overestimate the magnitude of homosexuality toward individuals favorably evaluated as belonging to the same social category. While the latter type of individual may be assumed to be more similar than dissimilar to the perceiver, Bramel (1963), in a partial replication of the original experiment, attempted to manipulate more explicitly the variable of similarity and dissimilarity. In this experiment, Bramel employed the same technique as before to make the experimental Ss believe that they had homosexual motivation by having them observe their own deceptively high galvanic skin responses when viewing photographs of good-looking men in states of undress. Before watching the galvanometer dial, the experimental Ss had been led to believe that high galvanometer needle readings indicated homosexual arousal. For the control Ss, the needle remained at the low end of the galvanometer dial. After all Ss viewed and recorded their own need readings for 15 male photographs, they rated the degree of homosexual tendencies of an individual telling stories to four TAT pictures. The actual stories contained no overt references to homosexual or heterosexual behavior. Before listening to the tapes of the TAT stories, half of Ss (the "student group") were told that the story teller was a student; the other half (the "criminal group") were told that the story teller was a criminal who had just been arrested for the third time after a series of armed robberies. In addition, all Ss rated themselves on homosexuality and how they compared themselves in similarity to the story teller. The latter ratings were performed to assess the adequacy of the induction of the two independent variables—homosexual arousal and the variable of similarity-dissimilarity. Bramel found that the experimental Ss ascribed more homosexuality to themselves, reflecting the adequacy of the experimental arousal of homosexuality; the Ss assigned to the student group rated themselves as more similar to the story teller than did those in the criminal group, indicating the adequacy of the similarity-dissimilarity induction. In conformity with the third postulate about projective techniques, Ss in the student group attributed more homosexuality to the story teller than those in the criminal group. Thus, supplementary projection takes place to stimulus figures perceived as similar to the perceiver, even though the attributed conscious trait is undesirable.

It is evident that the third postulate and its experimental evidence have profound implications for projective techniques. The fruitfulness of this assumption, over alternative ones, will now be considered with special reference to a sampling of related experimental and clinical problems in the field of projective techniques.

## 1. Hero Assumption

In the clinical use of thematic apperceptive techniques and doll play, it is sometimes assumed that the hero of a TAT story or the central identification figure in doll play reflects the characteristics of the subject and that the other figures in the story or doll play indicate how the subject perceives other individuals in his environment. Lindzey (1952) considers the hero assumption as a necessary feature of the clinical use of the TAT. On the other hand, Piotrowski (1952) has made the assumption that all figures in a story are equally revealing of the story teller's personality. The large-scale research endeavors of McClelland et al. (1953) on the achievement motive follow Piotrowski's assumption on this issue. Surprisingly, however, this important problem has generated very little direct research.

Lindzey and Kalnins (1958) undertook the only two studies on this problem, making the assumption that a distinction should be made between hero and nonhero figures in a TAT story. In the first of these studies, 30 undergraduate females were asked to evaluate the similarity between themselves and each character that they introduced into the six TAT stories they told. For the 180 stories, two independent raters agreed 90% in identifying the hero figure in each story. The main results of this study showed that the hero figures were more often perceived as similar to self than were nonhero figures. While Lindzey and Kalnins accepted this finding as offering modest support for the hero assumption, it must be pointed out that their study is not free from methodological criticism. In any valid test of the hero assumption versus alternative assumptions, it seems necessary to obtain independent evidence of the attributes of the subjects and then assess the extent to which these attributes are ascribed to heroes and nonhero figures. Without this kind of data, the Lindzey and Kalnins study is most difficult to interpret. If independent data on the story teller are obtained, then the hero assumption would predict that hero figures in TAT stories would be ascribed more of the story teller's attributes than would nonhero figures. Piotrowski's assumption would have to predict that these attributes be attributed equally to all figures. On the other hand, our third postulate would predict that attribution of traits would depend critically upon the perceived similarity of the story teller to the stimulus figures in the TAT pictures and the degree of consciousness of the attributes being projected. This type of experiment has yet to be done.

In the second study, Lindzey and Kalnins (1958) exposed the experimental $Ss$ to a complex frustration of social motives and compared their TAT protocols to those of unfrustrated controls. They hypothesized that the critical comparison between the hero assumption and Piotrowski's alternative assumption (i.e., that all figures are equally revealing) would be for the category of aggressive acts by nonhero figures in the stories. They argued that the hero assumption, in contrast to the aternative assumption, would predict no increase in aggression between nonhero figures. The data confirmed the prediction deduced from the hero assumption. However, our third postulate suggests that the results for the category of aggression by nonhero figures could be made to vary experimentally, provided the perceived similarity between these figures and the story teller were manipulated appropriately.

In light of the experimental findings that affects can be attributed to persons who are quite dissimilar to the perceiver, the hero assumption does not seem warranted in the interpretation of TAT stories. The inference from our postulate is that the story teller is quite likely to attribute affects to nonhero figures who are perceived as dissimilar to him. This observation should not be construed as implying that TAT protocol analysis should not attempt to distinguish between hero and nonhero figures. Quite the contrary. Attributes ascribed to nonheroes, provided they are dissimilar to the story teller, are likely to reflect unconscious states. Attributes attributed to heroes, provided they are similar to the story teller, are likely to indicate conscious states. In essence, clinical interpretation of any projective material must be based upon the meaning that stimuli have for patients.

### 2. Assumptions with Respect to Physical Similarity between Stimulus Figures and Projecting Individual

We turn now to the theoretical and practical problem of what type of stimulus figures an individual can most readily identify himself with, thereby facilitating maximum projection. Most of the research on this problem has been designed to test the premise that there is a monotonic relationship between amount of projection and increases in physical similarity between the story teller and the figures on apperceptive pictures. The reader will recall that Murray's (1943) original division of his pictures into sets for men, women, boys, and girls assumes that age and sex similarity of the TAT figures will facilitate identification and projective mechanisms. Since then, Murray's assumption has served as a useful model for many other apperceptive test constructors who have designed special sets of pictorial stimuli. In this connection, Henry's (1947) set of line drawings for Hopi and Navaho children, Thompson's (1949) series of pictures with Negro figures, the Michigan Picture Test (Hartwell, Hutt, Andrew, and Walton, 1951) for grade school children, the set of pictorial cards depicting nuns developed by Lasago y Travieso and Martinez-Arango (1946) for the personality assessment of nuns, and Kagan's (1956) 13 pictures to test aggression in boys between the ages of 10 and 13, may be cited as representative of authors who have, by varying degrees, accepted the Murray model.

Although a considerable amount of energy has been devoted to an examination of the assumed relation between physical similarity and projection, the obtained data present a problem in interpretation. In order to measure amount of projection attributable to differences in physical similarity between the projector and the stimulus figures in the pictorial stimuli, experimenters have commonly employed as their measures of the dependent variable, indices of story length, word counts, number of different themes, transcendence scores, level of productivity, and compliance with test instructions. However, there is little in the way of theoretical or experimental justification for the assumption that word counts and the like are valid or relevant measures of projection. Just because one set of pictorial figures evokes a higher word count or transcendence index than another set is by no means a relevant proof that the subjects are projecting more of their attributes to one of these sets. Such data, at least to this author, are irrelevant to the problem at hand. In order to test adequately the relation between physical similarity and projection, it is necessary either to induce personality states experimentally or to obtain independent evidence that the $Ss$ manifest certain personality characteristics. Then, it must be shown that one kind of stimulus material is a better reflector of these attributes than another type of material. As a consequence of the failure to obtain prior data on the attributes that individuals might project, the validity of the studies about to be reviewed is of questionable character. For organizational purposes, the studies will be grouped under the categories of identification with animals, color-of-skin identification, bodily similarity identification, and same-sex and opposite-sex identification. However, all studies deal directly or indirectly with the problem of the relation between the projector and the stimulus figures on pictorial stimuli (see also Murstein, 1961, 1963b).

a. *Identification with Animals.* Ever since Bellak designed the Children Apperception Test (CAT), experimenters have been unusually vigorous in testing a subsidiary premise upon which this test was built. Bellak made the assumption that young children would more readily identify with animal figures than human and it is this assumption which investigators have tested extensively. For obscure reasons, the central assumption of this technique, namely, that stimuli depicting eating, sibling rivalry, primal scenes, toilet settings, sleeping, and aggression evoke the cardinal problems of children, has remained untested.

In an early study with children between the ages of 5 and 10 years, Bills (1950) found that rabbit pictures instigated significantly longer stories than TAT cards. Moreover, the psychological inferences which might be drawn from these two tests appeared to be quite different. In a subsequent study, Bills, Leiman, and Thomas (1950) showed that neither the TAT nor the rabbit pictures produced material which agreed with data derived from play therapy sessions. In these two studies, adequate control was not exercised over the background features of the two sets of pictures.

In the first systematic attempt to control for the stimulus values of the human and animal pictures, Biersdorf and Marcuse (1953) had an artist construct six animal pictures similar to those on the CAT plus another six comparable pictures with humans substituted for animals. They attempted to ensure that the two sets of pictures were identical in emotional expression and in most other respects. When the two tests were given to 30 first graders, no differences were found between the techniques on such indices as number of ideas, number of words, reaction time, number of figures introduced into the stories who were not in the pictures, number of figures referred to in the pictures, and total response time. Two main criticisms of this kind of research are worth reiterating. First, it has already been pointed out that measures such as word count in no way indicate whether or not the Ss are projecting attributes which they possess. On this score alone, this and similar experiments do not provide a valid test of Bellak's proposition. Second, the human pictures indicate far more clearly to the Ss the sex of the figures than do Bellak's animal pictures. If animal and human pictures are to be matched, ambiguity with respect to sex of the figures must be constant.

Two additional studies have been conducted with the Marcuse pictures. Mainord and Marcuse (1954) gave the two sets of pictures to emotionally disturbed boys and girls whose mean age was 7 years. Again, simple quantitative indices showed no differences between the two kinds of pictures, although five clinicians indicated that the protocols based on the human pictures were clinically more useful than those based on the animal series. Interestingly enough, however, Budoff (1955) found that less well-adjusted children were more productive on the CAT pictures than on another set of comparable human pictures. In Budoff's study, normal children produced more revealing material on the human series. Furuya (1957) administered the Marcuse pictures to 72 Japanese children, with an age range of 6 to 12 years. On 20 tests of significance, the human pictures yielded better results than the animal pictures for four indices.

Light (1955) compared CAT cards with TAT cards, using 9- and 10-year-olds. While no significant differences in number of words occurred when the two sets of cards were compared, the CAT cards were more productive on a number of other criteria, such as expression of feelings, number of conflicts, and themes. Since this study failed to match the animal and human pictures on a number of critical stimulus dimensions, and contained no data on the personality attributes of the subjects which might be projected onto the respective figures, the findings are not pertinent to the general problem at issue. Using a group of intellectually superior children in the first, second, and third grade in a comparison between the CAT and a somewhat similar set of human pictures, Armstrong (1954) found that the human pictures elicited a significantly greater number of statements that went beyond picture description. There were no differences, however, between the two sets of pictures on word count.

In the most recent study on this proposition, Weisskopf-Joelson and Foster (1962) attempted to remove some of the deficiencies contained in the foregoing researches. They used 40 kindergarten children, with a mean age of 6 years, 2 months. While the CAT is designed for children between the ages of 3 and 10, Bellak and Adelman (1960) feel that the issue of animal *versus* human pictures should be tested on young children. Many of the other studies have used children close to the 10-year limit. In addition, this study avoided the use of a counterbalanced design in which all Ss receive each animal picture and its matching human picture. Counterbalanced designs may contaminate the results with strong differential carry-over effects from analogous pictures. In order to match four CAT pictures with similar human pictures, the investigators were forced to modify, probably in critical ways, the CAT pictures. For example, two important changes were the addition of clothes to the animals and the omission of the mouse in Card 3. While some children identify with the lion in Card 3, many take the mouse as the identification figure. While it would probably be inappropriate to design a picture with a human figure appearing out of a small hole in a baseboard, the omission of the mouse means that the investigators are no longer examining the CAT. It would have been better to use one of the remaining six cards. The results of this study showed that the mean transcendence index of the human pictures did not differ significantly from that of the animal pictures.

While most of these researches tend to show either no difference between animal and human pictures or that the human pictures are slightly more productive, the limitations of these studies prevent the acceptance of the proposition that children will identify as readily or more readily with human figures and will project more onto humans. As already stressed, none of these investigations had independent information on the attributes which may have been projected. Researchers have yet to show sufficient ingenuity in ensuring adequate control over background factors in designing their sets of pictures. Research has been largely limited to older children. Moreover, some studies have employed counterbalanced designs in which going from A to B may not be the same as going from B to A. In short, this writer adopts the strong position that no study has valid data. This conclusion should be contrasted with Murstein's (1963b) assertion that, after reviewing the same studies, he had "laid to rest" the assumption about identification with animals. Bellak's hypothesis is deserving of more inventive research and treatment than it has received up to this time.

Finally, it should be mentioned that no research has been conducted on the relative merits of animal and human stimuli in projective films. In contrast to still picture apperceptive techniques which commonly use human stimuli, filmed apperceptive techniques have primarily made use of puppets (Haworth, 1960; Lerner and Murphy, 1941) and animated cartoons (Gemelli, 1951). Apparently, the Test Filmique Thématique (Cohen-Séat and Rebéillard, 1955) is the only filmed technique that has exploited the possibilities of human stimuli. The research possibilities of filmed projective methods, contrasting the projective merits of various classes of stimuli figures, are almost limitless. Haworth (1960) should be consulted for a comprehensive review of films as a projective technique.

b. *Identification with Color of Skin.* The question of whether Negro Ss might more readily identify with Negro figures on an apperceptive test was raised by Thompson (1949). He hypothesized that sparsity of dynamically relevant material in the protocol data of Negroes might be due to the white figures on the TAT. Accordingly, he substituted Negro figures for the white ones on the TAT and gave the new set of pictures, along with the analogous 10 pictures from the original TAT, to a group of 26 Southern Negro college students. The students produced significantly longer stories on the Negro series than on the traditional TAT, suggesting that projection is facilitated by color-of-skin similarity between the story teller and the figures in the pictorial stimuli.

However, Thompson's modification of the original TAT for Negroes was quickly challenged. Riess, Schwartz, and Cottingham (1950) found no differences in story length between the Negro and white version of the

TAT for 30 Northern Negro and 30 Northern white college students. Analyzing the same data, Schwartz, Riess, and Cottingham (1951) showed that Negro students produce the same number of ideas to both sets of cards. Korchin, Mitchell, and Meltzoff (1950) contributed another study on the two versions of the test. Again, story length did not differ between the two versions for 80 Northern Negroes and 80 Northern whites. Similarly, Light (1955) did not find any differences in story length between the TAT and the Thompson modification for 26 students. In a more appropriate experimental design that avoids the difficulty of the counterbalanced designs used in the other studies, Cook (1953) tested one half of his Negro and white Ss with the Murray TAT and the remaining Ss with the Thompson modification. In agreement with other studies, Cook found no significant differences due to version of the test.

Aside from Thompson's initial study, the main conclusion of these studies appears to be that physical similarity of skin color does not increase projection. However, these investigations suffer from the same limitation as those dealing with the animal *versus* human identification problem. In point of fact, there is no evidence that the Ss are attributing any attributes to either version of the TAT. Moreover, the assumption that any simple manipulation of skin color will elicit perceptions of similarity and identification is tenuous, to say the least.

*c. Identification with Bodily Similarity.* A few investigators have attempted to test the formulation that bodily similarity between story teller and the central figure on TAT cards will increase the amount of projection. The measures of projection are usually word counts, transcendence indices, or level of productivity. The principal criticisms of these studies concern the correctness of the measures of projection and the crude manner of manipulating bodily similarity. As we have already indicated, the only way in which an experimenter can be sure that a subject is projecting is to have prior knowledge of the subject's attributes. The similarity variable is something that resides within the subject. That similarity is a psychologically mediated variable and not a physical variable is illustrated by the finding (Clark and Clark, 1947; Goodman, 1946) that Negro and white preschoolers identify more strongly with the white doll than the Negro doll when asked, "Which one looks like you?" Thus, the kind of person an individual perceives himself similar to may not correspond with the experimenter's preconceived notions. For example, when an experimenter draws a TAT figure as obese, there is no guarantee that an obese person will perceive himself or his body image as similar to the obese figure in a TAT picture. This kind of research requires phenomenal judgments from the subjects as to the kinds of individuals they perceive themselves similar to in specifically defined role situations.

Armed with such judgments, the researcher could then manipulate the similarity variable in role settings represented on TAT pictures. With these reservations in mind, the three studies which have dealt with the body similarity problem will be quickly reviewed.

Weisskopf and Dunlevy (1952) obtained no significant interaction for transcendence indices between type of subject variable (obsese, crippled, and normal) and type of central figure variable (obese, crippled, and normal). In a second study, Weisskopf-Joelson and Money (1953) investigated the effects of facial similarity between subject and central figure in the TAT on word counts and transcendence indices. In the neutral set of nine pictures, the facial features bore no resemblance to the subjects. In the experimental set, the facial features of the central figures were the photographic reproductions of the Ss' faces. The results showed that facial similarity between the S and the central figure did not produce a significant change either in word counts or transcendence indices. Greenbaum, Qualtere, Carruth, and Cruickshank (1953), in an investigation comparing TAT pictures and modified versions showing stimulus figures as physically handicapped, found that the unmodified TAT cards yielded a greater level of depth than the modified set.

When considered against the bench marks established for this kind of study, it must be concluded that adequate experimentation has yet to appear concerning the relation between perceived bodily similarity of the story teller and the central figure.

*d. Identification with Same-Sex and Opposite-Sex Figure.* At the level of theory, it is often assumed that Ss more readily identify with stimulus figures of their own sex. Primarily on the basis of developmental identification with the same-sex parent and the sex typing of behavior in socialization practices, this assumption appears tenable. Thus, it seems reasonable to hypothesize that an individual will project tension-producing affects of which he is aware onto the same sex stimulus. However, tension-producing affects of which he is unaware should be projected onto opposite-sex figures. Does this twofold supposition conform to the experimental findings?

In an early use of a filmed projective technique, McIntyre (1954) concluded that a viewer does not-increase projection to the like-sex film protagonist. A similar finding was obtained by Silverstein (1959), who administered two parallel sets of male and female apperceptive pictures and a shortened version of the Edwards Personal Preference Schedule to 40 male and 40 female college students. The thematic material and the Edwards schedule were scored for affiliation, aggression, autonomy, deference, exhibition, nurturance, sex, and succorance. The correlations between the Personal Preference Schedule scores and those from the thematic apperceptive pictures for the same-sex and opposite-sex figures were, in general, not significantly different from zero. Two major considerations vitiate any firm conclusions from these studies. Both used self-questionnaire data as the basis for information about the attributes of the subjects. Furthermore, the Ss in both studies did not seem to have identified with either sex figure in the projective material.

Moore and Schwartz (1963) have recently reported a comparison between two modified versions of the Rosenzweig P-F Study in which the sex of the frustrated figure was manipulated. Each version of the test consisted of 24 cartoons, with Form I so designed that a male figure was frustrated in the first 12 cartoons and a female figure was frustrated in the last 12 cartoons. In Form II, the female figures were frustrated in the first 12, and males in the next 12. Forty-eight males and 52 females received Form I and 52 males and 51 females responded to Form II. In contrast to the TAT, the P-F Study requires the S to identify with the frustrated person and to provide an appropriate response for him. The seven Rozenzweig scoring categories, when applied to the frustrated figures of the same sex and to those of the opposite sex, revealed no significant findings. The authors concluded that this contradicts the assumption of a relationship between attributes of the subject and pictorial stimuli. However, since the experimenters did not have any independent knowledge about the personality attributes of their Ss, their results are not germane to the assumption under consideration.

While the preceding studies have not yielded valid evidence on same-sex and opposite-sex identification, there are others which leave little doubt that sex of the stimulus figure is related to identification and projection.

Maccoby and Wilson (1957) carried out a study in which they tested the specific prediction that seventh grade pupils will identify with the like-sex character in a Hollywood feature ("The Tomboy"). This movie was thought to provide comparable opportunities in the choice of either a boy or a girl as the identificand. An identification index showed that the male viewers identified with the boy character and female viewers with the female character. Comparable results in another study (Albert, 1957) strengthen the supposition that Ss identify most strongly with same-sex stimulus figures.

However, it is possible for the individual to choose an identificand of dissimilar sex. While sex identity undoubtedly helps to mediate perceived similarity between the subject and stimulus figures, similarity cannot be measured by sex alone. The general role setting in which the figures are embedded, the sex typing of the behavior portrayed by the stimulus figures, the perceived consonance between the motives and actions of the stimulus figures and the subject, and the general adequacy of appropriate sexual identification within the subject are four important factors which we assume to mediate perceived similarity. These four variables must be taken into account before any adequate predictions can be made about identification with same-sex and opposite-sex figures. For example, if a male stimulus figure is engaged in sex-typed female activity, then a male subject may identify with an opposite sex figure, particularly if she is engaged in masculine activity. We also suspect that the identificand may be dissimilar in sex to the subject when tension-producing affects are not in awareness or when the subject's strongest developmental identification is to a member of the opposite sex.

It is these considerations that may help to clarify two of the most challenging and puzzling problems about achievement motivation in women. As a general background to research on the achievement motive, it should be mentioned that males have served as Ss in most of the studies that have demonstrated lawful relationships between achievement motive scores and performance variables. Studies on females have been few in number, largely because the preliminary research with females yielded equivocal data. As Lesser, Krawitz, and Packard (1963) have indicated, a comprehensive theory of the achievement motive should be able to incorporate the dynamics of achievement for both sexes. A theory of motivation, based on the findings of one sex, would be limited to approximately half the population.

In 1953, the two enigmas about the findings on the achievement motive for females were (a) why females did not increase in achievement under achievement-arousing operations, whereas males did; and (b) why women produced more achievement to pictures of males than to pictures of females. A decade ago, McClelland et al. (1953) reviewed three studies which showed that females did not show the expected increase in achievement as a consequence of achievement-involving instructions. Studies by Veroff (1950) and Veroff, Wilcox, and Atkinson (1953) indicated that female high school Ss and female college Ss manifest more achievement to male picture cues than to female ones. This finding occurred under neutral and achievement-oriented instructions, although neither study produced a significant increase in achievement motivation under arousal conditions. However, an examination of three recent studies with female Ss which have shown an increase in achievement with achievement-oriented instructions suggests an important interaction effect between the achievement motive and picture cues for females.

Angelini (1955) (reported on by Lesser et al., 1963) reported that competitive Brazilian college women showed a significant increase in achievement motive scores after achievement-arousal instructions which stressed appeals to leadership ability and intelligence. More significantly, perhaps, the Brazilian college women obtained higher achievement scores to pictures of males than did Brazilian college men to pictures of males. It is important to note that Angelini used only male card stimuli.

Alper (1957) showed that the sex of the central figure in a TAT card has an important influence on achievement for females. In her study, three groups of college girls were used, a group composed of 28 leaders who were tested under neutral instructions, a second group of 24 non-leaders who were tested under ego-oriented instructions, and a third sample of 24 nonleaders who were tested under relaxed conditions. Card 1 (boy and violin) of the TAT and Card 11G (young girl in empty classroom) from the Michigan Picture Test were used in the data analysis. Independent of pictures, Alper found that the nonleader ego-oriented group had significantly higher achievement scores than the relaxed non-leader group. The results for the male and female pictures showed (a) the leader group produced more achievement to the male picture than to the female picture, but no differences between the two pictures occurred for either the ego-oriented nonleaders or the nonleader relaxed group; (b) the male picture produced a significantly higher achievement score for the leader group than for the nonleader relaxed group, as it also did for the nonleader ego-oriented group in comparison with the nonleader relaxed group; (c) the female picture produced a significantly lower achievement score for the leader group than for the nonleader group, as it also did for the ego-oriented nonleaders in comparison with the nonleader relaxed group; and (d) the female picture produced significantly more achievement for the relaxed nonleaders than for the leaders. This complicated pattern of results indicates that a male picture is likely to arouse achievement more than a female for either female leaders or women who have been given achievement-arousing instructions. Since Alper did not have an achievement-aroused leader group for a direct comparison with a nonaroused leader group, this study merits replication with the addition of an aroused leader group.

The Lesser et al. (1963) study explored the interesting hypothesis that the failure of past investigators to arouse the achievement motive experimentally in females might be due to the fact that the women Ss who have been used were not overly concerned with achieving through means of intellectual skills. To test this hypothesis, they used 80 juniors and seniors from a high school for intellectually gifted girls. The admission to this school is competitive, and, once selected, the student is placed in a highly competitive environment which places stress on intellectual and scholastic achievement. The Ss were divided into two matched groups of 40 achievers and 40 underachievers. All Ss were exposed to neutral and to achievement-oriented instructions. Under each of the conditions, Ss wrote TAT stories to three pictures in which a male was the central figure and to three pictures in which a female was the central figure. While the main hypothesis of the study that the achievement instructions would yield an increase in achievement motivation was not confirmed, a significant interaction among groups, experimental treatments, and pictures was found. The interaction showed that "achieving girls did display the expected increase in achievement motivation scores under achievement orienting conditions, but only when responding to stimuli depicting females; underachieving girls also displayed the expected increase in achievement motivation scores under achievement orienting conditions, but only when responding to stimuli depicting males" (Lesser et al., 1963, p. 63). The authors applied a social role interpretation to their results. They made the assumption that achieving females conceive of intellectual achievement as an important part of their role, whereas underachieving girls perceive that the pursuit of intellectual achievement is part of the male role. In addition, they made the assumption that the attribution of the aroused motivation of achievement in the underachievers would be directed to male figures who are perceived as the proper agents for achievement expressions. Thus, achieving girls will attribute achievement to female figures and underachieving girls will attribute achievement to males. This social role explanation of the obtained results is most plausible and could be checked by obtaining role expectations that achieving and underachieving girls have for males and females. On the other hand, our third postulate would propose that achievement strivings are less in awareness for the underachievers than for the achievers. If this were the case, then it could be predicted that underachieving girls would project more of their achievement strivings onto male figures than female figures.

*Summary.* There is strong experimental evidence showing that individuals project their affects in accordance with the third postulate. The application of this postulate to the hero assumption and the assumption with respect to physical similarity between stimulus figures and the projecting individual was examined in great detail. Unfortunately, most of the studies on these assumptions suffer from methodological weaknesses. However, the evidence does indicate that type of stimulus figure on the TAT plays a critical role in controlling type of attribution.

### D. Postulate Four: Perceptual Dysfunctioning as a Function of Protusive Stimuli

*Acutely protusive stimuli will disrupt perceptual and cognitive organizing functions in individuals with weak decentering ability.*

Contemporary research on the development of perception and cognition (e.g., Piaget, 1950) shows that percepts and cognitions are initially under the control of the immediate stimulus environment. At birth and for sometime thereafter, objects possess no symbolic meaning, and consequently are perceived solely in terms of their color and shape. Early perceptual responsivity is immediate and spontaneously directed toward the environment. With increasing perceptual maturity, however, the impact of the immediate stimulus upon perceptions and cognitions becomes less and less. Proximal stimulation becomes subordinated to decoding systems and to abstract schemata. When a child has reached the stage of concrete and formal operations, he is no longer under the sway of the salient features of stimuli. He can decenter or refocus on various aspects of the immediate external and internal environment by highly flexible and balanced modes of perceiving.

From these notions, it follows that a large number of decoding systems and good decentering ability are the two most important factors that permit easy accommodation to protusive stimuli. While what constitutes a protusive stimulus for any individual can only be discovered by experimental techniques, it is suggested that any stimulus that cannot be readily assimilated into decoding systems is likely to function as a protusive cue. Kreezer's (1958) threshold technique for measuring the attention demand value of a stimulus is one possible operational method for determining protusive stimuli. Bright colors and affectively charged or threatening figures are two examples of stimuli which may be protusive for many individuals. For Ss with good decentering ability, such stimuli would, however, be incorporated into an existing decoding system. On the other hand, individuals with minimal decentering ability may find such stimuli hard to incorporate into a decoding system. In such a case, protusive stimuli are assumed to raise the individual's arousal level to such a point that it disrupts smooth perceptual functioning (see Section II, H and I, for a discussion of arousal level effects). It is further assumed that arousal level is lowered by resort to an early mode of perceptual responding, that is, by response immediately and directly toward the salient features of protusive stimuli.

This formulation implies that the effects of protusive stimuli are not likely to be shown on projective techniques unless individual differences in decentering ability are taken into account. If the decentering variable is overlooked in an experimental design, then the effects of protusive stimuli will not be manifest.

The bridge between these theoretical notions and projective methods will be limited to the possible effects of bright color as a generalized protusive stimulus. As applied to the Rorschach, it is predicted that protusive colors may cause perceptual dysfunctioning in individuals with weak decentering ability. The perceptual dysfunctioning is probably best assessed by combining the $C$ and $CF$ Rorschach determinants. Several factor analyses of the determinants have shown that the Rorschach does measure a lack of perceptual control factor. In both psychiatric and undergraduate students, Wittenborn (1950a, b) isolated a factor that involves a spontaneous perceptual approach to inkblots. The high loadings on $C$ and $CF$ indicate that spatial features of the inkblots are being minimized. The clustering of $C$ and $CF$ on a lack of perceptual control factor was also confirmed by Williams and Lawrence (1953). Inasmuch as the $FC$ determinant did not participate in the loadings on this factor, it would seem appropriate to treat the personality implications of the $FC$ response as different from $CF$ or $C$ responses.

Unlike many other hypotheses about color as a protusive variable, the present formulation is not rooted in the assumption that color evokes affective responses. In essential agreement with Schachtel (1943), Rickers-Ovsiankina (1943), and Shapiro (1960), the present hypothesis asserts that primitive color percepts represent a more immediate form of perception and is indicative of perceptual dysfunction. In basic agreement with Shapiro (1960), the present formulation remains theoretically neutral about the relation between color and affect.

### 1.  Evidence That Primitive Color Percepts Represent an Immediate Perceptual Mode and Are Reflective of Perceptual Dysfunctioning

While factor analyses of the Rorschach determinants indicate that protusive chromatic stimuli may produce a lack of perceptual control factor, is there more direct evidence to substantiate the hypothesis that individuals scoring high on such a factor manifest an immediate and spontaneous approach to the environment? A few studies (Mann, 1956; Singer and Spohn, 1954; Clark, 1948) have provided data that support the notion of a linkage between color responses and a spontaneous mode of perceiving. Research (Bills, 1954; Costello, 1958; Kohler and Steil, 1953; Wittenborn and Holzberg, 1951) has shown that depressive individuals make little use of color, indicating a lack of spontaneous and immediate reactions to protusive stimuli. In their factor analysis of Rorschach determinants and MMPI scales, Williams and Lawrence (1954) also obtained a significant negative correlation between the Depression scale and $CF$ and $C$ determinants. Superficially there was a finding in this study which would appear to contradict the present theoretical expectations, if ego strength is viewed as a reflector of a perceptual capacity to synthesize and inhibit excessive stimuli. This finding was the correlation of .50 between $CF$ scores and Barron's (1953) Ego-Strength ($Es$) scale. However, the construct validity of the $Es$ scale is open to question. For example, Gottesman (1959) found significantly higher *Es* scores for delinquents over normals. Barron (1956) likewise found that *Es* scores correlated with a cluster variable indicative of aggression. Moreover, in his original study Barron (1953) found that *Es* scores were positively correlated with the variables of outgoingness and spontaneity and negatively with introspection. Such data, if anything, indicate that the positive correlations between *Es* and *CF* support the present theoretical formulation.

## 2. *Experimental Manipulation of Color on the Rorschach*

The finding of Brosin and Fromm (1940) that color-blind neurotic individuals manifest "color shock" was the first report to raise the whole question as to whether color influences response performance. Our hypothesis suggests that color should have some effects. Since the early experimental endeavors of Wallen (1948) and Lazarus (1948, 1949), many investigators have studied color effects by comparing chromatic and achromatic versions of the Rorschach inkblots.

Since numerous other researchers (Allen, 1951; Allen, Manne and Stiff, 1951, 1952; Allen, Stiff and Rosenzweig, 1953; Barnett, 1950; Buker and Williams, 1951; Dubrovner, Von Lackum and Jost, 1950; Perlman, 1951; Sappenfield and Buker, 1949; Swartz, 1953) have followed the general methodological approach of Lazarus (1949), his test-retest experimental design merits critical evaluation. It involved (a) the administration of the standard Rorschach inkblots and their achromatic matches in a counterbalanced order to two groups of *S*s, and (b) a statistical comparison of the standard chromatic series and the achromatic version on various scores that are thought to be symptomatic of color disturbance. Many critics have raised cogent criticisms against the test-retest design, of which the following seem particularly crucial: (a) the assumption that an AB order of presentation involves the same memory and set effects as a BA order of presentation is highly questionable; and (b) since color may either inhibit or excite perceptual reactions, depending upon a critical interaction between kind of color and personality structure, the analysis of data based upon only one group will lead to a general cancellation effect. While recent investigators have usually avoided the counterbalanced design, only a few have attempted to take into account the possible interaction effects among kind of color, receptivity to color, and personality structure. It is for this reason that most of the research studies manipulating color on the Rorschach experimentally are not pertinent to the personality and perceptual hypotheses about the protusive role of color. In view of this deficiency, no attempt will be made to discuss most of these studies in any great detail. However, Baughman

(1958) should be consulted for the details of the studies conducted before 1958.

a. *Studies with Normal Subjects*. With the preceding reservation in mind, a brief review will be provided of the studies that have investigated the influence of color with normal Ss. Using 100 high school seniors, Lazarus (1949) found few differences between the achromatic series and the chromatic series. He did, however, find a higher $F\%$ and number of space responses on the noncolor cards. There was also a reduction in the number of $D$ responses to the achromatic version. Since this experiment, several similar experiments (Allen, 1951; Allen, Manne and Stiff, 1951, 1952; Barnett, 1950; Canter, 1951; Dubrovner, Von Lackum and Jost, 1950; Grayson, 1956; Meyer, 1951; Sappenfield and Buker, 1949) with normals have shown few or no differences in response performance between chromatic and achromatic versions of the Rorschach.

However, two recent studies indicate that color does have an influence on Rorschach performance. Exner (1959) investigated the role of chromatic and achromatic color on Card I of the Rorschach by constructing three different chromatic versions of this card by the monochrome-dye coupling method. The Ss, male and female students, were divided into four matched groups of one hundred cases each. The Ss in each group were administered a different version of Plate I. The chromatic versions of this card were blue, green, and brown and the achromatic version was the standard Card I. The data showed that the blue card yielded the greatest number of responses, the shortest reaction time, and significantly more wholes, small details, human movement, whole human figures, object content, "bell" content to Beck's $Dd24$, snow content, and animal face content than the other version of Card I. While it is a little disappointing that Exner did not include a red version of Card I, most of his data on the blue card is in keeping with the finding that blue is relaxing (Wexner, 1954), and produces less cortical and autonomic arousal than red (Gerard, 1958). The green card produced significantly fewer form determinants than any other version of Card I. These findings strongly support the conclusion that different colors have dissimilar effects. This conclusion, as Exner indicates, supports Crumpton's (1956) finding that a color perception on one Rorschach card may not indicate the same interpretation as a similar response on a different plate, and reaffirms the implications of the first postulate.

In the most comprehensive analysis of the stimulus structure of the Rorschach to date, Baughman (1959) prepared six different modifications of the standard Rorschach inkblots. His findings on color-achromatic comparisons will be limited to a discussion of plates II, III, VIII, IX, and X. On Plate II, the chromatic series yielded fewer movement and human percepts but more blood responses to the $D2$ area than any of the other card versions. On Plate III, color increased anatomical responses to the $D3$ area and lowered the number of responses to $D2$. Content analysis of Plate VIII showed that color depressed bear concepts, and catlike and landscape responses to the $D1$ area, and facilitated the butterfly, flower, and ice cream percepts to the $D2$ area. The chromatic series of Plate IX produced few minor details, but many whole percepts. Color also depressed the human percept to the $D4$ area. The colored version of Plate X produced an increased sensitivity to seed percepts to the $D3$ area, caterpillar or worm responses to the $D4$ area, rabbit head percepts to the $D5$ area, insect percepts to the $D8$ area, and flower percepts to the $D15$ area. While only a sampling of Baughman's data has been presented, two primary conclusions may be drawn: Color does influence Rorschach performance, especially the content categories; and color may either facilitate or inhibit responses.

The question now becomes one of accounting for individual differences in response to color. Conceptually, as already indicated, the studies of normals do not bear directly on the hypotheses relating color perception to personality variables. A design is required that will permit testing for the triple interaction effect among types of intrusive and non-compelling colors, receptivity to color, and personality structure.

*b. Studies with Neuropsychiatric Subjects.* Some researchers (Allen *et al.*, 1953; Baughman, 1954; Buker and Williams, 1951; Canter, 1958; Crumpton, 1956; Sterling, 1950; York, 1951) have attempted to escape the limitations of a normal sample by using psychiatrically disturbed *Ss*. However, studies with a single group of patients are no closer to an appropriate design than studies employing a single group of normals. Both designs overlook the requirement that interaction effects should be built into the experimental design.

With this qualification in mind, three studies (Allen *et al.*, 1953; Baughman, 1954; Buker and Williams, 1951) have shown that the removal of color does not seriously influence response performance on the Rorschach. Canter (1958) showed that an unshaded bright color version of Plates VIII, IX, and X produced an inhibition of color-dominant responses. Accuracy of form perception was impaired in the York (1951) study. With a sample of 10 psychotics, 10 neurotics, and 10 organics, Crumpton (1956) showed that color has no influence on color shock signs, productivity, reaction time, 8-9-10%, rejections, minus form quality of responses, $P\%$, $A\%$, avoidance of red area on Plates II and III, and irregularity of succession. However, color did have effects on content categories, supporting the findings of Baughman (1959) and Exner (1959) with normals. Whatever advantage these studies might have gained by the use of disturbed Ss was eliminated by failure to separate the patients in terms of personality variables hypothesized to be related to color perception. Thus, the findings from these studies cannot be related to any of the hypotheses about color on the Rorschach.

c. *Studies with Interaction Effects.* Five studies have contrasted normals and disturbed Ss on chromatic and achromatic versions of the Rorschach. Three (Brody, 1953; Perlman, 1951; York, 1951) of these studies have compared neurotics and normals on the two versions of the Rorschach and found that the effects of color are minimal or absent. While these studies approach the ideal design, they overlook the fact that the "crude" classification of normal or neurotic masks the individual differences within each of these groups which are likely to produce significant effects. It is well known that individual differences in autonomic and perceptual reactivity in neurotic and normal samples are likely to be large. Accordingly, the differences between each of the groups are likely to be canceled out, which ensures that they will not differ on most dependent variables. Rather than employing heterogeneous samples, one should use groups which are high and low on the specific personality variables assumed to be related to color perception, such as affect, inadequacy in perceptual decentering, and the like.

In a study that approximates the ideal design, Holtzman, Iscoe, and Calvin (1954) tested for relationships of type of color, anxiety, stimulus structure, presentation order, and examiner. Unfortunately, the high- and low-anxiety Ss were chosen on the basis of the Taylor Manifest Anxiety Scale (1953) and the Winne Scale of Neuroticism (1951). This means that the contrasting groups of college women were composed of those who admitted to neurotic symptoms and those who did not. In anticipation that type of color may produce an effect, the results of Plates II and III were analyzed together because their chromatic versions are both red and black. Similarly, Plates VIII and IX were grouped together because their standard versions involve multicolored pastel shades. A balanced experimental design was employed, in which each S received two chromatic and two achromatic inkblots in a predetermined order. Contrary to the theoretical expectations of some Rorschach workers, the findings did not support the assumed linkage between color and anxiety. Differences between the chromatic and achromatic versions were minimal or absent. Forsyth (1959) also found no significant differences when high anxious and low anxious male undergraduates were tested for differences on Elizur's content anxiety score. Anxiety was defined by the Welsh (1956) manifest anxiety scale and the comparisons were made between a chromatic, an achromatic, and a silhouette Rorschach series. A significant interaction effect showed that a moderately anxious group produced a low Elizur anxiety score on the colored cards and a high Elizur anxiety score on the achromatic and silhouette Rorschach series. While the Holtzman *et al.* and Forsyth studies are neatly conceived, their findings are only suggestive and do not provide critical evidence on the possible interaction effect among color type, color receptivity, decentering activity, and personality structure.

*d. Studies with Segments of the Rorschach.* The effects of color on Rorschach performance deserves one final methodological comment. In the studies reviewed to this point, the complete Rorschach inkblot has been used. There have been, however, a few studies (Siipola, 1950; Siipola, Kuhns and Taylor, 1950; Lazarus and Oldfield, 1955) in which segments of the usual details have been used. While results from these studies have indicated at least a modest effect of color on response performance, the results of such studies may not apply to intact inkblots.

*3. Experimental Manipulation of Color on the TAT*

Color has been shown to have effects on thematic apperceptive techniques in four of five studies. Brackbill (1951) found that neurotics, unlike control Ss, told more depressive stories to chromatic TAT pictures. Thompson and Bachrach (1951) found that both whites and Negroes gave significantly higher words on the chromatic version of the TAT. Lubin (1955) also found significantly higher word counts on a chromatic TAT for mentally retarded Ss, as did Lubin and Wilson (1956) for handicapped children. On the other hand, color did not influence the transcendence index in the Weisskopf–Joelson and Foster (1962) experiment when color and its absence were varied on the CAT. In general, these studies only demonstrate that color facilitates word productivity. In no way do they provide crucial information on the interaction effects among types of color, receptivity to color, perceptual decentering, and personality structure.

*Summary.* Only indirect evidence supports the validity of the fourth postulate, namely, the finding that color perception represents an immediate approach to the environment. While recent studies have shown that color influences response performance on the Rorschach and TAT, adequate experimental research remains to be done on the hypothesis that protusive stimuli disrupt perceptual activity in Ss with weak decentering ability.

E. POSTULATE FIVE: ANXIETY AS A FUNCTION OF CHIAROSCURO STIMULI

*Diffuse chiaroscuro stimuli evoke vague homogeneous perceptions which tend to be anxiety arousing.*

Working with Binder's (1933) interpretations of chiaroscuro responses on the Rorschach, Bohm (1960) and others have indicated that the two conditions necessary for the occurrence of a homogeneous sensory perception are similarity between stimulus elements and indistinct delineation. The latter condition is usually met by chiaroscuro stimuli. However, both conditions are met by exposing Ss to a homogeneous field (Ganzfeld). In order to achieve a Ganzfeld, similar to that described by Hochberg, Triebel, and Seaman (1951) and Kenny and Chappell (1963), Ss are required to wear eyecaps which are cut from table-tennis balls to fit the shape of the eye socket. A red light is projected onto the balls. Within a relatively short period of time, the initial red perception changes into an unpatterned gray visual field. It appears to the S that he is being stimulated by diffuse chiaroscuro stimuli and he may describe his perceptions as being foglike, cloudlike, or simply graylike. In short, the S has vague, homogeneous perceptions.

In terms of the present postulate, the induction of a Ganzfeld should be anxiety arousing. A recent experiment (Kenny and Chappell, 1963) has provided empirical support for this notion. Experimental Ss were subjected to a Ganzfeld for 20 minutes, and while still under this condition gave stories to six TAT card descriptions. A comparable control also told stories to the TAT card descriptions. The success of the Ganzfeld as an arouser of anxiety was assessed both by an anxiety questionnaire completed by the Ss after telling their stories and by scoring the TAT stories for anxiety effects. The anxiety questionnaire results showed the experimental Ss to be more anxious than the controls, and the TAT findings offered substantial support for the hypothesis that a continuous gray field is anxiety arousing. Six out of the 10 TAT anxiety indices showed significant differences in the predicted direction.

While this experiment offers evidence in support of the hypothesis that diffuse chiaroscuro stimuli evoke vague homogeneous perceptions which tend to be anxiety arousing, it only offers indirect support for any anxiety interpretation of chiaroscuro material on the Rorschach.

However, there is other evidence congruent with such an interpretation. In an analysis of the connotative meaning of the Rorschach, Rosen (1960) had his Ss make semantic judgments on the Rorschach inkblots and nine common Rorschach responses. The Ss rated the response "cloudiness" as bad, sad, hazy, cold, and dull. As Rosen indicates, such undesirable connotations are close to a description of generalized anxiety.

Ultimately, the validity of this postulate must be tested either by inducing anxiety or by using psychiatrically defined cases of anxiety and comparing their responses with those of matched controls. In terms of the notion of homogeneous perception, it would be desirable to limit the scoring of the shading material to Binder's *ChF* and pure *Ch* responses. With such a stipulation, it becomes extremely difficult to assess the validity of the fifth postulate through an examination of the research relating anxiety effects to the Rorschach, as investigators have used diverse scoring criteria for shading. If citation is limited to studies that come close to Binder's two scoring categories, the studies of Levitt (1957), Cox and Sarason (1954), and Levitt and Grosz (1960) support the proposition that shading responses are correlated with anxiety. Such findings buttress the present postulates, especially when it is noted that the three studies used different kinds of Ss and different external criteria of anxiety.

*Summary.* There is indirect evidence to support the notion that diffuse chiaroscuro stimuli instigate homogeneous perceptions which tend to be anxiety arousing. However, a great deal more experimental work is required on the present postulate before its validity status becomes known.

### F. Postulate Six: Idiosyncratic Responses

*If one rules out differential cultural experiences, response deviations (idiosyncratic responses) from the perceptual demands of the projective stimulus are indicative of significant personality characteristics.*

From a research and clinical point of view, two interlocking questions emerge from this general proposition:

1. Is reality-oriented behavior indicated by conformity to the demands of stimulus pull?

2. Are idiosyncratic responses more significant than usual responses?

To both questions, the answer appears to be affirmative. The first implies the assertion that the larger the response discrepancy from the stimulus pull of the projective material, the greater will be the impairment in the individual's ability to integrate perceptual and cognitive processes. Given the question on the Rorschach, "What might this be?," the individual has to attend to the stimulus, and, to the extent that the response is not stimulus bound, the inference may be drawn that perceptual and associational functioning are not being integrated. Putting this assertion the other way round, it is assumed that if the S is overresponding to his own associations and cognitions, then he is less likely to be attending to the reality demands of the stimulus situation. Lest the logic of this assertion be misunderstood, it should be stressed that it is not implied that compulsive adherence to the stimulus environment reflects ideal psychological health. The shape of the curve relating response adherence to stimulus demands and psychological health is undoubtedly nonmonotonic and close to an inverted U.

Many factors may reduce a subject's ability to integrate perceptual and cognitive processes. Clinically speaking, the three basic factors that probably produce idiosyncratic response are minimal decentering ability, neurophysiological dysfunctioning, and high levels of arousal in the presence of ambiguous cues. Strong motives per se should not impair an individual's respect for reality, unless some variable like cortical dysfunctioning is also present.

Before examining the research literature on this hypothesis, one methodological point is worth raising. In any rigorous test of the postulate, it would be most important to select stimuli that have highly predictable responses, that is, stimuli with few associations. If a stimulus evokes many different responses, the experimenter will have problems in establishing criteria for idiosyncratic responses. A control over the number of associations is also important in research which seeks to demonstrate that particular kinds of stimuli produce idiosyncratic responses in Ss with special kinds of conflict. For example, it has been commonly assumed that schizophrenics, relative to normals, produce a large number of idiosyncratic responses to emotional words in a word association test. Two studies (Deering, 1963; Jones, 1957) have found that schizophrenics do give more idiosyncratic associations to emotional stimuli than do normals. However, as Deering (1963) and Laffal (1955) both stress, the increase in number of unique responses may not be due to affect, but simply because emotional words evoke a larger number of associations than neutral words. In other words, emotional and neutral words should be matched in terms of number of associations they evoke, preferably by choosing words with a small number of associations.

Generally speaking, clinicians make the assumption that unusual themes or perceptual distortions to TAT cards are more revealing than usual themes or perceptual accuracy about personality. Only one study has examined this problem. Miller and Scodel (1955) obtained a usual and an unusual TAT story from each of 35 psychotherapy clients. Six judges then attempted "blind" matching of the 35 common and 35 unusual TAT stories to typescript records of the first two psychotherapy sessions of these patients. While the judges' matching was better than chance, the unusual stories were no better matched than the usual ones. Whether this negative finding provides critical evidence against the hypothesis is open to question, as the findings suffer from the fact that only early psychotherapy data were used. The definition of usual and unusual rested on clinical judgment rather than objective normative data.

At the present time, the ratio $(F + \%)$ between accurate and unclear form perception is the best measure of response deviations from the perceptual demands of the Rorschach inkblots. It is not within the scope of this paper to discuss the problems involved in specifying what constitutes good or poor form, although the solution to them ultimately hinges upon a statistical criterion of response frequency. Hypotheses about the validity of $F + \%$ have stimulated some research, most of which has involved a comparison of clinical groups. Korchin (1960) should be consulted for a brief review of some of these studies. It is sufficient to state that the main evidence concerning $F + \%$ tends to confirm the hypothesis that form accuracy is related to adequacy of perceptual contact with reality. Original research is required, however, in which inkblot stimuli are constructed with known variations in their difficulty level for yielding accurate form percepts. With material conforming to a cumulative homogeneity test model, the resulting threshold measure of contact with test stimuli should correlate significantly with external criterion data. Such a measure should also provide a purer measure of contact with reality than $F + \%$.

Finally, it should be noted that the Tomkins–Horn Picture Arrangement Test (Tomkins and Miner, 1957) rests explicitly upon the assumption that rare and homogeneous responses to similar test stimuli are indicative of significant personality characteristics. While the standardization of this test is excellent, more research is required on the validity of the scoring keys for personality. However, the diagnostic power of this test should ultimately prove to be high.

*Summary.* The validity of this postulate rests primarily upon form accuracy data of the Rorschach and, to a lesser extent, word association experiments. It is suggested that new material be specifically constructed in order to test its validity and for use in clinical situations.

### G. POSTULATE SEVEN: ANXIETY EFFECTS AS A FUNCTION OF STIMULUS GENERALIZATION

*With increasing perceived similarity between high-anxiety-evoking situations or figures and their stimulus representations on projective material, anxiety effects should increase by gradual increments.*

This postulate rests upon the validity of the phenomenon of stimulus generalization and the assumption that projective techniques will validly reflect anxiety effects. The fact of stimulus generalization seems well established, as does the assumption that anxiety effects are shown by projective instruments. Two recent studies (Walker and Atkinson, 1958; Kenny and Chappell, 1963) have shown that experimentally aroused anxiety is reflected in thematic apperceptive stories. While the ability of the Rorschach to reflect anxiety depends upon type of stress and determinants, Neuringer (1962) concluded, after a review of the literature, that laboratory stress induces lowered productivity, fewer $W$ and $P$ and more $m$ responses. Real life stress leads to more $F$ responses and a general reduction in the number of responses, $M$, $m$, and color responses.

Data from three studies are relevant to the present postulate. In connection with a study on the deviant family background of schizophrenics, Baxter and Becker (1962) hypothesized that poor premorbid male schizophrenics come from mother-dominated homes which are high in conflict and aggression and that good premorbid male schizophrenics come from father-dominated homes in which the mother was weak and the father was tyrannical. On the basis of this and related considerations, the authors predicted that poor premorbids should produce more anxiety to a maternal figure than to a paternal figure on the TAT, while good premorbids should manifest the reverse pattern. Cards 6BM (mother-son) and 7BM (father-son) of the TAT were given to 18 poor premorbid schizophrenics and 12 good premorbid schizophrenics. The predicted interaction between anxiety and parental figure was significant, with the poor premorbids showing more anxiety to the mother figure than to the father and the good premorbids showing the opposite pattern. This supports the notion that anxiety is generalized to pictorial representations of the original instigator of anxiety and again reinforces the notion that fruitful predictions must take into account the cue properties of stimulus figures.

Two studies by Epstein and Fenz are relevant to this postulate. In their first study (Epstein and Fenz, 1962), novice parachutists were tested on a word association test with four levels of stimulus relevance to parachuting and a set of general anxiety words. Two parallel forms of the word association test were constructed, since the test was administered on the day of the jump and on a control day. For eight $S$s the control day was 2 weeks after a jump and for another eight $S$s the control day was 2 weeks before a jump. Sixteen nonparachutists served as controls. In accordance with the notion of stimulus generalization, the results showed that the GSR and the mean reaction time in seconds for the parachutists increased monotonically as a function of stimulus relevance and was steeper on the day of the jump than on the control day. In their other investigation, Fenz and Epstein (1962) employed the same $S$s and experimental design. However, two sets of TAT-like stimulus cards were substituted for the word association test. The six pictures in each set contained four unrelated to parachuting, one slightly related, and one strongly related. Congruent with the findings from the word association study, the GSR to the initial impact of the pictures increased as a function of stimulus relevance and was steeper on the day of the jump. Reaction time on the day of the jump was similar between neutral and low-relevance pictures, but was significantly longer on the picture strongly related to parachuting. Another commonly used indicator of anxiety—frequency of pauses—showed similar results to the reaction time data. It should be pointed out that Epstein and Fenz did not employ the notion of stimulus generalization of fear to predict their results. On the basis of a *modified* version of Miller's (1948, 1959) model of approach-avoidance conflict, they assumed that the gradients of approach and avoidance drives may be added, without regard. to sign, to obtain a measure of conflict-instigated activation. Accordingly, they formulated the prediction that the activation gradient will increase as a function of increasing stimulus relevance. With the additional assumption that activation may be measured by autonomic reactivity indicators, such as the GSR, the obtained results also conform to their conflict model. Thus, it would appear that the results of both studies could be reconciled either to a stimulus generalization of fear concept or to a conflict model. In their first study, Epstein and Fenz (1962) argue that activation is shown by the gradient of GSR and not fear, on the grounds that parachutists on both the jump and control day produced larger GSR's to the high-relevance parachuting words than to the anxiety words. This argument is not persuasive on two grounds: (1) The anxiety words were included in the first place solely on the grounds of curiosity, and (2) through prior conditioning, fear may be more attached to high-relevance parachute words (e.g., target, jump, bailout) than to *a priori* chosen anxiety words (e.g., blackout, injury, hurt).

*Summary.* From these three studies, it would appear that anxiety does generalize as a function of perceived similarity between the original fear-producing situation and the stimulus representation of these events on projective tests.

### H. Postulate Eight: Drive-Stimulus Relevance

*For stimuli which have been scaled for a single drive, the following expectations should hold: (a) When only highly structured drive-stimulus material evokes thematic drive content, the individual possesses little or no drive represented by the stimulus material; (b) where minimal, moderate, and strong cues of the drive material evoke drive content, the individual is neurotically motivated and preoccupied with the goal of the drive; (c) when strong-drive Ss are compared with low-drive Ss, the magnitude of thematic drive content differences should gradually increase with increasing stimulus relevance to the drive; and (d) as the number of drive cues increase and the drive has anxiety attached to it, anxiety effects should mount.*

In attempting to provide a theoretical discussion of how the foregoing predictions are derived, the author will present a revised version of a model presented elsewhere (Kenny, 1961). The model makes the following assumptions: (a) Proximal stimuli evoke decoding reactions which are perceptual attempts by the individual to translate or decode proximal stimulation into distal objects; (b) drive stimuli, external or internal in origin, will increasé the probability that decoding reactions associated with the drive will occur, that is, drive stimuli narrow selectively the number of decoding reactions that are likely to occur; (c) as the number of decoding reactions instigated by stimuli increases, the arousal level of the person will also increase; (d) individuals seek to maintain moderate levels of arousal, avoiding high or low levels by filtering out stimuli that heighten or lower arousal level; (e) unless anxiety completely blocks the occurrence of decoding reactions related to a drive, anxiety level will interact with internal and external drive cues to increase drive-oriented schematic thought; and (f) drives are assumed to raise the gradient of stimulus generalization.

In terms of these assumptions, various predictions may be made about how individuals will function on projective tests. If a set of projective stimuli has been scaled along a dimension of increasing drive relevance, a random sample of Ss should show a gradual increment in thematic drive content as drive-stimulus relevance increases. Since drives are assumed to raise the entire gradient of stimulus generalization, Ss with high drive should give more thematic drive content to cues further down the dimension of drive relevance than low-drive Ss. Similarly, if a person only gives drive content to highly relevant cues, it may be inferred that drive level is low. On the other hand, if drive content is present to all levels of drive-stimulus relevance, then the inference may be made that drive is excessively high and there is marked preoccupation with the goal of the drive. It should be noted that McClelland et al. (1953) have made similar statements from an inductive base.

The preceding discussion has assumed that the drive state of the organism is not associated with anxiety. What happens to thematic drive content when the drive has anxiety associated with it? If the association of anxiety with drive cues is exceedingly high, there may be a complete blockage of thematic drive content to all stimulus representations of the drive. Since such an event is likely to be rare in permissive testing situations, the question becomes one of predicting what happens to thematic content when anxiety continues to operate. In terms of assumptions (b) and (e), above, highly structured drive stimuli should produce more thematic drive content than any other type of cue and should provide the best discrimination between low- and high-drive Ss. Of course, this prediction is bound to break down in the limiting case when cultural training has produced a strong communality of response to stimulus representations of drive states. In such a case, most Ss will respond in an identical manner, regardless of drive state.

The implication of the present model that highly structured drive stimuli are the best indicators of thematic drive content is exactly the opposite of that of Epstein and his associates (Epstein and Fenz, 1962; Fenz and Epstein, 1962). Their approach-avoidance conflict model makes the pivotal assumption that approach drives have less steep gradients than avoidance drives as a direct function of increasing stimulus relevance, and, as a consequence, approach or goal-relevant responses should increase to stimuli of low relevance and decrease to stimuli of high relevance. Our survey of the literature will investigate the validity of these two opposing predictions, as well as the other hypotheses.

Several studies have been concerned with the interaction between drive-stimulus relevance and drive level. It is difficult to evaluate the results of these studies because the stimulus properties of the projective stimuli and the precise range of the drive level are not clear. A strongly structured card for one researcher may be a moderately ambiguous card for another. What one investigator may call strong drive, another may call moderate. Until terminological differences between investigators are resolved and a methodology of defining drive-stimulus relevance is standardized, the task of comparing the findings of different studies is almost impossible. In spite of these problems, it does seem possible to draw tentative conclusions from a review of the studies in this area.

### 1. Drive-Stimulus Relevance and Aggression

Some doll play data, analyzed by Wurtz (1960), may be used to support the prediction that anxiety facilitates the expression of aggression. Making the assumption that more anxiety is aroused if aggression is expressed against parents than other children, Wurtz predicted that more direct and violent aggression will be expressed against parent dolls than child dolls. The doll play results of 150 children showed that the parent dolls were the objects of more violent aggression than child dolls, supporting the general proposition that anxiety interacts with drive to increase drive-oriented schematic thought.

In an attempt to evaluate the influences of maternal permissiveness on aggression, Weatherley (1962) divided female undergraduate students into two groups of 50 in terms of mother's reports as to the degree to which they permitted their children to express aggression as a child. Half of the Ss in each group told TAT stories after they had been aroused to aggression by insulting and depreciating comments, the other half in each group not being exposed to arousal conditions. Two levels of aggressive stimulus relevance were used, with cards 8BM and 18GF representing high cues and 2 and 6GF of the TAT representing low cues. The analysis of the data yielded a significant triple interaction among the variables of permissiveness, arousal, and stimulus relevance. A breakdown of this interaction effect showed that high maternal-permissive Ss manifested a significant increase in thematic aggression to high aggressive cue cards when they were under arousal conditions Low maternal-permissive Ss did not show this effect. If it is assumed that maternal permissiveness provides better opportunities for the reinforcement of aggression than does low maternal permissiveness, then the finding on the high maternal-permissive Ss confirms the theoretical expectations that highly structured drive stimuli are the best indicators of thematic drive content. Kagan's (1956) study of 118 elementary school children also showed that a picture most suggestive of aggression was more predictive of overt aggression than a less suggestive picture. While the least suggestive picture did not separate the aggressive from the nonaggressive children, more stories of aggressive fighting were produced by the aggressive Ss to the picture most suggestive of fighting than by nonaggressive Ss.

However, other studies on the aggressive drive only provide partial support for our theoretical expectations. Stone (1956) reported that TAT cards with moderate aggressive pull produced the greatest discrimination between assaultive and nonassaultive prisoners. High-aggressive pull pictures were not as discriminatory. In keeping with the present expectations, however, the moderate drive-relevance pictures were more discriminatory than the low-relevance pictures. Since the high-aggressive pictures (13MF, 18GF, and 19BM) have stimulus dimensions that can instigate themes other than aggression, the use of these cards leaves something to be desired. In a study (Hokanson and Gordon, 1958) involving 40 college students, half of the Ss were classified as high expressors of aggression and the other half as low expressors on the basis of a manifest hostility questionnaire. Within each group, half of the Ss were aroused to hostility by listening to a case history of a sadistic juvenile delinquent. Subsequent to arousal, all Ss told stories to a TAT card low in aggression (card 2) and one high in aggression (card 8BM). When the Ss were aroused, the low expressors showed more thematic hostility than the high expressors. With respect to cue relevance, the only significant finding was that the high card produced more thematic aggression than the low card for both groups. Saltz and Epstein (1963) divided male college volunteers into three experiment designs on the basis of self-report measures of hostility, guilt, and conflict over hostility. The three groups were composed of 20 Ss, each of whom scored at the extremes on each of these measures. All Ss were administered six TAT-type pictures, two of low relevance to aggression, one of high relevance to aggression, and four buffer pictures. In terms of their conflict model, Saltz and Epstein predicted that (a) hostile responses to low-relevance pictures are largely due to drive and hostile responses to high-relevance pictures are due to guilt, and (b) conflict over hostility will cause an overresponse to low-relevance pictures and an underresponse to high-relevance pictures. The data offered equivocal support for their first prediction and no support for the second prediction. More specifically, Saltz and Epstein concluded that the first part of their prediction (a) was confirmed by the findings of a positive relationship between the questionnaire measure of hostility and thematic hostility on the two pictures of low aggressive relevance. Since high relevance was only represented by one picture, the resulting error variance in the thematic score may have prevented any correlation between the high card and self-reported hostility. The second part of their first hypothesis (that guilt is best reflected by high-relevance pictures) was not supported by two of their three analyses of the questionnaire measures.

## 2. Drive-Stimulus Relevance and Sex

The preceding pattern of results in the Saltz and Epstein study are very similar to those found by Leiman and Epstein (1961) on the sex drive. In this study, 66 unmarried university students were first administered four TAT-like pictures of low-relevance to sex and two pictures of high relevance. They then filled out a questionnaire from which two indices of sexual drive and one index of guilt over sex were derived. One index of sexual drive was based on rate of orgasm, the other on deprivation. The data showed a positive relationship between thematic sex scores and the rate measure; however, no relationship occurred between thematic sexual responses and deprivation. The hypothesis that low-relevance pictures would provide the best measure of sexual drive and high-relevance pictures would be the best measure of guilt was not confirmed. However, a *post hoc* analysis of the individual cards did provide some support for this hypothesis. The other hypothesis of the authors that conflict effects would be shown by an overresponse to low-relevance pictures and an underresponse to high-relevance pictures was not upheld. Such a finding is congruent with the data from the Saltz and Epstein study on aggression.

## 3. Drive-Stimulus Relevance and Fear

The validity of Epstein's hypotheses about conflict effects, that drive is best measured by pictures of low relevance and that conflict is shown by an overresponse to low-relevance cues and an underresponse to high-relevance cues, is cast into further doubt by the two studies on parachuting (Fenz and Epstein, 1962; Epstein and Fenz, 1962) previously described. It will be recalled that in both studies novice parachutists were given a word association test and a thematic apperception test on the day of a jump and also on a control day. In the study (Fenz and Epstein, 1962) dealing with thematic pictures, the results showed that parachutists on the day of the jump manifested significantly more thematic *approach* responses to the high-relevance pictures than to the low-relevance pictures. Such a finding casts into doubt the notion that the gradient of avoidance is steeper than that of approach, a pivotal assumption in the conflict model. It should be noted that the obtained finding on the high-relevance picture supports the present author's formulation of stimulus relevance. In the word association study, Epstein and Fenz (1962) found their prediction that parachutists would give more parachute-relevant responses to stimulus words of low relevance and fewer such responses to stimuli of high relevance was not upheld. The parachutists on the day of the jump showed similar approach responses to all levels of stimulus relevance. In terms of their model, Epstein and Fenz also predicted that the number of perceptual misrecognitions of the stimulus words increase as a function of increasing stimulus relevance to parachuting. However, the opposite effect occurred; that is, on the day of the jump the parachutists showed a decrease in misperceptions as stimulus relevance to parachuting increased from low to high. This finding offers strong support for the present author's second assumption. In essence, it follows from this assumption that increases in drive will facilitate veridical perception for stimuli related to the drive.

### 4. Drive-Stimulus Relevance and Other Drives

Three other published studies also bear on the interaction effect between drive level and stimulus relevance. In examining the effects of about 86 hours' sleep deprivation on TAT stories, Murray (1959) found that the sleep-deprived group showed less thematic sleep content than did the control group and that they had significantly fewer sleep themes than the controls on a high sleep-suggestive card. The two groups did not differ in sleep themes to the low- and medium-sleep card. The experiment raises the general issue of whether sleep deprivation induces a drive. To this author, it seems more plausible to suggest that sleep deprivation will result in a general lowering of a person's arousal level. If this is the case, Murray's results may be expected in terms of our fourth assumption. In an early study on the interaction between the hunger drive and stimulus relevance, Epstein and Smith (1956) found that pictures of low stimulus relevance to hunger were better reflectors of the hunger drive than either a medium or a high picture-pull card. Unfortunately, only one picture was used at each of the high and moderate picture-pull levels. As already indicated, any findings based upon a single picture are likely to be unreliable.

Murstein (1963a) reported an experiment in which he tested an important part of Atkinson's (1958) theory of human motivation. In terms of this theory it may be predicted that, if the motive to achieve and the motive to avoid failure are held constant, achievement motivation will vary with the probability of success, with the highest possible motivation occurring when the probability is .5. In testing this prediction, Murstein found that a .5 group manifested more over-all achievement imagery than a .1 group; the difference between a .5 and .9 group was not significant. The major finding on stimulus relevance was the fact that pictures of moderate relevance to achievement produced the significant difference between the .5 and .1 group. If it can be safely assumed that the .5 group has a greater need to achieve than the .1 group, then such a finding is not in keeping with the present author's formulation of stimulus relevance. After reviewing the studies concerned with Atkinson's theory, Murstein (1963b) has concluded, however, that the empirical evidence in support of the assumption that a .5 group has the highest achievement motivation is "rather fragile."

*Summary.* Taken together, do the studies investigating the interaction effect between stimulus relevance and drive support the predictions of the eighth postulate? The investigations of Wurtz (1960), Kagan (1956), and Fenz and Epstein (1962) offer strong support for the model. Most of the other studies offer moderate support for the postulate. There is no support for the Epstein and Fenz hypothesis that conflict will cause an overresponse to low-relevance pictures and an underresponse to high-relevance pictures. Finally, their hypothesis that low-relevance pictures are the best measures of drive is seen to be most suspect when one views it against all the studies which have been reviewed in this section.

I. Postulate Nine: Arousal Level as a Function of Ambiguity

*For complex projective material, arousal level varies as a positive function of increasing ambiguity.*

It will be recalled that a distinction was made between projective techniques based upon the cumulative homogeneity model and those constructed on the pure relative frequency model. The Rorschach and TAT are the classic illustrations of the latter model. By complex projective material, we mean tests based on the pure relative frequency model. Before discussing the ninth postulate, it will be helpful to discuss the methodological approaches to the concept of ambiguity.

## 1. Definition of Ambiguity

Broadly speaking, there are two procedural techniques for defining the meaning of ambiguity. One may define a scale of increasing ambiguity in terms of increasing physical impoverishment. Some of the procedures that may be used to induce this kind of ambiguity would be reduction in time of exposure, photographic blurring, random or specific removal of stimuli, incomplete line tracings, reduction in illumination, and the like. Without any wish to imply that impoverishing techniques do not produce interesting experimental results, it is proposed that such operations in no way ensure that ambiguity has been manipulated. To this author, it does not seem to make sense to talk of an ambiguous physical stimulus. A stimulus is only ambiguous if it evokes different perceptual or decoding reactions. Impoverishment of the stimulus does not ensure that there will be an increase in the number of decoding reactions. In fact, their number might actually decrease under some conditions of physical impoverishment.

As this author (Kenny, 1961) proposed elsewhere, an adequate definition of ambiguity must be in terms of decoding reactions. A good quantitative index of ambiguity would take into account the number of alternative decoding reactions to a stimulus and the proportion of cases responding with any given decoding system. This author has proposed that the $\hat{H}$ measure of uncertainty from information theory takes into account these two factors. If we let $p(i)$ indicate the proportion of $Ss$ who give each of the different decoding reactions to a stimulus, then $\hat{H}$ is given by

$$\hat{H} = -\Sigma p(i) \log_2 p(i)$$

For example, if a projective stimulus elicits four different decoding reactions, with the proportion of individuals giving these reactions being .96, .02, .01, and .01, then $\hat{H}$ is equal to .2557. As $H$ increases, perceptual or decoding ambiguity increases. The original article (Kenny, 1961) should be consulted for a more extensive discussion and rationale of the $H$ measure, as might Murstein's (1963b) interesting application of it.

## 2. Ambiguity and Arousal Level

The assumption is made that increasing ambiguity heightens the arousal level of the individual and that $Ss$ attempt to hold to intermediate levels of arousal by avoiding high arousal levels. The additional operational assumption is made that arousal level can be roughly indicated by ratings on Osgood's (Osgood, Suci, and Tannenbaum, 1957) connotative factors of potency and activity and that high arousal levels will be judged as undesirable, as indicated by low ratings on the evaluative factor. In other words, ambiguity should correlate positively with potency and activity and negatively with evaluation. This theorizing should be contrasted with the often made assumption that ambiguity facilitates the expression of covert layers of personality. Any golden nuggets (Kenny, 1954, 1961; Kenny and Bijou, 1953; Bijou and Kenny, 1951; Murstein, 1958, 1963b; Gurel and Ullman, 1958; Laskowitz, 1963; Weisskopf, 1950a,b; Weisskopf-Joelson and Lynn, 1953) that such an assumption had in the early days of projective testing have been mined and it is now desirable to move on to a finer-grain analysis of psychological functioning on projective tests. The present postulate attempts such an analysis.

No published research on this postulate has yet appeared. However, this author and his associates (Barbara Long, Lynn Harvey, Atsuko Moriya, and H. Kuechler) have accumulated a large amount of data on the $\hat{H}$ measure and its correlates, which is being prepared for publication. While this is not the place to describe the details of the research, it may be in order to mention that the first phase of the research required various groups of Ss to examine 26 TAT cards for a 20-second period and to describe what they saw. On the basis of these perceptual statements, decoding categories were formed. In order to obtain an index of ambiguity for each card, the uncertainty measure has been applied to this data. The second phase of the research has sought to determine the correlates of the uncertainty measure. Only one finding of this research will be reported, that bearing on the present postulates.

Some unpublished data, collected by Atsuko Moriya under the author's guidance, offer confirmation of the postulate. Male and female university students served as Ss for the derivation of two $\hat{H}$ indices for each of 26 TAT cards, one for each of the sexes. Two other male and female groups rated each of the pictures on 9 bipolar concepts, three concepts for each of the three connotative factors. In order to investigate the predicted relationships, the uncertainty measure rank order of the 26 cards was correlated with each of the three rank orders of the cards based on the three semantic factors. For males, the rank order correlations between ambiguity and evaluation, activity and potency, were $-.46$, $.61$, and $.58$, respectively. For females the corresponding correlations were $-.52$, $.40$, and $.60$, respectively. All six correlations are statistically significant at less than the .05 level. These findings strongly indicate that ambiguity is correlated negatively with the evaluative factor and positively with the activity and potency factors, thereby supporting the postulate that ambiguity is arousal raising. However, a great deal more research is required before the postulate is viewed as anything other than a tentative formulation.

With some evidence in support of the notion that ambiguity is correlated with approximate indicators of arousal level, the next research question under investigation is, "How does arousal level interact with the existing personality structure within the individual?" An adequate conceptual and empirical answer to this most challenging question would take us far beyond the scope of this paper, which deals with stimulus functions in projective techniques.

## III.  Postscript

Traditionally the focus of projective techniques has been personality centered, with only a token recognition of the fact that the stimulus might have something to do with behavior. Throughout the review, an attempt has been made to come to grips with the stimulus problem. In order to make an interpretive pathway through a maze of diverse findings, a set of postulates as to how the stimulus articulates with personality functioning is proposed. Lest these postulates and the theorizing back of them cause premature closure, it should be stressed that the present formulation is presented in a tentative and cautious manner. A margin of error in the postulates is expected. It is hoped that they are worded in a sufficiently precise manner to be empirically tested. An extension of the present set of postulates into personality functioning is planned.

Much of the theorizing is not, of course, wholly original. In particular, an attempt has been made to establish a point of contact with recent developments in the perceptual and cognitive areas. Furthermore, it is hoped that the bridge offered between ambiguity and arousal will prove fruitful.

One final statement may be in order. If projective techniques are to survive in psychology, projective personologists must maintain contact with the rapidly expanding knowledge in many areas of psychology, especially perception, cognition, learning, motivation, and measurement theory, and modify their traditional instruments and interpretations in light of new information.

## References

Albert, R. S. The role of mass media and the effect of aggressive film content upon children's aggressive responses and identification choices. *Genet. Psychol Monogr.*, 1957, **55**, 221-285.

Allen, R. M. The influence of color in the Rorschach test on reaction time in a normal population. *J. proj. Tech.*, 1951, **15**, 481-485.

Allen, R. M., Manne, S. H., and Stiff, Margaret P. The role of color in Rorschach's test: a preliminary normative report on a college student population. *J. proj. Tech.*, 1951, **15**, 235-242.

Allen, R. M., Manne, S. H., and Stiff, Margaret P. The influence of color on the consistency of responses in the Rorschach test. *J. clin. Psychol.*, 1952, **8**, 97-98.

Allen, R. M., Stiff, Margaret P., and Rosenzweig, M. The role of color in Rorschach's test: a preliminary survey of neurotic and psychotic groups. *J. clin. Psychol.,* 1953, 9, 81-83.

Alper, Thelma G. Predicting the direction of selective recall: its relation to ego strength and achievement. *J. abnorm. soc. Psychol.,* 1957, 55, 149-165.

Andrew, G., Walton, R. E., Hartwell, S. W., and Hutt, M. L. The Michigan Picture Test: the stimulus values of the cards. *J. consult. Psychol.,* 1951, 15, 51-54.

Andrew, G., Hartwell, S. W., Hutt, M. L., and Walton, R. E. *The Michigan Picture Test.* Chicago: Science Research Associates, 1953.

Angelini, A. L. Um novo metodo para avaliar a motivacao humano. (A new method of evaluating human motivation.) *Bol. Fac. Filos. Cienc. S. Paulo.,* 1955, No. 207.

Armstrong, M. A. S. Children's responses to animal and human figures in thematic pictures. *J. consult. Psychol.,* 1954, 18, 67-70.

Arnheim, R. Perceptual and aesthetic aspects of the movement response. *J. Pers.,* 1951, 19, 265-281.

Arnheim, R. P. *Art and visual perception.* Berkeley: Univer. of California Press, 1954.

Atkinson, J. W. *Studies in projective measurement of achievement motivation.* Unpublished doctoral dissertation, Univer. of Michigan, Ann Arbor, 1950.

Atkinson, J. W. (Ed.), *Motives in fantasy, action and society.* Princeton, New Jersey: Van Nostrand, 1958.

Auld, F. The influence of social class on tests of personality. *Drew Univer. Studies,* 1952, No. 5, 1-16.

Auld, F., Eron, L. D., and Laffal, J. Application of Guttman's scaling method .o the TAT. *Educ. psychol. Measmt.,* 1955, 15, 422-435.

Barnett, I. *The influence of color and shading on the Rorschach test.* Unpublished doctoral dissertation, Univer. of Pittsburgh, Pennsylvania, 1950.

Barron, F. An ego-strength scale which predicts response to psychotherapy. *J. consult. Psychol.,* 1953, 17, 327-333.

Barron, F. Threshold for the perception of human movement in inkblots. *J. consult. Psychol.,* 1955, 19, 33-38.

Barron, F. Ego-strength and the management of aggression. In G. S. Welsh and W. G. Dahlstrom (Eds.), *Basic readings in the MMPI in psychology and medicine.* Minneapolis: Univer. of Minnesota Press, 1956, pp. 579-585.

Bartlett, F. C. *Remembering.* London: Cambridge Univer. Press, 1932.

Baughman, E. E. A comparative analysis of Rorschach forms with altered stimulus characteristics. *J. proj. Tech.,* 1954, 18, 151-164.

Baughman, E. E. The role of the stimulus in Rorschach responses. *Psychol. Bull.,* 1958, 55, 121-147.

Baughman, E. E. An experimental analysis of the relationship between stimulus structure and behavior on the Rorschach. *J. proj. Tech.,* 1959, 23, 134-183.

Baxter, J. C., and Becker, J. Anxiety and avoidance behavior in schizophrenics in response to parental figures. *J. abnorm. soc. Psychol.,* 1962, 64, 432-437.

Beck, S. J. Configurational tendencies in Rorschach responses. *Amer. J. Psychol.,* 1933, 45, 433-443.

Belden, A. W., and Baughman, E. E. The effects of figure-ground contrast upon perception as evaluated by a modified Rorschach technique. *J. consult. Psychol.,* 1954, 18, 29-34.

Bellak, L. *The Thematic Apperception Test and the Children's Apperception Test in clinical use.* New York: Grune & Stratton, 1954.

Bellak, L., and Adelman, Crusa. The Children's Apperception Test (CAT). In A. I. Rabin and Mary R. Haworth (Eds.), *Projective techniques with children.* New York: Grune & Stratton, 1960, pp. 62-94.

Berliner, A. The Rorschach determinant in terms of visual psychology. *Optom. Wkly.*, 1955, **20**, 13-17.

Biersdorf, K. R., and Marcuse, F. L. Responses of children to human and to animal pictures. *J. proj. Tech.*, 1953, **17**, 455-459.

Bijou, S. W., and Kenny, D. T. The ambiguity values of TAT cards. *J. consult. Psychol.*, 1951, **15**, 203-209.

Bills, R. E. Animal pictures for obtaining children's projections. *J. clin. Psychol.*, 1950, **6**, 291-293.

Bills, R. E. Self-concepts and Rorschach signs of depression. *J. consult. Psychol.*, 1954, **18**, 135-138.

Bills, R. E., Leiman, C. J., and Thomas, R. W. A study of the validity of the TAT cards and a set of animal pictures. *J. clin. Psychol.*, 1950, **6**, 293-295.

Binder, H. Die Hellunkeldeutungen im psychodiagnostischen experiment von Rorschach. *Schweiz. Arch. Neurol. Psychiat.*, 1933, **30**, 1-67.

Blum, G. S. A study of the psychoanalytic theory of psychosexual development. *Genet. Psychol. Monogr.*, 1949, **39**, 3-99.

Bohm, E. The Binder chiaroscuro system and its theoretical basis. In Maria A. Rickers-Ovsiankina (Ed), *Rorschach psychology.* New York: Wiley, 1960, pp. 202-222.

Brackbill, G. A. Some effects of color in thematic fantasy. *J. consult. Psychol.*, 1951, **15**, 412-418.

Bradburn, N. M. *N* achievement and father dominance in Turkey. *J. abnorm. soc. Psychol.*, 1963, **67**, 464-468.

Bramel, D. A dissonance theory approach to defensive projection. *J. abnorm. soc. Psychol.*, 1962, **64**, 121-129.

Bramel, D. Selection of a target for defensive projection. *J. abnorm. soc. Psychol.*, 1963, **66**, 318-324.

Brody, G. G. A study of the effects of color on Rorschach responses. *Genet. Psychol. Monogr.*, 1953, **48**, 261-311.

Brosin, H. W., and Fromm, E. O. Rorschach and color blindness. *Rorschach Res. Exch.*, 1940, **4**, 39-70.

Brosin, H. W., and Fromm, E. O. Some principles of gestalt psychology in the Rorschach experiment. *Rorschach Res. Exch.*, 1942, **6**, 1-15.

Bruner, J. S. Perceptual theory and the Rorschach test. *J. Pers.*, 1948, **17**, 157-168.

Bruner, J. S. Personality dynamics and the process of perceiving. In R. R. Blake and G. Ramsey (Eds.), *Perception: an approach to personality.* New York: Ronald Press, 1951, pp. 121-147.

Bruner, J. S. On perceptual readiness. *Psychol. Rev.*, 1957, **64**, 123-152.

Bruner, J. S., and Postman, L. Emotional selectivity in perception and reaction. *J. Pers.* 1947, **16**, 69-77.

Bruner, J. S., and Postman, L. Perception, cognition and behavior. *J. Pers.*, 1949, **18**, 14-31.

Brunswik, E. Distal focusing of perception: size constancy in a representative sample of situations. *Psychol. Monogr.*, 1944, No. 254.

Brunswik, E. *The conceptual framework of psychology.* Chicago, Illinois: Univer. of Chicago Press, 1952. (Int. Encyl. Unified Sci., Vol. I, No. 10.)

Brunswik, E. Representative design and probabilistic theory in a functional psychology. *Psychol. Rev.*, 1955, **62**, 193-217.

Budoff, M. *An investigation of the relative usefulness of animals and persons in a picture-story test for children.* Unpublished master's thesis, Univer. of Chicago, Chicago, Illinois, 1955.

Buker, S. L., and Williams, M. Color as a determinant of responsiveness to Rorschach cards in schizophrenia. *J. consult. Psychol.*, 1951, **15**, 196-202.

Canter, A. *An investigation of the psychological significance of reactions to color on the Rorschach and other tests.* Unpublished doctoral dissertation, Univer. of Iowa, Iowa City, 1951.

Canter, A. The effect of unshaded bright colors in the Rorschach upon the form-color response balance of psychotic patients. *J. proj. Tech.,* 1958, **22,** 390-393.

Carr, A. C. The relation of certain Rorschach variables to expression of affect in the TAT and SCT. *J. proj. Tech.,* 1956, **20,** 137-142.

Child, I. L., Frank, Kitty F., and Storm, T. Self-ratings and TAT: their relations to each other and to childhood background. *J. Pers.,* 1956, **25,** 96-114.

Chodorkoff, B. A note on Bitterman and Kniffen's "Manifest anxiety and perceptual defense." *J. abnorm. soc. Psychol.,* 1955, **50,** 144.

Clark, J. H. Some MMPI correlates of color responses in the group Rorschach. *J. consult. Psychol.,* 1948, **12,** 384-386.

Clark, K. B., and Clark, Mamie P. Racial identification and preferences in Negro children. In T. M. Newcomb and E. L. Hartley (Eds.), *Readings in social psychology.* New York: Holt, 1947, pp. 169-178.

Cohen-Séat, G., Rebéillard, M. Test filmique thématique. *Rev. int. Filmol.,* 1955, **6,** 111-118.

Cook, R. A. Identification and ego defensiveness in thematic apperception. *J. proj. Tech.,* 1953, **17,** 312-319.

Costello, C. G. The Rorschach records of suicidal patients. *J. proj. Tech.,* 1958, **22,** 272-275.

Cox, B., and Sargent, H. TAT responses of emotionally disturbed and emotionally stable children: clinical judgment versus normative data. *J. proj. Tech.,* 1950, **14,** 61-74.

Cox, F. N., and Sarason, S. B. Test anxiety and Rorschach performance. *J. abnorm. soc. Psychol.,* 1954, **49,** 371-377.

Crumpton, Evelyn. The influence of color on the Rorschach test. *J. proj. Tech.,* 1956, **20,** 150-158.

Deering, G. Affective stimuli and disturbance of thought processes. *J. consult. Psychol.,* 1963, **27,** 338-343.

Douvan, Elizabeth. Social status and success strivings. In J. W. Atkinson (Ed.), *Motives in fantasy, action and society.* Princeton, New Jersey: Van Nostrand, 1958, pp. 509-517.

Dubrovner, R. J., Von Lackum, W. J., and Jost, H. A. A study of the effect of color on productivity and reaction time in the Rorschach test. *J. clin. Psychol.,* 1950, **6,** 331-336.

Edmonston, W. E., and Griffith, R. M. Rorschach content and inkblot structure. *J. proj. Tech.,* 1958, **22,** 394-397.

Epstein, Marilyn. *The reliability and internal consistency of the Thematic Apperception Test.* Unpublished master's thesis, Univer. of British Columbia, Vancouver, Canada, 1964.

Epstein, S., and Fenz, W. D. Theory and experiment on the measurement of approach-avoidance conflict. *J. abnorm. soc. Psychol.,* 1962, **64,** 97-112.

Epstein, S., and Smith, R. Thematic apperception as a measure of the hunger drive. *J. proj. Tech.,* 1956, **20,** 372-384.

Eron, L. D. Frequencies of themes and identifications in the stories of schizophrenic patients and nonhospitalized college students. *J. consult. Psychol.,* 1948, **12,** 387-395.

Eron, L. D. A normative study of the Thematic Apperception Test. *Psychol. Monogr.,* 1950, **64,** No. 9 (Whole No. 315).

Exner, J. E. The influence of chromatic and achromatic color in the Rorschach. *J. proj. Tech.*, 1959, **23**, 418-425.

Fenz, W. D., and Epstein, S. Measurement of approach-avoidance conflict by a stimulus dimension in a test of thematic apperception. *J. Pers.* 1962, **30**, 613-632.

Feshbach, S. The effects of emotional restraint upon the projection of positive affect. *J. Pers.*, 1963, **31**, 471-481.

Feshbach, S., and Feshbach, Norma. Influence of the stimulus object upon the complementary and supplementary projection of fear. *J. abnorm. soc. Psychol.*, 1963, **66**, 498-502.

Feshbach, S., and Singer, R. D. The effects of fear arousal and suppression of fear upon social perception. *J. abnorm. soc. Psychol.*, 1957, **55**, 283-288.

Feshbach, S., Singer, R. D., and Feshbach, Norma. Effects of anger arousal and similarity upon the attribution of hostility to pictorial stimuli. *J. consult. Psychol.*, 1963, **27**, 248-252.

Fiske, D. W. Homogeneity and variation in measuring personality. *Amer. Psychologist*, 1963, **18**, 643-652.

Forsyth, R. P. The influence of color, shading, and Welsh Anxiety level on Elizur Rorschach content test analyses of anxiety and hostility. *J. proj. Tech.*, 1959, **23**, 207-213.

Framo, J. L. *Structural aspects of perceptual development in normal adults: a tachistoscopic study with the Rorschach technique.* Unpublished doctoral dissertation, Univer. of Texas, Austin, 1952.

Friedman, H. Perceptual regression in schizophrenia. An hypothesis suggested by the use of the Rorschach test. *J. proj. Tech.*, 1953, **17**, 171-186.

Furuya, K. Responses of school children to human and animal pictures. *J. proj. Tech.*, 1957, **21**, 248-252.

Gemelli, A. Le film, procédé d'analyse projective. *Rev. int. Filmol.*, 1951, **2**, 135-138.

Gerard, R. U. *Differential effects of colored lights on psychophysiological functions.* Unpublished doctoral dissertation, Univer. of California, Los Angeles, 1958.

Goodman, Mary E. *The genesis of race awareness and attitude.* Unpublished doctoral dissertation, Radcliffe College, Cambridge, Massachusetts, 1946.

Gottesman, I. I. More construct validation of the Ego-Strength scale. *J. consult. Psychol.*, 1959, **23**, 342-346.

Grayson, H. M. Rorschach productivity and card preferences as influenced by experimental variation of the color and shading. *J. proj. Tech.*, 1956, **20**, 288-296.

Greenbaum, M., Qualtere, T., Carruth, B., and Cruickshank, W. Evaluation of a modification of thematic Apperception Test for use with physically handicapped children. *J. clin. Psychol.*, 1953, **9**, 40-44.

Gurel, L., and Ullmann, L. P. Quantitative differences in response to TAT cards: the relationship between transcendence score and number of emotional words. *J. proj. Tech.*, 1958, **22**, 432-439.

Guttman, L. The basis for scalogram analysis. In S. A. Stouffer (Ed.), *Studies in social psychology in World War II. Vol. IV. Measurement and prediction.* Princeton, New Jersey: Princeton Univer. Press, 1950, pp. 60-90.

Haase, W. *Rorschach diagnosis, socio-economic class and examiner bias.* Unpublished doctoral dissertation, New York Univer., 1956.

Hartmann, H. Comments on the psychoanalytic theory of the ego. *Psychoanal. stud. Child*, 1950, **5**, 74-96.

Hartmann, H. *Ego Psychology and the problem of adaptation.* New York: International Univer. Press, 1958.

Hartwell, S. W., Hutt, M. L., Andrew, Gwen, and Walton, R. E. The Michigan Picture

Test: diagnostic and therapeutic possibilities of a new projective test for children. *Am. J. Orthopsychiat.*, 1951, **21**, 124-137.

Haworth, Mary. Films as a group technique. In A. I. Rabin and Mary R. Haworth (Eds.), *Projective techniques with children.* New York: Grune and Stratton, 1960, pp. 177-190.

Hemmindinger, L. Perceptual organization and development as reflected in the structure of Rorschach test responses. *J. proj. Tech.*, 1953, **17**, 171-185.

Hemmindinger, L. Developmental theory and the Rorschach method. In Maria Rickers-Ovsiankina (Ed.), *Rorschach psychology.* New York: Wiley, 1960, pp. 58-79.

Henry, W. E. The thematic apperception technique in the study of culture-personality relations. *Genet. Psychol. Monogr.*, 1947, **35**, 3-135.

Henry, W. E. *The analysis of fantasy.* New York: Wiley, 1956.

Hochberg, J. E., Triebel, W., and Seaman, G. Color adaptation under conditions of homogeneous visual stimulation (Ganzfeld). *J. exp. Psychol.*, 1951, **41**, 153-159.

Hokanson, J. E., and Gordon, J. E. The expression and inhibition of hostility in imaginative and overt behavior. *J. abnorm. soc. Psychol.*, 1958, **57**, 327-333.

Holt, R. R. A critical examination of Freud's concept of bound vs. free cathexis. *J. Amer. Psychoanal. Ass.*, 1962, **10**, 475-525.

Holtzman, W. H., Iscoe, I., and Calvin, A. D. Rorschach color responses and manifest anxiety in college women. *J. consult. Psychol.*, 1954, **18**, 317-324.

Holtzman, W. H., Thorpe, J. S., Swartz, J. D., and Herron, E. W. *Inkblot perception and personality.* Austin: Univer. of Texas Press, 1961.

Horiuchi, Haruyo. A study of perceptual processes of Rorschach cards by tachistoscopic method of movement and shading responses. *J. proj. Tech.*, 1961, **25**, 44-53.

Hull, C. L. *Principles of behavior.* New York: Appleton, 1943.

Jensen, A. R. The reliability of projective techniques: review of the literature. *Acta Psychologica*, 1959, **16**, 108-136.

Jones, R. A. *Some effects of emotion on the use of words by schizophrenics.* Washington, D. C.: Catholic Univer. American Press, 1957.

Kagan, J. The measurement of overt aggression from fantasy. *J. abnorm. soc. Psychol.*, 1956, **52**, 390-393.

Kagan, J. Thematic apperceptive techniques with children. In A. I. Rabin and Mary R. Haworth (Eds.), *Projective techniques with children.* New York: Grune and Stratton, 1960, pp. 105-129.

Kelly, E. L. Theory and techniques of assessment. *Annual Review of Psychology*, Vol. 5, Palo Alto: Annual Reviews, 1954, pp. 281-311.

Kenny, D. T. Transcendence indices, extent of personality factors in fantasy responses, and the ambiguity of TAT cards. *J. consult. Psychol.*, 1954, **18**, 345-348.

Kenny, D. T. A theoretical and research reappraisal of stimulus factors in the TAT. In J. Kagan and G. S. Lesser (Eds.), *Contemporary issues in thematic apperception methods.* Springfield, Illinois: Charles C Thomas, 1961, pp. 288-310.

Kenny, D. T., and Bijou, S. W. Ambiguity of pictures and extent of personality factors in fantasy responses. *J. consult. Psychol.*, 1953, **17**, 283-288.

Kenny, D. T., and Chappell, Marguerite C. Anxiety effects in thematic apperception induced by homogeneous visual stimulation. *J. proj. Tech. and Pers. Assess.*, 1963, **27**, 297-301.

Kenny, D. T., Harvey, Lynn, and Wilson, Barbara. Perceptual reactions to the TAT. Unpublished manuscript, 1961.

Kiesler, C., and Singer, R. D. The effects of similarity and guilt on the projection of hostility. *J. clin. Psychol.*, 1963, **19**, 157-162.

Klein, A., and Arnheim, R. Perceptual analysis of a Rorschach card. *J. Pers.*, 1953, **22**, 60-70.

Kohler, F. J., and Steil, A. The use of the Rorschach in involutional melancholia. *J. consult. Psychol.*, 1953, **17**, 365-370.

Korchin, S. J. Form perception and ego functioning. In Maria A. Rickers-Ovsiankina (Ed.), *Projective Psychology*. New York: Wiley, 1960, pp. 109-129.

Korchin, S. J., Mitchell, H. E., and Meltzoff, J. A. A critical evaluation of the Thompson Thematic Apperception Test. *J. proj. Tech.*, 1950, **14**, 445-452.

Kreezer, G. L. A threshold-method for measuring the attention-demand value of stimuli. *Amer. J. Psychol.*, 1958, **71**, 111-122.

Laffal, J. Response faults in word association as a function of response entropy. *J. abnorm. soc. Psychol.*, 1955, **50**, 265-270.

Lasaga y Travieso, J. E., and Martinez-Arango, C. Some suggestions concerning the administration and interpretation of the TAT. *J. Psychol.*, 1946, **22**, 117-163.

Laskowitz, D. Degree of pictorial ambiguity and fantasy evocation: an appraisal of the nonmonotonic hypothesis. *Perceptual and Motor Skills*, 1963, **16**, 187-193.

Lazarus, R. S. An experimental analysis of the influence of color on the protocol of the Rorschach test. *J. Pers.*, 1948, **17**, 182-185.

Lazarus, R. S. The influence of color on the protocol of the Rorschach test. *J. abnorm. soc. Psychol.*, 1949, **44**, 506-516.

Lazarus, R. S., and Oldfield, Margaret. Rorschach responses and the influence of color. *J. Pers.*, 1955, **23**, 356-372.

Leiman, A. H., and Epstein, S. Thematic sexual responses as related the sexual drive and guilt. *J. abnorm. soc. Psychol.*, 1961, **63**, 169-175.

Lennep, D. J. van. *Four-pictures test*. The Hague: Martinus Nijhoff, 1948.

Lerner, E., and Murphy, L. B. Methods for the study of personality in young children. *Monogr. Soc. Res. Child Developm.*, 1941, **6**, No. 4.

Lesser, G. S. Application of Guttman's scaling method to aggressive fantasy in children. *Educ. psychol. Measmt.*, 1958, **18**, 543-552.

Lesser, G. S., Krawitz, Rhode N., and Packard, Rita. Experimental arousal of achievement motivation in adolescent girls. *J. abnorm. soc. Psychol.*, 1963, **66**, 59-66.

Levine, R., Chein, I., and Murphy, G. The relation of intensity of a need to the amount of perceptual distortion: A preliminary report. *J. Psychol.*, 1942, **13**, 283-293.

Levitt, E. E. Alleged Rorschach indices in children. *J. proj. Tech.*, 1957, **21**, 261-264.

Levitt, E. E., and Grosz, H. D. A comparison of quantifiable Rorschach anxiety indicators in hypnotically induced anxiety and normal states. *J. consult. Psychol.*, 1960, **24**, 31-34.

Levy, D. M. Studies in sibling rivalry. *Res. Monogr. Amer. Orthopsychiat. Ass.*, 1937, No. 2.

Levy, E. Stimulus value of Rorschach cards for children. *J. proj. Tech.*, 1958, **22**, 293-296.

Light, B. H. A further test of the Thompson TAT rationale. *J. abnorm. soc. Psychol.*, 1955, **51**, 148-150.

Lindzey, G. Thematic Apperception Test: interpretive assumptions and relative empirical evidence. *Psychol. Bull.*, 1952, **49**, 1-25.

Lindzey, G. *Projective techniques and cross-cultural research*. New York: Appleton, 1961.

Lindzey, G., and Goldberg, M. Motivational differences between male and female as measured by the Thematic Apperception Test. *J. Pers.,* 1953, **22,** 101-117.

Lindzey, G., & Herman, P. S. Thematic Apperception Test: a note on reliability and situational validity. *J. proj. Tech.,* 1955, **18,** 36-42.

Lindzey, G., and Kalnins, D. Thematic Apperception Test: some evidence bearing on the "hero assumption." *J. abnorm. soc. Psychol.,* 1958, **57,** 76-83.

Little, K. B. Connotations of the Rorschach inkblots. *J. Pers.,* 1959, **27,** 397-406.

Loiselle, R. H., and Kleinschmidt, Ann. A comparison of the stimulus value of Rorschach inkblots and their percepts. *J. proj. Tech.,* 1963, **27,** 191-194.

Lubin, N. M. The effect of color in the TAT on productions of mentally retarded subjects. *Amer. J. ment. Defic.,* 1955, **60,** 366-370.

Lubin, N. M., and Wilson, M. O. Picture test identification as a function of "reality" (color) and similarity of picture to subject. *J. gen. Psychol.,* 1956, **54,** 31-38.

McArthur, C. Personality differences between middle and upper classes. *J. abnorm. soc. Psychol.,* 1955, **50,** 247-254.

McClelland, D. C. Methods of measuring human motivation. In J. W. Atkinson (Ed.), *Motives in fantasy, action, and society.* Princeton, New Jersey: Van Nostrand, 1958, pp. 7-42.

McClelland, D. C., Atkinson, J. W., Clark, R. A., and Lowell, E. I. *The achievement motive.* New York: Appleton, 1953.

Maccoby, Eleanor E., and Wilson, W. C. Identification and observational learning from films. *J. abnorm. soc. Psychol.,* 1957, **55,** 76-87.

McIntyre, C. J. Sex, age, and iconicity as factors in projective film tests. *J. consult. Psychol.,* 1954, **18,** 475-477.

Mainord, F. R., and Marcuse, F. L. Responses of disturbed children to human and to animal pictures. *J. proj. Tech.,* 1954, **18,** 475-477.

Mann, L. The relation of Rorschach indices of extratension and introversion to a measure of responsiveness to the immediate environment. *J. consult. Psychol.,* 1956, **20,** 114-118.

Mayer, J., and Binz, E. Stimulus values of Rorschach cards. *J. consult. Psychol.,* 1961, **17,** 186-187.

Meer, B., and Singer, J. L. A note on the "father" and "mother" cards in the Rorschach inkblots. *J. consult. Psychol.,* 1950, **14,** 482-484.

Meyer, B. T. An investigation of color chock in the Rorschach test. *J. clin. Psychol.,* 1951, **7,** 267-270.

Miller, J. S., and Scodel, A. The diagnostic significance of usual and unusual TAT stories. *J. consult. Psychol.,* 1955, **19,** 91-95.

Miller, N. E. Theory and experiment relating psychoanalytic displacement to stimulus response generalization. *J. abnorm. soc. Psychol.,* 1948, **43,** 155-178.

Miller, N. E. Liberalization of basic S-R concepts: extensions to conflict behavior, motivation and social learning. In S. Koch. (Ed.), *Psychology: a study of a science.* New York: McGraw-Hill, 1959, Vol. 2.

Moore, Mary E., and Schwartz, M. U. The effect of the sex of the frustrated figure on responses to the Rosenzweig P-F Study. *J. proj. Tech.,* 1963, **27,** 195-199.

Morgan, C. D., and Murray, H. A. A method for investigating fantasies: the Thematic Apperception Test. *Arch. Neurol. & Psychiat.,* 1935, **34,** 289-306.

Moriya, Atsuko. *The effects of culture on ambiguity and connotative meanings of Thematic Apperception Cards.* Unpublished master's thesis, Univer. of British Columbia, Vancouver, Canada, 1962.

Murray, E. J. Conflict and repression during sleep deprivation. *J. abnorm. soc. Psychol.,* 1959, **59,** 95-101.

Murray, H. A. The effect of fear on the estimates of the maliciousness of other personalities. *J. soc. Psychol.*, 1933, 4, 310-329.

Murray, H. A. *Thematic Apperception Test*. Cambridge, Massachusetts: Harvard Univer. Press, 1943.

Murstein, B. I. The relationship of stimulus ambiguity on the TAT to productivity of themes. *J. consult. Psychol.*, 1958, 22, 348.

Murstein, B. I. The role of the stimulus in the manifestation of fantasy. In J. Kagan and G. S. Lesser (Eds.), *Contemporary issues in thematic apperceptive methods*. Springfield, Illinois: Charles C Thomas, 1961, pp. 229-273.

Murstein, B. I. The relationship of expectancy of reward to achievement performance on an arithmetic and thematic test. *J. consult. Psychol.*, 1963, 27, 394-399. (a)

Murstein, B. I. *Theories and research in projective techniques:* Emphasizing the TAT. New York: Wiley, 1963. (b)

Neuringer, C. Manifestations of anxiety on the Rorschach test. *J. proj. Tech.*, 1962, 26, 318-326.

Osgood, C. E., Suci, G. J., and Tannenbaum, P. H. *The measurement of meaning*. Urbana: Univer. of Illinois Press, 1957.

Perlman, Janet A. Color and the validity of the Rorschach 8-9-10 per cent. *J. consult. Psychol.*, 1951, 15, 122-126.

Phillipson, H. *The object relations technique*. Chicago, Illinois: The Free Press, 1955.

Piaget, J. *Psychology of intelligence*. London: Routledge and Kegan Paul, 1950.

Piotrowski, Z. A. The Thematic Apperception Test of a schizophrenic interpreted according to new rules. *Psychoanal. Rev.*, 1952, 39, 230-251.

Postman, L., Bruner, J. S., and McGinnies, E. Personal values as selective factors in perception. *J. abnorm. soc. Psychol.*, 1948, 83, 148-153.

Postman, L., and Solomon, R. L. Perceptual sensitivity to completed and uncompleted tasks. *J. Pers.*, 1949, 18, 347-357.

Purcell, K. The TAT and antisocial behavior. *J. consult. Psychol.*, 1956, 20, 449-456.

Rabin, A. I. A contribution to the "meaning" of Rorschach's inkblots via the semantic differential. *J. consult. Psychol.*, 1959, 23, 368-372.

Rickers-Ovsiankina, Maria. Some theoretical considerations regarding the Rorschach method. *Rorschach Res. Exch.*, 1943, 7, 41-53.

Rickers-Ovsiankina, Maria. A synopsis of psychological premises underlying the Rorschach. In Maria A. Rickers-Ovsiankina (Ed.), *Rorschach psychology*. New York: Wiley, 1960, pp. 3-22.

Riess, B. F., Schwartz, E. K., and Cottingham, A. An experimental critique of assumptions underlying the Negro version of the TAT. *J. abnorm. soc. Psychol.*, 1950, 45, 700-709.

Riessman, F., and Miller, S. M. Social class and projective tests. *J. proj. Tech.*, 1958, 22, 432-439.

Rorschach, H. *Psychodiagnostics: a diagnostic test based on perception*. Bern, Switzerland: Huber, 1942 (1st ed. 1921).

Rosen, E. Symbolic meanings in the Rorschach cards: a statistical study. *J. clin. Psychol.*, 1951, 7, 239-244.

Rosen, E. Connotative meanings of Rorschach inkblots, responses and determinants. *J. Pers.*, 1960, 28, 413-426.

Rosenzweig, S. Idiodynamics in personality theory with special reference to projective methods. *Psychol. Rev.*, 1951, 58, 213-223.

Rosenzweig, S., and Fleming, Edith. Apperceptive norms for the Thematic Apperception Test: II. An empirical investigation. *J. Pers.*, 1949, 17, 483-503.

Rust, R. U. Some correlates of the movement response. *J. Pers.*, 1948, 16, 369-401.

Saltz, G., and Epstein, S. Thematic hostility and guilt responses as related to self-reported hostility, guilt, and conflict. *J. abnorm. soc. Psychol.*, 1963, **67**, 469-479.

Sanford, R. N. The effects of abstinence from food upon imaginal processes: A preliminary experiment. *J. Psychol.*, 1936, **2**, 145-159.

Sanford, R. N. The effects of abstinence from food upon imaginal processes: a further experiment. *J. Psychol.*, 1937, **3**, 145-149.

Sappenfield, B. R. Perception of masculinity-femininity in Rorschach blots and responses. *J. consult. Psychol.*, 1961, **17**, 373-376.

Sappenfield, B. R., and Buker, S. L. Validity of the Rorschach 8-9-10 per cent as an indicator of responsiveness to color. *J. consult. Psychol.*, 1949, **13**, 268-271.

Schachtel, E. On color and affect. *Psychiatry*, 1943, **6**, 393-409.

Schleifer, M. J., and Hire, A. W. Stimulus value of Rorschach inkblots expressed as trait and affective characteristics. *J. proj. Tech.*, 1960, **24**, 164-170.

Schwartz, E. K., Riess, B. F., and Cottingham, Alice. Further critical evaluation of the Negro version of the TAT. *J. proj. Tech.*, 1951, **15**, 394-400.

Seeman, W., and Marks, P. A. A study of some "test dimensions" conceptions. *J. proj. Tech.*, 1962, **26**, 469-473.

Shapiro, D. A perceptual understanding of color response. In Maria A. Rickers-Ovsiankina (Ed.), *Rorschach Psychology*. New York: Wiley, 1960, pp. 154-201.

Sherif, M. A study of some social factors in perception. *Arch. Psychol.*, 1935, No. 187.

Shneidman, E. S. Schizophrenia and the MAPS test. *Genet. Psychol. Monogr.*, 1948, **38**, 145-224.

Siipola, Elsa M. The influence of color on reactions to inkblots. *J. Pers.*, 1950, **18** 358-382.

Siipola, Elsa M., Kuhns, Florence, and Taylor, V. Measurement of the individual's reactions to color in inkblots. *J. Pers.*, 1950, **19**, 153-171.

Silverstein, A. B. Identification with same-sex and opposite-sex figures in thematic apperception. *J. proj. Tech.*, 1959, **23**, 73-75.

Singer, J. L., and Spohn, H. E. Some behavioral correlates of Rorschach's experiencer type. *J. consult. Psychol.*, 1954, **18**, 1-9.

Singer, R. D. A cognitive view of rationalized projection. *J. proj. Tech.*, 1963, **27**, 235-243.

Singer, R. D., and Feshbach, S. Effects of anxiety arousal in psychotics and normals upon the perception of anxiety in others. *J. Pers.*, 1962, **30**, 574-587.

Solomon, R. L., and Howes, D. H. Word frequency, personal values, and visual duration thresholds. *Psychol. Rev.*, 1951, **58**, 256-270.

Spivak, G., Levine, M., and Sprigle, H. Barron M threshold values in emotionally disturbed adolescents. *J. proj. Tech.*, 1958, **22**, 446-449.

Stein, M. I. Personality factors involved in the temporal development of Rorschach responses. *J. proj. Tech.*, 1949, **13**, 355-414.

Stein, M. I. Clinical psychology and the propaedeutic science. *J. proj. Tech.*, 1951, **15**, 401-404.

Sterling, M. E. *Color shock on the Rorschach test*. Unpublished doctoral dissertation, Univer. of Kentucky, Lexington, 1950.

Stone, H. The TAT aggressive content scale. *J. proj. Tech.*, 1956, **20**, 445-452.

Stone, L. J., and Fiedler, Mariam F. The Rorschachs of selected groups of children in comparison with published norms: II. The effect of socio-economic status on Rorschach performance. *J. proj. Tech.*, 1956, **20**, 276-279.

Stricker, G. Stimulus properties of the Blacky Pictures Test. *J. proj. Tech.*, 1963, **27**, 244-247.

Swartz, M. B. The role of color in influencing responses to the Rorschach test: an experimental investigation of the validity of the color shock hypothesis as a sign of neurotic disturbance and as a phenomenon induced by the color stimulus. Unpublished doctoral dissertation, New York Univer., New York, 1953.

Symonds, P. M. *Adolescent fantasy.* New York: Columbia Univer. Press, 1949.

Taniguchi, M., De Vos, G., and Murakami, E. Identification of mother and father cards on the Rorschach by Japanese normal and delinquent adolescents. *J. proj. Tech.*, 1958, **22**, 453-460.

Taylor, Janet A. A personality scale of manifest anxiety. *J. abnorm. soc. Psychol.*, 1953, **48**, 285-290.

Thompson, C. E. The Thompson modification of the Thematic Apperception Test. *Rorschach Res. Exch.*, 1949, **13**, 469-478.

Thompson, C. E., and Bachrach, J. The use of color in the Thematic Apperception Test. *J. proj. Tech.*, 1951, **15**, 173-184.

Tolar, A. The "meaning" of the Bender-Gestalt test designs: A study in the use of the semantic differential. *J. proj. Tech.*, 1960, **24**, 433-438.

Tomkins, S. S., and Miner, J. B. *The Tomkins-Horn pictures arrangement test.* New York: Springer, 1957.

Underwood, B. J. Stimulus selection in verbal learning. In C. N. Cofer and Barbara S. Musgrove (Eds.), *Verbal behavior and learning: problems and processes.* New York: McGraw-Hill, 1963, pp. 33-48.

Veroff, J. *A projective measure of achievement motivation in adolescent males and females.* Unpublished honors thesis, Wesleyan Univer., Middletown, Connecticut, 1950.

Veroff, J. Thematic apperception in a nationwide sample survey. In J. Kagan and G. S. Lesser (Eds.), *Contemporary issues in thematic apperceptive methods.* Springfield, Illinois: Charles C Thomas, 1961, pp. 83-111.

Veroff, J., Wilcox, S., and Atkinson, J. W. The achievement motive in high school and college age women. *J. abnorm. soc. Psychol.*, 1953, **48**, 108-119.

Veroff, J., Atkinson, J. W., Feld, Sheila C., and Guria, G. The use of thematic apperception to assess motivation in a nationwide interview study. *Psychol. Monogr.*, 1960, **74** (Whole No. 499).

Walker, E. L., and Atkinson, J. W. The expression of fear-relation motivation in thematic apperception as a function of proximity to an atomic explosion. In J. W. Atkinson (Ed.), *Motives in fantasy, action, and society.* New York: Van Nostrand, 1958, pp. 143-159.

Wallen, R. The nature of color shock. *J. abnorm. soc. Psychol.*, 1948, **43**, 346-356.

Weatherley, D. Maternal permissiveness toward aggression and subsequent TAT aggression. *J. abnorm. soc. Psychol.*, 1962, **65**, 1-5.

Weisskopf, Edith A. A transcendence index as a proposed measure in the TAT. *J. Psychol.*, 1950, **29**, 379-390. (a)

Weisskopf, Edith A. An experimental study of the effect of brightness and ambiguity on projection in the Thematic Apperception Test. *J. Psychol.*, 1950, **29**, 407-416. (b)

Weisskopf, E. A., and Dunlevy, G. P. Bodily similarity between subjects and central figure in the TAT as an influence on projection. *J. abnorm. soc. Psychol.*, 1952, **47**, 441-445.

Weisskopf-Joelson, Edith A., and Foster, Helen. An experimental study of the effect of stimulus narration upon projection. *J. proj. Tech.*, 1962, **26**, 366-370.

Weisskopf-Joelson, E. A., and Lynn, D. B. The effect of variations in ambiguity on projection in the Children's Apperception Test. *J. consult. Psychol.*, 1953, **17**, 67-70.

Weisskopf-Joelson, E. A., and Money, L. Facial similarity between subject and central figure in the TAT as as influence on projection. *J. abnorm. soc. Psychol.*, 1953, **48**, 341-344.

Welsh, G. S. Factor dimensions A and R. In O. S. Welsh and W. G. Dahlstrom (Eds.), *Basic readings on the MMPI in psychology and medicine.* Minneapolis: Univer. of Minnesota Press, 1956, pp. 264-281.

Werner, H. The concept of development from a comparative and organismic point of view. In D. Harris (Ed.), *The content of development.* Minneapolis: Univer. of Minnesota Press, 1957, pp. 125-148.

Wertheimer, M. Perception and the Rorschach. *J. proj. Tech.*, 1957, **21**, 209-216.

Wexner, Lois B. The degree to which colors (hues) are associated with mood tones. *J. appl. Psychol.*, 1954, **38**, 432-435.

Williams, H. L., and Lawrence, J. F. Further investigation of Rorschach determinants subjected to factor analysis. *J. consult. Psychol.*, 1953, **17**, 261-264.

Williams, H. L., and Lawrence, J. F. Comparison of the Rorschach and MMPI by means of factor analysis. *J. consult. Psychol.*, 1954, **18**, 193-197.

Winne, J. F. A peak of neuroticism. An adaptation of the Minnesota Multiphasic Personality Inventory. *J. clin. Psychol.*, 1951, **7**, 117-122.

Wittenborn, J. R. Some Thematic Apperception Test norms and a note on the use of the test cards in the guidance of college students. *J. clin. Psychol.*, 1949, **5**, 157-161.

Wittenborn, J. R. The implications of certain assumptions involved in the use of the Thematic Apperception Test. *J. consult. Psychol.*, 1950, **14**, 216-225. (a)

Wittenborn, J. R. A factor analysis of Rorschach scoring categories. *J. consult. Psychol.*, 1950, **14**, 261-267. (b)

Wittenborn, J. R. Level of mental health as a factor in the implications of Rorschach scores. *J. consult. Psychol.*, 1950, **14**, 469-472. (c)

Wittenborn, J. R., and Holzberg, J. D. The Rorschach and description diagnosis. *J. consult. Psychol.*, 1951, **15**, 460-463.

Woodworth, R. S. *Dynamics of behavior.* New York: Holt, 1958.

Wurtz, K. R. Some theory and data concerning the attenuation of aggression. *J. abnorm. soc. Psychol.*, 1960, **60**, 134-136.

York, R. H. *The effect of color in the Rorschach test and in selected intellectual tasks.* Unpublished doctoral dissertation, Boston Univer., Boston, Massachusetts, 1951.

Zax, M., and Benham, F. G. The stimulus value of the Rorschach inkblots as perceived by children. *J. proj. Tech.*, 1961, **25**, 233-237.

Zax, M., and Loiselle, R. H. The influence of card order on the stimulus value of the Rorschach inkblots. *J. proj. Tech.*, 1960, **24**, 218-221. (a)

Zax, M., and Loiselle, R. H. Stimulus value of Rorschach inkblots as measured by the Semantic Differential. *J. clin. Psychol.*, 1960, **16**, 160-163. (b)

Zax, M., Loiselle, R. H., and Karras, S. Stimulus characteristics of Rorschach inkblots as perceived by a schizophrenic sample. *J. proj. Tech.*, 1960, **25**, 439-443.

Zulliger, H. *Einführung in den Behn-Rorschach test.* Bern, Switzerland: Huber, 1946.

Zulliger, H. *Der Z-Test: ein formdent-Verfahren zur psychologischen Untersuchung von Gruppen.* Bern, Switzerland: Huber, 1948.

# AUTHOR INDEX

Numbers in italics indicate the pages on which the complete references are listed.

# SUBJECT INDEX

# ERICA SPINDLER

# IN SILENCE

MIRA®

MIRA

ISBN 1-55166-699-5

IN SILENCE

Copyright © 2003 by Erica Spindler.

Visit us at www.mirabooks.com

**Printed in U.S.A.**

First Printing: June 2003
10 9 8 7 6 5 4 3 2 1

"The cruelest lies are often told in silence."
—Robert Louis Stevenson

*Cypress Springs, Louisiana*
*Thursday, October 17, 2002*
*3:30 a.m.*

The one called the Gavel waited patiently. The woman would come soon, he knew. He had been watching her. Learning her schedule, her habits. Those of her neighbors as well.

Tonight she would learn the price of moral corruption.

He moved his gaze over the woman's darkened bedroom. Garments strewn across the matted carpeting. Dresser top littered with an assortment of cosmetic bottles and jars, empty Diet Coke and Miller Lite cans, gum and candy wrappers. Cigarette butts spilled from an overflowing ashtray.

*A pig as well as a whore.*

Twin feelings of resignation and disgust flowed over him. Had he expected anything different from a woman like her? An alley cat who bedded a new man nearly every night?

He was neither prude nor saint. Nor was he naive. These days few waited for marriage to consummate their relationship. He could live with that; he understood physical urges.

But excesses such as hers would not be tolerated in Cypress

Springs. The Seven had voted. It had been unanimous. As their leader, it was his responsibility to make her understand.

The Gavel glanced at the bedside clock. He had been waiting nearly an hour. It wouldn't be long now. Tonight she had gone to CJ's, a bar on the west side of town, one frequented by the hard-partying crowd. She had left with a man named DuBroc. As was her MO, they had gone to his place. To the Gavel's knowledge, this was a first offense for DuBroc. He would be watched as well. And if necessary, warned.

From the front of the apartment came the sound of the door lock turning over. The door opening, then clicking shut. A shudder moved over him. Of distaste for the inevitable. He wasn't a pred-ator, as some might label him. Predators sought the small and weak, either to sustain themselves or for twisted self-gratification.

Nor was he a bloodthirsty monster or sadist.

He was an honorable man. God-fearing, law-abiding. A patriot.

But as were the other members of The Seven, he was a man driven to desperate measures. To protect and defend all he held dear.

Women like this one soiled the community, they contributed to the moral decay running rampant in the world.

They were not alone, of course. Those who drank to excess, those who lied, cheated, stole; those who broke not only the laws of man but those of God as well.

The Seven had formed to combat such corruptions. For the Gavel and his six generals, it wasn't about punishing the sinful but about maintaining a way of life. A way of life Cypress Springs had enjoyed for over a hundred years. A community where people could still walk the streets at night, where neighbor helped neigh-bor, where family values were more than a phrase tossed about by political candidates.

Honesty. Integrity. The Golden Rule. All were alive and well in Cypress Springs. The Seven had dedicated themselves to ensuring it stayed that way.

The Gavel likened individual immorality to the flesh-eating bac-teria that had been in the news so much a few years back. A fish-erman had contracted necrotizing fasciitis through a small cut on his hand. Once introduced to the body, it ate its covering until only a putrid, grotesque patchwork remained. So, too, was the effect of individual immorality on a community. His job was to make certain that didn't happen.

The Gavel listened intently. The woman hummed under her breath as she made her way toward the back of the apartment and the bedroom where he waited. The self-satisfied sound sickened him.

He eased to his feet, moved toward the door. She stepped through. He grabbed her from behind, dragged her to his chest and covered her mouth with one gloved hand to stifle her screams. She smelled of cheap perfume, cigarettes. Sex.

"Elaine St. Claire," he said against her ear, voice muffled by the ski mask he wore. "You have been judged and found guilty. Of contributing to the moral decay of this community. Of attempting to cause the ruination of a way of life that has existed for over a century. You must pay the price."

He forced her to the bed. She struggled against him, her attempts pitiable. A mouse battling a mountain lion.

He knew what she thought—that he meant to rape her. He would sooner castrate himself than to join with a woman such as her. Besides, what kind of punishment would that be? What kind of warning?

No, he had something much more memorable in mind for her.

He stopped a foot from the bed. With the hand covering her mouth, he forced her gaze down. To the mattress. And the gift he had made just for her.

He had fashioned the instrument out of a baseball bat, one of the miniature, commemorative ones fans bought in stadium gift shops. He had covered the bat with flattened tin cans—choosing Diet Coke, her soft drink of choice—peeling back V-shaped pieces of the metal to form a kind of sharp, scaly skin. The trickiest part had been the double-edged knife blade he had imbedded in the bat's rounded tip.

He was aware of the exact moment she saw it. She stilled. Terror rippled over her—a new fear, one born from the horror of the unimaginable.

"For you, Elaine," he whispered against her ear. "Since you love to fuck so much, your punishment will be to give you what you love."

She recoiled and pressed herself against him. Her response pleased him and he smiled, the black ski mask stretching across his mouth with the movement.

He could almost pity her. Almost but not quite. She had brought this fate upon herself.

"I designed it to open you from cervix to throat," he continued, then lowered his voice. "From the *inside,* Elaine. It will be an excruciating way to die. Organs torn to shreds from within. Massive bleeding will lead to shock. Then coma. And finally, death. Of course, by that point you will pray for death to take you."

She made a sound, high and terrified. Trapped.

"Do you think it would be possible to be fucked to death, Elaine? Is that how you'd like to die?"

She fought as he inched her closer. "Imagine what it will feel like inside you, Elaine. To feel your insides being ripped to shreds, the pain, the helplessness. Knowing you're going to die, wishing for death to come swiftly."

He pressed his mouth closer to her ear. "But it won't. Perhaps, mercifully, you'll lose consciousness. Perhaps not. I could keep you alert, there are ways, you know. You'll beg for mercy, pray for a miracle. No miracle will come. No hero rushing in to save the day. No one to hear your screams."

She trembled so violently he had to hold her erect. Tears streamed down her cheeks.

"This will be your only warning," he continued. "Leave Cypress Springs immediately. Quietly. Tell no one. Not your friends, your employer or landlord. If you speak to anyone, you'll be killed. The police cannot help you, do not contact them. If you do, you'll be killed. If you stay, you'll be killed. Your death will be horrible, I promise you that."

He released her and she crumpled into a heap on the floor. He stared down at her shaking form. "There are many of us and we are always watching. Do you understand, Elaine St. Claire?"

She didn't answer and he bent, grabbed a handful of her hair and yanked her face up toward his. "Do you understand?"

"Y-yes," she whispered. "Anythi...I'll do...anything."

A small smile twisted his lips. *His generals would be pleased.*

He released her. "Smart girl, Elaine. Don't forget this warning. You're now the master of your own fate."

The Gavel retrieved the weapon and walked away. As he let himself out, the sound of her sobs echoed through the apartment.

# CHAPTER 1

*Cypress Springs, Louisiana*
*Wednesday, March 5, 2003*
*2:30 p.m.*

Avery Chauvin drew her rented SUV to a stop in front of Rauche's Dry Goods store and stepped out. A humid breeze stirred against her damp neck and ruffled her short dark hair as she surveyed Main Street. Rauche's still occupied this coveted corner of Main and First Streets, the Azalea Café still screamed for a coat of paint, Parish Bank hadn't been swallowed by one of the huge banking conglomerates and the town square these establishments all circled was as shady and lovely as ever, the gazebo at its center a startlingly bright white.

Her absence hadn't changed Cypress Springs at all, she thought. How could that be? It was as if the twelve years between now and when she had headed off to Louisiana State University in Baton Rouge, returning only for holiday breaks, had been a dream. As if her life in Washington, D.C., was a figment of her imagination.

If they had been, her mother would be alive, the massive, unexpected stroke she had suffered eleven years in the future. And her father—

Pain rushed over her. Her head filled with her father's voice, slightly distorted by the answering machine.

*"Avery, sweetheart... It's Dad. I was hoping...I need to talk to you. I was hoping—" Pause. "There's something... I'll...try later. Goodbye, pumpkin."*

If only she had taken that call. If only she had stopped, just for the time it would have taken to speak with him. Her story could have waited. The congressman who had finally decided to talk could have waited. A couple minutes. A couple minutes that might have changed everything.

Her thoughts raced forward, to the next morning, the call from Buddy Stevens. Family friend. Her dad's lifelong best friend. Cypress Springs' chief of police.

*"Avery, it's Buddy. I've got some...some bad news, baby girl. Your dad, he's—"*

Dead. Her dad was dead. Between the time her father had called her and the next morning, he had killed himself. Gone into his garage, doused himself with diesel fuel, then lit a match.

*How could you do it, Dad? Why did you do it? You didn't even say—*

The short scream of a police siren interrupted her thoughts. Avery turned. A West Feliciana Parish sheriff's cruiser rolled up behind her Blazer. An officer stepped out and started toward her.

She recognized the man by his long, lanky frame, the way he moved and held himself. Matt Stevens, childhood friend, high-school sweetheart, the guy she'd left behind to pursue her dream of journalism. She'd seen Matt only a handful of times since then, most recently at her mother's funeral nearly a year ago. Buddy must have told him she was coming.

Avery held up a hand in greeting. Still handsome, she thought, watching him approach. Still the best catch in the parish. Or maybe that title no longer applied; he could be attached now.

He reached her, stopped but didn't smile. "It's good to see you, Avery." She saw herself reflected in his mirrored sunglasses, smaller than any grown woman ought to be, her elfin looks accentuated by her pixie haircut and dark eyes, which were too big for her face.

"It's good to see you, too, Matt."

"Sorry about your dad. I feel real bad about how it all happened. Real bad."

"Thanks, I...I appreciate you and Buddy taking care of Dad's—" Her throat constricted; she pushed on, determined not to fall apart. "Dad's remains," she finished.

"It was the least we could do." Matt looked away, then back, expression somber. "Were you able to reach your cousins in Denver?"

"Yes," she managed, feeling lost. They were all the family she had left—a couple of distant cousins and their families. Everyone else was gone now.

"I loved him, too, Avery. I knew since your mom's death he'd been...struggling, but I still can't believe he did it. I feel like I should have seen how bad off he was. That I should have known."

The tears came then, swamping her. *She'd been his daughter. She was the guilty party. The one who should have known.*

He reached a hand out. "It's okay to cry, Avery."

"No...I've already—" She cleared her throat, fighting for composure. "I need to arrange a...service. Do the Gallaghers still own—"

"Yes. Danny's taken over for his father. He's expecting your call. Pop told him you were getting in sometime today."

She motioned to the cruiser. "You're out of your jurisdiction."

The sheriff's department handled all the unincorporated areas of the parish. The Cypress Springs Police Department policed the city itself.

One corner of his mouth lifted. "Guilty as charged. I was hanging around, hoping to catch you before you went by the house."

"I was heading there now. I just stopped to...because—" She bit the words back; she'd had no real reason for stopping, had simply responded to a whim.

He seemed to understand. "I'll go with you."

"That's really sweet, Matt. But unnecessary."

"I disagree." When she tried to protest more, he cut her off. "It's bad, Avery. I don't think you should see it alone the first time. I'm following you," he finished, voice gruff. "Whether you want me to or not."

Avery held his gaze a moment, then nodded and wordlessly turned and climbed into the rented Blazer. She started up the vehicle and eased back onto Main Street. As she drove the three-quarters of a mile to the old residential section where she had grown up, she took a deep breath.

Her father had chosen the hour of his death well—the middle of the night when his neighbors were less likely to see or smell the fire. He'd used diesel fuel, most probably the arson investigators determined, because unlike gasoline, which burned off vapors, diesel ignited on contact.

A neighbor out for an early-morning jog had discovered the still smoldering garage. After trying to rouse her father, who he'd assumed to be in bed, asleep, he had called the fire department. The state arson investigator had been brought in. They in turn had called the coroner, who'd notified the Cypress Springs Police Department. In the end, her dad had been identified by his dental records.

Neither the autopsy nor CSPD investigation had turned up any indication of foul play. Nor had any known motives for murder materialized: Dr. Phillip Chauvin had been universally liked and respected. The police had officially ruled his death a suicide.

*No note. No goodbye.*

*How could you do it, Dad? Why?*

Avery reached her parents' house and turned into the driveway. The lawn of the 1920s era Acadian needed mowing; the beds weeding; bushes trimming. Although early, the azaleas had begun to bloom. Soon the beds around the house would be a riot of pinks, ranging from icy pale to deep rose.

Her dad had loved his yard. Had spent weekends puttering and planting, primping. It all looked forlorn now, she thought. Overgrown and ignored.

Avery frowned. How long had it been since her father had tended his yard? she wondered. Longer than the two days he had been gone. That was obvious.

Further evidence of the emotional depths to which he had sunk. How could she have missed how depressed he had grown? Why hadn't she sensed something was wrong during their frequent phone conversations?

Matt pulled in behind her. She took a deep breath and climbed out of her vehicle.

He met her, expression grim. "You're certain you're ready for this?"

"Do I have a choice?"

They both knew she didn't and they started up the curving driveway, toward the detached garage. A separate structure, the garage nestled behind the main house. A covered walkway connected the two buildings.

As they neared the structure the smell of the fire grew stronger—not just of wood smoke, but of what she imagined was charred flesh and bone. As they turned the corner of the driveway she saw that a large, irregularly shaped black mark marred the doorway.

"The heat from the fire," Matt explained. "It did more damage inside. Actually, it's a wonder the building didn't come down."

A half-dozen years ago, while working for the *Tribune,* Avery had been assigned to cover a rash of fires that had plagued the Chicago area. It turned out the arsonist had been the estranged son of a firefighter, looking to punish his old man for kicking him out of the house. Unfortunately, the police hadn't caught him before he'd been responsible for the deaths of six innocent people—one of them an infant.

Avery and Matt reached the garage. She steeled herself for what would come next. She understood how gruesome death by fire was.

Matt led her to the side door. Opened it. They stepped into the building. The smell crashed over her. As did the stark reality of her father's last minutes. She imagined his screams as the flames engulfed him. As his skin began to melt. Avery brought a hand to her mouth, her gaze going to the large char mark on the concrete floor—the spot where her father had burned alive.

His suicide had been an act of not only despair but self-hatred as well.

She began to tremble. Her head grew light, her knees weak. Turning, she ran outside, to the azalea bushes with their burgeoning blossoms. She doubled over, struggling not to throw up. Not to fall apart.

Matt came up behind her. He laid a hand on her back.

Avery squeezed her eyes shut. "How could he do it, Matt?" She looked over her shoulder at him, vision blurred by tears. "It's bad enough that he took his own life, but to do it like that? The pain...it would have been excruciating."

"I don't know what to say," he murmured, tone gentle. "I don't have any answers for you. I wish I did."

She straightened, mustering anger. Denial. "My father loved life. He valued it. He was a doctor, for God's sake. He'd devoted his life to preserving it."

At Matt's silence, she lashed out. "He was proud of himself and the choices he'd made. Proud of how he had lived. The man who did that hated himself. That wasn't my dad." She said it again, tone taking on a desperate edge. "It wasn't, Matt."

"Avery, you haven't been—" He bit the words off and shifted his gaze, expression uncomfortable.

"What, Matt? I haven't been what?"

"Around a lot lately." He must have read the effect of his words in her expression and he caught her hands and held them tightly. "Your dad hadn't been himself for a while. He'd withdrawn, from everybody. Stayed in his house for days. When he went out he didn't speak. Would cross to the other side of the street to avoid conversation."

*How could she not have known?* "When?" she asked, hurting. "When did this start?"

"I suppose about the time he gave up his practice."

*Just after her mother's death.*

"Why didn't somebody call me? Why didn't—" She bit the words back and pressed her trembling lips together.

He squeezed her fingers. "It wasn't an overnight thing. At first he just seemed preoccupied. Or like he needed time to grieve. On his own. It wasn't until recently that people began to talk."

Avery turned her gaze to her father's overgrown garden. No wonder, she thought.

"I'm sorry, Avery. We all are."

She swung away from her old friend, working to hold on to her anger. Fighting tears.

She lost the battle.

"Aw, Avery. Geez." Matt went to her, drew her into his arms, against his chest. She leaned into him, burying her face in his shoulder, crying like a baby.

He held her awkwardly. Stiffly. Every so often he patted her shoulder and murmured something comforting, though through her sobs she couldn't make out what.

The intensity of her tears lessened, then stopped. She drew away from him, embarrassed. "Sorry about that. It's...I thought I could handle it."

"Cut yourself some slack, Avery. Frankly, if you *could* handle it, I'd be a little worried about you."

Tears flooded her eyes once more and she brought her hand to her nose. "I need a tissue. Excuse me."

She headed toward her car, aware of him following. There, she rummaged in her purse, coming up with a rumpled Kleenex. She blew her nose, dabbed at her eyes, then faced him once more. "How could I not have known how bad off he was? Am I *that* self-involved?"

"None of us knew," he said gently. "And we saw him every day."

"But I was his daughter. I should have been able to tell, should have heard it in his voice. In what he said. Or didn't say."

"It's not your fault, Avery."

"No?" She realized her hands were shaking and slipped them into her pockets. "But I can't help wondering, if I had stayed in Cypress Springs, would he be alive today? If I'd given up my career and stayed after Mom's death, would he have staved off the depression that caused him to do...this? If I had simply picked up the pho—"

She swallowed the words, unable to speak them aloud. She met his gaze. "It hurts so much."

"Don't do this to yourself. You can't go back."

"I can't, can I?" She winced at the bitterness in her voice. "I loved my dad more than anyone in the world, yet I only came home a handful of times in all the years since college. Even after Mom died so suddenly and so horribly, leaving so much unresolved between us. That should have been a wake-up call, but it wasn't."

He didn't respond and she continued. "I've got to live with that, don't I?"

"No," he corrected. "You have to learn from it. It's where you go from here that counts now. Not where you've been."

A group of teenagers barreled by in a pickup truck, their raucous laughter interrupting the charged moment. The pickup was followed by another group of teenagers, these in a bright-yellow convertible, top down.

Avery glanced at her watch. *Three-thirty. The high school let out the same time as it had all those years ago.*

*Funny how some things could change so dramatically and others not at all.*

"I should get back to work. You going to be okay?"

She nodded. "Thanks for baby-sitting me."

"No thanks necessary." He started for the car, then stopped and looked back at her. "I almost forgot, Mom and Dad are expecting you for dinner tonight."

"Tonight? But I just got in."

"Exactly. No way are Mom and Dad going to let you spend your first night home alone."

"But—"

"You're not in the big city anymore, Avery. Here, people take care of each other. Besides, you're family."

*Home. Family.* At that moment nothing sounded better than that. "I'll be there. They still live at the ranch?" she asked, using the nickname they had given the Stevenses' sprawling ranch-style home.

"Of course. Status quo is something you can count on in Cypress Springs." He crossed to his vehicle, opened the door and looked back at her. "Is six too early?"

"It'll be perfect."

"Great." He climbed into the cruiser, started it and began backing up. Halfway down the driveway he stopped and lowered his window. "Hunter's back home," he called. "I thought you might want to know."

Avery stood rooted to the spot even after Matt's cruiser disappeared from sight. Hunter? she thought, disbelieving. Matt's fraternal twin brother and the third member of their triumvirate. Back in Cypress Springs? Last she'd heard, he'd been a partner at a prestigious New Orleans law firm.

Avery turned away from the road and toward her childhood home. Something had happened the summer she'd been fifteen, Hunter and Matt sixteen. A rift had grown between the brothers. Hunter had become increasingly aloof, angry. He and Matt had fought often and several times violently. The Stevenses' house, which had always been a haven of warmth, laughter and love, had become a battleground. As if the animosity between the brothers had spilled over into all the family relationships.

At first Avery had been certain the bad feelings between the brothers would pass. They hadn't. Hunter had left for college and never returned—not even for holidays.

Now he, like she, had come home to Cypress Springs. Odd, she thought. A weird coincidence. Perhaps tonight she would discover what had brought him back.

CHAPTER 2

At six sharp, Avery pulled up in front of the Stevenses' house. Buddy Stevens, sitting on the front porch smoking a cigar, caught sight of her and lumbered to his feet. "There's my girl!" he bellowed. "Home safe and sound!"

She hurried up the walk and was enfolded in his arms. A mountain of a man with a barrel chest and booming voice, he had been Cypress Springs's chief of police for as long as she could remember. Although a by-the-books lawman who had as much give as a concrete block when it came to his town and crime, the Buddy Stevens she knew was just a big ol' teddy bear. A hard-ass with a soft, squishy center and a heart of gold.

He hugged her tightly, then held her at arm's length. He searched her gaze, his own filled with regret. "I'm sorry, baby girl. Damn sorry."

A lump formed in her throat. She cleared it with difficulty. "I know, Buddy. I'm sorry, too."

He hugged her again. "You're too thin. And you look tired."

She drew away, filled with affection for the man who had been nearly as important to her growing up as her own father. "Haven't you heard? A woman can't be too thin."

"Big-city crapola." He put out the stogie and led her inside, arm firmly around her shoulder. "Lilah!" he called. "Cherry! Look who the cat's dragged in."

Cherry, Matt and Hunter's younger sister, appeared at the kitchen door. The awkward-looking twelve-year-old girl had grown into an uncommonly beautiful woman. Tall, with dark hair and eyes like her brothers, she had inherited her mother's elegant features and pretty skin.

When she saw Avery she burst into a huge smile. "You made it. We've been worried sick." She crossed to Avery and hugged her. "That's no kind of a trip for a woman to make alone."

Such an unenlightened comment coming from a woman in her twenties took Avery aback. But as Matt had said earlier, she wasn't in the city anymore.

She hugged her back. "It wasn't so bad. Cab to Dullas, nonstop flight to New Orleans, a rental car here. The most harrowing part was retrieving my luggage."

"Big, tough career girl," Buddy murmured, sounding anything but pleased. "I hope you had a cell phone."

"Of course. Fully charged at all times." She grinned up at him. "And, you'll be happy to know, pepper spray in my purse."

"Pepper spray? Whatever for?" This came from Lilah Stevens.

"Self-protection, Mama," Cherry supplied, glancing over her shoulder at the older woman.

Lilah, still as trim and attractive as Avery remembered, crossed from the kitchen and caught Avery's hands. "Self-protection? Well, you won't be needing *that* here." She searched Avery's gaze. "Avery, sweetheart. Welcome home. How are you?"

Avery squeezed the other woman's hands, tears pricking her eyes. "I've been better, thanks."

"I'm so sorry, sweetheart. Sorrier than I can express."

"I know. And that means a lot."

From the other room came the sound of a timer going off. Lilah released Avery's hands. "That's the pie."

The smells emanating from the kitchen were heavenly. Lilah Stevens had been the best cook in the parish and had consistently won baking prizes at the parish fair. Growing up, Avery had angled for a dinner invitation at every opportunity.

"What kind of pie?" she asked.

"Strawberry. I know peach is your favorite but it's impossible to find a decent peach this time of year. And the first Louisiana berries are in. And delicious, I might add."

"Silly woman," Buddy interrupted. "The poor child is exhausted. Stop your yapping about produce and let the girl sit down."

"Yapping?" She wagged a finger at him. "If you want pie, Mr. Stevens, you'll have to get yourself down to the Azalea Café."

He immediately looked contrite. "Sorry, sugar-sweet, you know I was just teasing."

"Now I'm sugar-sweet, am I?" She rolled her eyes and turned back to Avery. "You see what I've put up with all these years?"

Avery laughed. She used to wish her parents could be more like Lilah and Buddy, openly affectionate and teasing. In all the years she had known the couple, all the time she had spent around their home, she had never heard them raise their voices at one another. And when they'd teased each other, like just now, their love and respect had always shown through.

In truth, Avery had often wished her mother could be more like Lilah. Good-natured, outgoing. A traditional woman comfortable in her own skin. One who had enjoyed her children, making a home for them and her husband.

It had seemed to Avery that her mother had enjoyed neither, though she had never said so aloud. Avery had sensed her mother's frustration, her dissatisfaction with her place in the world.

No, Avery thought, that wasn't quite right. She had been frustrated by her only child's tomboyish ways and defiant streak. She had been disappointed in her daughter's likes and dislikes, the choices she made.

In her mother's eyes, Avery hadn't measured up.

Lilah Stevens had never made Avery feel she lacked anything. To the contrary, Lilah had made her feel not only worthy but special as well.

"I do see," Avery agreed, playing along. "It's outrageous."

"That it is." Lilah waved them toward the living room. "Matt should be here any moment. All I have left to do is whip the potatoes and heat the French bread. Then we can eat."

"Can I help?" Avery asked.

As she had known it would be, the woman's answer was a definitive no. Buddy and Cherry led her to the living room. Avery sank onto the overstuffed couch, acknowledging exhaustion. She wished she could lean her head back, close her eyes and sleep for a week.

"You've barely changed," Buddy said softly, tone wistful. "Same pretty, bright-eyed girl you were the day you left Cypress Springs."

She'd been so damn young back then. So ridiculously naive. She had yearned for something bigger than Cypress Springs, something better. Had sensed something important waited for her outside this small town. She supposed she had found it: a prestigious job; writing awards and professional respect; an enviable salary.

What was it all worth now? If those twelve years hadn't been, if all her choices still lay before her, what would she do differently?

*Everything. Anything to have him with her.*

She met Buddy's eyes. "You'd be surprised how much I've changed." She lightened her words with a smile. "What about you? Besides being as devastatingly handsome as ever, still the most feared and respected lawman in the parish?"

"I don't know about that," he murmured. "Seems to me, these days that honor belongs to Matt."

"West Feliciana Parish's sheriff is retiring next year," Cherry chimed in. "Matt's planning to run for the job." There was no mistaking the pride in her voice. "Those in the know expect him to win the election by a landslide."

Buddy nodded, looking as pleased as punch. "My son, the parish's top cop. Imagine that."

"A regular crime-fighting family dynasty," Avery murmured.

"Not for long." Buddy settled into his easy chair. "Retirement's right around the corner. Probably should have retired already. If I'd had a grandchild to spoil, I—"

"Dad," Cherry warned, "don't go there."

"Three children," he groused, "all disappointments. Friends of mine have a half-dozen of the little critters already. I don't think that's right." He looked at Avery. "Do you?"

Avery held up her hands, laughing. "Oh, no, I'm not getting involved in this one."

Cherry mouthed a "Thank you," Buddy pouted and Avery changed the subject. "I can't imagine you not being the chief of police. Cypress Springs won't be the same."

"Comes a time one generation needs to make room for the next. Much as I hate the thought, my time has come and gone."

With a derisive snort, Cherry started toward the kitchen. "I'm having a glass of wine. Want one, Avery?"

"Love one."

"Red or white?"

"Whatever you're having." Avery let out a long breath and leaned her head against the sofa back, tension easing from her. She closed her eyes. Images played on the backs of her eyelids, ones from her past: her, Matt and Hunter playing while their parents barbecued in the backyard. Buddy and Lilah snapping pictures as she and Matt headed off to the prom. The two families caroling at Christmastime.

Sweet memories. Comforting ones.

"Good to be back, isn't it?" Buddy murmured as if reading her thoughts.

She opened her eyes and looked at him. "Despite everything, yes." She glanced away a moment, then back. "I wish I'd come home sooner. After Mom... I should have stayed. If I had—"

The unfinished thought hung heavily between them anyway. *If she had, maybe her dad would be alive today.*

Cherry returned with the wine. She crossed to Avery; handed her a glass of the pale gold liquid. "What are your plans?"

"First order of business is a service for Dad. I called Danny Gallagher this afternoon. We're meeting tomorrow after lunch."

"How long are you staying?" Cherry sat on the other end of the couch, curling her legs under her.

"I took a leave of absence from the *Post,* because I just don't know," she answered honestly. "I haven't a clue how long it will take to go through Dad's things, get the house ready to sell."

"Sorry I'm late."

At Matt's voice, Avery looked up. He stood in the doorway to the living room, head cocked as he gazed at her, expression amused. He'd exchanged his uniform for blue jeans and a soft chambray shirt. He held a bouquet of fresh flowers.

"Brought Mom some posies," he said. "She in the kitchen?"

"You know Mom." Cherry crossed to him and kissed his cheek. "Dad's already complained about the dearth of grandchildren around here. Remind me to be late next time."

Matt met Avery's eyes and grinned. "Glad I missed it. Though I'll no doubt catch the rerun later."

Buddy scowled at his two children. "No grandbabies *and* no respect." He looked toward the kitchen. "Lilah," he bellowed, "where did we go wrong with these kids?"

Lilah poked her head out of the kitchen. "For heaven's sake, Buddy, leave the children alone." She turned her attention to her son. "Hello, Matt. Are those for the table?"

"Yes, ma'am." He ambled across to her, kissed her cheek and handed her the flowers. "Something smells awfully good."

"Come, help me with the roast." She turned to her daughter. "Cherry, could you put these in a vase for me?"

Avery watched the exchange. She could have been a part of this family. Officially a part. Everyone had expected her and Matt to marry.

Buddy interrupted her thoughts. "Have you considered staying?" he asked. "This is your home, Avery. You belong here."

She dragged her gaze back to his, uncertain how to answer. Yes, she had come home to take care of specific family business, but less specifically, she had come for answers. For peace of mind—not only about her father's death, but about her own life.

Truth was, she had been drifting for a while now, neither happy nor unhappy. Vaguely dissatisfied but uncertain why.

"Do I, Buddy? Always felt like the one marching to a different drummer."

"Your daddy thought so."

Tears swamped her. "I miss him so much."

"I know, baby girl." A momentary, awkward silence fell between them. Buddy broke it first. "He never got over your mother's death. The way she died. He loved her completely."

She'd been behind the wheel when she suffered a stroke, on her way to meet her cousin who'd flown into New Orleans. For a week of girl time—shopping and dining and shows. She had careened across the highway, into a brick wall.

A sound from the doorway drew her gaze. Lilah stood there, expression stricken. Matt and Cherry stood behind her. "It was so...awful. She called me the night before she left. She hadn't been feeling well, she said. She had run her symptoms by Phillip, had wondered if she shouldn't cancel her trip. He had urged her to go. Nothing was wrong with her that a week away wouldn't cure. I don't think he ever forgave himself for that."

"He thought he should have known," Buddy murmured. "Thought that if he hadn't been paying closer attention to his patients' health than to his own wife's, he could have saved her."

Avery clasped her shaky hands together. "I didn't know. I...he mentioned feeling responsible, but I—"

*She had chosen to pacify him. To assure him none of it was his fault.*

*Then go on her merry way.*

Matt moved around his mother and came to stand behind her chair. He laid a comforting hand on her shoulder. "It's not your fault, Avery," he said softly. "It's not."

She reached up and curled her fingers around his, grateful for the support. "Matt said Dad had been acting strangely. That he had withdrawn from everyone and everything. But still I...how could he have done what he did?"

"When I heard how he did it," Cherry said quietly, "I wasn't surprised. I think you can love someone so much you do something...unbelievable because of it. Something tragic."

An uncomfortable silence settled over the group. Avery tried to speak but found she couldn't for the knot of tears in her throat.

Buddy, bless him, took over. He turned to Lilah. "Dinner ready, sugar-sweet?"

"It is." Lilah all but jumped at the opportunity to turn their attention to the mundane. "And getting cold."

"Let's get to it, then," Buddy directed.

They made their way to the dining room and sat. Buddy said the blessing, then the procession of bowls and platters began, passed as they always had been at the Stevenses' supper table from right to left.

Avery went through the motions. She ate, commented on the food, joined in story swapping. But her heart wasn't in it. Nor was anyone else's, that was obvious to her. As was how hard they were trying to make it like it used to be. How hard they were wanting to comfort with normalcy.

But how could anything be normal ever again? In years gone by, her parents had sat with her at this table. She, Matt and Hunter would have been clustered together, whispering or joking.

She missed Hunter, Avery realized. She felt the lack of his presence keenly.

Hunter had been the most intellectual of the group. Not the most intelligent, because both he and Matt had sailed through school, neither having to crack a book to maintain an A average, both scoring near-perfect marks on their SATs.

But Hunter had possessed a sharp, sarcastic wit. He'd been incapable of the silliness the rest of them had sometimes wallowed in. He had often been the voice of wry reason in whatever storm was brewing.

She hadn't been surprised to hear he had become a successful lawyer. Between his keen mind and razor-sharp tongue, he'd no doubt consistently decimated the opposition.

She brought him up as Lilah served the pie. "Matt tells me that Hunter's moved back to Cypress Springs. I'd hoped he would be here tonight."

Silence fell around the table. Avery shifted her gaze from one face to the next. "I'm sorry, did I say something wrong?"

Buddy cleared his throat. "Of course not, baby girl. It's just that Hunter's had some troubles lately. Lost his partnership in the New Orleans law firm. Was nearly disbarred, from what I hear. Moved back here about ten months ago."

"I don't know why he bothered," Matt added. "For all the time he spends with his family."

Cherry frowned. "I wish he hadn't come home. He only did it to hurt us."

"Now, Cherry," Buddy murmured, "you don't know that."

"The hell I don't. If he was any kind of brother, any kind of son, he would be here for us. Instead, he—"

Lilah launched to her feet. Avery saw she was near tears. "I'll get the coffee."

"I'll help." Cherry tossed her napkin on the table and got to her feet, expression disgusted. She looked at Avery. "Tell you the truth, all Hunter's ever done is break our hearts."

# CHAPTER 3

Talk of Hunter drained the joy from the gathering, and the remainder of the evening passed at a snail's pace. Lilah's smile looked artificial; Cherry's mood darkened with each passing moment and Buddy's jubilance bordered on manic.

Finally, pie consumed, coffee cups drained, Avery said her thanks and made her excuses. Cherry and Lilah said their goodbyes in the dining room; Buddy accompanied her and Matt to the door.

Buddy hugged her. "You broke all our hearts when you left. But no one's more than mine. I'd had mine set on you being my daughter."

Avery returned his embrace. "I love you, too, Buddy."

Matt walked her to her car. "Pretty night," she murmured, lifting her face to the night sky. "So many stars. I'd forgotten how many."

"I enjoyed tonight, Avery. It was like old times."

Avery met his eyes; her pulse fluttered.

"I've missed you," he said. "I'm glad you're back."

She swallowed hard, acknowledging that she'd missed him, too. Or more accurately, that she'd missed standing with him this way, in his folks' driveway, under a star-sprinkled sky. Had missed the familiarity of it. The sense of belonging.

Matt put words to her thoughts. "Why'd you leave, Avery? My dad was right, you know. You belong here. *You're* one of us."

"Why didn't you go with me?" she countered. "I asked. Begged, if I remember correctly."

Matt lifted a hand as if to touch her, then dropped it. "You always wanted something else, something more than Cypress Springs could offer. Something more than I could offer. I never understood it. But I had to accept it."

She shifted her gaze slightly, uncomfortable with the truth. That he could speak it so plainly. She changed the direction of their conversation. "Your dad and Cherry said you're the front-runner in next year's election for parish sheriff. I'm not surprised. You always said you were destined for great things."

"But our definitions of great things always differed, didn't they, Avery?"

"That's not fair, Matt."

"Fair or not, it's true." He paused. "You broke my heart."

She held his gaze. "You broke mine, too."

"Then we're even, aren't we? A broken heart apiece."

She winced at the bitter edge in his voice. "Matt, it...wasn't you. It was me. I never felt—"

She had been about to say how she had never felt she belonged in Cypress Springs. That once she'd become a teenager, she had always felt slightly out of step, different in subtle but monumental ways from the other girls she knew.

Those feelings seemed silly now. The thoughts of a self-absorbed young girl.

"What about now, Avery?" he asked. "What do you want now? What do you need?"

Discomfited by the intensity of his gaze, she looked away. "I don't know. I don't want to return to where I was, I'm certain of that. And I don't mean the geographical location."

"Sounds like you have some thinking to do."

*A giant understatement.* She turned to the Blazer, unlocked the door, then faced him once more. "I should go. I'm asleep on my feet and tomorrow's going to be difficult."

"You could stay here, you know. Mom and Dad have plenty of room. They'd love to have you."

A part of her longed to jump at the offer. The idea of sleeping in her parents' house now, after her father...she didn't think she would sleep a wink.

But taking the easy way would be taking the coward's way. She had to face her father's suicide. She began tonight, by sleeping in her childhood home.

He reached around her and opened her car door. "Still fiercely independent, I see. Still stubborn as a mule."

She slid behind the wheel, started the vehicle, then looked back up at him "Some would consider those qualities an asset."

"Sure they would. In mules." He bent his face to hers. "If you need anything, call me."

"I will. Thanks." He slammed the door. She backed the Blazer down the steep driveway, then headed out of the subdivision, pointing the vehicle toward the old downtown neighborhood where she had grown up.

Avery shook her head, remembering how she had begged her parents to follow the Stevenses to Spring Water, the then new subdivision where Matt and his family had bought a house. She had been enamored with the sprawling ranch homes and neighborhood club facilities: pool, tennis court and clubhouse for parties.

What had then looked so new and cool to her, she saw now as cheaply built, cookie-cutter homes on small plots of ground that had been cleared to make room for as many houses per acre as possible.

Luckily, her parents had refused to move from their location within walking distance of the square, downtown and her father's office. Solidly built in the 1920s, their house boasted high ceilings, cypress millwork and the kind of charm available only at a premium today. The neighborhood, too, was vintage—a wide, tree-lined boulevard lit by gas lamps, each home set back on large, shady lots. Unlike many cities whose downtown neighborhoods had fallen victim to the urban decay caused by crime and white flight, Cypress Springs's inner-city neighborhood remained as well maintained and safe as when originally built.

Despite the fact that most of Louisiana was flat, West Feliciana Parish was home to gently rolling hills. Cypress Springs nestled amongst those hills—the historic river town of St. Francisville, with its beautiful antebellum homes, lay twenty minutes southwest, Baton Rouge, forty-five minutes south and the New Orleans's French Quarter a mere two hours forty-five minutes southeast.

Besides being a good place to raise a family, Cypress Springs had no claim to fame. A small Southern town that relied on agriculture, mostly cattle and light industry, it was too far from the beaten path to ever grow into more.

The city fathers liked it that way, Avery knew. She had grown up listening to her dad, Buddy and their friends talk about keeping industry and all her ills out. About keeping Cypress Springs clean. She remembered the furor caused when Charlie Weiner had sold his farm to the Old Dixie Foods corporation and then the company's decision to build a canning factory on the site.

Avery made her way down the deserted streets. Although not even ten o'clock, the town had already rolled up its sidewalks for the night. She shook her head. Nothing could be more different from the places she had called home for the past twelve years— places where a traffic jam could occur almost anytime during a twenty-four-hour period; where walking alone at night was to take your life in your hands; places where people lived on top of each other but never acknowledged the other's existence.

As beautiful and green a city as Washington, D.C. was, it couldn't compare to the lush beauty of West Feliciana Parish. The heat and humidity provided the perfect environment for all manner of vegetation. Azaleas. Gardenias. Sweet olive. Camellias. Palmettos. Live oaks, their massive gnarled branches so heavy they dipped to the ground, hundred-year-old magnolia trees that in May would hold so many of the large white blossoms the air would be redolent of their sweet, lemony scent.

Once upon a time she had thought this place ugly. No, that wasn't quite fair, she admitted. Shabby and painfully small town.

Why hadn't she seen it then as she did now?

Avery turned onto her street, then a moment later into her parents' driveway. She parked at the edge of the walk and climbed out, locking the vehicle out of habit not necessity. Her thoughts drifted to the events of the evening, particularly to those final moments with Matt.

What *did* she want now? she wondered. Where did she belong?

The porch swing creaked. A figure separated from the silhouette of the overgrown sweet olive at the end of the porch. Her steps faltered.

"Hello, Avery."

Hunter, she realized, bringing a hand to her chest. She let out a shaky breath. "I've lived in the city too long. You scared the hell out of me."

"I have that effect on people."

Although she smiled, she could see why that might be true. Half his face lay in shadow, the other half in the light from the porch fixture. His features looked hard in the weak light, his face craggy, the lines around his mouth and eyes deeply etched. A few days' accumulation of beard darkened his jaw.

She would have crossed the street to avoid him in D.C.

How could the two brothers have grown so physically dissimilar? she wondered. Growing up, though fraternal not identical twins, the resemblance between them had been uncanny. She would never have thought they could be other than near mirror images of one another.

"I'd heard you were back," he said. "Obviously."

"News travels fast around here."

"This is a small town. They've got to have something to talk about."

He had changed in a way that had less to do with the passage of years than with the accumulated events of those years. The school of hard knocks, she thought. The great equalizer.

"And I'm one of their own," she said.

"It's true, then? You're back to stay?"

"I didn't say that."

"That's the buzz. I thought it was wrong." He shrugged. "But you never know."

"Meaning what?" she asked, folding her arms across her chest.

"Am I making you uncomfortable?"

"No, of course not." Annoyed with herself, she dropped her arms. "I had dinner with your parents tonight."

"And Matt. Heard that, too."

"I thought you might have been there."

"So they told you I was living in Cypress Springs?"

"Matt did."

"And did he tell you why?"

"Only that you'd had some troubles."

"Nice euphemism." He swept his gaze over the facade of her parents' house. "Sorry about your dad. He was a great man."

"I think so, too." She jiggled her car keys, suddenly on edge, anxious to be inside.

"Aren't you going to ask me?"

"What?"

"If I talked to him before he died."

The question off-balanced her. "What do you mean?"

"It seemed a pretty straightforward question to me."

"Okay. Did you?"

"Yes. He was worried about you."

"About me?" She frowned. "Why?"

"Because your mother died before the two of you worked out your issues."

Issues, she thought. Is that how one summed up a lifetime of hurt feelings, a lifetime of longing for her mother's unconditional love and approval and being disappointed time and again? Her head filled with a litany of advice her mother had offered her over the years.

*"Avery, little girls don't climb trees and build forts or play cowboys and Indians with boys. They wear bows and dresses with ruffles, not blue-jean cutoffs and T-shirts. Good girls make ladylike choices. They don't run off to the city to become newspapermen. They don't throw away a good man to chase a dream."*

"He thought you might be sad about that," Hunter continued. "She was. He hated that she died without your making peace."

"He said that?" she managed to get out, voice tight.

He nodded and she looked away, memory flooding with the words she had flung at her mother just before she had left for college.

*"Drop the loving concern, Mother! You've never approved of me or my choices. I've never been the daughter you wanted. Why don't you just admit it?"*

Her mother hadn't admitted it and Avery had headed off to college with the accusation between them. They had never spoken of it again, though it had been a wedge between them forever more.

"He figured that's why you hardly ever came home." Hunter shrugged. "Interesting, you couldn't come to terms with your mother's life, he her death."

She jumped on the last. "What does that mean, he couldn't come to terms with her death?"

"I would think it's obvious, Avery. It's called grieving."

He was toying with her, she realized. It pissed her off. "And when did all these conversations take place?"

Hunter paused. "We had many conversations, he and I."

The past two days, her shock and grief, the grueling hours of travel, the onslaught of so much that was both foreign and familiar, came crashing down on her. "I don't have the energy to deal with your shit, even if I wanted to. If you decide you want to be a decent human being, look me up."

One corner of his mouth lifted in a sardonic smile. "I didn't answer your question before, the one about my opinion of the local buzz. Personally, I figured you'd pop your old man in a box and go. Fast as you could."

She took a step back, stung. Shocked that he would say that to her. That he would be so cruel. After the closeness they had shared. She pushed past him, unlocked her front door and stepped inside. She caught a glimpse of his face, of the stark pain that etched his features as she slammed the door.

*Hunter Stevens was a man pursued by demons.*

To hell with his, she thought, twisting the dead-bolt lock. She had her own to deal with.

# CHAPTER 4

Hunter gazed at the row of unopened bottles: beer, wine, whisky, vodka. All sins from his past. Each a nail in the coffin of his life.

He kept them around to prove that he could. Such a strategy went counter to traditional AA teaching, but he was a masochistic son of a bitch.

Hunter thought of Avery and anger rose up in him in a white-hot, suffocating wave. Once upon a time they'd been the best of friends: him, Matt and Avery. Before everything had begun spinning crazily out of control. Before his life had turned to shit.

He pictured her sitting next to Matt at his family's dinner table. All of them laughing, swapping memories. Reveling in the good old days.

What part had he played in those memories? Had they shared stories that hadn't included him? Or had they simply plucked him out as if he had never existed?

Shut out again. Always the one on the outside, looking in. The one who didn't belong.

*"What's wrong with you, Hunter? What went wrong with you?"*

Good question, he thought, gazing at the bottles, squeezing his fists against the urge that swelled inside him. The urge to open a bottle and get stinking, fall-down drunk.

He'd been down that path; he knew the only place it would lead him was straight to hell.

A hell of his own making. One populated by children screaming in terror. One in which he was helpless to stop the inevitable. Helpless to do more than look on in horror and self-loathing. In despair.

Hunter swung away from the bottles. He sucked in a deep breath and moved deliberately away from the kitchen and toward the makeshift desk he had set up in the corner of his small living room. On the desk sat a computer, monitor glowing in the dimly lit room, fan humming softly. Beside it the pages of a novel. His novel. A story about a lawyer's spiral to the depths.

If only he knew the story's end. Some days, he thought his protagonist would manage to claw his way up from those depths. Other days, hopelessness held him so tightly in its grip he couldn't breathe let alone imagine a happy ending.

He pulled out the chair and sat, intent on channeling his energy and anger into his novel. Instead, he found his thoughts turning to Avery once more.

What caused a man to douse himself with a flammable substance and strike a match?

He knew. He understood.

He had been there, too.

The blinking cursor drew his attention. He focused on the words he had written:

*Jack fought the forces that threatened to devour him. To his right lay the laws of man, to his left the greatness of God. One wrong step and he would be lost.*

Lost. And found. He had come home to set things right. To start over. He had already begun.

And now, here was Avery.

All together again, he thought. He, Matt and Avery. The same as when his life had begun to implode. How would this affect his plans? The timetable of events he had carefully constructed?

It wouldn't, he decided. Things would be set right. His life would be set right. No matter how much it hurt.

CHAPTER 5

Avery bolted upright in bed, heart pounding, her father's name a scream on her lips. She darted her gaze to the bedroom door, for a split second a kid again, expecting her parents to charge through, all concerned hugs and comforting arms.

They didn't, of course, and she sagged back against the headboard. She hadn't slept well, no surprise there. She'd tossed and turned, each creak and moan of the old house unfamiliar and jarring. She had been up a half dozen times. Checking the doors. Peering out the windows. Pacing the floor.

In truth, she suspected it hadn't been the noises that had kept her awake. It had been the quiet. The reason for the quiet.

Finally, she'd taken the couple of Tylenol PM caplets she'd dug out of her travel bag. Sleep had come.

But not rest. For sleep had brought nightmares. In them, she had been enfolded in a womb, warm and contented. Protected. Suddenly, she had been torn from her safe haven and thrust into a bright, white place. The light had burned. She had been naked. And cold.

In the next instant flames had engulfed her.

And she had awakened, calling out her father's name.

*Not too tough figuring that one out.*

Avery glanced at the bedside clock. Just after 9:00 a.m., she noted. Throwing back the blanket, she climbed out of bed. The temperature had dropped during the night and the house was cold. Shivering, she crossed to her suitcase, rummaged through it for a pair of leggings and a sweatshirt. She slipped them on, not bothering to take off her sleep shirt.

That done, she headed to the kitchen, making a quick side trip out front for the newspaper. It wasn't until she was staring at the naked driveway that two things occurred to her: the first was that Cypress Springs's only newspaper, the *Gazette,* was a biweekly, published each Wednesday and Saturday, and second, that Sal Mandina, the *Gazette's* owner and editor-in-chief had surely halted her father's subscription. There would be no uncollected papers piling up on a Cypress Springs stoop.

*No newspaper? The very idea made her twitch.*

With a shake of her head, she stepped inside, relocked the door and headed to the kitchen. She would pick up the New Orleans *Times-Picayune* or *The Advocate* from Baton Rouge when she went into town that morning.

That trip might come sooner than planned, Avery realized moments later, standing at the refrigerator. Yesterday she hadn't thought to check the kitchen for provisions. She wished she had.

No bread, milk or eggs. No coffee.

Not good.

Avery dragged her fingers through her short hair. After the huge meal she'd consumed the night before, she could probably forgo breakfast. Maybe. But she couldn't face this morning without coffee.

A walk downtown, it seemed, would be the first order of the day.

After changing, brushing her teeth and washing her face, she found her Reeboks, slipped them on then headed out the front door.

And ran smack into Cherry. The other woman smiled brightly. "Morning, Avery. And here I was afraid I was going to wake you."

"No such luck." Avery eyed the picnic basket tucked against Cherry's side. "I was just heading to the grocery for a newspaper and some coffee. You wouldn't happen to have either of those, would you?"

"A thermos of French roast. No newspaper, though. Sorry."

"You're a lifesaver. Come on in."

Cherry stepped inside. "I remembered that your dad didn't drink coffee. Figured you'd need it this morning, strong."

*Her mother had been a coffee drinker. But not her dad.* Cherry had remembered that. But she hadn't. What was wrong with her?

"Figured, too, that you hadn't had time to get to the market." She held up the basket. "Mom's homemade biscuits and peach jam."

Just the thought had Avery's mouth watering. "Do you have any idea how long it's been since I had a real biscuit?"

"Since your last visit, I suspect," Cherry answered, following Avery. They reached the kitchen and she set the basket on the counter. "Yankees flat can't make a decent biscuit. There, I've said it."

Avery laughed. She supposed the other woman was right. Learning how to make things like the perfect baking powder biscuit was a rite of passage for Southern girls.

And like many of those womanly rites of passage, she had failed miserably at it.

Cherry had come prepared: from the basket she took two blue-and-white-checked place mats, matching napkins, flatware, a miniature vase and carefully wrapped yellow rose. She filled the vase with water and dropped in the flower. "There," she said. "A proper breakfast table."

Avery poured the coffees and the two women took a seat at the table. Curling her fingers around the warm mug, Avery made a sound of appreciation as she sipped the hot liquid.

"Bad night?" Cherry asked sympathetically, bringing her own cup to her lips.

"The worst. Couldn't sleep. Then when I did, had nightmares."

"That's to be expected, I imagine. Considering."

*Considering.* Avery looked away. She cleared her throat. "This was so sweet of you."

"My pleasure." Cherry smoothed the napkin in her lap. "I meant what I said last night, I've missed you. We all have." She met Avery's eyes. "You're one of us, you know. Always will be."

"Are you trying to tell me something, Cherry?" Avery asked, smiling. "Like, you can take the girl out of the small town, but you can't take the small town out of the girl?"

"Something like that." She returned Avery's smile; leaned toward her. "But you know what? There's nothing wrong with that, in my humble, country opinion. So there."

Avery laughed and helped herself to one of the biscuits. She broke off a piece. It was moist, dense and still warm. She spread on jam, popped it in her mouth and made a sound of pure contentment. Too many meals like this and the one last night, and she wouldn't be able to snap her blue jeans.

She broke off another piece. "So, what's going on with you, Cherry? Didn't you graduate from Nicholls State a couple years ago?"

"Harvard on the bayou to us grads. And it was last year. Got a degree in nutrition. Not much call for nutritionists in Cypress Springs," she finished with a shrug. "I guess I didn't think *that* through."

"You might try Baton Rouge or—"

"I'm not leaving Cypress Springs."

"But you'd be close enough to—"

"No," she said flatly. "This is my home."

Awkward silence fell between them. Avery broke it first. "So what are you doing now?"

"I help Peg out down at the Azalea Café. And I sit on the boards of a couple charities. Teach Sunday school. Make Mom's life easier whenever I can."

"Has she been ill?"

She hesitated, then smiled. "Not at all. It's just...she's getting older. I don't like to see her working herself to a frazzle."

Avery took another sip of her coffee. "You live at home?"

"Mmm." She set down her cup. "It seemed silly not to. They have so much room." She paused a moment. "Mama and I talked about opening our own catering business. Not party or special-events catering, but one of those caterers who specialize in nutritious meals for busy families. We were going to call it Gourmet-To-Go or Gourmet Express."

"I've read a number of articles about those caterers. Apparently, it's the new big thing. I think you two would be great at that."

Cherry smiled, expression pleased. "You really think so?"

"With the way you both cook? Are you kidding? I'd be your first customer."

Her smile faltered. "We couldn't seem to pull it together. Besides, I'm not like you, Avery. I don't want some big, fancy career. I want to be a wife and mother. It's all I ever wanted."

Avery wished she could be as certain of what she wanted. Of what would make her happy. Once upon a time she had been. Once upon a time, it seemed, she had known everything.

Avery leaned toward the other woman. "So, who is he? There must be a guy in the picture. Someone special."

The pleasure faded from Cherry's face. "There was. He— Do you remember Karl Wright?"

Avery nodded. "I remember him well. He and Matt were good friends."

"Best friends," Cherry corrected. "After Matt and Hunter...fell out. Anyway, we had something specia...at least I thought we did. It didn't work out."

Avery reached across the table and squeezed her hand. "I'm sorry."

"He just up and...left. Went to California. We'd begun talking marriage and—"

She let out a sharp breath and stood. She crossed to the window and for a long moment simply stared out at the bright morning. Finally she glanced back at Avery. "I was pushing. Too hard, obviously. He called Matt and said goodbye. But not me."

"I'm really sorry, Cherry."

She continued as if Avery hadn't spoken. "Matt urged him to call me. Talk it out. Compromise, but..." Her voice trailed helplessly off.

"But he didn't."

"No. He'd talked about moving to California. I always resisted.

I didn't want to leave my family. Or Cypress Springs. Now I wish..."

Her voice trailed off again. Avery stood and crossed to her. She laid a hand on her shoulder. "Someone else will come along, Cherry. The right one."

Cherry covered her hand. She met Avery's eyes, hers filled with tears. "In this town? Do you know how few eligible bachelors there are here? How few guys my age? They all leave. I wish I wanted a career, like you. Because I could do that on my own. But what I want more than anything takes two. It's just not fai—"

Her voice cracked. She swallowed hard; cleared her throat. "I sound the bitter old spinster I am."

Avery smiled at that. "You're twenty-four, Cherry. Hardly a spinster."

"But that's not the way I... It hurts, Avery."

"I know." Avery thought of what Cherry had said the night before, about loving someone to the point of tragedy. In light of this conversation, her comment concerned Avery. She told her so.

Cherry wiped her eyes. "Don't worry, I'm not going to do anything crazy. Besides," she added, visibly brightening, "maybe Karl will come back? You did."

Avery didn't have the heart to correct her. To tell her she wasn't certain what her future held. "Have you spoken with him since he left?"

Fresh tears flooded Cherry's eyes. Avery wished she could take the question back. "His dad's gotten a few letters. He's over in Baton Rouge, at a home there. I go see him once a week."

"And Matt?"

"They spoke once. And fought. Matt chewed him out pretty good. For the way he treated me. He hasn't heard from him since."

Avery could bet he had chewed him out. Matt had always returned Cherry's hero worship with a kind of fierce protectiveness.

"He's missed you, you know."

Avery met Cherry's gaze, surprised. "Excuse me?"

"Matt. He never stopped hoping you'd come back to him."

Avery shook her head, startled by the rush of emotion she felt at Cherry's words. "A lot of time's passed, Cherry. What we had was wonderful, but we were very young. I'm sure there have been other women since—"

"No. He's never loved anyone but you. No one ever measured up."

Avery didn't know what to say. She told Cherry so.

The younger woman's expression altered slightly. "It's still there between you two. I saw it last night. So did Mom and Dad."

When she didn't reply, Cherry narrowed her eyes. "What are you so afraid of, Avery?"

She started to argue that she wasn't, then bit the words back. "A lot of time's passed. Who knows if Matt and I even have anything in common anymore."

"You do." Cherry caught her hand. "Some things never change. And some people are meant to be together."

"If that's so," Avery said, forcing lightness into her tone, "we'll know."

Instead of releasing her hand, Cherry tightened her grip. "I can't allow you to hurt him again. Do you understand?"

Uncomfortable, Avery tugged on her hand. "I have no plans of hurting your brother, believe me."

"I'm sure you mean that, but if you're not serious, just stay away, Avery. Just...stay...away."

"Let go of my hand, Cherry. You're hurting me."

She released Avery's hand, looking embarrassed. "Sorry. I get a little intense when it comes to my brothers."

Without waiting for Avery to respond, she made a show of glancing at her watch, exclaiming over the time and how she would be late for a meeting at the Women's Guild. She quickly packed up the picnic basket, insisting on leaving the thermos of coffee and remaining biscuits for Avery.

"Just bring the thermos by the house," she said, hurrying toward the door.

It wasn't until Cherry had backed her Mustang down the driveway and disappeared from sight that Avery realized how unsettled she was by the way their conversation had turned from friendly to adversarial. How unnerved by the woman's threatening tone and the way she had seemed to transform, becoming someone Avery hadn't recognized.

Avery shut the door, working to shake off the uncomfortable sensations. Cherry had always looked up to Matt. Even as a squirt, she had been fiercely protective of him. Plus, still smarting from her own broken heart made her hypersensitive to the idea of her brother's being broken.

No, Avery realized. Cherry had referred to her brothers, plural. She got a little intense when it came to her *brothers.*

Odd, Avery thought. Especially in light of the things she had said about Hunter the night before. If Cherry felt as strongly about Hunter as she did about Matt, perhaps she'd had more interaction with Hunter than she'd claimed. And perhaps her anger was more show than reality.

But why hide the truth? Why make her feelings out to be different than they were?

Avery shook her head. Always looking for the story, she thought. Always looking for the angle, the hidden motive, the elusive piece of the puzzle, the one that broke the story wide open.

*Geez, Avery. Give it a rest. Stop worrying about other people's issues and get busy on your own.*

She certainly had enough of them, she acknowledged, shifting her gaze to the stairs. After all, if she got herself wrapped up in others' lives and problems, she didn't have to face her own. If she was busy analyzing other people's lives, she wouldn't have time to analyze her own.

She wouldn't have to face her father's suicide. Or her part in it.

Avery glanced up the stairway to the second floor. She visualized climbing it. Reaching the top. Turning right. Walking to the end of the hall. Her parents' bedroom door was closed. She had noticed that the night before. Growing up, it had always been open. It being shut felt wrong, final.

*Do it, Avery. Face it.*

Squaring her shoulders, she started toward the stairs, climbed them slowly, resolutely. She propelled herself forward with sheer determination.

She reached her parents' bedroom door and stopped. Taking a

deep breath, she reached out, grasped the knob and twisted. The door eased open. The bed, she saw, was unmade. The top of her mother's dressing table was bare. Avery remembered it adorned with an assortment of bottles, jars and tubes, with her mother's hairbrush and comb, with a small velveteen box where she had kept her favorite pieces of jewelry.

It looked so naked. So empty.

She moved her gaze. Her father had removed all traces of his wife. With them had gone the feeling of warmth, of being a family.

Avery pressed her lips together, realizing how it must have hurt, removing her things. Facing this empty room night after night. She'd asked him if he needed help. She had offered to come and help him clean out her mother's things. Looking back, she wondered if he had sensed how halfhearted that offer had been. If he had sensed how much she hadn't wanted to come home.

*"I've got it taken care of, sweetheart. Don't you worry about a thing."*

So, she hadn't. That hurt. It made her feel small and selfish. She should have been here. Avery shifted her gaze to the double dresser. Would her mother's side be empty? Had he been able to do what she was attempting to do now?

She hung back a moment more, then forced herself through the doorway, into the bedroom. There she stopped, took a deep breath. The room smelled like him, she thought. Like the spicy aftershave he had always favored. She remembered being a little girl, snuggled on his lap, and pressing her face into his sweater. And being inundated with that smell—and the knowledge that she was loved.

*The womb from her nightmare. Warm, content and protected.*

Sometimes, while snuggled there, he had rubbed his stubbly cheek against hers. She would squeal and squirm—then beg for more when he stopped.

*Whisker kisses, Daddy. More whisker kisses.*

She shook her head, working to dispel the memory. To clear her mind. Remembering would make this more difficult than it already was. She crossed to the closet, opened it. Few garments hung there. Two suits, three sports coats. A half-dozen dress shirts.

Knit golf shirts. A tie and belt rack graced the back of the door; a shoe rack the floor. She stood on tiptoe to take inventory of the shelf above. Two hats—summer and winter. A cardboard storage box, taped shut.

Her mom's clothes were gone.

Avery removed the box, set it on the floor, then turned and crossed to the dresser. On the dresser top sat her dad's coin tray. On it rested his wedding ring. And her mother's. Side by side.

The implications of that swept over her in a breath-stealing wave. He had wanted them to be together. He had placed his band beside hers before he—

Blinded by tears, Avery swung away from the image of those two gold bands. She scooped up the cardboard box and hurried from the room. She made the stairs, ran down them. She reached the foyer, dropped the box and darted to the front door. She yanked it open and stepped out into the fresh air.

Avery breathed deeply through her nose, using the pull of oxygen to steady herself. She had known this wouldn't be easy.

But she hadn't realized it would be so hard. Or hurt so much.

The toot of a horn interrupted her thoughts. She glanced toward the road. Mary Dupre, she saw. Another longtime neighbor. The woman waved, pulled her car over and climbed out. She hurried up the driveway, short gray curls bouncing.

She reached Avery and hugged her. "I'm so sorry, sweetie."

Avery hugged her back. "Thank you, Mary."

"I wish I'd gone to Buddy or Pastor Dastugue, but I...didn't. And then it was too late."

"Go to Buddy or Pastor about what?"

"How odd your daddy was acting. Not leaving the house, letting his yard go. I tried to pay a visit, bring him some of my chicken and andouille gumbo, but he wouldn't come to the door. I knew he was home, too. I thought maybe he was sleeping, but I glanced back on my way down the driveway and saw him peeking out the window."

Avery swallowed hard at the bizarre image. It didn't fit the father she had known. "I don't know what to say, Mary. I had no... idea. We spoke often, but he didn't...he never said...anything."

"Poor baby." The woman hugged her again. "I'm bringing some food by later."

"There's no need—"

"There is," she said firmly. "You'll need to eat and I'll not have you worrying about preparing anything."

Avery acquiesced, grateful. "I appreciate your thoughtfulness."

"I see I'm not the first."

"Pardon?"

The woman pointed. Avery glanced in that direction. A basket sat on the stoop by the door.

Avery retrieved it. It contained homemade raisin bread and a note of condolence. She read the brief, warmly worded note, tears stinging her eyes.

"Laura Jenkins, I'll bet," Mary Dupre said, referring to the woman who lived next door. "She makes the best raisin bread in the parish."

Avery nodded and returned the note to its envelope.

"You're planning a service?"

"I'm meeting with Danny Gallagher this afternoon."

"He does good work. You need help with anything, anything at all, you call me."

Avery promised she would, knowing that the woman meant it. Finding comfort in her generosity. And the kindness she seemed to encounter at every turn.

She watched the woman scurry down the driveway, a bright bird in her purple and orange warm-up suit, waved goodbye, then collected Laura Jenkins's basket and carried it to the kitchen.

The last thing she needed was more food, but she sliced off a piece of the bread anyway, set it on a napkin and placed it on the kitchen table. While she reheated the last of the coffee, she retrieved the cardboard box from the foyer.

She had figured the box would contain photos, cards or other family mementos. Instead, she found it filled with newspaper clippings.

Curious, Avery began sifting through them. They all concerned the same event, one that had occurred the summer of 1988, her fifteenth summer.

She vaguely remembered the story: a Cypress Springs woman named Sallie Waguespack had been stabbed to death in her apartment. The perpetrators had turned out to be a couple of local teenagers, high on drugs. The crime had caused a citizen uproar and sent the town on a crusade to clean up its act.

Avery drew her eyebrows together, confused. Why had her father collected these? she wondered. She picked up one of the clippings and gazed at the grainy, yellowed image of Sallie Waguespack. She'd been a pretty woman. And young. Only twenty-two when she died.

So, why had her father collected the clippings, keeping them all these years? Had he been friends with the woman? She didn't recall having ever met her or heard her name, before the murder anyway. Perhaps he had been her physician?

Perhaps, she thought, the articles themselves would provide the answer.

Avery dug all the clippings out of the box, arranging them by date, oldest to most recent. They spanned, she saw, four months— June through September 1988.

Bread and coffee forgotten, she began to read.

As she did, fuzzy memories became sharp. On June 18, 1988, Sallie Waguespack, a twenty-two-year-old waitress, had been brutally murdered in her apartment. Stabbed to death by a couple of doped-up teenagers.

The Pruitt brothers, she remembered. They had been older, but she had seen them around the high school, before they'd dropped out to work at the canning factory.

They'd been killed that same night in a shoot-out with the police.

How could she have forgotten? It had been the talk of the school for months after. She remembered being shocked, horrified. Then...saddened. The Pruitt brothers had come from the wrong side of the tracks—actually the wrong side of what the locals called The Creek. Truth was, The Creek was nothing more than a two-mile-long drainage ditch that had been created to keep low areas along the stretch from flooding but ultimately had served as the dividing line between the good side of town and the bad.

They'd been wild boys. They'd gone with fast girls. They'd drunk beer and smoked pot. She'd stayed as far away from them as possible.

Even so, the tragedy of it all hadn't been lost on her, a sheltered fifteen-year-old. All involved had been so young. How had the boys' lives gone so terribly askew? How could such a thing happen in the safe haven of Cypress Springs?

Which was the question the rest of the citizenry had wondered as well, Avery realized as she shuffled through the articles. They fell into two categories: ones detailing the actual crime and investigation, and the lion's share, editorials written by the outraged citizens of Cypress Springs. They'd demanded change. Accountability. A return to the traditional values that had made Cypress Springs a good place to raise a family.

Then, it seemed, things had quieted down. The articles became less heated, then stopped. Or, Avery wondered, had her father simply stopped collecting them?

Avery sat back. She reached for the cup of coffee and sipped. Cold and bitter. She grimaced and set the cup down. Nothing in the articles answered the question why her father had collected them.

She had lived through these times. Yes, her parents had discussed the crime. Everyone had. But not to excess. She had never sensed her father being unduly interested in it.

But he had been. Obviously.

She glanced at her watch, saw that it was nearly noon already. Perhaps Buddy would know the why, she thought. If she hurried, she should have plenty of time to stop by the CSPD before her two o'clock appointment with Danny Gallagher.

## CHAPTER 6

Cypress Springs police headquarters hadn't changed in the years she had been gone. Located in an old storefront downtown, a block off Main in back of the courthouse, it resembled a hardware store or feed and seed more than a modern law enforcement center.

Avery entered the building. The whirling ceiling fans kicked up fifty years of dust. The sun streaming through the front window illuminated the millions of particles. The officer on desk duty looked up. He was so young, he still sported a severe case of adolescent acne.

She stopped at the desk and smiled. "Is Buddy in?"

"Sure is. You here to see him?"

"Nope, just wanted to see if he was here."

The kid's face went slack for a moment, then he laughed. "You're teasing me, right?"

"Yes. Sorry."

"That's okay. Are you Avery Chauvin?"

She nodded. "Do I know you?"

"You used to baby-sit me. I'm Sammy Martin. Del and Marge's boy."

She thought a moment, then smiled. As a kid, he had been an absolute terror. Interesting that he had decided to go into law enforcement. "I never would have known it was you, Sammy. Last time I saw you, you were what? Eight or nine?"

"Eight." His smile slipped. "Sorry about your dad. None of us could believe it."

"Thanks." She cleared her throat, furious with herself for the tears that sprang to her eyes. "You said Buddy was in?"

"Oh, yeah. I'll tell him you're here." He turned. "Buddy! Got a visitor!"

Buddy shouted he'd be out in a "jiffy" and Avery grinned. "Fancy intercom system, Sammy."

He laughed. "Isn't it, though. But we make do."

His phone rang and she wandered away from the desk. She crossed to the community bulletin board, located to the right of the front door. Another one just like it was located in the library, the post office and the Piggly Wiggly. Cypress Springs's communications center, she thought. That hadn't changed, either.

She scanned the items tacked to the board, a conglomeration of community information flyers, Most Wanted and Missing posters and For-Sale-by-Owner ads.

"Baby girl," Buddy boomed. She turned. He came around Sammy's desk, striding toward her, boots thundering against the scuffed wooden floors.

"I was afraid you'd be at lunch."

"Just got back." He hugged her. "This is a nice surprise."

She returned the hug. "Do you have a minute to talk?"

"Sure." He searched her expression. "Is everything okay?"

"Fine. I wanted to ask you about something I found in my dad's closet."

"I'll try. Come on." He led her to his office. Cluttered shelves, battered furniture and walls covered with honorary plaques and awards spoke of a lifetime of service to the community.

Avery sat in one of the two chairs facing his desk. She dug out the couple of clipped articles she had stuffed into her purse and handed them to him. "I found a box of clippings like these in Dad's bedroom closet. I hoped you'd be able to tell me why he'd kept them."

He scanned the two clippings, eyebrows drawing together. He met her eyes. "Are you certain your dad collected them and not your mom?"

She hesitated, then shook her head. "Not one hundred percent. But Dad had removed everything else of Mom's from the closet, so why keep these?"

"Gotcha." He handed the two back. "To answer your question, I don't know why he saved them. Even considering the nature of the case, it seems an odd thing for him to do."

"That's what I thought. So, he wasn't involved with the investigation in any way?"

"Nope."

"Was he Sallie's physician?"

"Could have been, though I don't know for sure. I'd guess yes, just because for a number of years he was Cypress Springs's only general practitioner. And even after Bobby Townesend opened his practice, then Leon White, your daddy remained the town's primary doctor. People around here are loyal and they certainly don't like change."

She pursed her lips. "Do you remember this event?"

"Like it was yesterday." He paused, passed a hand over his forehead. "In my entire career, I've only investigated a handful of murders. Sallie Waguespack's was the first. And the worst."

He hesitated a moment, as if gathering his thoughts. "But the trouble started before her murder. From the moment we learned that Old Dixie Foods was considering opening a factory just south of here. The community divided over the issue. Some called it progress. A chance to financially prosper. A chance for businesses that had always fought just to survive to finally have the opportunity to grow, maybe even turn a profit.

"Others predicted doom. They predicted the ruination of a way of life that had stood for a century. A way of life disappearing all over the South. They cited other Southern communities that had been changed for the worse by the influx of big business."

He laid his hands flat on the desk. She noticed their enormous size. "The topic became a hot button. Friendships were strained. Working relationships, too. Some families were divided on the issue.

"I admit I was one of those blinded by the idea of progress, financial growth. I didn't buy the downside."

"Which was?"

"The influx of five hundred minimum-wage workers, many of them unmarried males. The housing and commercial support system that would have to be created to accommodate them. How they would alter the social and moral structure of the community."

"I'm not certain I understand what you mean."

"This is a community devoted to God and family. We're a bit of an anachronism in this modern world. Family comes first. Sunday is for worship. We live by the Lord's commandments and the Golden Rule. Put a couple hundred single guys on the street on a Friday night, money in their pockets and what do you think is going to happen?"

She had a pretty good idea—and none of it had to do with the Golden Rule. "And my father?" she asked. "Where did he stand on the issue?"

Buddy met her eyes. His brow furrowed. "I don't remember for sure. I'm thinking he saw the downside all along. He was a smart man. Smarter than me, that's for certain."

After a moment, he continued. "In the end, of course, the town had little recourse. The factory was built. Money began pouring into Cypress Springs. The town grew. And people's worst predictions came true."

He stood and turned toward the window behind his desk. He gazed out, though Avery knew there was little to see—just a dead-end alley and the shadow of the courthouse.

"I love this town," he said without looking at her. "Grew up here, raised my family here. I'll die here, I suspect. Those four months in 1988 were the only time I considered leaving."

He turned and met her eyes. "The crime rate began to climb. We're talking the serious stuff, the kind of crimes we'd never seen in Cypress Springs. Rape. Armed robbery. Prostitution, for God's sake."

He released a weary-sounding breath. "It didn't happen overnight, of course. It sneaked up on us. An isolated crime here, another there. I called them flukes. Pretty soon, I couldn't call them that anymore. Same with some of the other changes occurring in the community. Teenage pregnancies began to rise. As did the divorce rate. Suddenly, we were having the kind of trouble at the high school they had at big-city schools—alcohol, drugs, fighting."

She vaguely recalled fights, and somebody getting caught smoking pot in the bathroom of the high school. She had been insulated from it all, she realized. In her warm, protected womb.

"It must have been difficult for you," she said.

"Folks were scared. And angry. Real angry. The town was turning into a place they didn't like. Naturally they turned their anger on me."

"They felt you weren't doing enough."

It wasn't a question but he nodded anyway. "I was in over my head, no doubt about it. Didn't have the manpower or the experience to deal with the increased crime rate. Hell, our specialty had been traffic violations, the occasional barroom brawl and sticky-fingered kids shoplifting bubble gum from the five-and-dime. Then Sallie Waguespack was killed."

He returned to his chair and sank heavily onto it. "This town went ballistic. The murder was grisly. She was young, pretty and had her whole life ahead of her. Her killers were high on drugs. There's just nothing easy about that scenario."

"Why'd they kill her, Buddy?"

"We don't know. We suspect the motive was robbery but—"

"But," she prodded.

"Like I said, she was young and pretty. And wild. They ran in the same crowd, frequented the same kinds of places. The Pruitt boys knew her. Could have been that one—or both—of them were romantically involved with her. Maybe they fought. Maybe she tried to break it off. Won't know any of that for sure, but what I do know is, the evidence against them was rock solid."

He fell silent. She thought a moment, going over the things he had told her, trying to find where her father fit in. *If* he fit in. "What happened then, Buddy?"

He blinked. "We closed the case."

"Not that, I mean with the community. The crime rate."

"Things quieted down, they always do. Some good came of Sallie's death. People stopped taking the community, their quality of life, for granted. They realized that safety and a community spirit were worth working for. People started watching out for each other. Caring more. Service groups formed to help those in need. Drug awareness began being taught in the schools. As did sex education. Counseling was provided for those in need. Instead of condemning people in crisis, we began to offer help. The citizens voted to increase my budget and I put more officers on the street. The crime rate began to fall."

"My first thought upon driving into town was how unchanged Cypress Springs seemed."

"A lot of effort has gone into maintaining that." He smiled. "Would you believe, tourism has become our number one industry? Lots of day-trippers, people on their way to and from St. Francisville. They come to see our pretty, old-time town."

She wondered if that was a hint of cynicism she heard in his voice.

"What about the canning plant?"

"Burned a couple years back. Old Dixie was in financial difficulty and didn't rebuild. Without job opportunities, those without other ties to Cypress Springs moved. If you're looking for an apartment, there're plenty of vacancies."

Avery smiled. "I'll keep that in mind."

"Old Dixie went belly-up last year. The burned-out hulk's for sale. Myself, I can't see anyone buying it. It's a stinking eyesore on the countryside. And I mean that literally."

She arched an eyebrow in question and he laughed without humor. "Just wait. You haven't been here long enough to know what I'm talking about. When conditions are just right—the humidity's high, the temperature's warm and the wind's blowing briskly from the south, the sour smell of the plant inundates Cypress Springs. Folks close their windows and stay inside. Even so, it's damn hard to ignore."

"Makes it hard to forget, too, I'll bet." Avery wrinkled her nose. "Does the town have any recourse?"

"Nope, company's Chapter 7." He leaned toward her. "Can't squeeze blood out of a turnip. Waste of time to try."

Avery fell silent a moment, then looked at Buddy, returning to the original reason for her visit. "Why did Dad clip and save all these articles, all these years, Buddy?"

"Don't know, baby girl. I just don't know."

"Am I interrupting?" Matt asked from behind her.

Avery turned. Matt stood in the doorway, looking official in his sheriff's department uniform.

"What're you doing here, son?"

"Do I need a reason to pop in to see my old man?"

"'Course not." Buddy glanced at his watch. "But it's past lunch and the middle of a workday."

Matt shifted his gaze to hers. "You see why I chose the sheriff's department over the CSPD? He'd have been all over me, all day."

Buddy snorted. "Right. Nobody needs to sit on top of you and you know it. You practically breathe that job." He wagged a finger at his son. "Truth be told, I wouldn't have had you work for me— I'd never have gotten a moment's peace."

"Slacker." Matt strode into the room, stopping behind Avery's chair. "You have a woman call in a missing person last week?" he asked his dad.

Buddy's expression tensed. "Yeah. What about it?"

"Just got off the phone with her. She thinks you're not doing anything on the case, asked the sheriff's department to check it out."

The older man leaned back in his chair. "I don't know what she expects. I've done everything I can do."

"Figured as much. Had to ask anyway."

Avery moved her gaze between the two men. "Do I need to go?"

"You're okay." Matt laid a hand on her shoulder. "In fact, you're an investigative reporter, you give us your take on this. Dad?"

Buddy nodded and took over. "I got a call last week from a woman who said her boyfriend contacted her by cell phone from just outside Cypress Springs. He told her he broke down and was going to call a service station for a tow. She never heard from him again."

"Where was he heading?" she asked.

"To St. Francisville. Coming from a meeting in Clinton."

"Why?"

"Business. Meeting with a client. He was in advertising."

"Go on."

"I spoke with every service station within twenty miles. Nobody got a call. I asked around town, put up flyers, haven't gotten a nibble. I told her that."

Matt moved around her chair and perched on the edge of the desk, facing her. "So, what do you think? She's screaming foul play."

"So where's the body?" Avery asked. "Where's the car?"

"And not any car. A Mercedes. Tough to lose one of those around here." Matt pursed his lips. "But why would this woman lie?"

"We see a lot of that in journalism. Everybody wants their fifteen minutes of fame. To feel important. Or in this woman's case, maybe to rationalize why her boyfriend hasn't called."

She glanced at her watch and saw that it was nearly time for her meeting at Gallagher's. She stood. "I've got to go. Danny Gallagher is expecting me in at two." She looked at Buddy. "Thanks for taking all this time to talk to me, I appreciate it."

"If something comes to mind, I'll let you know." He came around the desk and kissed her cheek. "Are you going to be okay?"

"I always am."

"Good girl."

Matt touched her arm. "I'll walk you out."

They exited the station and stepped into the bright midday sun. Avery dug her sunglasses out of her handbag. She slipped them on and looked up to find him gazing at her.

"What were you and Dad talking about?"

"A box of newspaper clippings I found in Dad's closet. They were all concerning the same event, the Sallie Waguespack murder."

"That doesn't surprise me."

"It doesn't?"

"That's the story that blew this little burg wide open."

"I hardly remembered it until I read those clippings today."

"Because of Dad, I lived it." He grimaced. "The night of the murder, I heard him with Mom. He was...crying. It's the only time I ever heard him cry."

She swallowed past the lump in her throat. "I feel like such an ostrich. First Dad, now learning this. I wonder—" She bit the words back and shook her head. "I need to go. Danny's expecting—"

"You wonder what?" he asked, touching her arm.

She let out a constricted-sounding breath. "I'm starting to wonder just what kind of person I am."

"You were young. It wasn't your tragedy."

"And what of now? What about my dad? Was that my tragedy?"

"Avery, you can't keep beating yourself up about this. You didn't light that match. He did."

*But if she had been here for him, would he still have done it?*

"I've got to go, Matt. Danny's waiting."

She started off. He called her name, stopping her. She turned.

"Next Sunday? Spring Fest?"

"With you?"

He shot her his cocky smile. The one that had always had her saying yes when she should have been saying no. "If you think you could take an entire day of my company?"

She returned the smile. "I think I could manage it."

"Great. I'll give you a call about the time."

Pleased, she watched him head back to his cruiser. In that moment, he looked sixteen. Full of the machismo of youth, buoyed by a yes from the opposite sex.

*"If you're not serious, just stay away. Just...stay...away."*

Her smile slipped as she remembered Cherry's warning. Avery shook off the ripple of unease that moved over her. She was being ridiculous. Cherry was a sweet girl who was worried about her brother. Matt was lucky to have someone who cared so much about him.

# CHAPTER 7

The Gavel called the meeting to order. All six of his generals were in attendance. Ready to do battle. To lay down their lives for their beliefs and their community.

Each believed himself a patriot at war.

He surveyed the group, proud of them, of his selections. They represented both the old and new guard of Cypress Springs. Wisdom invigorated by youth. Youth tempered by the wisdom of experience. A difficult combination to beat.

"Good evening," he said. "As always, I appreciate the sacrifice each of you made to be here tonight."

Because of the nature of the group, because some would not understand their motives—even those who stood to benefit most from their efforts, indeed, their sacrifice—they met in secret and under cover of late night. Even their families didn't know the location or true nature of these meetings.

"I have bad news," he told the group. "I have reason to believe Elaine St. Claire has contacted a Cypress Springs citizen."

A murmur went around the table. One of his generals spoke. "How certain are you of this?"

"Quite. I saw the letter myself."

"This is bad," another said. "If she's brazen enough to contact someone in Cypress Springs, she very well might contact the authorities."

"I plan to take care of it."

"How? Isn't she living in New Orleans?"

"She can destroy us," another interjected. "To leave Cypress Springs is to lose the safety of our number."

The Gavel shook his head, saddened. New Orleans had been the perfect place for her. Sin city. Anything went.

But, it seemed, she hadn't been able to help herself. No doubt, the passing months had dimmed her fear, had lessened the immediacy of the danger. It was human nature, he acknowledged. He hadn't been surprised.

He was beginning to doubt the effectiveness of the warning system they had devised. Warnings rarely worked. Or only proved a short-term deterrent.

"She's in St. Francisville now," he said.

"Better," a general murmured. "We have friends there."

"We won't need them," the Gavel said. "I've planned a trap. A carefully executed trap."

"Lure her back to Cypress Springs," General Blue said. "Once here, she's ours."

"Exactly." He gazed from one face to another around the table. "Are we in agreement, shall I set the trap?"

The generals didn't hesitate. They had learned nothing good came with lack of conviction. Weakness opened the door to destruction.

The Gavel nodded. "Consider it done. Next? Any concerns?"

Blue spoke again. "A newcomer to Cypress Springs. An outsider. She's asking questions about The Seven. About our history."

The Gavel frowned. He'd heard, too. Outsiders always posed serious threats. They didn't understand what The Seven were fighting for. How seriously they took their convictions. Invariably, they had to be dealt with quickly and mercilessly.

Outsiders with knowledge of The Seven posed an even more significant danger.

Damn the original group, he thought. They'd been weak. They hadn't concealed their actions well. They hadn't been willing to take whatever measures were required, no matter the consequences to life or limb.

Too touchy-feely, the Gavel thought, lips twisting into a sneer. They'd bowed to internal fighting and the squeamishness of a few members. Bowed to a member who threatened to go to the American Civil Liberties Union and the Feds. And to any and all of those prissy-assed whiners who were sending this country to hell in a handbasket.

It made him sick to think about it. What about the rights of decent, law-abiding folks to have a safe, morally clean place to live?

That's where he and his generals differed from the original group. The Gavel had chosen his men carefully. Had chosen men as strong-willed as he. Men whose commitment to the cause mirrored his own in steadfastness and zeal.

He was willing to die for the cause.

He was willing to kill for it.

"The outsider," the Gavel asked, "anyone have a name yet?"

No one did. A general called Wings offered that she had just moved into The Guesthouse.

The Gavel nodded. Her name would be easy to secure. One call and they would have it.

"Let's keep an eye on this one," he advised. "She doesn't make a move we don't know about. If she becomes more of a risk, we take the next step."

He turned to Hawk, his most trusted general. The man inclined his head in the barest of a nod. The Gavel smiled. Hawk understood; he agreed. If necessary, they would take care of this outsider the way they'd taken care of the last.

Determination flowing through him, he adjourned the meeting.

# CHAPTER 8

The Azalea Café served the best buttermilk pancakes in the whole world. Fat, fluffy and slightly sweet even without syrup, Avery had never stopped craving them—even after twelve years away from Cypress Springs. And after a weekend spent preparing her childhood home for sale, Avery had decided a short stack at the Azalea wasn't just a treat—it was a necessity.

She stepped into the café. "Morning, Peg," she called to the gray-haired woman behind the counter. Peg was the third-generation Becnal to run the Azalea. Her grandmother had opened the diner when her husband had been killed in the Second World War and she'd needed to support her five kids.

"Avery, sweetheart." She came around the counter and gave Avery a big hug. She smelled of syrup and bacon from the griddle. "I'm so sorry about your daddy. If I can do anything, anything at all, you just let me know."

Avery hugged her back. "Thanks, Peg. That means a lot to me."

When the woman released her, Avery saw that her eyes were

bright with tears. "Bet you came in for some of my world-famous pancakes."

Avery grinned. "Am I that transparent?"

"You ate your first short stack at two years old. I remember your daddy and mama like to have died of shock, you ate the whole thing. Every last bite." She smoothed her apron. "Have yourself a seat anywhere. I'll send Marcie over with coffee."

The nine-to-fivers had come and gone, leaving Avery her choice of tables. Avery slipped into one of the front window booths. She looked out the window, toward the town square. They had begun setting up for Spring Fest, she saw. City workers were stringing lights in the trees and on the gazebo. Friday night it would look like a fairyland.

A smile tipped the corners of her mouth. Louisianians loved to celebrate and used any opportunity to do so: the Blessing of the Fleet on Little Caillou Bayou, the harvest of the strawberries in Pontchatoula, Louisiana's musical heritage in New Orleans at the Jazz Fest, to name only a few. Spring Fest was Cypress Springs's offering, a traditional Louisiana weekend festival, complete with food booths, arts and crafts, music and carnival rides for the kids. People from all over the state would come and every available room in Cypress Springs would be booked. She had gone every year she'd lived at home.

"Coffee, hon?"

Avery turned. "Yes, thanks."

The girl filled her cup, then plunked down a pitcher of cream. Avery thanked her, added cream and sugar to her coffee, then returned her gaze to the window and the square beyond.

The weekend had passed in an unsettling mix of despair and gratitude, tears and laughter. Neighbors and friends had stopped by to check on her, bringing food, baked goods and flowers. The last time she'd seen most of them had been at her mother's funeral and then only briefly. The majority had stayed to chat, reliving times past—sharing their sweet, funny, outrageous and precious memories of her father. Some, too, shared their regret at not having acted on his bizarre behavior before it had been too late. The outpouring of concern and affection had made her task less painful.

But more, it had made her feel less alone.

Avery had forgotten what it was like to live among friends, to be a part of a community. Not just a name or a P.O. box number, but a real person. Someone who was important for no other reason than that they shared ownership of a community.

Avery sipped her coffee, turning her attention to her dad's funeral. Danny Gallagher had recommended Avery wake her father Wednesday evening, with a funeral to follow the next morning. He had chosen that day so the *Gazette* could run an announcement in both the Saturday and Wednesday editions. The whole town would want to pay their respects, he felt certain. This would offer them the opportunity to do so.

Lilah had insisted on opening her home for mourners after the service on Thursday. Avery had accepted, relieved.

*Two days and counting.*

Would burying him enable her to say goodbye? she wondered, curving her hands around the warm mug. Would the funeral give her a sense of closure? Or would she still feel this great, gaping hole in her life?

The waitress brought the pancakes and refilled her coffee. Avery thanked her and not bothering with syrup, dug in, making a sound of pleasure as the confection made contact with her taste buds.

In an embarrassingly short period of time, she had plowed through half the stack. She laid down her fork and sighed, contented.

"Are they as good as you remember?" Peg called from behind the counter.

"Better," she answered, pushing her plate away. "But if I eat any more I'll burst."

The woman shook her head. "No wonder you're so scrawny. I'll have Marcie bring your check."

Avery thanked her and turned back toward the square. She began to look away, then stopped as she realized that Hunter and his mother were standing across the street, partially hidden by an oak tree, deep in conversation.

Not a conversation, Avery saw. An argument. As she watched, Lilah lifted a hand as if to slap her son but he knocked her hand away. He was furious; Avery could all but feel his anger. And Lilah's despair.

She told herself to look away. That she was intruding. But she found her gaze riveted to the two. They exchanged more words but as Hunter turned to walk away, Lilah grabbed at him. He shook her hand off, his expression disgusted.

Lilah was begging, Avery realized with a sense of shock. But for what? Her son's love? His attention? In the next moment, Hunter had strode off.

Lilah stared after him a moment, then seemed to crumble. She sagged against the tree and dropped her head into her hands.

Alarmed, Avery scooted out of the booth, hooking her handbag over her shoulder. "Peg," she called, hurrying toward the door, "could you hold my check? I'll be back later."

She didn't wait for the woman's answer but darted through the door and across the street.

"Lilah," she said gently when she reached the other woman. "Are you all right?"

"Go away, Avery. Please."

"I can't do that. Not when you're so upset."

"You can't help me. No one can."

She dropped her hands, turned her face toward Avery's. Ravaged by tears, stripped of makeup, she looked a dozen years older than the genteel hostess of the other night.

Avery held out a hand. "At least let me help you to your car. Or let me drive you home."

"I don't deserve your kindness. I've made so many mistakes in my life. With my children, my—" She wrung her hands. "God help me! It's all my fault! Everything's my fault!"

"Is that what Hunter told you?"

"I've got to go."

"Is that what Hunter told you? I saw you arguing."

"Let me go." She fumbled in her handbag for her car keys. Her hands shook so badly she couldn't hold on to them and they slipped to the ground.

Avery bent and snatched them up. "I don't know what he said

to you, but it's not true. Whatever's wrong with Hunter is not your fault. He's responsible for the mess of his life, not you."

Lilah shook her head. "You don't know... I've been a terrible mother. I've done everything wrong. Everything!"

Lilah attempted to push past; Avery caught her by the shoulders. She forced the woman to meet her eyes. "That's not true! Think about Matt. And Cherry. Look how well they're doing, how happy they are."

The older woman stilled. She met Avery's eyes. "I don't feel well, Avery. Could you take me home?"

Avery said she could and led Lilah to her sedan, parked on the other side of the square. After helping the woman into the front passenger seat, Avery went around to the driver's side, climbed in and started the vehicle up.

The drive out to the ranch passed in silence. Lilah, Avery felt certain, possessed neither the want nor emotional wherewithal to converse. Avery pulled the sedan into the driveway and cut the engine. She went around the car, helped Lilah out, up the walk and into the house.

At the sound of the door opening, Cherry appeared at the top of the stairs. She looked from her mother to Avery. "What happened?"

"I'm all right," Lilah answered, an unmistakable edge in her voice. "Just tired."

Cherry hurried down the stairs. She took her mother's arm. "Let me help you."

"Please, don't fuss."

"Mother—"

"I don't want to talk about it." She eased her arm from her daughter's grasp. "I have a headache and..." She turned toward Avery. "You're an angel for bringing me home. I hope I didn't interfere with your plans."

"Not at all, Lilah. I hope you feel better."

"I need to lie down now. Excuse me."

Cherry watched her mother make her way slowly up the stairs. When she had disappeared from view, she swung to face Avery, obviously distressed. "What happened?"

"I don't know." Avery passed a hand over her face. "I was at the

Azalea, in one of the window booths. I looked out and there was your mother and Hunter—"

"Hunter!"

"They were arguing."

Her expression tightened. "Son of a... Why won't he leave her alone? Why won't he just go away?"

Avery didn't know what to say, so she said nothing. Cherry shook with fury. She strode to the entryway table, yanked up the top right drawer and dug out a pack of cigarettes and a lighter. Her hands shook as she lit the smoke. She crossed to the front door, opened it and stood in the doorway, smoking in silence.

After several drags, she turned back to Avery. "What were they arguing about?"

"That I don't know. She wouldn't say."

Cherry blew out a long stream of smoke. "What *did* she say?"

"That she had made a mess of her life. Of her children's lives. That everything was her fault."

Cherry squeezed her eyes shut.

"I told her it wasn't true," Avery continued. "I told her Hunter's problems were his own."

"But she didn't believe it."

"Actually, it seemed to calm her."

"Hallelujah." Cherry moved out onto the porch, stubbed out her cigarette in an ashtray hidden under a step, then returned to the foyer. "There's a first."

"I take it this has happened before."

"Oh, yeah. He hadn't been back in Cypress Springs twenty-four hours before he started shoveling his shit her way. All of our way, actually. You wouldn't believe some of the things he said. The things he accused us of."

Cherry sighed. "It doesn't matter how well Matt and I are doing, all she can focus on is Hunter and his troubles. And somehow it's all her fault."

"What happened to him, Cherry? Hunter used to be so...kind. And funny."

She lifted a shoulder. "I don't know. None of us do."

"It began that summer, didn't it? That summer Sallie Wagues-pack was killed."

Cherry looked sharply at her. "Why do you say that?"

"Because it was that summer he and Matt started fighting. Just after they'd gotten their driver's licenses." She paused. "It's when Hunter seemed to...change."

Cherry didn't comment; Avery filled the silence. "I wouldn't have thought of it except for all the clippings I found in Dad's closet." She quickly explained how she had found the box, sorted through it then questioned Buddy about the contents. "Truthfully, I'd forgotten the incident."

"Why do you think one had anything to do with the other?"

"Excuse me?"

"Why do you think that murder has anything to do with Hunter?"

Avery blinked, surprised by the other woman's assumption. "I didn't. I was just placing it in a time frame."

Cherry rubbed the spot between her eyes with her thumb, in obvious discomfort. "I was just a kid, I hardly remember it all. But it was...a time of upheaval. Everybody was upset. All the time, it seemed."

She dropped her hand and met Avery's eyes. "For whatever reason, Hunter's changed. He's not one of us anymore. As much as it hurts me to admit, I can't imagine what it does to Matt. They're twins, for God's sake. Once they were as close as two people could be."

Cherry shivered slightly and closed the door. "To his credit, Matt's gone on. So have Daddy and I. But Mother can't seem to...let go." She paused. "It's been much worse since Hunter came back to Cypress Springs. Before, we could forget, you know? Out of sight, out of mind. Even Mom. I think she consoled herself with his professional success."

*Out of sight, out of mind.* Avery understood. In a way, she had done that with her father. She had told herself he was happy, that he had a nice comfortable life. Now she had to live with just how wrong she'd been.

"Then home he came," Cherry continued, "with a shitload of bad attitude and so many chips on his shoulder it's amazing he can walk upright."

"Why, Cherry? The other night your dad said Hunter almost lost his license to practice law. Do you know what happened?"

"Yeah, I know. He had it all and he blew it. That's what happened. Professional success. Money, brains. A family who loved him. And he's blown it all to hell.

"You know what he's doing?" she asked. "The man's gone from practicing corporate law at one of the top firms in the South to taking the odd divorce and bankruptcy case in Cypress Springs. I don't get it. He's working and living down in what used to be Barker's Flower Shop, one block off the square. At the corner of Walton and Johnson. Remember it?"

Avery indicated she did.

"You already know what I really think about why he came back to Cypress Springs." She didn't wait for Avery to reply. "He's come back to hurt us. To punish us for some imagined sin or slight against him."

Cherry glanced toward the stairway thinking, Avery knew, of her mother. "And what's really sad is, he's succeeding."

# CHAPTER 9

Avery left the ranch a short time later. Cherry told her to go ahead and take her mother's car—after one of these spells her mother didn't go out for days anyway.

As she drove through town, Avery couldn't stop thinking about what Cherry had said. About Hunter coming back to punish them. She'd dismissed Cherry's earlier claim, but now Avery couldn't put the image of Lilah's devastation out of her mind.

And the more she thought about it, the angrier she became. How could Hunter treat his family that way? All they had ever done was love and support him.

She didn't care if she had been gone for twelve years, she wasn't going to let him get away with it. The Stevenses were the closest thing to a family she had left, and she wasn't about to stand back and let Hunter hurt them.

She reached Walton Street, took a left, heading back toward Johnson. She found a parking spot a couple doors down from what had been Barker's Flower Shop. She angled into the spot and climbed out.

Barker's had been Cypress Springs's preferred florist during Avery's high-school years. Every corsage she'd worn had come from this shop.

And they'd all been from Matt, she realized. Every last one of them.

She reached the shop and felt a moment of loss at the empty front window. She used to love peering through at the buckets of cut flowers.

She tried the door. And found it locked. A cardboard clock face propped in the window proclaimed *Will Return At—*

Problem was the clock's hour hand was missing.

Cherry had said that Hunter used the front of the shop as his law office and lived in the back. If she remembered correctly, the Barkers had done the same. No doubt, the residence was accessed from the rear.

She went around back, to the service alley. Sure enough, the rear had been set up as a residential entrance.

She crossed to it and found the outer door stood open to allow fresh air in through the screen. She knocked on the door frame. "Hunter?" she called out. "It's Avery."

From inside came a scuffling, followed by a whimper. She frowned and knocked again. "Hunter? Is that you?"

The whimpering came again. She leaned closer and peered through the dirty screen. The room immediately beyond the door was a kitchen. It appeared empty.

From inside came a thud. Like something hitting the floor.

Something? Or someone?

Reacting, she tried the screen door, found it unlocked and pushed it open. She stepped through. Save for a handful of dishes in the sink, the kitchen was as neat as a pin.

Heart pounding, she made her way through the room. "Hunter?" she called again, softly. "It's Avery. Are you all right?"

This time, silence answered. No whimper, whine or scuffle.

*Not good.*

She rushed through the doorway to the next room and stopped

short. The biggest, mangiest dog she had ever seen blocked her way, teeth barred. The beast growled low in its throat and Avery's stomach dropped to her toes.

She took a step back.

Whimpering from behind the dog drew her gaze. On a blanket shoved into the corner lay a half-dozen squirming pups, so young their eyes weren't open yet.

"It's okay, girl," Avery said gently, returning her gaze to the mama. "I won't hurt your pups."

The dog cocked its head as if deciding if Avery could be trusted, then turned and loped back to her babies. She flopped onto her side on the floor and the pups began rooting for a teat. With a heavy sigh, she thumped her tail—which was as thick as a broom handle—once against the wooden floor.

Avery shook her head, feeling more than a little ridiculous. What an imagination she had. Big bad Avery, rushing in to save the day.

She turned away from the nursing dog to take in the room. Neat but spartan, she thought. A shabby but comfortable mishmash of furniture and styles. An ancient-looking couch in a shade that had probably once been a bright gold, but could now only be described as vomit colored. A beat-up coffee table. And a beautiful, butter-colored leather easy chair.

Left over from the good old days, she would bet. The piece he hadn't been able to get rid of.

She turned. A makeshift desk and file cabinet had been set up in the corner behind her. A computer rested atop the desk, screen dark. Beside the PC sat a stack of printer paper, a couple inches thick.

Curious, she crossed to the desk. A manuscript, she saw. She tipped her head to read. *Breaking Point.* A novel by Hunter Stevens.

Hunter was writing a novel? Why hadn't Matt or Cherry mentioned it?

Maybe they didn't—

"Come right in," Hunter said from behind her. "Make yourself at home."

Avery whirled around, hand to her throat. "Hunter!"

"You sound so surprised to see me. Were you expecting someone else?"

"This isn't how it looks. I didn't mean to—"

"To what?" he asked. "Break and enter?"

Cheeks burning, she tilted up her chin. "It wasn't like that. I can explain."

"Sure you can." He stalked past her, retrieved the manuscript and placed it in a file drawer. Avery noticed the way he handled the pages—carefully, with something akin to reverence.

"I didn't read anything but the title," she said softly. "And I didn't break in. The door was open."

He locked the drawer, pocketed the key then turned and faced her, arms folded across his chest. "How careless of me."

"I stopped by. And I heard a sound from inside. A...cry, then a thud. Like someone...falling. I thought you—"

At his disbelieving expression, she made a sound of frustration. "It was the dog and her pups I heard. I thought, you know, that something was wrong."

"Sarah?" He glanced over at the dog. At the sound of her name, the canine looked up and slapped her tail against the floor.

"See?" Avery said. "That's what I heard."

He smiled then, taking her by surprise. "You're right, that is a scary noise. Did you think the boogeyman had gotten me? Was big bad Avery going to rush in and save the day?"

The curving of his lips changed him into the young man she remembered from all those years ago and she returned his smile. "Why not? It could happen. I carry pepper spray. Besides, if you recall, I'm not one of those prissy, sissy girls like you dated in high school. Hunter," she mocked in an exaggerated drawl, "you're so big and strong. I don't know what I would do without you to protect me."

He laughed. "True, I would never call you prissy."

"Thank you for that."

"I'm sorry," he said. "For the other night. I acted like an ass."

"A bastard *and* an ass, actually. Apology accepted anyway."

The dog stood, shook off a last greedy pup and ambled over to

Hunter. She looked adoringly up at him. He squatted beside her and scratched behind her ears. She practically swooned with delight.

Avery watched the two, thinking Hunter couldn't be quite as heartless as he acted. "She seems devoted to you."

"It's mutual. I found her when she was as down and out on her luck as I was. Figured we made a good pair."

Silence fell between them. Avery longed to ask about the circumstances that had brought him to this place, but didn't want to spoil the moment of camaraderie.

She chose a safer topic instead, motioning the computer. "Your family didn't mention that you were writing a novel."

"They don't know. No one does. Unless like you, they make a habit of breaking and entering." He straightened. Sarah remained by his feet. "And I'd appreciate it if you didn't tell them."

"If that's what you want. But I'm sure if they knew they'd be nothing but supporti—"

"It is what I want."

"All right." She tilted her head. "The book, what's it about?"

"It's a thriller." He didn't blink. "About a lawyer who goes off the deep end."

"It's autobiographical then?"

"What are you doing here, Avery?"

She decided that beating around the bush would be a waste of time. "I want to talk to you about your mother."

"There's a shock."

She stiffened at his sarcasm. "I saw the two of you this morning. Arguing. She was really upset, Hunter. Hysterical, actually."

He didn't respond. Not with surprise or remorse. Not with concern or guilt. His impassive expression made her blood boil. "You don't have a comment about that?"

"No."

"She couldn't even drive, Hunter. I had to take her home."

"What do you want me to say? That I'm sorry?"

"For starters."

"That's not happening. Anything else?"

She stared at him, stunned. That he could be so unfeeling toward his mother. So careless toward those who loved him.

She told him so and he laughed. "That's rich. The pot calling the kettle black."

"What's that supposed to mean?"

"You know damn well what it means. Where have you been the last few years, Avery?"

She saw what he was doing and backed off, not about to let him divert the conversation. "We're not talking about me here, Hunter. We're talking about you. About you blaming everyone but yourself for your problems. Why don't you grow up?"

"Why don't you butt out, Ms. Big-City Reporter? Head back to your important job. Your life isn't here. It never was."

Stung, she struck back. "You're lucky you have such a great family. A family who loves you. One willing to stick by you even when you're such a colossal jackass. Why don't you show a little gratitude?"

"Gratitude?" He laughed, the sound hard. "Great family? For an investigative reporter you're pretty damn obtuse."

She shook her head, disbelieving. "No family is perfect. But at least they've stayed committed to one another. They've tried to be there for one another, through thick and thin."

"When did you become such an expert on my family? You've only been here, what? A week! Wait!" He brought his fingertips to his forehead. "I've got it! You're psychic?"

"It's senseless to even try to have a conversation with you." She started toward the door. "I'm out of here."

"Of course you are. That's your MO, isn't it, Avery?"

She froze, then turned slowly to face him. "Excuse me?"

"Where have you been the past twelve years?"

"In case you haven't noticed, Cypress Springs isn't exactly the place to have a career in journalism."

He took a step toward her. "You're a fine one to scold me about how I treat my mother. Look at how you treated yours. How many times did you visit her after you moved away?"

"I called. I visited when I could. I couldn't just take off whenever the mood struck."

"How long did you stay after her funeral, Avery? Twenty-four hours? Or was it thirty-six?"

She swung toward the door; he followed her, grabbing her arm when she reached it. "And where were you, Avery, when your dad was so depressed he set himself on fire?"

A cry spilled past her lips. She tugged against his hand. He tightened his grip. "Your dad needed you. And you weren't here."

"What do you know about my father! About how he felt or what he needed!"

"I know more than you could imagine." He released her and she stumbled backward. "I bet you didn't know that your dad and mine weren't even on speaking terms. That it had gotten so bad between them that if one saw the other coming on the street, he would cross to the other side to avoid making eye contact. I bet neither Matt nor Buddy told you that."

"Stop it, Hunter." She backed toward the door.

"I bet they didn't tell you that my parents haven't shared a bed in over a decade. Or that Mom's addicted to painkillers and booze." He laughed bitterly. "Dad's played the part of the jovial, small-town cop so long, he wouldn't recognize an authentic thought or feeling if it shouted his name. Matt's trying his damnedest to follow in the old man's footsteps and is so deeply in denial it's frightening. And Cherry, poor girl, has sacrificed her life to holding the dysfunctional lot together.

"Great family," he finished. "As American as apple pie and Prozac."

She stared at him, shaking with the force of her anger. "You're right. I wasn't here. And I hate myself for it. I would do anything, give anything, to change that. To bring them back. But I can't. I've lost them."

She grasped the door handle, fighting not to cry. Determined not to let him know he had won. "I didn't believe what Cherry told me. That you'd come back just to punish them. I believe it now."

He held out a hand. "Avery, I—"

"When did you become so cruel, Hunter?" she asked, cutting him off. "What happened to make you so hateful and small?"

Without waiting for an answer, she let herself out and walked away.

# CHAPTER 10

Gwen Lancaster stood at the window of her rented room and peered through the blinds at the gathering darkness. Lights in the buildings around the square began popping on. Gwen kept her own lights off; she preferred the dark. Preferred to watch in anonymity.

Did they know she was here? she wondered. Did they know who she was? That Tom had been her brother?

Had they realized yet that she would stop at nothing to find his killer?

As always, thoughts of her brother brought a lump to her throat. She swung away from the window, crossed to the desk and the Cypress Springs *Gazette* she had been reading. It lay open to the upcoming calendar of events. She had marked off those she planned to attend. First on the list was tonight's wake.

She shifted her gaze to the paper and the black-and-white image of a kindly-looking older man. The caption identified him as Dr.

Phillip Chauvin. Survived by his only child, a daughter, Avery Chauvin.

The entire town would be in attendance tonight. She had heard people talking about it. Had learned that the man had committed suicide. And that he had been one of Cypress Springs's most beloved brothers.

Suicide. Her lips twisted. Cypress Springs, it seemed, was just that kind of town.

Fury rose up in her. *They* would most probably be there. The bastards who had taken her brother from her.

Tom had been working toward his doctorate in social psychology from Tulane University. He'd been writing his dissertation on vigilantism in small-town America. A story he'd uncovered in the course of his research had brought him to Cypress Springs.

A story about a group called The Seven. A group that had operated from the late 1980s to the early 1990s, systematically denying the civil rights of their fellow citizens in the name of law and order.

After only a matter of weeks in Cypress Springs, Tom had disappeared without a trace.

Gwen swallowed hard. That wasn't quite true. His body had disappeared. His car had been found on the side of a deserted stretch of highway in the next parish. It had been in running order. There'd been no sign of a struggle or an accident. The keys had been gone.

Both the Cypress Springs police and sheriff's department had investigated. They'd combed her brother's car and the surrounding area for evidence. They'd searched his rented room, interviewed his fellow boarders, worked to reconstruct the last days of his life. Neither suspect nor motive had emerged.

They told her they believed he had been the victim of a random act of violence—that Tom had simply been in the wrong place at the wrong time. They had promised not to close the case until they uncovered what happened to him.

Gwen had a different theory about his disappearance. She believed his research into The Seven had gotten him killed. That he had gotten too close to someone or something. She had talked to him only days before he disappeared. He'd found so much more than he'd expected, he had told her. He believed that The Seven was not a thing of the past, but operating still. He had made an important contact; they were meeting the following night.

Gwen had begged him to be careful.

That had been the last time she'd heard his voice. The last time, she feared, she would ever hear his voice.

Although his research notes revealed nothing sinister, she hadn't a doubt his contact had either set him up or killed him.

Gwen brought the heels of her hands to her eyes. What if she was wrong? What if she simply needed someone—or something—she could point to and say they did it, that her brother was gone because of them. The therapist she had been seeing thought so. Hers was a common reaction, he'd said. The need to make sense out of a senseless act of violence. To create order out of chaos.

She dropped her hands, weary from her own thoughts. Chaos. That's what her life had become after Tom's disappearance.

She crossed back to the window. For several days city workers had been stringing lights in the trees. Tonight, it seemed, was the payoff. The thousands of twinkling lights snapped on, turning the town square into a fairyland.

It was so beautiful. Charming. A postcard-perfect community populated by the nicest people she had ever encountered.

It was a lie. An illusion. This place was not the idyllic paradise it seemed. People here were not the paragons they seemed.

And she would prove it. No matter what it cost her.

# CHAPTER 11

Gallagher's funeral home was housed in a big old Victorian on Prospect Street. The Gallagher family had been in the funeral game for as long as Avery could remember. She and Danny had gone to school together, and she remembered a report he had given in the seventh grade on embalming. The girls had been horrified, the boys fascinated.

Being the biggest tomboy in Cypress Springs, she had fallen in line with the boys.

Danny Gallagher met her at the front door of the funeral home. He'd been a lady-killer in school and although time had somewhat softened his chin and middle, he was still incredibly handsome.

He caught her hands and kissed her cheeks. "Are you all right?"

"As well as can be expected, I guess."

He looked past her, a frown wrinkling his forehead. "You drove yourself?"

She had. Truth was, half a dozen people had offered to drive her tonight, including Buddy and Matt. She had refused them, even when they had begged her to reconsider. She had wanted to be alone.

"I'm a city girl," she murmured. "I'm used to taking care of myself."

He ushered her inside, clearly disapproving. "If you need anything, let me or one of the staff know. I'm expecting a big crowd."

Within twenty minutes he was proved correct—nearly the entire town was turning out to pay their respects. One after another, old friends, neighbors and acquaintances hugged her and offered their condolences. Some she recognized right off, others had to remind her who they were. Again and again, each expressed their shock and dismay over her father's death.

Nobody actually said the word. But it hung in the air anyway. It was written on their faces, in the carefully chosen words and softly modulated tones. It was there in the things they didn't say.

*Suicide.*

And with that word, their unspoken accusation. Their condemnation. She hadn't been there for him. He had needed her and she had been off taking care of herself.

*"Where were you, Avery, when your dad was so depressed he set himself on fire?"*

Hunter's taunt from two days before was burned into her brain. She told herself he had meant to hurt her. That he was angry, hurting, just plain mean. She told herself he wouldn't win unless she let him.

But she couldn't tell herself the one thing she longed to: that the things he'd said weren't true. Because they were.

And in that lay their power.

Minutes ticked by at an agonizing pace. The walls began to close in on her. Her head became light; her knees weak. She felt as if she were suffocating on the smell of colognes and flowers, cloying, too sweet. Each vying for dominance over the other.

*She had to get some air.*

*The patio.*

She inched in that direction, fighting her mounting panic. She reached the doors, slipped through them and out into the unseasonably cool night air. She hurried to the patio's edge; grasped the railing for support.

"Keep it together, Avery. You can't fall apart yet."

From the other side of the patio came an embarrassed-sounding cough. She swung in that direction, realizing she wasn't alone. That she had been talking to herself.

A man she didn't recognize stood on the other side of the patio, smoking. She scolded herself for the spear of irritation she felt. It was she who was intruding. Not he.

He met her eyes. "Sorry about your dad, Ms. Chauvin. He was a fine man."

"Thank you," she said, fighting past the emotion that rose in her throat and crossing to him. "I'm sorry, but do I know you?"

He looked embarrassed. "We've never met." He extinguished the cigarette and held out a hand. "John Price. Cypress Springs Volunteer Fire Department."

She shook his hand. "Good to met you."

He looked away, then back, expression pure misery. "I was on call that morning. I was the first to...see your dad."

*He had seen her father.*

*He had been the first.*

A half-dozen questions popped into her head. She uttered the first to her tongue. "What did you do then?"

He looked surprised. "Pardon?"

"After you found him, what happened next?"

"Called my captain. He called the state fire marshal. They sent the arson investigator assigned to our region. He's a good guy. Name's Ben Mitchell."

"And he called the coroner."

"Yup." He nodded. "Parish coroner. Coroner called Buddy."

"That's how it works?"

He shuffled slightly. "Yeah. Our job's elimination and containment of the fire itself, as well as search and rescue. Once our job's done, we call the state fire marshal. He determines how the fire started."

"And calls the coroner?"

"Yes. If there are victims. He calls the PD. Chain of command."

She felt herself emotionally disengaging, slipping into the role of journalist. It was an automatic thing, like breathing. She found it comforting. "And my father was dead when you got there?"

"No doubt about that. He—" The man bit back what he was about to say.

"What?"

"He was dead, Ms. Chauvin. Absolutely."

She shut her eyes, working to recall what she knew of death by burning. The arson piece she'd done. Those two little victims; she had seen a picture. Charred cadavers. Entirely black. Generic fea—

"Avery? Are you okay?"

At Matt's voice, she opened her eyes. He stood in the doorway, Cherry hovering just behind him.

"Fine." As she said the word, she realized she felt a hundred percent better than when she'd stepped outside.

"People are looking for you."

She nodded and turned back to the fireman. "John, I'd like to talk to you more about this. Could I give you a call, set up something?"

He shifted his gaze, obviously uncomfortable. "Sure, but I don't know what I could tell you that would—"

"Just for me," she said quickly. "For closure."

"I guess. You can reach me through the dispatcher."

She thanked him, turned and crossed to where Matt and Cherry waited.

"Ms. Chauvin?" She stopped and glanced back at the fireman. "You might want to call Ben Mitchell, at the state fire marshal's office in Baton Rouge. He could tell you a lot more than I can."

"Thanks, John. I'll do that."

"What was that all about?" Cherry asked.

"Nothing. I needed some air."

Cherry frowned slightly and glanced over her shoulder, obviously annoyed with her answer. "Jill Landry married him. You remember Jill? Met him through her sister, in Jackson."

"He seems like a nice guy."

"I guess."

Avery stopped and looked at the other woman. "Are you trying to tell me something, Cherry?"

"No. I just thought you should know...he's not from around here, Avery."

"He found Dad," she said sharply. "I was asking him about it. Is that okay with you?"

"I didn't mean anything—" She glanced from Avery to her brother, expression wounded. "I just...I'm worried about you, that's all."

"I'm a big girl, Cherry. I don't need protecting."

"I see that." Color flooded her cheeks. "I won't make that mistake again. Excuse me."

"She was only trying to be your friend," Matt said softly, tone reproachful. "She cares about you. We all do."

Avery swore softly. "I know. I just reacted."

Matt laid a hand on her arm. "I understand. Just don't—" He paused.

"What?"

"You're hurting. I'm sympathetic to that. We all are. But don't push us away, Avery. We love you."

She swallowed hard, eyes burning. He was right. Alienating the people who cared about her would do nothing but leave her more alone than she already was.

She caught his hand, squeezed his fingers. "Thank you," she whispered. "Your friendship means more to me than I can say."

He curled his fingers around hers. "I'm here for you, Avery. I've always been here for you."

The moment was broken by three older women. Members of her mother's quilting group, she learned.

Matt greeted the women, then excused himself. She watched as he made his way through the crowded room, heading in the direction Cherry had gone. He meant to find and comfort his sister.

She would apologize later, Avery promised herself, turning back to the three, accepting their condolences. The Quilting Bees, as they called themselves, exited, leaving Avery momentarily alone.

She swept her gaze over the gathering, stopping on a group of men who stood at the far end of the room. They spoke to one another quietly, expressions intent. She recognized several of them; though by face not name. None had spoken to her tonight. As she watched, one of them nodded toward someone outside their circle. The others glanced in the direction he indicated.

She turned. They seemed to be discussing a woman she didn't recognize. Tall, slim and sandy-haired, she wore a simple black skirt and white, button-front blouse. She was alone, standing by a tall, potted fern. Something about her expression looked lost.

Avery frowned and shifted her gaze back to the men. They were definitely looking at the woman. One of them laughed. She didn't know why that struck her as wrong, but it did.

She darted another glance at the woman. Who was she? A friend of one of the men?

"Avery, honey, I'm so sorry."

She dragged her gaze from the group, meeting the eyes of the woman who had been Avery's first-grade teacher. She accepted the woman's condolences, hug and promised to call if she needed anything.

Avery turned back toward the group of men. They had dispersed. The woman they'd been talking about was gone as well. She checked out the thinning crowd, searching for her without luck. She wondered if she had imagined the whole thing.

It wouldn't surprise her, she acknowledged, glancing toward her father's closed casket and experiencing a moment of pure panic. Nothing would surprise her anymore.

CHAPTER 12

Hunter stared at his computer screen, the things he'd written swimming before his eyes. Mocking him. With a sound of disgust he hit the delete button and watched as the cursor ate one letter after another until nothing was left but the blank page.

How could he write when the words filling his head were ones he had flung at Avery? How could he envision his characters when her image crowded his mind? Her hurt expression. The accusation in her eyes.

She had looked at him as if he were some sort of monster.

*Dammit!* Hunter pushed away from the desk and stood. At the kitchen door, Sarah whined to go out. The dog had been antsy and agitated all evening—much as he himself had been.

He ignored her and made his way through the apartment and to the office in front. Empty, dark save for the blinking message light on his answer machine, he recalled the space as it had been: filled with the scent and color of flowers. Now it smelled as colorless as it looked. Like blank paper and law books.

He crossed to the front window and peered out at the dark street. From this vantage point he could see Gallagher's roof, one block over. They were all at Phillip's wake, he thought. His mother and father. Cherry. Matt. Most likely the entire town.

That's the kind of town this was.

He had figured Avery wouldn't care to see him. And he sure as hell hadn't wanted to see the Stevens clan. He wasn't certain he would have been able to hold his tongue.

And the last thing Avery needed was a confrontation.

He pressed the heels of his hands to his eyes. *Phillip. What a mess. Dammit.*

Hunter dropped his hands, acknowledging grief. Frustration. Truth was, he longed to be there. Longed to pay his respects to a man he had always admired. One who had become his friend. And who he now missed.

Some might have considered their friendship unusual, he supposed. After all, their ages had been separated by thirty years. But they'd had loneliness in common. Feelings of alienation. And a tremendous amount of history.

History that had included Avery.

*Yeah, great. Avery.* Some send-off for his friend. Flinging accusations at her. Hitting her where she was most vulnerable. Where she was already hurting.

She had called him hateful. And cruel.

Maybe she was right, he thought. Most probably she was.

What was it about him? Why was everything always black or white? Why couldn't he swallow his thoughts? Blur his personal line just a little? And who the hell was he to think he owned the high moral ground?

*Everything he touched turned to shit.*

Hunter glanced over his shoulder, toward the apartment. He longed for a drink. He needed one. The need clawed at him. He pictured himself walking to the kitchen, selecting the immediate poison of choice and drinking until he no longer possessed the ability to question the course of his life.

Drink to the point where he felt little but cynical amusement when someone he cared about called him hateful and cruel.

He swallowed hard against the urge. Wallowing instead in the pain. His anger and frustration. His feelings of loss. For they were real. Authentic. As much a part of life as breathing.

Never again, he promised himself, fisting his fingers. Never again would he anesthetize himself to life's highs and lows.

Sarah pawed at the kitchen door, then woofed softly. Hunter turned in that direction. She hadn't been out that long ago. Or had she? When he worked, he lost track of both time and the mundane details of life.

He exited the office and made his way to the kitchen. The dog whined. "Okay, girl." He grabbed the leash from the hook, snapped it to her collar and opened the door. She leaped forward, dragging him through the door and into the alley before he got a firm grip on the lead.

When he did, he yanked hard on it. Sarah heeled.

"What's up with you?" Hunter bent and scratched behind her ears. Instead of sinking on her haunches and sagging against him in grateful ecstasy, she stayed at attention, muscles taut. Quivering.

He frowned and turned his gaze in the direction of hers—the narrow, dark alley. "What is it, Sarah? What's wrong?"

She growled, low in her throat. The fur along the ridge of her back stood up.

"Anyone there?" he called.

Silence answered. He squinted at the darkness ahead, working to make out details, differentiate shape from shadow. Wishing for Sarah's acute sense of smell and hearing. He called out once more. Again, without answer.

Wondering at the wisdom of what he was about to do, he eased his grip slightly. The dog charged forward. Or tried to. He held her back, forcing her to proceed slowly, giving his eyes time to adjust to the dark.

As they reached the middle point of the alley, she angled right. Her growl deepened. Hunter drew back on the leash, struggling to hold her. The dog's muscles bunched and rippled as she fought him, digging in with each step.

Produce crates, he saw. A stack of them sent askew. From the

Piggly Wiggly around front. And tipped trash barrels, discarded bakery and deli items spewing out into the alleyway. Sarah began to bark. Not a high, shrill bark of excitement, but a fierce one. Deep, threatening.

"Sarah," he chided, "all this over a little spoiled chow?" He bent and thumped her side. "Or is the possum or coon that made this mess still hanging around?"

The sound of his voice did little to comfort her. As he moved to straighten, something peeking out from under the pile of crates and boxes caught his eye.

An animal's tail. No wonder Sarah was going bonkers. The creature that caused this messed had gotten itself trapped under one of the tipped crates. It could be hurt, maybe dead.

He glanced around, looking for something he could use to move the crates. No way was he about to use his hand. Cornered creatures defended themselves ferociously. Especially when hurt.

He spotted a broom propped in the opposite doorway. He retrieved it, then wedged its handle through the crate's wooden slats and tipped it up. His stomach rose to his throat. He took a step backward, Sarah's frenzied barking ringing in his ears.

*Not an animal's tail. Human hair.*

The woman it belonged to stared up at him, face screwed into a death howl.

# CHAPTER 13

Hunter stumbled backward, dragging Sarah with him. Bending, he propped his hands on his knees and dragged in deep breaths. *Steady, Stevens. Don't throw up. Dear God, don't—*

The image of the woman filled his head. He squeezed his eyes shut and sucked in another lungful of oxygen. *A woman....Jesus... What to do? What—*

*Make certain she's dead. Call the cops.*

Hunter expelled a long breath and straightened slowly. He turned his gaze toward the woman. She hadn't moved. She stared fixedly at him, mouth stretched into that horrible scream.

He hadn't a doubt she was dead. And that her death had been excruciating. But still, he should check her pulse. Shouldn't he? Wasn't that what they always did in the movies and on TV? That or fall completely apart.

*Not an option, Stevens.* He shortened his hold on Sarah's lead and inched closer. Carefully, he moved a couple of the toppled crates, revealing the woman's arm.

Sometime before she'd died, she'd polished her fingernails a bright, bloody red. Now, the contrast between the red polish and the fish-belly white of her skin affected him like a shouted obscenity.

Hunter moved closer. He circled his fingers around the woman's wrist. She was cold. Her skin spongy to the touch.

*No pulse. Not even a flutter.*

He yanked his hand back, instinctively wiping it against his blue jeans, and straightened.

*Get the cops. His dad. Or Matt.*

*They were all around the corner. At Phillip's wake.*

He considered his choices and decided he could notify them as quickly on foot as he could by calling the department. Decision made, he started forward at a run. As if sensing his urgency, Sarah stayed by his side. They cleared the alley, making the block to Gallagher's in less than three minutes.

He took the front steps two at a time, ordered Sarah to stay and burst through Gallagher's front door. Danny Gallagher stood just inside the door. His eyes widened. "Hunter, what—"

"Where are they?"

Danny pointed. "Number one, but—"

Hunter darted forward, not waiting for him to finish. He spotted his family the moment he entered the room. They stood in a tight clutch.

*Stevens clan against the world. Minus one, of course.*

He strode forward; the crowd parted silently for him. Conversations ceased. Expressions registered surprise. Then excitement. They expected a scene. They wanted one.

*He could liven things up, all right. Just not for the reason they thought.*

Hunter saw the moment his family became aware of his presence. They turned. Their gazes settled on him. Matt frowned; Buddy's eyebrows shot up even as his stance altered subtly, becoming defensive. Preparing for battle. His mother looked particularly pale, her eyes wide, alarmed. Cherry averted her gaze when he looked at her.

*As American as apple pie and Prozac.*

*Damn them all.*

"Dad," he said, not bothering with a greeting, "we need to talk."

Matt stepped forward, fists clenched. "You picked a hell of a time for one of your confrontations. Get out of here before Avery—"

"Back off," Hunter snapped. "This is an emergency, Dad. We need to speak privately."

"It'll have to keep, son. Tonight I'm honoring my best friend."

Hunter leaned toward him. He lowered his voice. "There's been a murder. Think that'll keep?"

From behind him came the sound of a sharply drawn breath. He turned. Avery had come up behind them, that she'd heard was obvious by her distraught expression.

She shifted her gaze from him to his dad, then Matt. "What's going on?"

Hunter held out a hand. "I'm sorry, Avery. I didn't mean to involve you in this."

Matt stepped between them. "Let's take this outside."

Hunter was happy to oblige. He followed his father and brother out front. Sarah thumped her tail against the porch when she saw him.

The two men faced him. Matt spoke first. "This better not be your idea of a sick—"

"Joke? I wish it was."

Quickly, Hunter explained, starting with Sarah pawing at the door and finishing with checking the woman's pulse.

Buddy and Matt exchanged glances, then met his eyes once more. Buddy took the lead. "Are you certain the woman was murdered?"

Hunter hesitated. He wasn't, he realized. She could have been a street person. Or someone who worked at one of the businesses on the alley. She could have had a heart attack, fallen into the crates, causing them to topple.

He pictured those ruby-colored nails and his relief died. Street people didn't get manicures. The businesses lining the alley all closed at five; if the woman worked in one of those businesses, wouldn't a loved one be looking for her by now? Wouldn't they think to check the alley?

Still, the woman could have died of natural causes.

"Hunter?"

He blinked, refocusing on his father. "I just assumed...because she was dead, in the alley..."

"Show us where she is."

Hunter did, leading the men to the spot. As he passed his door he could hear the puppies crying and stopped to put Sarah in. His dad and brother continued without him.

"Son of a bitch. Shit."

"Oh, goddamn."

*They'd found her. Their brief responses expressed volumes.*

Hunter made his way up the alley. He hung back a few feet, keeping his gaze averted as the other two men carefully shifted the crates to get a better look at the victim. He listened to their dialogue.

"This woman did not die of natural causes."

"No shit."

"Oh man, she's torn up bad."

That had come from Matt; he sounded weird, more than shaken. As if someone had a hold on his vocal cords and was squeezing. Hard.

"Slow down," his father warned. "We don't know what happened. We have to be careful not to destroy any evidence."

Hunter glanced at his brother. He saw him nod at his father's advice. Saw him trying to pull himself together. Saw the moment he got a grip on himself.

"Look, she's propped up on the right—" Matt squatted and peered closely at the corpse. "But no lividity on her left side."

"So she's been moved."

"Bingo."

It was human nature, Hunter supposed, that made him look her way. He immediately regretted it, but couldn't tear his gaze away. The woman's lower half was naked, her legs spread. It looked as if her panties had been ripped away, her mini skirt shoved up over her hips, bunching at her waist.

*Blood...everywhere. Smeared over her thighs, belly.*

Bile rose in his throat. He averted his gaze, struggling to breathe. Not to throw up.

"I've got to call this in," Buddy said, voice thick. "Get a crew here, ASAP."

"You need the sheriff's department's help on this one, Dad?" Matt sounded just as shaky. Hunter realized that for all their years in law enforcement, they had little experience with this kind of thing.

*This kind of thing? He was already dehumanizing it. Making it palpable.*

*Call it what it was. Murder. The violent extinguishing of a human life.*

"Hell yes," his father answered. "We're not equipped...this... It's Sallie Waguespack all over again."

Buddy and Matt made their calls. Within twenty minutes a crew consisting of both the Cypress Springs Police Department and the West Feliciana Parish Sheriff's Department had assembled at the scene.

Hunter stood back as a CSPD officer secured the scene with yellow tape. Another stood at each end of the alley to keep the curious away. The sheriff's department's crime scene guys had begun to do their thing: they'd set up portable spotlights to illuminate the alley so they could begin the painstaking job of collecting evidence. The police photographer was shooting the scene from every imaginable angle.

Except from the perspective of the victim, Hunter thought. Her eyes would never see anything again.

He turned his back on the scene and pressed the heels of his hands to his eyes. Still he pictured her, as if her image had been stamped on the inside of his eyelids. How long would it take to fade? he wondered. Would it ever?

"Need to ask you a few questions, Hunter."

The request came from Matt. Hunter dropped his hands and looked over his shoulder at his brother, realizing then how tired he was. Bone tired. "Figured. What do you want to know?"

"Tell us again the sequence of events that led to your finding the victim. As exactly as you can recall. Every detail."

*The victim.* Hunter angled a glance her way. "She have a name?"

"Yeah," Buddy answered. "Elaine St. Claire. Keep it to yourself for a couple hours until we notify her next of kin."

He wasn't surprised his father knew her name—he knew everybody in his town. "Who was she?"

"A local barfly. Party girl." Buddy glanced over his shoulder at her, grimaced and looked back. "Last I heard, she'd left town."

She hadn't gotten far. Poor woman. He sometimes thought of Cypress Springs as a spiderweb. Once tangled in its threads, there was no escape.

If the town was the web, who was the spider?

Matt made a sound of irritation. "Can we get on with it?"

"Sure." Hunter narrowed his eyes on his brother. "What do you want to know?"

His brother repeated his question and for the second time Hunter detailed how he had come upon Elaine St. Claire.

"And that's it? You're certain?" Buddy asked.

"Yes."

Matt frowned. "And you heard nothing, no commotion from the alley?"

"No. Nothing. I was working."

"Working?"

"At my computer."

"The dog, did she bark anytime during the evening?"

Hunter searched his memory. "Not that I noticed."

"A big dog like her must have a pretty big bark."

"I get preoccupied when I'm working. Tune out the world."

"What were you working on?"

Hunter hesitated. He didn't want his family to know about the novel. So he lied. "A divorce settlement."

Matt arched an eyebrow. "You don't seem so certain."

"No, I'm certain."

"Whose divorce?"

Hunter shook his head, disgusted. "That, as I'm sure you know, is confidential. And has nothing to do with why we're standing here."

Matt turned toward Buddy. "Could she have been here a while?"

"No way. The alley is busy during business hours. Employees out for a smoke, deliveries, kids skateboarding."

"That means she was dumped here sometime after the close of business today."

Buddy nodded. "I'll get one of my guys to talk to Jean about the crates, when they were put out." Jean, Hunter knew, was the owner of the grocery. "Make certain they were neatly stacked when she locked up."

"What about the trash barrels?" Matt asked. "Why aren't they depositing this stuff in the Dumpster?"

"I know the answer to that," Hunter offered. "If she's short staffed at the end of the day, she'll leave them in the barrels until morning." The two men looked at him. Hunter shrugged. "I ran into her one morning while walking Sarah."

"It seems this alley *is* a busy place."

Hunter frowned at Matt's tone. "Are we finished here? Can I go?"

"How much traffic does the alley see at night?"

"It's dead. Pardon the word choice."

"No traffic at all?" Matt questioned.

"Kids making out sometimes. Somebody turning in by mistake, realizing it and backing out. Me and Sarah, out for a walk. That's about it."

"You hear the kids, the cars, from your apartment?"

"Yeah. Most of the time."

"But tonight you didn't see or hear anything?"

Hunter stiffened at the sarcasm in his brother's voice. At his smirk. "If that's it, I'd like to go. It's been a rough night."

"Go on," Buddy said. "When we know more, we might need to speak with you again."

Hunter walked away, aware of his father's and brother's speculative gazes on his back. He longed to look back at them, to read their expressions. His every instinct shouted for him to do it.

He wouldn't give them the satisfaction. Wouldn't let them know just how weird this encounter had made him feel.

They'd treated him like a stranger.

A stranger whose sincerity they doubted.

"Hey, Hunter?"

He stopped, turned. Met his brother's gaze. "You remember anything else, it'd help. Give one of us a call."

## CHAPTER 14

The morning of her father's funeral dawned bright and warm. Turnout proved much smaller than the wake, mostly close family friends and neighbors. But Avery had expected that.

Lilah stood on her right, Buddy on her left. Each held her arm in a gesture of comfort and support. Lilah seemed much stronger than the night before, though she cried softly throughout the service. Matt stood behind his mother, Cherry beside him. Directly across from her stood Hunter. Alone. Expression resolute.

Avery's gaze went to his. She saw no grief there. No pity or sympathy. Only anger. Only the chip he carried on his shoulder. A shudder moved over her. Without compassion, what would a man become? What would such a man be capable of?

*He would be capable of anything.*

*He would be a monster.*

The pastor who had baptized her spoke warmly of the person her father had been, of the difference he had made in the community and to so many individuals' lives.

"He was a light in a sometimes dark world," the pastor finished. "That light will surely be missed."

She shifted her gaze to the casket, acknowledging dizziness. Conscious of rubberiness in her legs. A feeling of being disconnected from the earth.

"Ashes to ashes—"

*"He doused himself with diesel fuel and lit a match."*

"Dust to dust—"

*"Where were you, Avery, when your dad was so depressed he set himself on fire?"*

Avery couldn't breathe. She swayed slightly. Buddy tightened his grip on her arm, steadying her.

This wasn't right, she thought, a thread of panic winding through her. Her father couldn't have taken his own life. He couldn't be gone.

She hadn't said goodbye.

*It was her fault.*

Avery stared at the casket. Scenes of grief she had witnessed over the years played in her head: weeping widows; too-solemn children; despairing family, friends, neighbors, colleagues, all of humanity.

Death. The ultimate loss. The universal gut shot.

She fought the urge to throw herself on the casket. To scream and flail her fists and sob. She closed her eyes, fighting for calm. He would rest beside her mother, she told herself. His partner in this life and the next.

Or would he? Tears choked her. Would his sin separate them for eternity? Who would absolve him of it?

Who would absolve her?

"Avery, honey, it's over."

*Over. The end.*

*Ashes to ashes...doused himself in diesel fuel and lit a...where were you, Avery? Where were you when he...*

*Dust to dust.*

"Avery? Sweetheart, it's time."

She looked blankly at Buddy and nodded. He led her away from the grave. She shifted her gaze, vision swimming. It landed on the group of men from the wake. All in black. Standing together. Again.

Seven of them. They were staring at her. One of them laughed.

A sound passed her lips. She stumbled and Buddy caught her. "Avery, are you all right?"

She looked up at him, pinpricks of light dancing before her eyes. "Those men, that group over there. Who are they?"

"Where?"

"Over th—"

*They were gone.*

She shook her head. "They were just—" She swayed again. A roaring sound filled her ears. Blood, she realized. Rushing. Plummeting.

"Matt, quick! Give me a—"

When Avery came to, she lay on the ground looking up at the cloudless blue sky. A half-dozen people had gathered around her and were gazing down at her in concern.

"You fainted," someone said softly.

Buddy, she realized, blinking. She shifted her gaze. Matt. Cherry. Lilah. Pastor Dastugue. The world came into clear focus. The moments before she fainted filled her head.

Making a sound of dismay, she struggled to get up.

Matt laid a hand gently on her shoulder, holding her down. "Don't rush it. Take a deep breath, make certain you're steady."

She complied. A moment later, they allowed her to come carefully to a sitting position, then ease to her feet. Matt kept his arm around her, even though she assured him she was fine.

"I'm so embarrassed," she said. "I feel like an idiot."

"Nonsense." Lilah brushed leaves and other debris from her black jacket. "When's the last time you ate?"

She didn't know; she couldn't remember, couldn't seem to gather her thoughts. She wet her lips. "I don't know...lunch yesterday, I guess."

"No wonder you passed out," she said, distressed. "I should have brought you a meal."

Avery looked at Matt. "Did you see them?"

"Who?"

"That group of men. Standing together. There were seven of them."

Matt and Buddy exchanged glances. "Where?"

She pointed to the spot where the group had been standing. "Over there."

They looked in that direction, then back at her. "I don't recall seeing a group," Matt said. He looked at Cherry and Lilah. "Did either of you?"

The two women shook their heads no. Matt met her eyes. "Are you certain of what you saw?"

"Yes, I...yes. They were at the wake, too."

"Who were they?"

She rubbed her head, confused. At the wake, she had thought she recognized several of them. Now she couldn't recall who they had been.

*She was losing her mind.*

"I don't know. I..." Her words trailed off. She moved her gaze from one face to another, reading the concern in their expressions.

*They thought she was losing it, too.*

Lilah slipped an arm around her shoulders. "Poor baby, you've been through so much. Come now, I have finger sandwiches and cookies back at the house. We'll fix you right up."

Lilah did fix her up—as best as was possible anyway, considering the circumstances. She and the rest of the Stevens clan hovered around her, making certain she had plenty to eat, insisting she stay off her feet, shooing people off when she began to fade.

When the last mourner left, Matt drove her home. She laid her head against the rest and closed her eyes. After a moment, she opened them and looked at him. "Can I ask you something?"

He glanced at her, then back at the road. "Shoot."

"You really didn't see a group of men huddled together? Not at the wake or funeral?"

"I really didn't."

"I was afraid you were going to say that."

He reached across the seat, caught her hand and squeezed. "Stress and grief play havoc with the mind."

"I'd heard that."

He frowned slightly, looked at her again. "I'm worried about you, Avery."

She laughed without humor. "Funny you should say that, I'm worried about me, too."

He squeezed her fingers again, then returned his hand to the wheel. "It'll get better."

"Promise?"

"Sure."

They fell silent. She studied him, his profile, as he drove. Strong nose and chin. Nice mouth, full without being feminine. Kissable. She remembered that.

Damn handsome. Better-looking than he'd been all those years ago.

"Matt?" He cut another glance her way. "What was that about, with Hunter last night?"

"I don't think now's the time—"

"People were whispering about it at your mother's."

He turned onto her parents' street. "A woman was found murdered last night."

"Hunter found her?"

"Yes, in the alley behind his place."

In the places she had lived since leaving Cypress Springs, murders were commonplace. But here...

*Things like that weren't supposed to happen in Cypress Springs.*

*But neither were beloved physicians supposed to set themselves on fire.*

"How was she murdered?"

He reached her parents' house and eased up the driveway. At the top, Matt stopped, cut the engine. He angled in his seat to face her. "Avery, you don't need to know this. You have enough to deal with right now."

"How?" she persisted.

"I can't tell you. And I won't. I'm sorry."

"Are you?"

He caught her hand. "Don't be angry."

"I'm tired of everyone around here trying to protect me."

"Really? Beats the alternative, don't you think? I'm sure Elaine St. Claire would think so. If she were alive."

*The murdered woman. Obviously.* Heat stung Avery's cheeks. She sounded like a petulant child.

She curled her fingers around his. "I'm sorry, Matt. I'm not myself."

"It's okay. I understand." He brought their joined hands to his mouth, pressed a kiss to her knuckles, then released hers. "Are you sure you're going to be okay here alone?"

"There you go," she teased, "taking care of me again."

He returned her smile. "Guilty as charged."

"I'll be fine." She grabbed the door handle. Popped open the door. "I'm thinking nap. A long one."

He reached across the seat and caught her hand once more. She turned and met his eyes. His were filled with regret. "I really am sorry, Avery."

"I know, Matt. And that helps. A lot."

She climbed out of the vehicle, slammed the door and started toward the front walk. When she reached the door she glanced back. Matt hadn't made a move to leave.

She lifted her hand and waved. He returned the gesture, started up the vehicle and backed down the driveway. She watched as he disappeared from sight, then unlocked her door and stepped inside.

The phone was ringing. She hurried to answer it. "Hello?"

"Is this Dr. Phillip Chauvin's daughter?"

The voice was a woman's. Deep. Coarse-sounding. The voice of a lifelong chain-smoker.

"This is Avery Chauvin," she answered. "Can I help—"

"To hell with you," the woman spat. "And to hell with your father. He got what he deserved. You will, too."

In the next instant, the line went dead.

# CHAPTER 15

For the next twelve hours, Avery thought of little else but the woman's call. The things she'd said had played over in her head, a disturbing chant.

*He got what he deserved.*

*You will, too.*

At first she had been stunned. Shocked that someone could say such a thing about her father. Those emotions had given way to anger. She had tried dialing *69 only to discover her dad hadn't subscribed to the callback service. She had considered calling Buddy or Matt, then had discarded the thought. What could they do? Assure her the woman was just a crank? Advise her to get an unlisted number?

The woman could be a crank, that was true.

But what if she wasn't? What if the woman's call represented a legitimate threat?

Avery paced, thoughts whirling. Her father had been both a

Christian and physician. He'd believed in the sanctity of life. Had devoted his own life to preserving it.

What if her first reaction to his suicide had been the correct one? What if he hadn't killed himself?

Avery stopping pacing, working to recall word for word that last message he'd left her.

*"I need to talk to you. I was hoping— There's something... I'll...try later. Goodbye, pumpkin."*

When news of his suicide had reached her, she'd assumed that call had been a desperate plea for help. She'd assumed he'd called to give her a chance to talk him out of it. Or to say goodbye. She'd agonized over not taking that call ever since. She'd told herself that even if he hadn't spoken directly of suicide, she would have known. Would have picked up something in his voice. In her *if onlys* she would have been able to save his life.

*He got what he deserved.*

*You will, too.*

Those words, that threat, changed everything. Perhaps her dad had realized he was in danger. That he had an enemy. Maybe he had wanted to discuss it with her. Maybe he'd needed to bounce something by her.

He had done that a lot.

Avery acknowledged that what she was contemplating flew in the face of what everyone else believed to be true. People she trusted and cared about. Matt. Buddy. Lilah. The entire town.

Avery breathed deeply, battling her conflicting emotions: loyalty to people she loved, distrust of her own emotional state, suspicion for a criminal justice system that made mistakes, that often went with what looked obvious rather than digging for the truth.

But if he hadn't killed himself, that meant he'd been—

*Murdered.*

The word, its repercussions, ricocheted through her. A murderer in Cypress Springs? Two, she realized, thinking of the woman Hunter had found in the alley. Could they have been killed by the same person?

That hardly seemed likely, she acknowledged, becoming aware

of the fast, heavy beat of her heart. Just as unlikely, however, was the idea of two murderers in Cypress Springs.

Avery returned her thoughts to her father, his death. Who would have wanted to hurt her father? He'd been loved and respected by everyone.

Not everyone. He'd had an enemy. The woman's call proved that. Obviously, she herself had an enemy now as well.

*He got what he deserved.*

*You will, too.*

She crossed to the front window, inched aside the drape and peered out at the dark street. A few cars parked along the curbs, all appeared empty.

From what she could see. Which frankly, wasn't a hell of a lot.

Avery drew her eyebrows together. Had the woman called before, when Avery was out? She could have. Her father had neither caller ID nor an answering machine. Had she been watching Avery? Following her? Laying in wait? She could be anywhere. As close as a cell phone.

*Don't get paranoid, Chauvin. This is a story. Get the pieces. Figure it out.*

Avery released the drape, turned and headed for the kitchen. She glanced at the wall clock, registering the time: 1:27 a.m. She dug a message tablet and pen out of the drawer by the phone, laid it on the counter, then crossed to her newly purchased Mr. Coffee coffeemaker. She filled the glass carafe with water, measured coffee into the basket, then flipped on the machine.

While the coffee brewed, she searched her memory for what she knew of the act of murder. She had never worked the crime beat, but had managed to absorb a bit from sharing a cubicle with someone who did. He had been the zealous, self-important sort, had loved to hear the sound of his own voice and for some quirky reason, had thought crime scene details served as a sort of aphrodisiac for women.

Who would have thought she would ever be grateful for those four, long months of cubicle cohabitation?

The coffeepot burbled its last filtered drop and she filled a mug. She carried it, the tablet and pen to the big oak dining table and sat down. Obviously, if her father had been murdered, it hadn't been a random act of violence. That left a crime of passion or premeditated murder. Zealous Pete, her cubicle mate, had called love, hate and greed the Holy Trinity of murder. Meaning, most killers were motivated by one of those three.

She brought the mug to her mouth and sipped. Her hand shook slightly, whether from exhaustion or nerves she didn't know. She had a hard time imagining her gentle, kindhearted father being involved with anyone or anything that would lead to murder.

She squeezed her eyes shut. *Get outside the box, Avery. Let go of what you think you know.*

*Get the pieces. Then place them in the puzzle.*

She opened her eyes; picked up the pen. Her next step was to find out as much as she could about her dad's death. Talk to Ben Mitchell. The coroner. Buddy about his investigation.

And while she was at it, she would see what she could discover about Elaine St. Claire's murder to ascertain whether there was a connection between the two.

Later that morning, Avery paid a visit to Ben Mitchell at the state fire marshal's office in Baton Rouge. She had discovered that arson investigators were assigned by region, for the entire parish. Cypress Springs fell into region eight. She had also learned arson investigators had the authority to arrest those suspected of arson and to carry firearms.

Ben Mitchell, a middle-aged man with dark brown hair sprinkled with gray, was that investigator.

He greeted her warmly. "Have a seat, Ms. Chauvin."

She took the one directly across from his, laid her reporter's notebook on her lap and smiled. "Please, call me Avery."

He inclined his head. "Your dad was a good man."

"You knew him?"

"I think everybody in the parish did, in one capacity or another. He helped my sister through a tough time." He lowered his voice. "Cervical cancer. Even after she switched to an oncologist, he stood by her every step of the way."

*He'd been that kind of a doctor. It had always been about the patients as people, about their health. Never about money.*

"Thank you," she said. "I think he was a good man, too."

His gaze dropped to the tablet, then returned to hers. "How can I help you?"

She laced her fingers. "As I mentioned, I spoke with John Price at my father's wake. He suggested I contact you. I'm curious about...about my father's death."

"I don't understand."

She met his gaze evenly. "May I be completely honest with you?"

"Of course."

"Thank you." She took a deep breath, preparing her words, intending to be anything but completely honest. "I'm having some difficulty dealing with my father's death. With...understanding it. I thought if you could...share what you found at the scene...I might be able to...that it would help me."

His expression softened with sympathy. "What do you want to know."

"What you saw at the scene. The path your investigation took. Your official findings."

"Are you certain you want to hear this?" he asked.

She tightened her fingers. "Yes."

"Arson investigators study what caused a fire. Where it started and how long it burned. We can tell what kind of fuel was used by the fire's path, how hot and how long it burned."

"And what did my father's fire tell you?"

"Your father used diesel fuel, which, unlike gasoline, ignites on contact rather than on vapors. To do what he did, the diesel fuel was a better choice."

"Any other fuel do the same thing?"

"Jet fuel. JP-5 to the trade. Burns hotter, too. Harder to get." He paused as if to collect his thoughts. Or carefully choose his words. "Are you at all familiar with death by burning?"

"Refamiliarize me." He hesitated and she leaned forward. "I'm a journalist. Give me the facts. I can handle them."

"All right. First off, the human body doesn't actually burn to ash, the way it would if cremated. A house fire, for example, burns at about one thousand degrees. To completely incinerate, a body requires heat of around seventeen hundred degrees. The body maintains its form. The skin basically melts but doesn't disintegrate. It's not uncommon for areas of soft tissue to survive the fire.

"There's a shrinking that occurs," he continued. "For example, a two-hundred-pound man will weigh one hundred fifty pounds burned. The clothes, flesh and hair burn. The features, including the lips, remain. All solid black. Generic. Meaning the person no longer resembles themselves."

*Her father couldn't have done this. Could he?*

"How often do you see suicide committed this way?"

"Almost never."

"Why not?" she asked, though she had her own idea why. Through her profession she had learned the importance of not putting words in other people's mouths.

"Understand, I'm not a psychologist. I'm an expert on fire. Anything I offer would be my opinion, one not necessarily based on fact."

"I'd like to hear it anyway."

"Most people who choose to take their own life, want to get the job done. They want to go fast and as painlessly as possible."

"And burning to death is the antithesis of that."

"In my opinion."

"Yes." Avery glanced at her tablet, then back at the man. "Do you believe my father knew the difference in the way diesel fuel and gasoline burns?"

"Don't know. Could have been he chose the diesel fuel because he had it on hand."

"He siphoned the gas from his Mercedes."

"Yes."

"You ruled out arson? No question in your mind?"

He nodded. "As I mentioned earlier, following a fire's path tells us its story. With arson, the source of the fire is typically an outside perimeter. In addition, we find the gas can, rags, whatever the arsonist used to set the fire. People are funny, they think we won't find them or something. 'Course, some don't care."

"But my dad's case wasn't like that?"

"No. The fire started with your father and moved out from there. The remnants of the syphoning hose were found with him."

"Was there anything unusual about the scene? Anything that gave you pause?"

He drew his eyebrows together, as if carefully sifting through his memory. "Found one of your dad's bedroom slippers on the path between the house and the garage."

"And the other one?"

"There was no sign of it. I suspect he was wearing it."

"Where on the path?"

He thought a moment. "A few feet from the kitchen door."

Her dad had always worn slip-on-style slippers. He'd lost one just outside the door. Why hadn't he stopped for it? That didn't make sense. She wasn't an expert in human behavior, but it seemed to her that stopping for it would be an automatic response.

"You don't find that odd?" she asked.

"Odd?"

"Have you ever tried to walk in one shoe, Ben? It feels wrong. A kind of sensory disruption."

"But I imagine a man in your father's emotional state would be totally focused on what he intended to do. Although never in that position myself, I suspect it would be all consuming."

Avery wasn't convinced but dropped the subject anyway. "Anything else?"

He shifted his gaze slightly. "It appeared as if he crawled a couple feet toward the door. After he was aflame."

*He'd changed his mind. He tried to crawl for help.*

*It had been too late.*

She struggled to keep her despair from showing. Failing miserably, she knew.

"I'm sorry. I shouldn't have said—"

"No." She held up a hand. It trembled. "I appreciate your candor. It may be hard for you to understand, but knowing the facts will help me deal with this. I *have* to know exactly what happened."

"I do understand, being that kind of person myself." He glanced at his watch. "Have you talked to Buddy about his investigation? Or to the coroner about his findings?"

"Buddy, though not in great detail. I haven't spoken to the coroner yet. But I plan to."

He stood and held out his hand. "Good luck, Avery."

She followed him up. Took his hand. "Thanks, Ben. I appreciate the time." She started for the door, then stopped and looked back at him. "Ben, one last question. Do you have any doubt he committed suicide?"

From his expression she saw that the question surprised him. He hesitated, as if choosing his words carefully. "My job is to determine how and where a fire starts. Cause and circumstance of death fall to the coroner and police."

"Of course," she said, turning toward the door once more.

"Avery?" She looked back. "Buddy did a good job on this. I've never seen him so...shaken. He didn't want it to be true either."

*But even the most conscientious cop made mistakes. It happened, things went unnoticed, slipped through the cracks.*

But she didn't say those things to him. Instead, she thanked him again, turned and walked away.

## CHAPTER 16

Hunter hadn't set foot in the Cypress Springs Police Department in thirteen years. It hadn't changed, he saw. But then, in Cypress Springs nothing seemed to change, no matter how many years passed.

He had come today because he had remembered something about the other night that might prove useful to the St. Claire murder investigation.

And because since finding the dead woman thirty-six hours ago, he had been unable to think of much else. He couldn't put the image of the dead woman out of his head.

The front desk stood empty. Not for long, Hunter surmised by the steaming mug of coffee and half-eaten doughnut sitting on a napkin on its top. Hunter didn't wait, instead he strolled past as if he still had every right to do so.

He found the door to his father's office open, the room empty. Hunter stepped inside. It smelled like his dad, he realized. And like his childhood.

Hunter scowled at the thought, at the rush of memories that flooded his mind. Of playing under the big, old oak desk, of him and Matt staring openmouthed as their dad chewed out a couple underlings, of his last visit to the office, on his way to college.

Hunter had attempted, one last time, to broach his feelings of exclusion and alienation from his family.

*"Dad, just tell me what I've done. Tell me why you've shut me out. You and Mom, Matt and Cherry. It's like I'm not one of you anymore. Talk to me, Dad. I'll do whatever it takes to make it better."*

But his father hadn't had time for him. He had brushed him off, insisting Hunter was imagining it. That the fault lay with Hunter's perceptions, not reality.

Angry, hurt, he had left, promising that he would show them all, someday, somehow he would show them.

Hunter's gaze landed on the desk. A file folder stamped *Photos* lay on its top.

From the murder scene? he wondered, inching toward the desk. He saw immediately that they were; the file's tab bore the name St. Claire, Elaine.

"Hello, son."

*Son.* Hunter turned, feeling that one, quietly spoken word like a punch to his gut. He met his father's gaze. "Dad."

His father's shifted to the desk, then back to his. "What brings you in this morning?"

"The St. Claire murder."

The man nodded and ambled across to his desk. He motioned to the chair directly in front of it. "Have a seat."

Hunter would have preferred to stand, but he sat anyway. "Place hasn't changed a bit."

Buddy settled into his own chair. It creaked under his weight. "It's been a while."

"Thirteen years."

Hunter moved his gaze over the room. His Little League championship trophy was gone, as was the picture that had sat front and center on his dad's desk, of the two of them with the prizewinning fish at the Tarpon Rodeo. He scanned the shelves and walls, taking a quick, mental inventory.

He returned his gaze to the other man. "You've done some redecorating. Looks like you removed every trace of my existence."

"You left us, Hunter."

"Did I? Maybe I don't see it that way."

"Don't you ever get tired of the same old story, bro?"

Hunter twisted in his seat. The way Matt stood in the doorway, as if he owned the place, raised Hunter's hackles. "You're just in time for our little family reunion."

"Lucky me," Matt murmured.

"Hunter says he's here about the St. Claire investigation."

"That so?" Matt ambled in, stopping in front of the desk. He folded his arms across his chest and leaned against its edge.

"I walked Sarah around five forty-five, we took our usual route. Saw nothing out of the ordinary."

"And what's your usual route?"

"Walton to Main, around the square and back." He paused, then continued. "I was thinking, she...the victim, couldn't have been there yet. Because Sarah would have gone nuts. The way she did later."

"Why didn't you tell us this last night?" Matt asked.

"You didn't ask. And I didn't think of it until today."

Matt inclined his head. "Actually, it's fortuitous you dropped by. We had a couple more questions for you."

"Questions for me?" He shifted his gaze between the two men. "All right. Shoot."

"Did you know the victim?"

"No."

"Never heard the name Elaine St. Claire before?"

"Before last night, never."

"Where were you yesterday, between four in the afternoon and when you came to find us at Gallagher's?"

"Is that when she died?"

"Answer the question, please."

"You're kidding." He could tell by their expressions that they weren't. "Am I a suspect?"

"Standard investigative procedure. You found the body, that automatically makes you a suspect."

He got to his feet. "This is bullshit."

"Sit down, son," Buddy murmured, sending an irritated glance at Matt. "Answer the question. Where were you yesterday between the hours of four and eight?"

"I was working. Alone. Sarah was with me. Seems to me she should make a great alibi. She's certainly more loyal than most humans. Present company included."

"Other than taking Sarah for a walk, did you go out at all?"

"No."

"On the walk, did you speak with anyone?"

Hunter thought a moment. "No."

"Did anyone call during that time, someone who could substantiate your being home."

Again Hunter replied in the negative. "But that doesn't make me a killer, now, does it?"

"But it doesn't rule you out either."

Hunter longed to wipe the smug expression off his brother's face. "Can I go now?"

"Not quite yet." Matt glanced at his father, then back at Hunter. "You know how she died, Hunter?"

"Obviously not."

"A sharp or jagged instrument was repeatedly inserted—jammed really—into her vaginal canal."

Hunter went cold. "Oh, Christ."

"She bled to death from internal wounds. It was an excruciating, punishing death."

Buddy stepped in. "Do you have any idea who might have been capable of such a crime?"

"A psychopath."

"You got a name to go with that personality, bro?"

Hunter stiffened. "I wish I did."

"Why's that?" Buddy asked.

Hunter glanced at his father. "Obviously, so you could catch him before he hurts anyone else."

"Noble," Matt murmured. "What a guy."

Hunter stood and met his brother's gaze evenly. "You got a problem with me, Matt? This town too small for the two of us?"

"And here I thought I was the cowboy in the family."

"You didn't answer my question."

"I have a problem with disloyalty. And with cowards."

Hunter laughed without humor, throat tight. "And you see me as both."

"I do."

At times like this, he saw his brother so clearly. He'd always had to be right. Have the last word, have it his way. He had demanded the lion's share of their parents' attention. Adoration from the girls. He couldn't be simply part of the team, he'd had to be the *star.*

Hunter hadn't required adulation. He had been happy to let his twin have it.

But he had drawn the line when his brother had wanted him to stop thinking for himself. Matt had expected his brother to like who and what he did, to think like him. No, Hunter corrected, not expected. Required it of him. Of anyone who remained in his circle.

"You're not engaging me in this, Matt. There's no point in it."

"Like I said, bro, a disloyal coward."

"Because I won't fight with you?" Hunter demanded. "Or because I left, went on with my life? Because I didn't give one hundred percent loyalty to the great Matt Stevens? Is that it?"

"Boys—"

That one deeply uttered word shattered Hunter's veneer of control; anger burst through, white hot, blinding. Memories with it. His father had intoned that warning a million times growing up, from as early as Hunter could remember.

Only then, he had been one of them.

"You hate that I can think for myself, don't you, Matt? I'm not your dutiful little soldier and that makes you crazy."

"Whatever you need to tell yourself, bro."

"If you tried leaving your personal oyster shell, you would have realized you're not the be all and end all, Sheriff Stevens. But then, maybe that's why you never did."

Angry color flooded Matt's face. "You were always jealous of me. You still are. Because I got the girl."

"Leave Avery out of this."

"She's always been a part of it. You couldn't handle that it was me she wanted, not you."

Hunter met his eyes. "Wanted you? If that's so, where's she been all these years? Seems to me she left you behind."

Matt took a step toward him. Hunter curled his hands into fists, ready to throw the first punch. Eager.

Buddy stepped between them before he could. "Thanks for coming in, Hunter. We'll be in touch."

# CHAPTER 17

The West Feliciana Parish Coroner's office was located in St. Francisville. An elected official, Dr. Harris served all the parish, one of the smallest in Louisiana. The coroner examined the circumstances of death, performed toxicology tests, called time and manner of death and signed the certificate of death.

Avery had learned all this from the man's wife when she'd called to make an appointment. She had also learned that Dr. Harris had served for almost twenty-eight years. His office employed two deputy coroners, both physicians, and handled an average of eighty deaths a year. If he determined an autopsy was required to establish cause of death, the body was transported to Earl K. Long Hospital in Baton Rouge. There, a forensic pathologist would perform an autopsy. Unlike big parishes in the state, West Feliciana Parish didn't have the funding to employ its own forensic pathologist. That had surprised Avery.

Dr. Harris was a charming sprite of a man, with a wreath of thinning gray hair and a twinkle in his eye. Not what one expected from a parish coroner.

"Thank you for seeing me, Dr. Harris. I appreciate it." He smiled and she went on. "Your wife told me you've been the parish coroner for twenty-eight years."

"On and off. Took a hiatus to tend to my own practice, can't do it all, you know. Or so the wife tells me."

"But you came back."

"Being a perfectionist is a devil of a thing to be. Can't let go. Couldn't stand to see the job not being done right."

He leaned toward her, eyes twinkling with amusement. "They got a joker in here who called cause of every death cardiac arrest. Didn't look at medical records or any other circumstances surrounding the death. Several times the man had a nurse sign the certificates of death. Couldn't stand it. Agreed to come back. Twice."

He sat back, then forward again. "The thing is, ultimately we all have cardiac arrest, but that's not always what sends us off."

"Do things like that happen often?" she asked, thinking of her father. "Cause of death being miscalled because facts slip through the cracks?"

"Not when I'm in charge." He searched her gaze, then smiled gently. "How can I help you, Ms. Chauvin?"

"As I said on the phone, I'm looking into my father's death."

His expression puckered with sympathy. "I'm sorry for your loss."

"Thank you." She hesitated, searching for the right direction to proceed. "I learned from your wife that you handle about eighty deaths a year. And that you or one of your deputies go to the scene of every one."

"That's correct."

"She also told me that neither you nor your deputies perform autopsies, that those are done in Baton Rouge."

"Yes. By the forensic pathologist. Dr. Kim Sands."

"And you requested an autopsy on my father."

"I request one for every suicide. I have her report here."

"And she classified my dad's death a suicide?"

He nodded. "Her findings were consistent with mine."

Avery folded her hands in her lap to hide that they shook. "What did Dr. Sands call Dad's official cause of death?"

"Asphyxiation."

"Asphyxiation?" she repeated, surprised. "I don't understand."

"There's no reason you should," he said gently. "It's a little known fact that most victims of fire die of asphyxiation. In your father's case, with his first breath his airways would have filled with fuel vapors and flames. Death came quickly."

*He crawled a couple feet toward the door.* "Are you saying he died instantly?"

"Death is never instant. In forensics they speak of death coming in terms of seconds to minutes, minutes to hours, hours to days and so on. In your father's case we're looking at seconds to minutes."

She struggled to separate herself from her father's pain and focus on the medicolegal facts. "Go on."

"The presence of smoke and soot in the throat and lungs is one of the ways the pathologist determines the victim actually died in the fire."

"Or if he was dead before he was set on fire."

"Exactly."

"And Dr. Sands found both in his throat and lungs?"

"Yes." He reached for her father's file, flipped it open and read. "Yes," he repeated.

She cleared her throat. "What else would the pathologist look for in a case like my father's?"

"To confirm cause and manner of death?" She nodded. "Hemorrhages in the remaining soft tissue. Evidence of drugs or alcohol in the toxicology tests. We test blood, urine, bile and vitreous fluid. Each serves as a check for the other."

"And in my father—"

"We found trace amounts of the drug Halcion in his system. It's a sleep medication."

She straightened. "Sleeping pills? Are you certain?"

He looked surprised by her response. "You didn't know? I spoke with Earl, the pharmacist at Friendly Drugs in Cypress Springs. Your dad had been taking sleeping pills for some time."

"Who prescribed them?"

He thought a moment, then held up a finger, indicating she should wait. He referred to the file again. "There it is. Prescribed them for himself."

Avery didn't know what to say.

"Inability to sleep is not uncommon in people who are depressed."

She struggled to find her voice. *He hadn't been sleeping. Another thing she hadn't known about her father, his state of mind.*

*What kind of daughter was she?*

"Why would he do that?" she managed to say finally. "If he planned to kill himself the way he did, why take sleeping pills before?"

"Pill," he corrected. "The level of the drug in his bloodstream was consistent with having taking a .25-milligram tablet at bedtime. Which, by the way, was the dose he'd prescribed himself."

"I still don't understand, then—"

"Why?" he finished for her. "We can't be certain, of course. Could be he wanted to take the edge off, dull his senses. Or that he decided to act after he'd taken it."

*It appeared as if he crawled a couple feet toward the door.*

"Ms. Chauvin?"

She looked up. He held out a box of tissues. She hadn't realized she was crying. She plucked a tissue from the box and dried her eyes and cheeks, working to pull herself together. "Was there anything...suspicious about his death?"

"Suspicious?" He drew his eyebrows together. "I'm not certain I understand."

"Anything that suggested his death wasn't a suicide?"

When he spoke, his tone was patient. "If you discount leaving a death unclassified, there are only four classifications of death. Natural causes. Accident. Suicide or homicide. We can eliminate the first two. That leaves suicide. Or homicide."

"I realize that."

He frowned slightly. "What are you getting at, Ms. Chauvin?"

"I'm just—" She crumbled the tissue. "Frankly, I can't believe he did this. He didn't leave a note. In our conversations, and we spoke often, he gave no indication of being so depressed that he might take his own life."

Another man might have been offended, might have thought she was questioning his skill or professionalism; Dr. Harris was sympathetic. She suspected he dealt with grieving family members a lot.

"The Cypress Springs police did a thorough investigation. As did I. Dr. Sands is a top-notch forensic pathologist. Toxicology revealed nothing but the Halcion. I found nothing about the body to suggest homicide. Neither did Dr. Sands. Friends and neighbors described him as acting strangely for some time before his death. Reclusive. Depressed. That behavior seemed consistent with suicide. I understand, too, that your mother had died recently."

"A year ago," she murmured, shaken.

*He got what he deserved.*

*You will, too.*

Avery pressed her lips together.

He sat forward. "Is there something you think I should know? Something you're not saying?"

She met his eyes. What would he think if she shared her anonymous caller's message? Would he call it a sick joke—or a serious threat?

She shook her head. "No. Nothing."

"You're certain?"

"Absolutely." She stood and held out her hand. "You've been very helpful, Dr. Harris. Thank you for your time."

He followed her to her feet, took her hand. "If you need anything further, just call. I'm mostly here."

She started for the door. He called her name, stopping her. She looked back.

"I hope you'll forgive an old man for meddling, but I've done this job for a lot of years. Talked with a lot of grieving family members. I understand how difficult it is to accept when a loved one takes their own life. The guilt you feel. You tell yourself you should have seen it coming, that if you had, your loved one would be alive.

"The ones who do the best get on with living. They accept that the act wasn't about them, that it wasn't about anything they did or didn't do." He paused. "Time, Ms. Chauvin. Give yourself some time. Talk to someone. A counselor. Clergyman. Then get on with living."

*If only it were that easy. If only it all didn't feel so wrong.*

She forced a small smile. "You're very kind, Dr. Harris."

"Just so you know, I intend to tell your sister the same thing."

She stopped. Turned. "Excuse me?"

"Your sister. She called after you did. She's coming at three." At her expression, he frowned. "Is something wrong, Ms. Chauvin?"

"I don't have a sister, Dr. Harris."

## CHAPTER 18

Avery waited in the parking lot beside Dr. Harris's office, the SUV's windows lowered to let in the mild March breeze. She'd positioned the Blazer at the edge of the lot, alongside a dilapidated Cadillac Seville.

At two fifty-five, another vehicle pulled into the lot, a woman at the wheel. Avery slid low in her seat, not wanting the woman to spot her—yet. Not until she couldn't avoid coming face-to-face with Avery.

The woman parked her Camry, never even glancing Avery's way. She flipped down her sun visor, checked her appearance in the lighted mirror, then snapped it shut and got out of the vehicle.

Only then did Avery get a clear view of her. A small sound of surprise slid past her lips.

*The woman from her father's wake. The one the group of men had been staring at.*

Avery threw open her door and jumped out, slamming it behind her. The woman stopped. Turned toward her. Her face registered shock. Then dismay.

Avery closed the distance between them. "We need to talk."

"Excuse me?"

"Don't be coy. You were at my father's wake. And now you're here. Claiming to be my sister. I think you'd better tell me why."

She opened her mouth as if to deny the allegations, then shut it. She motioned to the picnic table at the rear of the building, set up under a sprawling old oak tree. "Over there."

They sat. The woman met her eyes. Tall and slender with short, curly blond hair, Avery judged her to be about the same age as she was.

"My name's Gwen Lancaster. I'm sorry if I've upset you. I know this is a difficult time. I...I lost my brother not long ago."

Avery gazed at her, unmoved. "Did you know my father?"

"No, I didn't."

"May I ask then, why you attended his wake and why you're here today?"

She paused a moment before answering. "I'm new to Cypress Springs. Pretty town."

"Yeah, it is." Avery narrowed her eyes. "Friendly, too."

Her lips twisted slightly. "Doesn't look so friendly from where I'm sitting."

"Do you blame me?"

She laughed, the sound short. Tight. "Actually, I don't." She glanced away, then back at Avery. "I've come to Cypress Springs to do some research. I'm working on my Ph.D. in social psychology. From Tulane University."

"Good for you," she said flatly. "So, what does that have to do with my father's death?"

"If I tell you, will you promise to keep an open mind?"

Avery leaned toward her. "I'm not promising you anything. I don't think I should have to."

Gwen held her gaze, then nodded. "At least allow me to begin at the beginning."

"Fair enough."

The woman folded her hands and laid them on the table's top, over a set of initials someone had carved in the wood. "I'm writing a thesis titled "Crime, Punishment and the Rise of Vigilantism in Small-Town America."

She paused. Avery wondered if she used the time to collect her thoughts—or to manufacture her answer. Avery had earned her right to suspicion, earned it through years of interviewing people with agendas that ran counter to the truth, people who manipulated and manufactured. People, she had learned, lied for a variety of reasons. Because it was easier than telling the truth. Or to shield themselves from punishment or incrimination. They lied to protect their reputations. Or as a way to keep from revealing who they really were.

"In my undergraduate studies, I became fascinated with the psychology of groups and group dynamics. What motivates a seemingly average, law-abiding citizen to take on the role of crusader? To take the law into their own hands or act outside the law?"

She lowered her eyes a moment, then returned them to Avery's, her blue gaze unblinking. "Vigilantes are strong believers in law and order. They're usually patriots and highly moral. It's a form of extremism, of course. And like all extremists, they turn their beliefs inside out and upside down."

Avery acknowledged being intrigued despite herself. "Like Timothy McVeigh, the Oklahoma City bomber."

"Exactly. He fit the profile to a T, although he acted alone. Remember, the thing that makes these people so dangerous is that they absolutely believe in their cause and are willing to die for it. Their beliefs aren't a way to justify their acts, in their minds those acts *are* justified by their beliefs."

Avery nodded, understanding. "So, you'd lump all extremists in this same category? Religious groups like Afghanistan's Taliban, political extremists like Al-Qaeda?"

"And white supremacists, survivalists or any other group that pushes its ideology to the extreme. No country, religion or race is immune. History is riddled with the bodies of those killed in the name of a cause."

"Why are you here?"

"A bartender told me a story about this picture-perfect Louisiana town. The town began to suffer an increase in crime. Instead of combating it through traditional law enforcement, they took the law into their own hands. They organized a group that policed the behavior of its citizens. They nipped in the bud behavior they considered aberrant. The crime rate fell, further justifying their actions in their own minds. I did some digging and found information that seemed to corroborate the story."

*She was talking about Cypress Springs.* Avery stared at her, waiting for the punch line. When it didn't come, she laughed. "A vigilante group? In Cypress Springs? You can't be serious."

"These types of groups are more likely to arise in communities like Cypress Springs. Insular communities, resistant to change, reluctant to welcome outsiders."

"This is ridiculous."

Avery made a move to stand; the woman reached out, caught her hand. "Hear me out. The group formed in the late 1980s as a reaction to the rapid increase in crime. They disbanded sometime later, beset by internal fighting and threats of exposure from within their own ranks."

*The 1980s? During the time before and after Sallie Waguespack's murder.*

The hair on the back of her neck stood up. If it weren't for the fact that she had just relived that time through her father's clippings and Buddy's recollections, she would have totally discounted the woman's assertions. She had learned during her years in investigative journalism that when one element of a story rang true, often others would, too.

But vigilantism? Could the people of Cypress Springs have been so concerned, desperate really, that they'd taken the law into their own hands? Could her father have been that desperate? Or Buddy? Their friends and fellow community leaders? She couldn't imagine them in the role of Big Brother.

"The core group was small, but they had an intricate network of others who monitored the activities of the citizens and reported to the group."

Avery frowned. "Spies? You're saying Cypress Springs citizens spied on each other?"

"Yes. The citizens were watched. Their mail read. What they ate, drank, read and watched was monitored. Where they went. If they worshiped. If need be, they were warned."

"Warned? You mean threatened?"

She nodded. "If the warnings went unheeded, the group took action. Businesses were boycotted. Individuals shunned. Property vandalized. To varying degrees, everyone was in on it."

"Everyone?" Avery made a sound of disbelief. "I have a hard time believing that."

"In groups such as these, responsibility for acts are disbursed throughout the group. What that means is, no one person carries the burden of responsibility for an act against another. It's the *group's* responsibility. By lessening the burden, the act becomes much easier to carry out. In addition, the individual's sense of responsibility shifts from the self to the group and its ideology."

Avery shook her head again. "I grew up here, I've never heard of any of this."

"It's not as outlandish as it sounds. It began as little more than a Neighborhood Watch-type program. A way to help combat crime. As unchecked good intentions sometimes do," the woman continued, "theirs spun out of control. Anyone who's actions fell outside what was considered right, moral or neighborly was singled out and warned. Before it was all over, they'd broken the civil rights of their fellow citizens in the name of righteousness, law and order."

"And nobody went to jail?"

"Nobody talked. The community closed ranks. Not untypical for this type of group." Gwen leaned toward Avery. Lowered her voice. "They called themselves The Seven."

*At her father's wake, the group of men. Watching Gwen.*

*Seven of them.*

A coincidence, she told herself, struggling to keep her thoughts from showing. To deny them. "And what exactly does all this have to do with my father? And you posing as my nonexistent sister?"

Gwen Lancaster didn't blink. "I'm trying to locate sources to verify the information I've gotten so far. Your dad fits the profile."

"My father's dead, Ms. Lancaster."

"Fit the profile," she corrected, flushing. "White. Male. Lifelong

Cypress Springs resident. A respected community leader during that time."

Her meaning sank in and Avery stiffened. "You're saying you believe my father might have been a part of this Seven?"

"Yes."

Avery stood. She realized she was shaking. "He wasn't," she said flatly. "He would never have been a part of something like that. Never!"

"Wait, please!" She followed Avery to her feet. "Hear me out. There's—"

"I've heard enough." Avery snatched her purse off the picnic bench. "There's a difference between thinking you're honorable and being honorable. And you know that, Ms. Lancaster. My father was a highly principled, moral man. A man others looked up to. A man who dedicated his life to helping others. To doing right, not to self-righteousness. It's an insult to his memory, to all he was, to suggest he would be party to this extremist garbage."

"You don't understand. If you would just—"

"I do understand, Ms. Lancaster. And I've listened quite enough." Avery backed away. "Stay away from me. If I find out you're prying into my father's life or death again, I'll go to the police. If I hear you're spreading these lies, I'll go to a lawyer."

Without waiting for the woman's reply, Avery turned and walked away.

# CHAPTER 19

Avery sat at the kitchen table, laptop open in front of her, hands curled around a mug of freshly brewed coffee. Early-morning sun streamed through the window. The screen glowed softly; the text blurred before her eyes.

She set the mug on the table and rubbed her eyes. Her head ached. She'd slept little. She'd left St. Francisville and driven blindly home, thoughts whirling. She'd been angry. Furious. That Gwen Lancaster could accuse her father of such despicable acts toward his fellow citizens. That she could suggest the people of Cypress Springs capable of spying on one another, punishing them for behavior that fell outside what a few had decided was acceptable.

Cypress Springs was a nice place to live. People cared about one another. They helped one another.

Gwen Lancaster, she had decided was either a liar or an academic hack. She had dealt with journalists like that. They started with a story someone told them, something juicy, outrageous or shocking. Like the one the bartender told Gwen Lancaster about a picture-perfect small town that turns to vigilantism to combat crime.

Great hook. A real grabber. They proceeded on the premise that it was true and began collecting the "facts" to prove it. Tabloid journalism cloaked in the guise of authentic journalism. Or in Gwen Lancaster's case, academia.

*The group of seven men at the wake. Watching Gwen Lancaster. The one laughing.*

Avery shook her head. A coincidence. A group of men, friends, standing together. Admiring an attractive woman. One making a sexual comment, then laughing. It happened all the time.

She turned her attention to the computer screen. She had realized she knew little more about vigilantism and extremism than what Gwen had told her and had spent the night researching both via the Internet.

She'd done searches on vigilantism. Crowd mentality and social psychology. Fanaticism. She had read about the Ku Klux Klan. Nazism. Experiments in group behavior.

Extremist groups had been much in the news since the September 11, 2001, attacks on the United States by the al-Qaeda terrorist organization. Her search had led her there and to pieces written in the aftermath of Timothy McVeigh's bombing of the Alfred P. Murrah Building in Oklahoma City in 1995. And others concerning the 1993 FBI shootout with the Branch Davidians in Waco, Texas.

What she'd found disturbed her. Any idea or belief, it seemed, could be taken to an extreme. The amount of blood spilled for God and country staggered. A chief motivator, she'd learned, was fear of change. The intense desire to keep the world, the order of things, the way it was.

*Folks were scared. And angry. Real angry. The town was turning into a place they didn't like.*

*People stopped taking their community, their quality of life for granted. They realized that safety and a community spirit were worth working for. People started watching out for each other.*

Avery stood and crossed to the sink. She flipped on the cold water, bent and splashed her face. How frightened had the people of Cypress Springs been? Enough to take the law into their own hands?

Could this be why her father had clipped and kept all those articles?

Avery ripped off a paper towel, dried her face, then tossed the towel into the trash. As much as she wanted to discount everything Gwen Lancaster had told her, she couldn't. Because of that damn box.

Gwen Lancaster knew something about her father that she wasn't telling. Why else would she have wanted to talk to the coroner about Phillip's death? Avery couldn't imagine he would have been able to shed any light on The Seven or her father's involvement in the group.

The coroner could answer questions about her father's death, not life.

That was it, Avery realized. Gwen Lancaster doubted the official explanation of Dr. Phillip Chauvin's death.

And Avery was going to find out why. First, she needed to locate the woman.

She crossed to the phone and dialed the ranch. Buddy knew everybody in this town, even outsiders. He answered.

"Hi, Buddy, it's Avery. Good morning."

"Baby girl. Good morning to you, too." Pleasure radiated from his voice. "How are you? We've been so worried, but wanted to give you some space."

"I'm hanging in there, Buddy. Thanks for your concern. How's Lilah?"

"She's good. Come by for dinner. Anytime."

"I will. Got a question. You know everyone around here, right?"

"Pretty much. Figure it's my job."

"I'm trying to find a woman named Gwen Lancaster. She's only been here a couple of weeks, tops."

"Pretty blonde? Writing some sort of paper?"

"That's her."

"You might check The Guesthouse. Why're you looking for her?"

Avery hesitated. She didn't want to lie. But she didn't want to let on what she was thinking. Not yet. She settled on a partial truth. "She was asking some questions about Dad, I want to find out why."

"That's odd. What kind of questions?"

"I thought it odd, too."

If he noticed her evasiveness, he didn't let on. "Good luck then. Let me know if you need anything else."

Avery thanked him and after promising to stop out for dinner in the next night or two, hung up. She started upstairs to dress. As far as she was concerned, there was no time like the present to call on Gwen Lancaster, ungodly hour or not.

A mere twenty minutes later, Avery crossed The Guesthouse's wide, shady front porch. The Landry family had owned The Guesthouse for as long as she could remember. They had converted the huge old Victorian, located right across from the square, into a guesthouse in the 1960s when they neither needed nor could afford to maintain the structure as a single-family residence.

The family occupied two-thirds of the first floor; the upstairs had been converted into four units consisting of a bedroom/sitting room combination, a kitchenette and bath. The remaining third of the main floor housed the same as the rooms above, with the addition of a small, separate parlor.

She stepped inside. The small registration area occupied the far end of the foyer. The young woman behind the desk looked up and smiled. The next-generation Landry, Avery thought. She was a mirror image of both Laurie, one of Avery's friends, and her older brother, Daniel.

"Hi," Avery said, crossing to the desk. "I bet you're Danny's daughter."

"I am." The teenager popped her gum. "How did you know?"

"I grew up here. Was a friend of your aunt Laurie's. You look just like your dad."

The girl pouted. "Everybody says that."

"I'm looking for Gwen Lancaster. I think she's staying here."

"She is. She's in 2C."

"Thanks." Avery said goodbye, then climbed the stairs. Room

2C was located on the left side of the hall, at the end. She reached the door and knocked, hoping it was still early enough to catch her in.

It was. Gwen opened the door, still bleary-eyed with sleep. She had awakened her, Avery realized without apology.

She laid a hand on the door, just in case the other woman tried to slam it on her. "Why are you so interested in my father's death? I want to know the truth. The whole truth."

The woman gazed unblinkingly at her a moment, then opened the door wider and stepped aside. "Come on in."

Avery did. Gwen shut the door behind her, then yawned. "Coffee?"

"No, thanks. I'm full up."

"Sorry, but I need a cup." She motioned toward the small seating area. "I'll be back in a jif."

True to her word, in less than five minutes Gwen sat across from her, cup clutched in her hands. Avery didn't even give her time to sip. "What you told me yesterday was bullshit. Talking to the coroner about my father's death would tell you nothing about his supposed role in The Seven. Obviously, you're interested in his death. Why?"

Gwen met her gaze. "Okay, the straight shit. I wonder if your dad's death was a suicide."

An involuntary sound slipped past Avery's lips. She brought a hand to her mouth and stood, turning her back to the other woman, struggling to compose herself.

"I'm sorry," Gwen murmured.

Avery shook her head but didn't turn. "Why?" she asked. "What makes you think—"

"For such a small town, Cypress Springs suffers a disproportionate number of suicides."

Avery turned. Met the woman's eyes. "Excuse me?"

"The population of Cypress Springs is around nine hundred. Correct?" Avery agreed it was. "In the last eight months, six of her citizens have taken their own lives. A rather large number, particularly for a community that purports to be such a great place to live. To give you an idea how huge that is, the annual total for Louisiana is 1.2 per thousand, per year. To stay within the state average, Cypress Springs should have about 1.2 suicides annually."

"Your figure can't be right."

"But it is. In addition," the woman continued, "there've been a number of strange disappearances."

"Disappearances?" Avery repeated.

"People picking up and moving in the night. No word to anyone. Not to family or friends." She took a sip of coffee. "The accidental death rate is also high. Hunting accidents. Car wrecks. Drownings. Most of them in the last year."

"And before that?"

"Much lower. All categories."

Avery struggled to assimilate the information. To place it in the framework of what she believed to be true. "I'll have to check this out myself."

"Be my guest."

She fell silent a moment. Craziness. What she was thinking was insanity. "Why would someone want to kill my father?"

"I don't know. I'm thinking he knew too much."

"About The Seven?"

"Yes."

"Then what about you?"

Gwen seemed startled by the question. "What do you mean?"

"It seems to me that *you* might know too much about this group. If it actually exists, that is."

"It exists," Gwen said, following her to her feet. Avery saw that she shook. "And they're getting bolder. Not even trying to cover up their work with an accident."

"What are you talking about?"

"The murder. Elaine St. Claire. I believe The Seven is responsible."

## CHAPTER 20

Avery left The Guesthouse. She angled across the square, making her way through the already thick throng of Spring Fest attendees. Though the festival ran from Friday evening through Sunday, Saturday's crowds were always the thickest. The smell of deep-fried crawfish pies and spicy shrimp étouffé floated on the morning air. Vendors preparing for the day laughed and called to one another.

Avery paid them little attention, instead reviewing the things she *knew* to be true. Her father was dead of an apparent suicide. An anonymous caller had threatened her, claiming her father had gotten what he deserved. That she would, too. A woman named Elaine St. Claire had been found murdered in the alley behind Walton Street. None of the official agencies that had investigated her father's death had found anything to suggest it had been other than a suicide.

And she was no longer alone in her belief that her father had been murdered. Gwen Lancaster believed it, too.

*Great. A conspiracy-theorist nutcase fell in line with her.
Reassuring.*

She would start with the facts, the place every good journalist began. Those facts would lead to others, which would either confirm or allay her suspicions. Hunter and the Elaine St. Claire murder seemed a good first step.

Avery stepped off the square onto Main Street, heading toward Johnson Avenue. It would be fruitless to approach Matt or Buddy; they were lawmen, they'd tell her nothing more than what was reported in the most recent issue of the *Gazette.*

But Hunter had been there. He'd discovered the body. Had been privy to Matt's and Buddy's reactions, he'd no doubt overheard some of their conversation at the scene.

She acknowledged excitement. A quickening of the blood that told her she was onto something, a high she experienced whenever she hit on the real thing—a powerhouse story with the ability to affect real change.

What change would this story precipitate if true?

Avery reached Johnson and turned down it. Moments later, she reached Hunter's law office. Peering through the window she saw the room was empty, so she went around to the alley entrance.

Hunter appeared at the door before she could knock. Sarah stood at his side. From inside she heard the whimpering of puppies.

He pushed open the screen door. She saw he was dressed in a T-shirt and running shorts.

"I was hoping we could talk," she said.

"About?" he asked, not looking at her. He clipped the lead onto Sarah's collar.

"About...stuff."

He met her eyes. "Stuff? Big-city journalists always use such technical words?"

"Smart-ass."

"Sarah and I are going for a run."

"I'll join you."

He skimmed his gaze over her. Unlike him, she had dressed for comfort—not exercise. She had, however, worn her athletic shoes. "Sorry. But this is our time."

"Our time? You and the dog's?"

"That's right. Haven't you heard the one about dog being man's best friend?"

"If you want an apology," she said, frustrated, "you've got it."

"For what?"

"Our argument."

One corner of his mouth lifted. "Seems to me that was a two-way street." He looked down at Sarah. "What do you think, girl? Can she keep up with us?"

As if she understood her master's question, the dog looked up at her. Avery returned the dog's baleful stare. "Come on, Sarah, give me a little credit. We girls have to stick together."

She seemed to nod, then swung her gaze to Hunter. He laughed. "No fair, you pulled the girl-solidarity thing on me."

Avery laughed. "Why not? It worked, didn't it?"

He stepped through the door, turned and locked it, then began to stretch.

"Where are we going?"

"Tiller's farm."

Tiller's farm was a forty-acre spread just east of Cypress Springs. Now used to raise mostly feeder cattle, the land had been in the Tiller family forever and old Sam Tiller refused to sell even an acre. Cypress Springs had built up around him. In retrospect, Tiller's refusal to budge had been one of the factors that had helped keep Cypress Springs small and pastoral.

*Three miles. There. And back.*

*Not good.*

Hunter glanced over at her. His lips lifted in amusement. "Want to back out now?"

"Not at all," she lied. "Just worried about that shotgun of his." Sam Tiller had not been happy when he'd discovered the shady, spring-fed pond on his property had become an oasis for Cypress Springs teenagers.

Buddy had dragged him in on a number of occasions for firing at the kids. Never mind that it'd only been buckshot and that the kids had been trespassing—shooting at teenagers was against the law.

"No worries, doll. I handled a legal problem for him, he gave Sarah and I carte blanche to visit anytime. Could even skinny-dip if we wanted."

She ignored the reference to a mercilessly hot August night when they had done just that. Hunter had promised not to look. She had believed him.

Then caught him staring.

"Ready?"

*As she would ever be.* "You bet."

They set off, the three of them, the pace relaxed. Warming up. Avery managed to keep up easily at first. Soon, however, she had to press to keep up, even though Hunter paced himself to accommodate her shorter legs.

After three-quarters of a mile, Avery was sweating. Out of breath. Her blue jeans and cotton blouse clung uncomfortably to her damp skin, twisting slightly, restricting her movement.

She'd give her kingdom for a pair of shorts and a sports bra, she decided, yanking her shirt from the waistband of her jeans as she ran. She unbuttoned the cuffs and rolled up the sleeves.

He glanced back. "You okay?"

"Fine," she managed to say, furious at herself. For her own pig-headedness. And for allowing herself to get so out of shape. In the past few months she had gone from a daily run to managing to fit one in once a week. Between that and the difference in their strides, she was hurting.

By the halfway point, however, her endorphins kicked in and the discomfort eased. Hunter drew ahead; she didn't try to keep up. Instead, she luxuriated in the pure pleasure of being outdoors, lungs, heart and muscles working in tandem.

"Meet me at the pond," he called over his shoulder.

She indicated she would, then watched as he pulled away.

When she arrived, Hunter was waiting for her, Sarah panting at his side. The way Avery figured it, she'd been about six minutes behind him.

He passed her a water bottle. "I'd forgotten that about you."

"What?" She accepted the bottle and took a long swallow.

"How determined you are."

She took another swallow, then handed the bottle back. "You mean pigheaded."

"Sometimes." His mouth twitched. "Personally, I believe determination is an admirable trait."

Sarah stood and wandered down to the pond. Avery watched longingly as she waded in for a drink. The water looked delicious.

"Go ahead," he said. "Take a dip. It's spring fed."

"In your dreams, Stevens."

"I didn't say skinny-dip. You, Ms. Chauvin, have a dirty mind."

"Actually, I don't think I'm the one with the dirty mind." She stood and crossed to the water's edge. Kneeling, she splashed water on her face, soaking her shirt in the process.

She glanced down at the now-transparent fabric. So much for modesty. Hell with it, she decided, unbuttoning the clinging fabric.

"Don't look," she ordered, glancing at him over her shoulder.

He rested back on an elbow. "Depends on what I'm going to miss."

"Hunter," she warned, narrowing her eyes at his cheesy smile.

"All right. No peeking, scout's honor."

She waited until he had dutifully turned his head, then peeled off her blouse.

"Very pretty."

She whirled around, wet blouse to her chest. "You looked."

"Of course I did." He laughed. "Can't stop a bird dog from hunting."

"Or a snake from striking."

He laid back, hands folded behind his head and gazed up at the blue sky. "Your honor's safe, doll. Most bathing suits reveal more than that bra, pretty as it is."

He had a point. She soaked her blouse in the chilly water, then draped the dripping fabric across her shoulders. The water sluiced over her shoulders and breasts, leaving trails of goose bumps in their wake.

She made her way back to where he rested. To his credit, he didn't look at her.

"What did you want to talk to me about?"

She hesitated, reluctant to ruin the warm, relaxed mood with talk of murder, then asked anyway. "Wondered if you could tell me anything about the St. Claire murder."

He didn't act surprised by her question. "What do you want to know?"

"The *Gazette* didn't say how she died."

"It's pretty grim."

"I think I can take it."

He tilted his face toward hers. "A sharp object was repeatedly inserted into her vaginal canal. Tore her insides to shreds. She bled to death."

Avery hugged herself, suddenly cold. "Who was she?"

"Dad knew her. Party girl. Heavy drinker. Spent a little time in jail."

*Anyone whose actions fell outside what was considered right, moral or neighborly was singled out.*

A woman like Elaine St. Claire fit that description. But she was also the kind who put herself in dangerous situations.

"They have any suspects?"

"Just me."

"Funny."

"I'm not laughing." He lay back again, draping an arm across his eyes. "Dad and Matt, in their infinite wisdom, are looking no further than the first to the scene."

"I find that difficult to believe."

He shrugged. "Could just be me, still chafing under Matt's interrogation. Wondered where I'd been that day between the hours of four in the afternoon and eight that night."

"And where were you?"

"Working on the novel. Nobody but Sarah for an alibi."

She didn't know what to say so she said nothing.

"Why so interested?" he asked.

*Good question. How did she answer it?* She decided on bluntness. "You have any doubt my dad killed himself?"

He sat up at that one. Looked at her. "Where did *that* come from?"

Ignoring the question, she tipped her face to the sky, then returned her gaze to his. "You'd become friends. Spent some time with him. Do you have any doubt he took his own life?"

For a long moment, he said nothing. When he spoke, his tone was heavy with regret. "No, Avery. I'm sorry."

A knot of tears clogged her throat. She pressed on. "Why?"

He looked at her. "Talking about this isn't going to change anyth—"

"Why, Hunter? Tell me."

"All right." He sat up. "I hadn't been back in Cypress Springs a week when your dad looked me up. I appreciated it. A lot. He didn't ask too many questions, didn't make me explain why or justify my actions. He did it for me, but I think, for himself, too. He needed somebody to talk to.

"Anyway, it worked for both of us and we started meeting every Friday morning for coffee. Then, one Friday, he didn't show. So I went by the house, found him still in his pajamas. All the blinds drawn. He insisted he had simply overslept, but he was acting... strange. Different."

"Different? What do you mean?"

"Jumpy, I guess. He didn't look me in the eye. After that, our meetings became sporadic. Our conversations...less comfortable. He began talking a lot about the old days. When your mom was alive and you were home. Never about the future, rarely about the here and now."

Hunter let out a long breath. "It should have rung a warning bell, but it didn't. I'm sorry," he said again.

She shook her head, as much in denial of his words as of the tears burning her eyes. "He lost a bedroom slipper that night, on his way out to the garage. The arson investigator told me that."

He didn't comment and her cheeks heated. "I think that's significant, Hunter. Walking in one shoe isn't natural. The path between the house and garage would have been cold, the stepping stones rough. He would have stopped and slid it back on."

"Avery," he said gently, "I hate that he did this, too. I know it hurts. I know—"

"No, you don't know. You *can't* know what I feel." Tears choked her; she fought them. "On fire, he crawled toward the door. He didn't want to do it, Hunter. He didn't."

"Avery, hon—" He made a move to take her into his arms and she jumped to her feet. "No," she said, more to herself than him. "No, I will not cry. No more."

She hugged herself, staring at the shimmering surface of the pond. In the tree behind her a couple of squirrels played tag. Sarah growled, low in her throat.

"Who would want your dad dead, Avery?" Hunter asked quietly. "Everyone loved him."

She couldn't take her gaze from the diamond-faceted surface of the water. "Not everyone. I got a call, this woman...she said Dad had gotten what he deserved. That I would, too."

"Who, Avery? What woman?"

"Don't know." Cocking her head, she moved toward the water. The surface was broken by a large, odd shadow. "She wouldn't identify herself and I didn't recognize her voice."

"Has she called again?"

"No." Avery reached the pond's edge, stopped and frowned.

"Most probably a crank," he said. "Someone with an ax to grind. Or someone in desperate need of attention. Even Cypress Springs is home to mentally unstable people."

"What's that?" She glanced over her shoulder at him. He was staring with unabashed admiration at her butt. Her cheeks warmed even as she motioned him to come. "Look."

He stood and ambled over, Sarah at his heels. She pointed. "A shape just beneath the water. See? Its edges are silvery."

He bent closer, then looked at her. "I think it's a car."

"A car?" She turned back to the pond. Made a sound of surprise as the shape that had caught her eye suddenly became clear to her. "I think you're right."

"One way to find out." He stripped down to his jogging shorts, then waded in. She watched as he took a deep breath, then dived under.

A moment later, he surfaced. "It is. And a fine car at that. A Mercedes coupe."

She frowned, something plucking at her memory.

"I'm going to take another look."

Hunter went under again. Sarah began to bark. This time when he reappeared he swam back, then climbed out. "I think we better call Dad."

## CHAPTER 21

Neither Avery nor Hunter had a cell phone. They decided the quickest route to a phone would be through the woods and across a pasture to Sam Tiller's place. The man caught sight of Hunter and broke into a broad smile, his weathered face creasing up like a Shar-Pei's hide.

He pushed open the screen door, smile faltering when he saw the condition they were in. "A bit early in the year to be swimming. Water'd be real cold." He shifted his gaze to her. "You're the doc's girl."

"Yes, sir. Good to see you."

"Damn shame about the doc. He was a good man." He turned to Hunter. "What's this all about?"

"We need to use a phone, Sam. To call Buddy." Hunter explained about jogging to the pond, Avery seeing the shadowy form of something under the water, then realizing it was an automobile.

The man scratched his head. "A car, you say? A Mercedes?

Damned if I can figure how it got there. Come on in, phone's this way."

They followed him inside. Sam's wife had died back when they were in high school and as far as Avery knew, the couple hadn't had children. The old farmhouse's interior begged for a little TLC. Fabrics were frayed, curtains dingy and any feminine touches had long since gone the way of the dinosaurs.

It reminded her of how her dad's house had begun to look.

Hunter dialed. Avery could tell by Hunter's side of the conversation that his father was surprised to be hearing from his son.

"You want me to call or— Fine. We'll meet you there."

Hunter hung up the phone. He turned to her and Sam. "Dad's calling Matt. The farm's outside the city limits and falls under the sheriff department's jurisdiction."

"Seeing it's in my pond," Sam said, "I think I'd better get a look at this thing. I'll drive us."

They all three crowded onto the bench seat of his battered old pickup truck; Sarah rode in back. The sky had begun to turn dark, fat black clouds forming to the south.

Within minutes they reached the turn for the pond. Hunter hopped out and unhooked the chain barricade; Sam eased the truck through. Avery wasn't surprised to see they had beaten both Buddy and Matt there.

Sam stopped the pickup; they climbed out. The farmer crossed to the water, squinted down at the cloudy surface. After a moment, he looked at Hunter. "Damned if it isn't a car. I'll be."

Just then, Matt pulled up, followed by Buddy. The younger Stevens climbed out, waited for his father, then crossed to the trio.

"What's the deal?" Matt asked.

Sam stepped forward. "A car," he said. "In my pond. Damned if I know where it came from."

Matt shifted his gaze briefly to her, then turned to Hunter. "You seem to be in the thick of everything these days."

"What can I say? Trouble finds me."

"How about you give me the sequence of events."

Hunter did. Matt shifted his gaze to hers. "You want to add anything to that?"

Dark clouds drifted over the sun; she shivered and shook her head. "I can't think of anything."

"How you goin' to get it out of there?" Sam asked.

"Call Bubba, get one of his wreckers over here, haul it out," Matt answered.

"You're certain it was a Mercedes?" Buddy asked.

"One hundred percent. Silver. A CLK 350."

The two lawmen exchanged glances. "But you say it was empty?"

"It appeared so," Hunter confirmed.

"But you're not certain?"

"No."

"If we need anything else, we'll be in touch." Matt looked at her. Something in his gaze had her folding her arms across her chest. "Storm's moving in," he said softly. "I suggest you take cover."

# CHAPTER 22

At the same moment the storm hit, Avery remembered what had eluded her before: the guy whose Mercedes had supposedly broken down outside of Cypress Springs, the one whose girlfriend had claimed he'd gone missing. She'd cried foul play, but without any evidence of a homicide, Buddy and Matt could only assume the story a fabrication or that the guy had wanted to disappear.

*They had their evidence now. Though a submerged vehicle did not a murder make.*

That's why Matt had asked twice about the vehicle being empty. He was looking for a body to go with the car.

"Here you are," Sam said, interrupting her thoughts. His pickup rattled as it crept up her driveway, then creaked to a stop.

She turned to him. "Thanks for the ride. I really appreciate it."

He peered out at the rain. A boom of thunder shook the truck. "I don't mind waitin' a minute, till it eases up out there."

"I appreciate that, Sam. But I'm already wet. A little more

water's not going to hurt me." She grabbed the door handle. "Thanks again for the—"

"It's not true," he said, cutting her off. "What they all say about him."

She stopped, looked back at him. "Pardon?"

"Hunter's a good man. Rock solid. Your father liked him."

Her mouth dropped. He motioned to the door. "Go on now. Before it gets any worse."

She did as she was told, hopping out into the downpour. Instantly soaked, she hurried to the front porch. There, she watched the old truck rumble off.

What who said about Hunter? His family? Others in the community?

*Your father liked him.*

She sank onto the porch swing and stared out at the rain. Her lips lifted with a curious kind of pleasure. The old farmer's comment shouldn't matter to her, but it did. It warmed her. She had always considered her father an excellent judge of character. Had turned to him for advice about people often, during both her adolescence and adulthood.

She liked Hunter, too, despite their recent clashes. She always had. As a young person, she had admired his intelligence and wit. His fine, dry sense of humor. She thought back, recalling the times he had helped her with math, the subject that had given her never-ending fits. She recalled how he'd had the ability to make her smile, even when she had not been in the mood to. She remembered the time, after a particularly upsetting disagreement with her mother, when he had held her and talked her through it. Quietly supporting her while getting her to see her mother's point of view as well.

Where had Matt been that day? she wondered. Busy? Or had she sought Hunter out because she'd known that he would be the one able to calm her?

And now, as an adult, she sensed a deep, abiding honesty in him—about himself and his shortcomings and about others. That made him difficult for some to take, she supposed. It made him confrontational.

Cypress Springs didn't embrace diversity. Round peg, round hole. PLUs—People Like Us. That made them feel safe. Secure.

She had always been the square peg. She hadn't realized it until now, but Hunter had been, too.

Lightning flashed, thunder shook the sky and the rain came down in blinding sheets. Avery turned her thoughts to Matt and Buddy at Tiller's Pond, arranging to have the vehicle hauled out. Standing in the rain, drenched and chilled. And she wondered if Hunter had made it home before the rain had come. He had eschewed Sam's offer of a ride in favor of completing his run.

She recalled Matt's comment to Hunter about being in the thick of everything of late. He'd been making reference to Hunter's having found Elaine St. Claire, now this car. His tone had been adversarial. Confrontational. To Hunter's credit, he hadn't taken the bait.

Matt had hardly looked at her, she realized. Neither had Buddy. Matt hadn't directed but one of the questions her way. His only comment to her had been about the approaching storm.

She glanced down at herself. The wet, white cotton was nearly transparent, her lilac-colored bra clearly visible. Her cheeks warmed. *Great, Chauvin. Very classy.*

She stood, took one last look at the rain and headed inside to change. The phone was ringing; she grabbed it.

She knew a split second before the woman spoke that it was her—the one who had called before. The heavy moment of silence when she picked up the phone tipped her off. She didn't give the woman a chance to speak. "Who are you? What do you want?"

"Damn you to hell," the woman said, laughing thickly, the sound mean. "Your father's already there."

"My father was a good man. He—"

"Was a liar and murderer. He got what he deserved."

"How dare you," Avery snapped, so angry she shook. "My father was a saint. He—"

The woman began to laugh, a witch's cackle. Pure evil.

With a cry, Avery slammed down the receiver. Without missing a beat, she picked it back up and punched in the Stevenses home phone. Cherry answered.

"Cherry," she said, "is Buddy there?"

"Avery? Are you all right?"

"Yes...I—" She sucked in a deep, calming breath, the woman's awful laugh, her words, still ringing in her ears. "Is he there?"

"No. He and Matt are out at Tiller's Pond. Do you need me to beep him?"

"No, it's not urgent. It's just...could you have him ring me when he gets in? It's important."

Cherry called Matt instead, Avery realized several hours later. He stood at her door, expression concerned. "What's wrong?"

"Cherry told you I called."

"She said you were upset."

Avery made a sound of embarrassment. In the hours that had passed, she'd put the incident into perspective. "I overreacted about something." She pushed open the door. "Come in."

He stepped inside. He'd changed out of his uniform and wore a pair of old, soft blue jeans and a white golf shirt. His arms and neck looked tan against the startling white.

He met her eyes. "What's up?"

"Did my father have any enemies?"

The question surprised him, she saw. "Enemies? Not that I know of. Why?"

"I've gotten a couple of unsettling anonymous calls. I got one this afternoon and it...I got upset. I called Buddy."

"The calls, were they from a woman or a man?"

"A woman."

"The nature of the calls?"

"Ugly." She folded her arms across her chest, then dropped them to her sides again. "The first time she called, she said that Dad had...gotten what he deserved. And that I would, too. This time she called him a—" she had to force the words out "—a murderer. And a liar."

"And you have no idea who the woman is?"

"No. None."

"You try *69?"

"Tried it. Dad didn't subscribe."

"You might want to add it or caller ID. Just in case she calls again."

Avery nodded. "I will."

He searched her expression. "She's just a crank, Avery. You know that, right?" When she hesitated, he shook his head. "We're talking about the doc here. Nobody had a higher moral character than your dad. I believe that. Black and white, no moral gray area."

"I know. But—" She clasped her hands in front of her. "I keep coming back to what she said, that he got what he deserved. Like maybe, he didn't kill himself. Like maybe somebody helped him out."

For a long moment, he said nothing. "You mean, somebody killed him?"

She met his gaze evenly. "Yes."

"Who would hurt your dad?" he asked.

"Someone who thought him a liar and murderer."

He caught her hands, rubbed them between his. She hadn't realized until that moment how cold they had been. "The CSPD did a thorough job. Dr. Harris is a crackerjack coroner who doesn't let anything slip by him. I reviewed everything as well, Avery." He gentled his tone. "I didn't want to believe it either."

Avery couldn't bring herself to look at him. He squeezed her fingers. "This caller is a mentally disturbed person. Or someone with an ax to grind, maybe with Buddy. Maybe someone trying to cause trouble through you. Why don't you take a look at Dad's report. It'll put your mind at rest."

"You don't think Buddy would mind?"

"No way." He smiled. "When it comes to you, Avery, Dad'll do anything."

She changed the subject. "How'd it go at the pond?"

He slid his hands into his front pockets. "Figured you might want an update."

"Car belonged to that guy who went missing, didn't it? The one you and Buddy were talking about the other day? The one reported missing by his girlfriend."

"Yup, sure did. His name was Luke McDougal."

"Was? He's dead?"

"Don't know. The vehicle's been hauled out. It's empty. Cell phone's in the car. Evidence team has it." He glanced at his watch. "The property's being searched, the pond dredged."

Avery shivered and rubbed her arms. "When will that be done?"

"The rain's slowed us down. Not until tomorrow, I suspect." He met her eyes, expression grim. "I need to ask you something, Avery. What were you and Hunter doing at Tiller's Pond?"

"I went to see him. He was going for a run. I joined him." She lifted a shoulder. "Ended up there."

He looked away, dragging a hand through his hair, swearing softly.

"What is it, Matt?"

He returned his gaze to hers. "I'm wondering why you went to see him in the first place."

"He and I were friends, I guess I still think of him that way. Does it matter?"

She saw by his expression that it did matter to him. It mattered a lot. She let out a pent-up breath. "I wanted to find out more about the St. Claire murder. Since he had been at the scene, I figured he could tell me what I needed to know."

"You could have come to me. I would have answered your questions."

"Matt," she chided, "I'm a journalist. I'm experienced enough to know what the police will, or will not, share."

He tipped his face toward the ceiling, the picture of frustration. "Help me out here, Avery. I feel like a jerk."

She smiled. "You're jealous?"

"Don't laugh." He glowered good-naturedly at her. "Hell, yes, I'm jealous. I know the kind of things that went on at Tiller's Pond."

Flattered, she closed the distance between them, stopping inches from him. She tilted her face to his, shamelessly flirting. "Yeah, but all those things happened with you."

Something flickered in his eyes, some strong emotion. One that stirred her blood. "Dammit, your shirt was wet."

"I was hot. The water was cool."

He cupped her cheeks in his palms, grip just short of painful. "Be careful, okay? Hunter's not...he's not the boy you knew."

*It's not true what they say about him. Hunter's a good man.*

"I'm a big girl, not a teenager, Matt." He didn't smile. Hers wavered. "Is there something you're not telling me?"

He bent, pressed his mouth to hers in a quick, hard kiss. "I'll pick you up for Spring Fest tomorrow at three."

Without another word, he left. She watched as he crossed to his cruiser, climbed in and backed down the driveway. She brought a hand to her mouth, to the imprint of his lips against hers. Their date, she realized. Spring Fest, she had forgotten all about it.

A date with Matt Stevens. After all these years. She eased the door shut, locked it, but didn't move from the foyer. What was she getting herself into? What did he want from her?

More than friendship, more than a stroll down memory lane. That was obvious. But what of her feelings? What did she want?

She enjoyed his company, reliving the past. When with him she became the girl she had been back then.

She thought of Hunter, his image slipping into her head, filling it. There was something between her and Hunter as well, she realized. Something strong. Something that caused her to think of him when she shouldn't.

But what? Concerned friendship? Attraction? Sexual awareness?

Or suspicion?

What had Matt meant when he'd said she didn't know Hunter as well as she thought? When he had warned her to be careful?

Moody and aggravating as Hunter could be, she hadn't felt threatened around him. Even when they had clashed. The only thing that had seemed in any imminent danger had been her reputation.

So why his real, nearly palpable concern?

# CHAPTER 23

Spring Fest was much as Avery remembered it. The atmosphere of celebration, the sound of children laughing mingling with the smells of good Louisiana food and the warmth of the sun on the back of her neck.

She and Matt did it all: rode the Ferris wheel and Tilt-A-Whirl; sampled foods from all the vendors, so much that she longed to unsnap the top button of her shorts; wandered through the arts and crafts booths; and from the blanket they'd spread under the canopy of the square's biggest oak tree, listened to the various bands scheduled throughout the day.

The day should have been perfect, Avery told herself. She should be relaxed, totally content. Hard to be either, however, when news of Luke McDougal's car being found in Tiller's Pond and the St. Claire murder was on everyone's lips. Hard to feel carefree when she couldn't shake her suspicions about her father's death. When she couldn't discount what Gwen Lancaster had told her about The Seven and the disproportionate number of suicides in Cypress

Springs. Or that she believed her dad had been killed because he had known too much about The Seven.

Avery found herself trying to read people's expressions, trying to see beyond what they were saying to what they weren't. Every glance from one person to another became a signal of some sort. She found herself listening to the conversations around her, hoping to recognize the voice of her anonymous caller.

She hated feeling this way, suspicious and on edge. Distrustful to the point of paranoia.

"Thirsty?"

Avery turned and found Matt's gaze on her. They sat on the blanket; the sun had set and the final band of the day had just finished their first song. "What did you have in mind?"

"Beer?"

"Why not?"

He frowned slightly. "Are you all right?"

"Fine. A little tired."

He opened his mouth as if to say something further, then seemed to change his mind and stood. "Don't disappear on me."

"I won't." As he walked away, her smile faded. Luke McDougal had disappeared. According to Gwen Lancaster, so had a number of Cypress Springs citizens, picking up and moving in the night. No word to anyone.

"Where'd that no-good kid of mine go?"

Avery looked up at Buddy and smiled. Dressed in his uniform, complete with service weapon and nightstick, there was no doubt he was on duty. "Beer run."

"A cold one sure would hit the spot right now."

She made a sound of sympathy. "No rest for the wicked, I see."

"Love Spring Fest. And hate it. With so many visitors in town and so much drinking going on, there's always some sort of commotion." He looked in the direction Matt had gone.

Avery patted the blanket. "Have a seat."

"I'd rather dance. Care to cut a rug with an old man like me?"

She smiled affectionately and stood. "I'd love to."

He led her toward the makeshift dance floor, in front of the bandstand. He held out his arms. She took his hand and they began to move in time to the music, a Cajun two-step. "I've been waiting for a chance to get you alone. Matt's not left your side all day."

"Matt's grown into a good man," she said. "You must be proud."

He shifted his gaze, a sadness crossing his features. Sensing he was thinking of his other son, she murmured, "Hunter's going to be okay. He will, I'm certain of it."

He met her eyes once more, the expression in his gentle. "Thank you, Avery. That means the world to me."

The music's pace shifted, Buddy adjusted smoothly. For such a big man, he was light on his feet, graceful. She told him so.

"Lilah made it clear when we were dating, if I wanted to win her hand, I had to know how to dance. So I learned. It wasn't easy, let me tell you." He chuckled. "Two left feet is my natural inclination."

She smiled at the story. "Where is Lilah tonight? I haven't seen her or Cherry."

"Lilah's home. Under the weather. Cherry elected to stay with her."

"I'm sorry to hear she's not feeling well."

"She suffers horribly this time of year with her allergies."

"Is there anything I can do?"

"Pay her a visit." He smiled, the picture of fatherly affection. "I'm so pleased you're home, Avery."

She kissed his cheek. "I am, too, Buddy. I didn't realize how much I missed this place. The people."

"It's a good place. Good people."

*Anyone whose actions fell outside what was considered right, moral or neighborly was singled out.*

Her smile faded. "What's wrong?" he asked.

"Buddy, can I ask you something?"

"Sure, baby girl."

"You ever heard of a group called The Seven?"

His steps faltered; he drew his eyebrows together. "When you asked about her, I was afraid this might happen."

"Who?"

"That Gwen Lancaster."

"You know her?"

"Of her," he corrected, expression tight. "She's been going around Cypress Springs spreading lies. Starting rumors."

"So the group never existed?"

"They existed, all right. Just not the way she's portraying them. To hear her talk, they were a bunch of hatemongers and murderers."

He let out a heavy-sounding breath. "They called themselves Seven Citizens Who Care. The group organized in an attempt to stem the tide of social ills that had beset our town. Their feeling was, stop crime before it happened. They began a drug and alcohol awareness program in the schools. They organized a chapter of Planned Parenthood. They arranged counseling for families in crisis. They began a campaign to get families back to church."

Avery remembered suddenly being required to take sex education in the tenth grade, remembered the addition of films about the dangers of alcohol and drugs in health class—subjects that had never been broached in school before.

"They weren't high-profile. They weren't in it for acclaim or notoriety. They were simply citizens willing to take a stand for this community. Lilah belonged. So did Pastor Dastugue."

"I feel like an idiot. I didn't know."

"I wish they had been more public. Then people like Gwen Lancaster couldn't spread their lies."

"What's going on here, Dad? You trying to steal my girl?"

Buddy's expression cleared. "I think your mother would have something to say about that, son."

A commotion by the bandstand interrupted their banter. Buddy glanced in that direction, then swore softly. "Excuse me, kids. Duty calls."

They watched him go. The band struck up another tune. "Dance with me?"

Matt held out his arms; Avery stepped into them. Her talk with Buddy had changed everything, she realized. She felt as if a thousand-pound weight had been lifted from her shoulders. How could she have trusted a stranger over people she knew and loved?

"You and Dad have a nice talk?" he asked.

"Really nice."

"He loves you a lot, you know. As much as me or Cherry."

*But not Hunter. Never Hunter.*

"You're thinking of my brother, aren't you?"

How did he so easily read her mind? Did he know her so well, still, after all these years?

"Yes," she said.

"He did this to himself, Avery. He removed himself from our lives."

"But why? I guess I just...don't understand. We were all so close."

"I wish to God I knew what went wrong. You can't imagine—" He looked away, then back, expression in his eyes anguished. "I've never been closer to anybody than I was my brother. He's my other half, Avery. When we were kids...I couldn't have imagined this. That we wouldn't be best friends anymore. That we wouldn't even speak to one another, for God's sake."

"Have you tried to reconcile?"

He laughed, the sound tight. "Are you kidding? We all have. Tried and been rebuffed. Time and again."

"Hunter said something about Dad and Buddy's relationship. That they didn't even speak anymore. That it had become so bad between them, Dad would cross the street to avoid their coming face-to-face. Is that true?"

"Son of a bitch," he muttered, expression tightening. "That prick."

"So, it's not true?"

"Only partially. In the last months before his suicide. I believe he avoided Dad because he knew Dad would realize how bad off he was and stop him."

"Oh," she murmured, feeling small and gullible.

"Did he say anything else about us?"

*Nothing she was about to repeat.* She shook her head. "He seems so serious now. As if he's facing—"

"I don't want to talk about my brother, Avery. Not tonight." Matt drew her closer against him. "Did today bring back memories?"

She tilted her face up to his. "Good ones."

"Remember the Spring Fest we sneaked off to make out? We were all of thirteen."

"Your dad caught on. Followed us. Made you apologize to me."

"Lectured me about how to treat a lady."

She laughed. "Little did he know, it was the lady's idea."

*And three years later, sneaking off to Tiller's Pond had also been her idea. And there, under the star-sprinkled sky they had consummated their passion for one another.*

"We were so bad," she said.

"We were in love." His gaze held hers. Her mouth went dry. "I couldn't get enough of you, Avery. Of touching you. Of being with you."

The blood rushed to her head. He dropped a hand to the small of her back, began moving his fingers in slow, rhythmic circles.

She melted against him. Memories swamped her. Of past moments like this. Of hot, urgent hands and mouths. Of the dizzying rush of their newfound sexuality.

He brought his mouth to her ear. "Seeing you with Hunter yesterday like that, it made me crazy. I couldn't look at you. I was afraid of what I might do. To you. To him."

What would it be like to make love with Matt? Avery wondered. Without the potency of young love, without the heady rush of their burgeoning sexuality? They weren't kids anymore but consenting adults. They'd had other lovers, they had hurt and been hurt. They wouldn't have to hurry, wouldn't need to worry about getting home before curfew or being caught. She knew how to please a man; he to please a woman.

With Matt she could have what she had lost. She could be the girl who was otherwise gone forever.

Cherry's warning to stay away from her brother unless she was serious ran through her mind, as did the assertion that Matt had never loved anyone but her.

Until she knew what she wanted, they couldn't go there. Much as she longed to.

"What are you thinking?" he asked.

"About the past. The way it was between us."

"I'm glad." He dropped his face close to hers. "Because it was good. And it could be good again. Very good."

"I wish I could be as certain. So much has changed, Matt. We've cha—"

He brought a finger to her lips. "I'm a patient man. I've waited this long, I can wait a little longer."

CHAPTER 24

Gwen stared at the front page of the *Gazette*'s Wednesday edition, her morning cup of coffee cooling on the bedstand. Not the headline story about Peggy Trumble's winning entry in the annual Spring Fest bake-off, but the one at the bottom, tucked into a corner, almost an afterthought: Car Hauled Out of Tiller's Pond.

She skimmed the piece for the third time. The story—hardly more than a blurb—went on to report how Avery Chauvin and Hunter Stevens had discovered a car abandoned in Tiller's Pond. The vehicle had been hauled out and found to be empty.

It was the last line of the piece that shook her to the core.

The owner of the vehicle, New Orleanian Luke McDougal, who had been heading from nearby Clinton to St. Francisville, had been reported missing by his girlfriend three weeks before. Anyone with information should call the West Feliciana Parish Sheriff's Department.

*No body. Just like her brother.*

Gwen's legs shook so badly she had to sit. She sank onto the edge of the bed and brought a hand to her mouth. A suicide. A murder. And two disappearances. The Seven were responsible for all three, she hadn't a doubt. Dr. Phillip Chauvin had been killed because he'd known too much about The Seven. Elaine St. Claire had been killed because of her lifestyle. Her brother had gotten too close to the group.

What about Luke McDougal? She shifted her gaze to the *Gazette.* According to the article, he had been passing through town. So what was his connection to the group? Was there a connection?

There had to be. McDougal's disappearance was too similar to her brother's. Car found, seemingly abandoned. No sign of its owner or of foul play.

Avery Chauvin had been at the scene. So had Hunter Stevens. Gwen drew her eyebrows together, curious. She had seen the man's name in connection with another news piece recently. She searched her memory a moment.

*He had found Elaine St. Claire's body.*

That was odd, even for a community as small as Cypress Springs. It seemed to her that the coincidental and unexplainable were piling up. As were the bodies—even if no one but she saw it.

*She could be next.*

Avery Chauvin had told her the same thing, though at the time it hadn't frightened her. Now she wondered if the woman meant the words as a warning. Or a threat.

Gwen fought the urge to flee. Fought to come to grips with the overwhelming sensation of being trapped. She had trusted Avery, even though she had known nothing about her. She had automatically assumed she could because Avery had only recently returned to Cypress Springs. And because of her father's suicide.

That hadn't been smart. Avery Chauvin could be sympathetic to The Seven. Their cause. Her father very well may have taken his own life, she had no physical evidence proving otherwise, just a gut feeling.

Gwen recalled Avery's surprise and denial to her assertions about The Seven. Her obvious, nearly palpable relief when Gwen had suggested her father's death might have been other than suicide. As if relieved to have an ally.

Avery could be in cahoots with The Seven, but she thought not.

Gwen stood and crossed to the window, lifted one of the blind's slats and peered out at the brilliant morning. People moved about— on their way to school, work, on errands. City workers were still cleaning up from the weekend festival, removing lights, combing the square for the last remnants of trash.

Though no one as much as glanced her way, she felt as if she was being watched. Her comings and goings recorded. Who she spoke with noted.

*Action against her was being planned.*

Shuddering, she stepped away from the window. She brought the heels of her hands to her eyes. She had been too vocal about The Seven. Had asked too many questions of too many people. She hadn't used caution.

In her zeal to uncover her brother's fate, she had put herself in harm's way. Just as her brother, in his zeal to prove his thesis, had. Would she, like Tom, simply disappear? Who would come looking for her if she did? Or would her end come via suicide? She could see the headline now: Sister, Despondent Over Disappearance of Brother, Takes Own Life.

Who would doubt she'd done it? Not her mother, who had slid so deeply into depression herself that she could hardly get out of bed in the morning. Not the shrink she had seen, who had prescribed antidepressants, then lectured her for not taking them.

*Don't get paranoid. Just be careful.*

She needed an ally. She needed someone she could trust. Someone who belonged here, in this community. Someone the citizens of Cypress Springs trusted. Who could poke around and ask questions. Someone skilled at ferreting out facts. A person who had a compelling, personal reason for wanting to help her.

Only one such person came to mind.

Avery Chauvin.

## CHAPTER 25

Gwen quickly showered and dressed. She towel-dried her hair, grateful for her no-fuss cap of curls, slapped on a touch of makeup, grabbed her handbag and darted out. Avery, she'd noted, had taken to jogging early then stopping for breakfast at the Azalea Café.

It was a bit late, but if she was lucky she would catch Avery as she was leaving the café.

She was better than lucky, Gwen saw, spotting Avery through the café's picture window—it looked as if the other woman had just gotten her pancakes. She was deep in an animated conversation with Peg, the Azalea's owner.

Gwen stepped into the restaurant. At the jingle of the door opening, both the café's owner and Avery looked her way. Avery's smile faded.

Gwen pasted on a friendly smile and crossed to the booth. "Morning, Avery."

"Morning." She returned her attention to the other woman in an obvious rebuff.

*They'd ended their last conversation if not on a friendly note, then one of growing respect. Avery had begun to believe in The Seven.*

*What had changed since then?*

"Sit anywhere, hon," Peg interjected. "I'll be right with you."

Gwen hesitated, then nodded, choosing the table across the aisle from Avery. When the woman finished, she turned and took Gwen's order.

She asked for an English muffin and coffee, then watched Peg make her way back to the counter. When she reached it, she glanced back at Gwen, frown marring her forehead. Finding Gwen watching her, she smiled cheerfully and headed for the kitchen.

When the woman disappeared through the swinging doors, Gwen turned to Avery. "I was hoping I'd find you here."

Avery dug into her pancakes, not glancing her way.

"I really need to talk to you. It's important."

Avery looked at her then. "I don't want to talk to you. Please leave me alone."

"Did you have the chance to check out the facts I gave you when we spoke last?"

"I didn't realize you gave me any facts. I seem to remember un-substantiated opinion and half-truths."

"If you would check—"

"I don't care to discuss this."

"Did they get to you? Is that what's happened? Did they threaten you with—"

Avery cut her off. "I don't know if you're delusional or just mean-spirited, but I've had enough."

"I'm neither, I promise you that. As a journalist—"

"I'm a good journalist. I test premise against facts. I don't twist the facts to make them sensational. I don't bend them to fit my own personal needs."

"If you would just listen."

"I listened too much already." Avery leaned toward her. "What you told me about The Seven were untruths. Yes, The Seven existed, but not as you described them. Yes, they were a group of civic-minded residents. But not a secret tribunal that spied and passed judgment on their fellow citizens. They called themselves Seven Citizens Who Care. They started a drug and alcohol awareness program in the schools and tried to get families back to church. My pastor was a member, for heaven's sake. So was Lilah Stevens. I suggest *you* check your facts, Ms. Lancaster."

"That's not true! Who told you this? Who—"

"It doesn't matter." Avery tossed her napkin on the table and slid out of the booth, pancakes hardly touched. "Put it on my tab, Peg," she called. "I need some fresh air."

Gwen stifled a sound of distress, jumped up and started after her, nearly colliding with Peg. The woman jumped back. The coffee she carried sloshed over the cup's side. With a cry of pain, she dropped the cup; it hit the floor and shattered.

Gwen apologized, but didn't stop. She made it out of the restaurant and onto the street moments after Avery.

"Wait!" she shouted. "I haven't told you everything."

Avery stopped and turned slowly. She met Gwen's gaze, the expression in hers resigned. "Don't you get it? I don't want to hear anything else you have to say. I love this town and the people who live here."

"Even if they killed your father? Would you love them then?"

For the space of a heartbeat, the other woman didn't move, didn't seem to breathe. Then she shook her head. "I see now how desperate you are. To stoop that low. Be so...cruel. I feel sorry for you, Gwen Lancaster."

"I can ask that question," Gwen went on, knowing her time was limited, that the other woman would bolt any moment, "because they killed my brother."

"Nice try, but—"

"It was the same as with Luke McDougal. His car was found. No sign of violence. He was just...gone."

Gwen became aware of the volume of her voice, of the number of people around. Of who might be watching...and listening. She closed the distance between them.

"Tom Lancaster," she continued softly. "The *Gazette* ran a piece about his disappearance. It was about the size of the one they ran about McDougal's. Wednesday, February 6, this year. I have my

own copy but you'd probably think I found some way to manufacture it."

Gwen glanced at the café's front window and found Peg there,
peering out at them. She shifted her gaze. A CSPD patrolman
seemed to be paying more attention to them than to the driver he
was ticketing; she glanced toward the square. The old man on the
bench across the street was openly watching them over the top of
his newspaper.

She lowered her voice even more. "That's how I know about The
Seven, from Tom. The thesis was his. He was here researching. He
got too close."

"I think you're unstable," Avery said, voice shaking. "I think you
should get some help."

"Check it out. Come see me when you believe."

## CHAPTER 26

Just past dawn the next morning, Avery lay awake, staring at the ceiling. Fatigue pulled at her. A headache from lack of sleep pounded at the base of her skull. Gwen Lancaster's baldly stated question had played over and over in her head, making rest impossible.

*"Even if they killed your father? Would you love them then?"*

Avery rolled onto her side, curling into a tight ball. She wished she had never met the woman. She wished she could find a way to find and hold on to the peace of mind she had felt the other night after speaking with Buddy.

Why couldn't she simply believe in Buddy and Matt and the other people she loved and trusted? Why couldn't she put her faith in the various agencies that had investigated her father's death and determined it to be a suicide?

*"I can ask that question, because they killed my brother."*

"Dammit!" Avery sat up. She balled her hands into fists. Desperate people resorted to desperate measures to get their way.

Gwen Lancaster was desperate, that had been obvious. So why should she believe her? Why not write her off as either a nut or a liar?

That very desperation. It rang true. Gwen Lancaster believed what she was saying. She was frightened.

Avery flopped onto her back, staring up at the ceiling once more. Gwen could be suffering from a psychotic disorder. Schizophrenics believed the voices they heard in their heads; their visions, the people who populated them, were as real to them as Matt and Buddy were to her. Paranoid schizophrenics believed that others plotted against them. Some functioned for years without detection.

But that didn't explain her anonymous caller. It didn't explain Luke McDougal's disappearance or Elaine St. Claire's murder.

And it certainly didn't assuage her feeling that her father could take his own life.

She threw back the covers and climbed out of bed. She crossed to the window and nudged aside the curtain. Cypress Springs had not yet awakened. She saw not a single light shining.

Headlights cut across the road, slicing through the dim light, bouncing off the trees and morning mist. A police cruiser, she saw. It slowed as it reached her property line, inching past at a snail's pace. Instinctively, she eased away from the window, out of sight.

Silly. Without a light inside, they wouldn't be able to see her. Besides, the cruiser was no doubt Buddy's doing.

Playing daddy. Watching out for her.

She rubbed her face, acknowledging exhaustion. She *was* being silly. Losing sleep over this. Letting it tear her apart. She should be able to go on faith. Should be able to, but couldn't. She wasn't built that way. As an investigative reporter, she tested premise against facts, day in and day out.

If she wanted to regain her peace of mind, she would have to disprove Gwen Lancaster's claims.

Avery turned away from the window and began to pace, mind working, the skills she used on her job kicking in. If this were a story she was considering, what would she do?

Begin with a premise. One she thought had merit, that would

not only make a good story but also make a difference. Remedy a problem.

Like the story she had done about the flaws in the foster care system. She had exposed the problems. By doing so, she'd helped future children caught in the system. Hopefully. That had been her aim; it was the aim of all good investigative reporting.

She stopped. So what was her premise? A group of small town citizens, frightened over the growing moral decay of their community, take the job of law and order into their own hands. Their actions begin benignly enough but unchecked, become extremist. Anyone who's actions fall outside what is considered right, moral or neighborly is singled out. They break the civil rights of their fellow citizens in the name of righteousness, law and order. Before it's all over, they resort to murder, the cure becoming worse than the illness, the judges more corrupt than the judged.

It was the kind of premise she loved to sink her teeth into. One that would make a startling, eye-opening story. It spoke to her on many levels. She loved her country and believed in the principles on which it had been founded. The freedoms that had made it great. Yet, she also bemoaned the loss of personal safety, the ever-decaying American value system, the inability of law enforcement and the courts to adequately deal with crime.

But this wasn't some anonymous story she was following up, Avery reminded herself. Her role wasn't that of uninvolved, cool-headed journalist. This was her hometown. The people involved her friends and neighbors. People she called family. One of the dead was her father.

She was emotionally involved, all right. Up to her eyeballs.

Premise against facts, she thought, determination flowing through her. She wouldn't let her emotions keep her from being objective. She would stay on her guard, wouldn't be blinded by personal involvement.

And same as always, she would uncover the truth.

# CHAPTER 27

A very decided her first stop of the morning would be at the office of the Cypress Springs *Gazette,* located in a renovated storefront a block and a half off the square. Founded in June 1963, just months before the assassination of President John F. Kennedy, a picture of the former president still hung in the front waiting area.

She stepped through the door and a bell tinkled, announcing her presence. The front counter stood empty.

A tall, sandy-haired man appeared in the doorway to the newsroom. Behind his Harry Potter spectacles, his eyes widened. "Avery Chauvin? I was wondering if you were going to stop by for a visit."

"Rickey? Rickey Plaquamine? It's so good to see you."

He came around the counter and they hugged. She and Rickey had been in the same grade and had gone to school together all their lives. They had worked together on the high-school newspaper, had both pursued journalism and attended Louisiana State University in Baton Rouge. He, however, had opted to return to Cypress Springs after graduation, to report for the local paper.

"You haven't changed a bit," she said.

He patted his stomach. "Not if you ignore the thirty pounds I've gained. Ten with each one of Jeanette's pregnancies."

"Three? Last I heard—"

"We just had our third. Another boy."

"Three boys." She laughed. "Jeanette's got her hands full."

"You don't know the half of it." His smile faded. "Damn sorry about your dad. Sorry we didn't make the service. The new one's got colic and the entire household's been turned upside down."

"It's okay." She shifted her gaze toward the newsroom. "Where's Sal?"

He looked surprised. "You didn't know? Sal passed away about six months ago."

"Passed away," she repeated, crestfallen. Sal had been a big supporter of hers and had encouraged her to go into journalism. With each advancement of her career, he'd written her a note of congratulations. In each, his pride in her accomplishments had come shining through. "I didn't know."

His mouth thinned. "Hunting accident."

Avery froze. Goose bumps crawled up her arms. "Hunting accident?"

"Opening day of deer season. Shot dead. In fact, the bullet took half Sal's head off."

Her stomach turned. "My God. Who was the shooter?"

"Don't know, never found the guy."

"Sounds like it could have been a homicide."

"That's not the way Buddy called it. Besides, who'd want Sal dead?"

Her father. Sal Mandina. Two men who had been pillars of the community, men the entire town had looked up to. Both dead in the past six months. Neither from natural causes.

Rickey cleared his throat. She shifted her attention to the task at hand. "I was doing a little research and wondered if I could take a look at the archived issues of the *Gazette*."

"Sure. What're you looking for?"

"The Waguespack murder."

"No kidding? How come?"

She debated a moment about her answer then decided on incomplete honesty, as she called partial truth. "Dad saved a bunch of clippings... I'd forgotten the entire incident and wanted to fill in the blanks." She smiled brightly. "You mind?"

"Not at all. Come on." He led her back into the newsroom. From there they headed up to the second floor. "Biggest local news story we ever carried. I'm not surprised your dad kept clippings."

"Really? Why?"

"Because of the furor the murder caused in the community. Nobody escaped unchanged."

"That's what Buddy said."

"You talked to Buddy about it?"

Was that relief she heard in his voice? Or was she imagining it? "Sure. After all, he and Dad were best friends."

He unlocked the storage-room door, opened it and switched on the light. She stepped inside. It smelled of old newspapers. The room was lined with shelves stacked with bound volumes of the *Gazette.* At the center of the room sat a long folding table, two chairs on either side. Her throat began to tickle, no doubt from the dust.

"Call me if you need me. I'm working on Saturday's edition. The spring Peewee soccer league is kicking into high gear. Pardon the pun." He pointed toward the far wall. "The 1980s are over there. They're arranged by date."

Avery thanked him, and when she was certain she was alone, she crossed to issues from the past eight months. She carried a stack to the table and sat. From her purse she took a steno pad and pen and laid them on the table.

She opened the volume for Wednesday, February 6 of this year. And found the story just where Gwen had said she would.

### Young Man Missing

Tom Lancaster, visiting grad student from Tulane University, went missing Sunday night. Sheriff's department fears foul play. Deputy Sheriff Matt Stevens suspects Lancaster a victim of a random act of violence. The investigation continues.

Avery sucked in a shaky breath. One truth did not fact make, she reminded herself. The best lies—or most insidious delusions—contained elements of truth. That element of believability sucked people in, made them open their wallets or ignore warning signs indicating something was amiss.

She found a number of stories about Sal's death. Since he'd been the *Gazette's* editor-in-chief, the biweekly had followed it closely. As Rickey had told her, he had been shot on the opening day of deer season. The guilty party had never been found, though every citizen who'd applied for a hunting license had been questioned.

Buddy had determined Sal had been shot from a distance with a Browning .270-caliber A-bolt rifle. Both it and the Nosler Ballistic Tip bullet were local hunters' favorites. Closed-casket services had been held at Gallagher's.

Rickey had been wrong about one thing: Buddy had classified the death as a homicide.

For the next two hours she picked her way through the archived issues. What she found shook her to the core.

*Gwen Lancaster hadn't been fabricating.*

Avery picked up her notepad, scanning her notes. She had listed every death not attributed to natural causes. Kevin Gallagher had died this year, she saw. Danny Gallagher's dad. A car wreck on Highway 421, just outside of town. His Lexus had careened off the road and smashed into a tree. He hadn't been wearing a seat belt and had gone through the windshield.

Deputy Chief of Police Pat Greene had drowned. A woman named Dolly Farmer had hung herself. There'd been a couple more car wrecks, young people involved—both in the same area Sal had died. The city, she saw, had commissioned the state to reduce the speed limit along that stretch of highway.

She frowned. Another hanging—this one deemed accidental. The kid, it seemed, had been into autoeroticism. Another young person had OD'd. Pete Trimble had fallen off his tractor and been run over.

Avery laid the notepad on the table and brought a trembling hand to her mouth. Eight months, all this death. Ten of them. Thirteen if she tossed in Luke McDougal, Tom Lancaster and Elaine St. Claire.

She struggled for impartiality. Even so, Gwen had not presented the facts accurately: she had claimed there'd been six suicides—including her father's—in the past eight months. She saw two.

"You okay up here?"

Avery took a second to compose herself and glanced over her shoulder at Rickey. She forced a smile. "Great." She hopped to her feet. "Just finished now."

She tucked the notebook into her purse, then grabbed up the volume she had been studying. She carried it to the section that housed the 1980s, hoping he wouldn't notice she was shelving it incorrectly.

She wasn't that lucky.

"That doesn't go there." He crossed the room. "Wrong color code."

He slid the volume out, checked the date, frowning. "Thought you wanted to look at stuff from 1988."

"Caught me." She hiked her purse strap higher on her shoulder. "I did, I just—" She looked away then back, working to capture just the right note of sincerity. "It's so maudlin, really. But Dad's...his death...I—"

He glanced down at the volume as the date registered. "Geez, Avery, I'm sorry."

"It's okay." She manufactured a trembling smile. "Want to walk me out?"

He did just that, stopping at the front door. "Avery, can I ask you something?"

"Sure."

"Rumor on the street is you're staying. Is that so?"

She opened her mouth to deny the rumor, then shut it as she realized she didn't know for certain what she was doing. "I haven't decided yet," she admitted. "But don't tell my editor."

He smiled at that. "If you stay, I'd love to have you on the *Gazette* staff. A big step down, I know. But at the *Post* you've got to put up with the city."

"You're right about that." She smiled, pleased by the offer. "If I stay, there's no one I'd rather work with."

"Stop by and see Jeanette. Meet the kids. She'd love it."

"I would, too." She crossed to the door. There she glanced back. "Rickey? You ever hear of a group called The Seven?"

His expression altered subtly. He drew his eyebrows together, as if thinking. "What kind of group? Religious? Civic?"

"Civic."

"Nope. Sorry."

"It's okay. It's something Buddy mentioned. Have a great day."

She stepped out onto the sidewalk. Squinting against the sun, she dug her sunglasses out of her purse, then glanced back at the *Gazette's* front window.

Rickey was on the phone, she saw. In what appeared to be a heated discussion. He looked upset.

Rickey glanced up then. His gaze met hers. The hair on the back of her neck prickling, she lifted a hand in goodbye, turned and walked quickly away.

# CHAPTER 28

Avery went home to regroup and decide on her next step. She sat at her kitchen table, much as she had for the past hour, untouched tuna sandwich on a plate beside her. She stared at her notebook, at the names of the dead.

Such damning evidence. Didn't anyone in Cypress Springs find this rash of deaths odd? Hadn't anyone expressed concern to Buddy or Matt? Was the whole town in on this conspiracy?

*Slow down, Chauvin. Assess the facts. Be objective.*

Avery pushed away from the table, stood and crossed to the window. She peered out at the lush backyard, a profusion of greens accented by splashes of red and pink. What did she actually have? Gwen Lancaster, a woman who claimed that a vigilante-style group was operating in Cypress Springs. A number of accidental deaths, suspicious because of their number. Two missing persons. A murder. A suicide. And a box of newspaper clippings about a fifteen-year-old murder.

Accidents took lives. People went missing. Murders happened, as tragic a fact as that was. Yes, the suicide rate was slightly higher than the state average, but statistics were based on averages not absolutes. It might be two years before another Cypress Springs resident took his own life.

And the clippings? she wondered. A clue to state of mind or nothing more than saved memorabilia?

If the clippings were evidence to a state of mind, wouldn't her dad have saved something else as well? She thought yes. But where would he have stored them? She had emptied his bedroom closet and dresser drawers, the kitchen cabinets and pantry and the front hall closet. But she hadn't even set foot in his study or the attic.

Now, she decided, was the time.

Two and a half hours later, Avery found herself back in the kitchen, no closer to an answer than before. She crossed to the sink to wash her hands, frustrated. She had gone through her father's desk and bookshelves, his stored files in the attic. She had done a spot check of every box in the attic. And found nothing suspicious or out of the ordinary.

She dried her hands. What next? In Washington, she'd had colleagues to brainstorm with, editors to turn to for opinions and insights, sources she trusted. Here she had nothing but her own gut instinct to guide her.

She let it guide her now. She picked up the phone and dialed her editor at the *Post*. "Brandon, it's Avery."

"Is it really you?" He laughed. "And here I thought you might be hiding from me."

He appreciated bluntness. He always preferred his writers get to the point—both in their work and their pitches. The high-stress business of getting a newspaper on the stands afforded no time for meandering or coy word games.

"I'm onto a story," she said.

"Glad to hear your brain's still working. Though I'm a bit surprised, considering. Tell me about it."

"Small town turns to policing its citizens Big Brother-style as a way to stop the ills of the modern world from encroaching on their way of life. It began when a group of citizens, alarmed by the dramatic increase in crime, formed an organization to counter the tide. At first it was little more than a Neighborhood Watch-type program. A way to help combat crime."

"Then they ran amok," he offered.

"Yes. According to my source, the core group was small, but they had an intricate network of others who reported to the group. Citizens were followed. Their mail read. What they ate, drank and watched was monitored. Where they went. If they worshiped. If the group determined it necessary, they were warned that their behavior would not be tolerated."

"Goodbye civil rights," Brandon muttered.

"That's not the half of it. If their warnings went unheeded, the group took action. Businesses were boycotted. Individuals shunned. Property vandalized. To varying degrees, everyone was in on it."

He was silent a moment. "You talking about your hometown?"

"Yup."

"You have proof?"

"Nope." She pulled in a deep breath. "There's more. They may even have begun resorting to murder."

"Go on."

"The deaths are masked as suicides or accidents. A drowning during a fishing trip, a farmer falling under his tractor, a hanging, a—"

"—doctor setting himself on fire."

"Yes," she said evenly. "Things like that."

"Avery, you're not up to this. You're not thinking clearly right now."

"I can handle it. I haven't lost my objectivity."

"Bullshit and you know it."

She did, but she wasn't about to admit that. "I just want to find out the truth."

"And what is the truth, Avery?"

"I'm not certain. The story could be a work of fiction. My source is—"

"Less than credible? Unreliable? His motivations questionable?"

"Yes."

"They always are, Avery. You know that. And you know what to do."

*Follow leads. Find another source. Prove information accurate.*

"Not as easy as it sounds," she said. "This is a small community. They've closed ranks. Others, I suspect, are frightened."

"I think you should come back to Washington."

"I can't do that. Not yet. I have to pursue this."

"Why's that, Avery?"

*Because of her dad.* "It'd make a good story," she hedged. "And if it's true, somebody's getting away with murder."

"It would make a good piece, but that has nothing to do with why you want to go after it. We both know that."

In her editor's vernacular, admitting the story had potential equaled a green light. "It's the stuff Pulitzers are made from," she teased.

"If what you're telling me is true, it's the stuff that fills morgues. I want you back at your desk, Avery. Not laid out on a slab."

"You worry too much. Got any suggestions?"

"Look closely at the facts. Double-check your own motivations. Then go to people you trust." He paused. "But be careful, Avery. I wasn't kidding when I said I wanted you back alive."

# CHAPTER 29

Avery took her editor's advice to go to people she trusted. She decided to start with Lilah, who she had been meaning to pay a visit to anyway.

She parked her rental in the Stevenses' driveway and climbed out. Their garage door was open; Avery saw that both Lilah's and Cherry's cars were parked inside.

Avery made her way up the walk, across the porch to the door. She rang the bell. Cherry answered.

"Hey," Avery said.

The other woman didn't smile. "Hey."

"I stopped by to see how Lilah was feeling."

Cherry didn't move from the doorway. "She's better, thanks."

Avery had been meaning to call Cherry and apologize for the way she'd snapped at her at her father's wake, but hadn't. Until that moment, Avery hadn't realized just how badly she had hurt the other woman. Or how angry she was. Her reaction seemed extreme to Avery, but some people were more sensitive than others.

"Cherry, can we talk a moment?"

"If you want."

"I'm sorry about the other night. At the wake. I was upset. I shouldn't have snapped at you. I've been kicking myself for it ever since."

Cherry's expression softened. In fact, for the space of a heartbeat, Avery thought the other woman might cry. Then her lips curved into a smile. "Apology accepted," she said, then pushed open the screen door.

Avery stepped inside and turned to the younger woman who motioned toward the back of the house. "Mother's on the sunporch. She'll be delighted to see you."

She was. "Avery!" the older woman exclaimed, setting aside her novel. "What a pleasure."

Lilah sat on the white wicker couch, back to the yard and its profusion of color. Sun spilled through the window, bathing her in soft, white light—painting her the picture of Southern femininity.

Avery crossed, bent and kissed the woman's cheek, then sat in the wicker queen's chair across from her. "I've been worried about you."

She waved aside her concern. "Blasted allergies. This time of year is such a trial. The headaches are the worst."

"Well, you look wonderful."

"Thank you, dear." Lilah shifted her gaze to her daughter. "Cherry, could you bring Avery an iced tea?"

Avery started to her feet. "I can get it."

"Nonsense," Lilah interrupted. "Cherry's here. Would you mind, sweetheart? And some of those little ginger cookies from the church bake sale."

"No problem," Cherry muttered. "Got to earn my keep, after all."

Avery glanced at the girl. Her features looked pinched. Avery cleared her throat. "Really, Lilah, I can get my own dri—"

Cherry cut her off. "Don't worry about it, Avery. I'm used to this."

After Cherry left the room, Lilah made a sound of frustration. "Some days that girl is so testy. Just miserable to live with."

"We all have bad days," Avery said gently.

"I suppose so." Lilah looked down at her hands, clasped in her lap. When she lifted her eyes, Avery saw that they sparkled with tears. "It's been...difficult for Cherry. She shouldn't be taking care of us. She should have a family of her own. Children to care for."

"She will, Lilah. She's young yet."

The woman continued as if Avery hadn't spoken. "After Karl left, she changed. She's not happy. None of my children—"

Lilah had been about to say that none of her children were happy, Avery realized. Hunter she understood. And to a degree, Cherry. But what of Matt?

Avery reached across the coffee table and caught Lilah's hand. She squeezed. "Happiness is like the ocean, Lilah. Sometimes swelling, sometimes retreating. Constantly shifting." She smiled. "Sudden swells are what make it all so much fun."

Lilah returned the pressure on her fingers. "You're such a dear child, Avery. Thank you."

"Here you go," Cherry said, entering the room with a tray laden with two glasses of tea, sugar bowl and plate of cookies. Each glass sported a circle of lemon and sprig of mint.

She set the tray on the coffee table. The cookies, Avery saw, were arranged in an artful fan, atop a heart-shaped doily. "How lovely," Avery exclaimed. "Cherry, you have such a gift."

She flushed with pleasure. "It was nothing."

"To you, maybe. I could no sooner put this tray together than run a marathon in world record time."

"You're too sweet."

"Just honest. Join us?"

"I'd love to but there are some things I wanted to do this afternoon. And if I don't get to them, it'll be dinnertime and too late." Cherry turned to her mother. "If you don't need anything else, I'll get busy?"

Lilah waved her off, and for the next few minutes Avery and the older woman chatted about nothing more weighty than the weather. When the conversation lulled, Avery brought up the subject most on her mind. "Buddy told me that back in the eighties you were part of a civic action group called Seven Citizens Who Care."

She drew her eyebrows together. "Why in the world did he do that?"

"We were talking about Cypress Springs. How it's such a great place to live." Avery reached for a cookie, laid it on her napkin without tasting. "Said you enacted real change in the community."

"Those were difficult times." She smoothed the napkin over her lap. "But that's ancient history."

Avery ignored her obvious bid to change the subject. "He said Pastor Dastugue was part of the group. Who else was a member of The Seven?"

"What did you say?"

"The Seven, who else—"

"We didn't call ourselves that," she corrected sharply. "We were the CWC."

She had struck a nerve, no doubt about it. Ignoring the prickle of guilt, she pressed on. "I'm sorry, Lilah. I didn't mean to upset you."

"You didn't." She smoothed the napkin. Once. Then again. "Of course you didn't."

"Was there another group called The Seven?"

"No. Why would you think that?"

"Your response...it seemed like The Seven might be something you didn't want to be associated with."

She went to work on the napkin. "Silly, Avery. Of course not."

"I stopped by the *Gazette* this morning," Avery said. "Rickey Plaquamine offered me a job."

"Outstanding." Lilah leaned forward, expression eager. "And? Did you take it?"

"Told him I'd think about it."

She pretended to pout, though Avery could see she was delighted she hadn't outright declined the offer.

"We'd all be thrilled if you decided to make Cypress Springs your home, Avery. But no one more than Matt." She brought her tea to her lips, sipped then patted her mouth with her napkin. "Buddy told me you and Matt seemed to be enjoying yourselves at Spring Fest."

Avery thought of the other night, of dancing with Matt under the stars. Of how comfortable she had felt, how relaxed. Although she hadn't seen him since, he had called every day to check on her.

She smiled. "We did. Very much."

Avery offered nothing further, though she could tell the woman was eager for details. And assurances, Avery supposed. About her and Matt's future. Ones that she was unable to make.

"Rickey looked great. He said he and Jeanette just had their third."

"A handsome boy. Fat. All their babies have been fat." Lilah leaned toward Avery, twinkle in her eyes. "It's all the ice cream Jeanette eats during her last trimester. Belle from the Dairy Barn told me Jeanette came every day, sometimes twice a day, for a double-swirl hot-fudge sundae."

A smile tugged at Avery's mouth. Poor Jeanette. Small-town living—life in a fishbowl.

Avery refocused their conversation. "Until today, I hadn't known Sal was gone. I was so shocked. Dad knew how I felt about Sal, I'm surprised he didn't tell me."

Lilah opened her mouth, then shut it. "This year," she began, struggling to speak, "it's been difficult. Our friends...so many of them...passed away."

Avery stood and crossed to the woman. She bent and hugged her. She felt frail, too thin. "I'm sorry, Lilah. I wish I could do something to help."

"You already have, sweetheart. By being here."

They chatted a couple moments more, then Lilah indicated she needed to rest. They stood. Avery noticed the woman wasn't quite steady on her feet. It alarmed her to see her this way. Just over two weeks ago, she had seemed the picture of health.

They reached the foyer. Lilah kissed Avery's cheek. "Stop by again soon."

"I will. Feel better, Lilah."

Avery watched as the woman made her way up the stairs, noticing how tightly she gripped the handrail, how she seemed to lean on it for support. She found it hard to believe that seasonal allergies would cause this dramatic change in the woman, though she had no real frame of reference for that belief since she had been one of the lucky ones who had been spared them.

Hunter had claimed his mother was addicted to painkillers and booze. Substance abuse took a terrible toll on health and emotional stability. Could that be what she was seeing?

Cherry appeared in the study doorway, to Avery's left. "Mother's going up to nap?" she asked.

"Mmm." Frowning, Avery shifted her gaze to Cherry. "Is she all right?"

"She's fine. The allergy medicine takes it out of her."

"You're certain? She's not having any other problems, is she?"

"Of course not. Why do you ask?"

"I'm concerned. She was so strong just two weeks ago."

"Her bouts are like this." Cherry shrugged. "Mom just doesn't bounce back like she used to."

Avery lowered her gaze. Cherry held a gun, some sort of revolver. She returned her gaze to the other woman's. "Not to be too nosy, but why the—"

"Gun? I'm heading out to the practice range."

"The practice range?" Avery repeated, surprised. Girls in rural Louisiana grew up around hunting and guns, though they were less likely to know how to use one than to bake a peach pie from scratch. "You shoot?"

"Are you kidding? With Matt and Dad as role models? How about you?"

"I'm a bunny-hugging pacifist."

"You want to come along anyway?"

"Why not?"

Avery followed Cherry into her father's study. His gun closet stood open. It held no less than a dozen guns and rifles. Cherry helped herself to a box of bullets, closed and locked the closet. She slipped the key into her pocket, fitted her revolver in its case and snapped it shut.

"Ready?"

She nodded and they headed out, Avery following in her own car. The gun range was actually a cleared field ten miles outside of town, not far from the road to the canning factory. On the edge of the field sat a dilapidated chicken coop and three bales of straw, each set a dozen feet apart, standing on end. The land looked what it was: abandoned and overgrown.

They climbed out of their cars. "This was part of the Weiners' farm, wasn't it?" Avery asked.

"Yup. Sold the whole thing to Old Dixie Foods. Moved up to Jackson."

Avery wrinkled her nose. "What's that smell?"

"The canning factory. Wind's just right for it today." Cherry opened the gun case, took out the gun and began to load it. "Give it a minute, you get accustomed to the smell."

Avery had a hard time believing that. "What kind of gun is it?"

"Ruger .357 Magnum with a six-inch barrel."

"The Dirty Harry gun, right? From the films?"

"Close. Detective Harry Callahan carried the .44 Magnum." She laughed. "Even *I* don't need that much firepower."

Avery watched as Cherry slid six bullets into the chamber, then snapped it shut. "What do you shoot at?" she asked.

"Whatever. The chicken coop, tin cans, bottles. Dad has a hand-operated skeet thrower, sometimes we shoot skeet. For that we use a hunting rifle or shotgun."

To that end she popped open her trunk and took out a cardboard box filled with tin cans. While Avery watched, she crossed the field and set the cans on top of the straw bales and along the chicken coop's window ledges and roof.

She jogged back. She checked her gun, aimed and fired, repeating the process six times. The cans flew. She missed the last and swore.

She glanced at Avery. "I heard what you asked Mom about. That old group, the CWC."

"Do you remember it?"

"Sure. I remember everything about that time."

Avery frowned. "It's so weird, because I don't."

Cherry reloaded the revolver's chamber. "That's not so weird. My family's the reason I remember so clearly."

"It was a rough time, your dad said."

"Rough would be an understatement."

She fell silent a moment, as if lost in her own thoughts. In memories of that time.

"Can I ask you a question?"

"Shoot." Cherry grinned. "Sorry, I couldn't help myself."

"Did you know Elaine St. Claire?"

"Who?"

"The woman who was murdered."

Cherry sighted her mark. She pulled the trigger. The bullet exploded from the gun. She repeated the process five more times, then looked at Avery. "Only by reputation."

"What do you mean?"

Cherry cocked an eyebrow. "Come on, Avery. *By reputation.* She'd seen more mattresses than the guy down at the Sealy Bedding Barn."

Avery made a sound of shock. "The woman's dead, Cherry. It seems so callous to talk about her that way."

"I'm being honest. Should I lie just because she's dead? That would make me a hypocrite."

"Ever hear the saying 'Live and let live'?"

"That's big-city crapola, propagated by those intent on maintaining status quo and contentment of the masses. You have to live with the bottom-feeders."

"And you don't?"

She looked at Avery, expression perplexed. "No, we don't. This is Cypress Springs not New Orleans."

"You're saying Elaine St. Claire got what she deserved? That you're glad she's dead?"

"Of course not." She flipped open the .357's chamber, reloaded, then snapped it shut. "Nobody deserves that. But am I sorry she's not spreading her legs for every dick in town, no I'm not."

Avery gasped; Cherry's smile turned sly. "I've shocked you."

"I didn't think Matt's little sister could talk that way."

"There's a lot you don't know about me, Avery."

"Sounds ominous."

She laughed. "Not at all. You've been gone a long time, that's all." Without waiting for a response, she sighted her tin prey and fired. One shot after another, ripping off six. Hitting her target each time.

Avery watched her, both surprised and awed by her ability. Unnerved by it as well. Particularly in light of their conversation. She shifted her gaze to Cherry's arms, noticing how cut they were. The way her biceps bulged as she gripped the gun, how she hardly recoiled when it discharged.

She'd never noticed what good shape the other woman was in. How strong she was. How strongly built. Avery supposed that was because compared to her, everybody looked big.

Truth was, she'd always thought of Cherry as a girlie-girl, like Lilah. And like her own mother had been. Avery had been the tomboy. The one who hadn't quite fit the mold of Southern womanhood. And now here was Cherry, all buff and macho, blasting the crap out of tin cans.

Cherry reloaded, turned and offered the gun to Avery, grip out. "Want to give it a try?"

Avery hesitated. She disliked guns. Was one of those folks who thought the world would be a better place if every weapon on the planet was collected and destroyed and people were forced to sit across a table from one another and work out their differences. Maybe over a latte or caffe mocha.

Cherry's smug grin had her reaching for the gun. "Okay," she said grimly, "walk me through this."

"It helps to plant your feet. Like this." Cherry demonstrated. "Wrap both hands around the grip. That's right," she said as Avery followed her directions.

"I feel like an idiot," Avery said. "Like an Arnold Schwarzenegger wannabe."

"I felt that way at first. You'll grow to like it."

*When pigs fly.* "What now?"

"Point and shoot. But be careful, it's got some kick."

Avery aimed at the can that looked closest to her and pulled the trigger. The force of the explosion sent her stumbling backward. She peeked at the target. "Did I hit it?"

"Nope. You might try keeping your eyes open next time."

"Shit."

"Try again."

Avery did. And missed cleanly. After her sixth attempt, she handed the gun back. "My career as a shooter is officially over."

"You might change your mind. If you stay in Cypress Springs."

"Don't hold your breath." She watched Cherry handle the weapon with a sort of reverence completely foreign to Avery. "What's the allure? I don't get it."

Cherry thought a moment. "It makes me feel powerful. In control."

"That's an odd answer."

"Really? Isn't that what weapons are all about? Power and control. Winning."

"And here I always thought they were about killing."

"There are always going to be bad guys, Avery. People determined to take away what you hold dear. People without morals or conscience. Guns, the ability—and willingness—to use them are a necessary deterrent."

Avery had argued this one before and knew she couldn't win. And a part of her knew Cherry spoke the truth. The current truth. But she was idealist enough to believe there was another way. "The only way to fight violence is with violence, that's what you're saying? React to force with greater force until we've blown the entire planet to hell?"

"The one with the biggest *boom* wins."

Moments later, Avery drove off. She glanced in her rearview mirror. The sun was setting behind her, the sky a palette of bloody reds and oranges. Cherry stood where she had left her, standing beside her car, staring after Avery.

Her outing with the younger woman had left her feeling uncomfortable, as if she had been party to something unclean. As if she had witnessed something ugly and had done nothing to stop it.

The things Gwen Lancaster had told her about The Seven played through her head.

*Anyone whose actions fell outside what was considered right, moral or neighborly was singled out and warned. Before it was all over, they'd broken the civil rights of their fellow citizens in the name of righteousness, law and order.*

Could the woman she had just spent the past hour with be party to that?

Absolutely. Avery didn't have a doubt about it. What she was less certain of, however, was how to reconcile the Cherry Stevens she had been witness to today with the one who had brought her breakfast her first morning in Cypress Springs. The one who had been caring, sweet-natured and sensitive.

Today, nothing about Cherry had rung true to her, from the things she had said about Elaine St. Claire to the subtly sly tone she had assumed with Avery.

But why would she have affected such an attitude with her? It didn't make sense. Why either alienate her or, if part of The Seven, be so open about her beliefs? Surely those involved hadn't maintained their anonymity with such transparency.

Avery drew to a stop at the crossroads, stunned with the course of her own thoughts. She was thinking as if The Seven was a given. As if they had and did exist, as if anyone could be a part of their numbers.

An ill feeling settling in the pit of her stomach, she dug through her purse, found the card with Gwen's phone number on it. She punched the number into her cell phone; on the third ring the woman's recorder answered.

"It's Avery Chauvin," she said. "You've got my attention now. Call me." She left the number for both her cell and parents' home phone, then hung up.

Through the open window came the sound of a gun discharging. Avery jerked at the sound. She closed the window against it and the sour-smelling breeze.

## CHAPTER 30

The Gavel entered the war room. It had been difficult to get away this Friday evening—he was late. His generals were all in place, assembled around the table. Two held the rapt attention of the others as they complained about the Gavel's leadership and the way he had handled Elaine St. Claire.

One by one they became aware of his presence. Nervous silence fell over them. Guilty silence.

He crossed to his place at the table's head, working to control his anger. He shifted his gaze from one of his detractors to the other. Their discomfort became palpable. "You have a problem, Blue? Hawk?"

Blue faced him boldly. "The situation with the outsider is worsening. We must take action."

"Agreed." He turned his gaze to the other. "Hawk?"

"The handling of St. Claire was a mistake."

Shock rippled through the group. Hawk was the Gavel's biggest supporter. His ally from the beginning. His friend.

Fury took the Gavel's breath. A sense of betrayal. He kept a grip on his emotions. "What should we have done, Hawk? Allowed her to continue to sully the character of this town? To tear at its moral fiber thread by thread? Or allowed her to go to the authorities? Have you forgotten our pledge to one another and this community?"

The other man squirmed under his gaze. "Of course not. But if we'd...taken care of her as we have the others, no one would be the wiser. To have so openly disposed of her—"

"Has sent a message to others like her. We will not be discovered, I promise you that."

Hawk opened his mouth as if to argue, then shut it and sat back, obviously dissatisfied. The Gavel narrowed his eyes. He would speak with him privately; if he determined Hawk a risk, he would be removed from the high council.

"What of the reporter?" Blue asked.

"Avery Chauvin? What of her?"

"She's been talking to the other one. The outsider."

"And asking questions," another supplied. "A lot of questions."

He hesitated, surprised. "She's one of us."

"Was one of us," Blue corrected. "She's been away too long to be trusted. She's become a part of the liberal media."

"That's right," Hawk supplied. "She doesn't understand what we cherish. What we're fighting to save. If she did, she would never have left."

A murmur of agreement—and concern—went around the table. Voices rose.

The Gavel struggled to control his mounting rage. Although he didn't let on, he had begun to have doubts about Avery Chauvin's loyalty as well. He, too, had become aware of her snooping. Nosing around things she didn't—and couldn't—understand.

But he was the leader of this group and he would not be questioned. He had earned that right. If he determined Avery Chauvin represented minimal risk, he expected his generals to fall in line.

He held up a hand. His generals turned their gazes to his. "Must I remind you we are only as strong as our belief in our cause? As our willingness to do whatever is necessary to further that cause?

Or that dissension among our number will be our undoing? Just as it was the undoing of our fellows who came before?"

He paused a moment to let his words sink in. "We are the elite, gentlemen. The best, the most committed. We will not allow—I will not allow—anyone to derail us. Even one of our own sisters."

The generals nodded. The Gavel continued. "Leave everything to me," he said. "Including the reporter."

CHAPTER 31

Avery had expected Gwen to return her message Thursday evening, within hours of her leaving it. Instead, the next day came and went without word from her, and Avery began to worry. She tried her again. And left another message.

Just as she decided to pay a visit to The Guesthouse, her doorbell rang. Certain it was Gwen, she hurried to answer it. Instead of the other woman on her doorstep, she found Buddy.

He smiled as she opened the door. She worked to hide her dismay even as she scolded herself for it. "Hello, Buddy. What a nice surprise."

"Hello, baby girl." He held up a napkin-covered basket. "Lilah asked me to run these by."

She took the basket, guilt swamping her. "What are they?"

"Lilah's award-winning blueberry muffins."

Even as he answered, their identifying smell reached her nose. Her mouth began to water. "How is she?"

"Better. Back in the kitchen." He mopped the back of his neck with his handkerchief. "Hot out there today. They say it's going to break records."

"Come on in, Buddy. I'll get you a cold drink."

"I'm not going to lie, some ice water would be great."

He stepped inside; she motioned for him to follow her. The air conditioner kicked on. He looked around as they made their way to the kitchen, obviously taking in the disarray, the half-emptied shelves, the stacks of boxes. "Looks like you're making some headway," he said.

"Some." She reached into the freezer for ice, then dropped a couple cubes into a glass. She filled it with water and handed it to him. "I'm not spending as much time on it as I should be. The Realtor is champing at the bit. She has a client looking for a house like this one."

He took a long swallow of water. "It's a great house. Great location. I hate to see—"

He bit the words back, then shifted the glass from one hand to the other, the nervous gesture unlike him. "Have you given any thought to keeping it? To staying in Cypress Springs? I'm growing accustomed to having you around. We all are."

She met his eyes, touched by the naked yearning she saw in them. Torn. How could she on the one hand feel such affection for these people and this community, and on the other suspect them of being party to something as despicable as murder? What was wrong with her?

"I've been thinking about it a lot," she said. "I haven't made a decision yet."

"Anything I can do to sway you?"

"Just being you sways me, Buddy." She stood on tiptoe and kissed his cheek.

He flushed with pleasure. "Lilah told me you stopped by."

"I did." Avery poured herself a glass of water. "We had a nice visit."

"And you spent some time with Cherry as well."

She felt her smile slip. He saw it and frowned.

"What's wrong?"

"Nothing. She's turned into a damn good shot. I was awed."

"She has at that. Personally, I think she would have made a good lawman."

That surprised her. "You encouraged her?"

"I did." He sighed. "But you know how it is down here, sexual stereotypes run deep. Women are supposed to get married and have babies. And if they work, they choose a womanly profession."

Like catering. Not law enforcement. Or journalism. Her own mother had done her damnedest to convince her of that very thing.

"I do know, Buddy."

His expression softened. "You look tired."

She averted her gaze. "I'm not sleeping well." That at least was true. It was *why* she wasn't sleeping that ate at her.

"That's to be expected. Give yourself some time, it'll get better."

Silence fell between them, broken only by the click of the ice against the glass as Buddy took another swallow of his water. "Rickey told me you stopped by the *Gazette.*"

She looked at him. He lowered his eyes to his hat, then returned them to her. In his she saw sympathy. "Did you get the answers you were searching for?"

Rickey had called Buddy, she realized. He knew what she had been looking at. That she had asked about The Seven.

He probably knew she had spoken with Ben Mitchell and Dr. Harris as well. Small towns kept no secrets.

*Except if what she suspected was true, this town had kept a secret. A big one.*

"Talk to me, Avery," he urged. "What's going on with you? I can't help if I don't know what's wrong."

She thought of what her editor had said, that she should go to the people she trusted.

She trusted Buddy. He would never hurt her, she believed that with every fiber of her being.

"Buddy, can I...ask you something?"

"You can ask me anything, baby girl. Anytime."

"I spoke with Ben Mitchell, the arson investigator from the fire marshal's office. Something he said has been bothering me."

"Go on."

She took a deep breath. "He found one of Dad's slippers on the path between the house and the garage. He speculated he was wearing the other one and that it burned in the fire. Do you recall that to be true?"

Buddy drew his eyebrows together in thought. "I do. If you want the specifics, we can check my report."

"That's not—" She thought a moment, searching for the right words. "Does anything about that seem wrong to you?" At his blank expression, she made a sound of frustration. "Obviously not."

"I don't understand." He searched her gaze. "What are you thinking?"

"I don't know. I—"

*That was a lie. She did know.*

*Say it, Avery. Get it out there.*

"I don't think Dad killed himself."

The words, the ramifications of them, landed heavily between them. For a long moment Buddy said nothing. When he met her eyes, the expression in his was troubled. "Because of this slipper thing?"

"Yes, and...and because I knew my dad. He couldn't have done it."

"Avery—"

She heard the pity in his voice and steeled herself against it. "You knew him, too, Buddy. He loved life. He valued it. He couldn't have done this, not in a million years."

"You realize," he said carefully, "if you believe this, you're saying he was murdered?"

Heat flooded her cheeks. Standing with him, looking into his eyes, she felt like a fool. She couldn't find her voice, so she nodded.

"Do you doubt I did a thorough investigation?"

"No. But you could have missed something. Dr. Harris could have missed something."

"I could make my report available to you, if that would help."

Gratitude washed over her. "It really would. Thank you, Buddy."

He was silent a moment, then as if coming to a decision, sighed deeply. "Why are you doing this, baby girl?"

"Pardon?"

"Your dad's dead. He killed himself. Nothing's going to bring him back."

"I know, I just—"

"We love you. You belong here, with us. You are one of us. Don't you feel it? Don't you feel like you belong?"

Tears swamped her. The people of Cypress Springs were her friends. They had been nothing but kind to her, welcoming her back unconditionally. The Stevenses were her second family. Now, her only family.

Being back had been good. For the first time in a long time she had felt as if she belonged. She didn't want to lose that.

She told him so, then swallowed hard. "If only I could accept...if only I didn't feel so—" She bit the last back, uncertain how she felt—or rather, which she felt most. Confused? Conflicted? Guilty?

*She felt as if the last might eat her alive.*

Buddy set his glass on the counter and crossed to her, laid his hands on her shoulders. She lifted her eyes to his, vision swimming. "You are not responsible for your father's death. It's not your fault."

"Then why...how could he have done it?"

He tightened his fingers. "Avery," he said gently, "you may never know exactly what happened. Because he's gone and we can't be party to his thoughts. You have to accept it and go on."

"I don't know if I can," she answered helplessly. "I want to. Lord knows—"

"Give yourself some time. Be good to yourself. Stay away from people like Gwen Lancaster. She doesn't have your best interests at heart. She's unstable."

Avery thought of the other woman. Of her accusations. Her desperation. Their very public discussion outside the Azalea Café.

"Matt's worried about you, too," Buddy continued. "He's working around the clock on the McDougal disappearance. McDougal wasn't the first. A couple months back, another man disappeared."

"Tom Lancaster."

"Yes." He dropped his hands, stepped away from her. "The cases are too similar for them not to be related. And the St. Claire murder coming so close on their heels...it seems a stretch to connect that as well, but we're looking at every possibility. After all, these sorts of things don't happen in Cypress Springs."

"But other sorts of things do."

He frowned. "Excuse me?"

"Haven't you noticed the high number of unexpected deaths around here in the past eight months? The accidents and suicides?"

His frown deepened. "Every town has its share of accidental deaths. Every town has—"

"What about Pete Trimble's death? He was a farmer all his life. How could he fall under his tractor?"

"We found a nearly empty fifth of Jack Daniel's in the tractor's cab. His blood alcohol level was sky high."

"What about Dolly Farmer? The *Gazette* reported she hung herself? From what I read, she seemed to have everything to live for."

"Her husband had run off with his young secretary. The *Gazette* didn't print that."

"What about Sal?"

"Somebody who had no business with a rifle shot him. In their inexperience, they mistook him for a deer. When they discovered their mistake, they ran off."

"So many deaths, Buddy," she said, hearing the edge of hysteria in her own voice. "How can there be so many...deaths?"

"That's life, baby girl," he said gently. "People die."

"But so many? So close, so tragically?"

He caught her hands, squeezed her fingers. "If not for your father, would any of this seem out of the ordinary to you? If not for the imaginings of a woman in the throes of grief, would any of those deaths have seemed suspicious?"

*Was that woman Gwen Lancaster? Or her?*

*Dear God, how far gone was she?*

Her eyes welled with tears. She fought them from spilling. One slipped past her guard and rolled down her cheek.

Buddy eased her against his chest and wrapped his big, bearlike arms around her. "Gwen Lancaster is in a lot of pain. Her brother disappeared and is more than likely dead. I feel for her, I do. Lord knows how much losing my best friend hurt, I can only imagine how she must feel."

He drew slightly away, looked into her eyes. "People in pain do things, believe in things...that just aren't true. As a way to lessen the pain. To justify their own actions or ease their own guilt. Trust the people you love. The people who love you. Not some woman you don't even know."

He brushed a tear from her cheek with his thumb. "This is a small town, Avery. People around here get their backs up easily. Stop playing the big-city investigative reporter or they'll forget you're one of them and start treating you like an outsider. You wouldn't like that, would you?"

Avery swallowed hard, confused. His words, gently spoken though they had been, smacked of a threat. A warning to cease and desist. "I don't understand. Are you saying—"

"A bit of friendly advice, baby girl. That's all. A reminder what small-town folks are like." He dropped a kiss on her forehead, then stepped away from her. "You're family, Avery, and I just want you to be happy."

# CHAPTER 32

Avery stood at her front door for a long time after Buddy left. She felt numb, disconnected. She gazed out at nothing, the things Buddy had said playing over in her head.

Would anything Gwen said to her have made her suspicious if she hadn't be in the throes of grief? Sal's death would have been a terrible tragedy, one of those freak occurrences that made one ask, "Why?" Dolly Farmer another victim of the breakdown of the family, Pete Trimble a drunk-driving statistic.

What did *she* believe? She rubbed her throbbing temples. How could she be so easily swayed? One moment believing the people of Cypress Springs were involved in a conspiracy of discrimination and murder, the next sucked in by an emotionally unstable woman with a questionable agenda. She had always been so firm in her beliefs, so self-confident. She had been able to access the facts, make a decision and move on.

Avery dropped her hands. Is this how a breakdown began? One small confusion at a time? A bout of tears, mounting indecision, a feeling of drowning that passed only to return without a moment's notice?

Becoming aware that the air-conditioning was being wasted, she closed the door, turned and wandered back to the kitchen. Her gaze landed on Buddy's nearly empty water glass.

What did she want to believe?

In the people she loved and trusted. In those who loved her.

And that her father hadn't taken his own life.

Therein lay the source of her conflict.

The phone rang. She turned toward it but made no move to pick it up. The caller let it ring nine times before hanging up. A moment later it rang again. Someone needed her. To speak to her.

Her father had needed to speak to her.

She hadn't taken his call.

She leaped for the phone, snatching the receiver off the base. "Hello?"

"Avery? It's Gwen."

*Not now. Not her.* She fought the urge to slam down the phone.

"I just got your message," the woman continued. "I drove to New Orleans to see my mother." She paused. "Avery? Are you there?"

"Yes, I'm here."

"I'd like to get together as soon as possible. When can you—"

"I'm sorry, Gwen, I can't talk about this just now."

"Are you all right?"

*If she could call falling apart at the seams all right.* "Yes, fine. I just...this isn't a good time."

"Are you alone?"

Avery heard the concern in the other woman's voice. She could imagine what she was thinking. "Yes."

"You sound strange."

"I think I made a mistake."

"A mistake? I don't understand."

"I can't do this. I feel for you, Gwen, I do. I understand loss, I'm swimming in it myself. But I can't be party to your far-fetched notions. Not anymore."

"Far-fetched? But—"

"Yes, I'm sorry."

"I'm all alone, Avery. I need your help." The other woman's voice rose. "Please help me find my brother's killer."

Avery squeezed her eyes shut. Against the desperation in the other woman's voice. The pain.

*Trust the people you love. The people who love you.*

"I wish I could, Gwen. My heart breaks for you, but—"

"Please. I don't have anyone else."

She felt herself wavering; she steeled herself against sympathy. "I really can't talk right now. I'm sorry."

Avery hung up. She realized she was shaking and drew in a deep breath. She had done the right thing. Pain shaped reality—her pain, Gwen's. The woman had focused her energy on this conspiracy theory as a way to lessen her pain. To turn her attention away from grief.

Avery had been drawn in for the same reason.

The phone rang again. *Gwen. To plead her case.* As much as she preferred to avoid the woman, she needed to face this. This was part of getting her act together.

She answered without greeting. "Look, Gwen, I don't know how to make it more plain—"

"How does it feel to be the daughter of a liar and murderer?"

The breath hissed past Avery's lips, she took an involuntary step backward. "Who is this?" she demanded, voice quaking.

"I'm someone who knows the truth," the woman said, then laughed, the sound unpleasant. "And there aren't many of us left. We're dropping like flies."

"You're the liar," Avery shot back. Outrage took her breath, fury on its heels. "My father was an honorable man. The most honest man I've ever known. Not a coward who's too afraid to show her face."

"I'm no coward. You're the—"

"You are. Hiding behind lies. Hiding behind the phone, making accusations against a man who can't defend himself."

"What about my boys!" she cried. "They couldn't defend themselves! Nobody cared about them!"

"I don't know who your boys are, so I can't comment—"

"Were," she hissed. "They're dead. Both my boys...dead. And your father's one of the ones to blame!"

Avery struggled not to take the defensive. To remain unemotional, challenge the woman in a way that would draw her out, get her to reveal her identity. "If you had any proof my dad was a murderer, you wouldn't be hiding behind this phone call. Maybe if I knew your sons' names I'd be more likely to think you were more than a pathetic crank."

"Donny and Dylan Pruitt," she spat. "They didn't kill Sallie Waguespack. They didn't even know her."

*The Waguespack murder.*

*Dear God, the box of clippings.*

Avery's hands began to shake. She tightened her grip on the receiver. "What did my father have to do with this?"

"Your daddy helped cover up for the real killer." The woman cackled. "So much for the most honest man you've ever known."

"It's not true," Avery said. "You're a liar."

"Why do you think my boys never stood trial?" she demanded. "'Cause they didn't do it. They was framed. None of it would have stood up to judge and jury. And all of them, those hypocrite do-gooders, would have gone to jail!"

"If you had any proof, you'd show it to me."

"I have proof, all right. Plenty of proof."

"Sure you do."

At the sarcasm, the woman became enraged. "To hell with you and your dead daddy. You're like the rest of 'em. Lying hypocrites. I tell you what I got and you'll bring the authorities down on me like white on rice."

Avery tried a different tack. "Why do you think I left Cypress Springs? I'm not one of them. I never was." She let that sink in. "If what you're telling me is true, I'll make it right."

"What's in it for you?"

"I clear my father's name."

The woman said nothing. Avery pressed on. "You want justice for your boys?"

"In this town? Ain't no justice for a Pruitt in this town. Hell, ain't no real justice to be had in Cypress Springs."

"Show me what you've got," Avery urged. "You've got proof, I'll make it right. I promise you that."

She was quiet a moment. "Not over the phone," she said finally. "Meet me. Tonight." She quickly gave an address, then hung up.

CHAPTER 33

Magnolia Acres trailer park was located on the southern boundary of Cypress Springs, just outside the incorporated area. Avery turned into the park, noting that the safety light at its entrance was burned out.

Or had been shot out by kids with BB guns, she thought, seeing that all the park's safety lights were dark.

She made her way slowly down the street, straining to make out the numbers. Even the dark couldn't soften the forlorn, abandoned look of the area. The only thing the neighborhood had going for it, Avery thought, was the large lot given each residence. But even those had a quality of runaway disrepair about them. The weeds were winning.

She found number 12 and parked in front. Avery climbed out. Music came from several directions: rap, rock and country. From an adjacent trailer came the sound of a couple fighting. A child crying.

Avery slammed the car door and started toward the trailer, scanning the area as she did, noting details. Dead flowers in the single window box. A pitiable attempt at a garden: a few shrubs that badly need trimming, weeds, a rock border, half overgrown. Three steps led up to the front door. A concrete frog sat on the top step.

She neared the door, saw that it stood slightly ajar. Light spilled from inside. As did the smell of fried food.

She climbed the steps, knocked on the door and it swung open. "Mrs. Pruitt," she called. "It's Avery Chauvin."

No answer. She knocked and called out again, this time more loudly.

Again, only silence answered.

She stepped inside. The place was in a shambles. Furniture overturned, newspapers and take-out boxes strewn about, lamp on its side on the floor, light flickering. Her gaze landed on a dark smear across the back wall.

Avery frowned and started toward it. A radio in the other room played the classic "Strangers in the Night." Avery laughed nervously at how weirdly appropriate that was.

She reached the back wall. She squinted at the stain, touched it. It was wet. She turned her hand over. And red.

With a growing sense of horror, Avery turned slowly to her left. Through the doorway to the kitchen she saw a woman stretched out on the floor, back to Avery.

"Mrs. Pruitt?"

Swallowing hard, she crept forward. She reached the woman. Squatted beside her. Stretched out a hand. Touched her shoulder.

The woman rolled onto her back. The woman's eyes were open but it was her mouth that drew Avery's gaze—blood-soaked, grotesquely stretched.

With a cry, Avery scrambled backward. She slipped on the wet floor, lost her balance, landing on her behind. Blood, she realized, gazing down at herself. She had slipped in it, splattering herself, smearing it across the floor.

A sound drew her gaze. The woman blinked. Her mouth moved. She was alive, Avery realized. She was trying to speak.

Avery righted herself and crept closer. Heart thundering, she knelt beside her, bent her head toward the woman's. A small sound escaped her—little more than a gurgle of air.

"What?" Avery asked, searching her gaze. "What are you trying to tell me?"

Her mouth moved again. She inched her hand to Avery's, fingers clawing.

From the front room came the sound of footsteps. Avery froze. She swung her gaze to the doorway, heart thundering.

*The person who had done this could still be in the house.*

The sound came again. Terrified, she jumped to her feet. She looked wildly around her. *No back door. Small window above the sink.*

*No way out.*

Her gaze landed on the phone. She lunged for it.

"Police!"

Avery whirled around and found herself staring down the barrel of a gun. Her cry of relief stuck on her tongue.

"Get your hands up," the sheriff's deputy said, voice steely. She obeyed the order. Keeping his weapon trained on her, he bent and checked the woman's pulse.

"She's alive," Avery said, fighting hysteria. "She was trying to tell me something. When I heard you, I thought you were the one....the one who did this."

He unhooked his radio, called the incident in and requested an ambulance, never taking his gaze or aim off her.

"Turn around. Hands on the wall."

She did as he ordered, the scream of sirens in the distance. Her bloody hands would leave marks on the wall, she thought, a cry rising in her throat.

The officer came up behind her. "Feet apart."

"You have the wrong idea. I found her this way." When she twisted to plead her case to his face, she found herself shoved flat against the wall, his hand between her shoulder blades. Gun to her head.

"Back off, Jones! Now!"

At the sound of Matt's voice, the deputy reacted instantly, dropping his hands, stepping back.

"Matt!" Avery cried. She ran to him, and he folded her in his arms.

"Sweetheart, are you all right?"

Avery clung to him, shaking. She managed a nod, eyes welling with tears. "The woman...is she...I thought...I heard a noise and—" She buried her face in his shoulder. "I thought whoever had done this, that he was still here."

He tightened his arms around her. "Deputy Jones?"

"Received a call from a neighbor. They heard a commotion. What sounded like a gunshot. When I arrived, I found the door open and interior ransacked. I called for assistance and made my way in here. I found the suspect kneeling over the victim."

"I found her this way!" Avery looked up at Matt. "The door was open...I called her name. She didn't answer, so I made my way in. I—"

The paramedics arrived then, interrupting her, shouting orders, pushing her and Matt toward the door. Behind them waited several more deputies, ready to process the scene the moment the paramedics gave the okay.

Holding her close to his side, Matt led her from the kitchen through the living room and outside. As they made their way out, her toe caught on the frog and it toppled into the garden. They descended the steps and crossed to two rickety lawn chairs set up around a kid's inflatable wading pool. Yellow crime scene tape had already been stretched around the perimeter of the trailer; a deputy stood sentinel, watching the group of neighbors who had come out to gawk.

"Sit," Matt said. "I have to go now. I need you to wait here. We're going to need to question you." He searched her expression. "Will you be all right?"

She nodded. "I'll be okay."

He squeezed her hands, then turned toward the deputy. "Make sure nobody bothers her. If she has any problems, come get me."

Avery watched him go, an intense sense of loss settling over her. She bit her bottom lip to keep from calling him back and sank onto the chair, the woven seat sagging dangerously.

"You all right?"

She glanced at the deputy, a baby-faced young man who hardly looked old enough to be out past ten, let alone to carry a weapon. She nodded. "The woman...is she Trudy Pruitt?"

The kid looked surprised by her question. And rightly so, she supposed, considering the circumstances. He answered anyway. "Uh-huh. Waitresses over at the Hard Eight."

*The pool hall.*

Avery hugged herself, the woman's image filling her head. Her vacant stare. Her slack mouth. The feel of her fingers clawing at Avery's.

She squeezed her eyes shut tightly, attempting to block out the images. They played on anyway. The woman's bloody mouth moving, the tiny puff of breath against her cheek. Blood, everywhere.

The paramedics came out. Avery opened her eyes at the sound. One looked her way. Their eyes met. In his she saw regret. Apology.

Her breath caught. She shifted her gaze. *No stretcher.*

They passed her. Climbed into the ambulance. Slammed the doors shut, the sound heavy. Final.

"Avery?"

She turned. Matt stood in the trailer doorway. She got to her feet; he started toward her.

"She didn't make it," she said when he reached her.

"No."

He caught her hands. "What are you doing here, Avery?"

She blinked, confused. "Pardon?"

"Tonight, what brought you here?"

"The woman, Trudy Pruitt. She said she had proof...about my father. And Sallie Waguespack."

His forehead creased. "Avery, sweetheart, you're not making any sense. Start at the beginning."

She drew in a deep breath, working to collect her jumbled thoughts. To fight past twin feelings of panic and confusion. "I need to sit."

He nodded and she did. He swung the second chair to face hers, then sat. He took out a small notepad. "Ready?"

She nodded. "The day of Dad's funeral I got an anonymous call. From a woman. She said that Dad had...gotten what he deserved. That I would, too. Then she hung up."

His expression tightened. "The caller you told me about the day

McDougal's car was discovered in Tiller's pond?" She nodded. "Go on."

"She called again just this afternoon. She said Dad had helped cover up a crime, a murder."

"Sallie Waguespack's."

"Yes. She called him a liar. And a murderer."

"And that woman was Trudy Pruitt."

"She said she had proof. She was...going to show it to me tonight."

"Did she tell you that her sons—"

"She said they didn't do it. That they were framed."

He passed a hand over his face. "Dammit, Avery...I wish you'd called me. Trudy Pruitt has been proclaiming her sons' innocence for fifteen years, to anyone and everyone who'd listen. Twice she hired investigators to review the evidence, neither investigator found anything to suggest killers other than Donny and Dylan.

"Trudy Pruitt was an alcoholic and drug abuser. Before and after her sons' deaths. She's spent her life between jail and rehab, a bitter and desperately unhappy woman."

Avery clasped her hands together. "Why my dad, Matt? Why me? Why did she choose...us?"

"Why does someone like Trudy Pruitt do anything? My guess is, your dad's wake and funeral stirred up memories. The overwhelming love and community support for you fed her bitterness. Unfortunately, we'll never know for sure what her motivations were, not now."

*Because she was dead.*

*Murdered.*

The full impact of that hit her with the force of a wrecking ball. Elaine St. Claire. Luke McDougal. Tom Lancaster. Now Trudy Pruitt.

"Who did this, Matt?"

"I don't know," he said grimly. "Not yet. I need your help, Avery."

"How? What can I do?"

"I need you to tell me exactly what happened tonight. What you saw and heard. Every detail, no matter how insignificant it might seem to you."

"All right." She paused a moment, collecting her thoughts, then began with arriving at the trailer park right around 10:00 p.m. "I noticed how dark the park was, that all the safety lights were out."

He made a note. "Did you pass another car on your way in?"

She shook her head. "I found Mrs. Pruitt's trailer and climbed out. I could hear music coming from a number of directions."

"Where?"

"I don't know. I assumed other trailers. I heard the couple next door fighting, a child crying."

"Next door? You're certain?"

Avery glanced in the direction of the nearest trailer. A man, woman and child stood in the doorway, staring her way. "Fairly certain."

Again he made a notation on the pad. "What about inside Trudy Pruitt's?"

"I found the door partially open. I knocked and called out. When she didn't answer, I poked my head inside. Called out again." She closed her eyes, remembering. "The living room was a mess. At first I...I thought she was a slob. I didn't...until I saw the blood...on the back wall, I didn't realize anything was wrong." She pulled in a shaky breath. "And then I saw her. Lying there."

"Did you touch anything?"

She thought a moment. "The blood on the wall. That's when I realized what it was."

"Go on."

"I went to her, reached out and touched her shoulder. She rolled onto her back."

"She was on her side?"

"Yes. She tried to speak to me."

He straightened slightly. "What did she say?"

Avery's eyes welled with tears. "She never...I couldn't make anything out. I heard a noise...and got frightened. I thought maybe the killer was still in the house and now—" She struggled past the emotion welling up in her. "Her hand...she—"

Avery glanced down at her hands. Blood stained the tops of the fingers of her right hand. "Touched mine. Like she needed my attention. Like she needed to tell me something important."

"It might have been nothing more than the need for human contact," he said gently. "She was dying, Avery."

"Now we'll never know."

"Other than Deputy Jones, did you hear anything?"

"The radio playing."

"And that's it?"

She couldn't tear her gaze from her bloodstained fingers. "Yes."

"If you think of anything else, call me. No matter how insignificant you might believe it is." He closed the notepad. "Promise?"

"I will."

"Avery?" She looked up. "Call me if you need anything else. Even just to talk. I'm here for you."

She swallowed hard. "Thank you, Matt."

"I'll have one of my deputies follow you home. Are you up to driving?"

She said she was and Matt called one of his deputies over, gave him directions, then accompanied her to her vehicle.

"I was by your house earlier. Dropped something off."

"For me?"

"In light of this, I wish to hell I..." He swore. "My timing stinks." He opened her car door. "I'll call you tomorrow."

She found what Matt had referred to on her front porch. Flowers. A beautiful spring bouquet. The card read:

*Thinking of you and me. Dancing under the stars. Matt.*

A hysterical-sounding laugh slipped past her lips. She laughed until she cried.

CHAPTER 34

Avery slept little that night. Every time she'd closed her eyes, she'd seen Trudy Pruitt lying in a pool of red, eyes wide and pleading, blood-soaked mouth working. Finally, Avery had given up and climbed out of bed. After brewing a pot of coffee, she'd dragged out the box of newspaper clippings and had begun poring over them, looking for anything that didn't fit, anything that might suggest a cover-up.

Nothing in the news stories jumped out at her.

What had Trudy Pruitt been trying to tell her? What proof of her father's involvement in the Sallie Waguespack murder did she have? Had she been the bitter, unstable drunk Matt purported her to be? One who had simply chosen Avery as a vehicle for venting her unhappiness?

Avery shifted her gaze to the box of clippings. *Dammit.* If not for these she might be able to believe that. *Why, Dad? Why did you save these?*

Only one person could answer that question.

Buddy.

Twenty-five minutes later Avery found herself at the ranch. She rang the bell, praying she had caught him before he left for church. If she remembered correctly, the Stevenses had most often chosen to attend the late service. They had today as well, she saw as Lilah opened the door.

"Avery," the woman exclaimed, "I heard about what happened. Are you all right?"

She nodded. "Just shaken. Is Buddy here?"

"And Matt. We're having breakfast."

"I'm sorry, I should have called—"

"Nonsense." She caught her hands and drew her inside. The house smelled of bacon and biscuits. "Come on in. I'll set you a place."

Before Avery could tell her not to bother, she was calling out for Cherry to do just that.

The men stood when she entered the kitchen. Matt took one look at her and came around the table. He caught her hands. "Are you okay?"

She forced a weak smile. "Hanging in there. Barely."

He led her to the chair next to his. Cherry set a plate, napkin and utensils on the blue-and-white-checked place mat in front of her. "Coffee?"

"Thanks."

The younger woman filled a mug and handed it to her. "Matt told us about last night. How horrible for you."

Lilah passed her the tray of biscuits. "I can't imagine. I'm quite sure I would have fainted."

Avery took a biscuit, though the thought of eating made her queasy. She swallowed hard, shifting her gaze to Matt. "How's the investigation coming?"

"We canvassed the trailer park for witnesses. The kid next door says she saw a car pull up with its lights off. Then her folks began fighting."

"So she never saw who got out," Avery said, disappointed.

"Or when it drove off. The crime scene techs have done their thing, but it's too soon for the evidence report. As soon as I'm done here, I've got to get back."

"If you need any assistance from our department, son, we're ready."

"Thanks, Dad. I appreciate that."

Cherry spread strawberry jam on her biscuit. "What were you doing at that awful woman's house, Avery? Why were you there?"

The table went silent. All eyes turned to her. Uncomfortable, Avery opened her mouth then shut it as Matt squeezed her knee under the table.

"I've asked Avery not to talk about that just now," he said quietly. "As difficult as that request is, she's agreed."

Avery silently thanked him.

Cherry pouted. She lifted her right shoulder in a disinterested shrug. "I didn't mean anything by it, I just couldn't imagine, that's all."

Aware of the minutes ticking past, Avery looked at Buddy. "I need your help with something, Buddy. Could we talk privately?"

His forehead creased with concern. "Sure, baby girl. I was done here. Let's go to my office."

She turned to Matt, finding the moment awkward. Feeling Cherry's and Lilah's curiosity. "If you'd like to join us—"

"You guys go on. I'll check in on my way out."

She sent him a grateful glance, for the second time that morning touched by his understanding. By the way he seemed to know what she needed without her having to ask. He made her feel safe. Cared for.

She stood and followed Buddy to his office. He closed the door behind them and motioned to the love seat. She sat and looked up at him. "Matt told you why I was at Trudy Pruitt's last night? He told you about the calls?"

"Yes." His frown deepened. "Why didn't you tell me this was going on?"

"What could you have done? Someone was making crank calls to me. I figured you would tell me to ignore them or change to an unlisted number."

"When you found out who the anonymous caller was, you

should have contacted me immediately." He leaned toward her, expression grave. "Avery, if you had shown up fifteen minutes earlier, you might be lying beside Trudy Pruitt in the morgue."

A chill washed over her. She shuddered. She had never considered that fact.

"Trudy Pruitt ran with a rough crowd. Always did. Don't know yet who killed her, but I'll bet money it was one of them."

Matt tapped on the office door, then poked his head in. "I'm leaving."

Buddy waved him inside. "Come in, son."

Matt did, shutting the door behind him and sat down.

"She said her boys didn't kill Sallie Waguespack," Avery continued. "Said my dad was involved in a cover-up. She said she had proof."

"And you believed her?" Buddy said.

"Frankly, I didn't want to, but I...don't you think it's weird that the same night she was going to show me proof her sons were innocent of Sallie Waguespack's murder, she was killed?"

Matt's mouth thinned. "Trudy Pruitt was involved with some dangerous characters. That involvement got her killed."

"But—"

Matt stood. "Look, Avery, there are things you don't know. Things we've uncovered that I can't share with you. I wish I could. I hate to see you tearing yourself up over this, but I can't. I'm sorry."

He bent and brushed his lips against hers. "I've got to go."

Avery stared after him, surprised. Disoriented by the intimacy of the move. Disoriented, she admitted, but not displeased.

Buddy broke the silence, tone soft. "If Trudy Pruitt had this supposed proof, why did she wait until now, until you, to bring it forward?"

Avery turned back to him. She didn't have an answer for that. "She never...came to you with—"

"Of course she did. And the district attorney. And the sheriff's department. And anyone else who would listen. She had nothing, not one scrap of evidence, to support her claim of her sons' innocence."

"I have a favor to ask, Buddy. For my own peace of mind, may I look at your files of the Waguespack murder investigation?"

"Avery—"

"She called Dad a liar, Buddy. And a murderer. Why would she do that?"

"Your daddy was the most honest, upright man I've ever known. I was proud to call him my friend."

"Then you must understand. I feel like I have to uphold his honor. Prove him innocent."

Buddy leaned forward. "Innocent to who, Avery?"

Not liking the answer, she curled her hands into fists. "Why did he keep that box of newspaper clippings, Buddy? Why did he kill himself?"

Buddy sighed heavily and stood. He crossed to her and laid a hand on her shoulder. "If it'll help you, baby girl, of course you can look at the files. Just let me tell Lilah to go on to the service without me."

# CHAPTER 35

Three hours later, Avery thanked Buddy for his help. "I'm sorry I messed up your Sunday," she said.

"You couldn't, baby girl." He kissed her cheek. "Do you feel better now?"

She didn't. She lied.

The information in the file should have reassured her. Everything appeared to be in order. At 10:30 p.m. on the night of June 18th, 1988, Pat Greene, one of Buddy's deputies, called in, requesting assistance. Making rounds, he had seen a couple of young men fleeing Sallie Waguespack's home. He'd investigated and found the woman murdered.

From the deputy's description of them, Buddy had suspected the Pruitt boys. Donny and Dylan, who had been in trouble since they were old enough to steal their first candy bar, had been brought in on suspicion of dealing just the week before. The evidence hadn't supported charges, but it had only been a matter of time.

When Buddy and Pat had found the two young men, Donny and

Dylan were high. When confronted, the boys had initiated a shoot-out and were killed. After the fact, the murder weapon was found in the drainage ditch behind their trailer, Donny's prints on it.

The CSPD had launched a full investigation, discovering that Donny and Dylan had been frequenting the bar where Sallie was a cocktail waitress. Drugs had been found in Sallie's house and the Pruitt boys' apartment.

It had been determined that the boys had been dealing; Sallie Waguespack had been buying. A drug deal gone bad, they'd figured. The woman had owed them money or threatened them with the cops. One witness had claimed the three had been sleeping together, further complicating the scenario. Jealousy may have been a motive. Certainly, from the way she had been killed—hacked at with a kitchen knife—it had been a crime of passion.

Avery stopped at Buddy's office door and looked back at him. "Did you ever doubt Donny and Dylan Pruitt's guilt?" she asked. "Even for a moment?"

"Never." He ran a hand over his face, looking every one of his sixty-six years. "The murder weapon was found behind their trailer, Donny's prints on it. Sallie Waguespack's blood was found on the bottom of Dylan's shoe. Drugs were involved. We had Pat Greene, who placed them at the scene. Physical and circumstantial evidence. Can't get a much cleaner case than that."

He was right about that. She knew enough about police work to understand the process, from arrest to prosecution.

She started through the door, then stopped and turned back once more. "I didn't see an autopsy report."

His face puckered with confusion. "It should be there."

"It wasn't."

He shuffled through the folder, then returned his gaze to hers. "It's misfiled. I'll look around, give you a call when I locate it."

"Thanks, Buddy." She forced a smile. "Enjoy the rest of your day off."

Avery left the CSPD and minutes later found herself at Hunter's door. Without pausing to question her own motivation, she rapped on the frame.

Sarah began to bark, the puppies to yip. Hunter appeared at the door. He looked tired. Disheveled. Irritated at having been disturbed.

"You were working," she said. "I'm sorry."

"What do you want, Avery?"

She hesitated, put off by his surliness. "May I come in?"

He pushed opened the screen, moved aside. She stepped into the kitchen—and was immediately surrounded by squirming puppies. Sarah stood by her master's side, eyes pinned on Avery.

"They're getting big," Avery murmured. She squatted and the puppies charged her, licking her hands, butting each other out of the way. "They're so cute."

"If there's a point to your visit I'd appreciate your getting to it."

Her cheeks heated. She straightened. Met his eyes. "Did you hear what happened?"

"You mean Trudy Pruitt's murder?"

"Yes. And that I was there."

"I heard." His mouth thinned. "Even those of us who reside outside the chosen circle are part of the gossip chain."

"Never mind. You're such an asshole." She swung around to go. "I'm sorry I came here."

He caught her arm. "Why did you, Avery? Why do you keep coming around?"

"Let go of me."

He tightened his grip. "You came for something. What do you want from me?"

*She didn't know, dammit.* She tilted up her chin, furious. At herself. At him. "I don't want anything from you, Hunter. Maybe I'm here because unlike everyone else, I'm not willing to give up on you. Maybe I still see something in you that everyone else has forgotten."

"Bullshit."

"Believe what you want." She yanked her arm free, took a step toward the door.

He blocked her path. "I'd pegged you for being more honest than this, Avery. You want something from me. Spit it out."

"Stop it, Hunter. Let me go."

He moved closer, crowding her. "Why not run to Matt? Isn't he your *boyfriend?*"

He put a nasty emphasis on the last. She wanted to slap him. "Shut up."

He took another step forward; she back. She met the wall. "What would you give to have your father back, Avery?"

His question took her by surprise. Disarmed, she met his eyes. "Anything. I'd give anything."

"What do you want, Avery?" he asked again. He cupped her face in his palms. "Do you want me to tell you he loved you? Do you want me to tell you it's not your fault? Absolve you of guilt? Is that why you're—"

"Yes!" she cried. "I want to wake up to discover this has all been a nightmare. I want to have taken my father's call that last day...I want to stop hating...myself for...I want—"

The words stuck in her throat; she brought her hands to his chest. Curled her trembling fingers into his soft T-shirt. "I want what I can't have. I want my father back."

For long seconds, he gazed at her, expression dark with some strong emotion. Finally, he swore and dragged in a shaky breath. "He loved you, Avery. More than anything. Every time we were together, he talked about you. How proud he was of you. Proud that you'd had the guts to follow your dreams. That you'd done so well. He took pride in your courage. Your strength of will."

A cry slipped past her lips. One of relief. Of an immeasurably sweet release from pain. Tears flooded her eyes.

"His suicide, it wasn't about you, Avery," he went on. "He was at peace with where you were in your life."

He dropped his hands, stepped back. "Go on. Get out of here. You got what you wanted. I can't give you anything else."

She hesitated, reached a hand out. Laid it on his forearm. "Hunter?" He met her eyes. "Thank you."

He didn't reply. She dragged her hand down to his, laced their fingers. Slowly, deliberately, she brought his hand to her mouth, opened it and pressed a kiss to his palm.

He trembled. Ever so slightly. Revealing himself. What he wanted.

He wanted her.

And in that moment, she realized she wanted him as well. Without thoughts of consequences or tomorrows, she drew him closer, against her. She tilted her face up to his.

She saw the desire in his dark gaze. And the vulnerability. The combination took her breath.

She brought his hand to her chest, just above the swell of her left breast.

"Avery, I don't—"

"Yes, you do." She leaned closer. "And I do, too."

She kissed him then. Deeply. Without hesitation. She wanted him, he wanted her. Simple.

He kissed her back. In a way that left no question who would lead. Not breaking their kiss, he lifted her. She wrapped her legs around his waist, her arms around his neck. He carried her to his bed, laid her on it. For a moment, he stood above her. Holding her gaze.

Her lips tipped into a small, contented smile. She reached up, caught his hands and drew him down to her.

That moment proved the calm before the storm. Passion exploded between them. They tugged at one another's clothes, zippers and buttons, clinging panties. Greedy. Impatient to feel the other's naked body against their own.

They made love, she on top of him. She orgasmed with a cry she worried might be heard at the Piggly Wiggly next door.

She collapsed against his chest. Beneath her cheek his heart thundered. She had always wondered, all those years ago, what kissing Hunter would be like. What being with him would be like.

Now she knew. And she wondered why she had waited so long to find out.

"I hated that."

She lifted her head and met his eyes. "Me, too."

His eyes crinkled at the corners with amusement. "I could tell."

She rubbed her forehead against his bristly chin. "You have anything to eat in this place?"

"A loaded question."

"Funny. Got any homemade chocolate cake?"

"Sure. Baked it this morning."

She grinned, feeling young, randy and totally irresponsible. "How about a PB&J?"

"Got something even better."

He rolled them both out of bed. He gave her one of his T-shirts to wear. The soft white fabric swallowed her. She glanced at its front. "Party hard on Bourbon Street?"

"From the old days."

She followed him to the kitchen, Sarah at their heels, the puppies on hers. Avery leaned against the counter while he made them both PB&M—peanut butter and marshmallow cream—sandwiches, then poured two big glasses of cold milk.

Whole milk, she saw. *Talk about irresponsible.*

They sat at the tiny dinette and dug in. "My God, this is good," she said, mouth full. She washed it down with a long swallow of the creamy milk.

"Awesome, isn't it? Worth shouting about."

He wasn't talking about the milk. Or the sandwiches. She flushed and shifted her gaze. He laughed softly, stood and went to make himself another sandwich.

"Want another?" he asked.

"Not if I want to be able to snap my pants tomorrow. But thanks."

He fixed his and sat back down. "Earlier, you said something about wishing you had taken a call from your dad. What did you mean?"

She laid the last of her sandwich carefully on the plate. "That last day, before Dad...died, he called. I was on my way out. Meeting a source, one who'd finally agreed to talk to me."

Her voice thickened; she cleared it. "I heard Dad's voice on the recorder and I...I thought, I'd call him later. My source couldn't wait, but my father...he'd always be there."

Hunter reached across the table and touched her hand. "I'm sorry, Avery."

"If only I could go back, take that call."

"But you can't."

Silence fell between them. Hunter broke it. "Why were you at Trudy Pruitt's last night?"

"Remember the caller I told you about? The woman who said

Dad got what he deserved?" He nodded. "She called again. A couple of times. She said Dad was a liar. And a murderer."

"Your dad? Avery, you can't honestly belie—"

She stopped him. "That woman was Trudy Pruitt. Donny and Dylan Pruitt's mother."

"They're the ones who killed that woman."

"Sallie Waguespack." Sarah whined and laid her head on Avery's lap. Avery scratched her behind the ears. "She claimed they didn't do it. That they were framed."

"Of course she did. She was their mother."

"She said Dad was part of the cover-up. That she had proof."

"And?"

"She was killed before she could give it to me."

"And you think she was murdered because of that proof?"

"It's crossed my mind. It's an awfully big coincidence, she lives all these years, contacts me and gets herself killed."

He was silent a moment. "And you believe whoever was involved with your dad in this frame-up killed him then Trudy Pruitt?"

She leaned forward. "You ever heard of a group called The Seven?"

He frowned. "My mother was part of a civic organization called The Seven something or other."

"How about a woman named Gwen Lancaster? Ever heard of her?" He shook his head. "Her brother, Tom Lancaster?"

His expression altered subtly. "That name's familiar but I can't place from where."

"He disappeared in February this year. Similar situation to McDougal. A Cypress Springs outsider. No sign of violence, but the police suspected foul play. The *Gazette* ran the story on the sixth."

"That's right." He paused as if remembering. "The big difference between the two, of course, was the car. Lancaster's was left out in the open. McDougal's had been hidden. Which to me suggests the two are unrelated."

"Unrelated? Two young men disappear from the same small community, barely eight weeks apart and you don't think those disappearances are related?"

"Modus operandi, Avery. Criminals tend to repeat their crimes, how they carry out those crimes. If a murderer leaves a body out in the open the first time, they'll do it the second, then the third. Basic investigative technique."

She shook her head. "Trudy Pruitt, Elaine St. Claire, Tom Lancaster, Luke McDougal. If I accept your definition, we're dealing with four different killers."

"McDougal may very well have chosen to go missing. People do it all the time. Coming on the heels of Lancaster is a coincidence. Or clever planning from a man intent on disappearing."

"For heaven's sake." She made a sound of frustration. "Three killers then. In a town that has had only a couple of murders in a decade?"

He pushed his plate away. Sat back. "Okay, you're obviously up to your elbows in this. You tell me."

She began at the beginning, with Gwen Lancaster. She told him about how they'd met, the things she had told Avery about a group called The Seven. And about her brother Tom, who had disappeared while researching the group.

"At first I didn't believe her. The idea of a vigilante-style group operating in Cypress Springs seemed ludicrous. According to Gwen, the original group disbanded after only a few years, but are operating again. Willing to murder to achieve their goals."

"You'll forgive me if I chuckle under my breath."

"I felt the same way." She leaned toward him. "She dared me to check out her facts. I did, Hunter. What I found stunned me. In the past eight months there have been ten unexpected deaths. Not counting Elaine St. Claire, Trudy Pruitt or McDougal and Lancaster. Cypress Springs is a community of about nine hundred, Hunter. That's a lot of deaths."

"Accidents happen."

"Not like that they don't." She paused, then drew a deep breath. "Gwen claims The Seven are responsible for her brother's death. He got too close and they killed him."

"And she hooked you by claiming they're responsible for your father's death as well."

She held his gaze despite the pity she read in his. "Yes."

"Avery, the woman was trying to pass herself off as your father's daughter. Doesn't that tell you something?"

"I know. I thought the same thing at first but—"

"But you want to believe it."

"No." She shook her head. "That's not it."

"Have you talked to Dad about this?"

"I talked to him about The Seven. He says no such group exists—now or ever."

"But you don't believe him?"

Just considering the question felt like a betrayal. "It's not that, I just...I'm thinking he's out of the loop."

"Dad? Out of the loop in this town?"

"Listen to me, Hunter. The day I drove into Cypress Springs, the first thing I thought was that the town hadn't changed. Like it hadn't been touched by time." She paused, then went on. "Since then, what's struck me is how homogeneous this town is. Look in the phone book. How many names do you recognize? It's all the same families as when we were kids."

"What are you getting at, Avery?"

"What does it take to keep time from marching on, Hunter? What does one have to do?"

For a long moment he said nothing. His expression revealed nothing of his thoughts. When he finally spoke, his tone was measured.

"Avery, listen to me. I want you to think about what I'm about to ask you. What would you get out of this? If it's true."

"I don't understand."

"If your dad was killed by this...Seven, what would you get out of it?"

She began to tell him she would get nothing out of it, then swallowed the words.

*If he hadn't taken his own life, she would be absolved from guilt.*

Avery fisted her fingers, furious at the thought. At the longing that accompanied it. She pushed both away. "You think I want Dad to have been murdered? You think I want Cypress Springs to be home to some murdering, extremist group?"

His expression said it all and she shook her head. "I don't, okay? How awful, how—"

She bit those words back, searching for others, though whether to convince him or herself she didn't know.

"I was always on the outside, Hunter. I never fit in here, never felt like I really belonged. Now I do. Now Cypress Springs feels like home."

He stood. Crossed to her. Cupped her face in his hands. "Grief twists reality."

"I know, but—"

"Don't do this to yourself, Avery."

"I have to know. For sure. I wish I could trust...I know I should, but I can't."

"Then get your proof. Of innocence or guilt. If that's what you need, get it."

## CHAPTER 36

Gwen glanced at her dashboard clock. The amber numbers read 10:45. A knot of fear settled in her belly. She gripped the steering wheel tighter, her palms slippery on the vinyl.

*The woman had warned her to come alone. She had promised information about The Seven, past and present.*

*Information about Tom.*

Gwen acknowledged that she was scared shitless. She pressed her lips together. They trembled. Tom had disappeared on just such an errand, on just such a promise. Like hers, his meeting time had been a late hour, his destination a deserted spot off an unnamed country road.

*If not for Tom, she wouldn't go. She would simply keep driving, not stopping until she reached the lights of New Orleans.*

She had grown to hate Cypress Springs. The quaint buildings and town square, the people whose welcoming smiles hid judgment and suspicion. The sour smell that inundated the community when the wind shifted from the south. The way people went about their business, pretending it didn't exist.

Gwen realized she was holding her breath and released it. She drew another, deeply, working to calm herself. She was alone. No allies. No one to share her fears with. Avery Chauvin had been her last hope for that.

That hope had been abruptly squashed.

*Another dead. Trudy Pruitt.*

*They had cut out her tongue.*

Gwen had heard that this morning, while breakfasting at the Azalea Café. She had been devastated.

The woman had been killed only a matter of hours after having met with Gwen. After having confirmed the past and present existence of The Seven. After confirming all of Gwen's suspicions: that a group of citizens met in secret and passed judgment on others, that they delivered one warning, that if it wasn't heeded, they took action, that they had never really disbanded—simply gone deeper underground. That in the past months they had become more active. And it seemed, more dangerous.

Guilt, a sense of responsibility, speared through her. If she hadn't come to Cypress Springs, if she hadn't tracked Trudy Pruitt down, would the woman be alive today?

*Go, Gwen. Run. As fast as you can.*

She flexed her fingers on the steering wheel. Other than putting her own life and the lives of others in jeopardy, what was she accomplishing? She couldn't help her brother now. Anyone who might have been willing to talk would be too frightened to do so after Trudy Pruitt.

But if she ran, she would never know what happened to Tom.

And she didn't think she could go on with her life until she did.

So, here she was. Gwen focused her attention on the upcoming meeting. The woman's call had come late this afternoon. She had refused to identify herself. Her voice had been unsteady, thick-sounding. As if she had been crying.

Or was trying to disguise her identity.

She had claimed to have information about The Seven and

Gwen's brother. Gwen had tried unsuccessfully to get more out of her.

Quite possibly, tonight's rendezvous would prove a setup.

Or an ambush.

Gwen squared her shoulders. She wouldn't go without a fight. She glanced at her windbreaker, lying on the seat beside her. Nestled in the right pocket was a .38-caliber Smith & Wesson revolver. Hammerless, with a two-inch barrel, the salesman had called it the ladies' gun of choice. He had assured her it would be plenty effective against an attacker, particularly, she knew, if she had surprise on her side.

She had taken other precautions as well, sent e-mails to the sheriff's department, her family lawyer and her mother. She had updated each with what she had uncovered so far, where she was going tonight and why. She found it hard to believe that both a brother and sister disappearing from the same small community would fly.

Even if she was killed, she had turned up the heat.

Their rendezvous point, Highway 421 and No Name Road loomed before her. The woman had instructed her to turn onto No Name Road and drive a quarter mile to an unmarked dirt road. She would recognize it by the rusted-out hulk of a tractor at the corner. There, she was to take a right and drive another quarter mile to an abandoned hunting cabin.

Gwen turned onto No Name Road. Her headlights sliced across the roadway. Heavily wooded on either side, the light bounced off and through the branches of the cypress, pine and oak trees.

Some small creature darted in front of her vehicle. Gwen slammed on the brakes. Her tires screamed; her safety harness yanked tight, preventing her from hitting the steering wheel. The creature, a raccoon, she saw, made the side of the road and scurried into the brush.

Legs shaking, she eased the car forward, the dark seeming to swallow her. She strained to see beyond the scope of the headlights. The woman had warned her not to be late. It was nearly eleven now.

The drive came into view. She turned onto it, gravel crunching under her tires.

The cabin lay ahead, illuminated by her headlights. An Acadian, with a high, sloping roof and covered front porch. It looked a part of the landscape, as if it had been here forever. Rustic. Made of some durable wood, most probably cypress.

She drew her vehicle to a stop, searching the area for other signs of life. She found none. Not a light, vehicle or movement. She lowered her window a crack, shut off her engine and listened. The call of the insects and an owl, chirping frogs. Some creature running through the brush.

Nothing that spoke to the presence of another human.

*Show time.*

Gwen took a deep breath. Her heart beat hard against the wall of her chest. She struggled for a semblance of calm. She had to keep her head. Her wits about her. How could she hope to outsmart a killer if she couldn't think? If she couldn't accurately aim the gun because her hands shook?

She retrieved her jacket, put it on. She slipped her hand into the right pocket to reassure herself the gun was there. The metal was smooth and cool against her fingertips.

She opened the car door, choosing to leave the keys in the car's ignition. She wanted them there in case she needed to make a quick escape.

Gwen stepped out. The wind stirred the mostly naked branches of the oak and gum trees. The sound affected her like the scrape of fingernails on a blackboard.

She rubbed her arms, the goose bumps that raced up them. "Hello," she called. An owl returned the greeting. She waited. The minutes ticked past. She shifted her gaze to the cabin.

*Her caller could be there. Waiting.*

*She could be dead. Another Trudy Pruitt.*

Gwen didn't know why that thought had filtered into her brain, but it had. And now, planted there, she couldn't shake it.

Minutes passed. Eleven o'clock became eleven-fifteen. Eleven-thirty.

Midnight.

*Do it. Check out the cabin.*

*Or go. And never know.*

She turned to the building. She stared at it, knees rubbery with fear. She couldn't not check. What if the woman was there and hurt; she would need help.

Gwen put her hand in her pocket, closed her fingers around the gun's grip and started forward, acknowledging terror. The Lord's Prayer ran through her head, the familiar words comforting.

*Our Father who art in heaven*
*Hallowed be thy name*

She reached the porch steps. She saw then that they were in disrepair. She grabbed the handrail, tested it, found it sturdy and began to pick her way up the steps.

She reached the porch. Took a step. The wood groaned beneath her weight. She quickly crossed. Made the door. Hand trembling, she reached out, grasped the knob and twisted.

*Thy kingdom come, Thy will be done*
*On earth as it is in—*

The door swung open. Taking a deep breath, she peered inside. Called out, voice barely a whisper. She waited, listening. Letting her eyes adjust to the absolute dark.

As they did, several large forms took shape. Furniture, she realized, taking a tentative step inside. A couple broken-down chairs. A shipping crate serving as a coffee table. Things left behind by previous residents, she decided.

She picked her way inside, blindly, calling herself a dozen different kinds of idiot. What was she trying to prove? Nobody was here. She had been sent on a wild-goose chase. Somebody's idea of a joke. A sick joke.

She turned. A baglike white shape in the doorway up ahead caught her eye. She made her way cautiously toward it. Not a bag, she saw, a white sheet, drawn up and knotted to form a kind of pouch.

She gazed at the package with a sense of inevitability. Of predestination. Whoever had contacted her had predicted her every step. Keeping the rendezvous. Waiting. Coming into the cabin. Finding this package.

*And opening it.*

She squatted and with trembling fingers untied the knot, peeled away the sheet.

Revealing a cat. Or rather, what had been a cat. A tabby. It had been slit open and gutted. Gwen brought a hand to her mouth; stomach lurching to her throat. The creature's sandy-colored fur was matted with blood, the sheet soaked.

She reached out. And found the blood was tacky.

This had been done recently. Just before she had been scheduled to meet her informant.

*The Seven gave one warning. If it wasn't heeded, they took action.*

*She had gotten her warning.*

Something stirred behind her. *Someone.* Gwen sprang backward, whirled around. The cabin door stood open; nothing—or no one—blocked her path. Panicked, she ran forward. Through the main room and onto the porch. Her foot went through a rotten board. She cried out in pain, stumbled and landed on her knees.

Clawing her way to her feet, she darted toward her car. She reached it, yanked open the door and scrambled inside. Sobbing with relief, she started the vehicle, threw it into Reverse and hit the gas. When she reached the main road, she dared a glance back, terrified at what she would see.

The deserted country road seemed to mock her.

# CHAPTER 37

Avery parked her car around the corner from The Guesthouse. She cut her lights, then the engine as she glanced quickly around. The square appeared deserted, its surrounding businesses dark. Cypress Springs retired early and slept soundly.

Just as she had planned for.

She meant to collect Gwen and head to Trudy Pruitt's trailer to have a look around. If Gwen refused, which was entirely possible, considering how Avery had treated her, she would go alone.

Avery had decided on this course of action after leaving Hunter. He had told her to get her proof and that's just what she meant to do. She had planned carefully. Had assembled everything she and Gwen would need: latex gloves, penlights, plastic Ziploc bags. And finally, her courage.

Now, to convince Gwen they were on the same team. She had tried the cell phone number the woman had given her. She had repeatedly gotten a reply stating the cell number she had called was no longer in service. Contacting the other woman by land line re-

quired having The Guesthouse management ring her room or calling the pay phone in the hall. She hadn't wanted to do either.

Nor had she wanted to be seen paying her a visit. Which left a
chance encounter or stealth.

During the drive there, she had kept careful watch in her
rearview mirror. She had not wanted to be followed. She had not
wanted the wrong set of eyes to see her arriving at Gwen's.

*The wrong set of eyes? Cloak-and-dagger driving maneuvers?*
*Secret meeting?*

She was losing her mind. Spiraling into a kind of paranoid
schizophrenia, one in which she suspected her home of being
watched, her phone of being bugged. One in which every smiling
and familiar face hid a secret agenda.

A nervous laugh flew to her lips. She wanted the truth. No, she
needed it. And she would do whatever was necessary to get it.

She thought of Hunter. Of the afternoon spent with him, in his
bed. The experience felt surreal to her. As if she had dreamed it.

What had she done? Consummated some ancient passion she
hadn't even consciously acknowledged? How could she be with
Hunter when Matt was the one she had always wanted? What had
she been thinking?

Obviously, she hadn't been thinking. She had acted on emotion.
And physical urges.

She closed her eyes, thinking of the past, her relationship with
Hunter. With Matt. All those years ago, had she chosen Matt because Hunter took her out of her safety zone? Because he had always pushed her, both emotionally and intellectually?

She had always been comfortable with the outgoing Matt. She
had known where she stood all the time. Had never felt out of control. Weren't control and comfort good things? What did she really want?

Avery shook her head, refocusing on this moment. On what she
had set out to do. Thoughts of Hunter, Matt and her future would
have to wait.

She slipped out of the Blazer. Dressed entirely in black, she
hoped to meld with the shadows. She eased the door shut and

quickly made her way to the corner, hanging close to the inside edge of the sidewalk, near the shrubs and trees.

Until they had drifted apart their junior year of high school, Laurie Landry had been one of her best friends. Laurie had taught Avery that her parents kept a spare house key tucked inside the covered electrical outlet to the right of the front door. She and Laurie had used it many times over the years to slip in and out at all times of the night.

If it wasn't there, she wasn't certain what she would do.

She needn't have worried. The Landrys kept the key in the same place they had twelve years ago. A testament to how slowly some things changed in Cypress Springs. How safe a place to live it was.

Unless, of course, you were targeted by The Seven for behavior modification.

Permanent behavior modification.

Avery retrieved the key, opened the door and stepped into The Guesthouse's main hall. Turning, she relocked the door, slipped the key into her pocket and started up the stairs. The desk closed at 8:00 p.m.; each guest was given a key to come and go as they pleased.

Neither the Landry family nor a guest would give a second thought to the sound of someone moving about.

Avery quietly climbed the stairs. She reached the top landing and turned left. Gwen occupied the unit at the far end of the hall. Avery reached it and stopped, a dizzying sense of déjà vu settling over her.

Gwen's door stood ajar.

*Not again. Please God, not again.*

With the tips of her fingers, Avery nudged the door the rest of the way open. She called Gwen's name, her voice a thick whisper.

Gwen didn't reply.

But she hadn't expected her to. She expected the worst.

Avery reached into her pocket and retrieved her penlight. She switched it on and stepped fully into the room, the slim beam of light illuminating the way. The place had been ransacked. Drawers and armoire emptied. Dresser mirror shattered. Lamps toppled.

She moved through the room, sweeping the light back and forth in a jittery arc. No bloody prints. No body. Swallowing hard, she crossed to the made bed. Bending, she lifted the bed skirt, pointed the light and peered underneath.

*Nothing. Not even a dust bunny.*

She dropped the skirt and straightened. Turned toward the armoire. Its doors hung open, contents emptied onto the floor in front. Avery pivoted toward the bathroom's closed door, then glanced back at the hallway. She shouldn't be handling this alone. She should call Buddy, the CSPD. Get them over here. Let them search for Gwen.

She couldn't do that. How would she explain being here? Latex gloves and penlight in her pocket? Last night at Trudy Pruitt's and tonight at Gwen Lancaster's—

*Get the hell out. Call the cops from the car. Or better yet, from a pay phone on the other side of town.*

Instead, Avery took a step toward the bathroom. Then another. As she neared it, she heard what sounded like water running.

She grasped the knob, twisted it and pushed. The door eased open. She inched closer, shone her light inside.

The room was small—a pedestal sink, medicine cabinet, claw-footed tub with pink, flowered shower curtain circling it. The floor clear.

The sound she'd heard was the toilet running. She crossed to it, jiggled the handle. It stopped filling.

*So far so good.*

She returned her gaze to the tub. To that flowered curtain. *She had to look. Just in case.*

She sidled toward it. As if a less direct approach might influence what she found. She stopped within arm's reach of the curtain. Her heart thundered in her chest. Her mouth went dry, her pits and palms were wet.

*Do it, Chauvin.*

She forced herself to lift her arm, grab a handful of the vinyl and yank it away.

"Don't move a muscle or I'll blow your fucking head off!"

Avery froze. Gwen, she realized. She was alive!

"Hands up!" Gwen snapped. "Then turn around. Slowly."

Avery did. Gwen stood in the doorway, face white as a sheet. She held a gun, had it trained on her.

"It's me, Gwen. Avery."

"I have eyes."

"This isn't how it looks. Your door was open...I found the place like this."

"Sure you did."

"It's true. I needed to reach you...your cell number wasn't working and I couldn't call here because I didn't want anyone to know we were in contact."

The gun wavered. Gwen narrowed her eyes. "You needed to reach me? I seem to remember you telling me you wanted nothing to do with me."

"That was before Trudy Pruitt."

Her already ashen face paled more. "What do you know about Trudy—"

"I was there last night. She called me, set up a meeting. When I got there her door was open, her trailer ransacked. I found her in the kitchen...on the floor. When I saw your door...your place, I...I thought they'd gotten you, too."

For a long moment Gwen simply stared at her. As if evaluating her words, deciding if she was being truthful. Then with the tiniest nod, she lowered the gun.

"Thank you." Avery let out a shaky breath. "That's twice in two days I've found myself staring down the barrel of a gun."

From the hallway came what sounded like someone climbing the stairs. They both swung in that direction. Gwen darted toward her door and shut it. She locked the dead bolt, then looked at Avery. She held a finger to her lips and pointed at the bathroom.

Avery indicated she understood. A moment later Gwen closed them in it, crossed to the tub and started the shower. White noise, Avery realized. To muffle their words, in case someone was listening.

That done, Gwen crossed to the toilet, lowered the lid and sank onto it. She dropped her head to her hands.

After several moments Gwen lifted her head and looked at Avery. "I thought I was dead."

Her voice shook. So, Avery saw, did her hands. She clasped them together.

"A woman called," Gwen continued. "She said she had information about The Seven and about Tom. We were supposed to meet tonight."

"She didn't show."

"No. She was a decoy."

"A decoy? You mean to lure you away from here?"

"To deliver my warning."

"I don't understand."

"I interviewed Trudy Pruitt yesterday. She told me The Seven exist. Past and present. She said they killed Elaine St. Claire. That they always deliver a warning before taking action. A terrible threat."

"Elaine St. Claire was warned?"

"Yes. She and Trudy were friends. They both served drinks down at Hard Eight. One day Elaine just up and disappeared."

"She took the warning seriously and left Cypress Springs?"

"Yes. A couple months later, Trudy got a letter from the woman. Apparently a representative of the group had paid St. Claire a late-night visit. He had made this weapon...a phallus with sharp spines and a knife blade imbedded in its tip.

"The man told her she had been judged and found guilty—of moral corruption. Because she slept around. A lot, apparently. He told her he would give her what she loved—that he would fuck her to death."

Avery pressed her lips together to hold back a sound of horror. She recalled what Hunter had told her about Elaine St. Claire's death. The two stories jibed.

Gwen stood. Avery sensed she was too jumpy to remain seated. "They warned me tonight. A cat...they gutted it, left it for me. At the meeting place. They meant to frighten me."

"And they succeeded."

"Hell, yes. I'm terrified."

"You've got to get out of Cypress Springs. Now. Tonight. I'll keep in touch, let you know what I find out."

"What makes you think you're immune?"

"I don't understand."

"You're not one of them anymore, Avery. If they discover you're onto them, they'll kill you."

"I'll make sure they don't find out."

Gwen laughed, the sound hard, humorless. "It's too late for that. They've seen us talking. You've asked questions around town. They see everything, Avery. *Everything.*"

"I'm not leaving until I know the truth about my dad's death."

Gwen looked at her. Avery understood. Gwen wouldn't leave until she knew what had happened to her brother.

"We're in this together then," Avery said.

"Guess so."

Avery rubbed her arms, chilled. "In the interview, did Trudy Pruitt say anything about me or my father? Did she say anything about Sallie Waguespack?"

Gwen shook her head. "She talked exclusively about The Seven. I've got it all in my... Oh, no."

"What?"

"My notes!"

Gwen leaped toward the door, yanked it open and raced into the bedroom.

Avery followed. Watched as she tore through the debris littering the floor, looked under the bed and in the armoire, expression frantic.

"Gone. Everything is gone. My notes. Interview tapes." She sank to her knees. "They get away with murder."

"No, they don't. We won't let them." Avery crossed to the woman. "I believe you. God help me, but I do. Together, we can beat them."

Gwen shook her head. "We can't beat them. No one can."

"That's what they want us to believe. That's how they've gotten away with this for so long." She held out a hand to help the other woman up. "Tell me exactly what happened tonight, everything you've learned so far. I'll do the same. Together, we'll figure this out. We'll go to the state police or the FBI. We can do it, Gwen. Together."

"Together," Gwen repeated, taking Avery's hand, getting to her feet, returning with her to the bathroom. There, Gwen explained the events of the day, from the woman's call to finding the gutted cat and running for what she assumed was her life.

Avery thought a moment. "And you have no idea who the woman was?"

"None."

"Did she call on the pay phone in the hall?" Gwen shook her head. "So she had to go through the front desk. Did you ask—"

"Yes. They said they didn't know who it was. Said they assumed it was a friend of mine from out of town."

"But you don't believe that?"

"I don't believe anything anymore." She laced her fingers. "What about you?"

Avery began with the first anonymous call. "She said Dad got what he deserved. That I would, too. Before that call I was struggling with the idea of Dad killing himself. After it—"

"You didn't buy it at all."

"Yes. She called a couple more times. She accused Dad of being a liar and a murderer, of helping frame her boys for Sallie Waguespack's murder. She said she had proof."

"Why did you believe her? Everything you've told me about your dad—"

"I found this box of newspaper clippings in Dad's closet. They were all from the summer of 1988. All concerning Sallie Waguespack's murder."

"His having them supports Trudy Pruitt's claim."

"Not necessarily. Her murder was the biggest thing to ever hit this town. It was a shock, a wake-up call. He was civic-minded. He probably followed the story because he—"

"Avery," she interrupted gently, "he clipped all those newspaper articles and kept them for fifteen years. There has to be a reason. Something personal."

Avery knew she was right. She had thought the same all along. But no way had he been an accomplice to murder. No way. She told Gwen so.

The other woman didn't argue. "When did you learn your caller was Trudy Pruitt?"

"The same afternoon she was killed. I goaded her into telling me her name. I promised that if she showed me proof of her claims, I'd make it right. That I'd find a way to exonerate Donny and Dylan. We set up a meeting for that night."

Avery pulled in a deep breath. "She was still alive...she tried to tell me something but died before she could."

Gwen's expression altered. "Didn't you know? They cut out her tongue."

"Are you...that can't..." But it was true, Avery realized, picturing the woman's face, her bloody mouth.

They fell silent. Gwen broke it first. "Seems to me that shoots the whole random-act-of-violence thing to hell."

Avery winced at her sarcasm. Shifted the subject. "Buddy let me look at his records of the Waguespack murder. Everything seemed in order, but I keep coming back to that box of clippings. And my belief that Dad wouldn't take his own life. And now, all the deaths." A lump formed in her throat; she swallowed past it. "Who are these people, Gwen? Who are The Seven?"

"Put it together, Avery." She leaned toward her. "You're a reporter...who fits the profile?"

When Avery didn't respond, Gwen filled in for her. "They're probably all men. Though, obviously, since a woman lured me out tonight, women are part of the group. They're no doubt longtime Cypress Springs residents. Pillars of the community. Men who are looked up to. Ones in influential positions or ones who have influence." She paused. "Like your dad."

"He would never have been party to this. Never, he—"

Gwen held up a hand, stopping her. "It's the only way this would work. I guess them all to be mature, forty and up. Maybe way up, if the members of today's Seven are the same, or partly the same, as the past's.

"And," she finished, "if today's group mirrors the one of the 1980s, they have many accomplices in the community. Like-minded citizens willing to spy for them. Break the law for them."

Avery frowned. "The past and the present, they're intertwined. The group from the 1980s, Sallie Waguespack's death. I just don't know how."

"What do you think Trudy Pruitt's proof was?"

"I don't know. But if it was for real, the way I figure it, there's a chance it's still in her trailer."

Gwen moved her gaze over Avery, her expression subtly shifting to one of understanding. "And you're thinking we should go find it?"

"If you're up for it."

"At this point, what do I have to lose?"

*They both knew, both were acutely aware of what they could lose. Their lives.*

"Besides," Gwen murmured, smile sassy, "I've got a pair of black jeans I've been dying to wear."

CHAPTER 38

Avery parked the SUV just outside the trailer park and they walked in. Neither spoke. They kept as much as possible to the deepest shadows. Unlike the previous evening, Avery was grateful for the blown-out safety lights.

They reached Trudy Pruitt's trailer. The yellow crime scene tape stretched across the front, sagging in the center, forming an obscene smile. Avery shivered despite the warm night.

"How are we going to get in?"

"You'll see." She quickly crossed to the trailer. Instead of climbing the steps, she stepped into the garden. The frog figurine was just where she had expected it to be. She picked it up, turned it over, opened the hidden compartment and took out a key. "My bet is, this is a key to her front door."

"How did you know that was there?"

"I noticed the figurine, thought it was concrete until I accidentally knocked it off the porch. Why else would someone have a fake concrete frog on the front steps?"

"Good detective work."

Avery lifted a shoulder. "Journalists notice things."

They climbed the steps, let themselves in. Avery retrieved her penlight, switched it on. Gwen did the same. No one had cleaned up the mess. In all likelihood, even when the police gave the okay, there would be no one to clean it up. She averted her gaze from the bloody smear on the back wall.

From her back pocket, she took the two pairs of gloves she had picked up at the paint store that afternoon. She handed a pair to Gwen. "This is still a crime scene. I don't want my prints all over the place."

Gwen slipped them on. "We get caught, we're in deep shit."

"We're already in deep shit. Let's start in the bedroom."

They made their way there, finding it in the same state of chaos as the front room: the bed was unmade, the dresser drawers hung open, clothes spilling out. Beer cans, an overflowing ashtray, newspapers and fashion magazines littered the dresser top and floor.

They exchanged glances. "Wasn't a neat freak, was she?" Gwen murmured.

Avery frowned. She moved her gaze over the room, taking in the mess. "You're right, Gwen. The killer didn't make this mess, Trudy Pruitt was simply a slob."

"Okay. So?"

"Last night I thought the place had been ransacked. Now I realize that wasn't the case. Why search the living room but not the bedroom?"

"What do you think it means?"

"Maybe nothing. Just an observation. Let's get started."

"What are we looking for?"

"I'll know it when I see it. I hope."

They began to search, carefully examining the contents of each drawer, then the closet, finally picking through items on the dresser top. Avery shifted her attention to the floor.

The *Gazette,* she saw. Strewn across the floor. Avery squatted beside it. Not a current issue, she realized. The issue reporting her father's death. Trudy Pruitt had drawn devil horns and a goatee on his picture.

"What?"

Avery indicated the newspaper. Gwen read the headline aloud. "'Beloved Physician Commits Suicide. Community Mourns.'" She met Avery's eyes. "I'm sor—" She stopped, frowning. "Look at this, Avery. Trudy made some sort of notations, here in the margin."

The woman had used a series of marks to count. Four perpendicular hatchet marks with another crosswise through them. Beside it she had written "All but two."

"Five," Gwen murmured. "What do you think she was counting?"

"Don't know for certai—" She swallowed, eyes widening. "My God, five plus two—"

"Equals seven. Holy shit."

"She was counting the dead. Dad was number five. There are, or were, two left."

"But who were they?"

"On the phone she said there weren't many of them left. That they were dropping like flies."

"People who knew the truth."

"Gotta be."

Avery carefully leafed through the remaining pages of the paper. Nothing jumped out at her. She carefully folded the page with her father's photo and Trudy Pruitt's notations, then slipped it into a plastic bag.

They searched the living room next, checking the undersides and linings of the chairs and sofa, behind the few framed photos, inside magazines. They found nothing.

"Kitchen's next," Avery murmured, voice thick.

"That's where...it's going to be bad." Gwen paled. "I've never—" They exchanged glances, and by unspoken agreement, Avery took the lead.

Using tape, the police had marked where Trudy had died. A pool of blood, dried now, circled the shape. Several bloody handprints stood out clearly on the dingy linoleum floor.

Her handprints.

Avery started to shake. She dragged her gaze away, took a deep, fortifying breath. "Let's get this over with."

Avery checked the freezer. It was empty save for a couple unopened Lean Cuisine frozen meals and a half-dozen empty ice trays. The cabinets and pantry also proved mostly bare. They found nothing taped to the underside of shelves, the dining table or trash barrel.

"Either she never had any proof or the killer already picked it up," Avery said, frustrated.

"Maybe her proof was in her head," Gwen offered. "In the form of an argument."

"Maybe."

Gwen frowned. "No answering machine."

Avery glanced at her. "What?"

"Everybody's got an answering machine these days." She pointed at the phone, hanging on the patch of wall beside the refrigerator. "I didn't see one in the bedroom, either. Did you?"

Avery shook her head and crossed to the phone, picked it up. Instead of a dial tone, a series of beeps greeted her. She frowned and handed the receiver to the other woman.

"Memory call," Gwen said. "It's an answering service offered through the phone company. I have it."

"How do you retrieve the messages?"

"You dial the service, then punch in a five-digit password. The beeps mean she has a message waiting."

"What's the number?"

"Mine's local. It'd be different here. Sorry."

Avery glanced around. "My guess is, Trudy wrote that number down, that it's here, near the phone. So she wouldn't have to remember it." She slid open the drawers nearest the phone, shuffled through the mix of papers, flyers and unopened mail.

"Look on the receiver itself," Gwen offered. "Until I learned mine, that's where I taped it."

Avery did. Nothing had been taped to either receiver or cradle. She made a sound of frustration and looked at Gwen. "No good."

"Tom had the service," she murmured. "He programmed it into his—"

"Speed dial," Avery finished for her, glancing at the phone. Sure enough, the phone offered that feature, for up to six numbers. She tried the first and was connected to the Hard Eight.

She gave Gwen a thumbs-up, then tried the second programmed number, awakening someone from a deep sleep. She hung up and tried again.

The third proved the winner. A recording welcomed her to "her memory call service."

"Got it," Avery said, excited. "Take a guess at a password."

"1-2-3-4-5."

Avery punched it in and was politely informed that password was invalid. She tried the same combination, backward. She punched in several random combinations.

All with no luck. She hung up and looked at Gwen. "What now?"

"Most people choose passwords they can easily remember, their anniversary, birthday, kid's birthday. But we don't know any of those."

"Oh yes we do," Avery murmured. The date Trudy Pruitt had never forgotten. The one she might use as a painful, self-mocking reminder. "June 18, 1988. The night Sallie Waguespack was murdered and her sons were killed in a shoot-out with the police."

Avery connected with the answering service again, then punched in 0-6-1-9-8-8. The automated operator announced that she had five new messages waiting and one saved message.

Avery gave Gwen another thumbs-up, then pressed the appropriate buttons to listen to each. The recording announced the day, date and time of call, then played the message. The woman's boss at the bar, pissed that she hadn't shown up for work. Several hang-ups. A woman, crying. Her soft sobs despairing, hopeless. Then Hunter. He said his name, gave his number and hung up.

Avery's knees went weak. She laid her hand on the counter for support. *Hunter had called Trudy Pruitt the last afternoon of her life. Why?*

"What's wrong?"

Avery looked at Gwen. She saw by the other woman's expression that her own must have registered shock. She worked to mask it. "Nothing. A...a woman crying. Just crying. It was weird."

"Replay it."

Avery did, holding the phone to both their ears, disconnecting the moment the call ended.

"The woman who called me sounded as if she had been crying," Gwen told her. "What if they were one and the same?"

"What time did she call you?"

Gwen screwed up her face in thought. "About five in the afternoon."

Avery dialed, called up the messages again. The woman had called Trudy Pruitt at four forty-five. Avery looked at Gwen. "A coincidence?"

"A weird one." Gwen frowned. "What do you think it means?"

"I don't know. I wonder if the police have listened to the messages."

"They could be retrieving them directly from the service. After all, the calls could be evidence."

"Or the police might have missed them, same way we almost did. Let's get out of here," Avery said.

They left the way they'd come, reaching the SUV without incident. Avery started the engine and they eased off the road's shoulder. She didn't flip on her headlights until they'd gone a couple hundred feet.

She couldn't stop thinking about Hunter having called Trudy Pruitt. Why? What business could he have had with the woman? And on the last day of her life? And why hadn't he mentioned it when they'd discussed the woman's death?

The answers to those questions were damning.

"Something's bothering you."

She glanced at Gwen. She should tell her. They were partners now, in this thing together. If Gwen had been one of her colleagues at the *Post,* she would.

But she couldn't. Not yet. She had to think it through.

"I'm wondering why people like Trudy Pruitt stayed in Cypress Springs? Why not leave?"

"I asked her that. She said some did leave. For others, for most, this was their home. Their friends were here. Their family. So they stayed."

"But to live in fear. To know you're being watched. Judged. It's just so wrong. So...un-American."

Avery realized in that moment how carelessly she took for granted her freedoms, the ones granted by the Bill of Rights. What if one day they were gone? If she woke up to discover she couldn't express her views, see the movies or read the books she chose to. Or if skipping worship Sunday morning or drinking one too many margaritas might land her on a Most Wanted list.

"It's not been until recently that things have gotten really weird," Gwen continued. "For a long time before that it was quiet."

"Recently? What do you mean?"

"In the last eight months to a year. About the time the accidents and suicides began. Trudy said that after Elaine disappeared she thought about going. But she couldn't afford to leave."

Avery hadn't considered that. It cost money to pick up and move. One couldn't simply carry a trailer on their back. Apartments required security deposits, first and last month's rent, utility deposits. Then there was the matter of securing a job.

Not like the moves she had made, ones where she'd lined up a job, and her new employer had covered her moving expenses. She'd had money in the bank to fall back on, a father she could have turned to if need be.

To a degree, people like Trudy Pruitt were trapped.

Now she was dead.

"According to what Trudy told me, most of the citizens fell in like sheep. They were frightened of what Cypress Springs was becoming, only too happy to head back to church, rein in their behavior or spy on their neighbors if it meant being able to leave their house unlocked at night."

"What about her? She didn't fall in line with the rest."

Gwen's expression became grim. "I don't think she knew how to be any different. And...I don't think she felt any motivation to change. She hated this town, the people. Because of her boys."

"But she didn't say anything about them? About their deaths, Sallie Waguespack's murder?"

"Nothing except that they didn't do it. That they were framed."

"How about Tom? Did she say anything about him?"

"I asked. She didn't know anything about him but what she'd read in the paper. She told me she didn't have a doubt The Seven killed him."

"He hadn't interviewed her?"

"Nope. She found me, actually."

Avery pulled to a stop at a red light. She looked at Gwen. "Did she say who The Seven were?"

"No. She said revealing that would get her dead."

*She got dead anyway.* The light changed; Avery eased forward.

The square came into view up ahead. "Drop me at that corner," Gwen said.

"You're sure? I could park around the corner, give you a hand cleaning up?"

"It's better this way. The less possibility of us being seen together, the better."

Avery agreed. She stopped at the next corner. "Call me tomorrow."

Gwen nodded, grabbed the door handle. "What's next?"

"I'm not sure. I need to think about it. Lay out the facts, decide which direction to go."

Gwen opened her car door and stepped out. Avery leaned across the seat.

"Gwen?" The other woman bent, met her eyes. "Be careful."

She said she would, shut the door and walked quickly off. Avery watched her go, a knot of fear settling in her chest. She glanced over her shoulder, feeling suddenly as if she was being watched, but seeing nothing but the dark, deserted street.

But they were out there. The Seven, their spies. A killer.

Being careful wasn't going to be enough to keep either of them safe, she thought. Not near enough.

CHAPTER 39

The Gavel stood alone in his dark bathroom. Naked. Trembling. He stared at his reflection in the mirror above the sink. The man who stared back at him barely resembled the one he knew himself to be.

He was sweating, he realized. He pushed the hair off his forehead. He leaned closer to the mirror. Were those tears in his eyes?

He stiffened, furious. He wasn't a child. Not some weak-bellied girl who fell apart anytime the going got tough. He was the strong one. The one whose will, whose determination, carried them all.

Without him, Cypress Springs would have been lost. They all would have been lost.

He bent, splashed his face with cold water, then straightened. Rivulets of water ran over his shoulders, down his belly, beyond. He breathed deeply through his nose. His chest expanded; he felt the oxygen feed his blood, the blood his muscles. He swelled in size, stature.

He smiled. Then laughed. They didn't understand. His eyes

were everywhere. While his generals scurried pathetically about, he saw everything, knew everything. Did they think he didn't hear them whispering to one another, exchanging furtive, knowing glances? Making their plans?

His enemies, it seemed, were growing in number.

Rage welled up in him. Those he trusted turning on him. Those he had turned to for support—indeed, for love—planning his demise. He had given his life for them. The things he had done, the chances he had taken—that he continued to take—to make their lives, their world, a better place. All he had done for them.

Was absolute loyalty too much to ask for in return?

He narrowed his eyes. Apparently so. And for that, they would pay dearly.

This was his town. He was their leader. Nothing and no one would change that.

Not Gwen Lancaster. Not Avery Chauvin.

Tonight, he had stood in the shadows and watched as the two women formed an unholy alliance. One of Cypress Springs's favored daughters had proved herself an outsider. And traitor.

A spear of sadness pierced his armor, he fought it off. The urge to open his arms again, to forgive. Forget. Such emotions were for the weak. The self-indulgent. The unencumbered.

None of those applied to him.

His every instinct told him to silence Gwen Lancaster, do it quickly, before she caused more damage. But there were rules to be followed, a proven system to be adhered to. To willfully ignore either would be a step toward anarchy.

It only took one, he thought grimly. One spoiled fruit. One self-indulgent individual on a misdirected campaign.

How was it that only he had great resolve? Why had he been cursed with this perfect vision? This absolute knowledge? He had been born to lead. To show others the way.

It was lonely. He longed to turn from his gift, his call, but how could he? He opened his eyes each day and saw the truth.

He didn't enjoy killing. He had hoped, prayed, that each of those found guilty would take his warning to heart. His lips twisted. But they had been stupid. Ignorant and small-minded.

*Liar.* Killing the last had been a blessing. A pleasure. The woman had left him no other option. Meeting with outsiders, calling insiders. She had forced his hand. She should have been silenced years ago. He had allowed others to sway him.

A mistake. One of several recent mistakes his generals loved to discuss. That they used against him. Who did they plan to replace him with? Blue? Hawk?

Laughable. He would show them. Soon they would see.

They would all see.

# CHAPTER 40

Hunter sat bolt upright in bed, the sound of children's screams echoing in his head. For a moment he couldn't think. Couldn't separate himself from the nightmare.

With his mind's eye he saw the car careening out of control. The fence going down. The children's terror. The one child standing frozen in the path of his two thousand pounds of steel and glass.

The woman, throwing herself at the child. Saving the boy. Sacrificing herself.

He became aware of the light streaming through the blinds. The soft hum of traffic, of the Monday-morning delivery trucks in the alley. Sarah's puppies whimpering, hungry.

Hunter leaned over the side of the bed and looked at her. It seemed to him she was doing her best to block out their cries. "You're being paged," he said to her.

She lifted her head, looked at him.

"I'll get up if you will."

She stared at him a moment, then thumped her tail once. "I'll take that as a yes," he said and climbed out of bed.

He pulled on a pair of shorts and headed to the bathroom. Teeth brushed, bladder emptied, he beelined for the kitchen. Sarah beat him there. She stood at the door, anxious but patient. He grabbed her lead off the hook, clipped it onto her collar and then together they stepped out into the bright, warm morning.

He and Sarah had their routine. A quick trip out to the nearest patch of grass to take care of her immediate needs, then back for her to feed her pups and him to guzzle coffee. Later, they would take a longer walk or a run.

Sarah did her business and they started back. They rounded the corner. His steps faltered. The dog whined.

Avery waited at his door.

She turned. Their eyes met. He sent her a sleepy, pleased smile. "No breaking and entering today?"

She didn't blink. "We need to talk."

"Guess not." Hunter crossed to the door, pushed it open. From the corner of his eye, he saw her bend and scratch Sarah behind the ears. "Come on in. I need coffee."

He headed for the coffeemaker. She didn't wait for him to reach it. "You called Trudy Pruitt the day she was killed. Why?"

*Son of a bitch. Not good.*

"A little intense for this time of the morning, aren't we, Avery? It's not even eight."

"I asked you a question."

He filled the coffeemaker's carafe with water, then poured it into the reservoir. "Yeah, but you didn't ask it very nicely."

"I'm not playing a game here."

He turned, met her eyes. "She called me. I don't know why because she got my machine. I returned her call. That's it."

He measured dark roast into the filter, slid the basket into place and switched on the machine. That done, he crossed to stand directly in front of her. "And where, exactly, did you get that information? From Matt? Was he trying to poison your mind against me?"

"You don't need any help in that department."

"And here I thought you'd still respect me in the morning."

Angry color shot into her cheeks. "We talked about her, Hunter. You and I, we talked about her calls to me...that I was there that night. You never said anything. Do you have any idea how damning that looks?"

"I don't really care how it looks, Avery."

She curled her hands into fists. "You don't care, do you? You wear your indifference like some twisted badge of honor."

The coffeemaker gurgled; the scent of the brew filled the air. "What do you want me to say?"

"I want you to tell me the truth."

"I was writing. She called, left a message. Truthfully, I didn't remember she was Dylan and Donny's mother. Not until later. I assumed she was calling about legal representation. Why else? Other than a vague recollection of the name, I didn't have a clue who she was. That's the truth, believe it if you want."

"Why didn't you mention she called, when we were talking about her? She was murdered, Hunter!"

He laid his hands on her shoulders. "What would it have brought to the equation? I never even spoke to the woman."

She shrugged off his hands. Took a step away. "You told me to get my proof, Hunter. I went there, to her trailer to look for it."

"When?" he asked, her words, the ramifications of them hitting him like a sledgehammer.

"Last night. Late."

He made a sound of disbelief. "Do you know how stupid that was, Avery? A woman was murdered there. What if the killer had come back? Looking for the same thing you were. Or to relive the kill?"

He pressed his point, seeing that it was having its intended effect—scaring her. "The percentage of killers who do just that is high, so high that police manuals suggest staking out a murder scene as an effective investigative strategy."

She looked shaken, but didn't back down. "I found your message. It's on her machine, okay? The woman saved it."

He thought of Matt. His brother was already hot to pin Elaine St. Claire's murder on him. Why not this murder as well?

He looked at the ceiling. "Shit."

"Care how things look now, Hunter?"

He swung away from her, crossed to the cupboard. He selected a mug, then filled it. Took a sip. He glanced over his shoulder at her. "Was there anything else you wanted to grill me about this morning?"

She opened her mouth as if to answer, then shut it, turned and started for the door.

He followed her. "I take it you're not staying for coffee."

"Go to hell."

*Careening out of control. Children screaming.*

"Been there, done that."

Her steps faltered. She stopped but didn't turn.

He stood directly behind her, so close he could hear her breathing, smell the fruity shampoo she used. He longed to touch her. To coax her back into his arms. Tell her everything, anything that would convince her to stay.

"And that's supposed to make me feel what?" she asked softly, voice vibrating with emotion. "Sorry for you? You think there's anyone alive who hasn't experienced real pain? Personal tragedy?"

"I wasn't asking for your pity. I was being honest."

"Well, bully for you."

She pushed the screen door open. Stepped out into the alley. And ran smack-dab into Matt.

"Avery!" Matt caught her arm, steadying her. "What are you doing here?"

"Ask your brother." She glanced back at Hunter, standing at the door. "Maybe he'll give *you* a straight answer."

"I don't understand."

She shook her head, stood on tiptoe and kissed Matt's cneek. "Call me later, Matt. I've got to go."

CHAPTER 41

Hunter watched Avery go. She had asked Matt to call her later. Why? To make certain he knew about the call on Trudy Pruitt's answering machine? Or because they were sleeping together?

"What was Avery doing here?"

Hunter faced his brother. "Nothing kinky. Unfortunately."

A muscle in his brother's jaw twitched. "Prick."

"So I've been called on more than one occasion." One corner of his mouth lifted. "This seems to be my morning for visitors. Lucky me."

Matt moved his gaze over him, taking in the fact he wore nothing but a pair of shorts, that he had obviously not been out of bed long. "What did she mean, about getting a straight answer out of you?"

Hunter leaned against the door frame, mug cradled between his palms. "I haven't a clue."

"Bullshit."

He lifted the mug to his lips, sipped. "Believe what you will. It's a free country."

"How free?"

"I don't follow."

"Maybe you're one of those Americans who believe your personal freedoms entitle you to trample on the freedoms of others? Maybe even take the law into your own hands? Or take a life?"

Hunter laughed. "I'm a lawyer. I uphold the law."

"Funny, that's what I do, too."

"What can I do for you, Matt?"

"I'm here on official business, Hunter."

"And here I'd thought you might be wanting a brotherly chat. I'm devastated."

Matt ignored his sarcasm. "May I come in?"

Wordlessly, he stepped away from the door. Matt entered the kitchen. He moved his gaze over the room, then brought it back to Hunter. "Where were you night before last? Between nine and ten-thirty?"

*The night Trudy Pruitt was murdered.*

Hunter folded his arms across his chest. "I was here. Working."

"Alone?"

"With Sarah."

"Sarah?"

Hunter nodded in the direction of the dog. "And her pups."

A look of annoyance passed over his brother's face. "You seem to spend an awful lot of time here, alone."

"I like it that way."

"You hear about Trudy Pruitt?"

"Yeah."

"You know the woman?"

"Nope. Not personally."

"Not personally. What does that mean?"

"I'd heard of her. I knew who she was. Who her kids were."

Hunter waited. This was where Matt would call Hunter a liar, challenge his story, throw up the message on the recorder. *If* he had checked Pruitt's answering machine.

And if he did, this was where Hunter would lawyer-up.

"Mind if I have a look around?"

Hunter laughed, the sound humorless. His brother and his crew of small-town constables had just flunked crime scene investigation 101. "Yeah, I mind. You want a look around, you get a search warrant."

"Expect it."

"Want to tell me why you're so interested in me?"

"You'll know soon enough."

"Right. You don't have dick. Go fish someplace else."

Matt shook his head. "For a lawyer, you're not very smart."

"And for a cop, you're not very observant."

"I don't have time for this." Matt made a sound of disgust and turned toward the door. "I'll see you when I've got that warrant."

"You'd love to pin this on me, wouldn't you, Matt? For a lot of different reasons, all of which have nothing to do with guilt or innocence."

His brother stopped. But didn't turn. "Name one."

"Avery."

The barb hit his mark, Hunter saw. His brother stiffened. Swung to face him. "Stay away from her. She's too good for you."

"At least we agree on something. A miracle."

"You're such an asshole. I can't believe you're my brother."

"Your twin," Hunter corrected. "Your other half."

Matt laughed, the sound tight. "We're nothing alike. I believe in family and community, hard work, loyalty."

"Just that I'm alive pisses you off, doesn't it?"

"Stay away from Avery."

"Why should I? She doesn't belong to you anymore. You let her go."

Matt flexed his fingers, longing, Hunter knew, to take a swing at him. How many times as kids had they argued, then come to blows, determined to beat the other senseless.

Even so, they had been a team then. Now, they were adversaries.

"What do you have to offer her?" Matt challenged. "Nothing. You're a broken-down drunk who—"

"A former drunk. There's a difference, brother." He took a step toward the other man. "Don't you see it? She and I are the same. We never fit in here. We never will."

Matt trembled with fury. This time it was he who took a step forward. "All these years, is this what it's been about, Hunter? Avery? Jealousy? Over what I am and what I had?"

"Had. You said it, Matt. No longer. You chose Cypress Springs over her."

"Shut up! Shut the fuck up!"

Hunter closed the remaining distance between them. They stood nose to nose, his twin's fury, his lust for blood palpable. Hunter recognized it because the same emotion charged through him.

"Make me," Hunter said.

"You'd love that. You'd scream police brutality. Get my badge."

"I'm not built that way. Take a punch. It's on me."

His brother didn't move. Hunter knew exactly where to push, how. They'd grown up together, knew each other's strengths—and weaknesses. Ever so softly, he clucked.

"Afraid?" he taunted. "Chicken? Remember when we were kids? You wouldn't fight unless you knew you could win. Guess the big tough sheriff's not so tou—"

Matt's fist caught the side of Hunter's nose. Blood spurted. Pain ricocheted through his head, momentarily blinding him.

With a sound of fury, Hunter charged his brother. He caught him square in the chest, sending them both flying backward. Matt slammed into the refrigerator. From inside came the sound of items toppling.

"You son of a bitch!" Matt shoved him backward. "You have nothing to offer her! You threw away everything you ever had. Your family and community. Your career. Reputation. You're pathetic!"

"I'm pathetic? That's the difference between us, bro. The way I look at it, you threw away the only thing that really mattered."

Hunter twisted sideways, destabilizing the other man. They went down, taking the assortment of plates and glasses that had been drying on the rack by the sink with them. They crashed to the floor, the crockery raining down on them.

Hunter reared back, smashed his fist into his brother's face. Sarah barked, the sound high, frenzied. Matt grunted in pain; retaliated, catching Hunter in the side of his head.

Sarah's bark changed, deepened. She growled low in her throat.

The sound, what it meant, penetrated; Hunter glanced toward the circling dog. "Sarah!" he ordered. "Heel!"

Matt used the distraction to his advantage, forcing Hunter onto his back. Glass crunched beneath his bare shoulders. A hiss of pain ripped past his lips as the shards pierced his skin. Sarah made her move.

She leaped at Matt, teeth bared. In a quick move, Matt rolled sideways, unsheathed his weapon and aimed at the dog.

"No!" Hunter threw himself at Sarah, plowing into her side, knocking her out of harm's way. They landed in a heap; she whimpered in pain, then scrambled to all fours.

Hunter jumped to his feet, shaking with rage. "You're a maniac."

Matt eased to his feet, holstered his weapon. "It would have been self-defense. The bitch could have torn me apart."

"Get the hell out of here." Hunter wiped his bloody nose with the back of his hand, aware of blood running in rivulets down his back. "You're not worth it, Matt. Not anymore."

Expression impassive, Matt tucked in his shirt, smoothed back his hair. "Two was always too many, wasn't it, Hunter? Two of us, just alike?"

"That's bullshit." He crossed to the sink. Yanked a paper towel off the roll, soaked it in cold water, then looked back at the other man. "You're blind, Matt. You don't have a clue."

"You're the one who's blind. Blinded by jealousy. For me, my relationship with Mom and Dad. Because of Avery."

Hunter's gut tightened at the grain of truth. Matt had always been the leader of the two, the charismatic one, the one everybody gravitated to: girls, the other kids, teachers. Even their parents and Cherry.

"I always loved you," Hunter said softly. "No matter what. I was proud you were my brother."

"Now who's shoveling the shit?"

"You've got to open your eyes, Matt. When it comes to Dad, our family, this town, you don't see anything as it really is."

"Better being a blind man than a dead one."

"Is that a threat, Sheriff Stevens?"

Matt laughed. "I don't have to kill you, Hunter. You're already dead."

# CHAPTER 42

Avery decided to spend the morning going through her parents' attic, separating things she wanted to save from those she would donate to charity or toss. If she ever intended to put the house up for sale, it had to be done. Besides, she needed something to occupy her hands while she mentally reviewed the events of the past few days.

The pieces fit together; she just hadn't figured out how. Not yet. This was no different from any story she had ever tackled. A puzzle to be solved, assembled from bits of information gleaned from a variety of sources. The meaning of some of those bits obvious, others obtuse. Some would prove unrelated, some surprisingly key.

In the end, every story required a cognitive leap. That *ah-ha* moment when the pieces all fell into place—with or without the facts to back them up. That moment when she simply *knew*.

Avery climbed the stairs. When she reached the top, she glanced toward her parents' bedroom. At the unmade bed. She stared at it a moment, then turned quickly away and started toward the end of the hall and the door to the attic stairs. She unlocked and opened the door, then headed up.

It was only March, but the attic was warm, the air heavy. During the summer months it would be unbearable. She moved her gaze over the rows of neatly stacked boxes, the racks of bagged clothes. From hooks hung holiday decorations: wreaths, wind socks and flags, one wall for each season. Evenly spaced aisles between the boxes.

So neatly organized, she thought. Her mother had been like that. Precise. Orderly. Never a hair out of place or social grace forgotten. No wonder the two of them butted heads so often. They'd had almost nothing in common.

Avery began picking through the boxes. She settled first on one filled with books. While she sorted through them, she pondered the newspaper she and Gwen had found in Trudy Pruitt's bedroom, the woman's cryptic notation. The hatchet marks. The words *All but two*. Trudy Pruitt had been counting the dead. Avery felt certain of that.

All but two who knew the truth about the Waguespack murder? It made sense in light of what she had said on the phone, that those who knew were dropping like flies. But, she could also have been counting the passing of people she hated. Or ones she feared. Or people she believed responsible for her sons' deaths.

The last rang true, made sense. Trudy Pruitt had been consumed by that event, that had been obvious to Avery. Had she found the note that had been written on the article about her father's suicide before the woman's murder, she would have considered Trudy Pruitt a suspect in his death as well as that of the others.

But she hadn't. Nor did she believe the woman had been smart or sophisticated enough to have pulled off the murders. Not alone, anyway.

Avery's fingers stilled. An accomplice. That could be. Perhaps the accomplice had decided Trudy Pruitt had outlived her usefulness. Or had become a liability.

*Hunter.* He'd left a message for her. Had he simply been returning the woman's call, as he claimed?

His explanation was plausible. She wanted it to be true. Wanted it in a way that was anything but uninvolved. Anything but unemotional.

Avery squeezed her eyes shut, struggling to recall exactly what he'd said in the message. His full name and phone number. Not that he was returning her call.

But if they had been accomplices, surely he wouldn't have had to identify himself, the woman would have recognized his voice. And surely he wouldn't have identified himself with his full name, Hunter Stevens. Nor, she supposed, would he have had to give her his number.

She frowned, shifting absently through the box of books, most of them westerns. Her dad had loved the genre. He'd eaten them up, chewing through the paperback novels as fast as publishers could put them out.

Her mother had read, too. Not as voraciously, however. In truth, the book Avery remembered seeing her mother with most had been her journal. She had carried one everywhere, doggedly recording the moments and events of her life.

Her mother had dreamed of being a writer. She had shared that before Avery left for college. They had been arguing about Avery's decision to leave Cypress Springs—and Matt—behind.

At the time, Avery hadn't believed her mother. Now, she wondered.

She recalled the scene clearly. Her mother had shared that tidbit in the context of making choices in life. She had expected her daughter to follow in her footsteps—be the traditional Southern woman, wife and mother, community volunteer. She had expected Avery to acknowledge what was important.

Chasing a dream wasn't. A career wasn't.

She had urged her to marry Matt. Start a family. Look at her, she had said. Where would Avery be if she had chased a career instead of marrying her father?

Perhaps she and her mother had had something in common, after all.

A headache started at the base of Avery's skull. She brought her hand to the back of her neck and rubbed the spot, recalling how their conversation had ended. They'd fought. It had been ugly.

*"You took the easy way, Mom. You settled. I'm not going to be like you!"*

And then, later, *"You never loved me, Mother. Not for me. You always tried to change me, make me like you. Well, it didn't work."*

Avery cringed, remembering the hateful words, recalling her mother's devastated expression. She had never taken those words back. Had never apologized.

And then it had been too late.

"Shit," Avery muttered, regret so sharp and bitter she tasted it. She thought of what Hunter had said, that her father believed her unresolved issues with her mother had been the reason she'd visited so rarely. Had he been right? Had she been waiting for an apology? Or had she stayed away because she knew how badly she had hurt her mother and hadn't wanted to look her in the—

*She had carried a journal everywhere, doggedly recording the moments and events of her life.*

Of course, Avery thought. Her mother's journals. She would have noted Sallie Waguespack's death, its effect on the community and if her husband had somehow been involved.

But where were they? Avery had searched the house, emptied closets and drawers and bookcases. She hadn't seen even one of the journals. So, what had her father done with them?

Up here. Had to be.

Although she had already done a perfunctory search of the attic, she started a more complete one now. She not only checked the notations on each box, she opened each to make certain the contents matched the labels.

By the time she had checked the last carton, she was hot, dirty and disappointed. Could her father have disposed of them? Or her mother, sometime before she died?

Maybe Lilah would know. Checking her watch, Avery headed downstairs to the phone. She dialed the Stevenses number and Lilah answered immediately.

"Hi, Lilah, it's Avery."

"Avery! What a pleasant surprise. What are you up to this morning?"

"I'm working on the house, packing things up, and realized Mother's journals are missing."

"Her journals? My goodness, I'd forgotten she used to do that."

"So had I. Until this morning."

"At one time she was quite committed to it. Remember the Sunday she pulled her journal out during Pastor Dastugue's sermon? We were all sitting right up front, he was so pleased." The woman laughed lightly. "He thought she was taking notes."

"What do you mean, she had been committed to it? Did she give it up?"

"Yes, indeed. Let me think." The woman paused. "About the time you went off to university."

Avery felt the words like a blow. About the time she went off to L.S.U. After their fight. After her mother had confided in Avery—and been met with disbelief and disdain.

"She never said anything, you understand," Lilah continued. "I just noticed she didn't have one with her. When I asked, she said she had given it up."

"Lilah, would you have any idea where she or Dad might have stored them?"

"Stored them?" The other woman sounded confused. "If they're not at the house, I imagine she got rid of them. Or your father, with the rest of her things."

Avery's stomach fell at the thought. "I just can't imagine either of them—"

"We all thought him so strong, clearing out her things the way he did. The reminders were just all too painful."

The doorbell rang. Avery ended the call and hurried to answer it.

Hunter stood at her door. She gazed at him through the screen, taking in his battered face. "My God, what happened to you?"

"Long story. Can I come in?"

"I don't think that's such a good idea."

He looked away, then back at her. "I've got this problem, Avery. And it has to do with you."

She folded her arms across her chest. "With me?"

"This morning Matt called me a dead man. And I realized it was true." He paused. "Except when I'm with you."

His words crashed over her. She laid her hand against the door frame for support, suddenly unbalanced. Light-headed. One second became two, became many.

"Avery," he said softly. "Please."

Wordlessly, she swung the screen door open. Was she letting in friend or foe? She didn't know, was simply acting on instinct. Or, if she was being honest, on longing. She moved aside as he entered and with shaky hands closed the door, using the moment to break their eye contact as she attempted to regain her equilibrium. She turned the dead bolt, took a deep breath and faced him. "I'll make us an iced tea."

Without waiting for a response, she started for the kitchen.

Avery was acutely aware of him following her, watching her as she poured them both an iced tea, as she added a wedge of lemon. She cleared her throat, turned and handed him the glass.

Their fingers brushed as he took the glass. He brought it to his lips; the ice clinked against its side as he drank.

She dragged her gaze away, heart thundering. "You and Matt got into it this morning."

It wasn't a question. He answered anyway. "Yes. We fought about you."

"I see."

"Do you?"

She shifted her gaze. Wet her lips.

"He wanted to know where I was night before last."

"And did you tell him?"

"Of course. I was home working. Alone." He set his glass on the counter. "I told you the truth this morning, Avery. Trudy Pruitt called me. I don't know why, but I assumed it was for legal counsel. I returned her call. I never even met the woman let alone killed her."

"Is that what Matt thinks, that you killed her?"

"That's what he wants to think."

She defended the other man. "I doubt that, Hunter. You're brothers. He's just doing his job."

"Believe that if it makes you feel better." He glanced away, then
back. "He didn't think to check the woman's recorder. Yet, anyway. Are you going to tell him about the message?"

She wasn't, she realized. And not only because doing so would
mean admitting to having broken and entered a posted crime scene.

She shook her head. "No."

"I have to ask you something."

"All right."

"Are you sleeping with him?"

She met his gaze. "That's a pretty shitty question, considering."

"He's acting awfully possessive."

"So are you."

He took a step toward her. "But we *are* sleeping together."

Her mouth went dry. "Did," she corrected. "One time. Besides,
would it matter to you if we were?"

"Ditto on the pretty shitty question."

"No," she answered. "I'm not."

He brought a hand to the back of her neck and drew her toward
him. "Yes," he murmured. "It would."

Heart thundering against the wall of her chest, she trailed her
fingers across his bruised jaw. "Who threw the first punch?"

"He did. But I goaded him into it."

She laughed softly. Not because it was funny, but because it was
so true to the boys she had known all those years ago. "Well,
frankly, you look like he kicked your ass."

"Yeah, but you should see him."

Avery laughed again. "By the way," she murmured, "I believe
you. About your call to Trudy Pruitt."

"Thank you." A smile tugged at his mouth. "Does this mean
we can revisit the sleeping-together versus the slept-together
thing?"

"You're awful."

His smile faded. "Matt accused me of being jealous of him. Of
his relationship with you. With our parents. Jealous of his ability
to lead. He suggested envy was at the root of everything that's hap-

pened between the two of us. That I withdrew from the family because of it."

She rested her hands on his chest, her right palm over his heart. "And what did you tell him?"

"That it was bullshit." He cupped her face in his palms. "I always wanted you. But you chose Matt. And he was my brother."

The simple honesty inherent in those words rang true. They touched her. They spoke to the man he was. And the relationship he and Matt had shared.

In light of her intense feelings for Hunter, she wondered what would have happened all those years ago if Hunter had made a play for her. She wondered where they would all be today.

"What about now, Avery? I have to know, do you still belong to my brother?"

She answered without words. She stood on tiptoe, pressed her mouth to his, kissing him deeply. She slid her hands to his shoulders. He tensed, wincing.

She drew away. "You're hurt."

"It's nothing. A few cuts."

"Turn around." When he tried to balk, she cut him off. "Now, please."

He did. She lifted his shirt and made a sound of dismay. Cuts riddled his back and shoulders, some of them jagged and ugly. "How did this happen?"

"It's no big deal."

"It is. A very big deal." She lightly touched a particularly nasty cut with her index finger. "Some of these look deep. You need stitches."

"Stitches are for sissies." He looked over his shoulder and scowled at her. "I picked out the pieces. As best I could, anyway."

Frowning, she examined his back. "Most of them, anyway."

"Come on." She led him to the bathroom and ordered him to sit, pointing to the commode. "Take off your shirt."

He did as he was told. From the medicine cabinet she collected bandages of varying sizes, disinfectant and a pair of tweezers.

He eyed the tweezers. "What do you plan to do with those?"

She ignored the question. "This might hurt."

He nearly came off the seat and she began probing with the tweezers. "Might hurt! Take it easy."

She held up the sliver of glass, pinned between the tweezer's prongs. "How did you say this happened?"

"Matt and I were going at each other like a couple of jackasses, broke some gla— Hey! Ow!"

"Big baby." She dropped another sliver into the trash. "So you two broke some glass and rolled around in it."

"Something like that."

"Bright."

"You had to be there."

"No thanks." She examined the rest of his injuries, didn't see any more glass and began carefully cleaning the cuts. Each time she touched him with the disinfectant-soaked cotton, he flinched.

"I don't get it," she murmured, being as gentle as she could. "You can roll on a bed of glass, but a little Betadine and you're ready to tuck tail and run."

"Tuck tail? No way. It's a guy thing."

"And I say, thank God for the female of the species." She fitted a bandage over the last wound. "There, all done."

He grabbed her hand and tumbled her onto his lap. She gazed up at him, surprised, heart racing.

"I agree," he murmured, voice thick. "Thank God."

They made love there, in the bathroom, against the back of the door. It shouldn't have been romantic, but it was. The most romantic and exciting sex she had ever had. She orgasmed loudly, crying out. He caught her cries with his mouth and carried her, their bodies still joined, to the bed. They fell on it, facing one another.

He brought her hand to his chest, laid it over his wildly pumping heart. "I can't catch my breath."

She smiled and stretched, pleased. Satisfied beyond measure. "Mmm...good."

They fell silent. Moments ticked past as they gazed at one another, hearts slowing, bodies cooling.

Everything about him was familiar, she realized. The cut of his strong jaw, the brilliant blue of his eyes, the way his thick dark hair liked to fall across his forehead.

And everything was foreign as well. The boy she had known and liked had grown into a man she desired but didn't know at all.

"I'm sorry," he said softly. "About this morning. I acted like an ass. Another one of my problems."

She trailed a finger over his bottom lip. "What happened, Hunter? In New Orleans? Why'd you come home?"

"Home?" he repeated. "After all these years, you still call Cypress Springs home?"

"Don't you?"

He was silent a moment. "No. It ceased being home the day I walked away."

"But you've returned."

"To write a book."

"But why here?" He didn't reply. After a moment she answered for him. "Maybe because you felt safe here? Or felt you had nowhere else to go? Both could be called definitions of home."

He laughed scornfully. Humorless. "More like returning to the scene of the crime. The place my life began to go wrong."

She propped herself on an elbow and gazed down at him. He met her gaze; the expression in his bleak. "Talk to me," she said quietly. "Make me understand."

He looked as if he might balk again, then began instead. "New Orleans, my time at Jackson, Thompson and Witherspoon, passed in a blur. I was good at what I did. Too good, maybe. I moved up too fast, made too much money. I didn't have to work hard enough."

*So he didn't respect it. Or himself.*

"I became counsel of choice for New Orleans's young movers and shakers. Not the old guard, but their offspring. Life was a party. Drugs, sex and rock 'n' roll."

Avery cringed at the thought. She certainly wasn't naive. Her years in journalism had been...illuminating. But she had been lucky enough—strong enough—to resist falling into that particular pit.

"The drugs were everywhere, Avery. When you're dealing with the rich and famous, everything's available. Anything. Alcohol remained my drug of choice, though I didn't turn down much of anything."

He rolled onto his back and gazed up at the ceiling. Retreating from her, she knew. And into the past. "At first, the firm looked the other way. I was a hot commodity. Staying on top of my cases and clients despite my after-hours excesses. Substance abuse is not unheard of in lawyers. A by-product of the stresses of the job and the opportunity for abuse.

"Then the line blurred. I started using during the day. Started screwing up at work. A missed court date here and forgotten deadline there. The firm made excuses for me. After all, if word got out that one of their junior partners was a drunk, their exposure would have been huge. When I showed up drunk for a meeting with an important client, they'd had enough. They fired me.

"Of course, I was in denial. It was everybody's problem but mine. I could handle the alcohol. The drugs. I was a god."

Avery hurt for him. If was difficult to reconcile the man he described with the one she had known as a teenager—or the one she lay beside now.

"I went on a binge. My friends deserted me. The woman I was living with left. I had no more restraints, no one and nothing to hold me back."

He fell silent a moment, still deeply in the past. Struggling, Avery suspected, with dark, painful memories.

When he resumed, his voice shook slightly. "One morning I lost control of my vehicle by an elementary school. The kids were at recess. My car windows were open, I heard their laughter, squeals of joy. And then their screams of terror.

"I was speeding. Under the influence, big time. I crashed through the playground fence. There was nothing I could do but watch in horror. The children scattered. But one boy just stood there...I couldn't react."

He covered his eyes with his hands as if wanting to block out the memory. "A teacher threw herself at him, knocking him out of the way.

"I hit her. She bounced onto the hood, then windshield. The thud, it—" He squeezed his eyes shut, expression twisted with pain. "Miraculously, she wasn't killed. Just a couple broken ribs, lacerations...I thank God every day for that.

"The fence and the tree I clipped had slowed my forward momentum. Still, if I'd hit that boy, I would have killed him."

He looked at her then, eyes wet. "She came to see me. *Me,* the man who— She forgave me, she said. She begged me to see the miracle I had been offered. To use it to change my life."

Avery silently studied him. He had, she knew, without his saying so. The novel was part of that change. Coming back to Cypress Springs. Going back to move forward.

"That boy, I wonder if he finds joy in the playground now. I wonder if any of them can. Do they wake up screaming? Do they relive the terror? I do. Not a day goes by I don't remember. That I don't see their faces, hear their screams."

"I'm sorry, Hunter," she said softly. "I'm so sorry."

"So you see, I'm both cliché and a cautionary tale. The drunk driver barreling into a schoolyard full of children, the one lawyers like me argue don't exist."

He said the last with sarcasm, then continued, "I was charged with driving under the influence and reckless endangerment. The judge ordered me into a court-monitored detox program. Took away my license for two weeks. Slapped me with a ridiculously low fine and ordered me to serve a hundred hours of community service."

*If someone had been killed he would have been charged with vehicular homicide. He would have served time.*

*Hunter was already serving time.*

"I haven't had a drink since," he finished. "I pray I never will again."

She found his hand, curled her fingers around his.

Moments ticked past.

"Matt's still in love with you."

She started to deny it, he stopped her. "It's true. He never stopped."

"Why are you telling me this?"

"I goaded him into losing control today, into throwing the first punch. The sick thing is, I took so much pleasure in doing it. In being able to do it. Perverse SOB, aren't I?"

"You're not so bad." Her lips lifted slightly. "Not as bad as you think you are, not by a long shot."

He turned his head, met her eyes. "Run, Avery. Go as fast as you can. I'm no good for you."

"Maybe I should be the judge of that."

His smile didn't reach his eyes. "That'd be risky. We both know you've never been that great a judge of character."

"Is that so?" She sat up, feigning indignation. "Actually, I'm a pretty damn good judge of— You're bleeding again."

"Where?" He sat up, craning to see over his shoulder.

"Here." She twisted to grab a couple of tissues from the box on her bed stand, then dabbed at the trickle of blood seeping from the bandage under his left shoulder blade. She remembered it had been the ugliest of the gashes.

Avery climbed out of bed, dragging the sheet with her. Wrapping it around her, toga style. "I'll bet there are some heavy-duty bandages in Dad's bathroom." She wagged a finger at him. "Stay put."

"Yes, Nurse Chauvin."

Avery padded into the hallway, heading toward her parents' bedroom. The door stood open, giving her a clear view of the bed. She should make it, she thought. Or strip it. Seeing it like that, day after day, reminded her of the last night of her father's life. And in doing so, it reminded her of his death.

*The last night of his life.*

*The unmade bed.*

Avery brought a hand to her mouth. Her dad had been in his pajamas. He had taken sleep medication. Obviously, he had either been asleep or had climbed into bed. Why put on his pj's if he meant to kill himself? Why climb into bed, under the covers? Only to get out, step into his slippers and head to the garage to kill himself?

*It didn't make sense to her. Even considering her father's state of mind as described by his friends and neighbors.*

She closed her eyes, thoughts racing, assembling another scenario. Her father in bed. Sleep aided by medication. Someone at the door. Ringing the bell or pounding.

The coroner had found trace amounts of the drug Halcion in his bloodstream. She had taken a similar medication before, to help her sleep on international flights. She had been easily roused. The medication had simply relaxed her, aided her ability to sleep.

Her dad had been a physician. Had spent his working life on call. Someone pounding on the door would have awakened him, even from a deep, medicated sleep.

So he had climbed out of bed. Stepped into his slippers and headed down to the front door. Or side door. There the enemy had waited. In the guise of a friend, she thought. Someone he had recognized and trusted.

So, he had opened the door.

Avery realized she was shaking. Her heart racing. It hurt, but she kept building the scenario, fitting the pieces together.

He would have been groggy. Easy to surprise and overpower, especially by someone he trusted.

How had they done it? she wondered. She flipped through the possibilities. Neither the coroner nor police had found any indication of foul play. No marks. No fractures. No detectable signs of a struggle, not at the scene or on the body.

She recalled what she had learned about death by fire—that the flesh basically melted but the body didn't incinerate. An autopsy could be performed. A blow to the head with enough force to disable a man would leave evidence for the pathologist.

Could his assailant have subdued him, secured him with ropes and carried him to the garage? She shook her head, eliminating the possibility. According to Ben Mitchell, her dad had crawled a few feet toward the door, impossible if bound.

So, how did one subdue a man without leaving a detectable mark on the body or in the bloodstream?

Then she had it. A friend in D.C. had carried a stun gun instead of pepper spray. She had sung its praises and tried to convince Avery to purchase one. What had she told Avery? That it delivered a high-voltage electrical charge that would immobilize an attacker for up to fifteen minutes. With no permanent damage. And no detectable mark on the body.

It would have paralyzed her father long enough for his murderer to carry him out to the garage, douse him with fuel and toss a match.

*His slipper had fallen off on the path between the house and garage.*

That's why he hadn't stopped to slip it back on. He hadn't been walking. He'd been carried. She pictured the murderer dumping him in the garage. He'd had the fuel there, ready. Diesel fuel lit on contact. No flashover. The murderer could have tossed the match and walked away.

While her father burned alive. By the time he had been able to respond, it had been too late.

"What's wrong?"

She turned. Hunter had come up behind her. "I know how it happened. With Dad. I know how they killed him."

## CHAPTER 43

Hunter awakened to realize he was alone in bed. He glanced at Avery's bedside clock. Just after 5:00 p.m. They had slept the afternoon away.

At least he had.

He sat up. The pillow next to his still bore the imprint of Avery's head. He laid his hand in the indention and found it cold. He shifted his gaze to the window. The light had changed, lost the brilliance of midday and taken on the violet of early evening.

He ran a hand absently across his jaw, rough with a five o'clock shadow, thoughts on Avery. She had shared her theory with him— that her father had been awakened by a trusted friend at the door. That a stun gun had been used to immobilize him. That her father had dragged himself to the door, but that his effort had been too late.

Afterward, Hunter had held her while she cried. Her weeping had broken his heart and he had tried to comfort her by poking holes in her theory. Why would someone have killed her father? he'd asked. What could their motive have been?

Nothing he said had helped, so he had simply held her until her tears stopped. And then he'd led her to the bed and lay with her until they had both drifted off.

Hunter threw the coverlet aside and climbed out of bed. After retrieving his jeans from the floor, he went in search of Avery.

He found her in the kitchen. She stood at the sink, gazing out the window behind it. The portable phone lay on the kitchen table. Beside it a steno-size spiral notebook and a folded newspaper.

*She had been up for some time.*

He approached silently. She wore a white terry-cloth robe, cinched at the waist. It swallowed her, accentuating her diminutive stature. With her little-boy haircut and pixie features she looked like a child dressed up in her mother's things.

Those who underestimated her because of her petite size made a big mistake. She possessed a keen mind and the kind of determination that sometimes bordered on pigheadedness. He'd always admired her, even when she'd dug in her heels about something that to his mind had made no sense.

He'd admired her character, as well as her sense of fair play. She had stood up to the bullies. Had taken the side of the underdog, befriended the new kids and odd ones, championed the outsiders. It hadn't made her popular, but for the most she hadn't cared about popularity.

Truth was, he had always been in awe of her strength.

He had always been a little bit in love with her.

Was that what was going on now? he wondered. Had she decided to befriend the underdog? Champion him, the outsider?. No matter what others thought?

She became aware of his presence and looked at him. The barest of smiles touched her mouth. "It's going to storm."

He crossed to stand beside her. The wind had begun to blow, he saw. Dark clouds tumbled across the evening sky. "It's spring. We need the rain."

"I suppose."

He touched her cheek lightly. "Are you all right?"

"Hanging in there." She tilted her head into his hand. "Hungry?"

"Starving. We could order out."

She shook her head. "I have eggs. And cheese."

"Sounds like an omelette."

They worked together, playfully arguing over what ingredients to include. Onions were out. Bell peppers in. Mushrooms were a must. Lots of cheese. A bit of cayenne pepper.

"I'll make toast," he offered.

"I have English muffins. In the fridge."

"Even better." He retrieved them along with the orange juice and butter. After splitting two of the muffins and popping them into the toaster, he rummaged around in the cabinets and drawers, collecting flatware, plates, glasses and napkins.

Hunter carried them to the oak table. He moved the phone and newspaper; as he did, he saw it was the issue of the *Gazette* that had reported her dad's death. He frowned, shifting his gaze to the spiral notebook that lay beside it. A column of names with a date beside each ran down the page. *Pat Greene. Sal Mandina. Pete Trimble. Kevin Gallagher. Dolly Farmer.* Her father's name was there. At the bottom, Trudy Pruitt's.

"What's this?"

She didn't look at him. "Something I'm working on."

"Working on?" he repeated. "It looks like a list of people who have died in—"

"The past eight months," she finished for him. "Here in Cypress Springs."

She wouldn't have the list out if she hadn't wanted him to see it. "This is about those things Trudy Pruitt said to you, isn't it? About your dad being involved in Sallie Waguespack's death?"

She turned the omelette. "Yes. And about the clippings I found in his closet. And two murders and two disappearances in the past six weeks. And a group called The Seven."

He frowned. "I'm not going to be able to deter you from this, am I?"

She looked over her shoulder at him. "No."

*Determined to the point of pigheaded. She wouldn't let this go until she was satisfied she knew the truth. Beyond-a-shadow-of-a-doubt truth.*

*No wonder she was such a good investigative reporter.*

"Dammit, Avery. You drive me crazy."

She lifted a shoulder. "Forget it then if it'll make you feel better."

"Like hell. You think I'm going to leave you to track down a killer yourself? Two women have already been murdered. I don't want you to be the third."

She smiled and batted her eyelashes at him in exaggerated coquetry. "That's so sweet, Hunter."

"This isn't funny. There's a killer out there."

"That's right. And he may have killed my father."

"Would you like my help?" he asked, resigned.

She thought a moment, then nodded. "I think I would. Eggs are ready."

She slid the omelettes onto plates. He buttered the English muffins and set them on the table. While they ate, Hunter curbed his impatience. This was her party, after all.

When they had finished, she stood, cleared the plates then sat back down. She met his eyes. "As you know, last night I went to Trudy Pruitt's trailer. The woman had accused my father of being involved in Sallie Waguespack's murder. Of helping the police to frame her sons. She said she had proof, but she was killed before she could give it to me."

"So you went looking for it. Gwen Lancaster was with you."

"How did you—?"

"Good guess."

"What you don't know is that Gwen had interviewed Trudy about The Seven just hours before Trudy's death."

Hunter straightened. "She interviewed Trudy Pruitt?"

"Yes. The woman confirmed the existence of The Seven. She claimed the group was responsible for Elaine St. Claire's murder."

"Avery," Hunter said, frowning, "word is, the woman was an unstable drunk. Because of her boys, she had an ax to grind with this town. I wouldn't put too much stock in what she had to say."

"You sound like Matt. Buddy, too."

"They're right. You should listen."

She looked frustrated. "What about Gwen? Her place was ransacked. All her notes stolen. Someone lured her out to a hunting camp off Highway 421 and No Name Road. They left her a gutted cat."

"Try that again."

"A woman phoned Gwen. She told her she had information about Gwen's brother's disappearance. She arranged a meeting at the hunting camp."

"But she didn't show."

"Right. Instead, Gwen found the cat. It was a warning. To cease and desist. That's the way The Seven works. One warning, then they act."

Hunter listened, his sense of unease growing. "How do you know any of that's true, Avery? She could have ransacked her own place, lied about the cat, the phone call and notes. All in an effort to convince you it was true. To gain your trust."

She shook her head. "I was at The Guesthouse when she returned. She was frightened, Hunter. Terrified."

She slid the piece of newspaper across the table. "Last night Gwen and I found this. On Trudy Pruitt's bedroom floor."

Hunter gazed at the clipping. The woman had drawn devil horns and a goatee on the picture of Avery's father, yet Avery seemed so matter-of-fact about the item it was as if finding such an upsetting thing in a murdered woman's bedroom was an everyday occurrence.

"Look here, in the margin," she continued. "She was tallying something, keeping score."

"'All but two,'" he murmured. "What do you think it means?"

"I believe she was counting the dead so far. My dad was number five."

"Plus two equals seven."

"I noticed that."

"Okay, you have my full attention."

She tapped the page. "The way I figure it, these were either people she believed had been involved in the cover-up of Sallie Waguespack's murder or ones who knew the truth about it."

"Presuming there was a cover-up."

"Yes." She stood and began to pace. "You're a lawyer... Who would have been involved in the investigation?"

"I'm not a criminal attorney, but obviously you've got a murderer and a victim. Person or persons who discovered the body. First officer. Detectives, criminalists. The coroner or his deputy."

"Witnesses, if any."

"Right."

"Your dad let me read the file," she said. "Officer Pat Greene was out on patrol. He saw the Pruitt boys leaving Sallie Waguespack's. The boys had a history of trouble with the law, so he decides he'd better check it out. He finds the woman dead, then calls Buddy."

She stopped, expression intent, as if working to recall the exact sequence of events. "From Pat's description, Buddy figures it was the Pruitt brothers Pat saw. He and Pat go looking for them. The meeting ends in a shoot-out that left the boys dead."

"They left the murder scene untended?"

She thought a moment. "I can't remember. They may have waited for the coroner, but I don't think so. According to the file, no other officer was called to the scene."

"Go on."

"The murder weapon was found in the ditch behind the Pruitt's trailer. Donny's prints were on it. One of the boys had the victim's blood on his shoe. They opened fire on the police when approached and Pat Greene had already placed them at the scene. Case closed. No need for further investigation, nice and neat."

"Too nice and neat, you're thinking?"

"Maybe."

"What about the autopsy? As I understand it, an autopsy is always requested in a murder case."

"It wasn't in the file. Buddy thought it had been misplaced and promised to locate it for me. I'll give him a call tomorrow."

Silence fell between them. Hunter sensed her doing the same as he, considering the possibilities, doing a mental tally. The numbers didn't add up.

"Let's count who could have been involved," he said. "You've got two officers at the scene, Dad and Pat Greene. You've got the coroner. That's three. Throw in the victim and the Pruitts you've got six. Your dad could be number seven, though how he fit in I'm not certain."

He drummed his fingers against the tabletop. "Maybe she was counting the deaths of The Seven? Maybe she was the one bumping them off? Maybe one of the last two killed her first?"

"Maybe, but I don't think so. Unless she had an accomplice. These deaths were made to look like accidents. There was a level of sophistication I don't believe Trudy Pruitt capable of."

"If she had an accomplice, who would that be? Someone who thought as she did. Someone with an ax to grind against Cypress Springs or a group of her citizens."

Avery thought a moment, then shook her head. "Then who killed Elaine St. Claire? Not Trudy Pruitt, they were friends. She told Gwen that The Seven were responsible for Elaine's death."

"Maybe The Seven are the ones who killed Sallie Waguespack."

"That doesn't work because the way I understand it, the Waguespack murder was the catalyst for the formation of The Seven."

"But you don't know that for sure."

She made a sound of frustration. "No, dammit. All I have is speculation."

"And a growing number of dead." He stood and crossed to her. "Let's back up again. Who could have known the truth about Sallie Waguespack's death?"

"The Pruitt boys. Buddy. Pat Greene. My dad, because Trudy Pruitt implicated him."

"Trudy herself," he offered. "Maybe whoever prepared Sallie for burial."

"Oh my God."

"What?"

She crossed to the counter, to her notebook. She ran a finger down the column of names, mouth moving as she silently read them.

He watched her, a sinking sensation in the pit of his stomach. "What?"

She lifted her gaze to his. "Everyone we named is dead, Hunter. Except your dad."

The words landed heavily between them. Hunter stared at her, his world shifting slightly. "That can't be."

"It is." She held the steno pad out and he saw that her hand trembled. "Take a look."

He shook his head, but didn't reach for the notebook. "Do you realize what you're saying?"

She nodded slowly, face pale.

*Either Buddy Stevens was a killer. Or next in line to die.*

"Look at the list," she said again. "Pat Greene, Dad, Kevin Gallagher, Trudy Pru—"

"I don't give a damn about your list!" The words exploded from him. "You've gone around the bend with this thing, Avery. Way past rational."

She took a step back, expression hurt. "This doesn't mean your dad's the one. He could be in danger, Hunter. If so, we need to warn him."

*It was bullshit. Nothing went on in this town without his dad knowing, never had. Who better than the chief of police to orchestrate a cover-up? Who better than a lawman to arrange deaths to look like accidents?*

Hunter tipped his face to the ceiling, thoughts racing. Reviewing the things they had discussed, the key players in the Waguespack investigation.

*But why? After all these years? Had someone threatened to blow the whistle on them all?*

That didn't make sense. His father killing old friends in an effort to quiet them fifteen years after the fact didn't make sense.

*Someone else was the perpetrator.*

*His dad was in danger.*

He looked at Avery. "What about the coroner? Is he on your list?"

"Dr. Harris. No, he's not." She glanced at the steno pad as if to reconfirm her answer, then looked back at him. "Dr. Harris has been the parish coroner on and off for twenty-eight years."

"Was he coroner in 1988?"

"I don't know. If he was—"

"Then Dad's not the last."

## CHAPTER 44

Gwen's eyes snapped open. Heart pounding, she scrambled into a sitting position. She had been dreaming about her brother. He had been trying to warn her.

As the effects of the dream began to fade, a chill slid down her spine.

*Something was wrong.*

Gwen moved her gaze over the dark room, stopping on the window. From outside came the sound of rain. A sudden, blinding flash of light.

She jumped, then laughed softly at herself. At her jitters. The storm had awakened her. She glanced at the bed stand. The clock's face, usually a reassuring glow in the night, was dark.

The power had gone out.

Gwen climbed out of bed, heading for the bathroom.

She stopped as her foot landed in something wet. She looked down at the floor, confused. How—

A breeze stirred against her ankles. She looked back at the window. It was closed. Locked.

*The bathroom window. It faced the side yard. The big oak tree.*

Lightning illuminated the room. She lowered her gaze. Water, she saw. A trail of it from the bathroom to the bed. She glanced over her shoulder at the half-open bathroom door. The darkness beyond.

*Someone, waiting.*

A cry spilling past her lips, she bolted forward. He burst from the bathroom. Grabbed her from behind. One strong arm circled her waist; a gloved hand covered her mouth. Tightly. She was dragged backward.

He held her pinned against his chest. She fought as best she could, kicking out, trying to twist free of her assailant's grasp. He was too strong. His grip was so tight over her nose and mouth she couldn't breathe. She grew light-headed. Pinpricks of lights danced before her eyes.

He bent his head close to hers. His labored breath was hot against her ear. He wore a ski mask. The fuzzy knit tickled her cheek.

"You have been judged, Gwen Lancaster. Judged and found guilty."

*The Seven. They had come for her.*

*As they had come for Tom.*

Terror exploded inside her. It stole her ability to think. To resist. Was this what it had been like for Tom? In the moments before the end, had he thought of her? Their parents? Or had the fear stolen his ability to do that as well?

*Don't give in, Gwen. Keep your head.*

It was as if Tom had spoken to her. The sound of his voice moved over her, calming, steadying. She had to keep her wits about her, not fall apart. Everybody made mistakes. Slipped up. He would, too.

She needed to be able to act at that moment. She forced herself to relax.

"We warned you," he hissed. "Why didn't you go? Why did you have to involve others? Now it's too late for you."

*Others.*

*Avery.*

She heard what sounded like regret in his voice. She tried to respond, to apologize, to beg for one last chance. Her words came out in pitiable whimpers against his hand.

"I really am sorry," he murmured, forcing her forward, toward the bathroom. "Sorry for the abominable state of the world that makes this necessary. Sorry you were dragged into something that wasn't your battle. But this is war. In war collateral damage is inevitable."

*Collateral damage. The unfortunate but unavoidable loss of life. Had he said the same to Tom? The others?*

They reached the bathroom. He forced her through the door, shutting it behind them. Lightning flashed. What it illuminated sent fear spiraling through her. A black plastic drop cloth laid out in the old-fashioned claw-footed tub. Several lengths of rope. A knife, its jagged edge gleaming against the black plastic.

She dug in her heels, fighting him in earnest. The mistake wasn't coming, she realized. He had thought this through, every detail.

What of Avery, she thought dizzily. Had she been killed already? Had she suffered the knife as well?

*She didn't want to die.*

Tears flooded her eyes. Her vision blurred. *She didn't want to die this way.*

He made a sound of disappointment. "This isn't about me. Or you. It's so much bigger than either of us." He forced her closer to the tub. "I know what you're thinking. That Cypress Springs is too small and inconsequential for what happens here to make a difference in the world. You're wrong. Consider what happens when you toss a pebble in the pool, how that little plunk affects the entire pool in ever-widening ripples. So too with us.

"Our influence is spreading. We're branching out into other small communities. Finding others who think as we do. Others who are sick of the filth. The drugs. The moral decay that has spread to every nook and cranny of this country. Others who believe the end justifies the means."

Gwen began to cry. She shook her head, unable to take her eyes off the knife.

"Time for sentencing, Gwen Lancaster."

He turned quickly, dragging her with him, propelling her forward. Before she could grasp what was happening, her head smashed into the doorjamb.

Pain exploded behind her eyes. Her world went black.

## CHAPTER 45

Avery gazed out at the rain-soaked morning. Leaves and branches littered the yard; a limb from the neighbor's tree had fallen and partially blocked her driveway.

Hunter had left hours ago, sometime before the storm hit. He'd used Sarah as an excuse. She had known the truth to be otherwise; he had wanted to be alone. To sort through his thoughts, come to grips with them.

Whatever they were. She wasn't certain. He had been shaken, that she knew. But noncommittal. Almost secretive.

They'd gone over the list again. And again. With the possible exception of the coroner, every person involved with the investigation had died recently. And unexpectedly.

She closed her eyes, picturing the notations Trudy Pruitt had made on the newspaper—*All but two.*

*Was Buddy Stevens one of those two? Was his life in danger? Or was he a killer?*

Avery turned away from the window. Buddy Stevens was a good

man. The very epitome of law and order. To imagine him as otherwise was to ponder the ridiculous.

.Then why did she have this heavy feeling of dread in the pit of her stomach?

No. She squeezed her eyes shut. Buddy wasn't a part of this. And she wouldn't lose him to a killer.

Avery made her way to the kitchen. She and Hunter had agreed that she would call Dr. Harris and Buddy this morning. The clock on the microwave revealed that it was not quite eight. She would wait a few more minutes before trying the man.

And before trying Gwen. Again.

Gwen hadn't called yesterday, neither Avery's home line nor her cell. So Avery had tried the woman's cell while Hunter slept. The number had worked, but Gwen hadn't answered. She had tried early this morning with the same result.

Avery sank onto one of the kitchen chairs then returned to her feet, too antsy to sit. She began to pace. Neither time she had left a message; now she wished she had. At least Gwen would know they were still on the same side. And that she was okay.

Where was her friend? Why hadn't she called?

Avery stopped, picked up the phone and brought it to her ear, checking for a dial tone. At the welcoming hum, she hesitated then punched in the woman's cell number. It went straight to her message service, indicating she didn't have the device on.

"Gwen, hi. It's Avery. I have information. Call me."

She replaced the receiver. Now what? Call The Guesthouse, going through the operator? Try the hall pay phone? Or wait?

She decided on the last. In the meantime she would call Dr. Harris.

The coroner answered the phone himself, on the first ring. "Dr Harris. It Avery Chauvin."

"Ms. Chauvin," he said warmly. "How are you?"

"Better," she said. "Thank you for asking."

"Glad to hear it. What can I do for you this morning?"

"I'm working on a story about the Sallie Waguespack murder."

"Did you say Waguespack?"

"I did."

"My, that's an old one."

"Yes—1988. Were you coroner at that time?"

"Nope. That was during one of my hiatuses. Believe Dr. Bill Badeaux was coroner then."

"Would you know how I could contact him?"

"I'm afraid that'd be tough, seeing he passed on."

*That left Buddy. He was the last one.*

"I'm sorry to hear that," she said, forcing normalcy into her tone. "Did he pass away recently?"

"A year or so ago. Heard through the grapevine. He'd moved away from the parish way back."

*A year or so. Maybe he had been the first.*

Her legs began to shake. She found a chair and sank onto it.

"Ms. Chauvin? Are you okay?"

"Absolutely." She cleared her throat. She wanted to ask how the man had died, but didn't want to arouse his suspicions, especially in light of what she intended to ask next. "Did Buddy Stevens get in touch with you?"

"Buddy? No, was he supposed to?"

"He couldn't find the Waguespack autopsy report. He was going to give you a call. Probably slipped his mind."

"'Course, the autopsy would have been done in Baton Rouge, but I'd have a copy. I tell you what, I'll pull it and give you a call back."

"Could you do it now, Dr. Harris? I'm sorry to be such a pest, but my editor gave me an unreal deadline on this story."

"I can't." He sounded genuinely sorry. "I was on my way over to the hospital when you called and it's going to take a few minutes to locate the file."

"Oh." She couldn't quite hide her disappointment.

"I tell you what, I should be back in a couple hours. I'll take care of it then. What number should I call?"

To ensure she wouldn't miss him, Avery gave him her cell number. "Thank you, Dr. Harris. You've been a big help."

She hung up, then dialed Hunter. He answered right away.

"It's Avery," she said. "A Dr. Bill Badeaux was West Feliciana Parish coroner in 1988. He died about a year ago."

"Shit. How?"

"I was afraid to come off too nosy. I figured it wouldn't be too hard to find out. One trip over to the *Gazette*—"

"I'll do it."

"But—"

"But nothing. You've already poked around over there. I don't want you drawing any more attention to yourself."

"You think I'm right, don't you? About The Seven?"

She heard a rustling sound from the other end of the phone, then Sarah began to bark. "I'll let you know," he said. "Where are you going to be?"

His voice had changed. Become tight. Angry-sounding. "Are you all right?" she asked.

"Fine."

In the background Sarah was going nuts. A thought occurred to her. "Are you alone?"

"Not completely."

"I don't understand. I—"

"Stay put. I'll call you back."

"But—"

"Promise."

She hesitated, then agreed.

The next instant, the phone went dead.

# CHAPTER 46

Avery showered and dressed. Made her bed and separated her laundry before throwing a load of whites in the washer. Then she foraged through the refrigerator and checked her e-mail via her laptop. She responded evasively to her editor's query about progress on her story and figured everyone else could wait.

Time ticked past at an agonizing pace. She glanced at the clock every couple of minutes. After nearly an hour, she acknowledged she couldn't stand another minute of inactivity.

Bringing both the portable and cell phone with her, she headed upstairs. As she reached the top landing, her gaze settled on the framed photographs that lined the long hallway wall. She had always jokingly called it her parents' wall of fame.

How many times had she walked past all these photos without looking at them? Without considering the fact that she was pictured in almost every one? How could she have taken her parents' love so for granted?

She stopped, pivoted to her right. Her gaze landed on a photo of her as a toddler. Her first steps, Avery thought, taking in her mother on her knees on the floor, arms out. Coaxing and encouraging her. Promising she would be there to catch her.

Avery moved her gaze across the wall. Baby pictures, school portraits, pictures from every imaginable holiday and event of her life. And in a great number of them, there stood her mother, looking on with love and pride.

She took in the photograph of her first steps once more, studying her mother's expression. The truth was, she hadn't known her mother at all. What had been her hopes, dreams and aspirations? She had longed to be a writer. Yet Avery knew nothing of her writing.

She had always blamed her mother for their distant relationship, but perhaps the fault had been hers. She'd had her father, and loving him had been so easy.

She, it seemed, was the one who had taken the easy way. The one who had settled—for a loving relationship with one parent instead of two. If only she had her mother's journals. In them resided her mother's heart and soul. Her beliefs and wishes, disappointments and fears. The opportunity to know her mother.

Her father wouldn't have thrown them out. Her mother—the woman pictured in these photographs—would not have destroyed them, even if she had given up on them.

They were here. Somewhere.

Avery started for the attic, a sense of urgency settling over her. A sense that time was running out.

She reached the attic. Scanned the rows and stacks of cartons. In one of these boxes she would find the journals. Stored with other items. Hidden beneath.

She began the search, tearing through the cartons—her mother's clothing, personal items, other books, family memorabilia.

She found them in the box housing Avery's doll collection. The dolls her mother had insisted on buying and lining Avery's bedroom shelves with—despite Avery's disdain for them.

Her mother had packed the volumes neatly, arranging the books in chronological order. The first one was dated 1965. Her mother had been seventeen. The last one dated August 1990—just as Lilah had said, her mother had given up journaling the August when Avery had gone off to university.

Avery trailed a finger over the spines with their perfectly aligned, dated labels. She stopped on the one dated January through June 1988.

All the answers she sought were here, she thought, pulse quickening. About Sallie Waguespack's death and her father's part in it. Perhaps ones about The Seven, their formation.

But other answers were here as well. Ones to personal questions, personal issues that had plagued her all her life.

Sallie Waguespack could wait, she decided, easing the volume dated 1965 from its slot. Her mother could not.

Avery began to read. She learned about a girl raised by strict, traditional parents. About her dreams of writing. She learned that her mother had been a deeply passionate woman, that she had often been afraid, that in her own way she had rebelled against her parents' strict upbringing.

Through her mother's words, Avery relived the day she met Phillip Chauvin, their first date. Their courtship, wedding. The first time they made love. Avery's birth.

Avery struggled to breathe evenly. She realized her cheeks were wet with tears.

Her mother had given up a lot to be a wife and mother.

But what she had gotten in return had been huge.

She had loved being a mother. Had loved being Avery's mother. She had described with pride her daughter's determination. That she was different from the other girls—that she seemed insistent on marching to her own tune.

She baffles me. I put a bow in her hair and when I'm not looking, she rips it out.

Today Avery won first prize in the parish-wide essay contest. She read her essay to the class. I hid my tears. Her talent takes my breath away. Secretly, I smile and think, "She got that from me. My gift to my precious daughter."

Avery wiped tears from her cheeks and read on, this time from the 1986 journal.

She breaks my heart daily. Doesn't she know I want the world for her? Doesn't she know how frightened I am of losing her?

And then later she poured out her heart.

I've lost her. She and I have nothing in common. She turns to her dad, always. They laugh together, share everything. I often think I made a huge mistake. If I'd pursued my writing, we would have had something in common. Maybe then she wouldn't look at me as if she thought I had no purpose in her life. That I had wasted my life.

Avery selected the last volume next—1990, the year she had graduated from high school.

Where did I go wrong? How did she and I grow so far apart? She's leaving Cypress Springs. I begged her to stay. Even as I thought of my own choices, my mistakes and regrets, I pleaded with her. I shared my dreams, but it is too late.

Avery closed the book, hands shaking, fighting not to fall apart. She had accused her mother of not loving her. But her mother had loved her deeply. Avery had accused her of trying to change her, of trying to mold her into someone different, something other than who she was.

But her mother had understood and admired her for the person she was, different from the other girls, the one who had never fit in.

In truth, her mother had never fit in either. Not with her own parents. Not with her community. Not with her daughter.

*She and her mother had been just alike.*

Avery pressed her lips together, holding back a sound of pain. If only she had read the journals before her mother died. If only she had let go of her pride.

She had wanted to. She'd been sorry for the way she'd acted, the way she had hurt her mother. Instead of acting on the emotion, she had let pride control her. She had been so certain she was right.

So, she had stayed away. Nursed her feeling of self-righteous indignation.

And had missed out on so much. Time with her mother and father. Now it was too late.

To be with them. But not for justice for Sallie Waguespack and the Pruitt brothers.

She located the appropriate volume and flipped through to the entry for June 19, the day after Sallie Waguespack's murder.

> That poor woman. And pregnant, too. It's too horrible to contemplate.

Her mother had then gone on to describe other, mundane events.

Avery frowned, her investigative instincts kicking into overdrive. Pregnant? Nothing else she had read had mentioned the woman being pregnant. Avery flipped ahead, looking for another reference.

She didn't find one. Could her mother have been mistaken? That didn't seem likely. Where had she gotten her information?

Maybe from her husband, Avery thought. The local general practitioner. Perhaps Sallie Waguespack's physician. Probably.

So why had that information been kept from the public?

Avery read on, heart racing, realizing that all the answers she sought were here, in her mother's words.

> Phillip was quiet today. Something is terribly wrong but he won't speak of it.

And then later,

> Phillip and Buddy argued. They aren't speaking and it pains me that such good friends are being torn apart by something like this.

Something like what? Avery wondered. Sallie Waguespack's murder? Had they been on opposite sides of the tide of public opinion?

Avery found no further mention of conflict between the two

friends or about the murder or investigation until a passage that
caused her heart to skip a beat.

> Buddy has involved himself in something...a group. There's
> seven of them. Something secret. I heard him trying to con-
> vince Phillip to join.

Avery stopped, working to collect her thoughts. Buddy a member of the original Seven? Trying to convince her father to join?
She read on.

> Phillip went out tonight; he met with that group, The Seven.
> He seemed troubled when he returned. I'm concerned...
> Everything is different now. Everything has...changed.

Avery glanced at her watch, shocked to see that nearly two hours
had passed already. There were so many journals yet to read. She
needed another pair of eyes.

Hands shaking, she dug in her pocket for the paper she had
scrawled Gwen's cell number on. She dialed the number, left a
message and stood, a ripple of unease moving over her. Where was
Gwen?

To hell with stealth, she decided, hurrying for the attic stairs,
stopping when she reached them. Turning, she darted back to the
boxes of journals. She bent, collected the ones from 1988 and
1990, then ran for the stairs.

Minutes later, journals stuffed into her handbag, she backed her
SUV down the driveway. She reached The Guesthouse in no time
at all, parked in front and hurried up the walk. As she made a move
to grab the doorknob, the door opened.

Avery jumped backward, making a sound of surprise.

Her old friend Laurie stepped through.

"Avery," she said, looking startled. "This is so weird. I was just
thinking about you. I've meant to call or stop by, but it's been nuts
around here what with Fall Festival and—"

"Don't worry about it. It's good to see you."

Laurie glanced at her watch. "I'd love to chat, but I'm late."

"Actually, I stopped by to see Gwen Lancaster. Is she in?"

Laurie drew her eyebrows together. "Gwen Lancaster? The woman in 2C?"

"Yes. Is she here?"

"I don't know. I haven't seen her today."

"When's the last time you did see her? It's important."

The other woman frowned. "I don't know...I don't keep tabs on our guests."

Realizing how she sounded, Avery forced a laugh. "Of course you don't. If she's not there, could I leave her a note?"

"Sure, Avery. No law against that." She hitched her purse strap higher on her shoulder, started off, then stopped and looked back at Avery, eyes narrowed. "Gwen Lancaster's not from around here. How do you know her?"

Avery lifted a shoulder in feigned nonchalance. "We met down at the Azalea Café. Hit it off."

"Oh." Laurie frowned slightly. "Her brother's the one who disappeared. Tom. He stayed with us, too."

"I'd heard that."

"A girl can't be too careful, Avery."

Chill bumps raced up her arms. Had that been a warning? A threat?

Or nothing at all but small-town gossip?

"It seems that in this case," Avery murmured, "a guy can't be too careful, either."

The woman hesitated, then laughed, the sound lacking warmth. "I've got to go," she said. "See you around."

Avery watched her walk away, then turned and headed inside. The front desk was empty; she trotted up the stairs, to the end of the hall.

She half expected to find Gwen's door as she had last time—propped open, chaos inside.

It was closed tight. She knocked, waited a moment, then knocked again. "Gwen," she called softly. "It's Avery."

Still no answer. From downstairs came the sound of the front door opening and closing. She glanced over her shoulder, saw she was alone, then tried the door. And found it locked.

Reassured, she took the notepad and pen out of her purse, scrawled a brief note asking Gwen to call her on her cell, ASAP, telling her she had found something important. She wrote the number, bent and slid the note under the door.

She turned and found Laurie standing a dozen feet behind her. Avery laughed nervously. "You surprised me, Laurie. I thought you'd left."

"This is a nice place to live, Avery," the woman said. "You don't know, you've been away."

"Pardon me?"

"Folks around here like things the way they are. I thought you should know that."

Avery stared at her old friend, heart thundering. "You're referring to The Seven, aren't you?"

"I don't know what you're talking about."

"Yes, you do. The Seven. The ones who keep Cypress Springs a nice place to live. By whatever means necessary."

"Gwen Lancaster is a troublemaker. An outsider." Laurie took a step back. "We take care of our own. You should know that. You used to be one of us, too."

# CHAPTER 47

"Hunter!" Avery called, rapping on his door. "It's me. Avery."

When he didn't answer after a moment, she called out again, urgency pressing at her. Time was running out. She had found the clues to the past and Sallie Waguespack's murder. She had proof The Seven existed. She had figured out how her father had been killed. She knew from experience that once the pieces of a story began falling into place, anything could happen. And it usually happened fast.

She needed to uncover the killer's identity. Why he had done it. Before it was too late. Before he killed again.

*If he hadn't already.*

Sarah whined and pawed at the door. Avery peered through the window at the obviously empty kitchen. Where was Hunter? It had been several hours since they'd spoken; he'd said he would get back to her. Why hadn't he?

She checked her watch, frowning. He could have gone for a run.

To the grocery or out for lunch. He could be over at the *Gazette,* researching how Dr. Badeaux had died.

Sure, she reassured herself. That was it. He was fine. He—

He'd sounded strange when they spoke. Sarah had been going nuts in the background. Barking. Growling.

*Are you alone?*

*Not completely.*

Panicked, she tried the door. She found it unlocked and stumbled inside. "Hunter," she called. "Hunter!"

She moved her gaze over the kitchen. Nothing appeared out of order and she hurried to the living room. Hunter's computer was on, a document on the screen. She swung to the right. The puppies slept in the pen Hunter had constructed for them, a heap of soft, golden fur.

*Nothing out of place.*

Turning, she crossed to Hunter's bedroom. And found it much as she had the rest of the apartment. Feeling more than a little neurotic, she checked under the bed and in the closet.

*Nothing. Thank God.*

She laughed to herself and turned. Her gazed landed on Sarah. The dog sat at the closed bathroom door, nose pressed to the crack. She whined, pawed at the door.

The breath hissed past Avery's lips; her knees went weak.

Screwing up her courage, she inched toward the closed door. She reached the dog. Hand visibly trembling, Avery reached for the knob, grasped it and twisted.

The door eased open. Sarah charged through. Avery stumbled in after. Something brushed against her ankles and a scream flew to her throat.

A puppy, Avery realized. One of Sarah's pups had gotten locked in the bathroom.

Avery crossed to the commode, sank onto it. She dropped her head into her hands. She was losing it. Going around the bend at the speed of light.

As if sensing her distress, Sarah laid her head in Avery's lap. Avery stroked the dog's silky head and ears, then patted her side. "I bet I look pretty silly to you."

The dog thumped her tail against the tile floor.

"Where'd he go, girl?"

Sarah lifted her head, expression baleful. Avery pressed her forehead to the dog's. "Right. He didn't take me either. How about we wait together?"

Sarah wagged her tail, collected her wayward pup by the scruff of its neck and carried it back to its brothers and sisters.

Avery followed, thoughts racing. Hunter had left his computer on, document up. She crossed to his desk, sat and closed the document. She saw that he had last saved at 7:37 that morning. Right about the time she had called. Just before. That meant that he hadn't written since they'd spoken. She glanced at her watch. Five hours ago.

She frowned. Computer on. Document up. Door unlocked. Where could he have gone?

A scrap of paper peeking out from the keyboard caught her eye. She inched it out.

*Gwen's name. Her room number at The Guesthouse.*

Avery gazed at the notation. At Hunter's bold print. A tingling sensation started at her fingertips and spread. Why had he written this? Why would he have needed to know her room number?

Hunter had left before the storm hit. Because of Sarah, he'd said. How did she know he'd even gone home? Maybe he had left her and gone to Gwen's?

She had told him about Gwen. Everything. How they had met. About her brother. The gutted cat. That she had interviewed Trudy Pruitt.

He had stopped on that, she recalled. He had looked strange, she remembered. Shaken.

*Hunter's voice on the answering machine.*

Avery brought a hand to her mouth, thoughts tumbling one over another. Hunter had returned to Cypress Springs about ten months ago.

About the time the rash of unexpected deaths had started.

*No.* She shook her head. *Not Hunter.*

Cherry's words rang in her head. *He's come home to hurt us. To punish us.*

Someone her father had trusted, someone he would open the door to in the middle of the night.

*"Your father and I had become friends. Every time we were together, he talked about you."*

*Run, Avery. Go as fast as you can.*

With a sense of inevitability, Avery reopened the computer document and read:

His thoughts settled on vengeance. On the act he had just carried out. Some thought revenge an ugly, futile endeavor. He fed on it. On thoughts of the pain he could inflict. Punishment deserved—

Avery leaped to her feet. The chair went sailing backward. *Not Hunter! It couldn't be true.*

She took a deep breath, fighting for calm. A clear head. Her gaze settled on the desk once again, its drawers. She tried them. And found them locked.

She had found the paper with Gwen's name on it, maybe she would find something else.

She hoped to God she didn't.

Turning, she headed for the bedroom. She went to the closet, rifled through it, then turned to the dresser. There, underneath some sweaters, she found a plastic storage bag. With trembling fingers she eased it from under the garments and held it up.

Tom Lancaster's Tulane University ID card. A cheap gold crucifix. A man's class ring.

A cry of disbelief slipped past her lips. She dropped the bag, turned and ran blindly for the door. What to do? Where to go? Buddy? Matt?

Gwen. Dear God, let her be all right.

Even as the prayer ran through her head, fear clawed at her. The sense of impending disaster. That it was too late. That the clock had just stopped.

*She had been sleeping with the enemy.*

She made it to her car. Fighting hysteria, she unlocked it and climbed inside. It took her three tries, but she finally got the keys into the ignition and the vehicle started.

She glanced out her window. Several people on the sidewalk had stopped and were staring at her.

She jerked away from the curb—a kid on a bike appeared before her and she slammed on the brakes. The momentum of the vehicle jerked her against the safety harness, knocking the wind out of her.

The kid whizzed by. She collected herself and merged into traffic, gripping the steering wheel so tightly her fingers went numb. The sound of a siren penetrated her panic. She glanced in the rearview mirror. A sheriff's cruiser, cherry lights flashing.

*Matt!* She pulled over. Tumbled out of the vehicle and ran to him. He met her halfway. Caught her in his arms.

"Avery, thank God you're safe." He held her tightly to his chest. "When I heard, I was so afraid—"

She clung to him. "How did you know about Hunter? When did you find out?"

"Hunter?" He frowned, searching her gaze, his concerned. "What are you talking about?"

"But I thought...the way you pulled me over..."

Her words trailed off. She went cold with dread. "What's wrong, Matt? What's happened?"

"Your parents' house is on fire. I just got the call."

# CHAPTER 48

Avery left her car and rode with Matt. She smelled the fire a block before she saw the flames. Saw the smoke billowing up into the pristine blue spring sky. The two trucks came into view next, the pumper and water truck, lights flashing. Half a dozen guys had turned out, the firefighters in their chartreuse coats and helmets, hoses spewing water at the dancing flames.

Then she caught sight of the house. The fire had completely engulfed the structure. A cry ripped past her lips. Until that moment, she had hoped—prayed—Matt was wrong. That it was a mistake.

Matt stopped the car and she stumbled out. The heat slammed into her, the acrid smell of smoke. Her eyes and throat burned. She brought a hand to her mouth, holding back a cry.

Neighbors clustered around the perimeter of the scene, huddling together, their expressions ranging from fear and disbelief to horrified fascination. They glanced at her, then looked away. As if ashamed. As if in meeting her eyes, her tragedy became theirs.

And because they were so very grateful this had happened to her not them.

*If they looked away, maybe they could pretend it hadn't happened.*

She hugged herself, chilled despite the heat. Lucky them. She wished she could pretend. That her childhood home wasn't in flames. Gone, she thought. All her parents' things. Mementos. The photographs she had looked at that very morning. Gone. Forever.

She had nothing left to remember them by.

"Wait here," Matt said. "I'm going to see if I can help." He hesitated, searching her expression, his concerned. "Are you going to be all right?"

A hysterical-sounding laugh raced to her lips. Oh sure, she thought. Just dandy.

"Fine," she managed to say. "Go."

He squeezed her hand, then disappeared. She watched him, and turned at the sound of her name. Buddy had arrived and was hurrying toward her.

She ran to him. He enfolded her in his arms, holding her tightly. "When the call came in, I was so frightened. No one knew if you were in the house. Thank God you're all right. Thank God."

She clung to him. "What am I going to do, Buddy? I've lost everything."

"Not us, baby girl," he said fiercely. "You haven't lost us."

"Where will I go? Where is home now?"

"You will stay with us as long as you like. We're your family now, Avery. That hasn't changed. It will never change."

"Ms. Chauvin?"

She glanced over her shoulder at John Price, the firefighter she'd met at her father's wake. He took off his helmet. His dark hair was plastered to his head with sweat, his face black with soot. "I'm sorry we couldn't save it, Ms. Chauvin. I'm really...sorry."

She nodded, unable to speak. She shifted her gaze. Ben Mitchell, the arson investigator, had arrived; he was conferring with Matt. They disappeared around the side of the house.

"Do you know how this happened?" she asked.

The fireman shook his head. "Arson takes over from here."

"I don't understand how...I was home this morning. I used my laptop, made some coffee, everything was fine."

The man shifted his helmet from one hand to the other, expression uneasy. "You have to know how odd this is, considering your father's death."

*Her dad had burned. Now his house.* A small sound passed her lips. Until that moment she hadn't made that connection.

One of his colleagues called him. "I've got to go. Ben's good, he'll figure it out."

Buddy put an arm around her shoulder. "Here comes Matt and Mitchell."

Avery turned. Waited. When they reached her, Matt and his dad exchanged glances, their expressions grim.

"Looks like arson, Avery," Matt said. "Whoever did it left the fuel can."

"Arson," she repeated. "But why...who—"

"Can you account for your whereabouts for the last few hours?" Ben Mitchell asked.

"Yes, I—"

*The journals. Going to The Guesthouse, looking for Gwen. Leaving the note.*

*Hunter. Gwen's name and room number scrawled on paper by his computer.*

"Avery?" Matt laid his hands on her shoulders. "Earlier, you said something about Hunter. You asked me how I had found out. What were you talking about?"

She stared at her friend, mouth working. She fought to think clearly. To focus. Not to panic.

*Her mother's journals. Evidence of The Seven. Of something wrong with the Waguespack murder investigation.*

All destroyed in the fire. All but...

But she hadn't told anyone about the journals.

"Avery?" Matt shook her lightly. "Avery, what—"

"You have to help me, Matt." She caught his hands. "You have to come with me now."

"Avery," Buddy said softly, "you're in shock. You need to rest. Come home with me and—"

"No!" She shook her head. "A friend. Gwen Lancaster, she's in trouble." Her voice rose. "You have to help me!"

"Okay," Buddy said softly, tone soothing. "I'll help you. We'll go find this friend of yours. Everything will be fine."

"I'll go, Dad." Matt looked from Avery to her father. "You've got your hands full here."

Buddy looked as if he wanted to argue, then nodded. "Okay, but keep me posted. And bring her back to the ranch. Lilah and Cherry will get her fixed up for the night."

Matt agreed and they walked to his cruiser. He helped her into the vehicle, went around and climbed behind the wheel. He looked at her. "Where are we going?"

"The Guesthouse. I think there might have been another murder."

## CHAPTER 49

Matt flipped on the vehicle's cherry lights and siren and threw the cruiser into gear. He flew through the streets, handling the vehicle like a professional driver, the only indication of his distress the muscle that jumped in his jaw.

"What the hell's going on, Avery?" He didn't take his eyes from the road. "How do you know Gwen Lancaster?"

"It's a long story." She wrapped her arms around her middle. "Do you know her?"

"Yes, because of her brother. I worked on the investigation." He paused. "I felt real bad for her. She seemed like a nice person."

"And now she's dead, too."

"We don't know that."

"Then where is she?" Her voice rose, hysteria pulling at her. "We were supposed to talk. She didn't call. She wouldn't have left without—"

"Stop it," he said sharply. "We don't know she's dead. Until there's a body, we'll presume she's alive. Okay?"

They arrived at The Guesthouse. He screamed to a stop; they piled out and hurried up the walk. Unlike earlier, Laurie sat at the front desk. She stood as they entered. "Matt, Avery, what—"

"Have you seen Gwen Lancaster today?"

Her gaze moved between them. "No, I—"

"Mind if we go upstairs?" She shook her head. "We may need you to open the door."

It was only the second time Avery had seen Matt acting in an official capacity and she acknowledged being impressed. And a bit taken aback. Gone was the aw-shucks small-town sheriff, replaced by a determined lawman whose tone left no doubt he meant business.

The three hurried up the stairs. Matt rapped on Gwen's door. "Sheriff, Ms. Lancaster." When he repeated the process without answer, he turned to Laurie. "Open it, please."

Laurie nodded, face deathly pale. She took out a master key, unlocked the door and stepped back.

"Wait downstairs for now. But don't leave the premises, I may need to question you." He softened his tone. "Please, Laurie."

The woman hesitated for a fraction of a moment, then backed toward the stairs. Avery watched her, frowning. She looked frightened.

*Did she know more than she was telling? Had she played some part in Gwen's disappearance?*

Matt unsheathed his service weapon. "Stay put, Avery." He stepped across the threshold, Colt .45 out. "Sheriff!" he called.

He disappeared into the unit, reappearing several moments later, features tight.

"Is she—"

"No."

Avery brought a hand to her chest, relieved. "Thank God. I was so worried."

"I'd like you to look around. You might see something I missed." He paused. "But don't touch anything. Take as few steps as possible."

"I don't understand."

"The fewer people through a crime scene the better."

"But you said she...wasn't dead. You said you didn't find evidence of..."

Her words trailed off. He hadn't said either of those things, she realized.

*"Until we find a body, we presume she's alive."*

Obviously, he hadn't found a body.

But he had found something else.

She stepped inside. Moved her gaze over the room. "She's cleaned up. The last time I was here, the place had been ransacked."

"Ransacked?" he repeated, scowling at her. "Just how much haven't you told me?"

She met his eyes, feeling like an idiot. "A lot."

His mouth thinned, but he didn't comment. Instead, he motioned to the room. "Anything else?"

She carefully studied the interior. The unmade bed, robe thrown over the foot. Blinds open, Gwen's running shoes on the floor by the bed.

Her gaze stopped at what appeared to be a puddle. "The floor's wet."

"Excuse me?"

"Look."

She pointed. He crossed to the spot, squatted, dipped his middle and index fingers into the liquid and brought his fingers to his nose. "Water."

He shifted his gaze toward the bathroom. "There's another."

In all they found three in what appeared to be a line from the bathroom to the bed.

"What do you think it means?" she asked.

"Don't know yet." He touched her arm. "I need you to take a look at this."

He led her to the bathroom. A circular-shaped bloodstain marred the white wooden door. Splatters radiated from the circle, drips from the bottom of the stain.

Avery stared at the mark, pinpoints of lights dancing in front of her gaze.

"Blood's dry." He leaned close, examining the mark but not touching it. "A few strands of hair," he murmured. "Maybe some tissue."

"I don't feel so good," she said, swaying slightly.

He caught her arm, steadying her. "Are you okay?"

"No."

He led her out of the unit and into the hall. He ordered her to sit.

She did, lowering her head to her knees. She breathed deeply through her nose until she felt steady enough to lift her head.

"My note's gone," she said.

"You left a note?"

"Slid it under her door. Around noon." She realized what that meant and brought a hand to her chest, relieved. "If she picked it up, she's alive."

"*If* she picked it up. Someone else may have."

"But who? The door was locked." She shook her head, refusing to acknowledge he had a point. "No, she got it."

"Avery—" He squatted in front of her, caught her hands, gripping them tightly. "The blood's completely dry. It's been there a while."

"I don't understand what you're..." Her words trailed off as she got it.

"I'm sorry, Avery. I really am."

She brought her head to her knees once more.

"She could have fallen," he said softly. "Have you checked the hospitals?"

She looked up, hopeful. "No."

"I'll do it. I need to make a few calls, including one to Dad. Order an evidence crew over. Talk to Laurie, her family. The other guests. But first, I think we should talk."

"Talk," she repeated weakly. "Now?"

"It's important." He rubbed her hands between his. "I need you to tell me everything. Are you up to it?"

She managed a nod. "I'll try."

"That's my girl. First, how did you become involved with Gwen Lancaster?"

As quickly and as succinctly as she could, Avery filled him in on how she and Gwen had become acquainted. She explained about Gwen coming to her with proof of The Seven's existence. The suicides, the freak accidental deaths. "I didn't believe her until I researched at the *Gazette*. When I saw all the deaths...there...in black and white, I couldn't ignore her. Plus, she believed my father was murdered."

"And that's what you believed?"

She laced her fingers. "I just couldn't accept he had killed himself."

"Go on."

"So we joined forces."

He paused a moment as if mulling over what she had told him, putting the various pieces together, filling in the blanks. "Why did you believe she had been murdered?"

"Because we had arranged to speak by phone and I wasn't able to reach her. And because The Seven knew she was onto them. They had given her a warning."

He frowned. "What kind of warning?"

"A gutted cat. They ransacked her room. Stole her notes and interview tapes." When he simply stared at her, she stiffened her spine. "You think I'm making all this up, don't you? You think I'm losing my mind."

"I wish I did. As unbelievable as this all is, I can't discount it." He pointed. "That bloodstain is stopping me. The fact that she's missing. And that two other women are dead."

He paused. "The note you left, what did it say, Avery?"

"To call me. That I had found some evidence." It seemed a lifetime already since this morning, so much had happened. "Sallie Waguespack was pregnant, Matt."

He looked startled. "Are you certain?"

"It was in my mother's journals. She had...boxes of—" Her voice broke.

*All gone. Her parents. Her childhood home. Every memento of growing up, ash now.*

"He burned my house down. Because of the journals. He found out somehow. He killed Gwen. And the others. I found evidence. Trophies."

Matt leaned toward her. "Who, Avery? Who did it?"

"Hunter," she said, words sticking in her throat. "I think Hunter did it."

## CHAPTER 50

After the sheriff's department criminalists arrived at the scene, Matt drove her out to his parents' house. As they drove across town, she detailed everything that had happened in the past few days—about her and Gwen going to Trudy Pruitt's trailer and finding Hunter's message on the woman's voice mail; discovering Gwen's name and room number scrawled on a paper by his computer; realizing that all the deaths had begun after Hunter's return to Cypress Springs; and then finding the Ziploc bag of personal items that had obviously belonged to the victims.

"It's my fault," she said as he drew the vehicle to a stop in the driveway. "I told him about Gwen. About what we discovered. That she had interviewed Trudy Pruitt." Her voice thickened. "I trusted him, Matt."

He turned and drew her into his arms. Held her tightly. When he released her, she saw that his eyes were bright with unshed tears.

She realized how hard this must be for him. Hunter was his brother. His twin.

His other half.

She brought a hand to his cheek. "Matt, I don't know what to say. I wish—"

"Shh." He brought her hand to his mouth. "We'll have time for this later. I have to go. Are you going to be all right?"

She forced lightness into her tone. "With Lilah and Cherry cooing and clucking over me, are you kidding?"

He glanced toward the doorway where his mother and sister waited. "I'll come by later. Okay?"

She said it was and climbed out of the cruiser. She watched him back out of the driveway, then turned and started toward the two women.

Lilah hugged her. "Avery, honey, I don't know what to say. I'm devastated."

Cherry touched her arm. "Don't worry about a thing, Avery. If I don't have something you need, I'll go out and buy it."

"Buddy called. He said it was arson." Lilah shuddered. "Who would do such a thing?"

Avery didn't want to talk about it. Truth was, she had neither the energy nor heart for it.

There would be time for talking, hashing and rehashing. Time to break it to Lilah what her son had become. She prayed she wasn't around when that happened.

"Would you mind terribly if we didn't talk about it right now? I'm just...overwhelmed."

"Poor baby. Of course I don't mind." The woman's cheeks turned rosy. "Maybe you should lie down, take a little nap. I know everything is clearer when I'm rested."

"Thank you, Lilah. You're so good to me."

The woman looked at her daughter. "Why don't you take Avery up to the guest room. I'll get some towels and soap for the guest bath."

"Sure." She smiled sympathetically at Avery. "I'll grab you a change of clothes, in case you want to clean up."

"Thanks," Avery said, realizing then that she smelled of smoke.

They started upstairs. Halfway up, Lilah stopped them. Avery glanced back. "I'm fixing baked macaroni and cheese for supper. With blueberry pie for dessert. We'll eat about six."

Avery managed a small smile, though thoughts of eating couldn't be farther from her mind.

Cherry left her at the guest room, then returned moments later with clothes and a basket of toiletries, including a new toothbrush. Cherry held the items out. "If you need anything else, just ask."

Avery saw real concern in her eyes. She experienced a twinge of guilt for her former suspicions about the other woman. "Thank you, Cherry, I...really appreciate this."

"It's the least I—" She took a step backward. "Bathroom's all yours."

"Thanks." Avery hugged the items to her chest. "I think I...a shower will be nice."

"Are you going to be all right?"

"I'll manage. Thanks for worrying about me. It means a lot."

Avery watched Cherry hurry down the hall, then retreated to the silence of her room. As that silence surrounded her, the smell of the fire filled her head.

With it came the image of her family's home being engulfed in flames. And a feeling of despair. Of betrayal.

*Hunter, how could you?*

Turning, she carried the toiletries and clothes to the guest bath, which was accessible from the bedroom. A Jack and Jill-style bath, consisting of one bath and commode area, flanked on either side by individual sink and dressing areas. She locked the door that led to the other bedroom's dressing area.

A half hour later she stepped out dressed in the pair of light-weight, drawstring cotton pants and white T-shirt Cherry had lent her, the smell of the fire scrubbed from her hair and skin. She towel-dried and combed her hair, then crossed to the bed. Sank onto a corner.

She closed her eyes. Her head filled with images—of fire engulfing her home, of Gwen's name and room number scrawled on a paper by Hunter's manuscript, of blood smeared across the wall of Trudy Pruitt's trailer.

Her cell phone rang.

She jumped, startled, then scrambled across the bed for her purse. She grabbed it, dug inside for the device. She answered before it rang a third time. "Gwen, is that—"

"Ms. Chauvin?"

Her heart sank. "Yes?"

"Dr. Harris. I apologize for it having taken so long for me to get back to you, I had some trouble locating the information you needed."

Avery frowned, confused. *Dr. Harris? Why was he—*

Then she remembered—the autopsy report. Her call to the coroner that morning seemed a light-year ago.

"Ms. Chauvin, are you there?"

"Yes, sorry. It's been a rough day."

"And I'm afraid my news won't make it any better. There was no autopsy performed on Sallie Waguespack."

"No autopsy," she repeated. "Aren't autopsies always performed in the case of a murder?"

"Yes, I'm surprised as well. That said, however, because of the circumstances, the coroner determined an autopsy unnecessary."

"The coroner has that option?"

"Certainly." He paused a moment. "With a typical homicide, the lawyers will require one. The police or victim's family."

"But the Waguespack murder wasn't a typical homicide."

"Far from it. The perpetrators were dead, there would be no trial. No lawyers requiring proof of cause of death. The police had plenty of evidence to support their conclusion, including the murder weapon."

"An open and closed case," she murmured. *Perfect for a setup. Everything tied up nice and neat.*

"Would you have made that call, Dr. Harris?"

"Me? No. But that's my way. When it comes to the cessation of life, I don't take anything for granted." He paused, cleared his throat. "I have one more piece of information that's going to surprise you, Ms. Chauvin. Dr. Badeaux wasn't the coroner on this homicide."

She straightened. "He wasn't. Then who—"

"Your father was, Avery. Dr. Phillip Chauvin."

# CHAPTER 51

Avery sat stone still, heart and thoughts racing, cell phone still clutched in her hands. Dr. Harris had explained. Dr. Badeaux had employed two deputy coroners, all West Feliciana Parish physicians, all appointed by him. The coroner or one of his deputies went to the scene of every death, be it from natural causes, the result of accident, suicide or homicide.

The night of the Waguespack murder, Dr. Badeaux had been winging his way to Paris for a second honeymoon. Her dad had been the closest deputy coroner. When Dr. Badeaux had returned, Sallie Waguespack had been in the ground. He had accepted his deputy's call and it had stood for fifteen years.

*"My boys didn't kill that Sallie Waguespack. They was framed."*

*"Your father got what he deserved."*

Trudy Pruitt had been telling the truth. Her sons had been framed. And her father had been a part of it.

Betrayal tasted bitter against her tongue. She leaped to her feet, began to pace. She couldn't believe her father would do this. She'd thought him the most honorable man she had ever known. The most moral, upright.

The box of clippings, she realized. That was why he had saved them all these years. As a painful reminder.

What he'd done would have eaten at him. She hadn't a doubt about that. All these years...had he feared exposure? Or had he longed for it?

That was it, she thought. The why. He hadn't been able to live with his guilt any longer. But he hadn't killed himself. He had decided to come clean. Clear the Pruitt boys' names.

And he had been murdered for it.

But why had he done it? For whom had he lied?

*His best friend. Sheriff Buddy Stevens.*

Avery squeezed her eyes shut. Buddy had lied to her. The day she'd gone to see him, about having found the clippings. She had asked him why her father would have followed this murder so closely, why he would have kept the box of news stories all these years. She had asked if her dad had been involved with the investigation in any way.

Buddy had claimed he hadn't had a clue why her father would have clipped those stories, that her father hadn't been in any way involved in the investigation.

He'd been up to his eyeballs in this. They both had been.

She recalled the words in her mother's journal. That after the murder everything had been different. That her father and Buddy's relationship had been strained. Hunter had claimed that their fathers never even spoke anymore.

What could cause such a serious rift between lifelong friends?

The answer was clear. For a friend, her dad had gone against his principles. Afterward, he had hated both himself and his friend for it.

*That poor woman. And pregnant, too.*

Pregnant. With whose baby?

Avery didn't like what she was thinking. She glanced toward the doorway. Lilah was in the kitchen, preparing dinner. She would know. Like her mother, she had lived through it. Had watched as best friends grew distant, then to despise one another.

Avery grabbed her handbag, with the two journals tucked inside, and slipped into her shoes. She went to the bedroom door and peeked out. The house was quiet save for sounds coming from the kitchen.

She slipped into the hall and down the stairs. From the study came the sound of Cherry and Buddy, talking softly. Avery tiptoed past the closed door and headed to the kitchen.

Lilah glanced over her shoulder at her and smiled. Avery saw that she was grating cheese. She wore a ruffled, floral apron—a flour smudge decorated her nose and right cheek. The blueberry pie, pretty as a picture from *Bon Appétit,* sat cooling on a rack by the oven.

"You look refreshed," she said brightly.

"At least I don't reek of smoke anymore."

"There's something to the whole comfort-food thing, don't you think?" She turned back to her grating. "Macaroni and cheese, chicken pot pie, tuna casserole. Good, old-fashioned stick-to-your-ribs stuff. Just thinking about it makes one feel better."

If only it was so easy, Avery thought, watching her work. If only life were so simple. Like something out of *Life* magazine in the 1950s. Or an episode of an old TV show.

Life wasn't like that, no matter how much she longed for it to be. The picture Lilah presented was wrong. She saw that now. A deception. An illusion.

A picture-perfect mask to hide the truth from the world.

But what was the truth?

Avery opened her handbag and drew out the journal from 1988. "Lilah," she said softly, "I need to ask you something. It's important."

The woman glanced at her. Her gaze dropped to Avery's hands. "What's that?"

"One of my mother's journals. I found it in my parents' attic."

"But I thought your father had gotten rid of them."

"No. Mother had packed them away. They were almost all lost in the fire."

Lilah's expression altered slightly. Her gaze skittered from Avery's to the journal. "Not that one."

"No. Or one other."

"Thank God for that."

"Yes." Avery carefully slid it back into her purse. "I discovered something interesting in this journal, Lilah. I wanted to ask you about it."

"Sure, hon." She went to the refrigerator and retrieved a jug of milk. She filled a measuring cup full. "What do you need to know?"

"Whose baby was Sallie Waguespack carrying?"

The measuring cup slipped from her fingers. It hit the countertop and milk spewed across the country-blue Formica. With a small cry, she began mopping up the mess.

"Lilah?"

"I don't know what you're talking about."

"Yes, you do. Whose baby was it?"

Lilah's movements stilled. The kitchen was silent save for the steady drip drip of milk dropping onto the tile floor.

"They're all dead now, Lilah. Everyone connected with the Waguespack murder investigation. All of them but Buddy. Do you know how damning that is?"

Lilah whimpered. Avery took a step toward her. "What really happened that night? Buddy, my dad, Pat Greene, they were all in on it. All covering up for somebody. Who was it, Lilah? Who?"

Avery grabbed her arm. "Those boys were framed, weren't they? They didn't kill Sallie Waguespack."

Lilah's mouth moved, but no sound emerged. Avery shook her. "Those boys were sacrificial lambs. It's in the journal, Lilah! I discovered it this morning. You were the only person I mentioned the journals to. Who did you tell? That's why my house was torched, to destroy the evidence!"

A sound of pain escaped Lilah's lips. "No. Please, it's not—"

"Stop protecting him, Lilah. You have to come clean. You have to make this right." She lowered her voice, pleading. "Only you can do it, Lilah. Only you can—"

"It was Buddy's baby!" she said, the words exploding from her. "He betrayed me, our children. This town. By day, Mr. Morality. Lecturing about how the citizens needed to take action, restore Cypress Springs to a God-fearing, law-abiding place to live. By night fornicating with that...with that cheap whore!"

Her tears came then, deep wrenching sobs. She doubled over. Her small frame shaking with the force of her despair.

"And she became pregnant."

"Yes." Lilah looked up, expression naked with pain. "That's when Buddy confessed to me what had been going on, that the woman was pregnant. I hadn't...I never—"

She bit the words back but they landed between them— *She hadn't known. She never suspected.*

Avery's heart went out to the other woman. She had always thought the Stevenses had the perfect marriage. Apparently, Lilah had thought so, too.

"She was going to make trouble for him. She wanted to ruin him. Make it public. Shame him...all of us."

Lilah met Avery's gaze, calm seeming to move over her. "I couldn't have that. I couldn't have my family exposed to his filth. I couldn't let that happen."

"What did you do?" Avery asked softly, though she already knew.

"I went to see her. To beg her to keep quiet. To do the right thing." An angry sound escaped her. "The right thing? I was so naive. Sallie Waguespack wouldn't know the right thing if it hit her with a sledgehammer.

"She laughed at me. Called me pathetic. The stupid little *housewife.*" Lilah fisted her fingers. "She bragged about how she seduced him, about the...sex they had. She bragged about being pregnant. She promised that before she gave up Chief Raymond 'Buddy' Stevens, she would drag him and his family through the mud.

"We were in the kitchen. I was crying, begging her to shut up. I saw a knife on the counter." Lilah's eyes took on a glazed look. "I didn't do it on purpose. You have to believe me."

"Go on, Lilah. Tell me everything."

"I picked up the knife and I...stabbed her. Again and again. I didn't even realize...until...the blood. It was everywhere."

Avery took a step back, found the counter, leaned on it for support. "So Buddy took care of it for you," Avery whispered.

"Yes. I didn't ask him to. He told me to stay put, that he would take care of everything. But I didn't understand what that meant... didn't know until...the next day."

*He framed the Pruitt boys. Manufactured the evidence against them and covered up the evidence against his wife.*

*He called upon his best friend to help. Pat Greene and Kevin Gallagher, too.*

"I've had to live with that all these years. The guilt. The self-hatred. Those boys...what I did—"

She curved her arms around her middle, seeming to fold in on herself. "We were all so close back then. The best of friends. Buddy begged your daddy to lie, to make the medical facts agree with the evidence. To not request an autopsy. It was easy because the Pruitt boys were dead."

"And nothing would have to stand up to the scrutiny of a trial."

"Yes. Phillip couldn't live with the guilt at what he'd done. That's why he did it. Why he killed himself. I wish to God I had the guts to do the same! My children...my friends, I ruined every-thing!"

The kitchen door flew open. Buddy charged through, Cherry behind him, expression stricken.

"Enough!" he roared, face mottled with angry color.

Lilah cringed. Cherry rushed to her mother's side, drew her protectively into her arms.

Avery turned to the man she had once thought of as a second father. "It's too late, Buddy. How could you?"

"I never wanted you to know, Avery," he said, tone heavy with regret. "Your father didn't want you to know."

Avery trembled with anger. With betrayal. "How do you know what my father wanted? You used your friendship to force him to lie!"

He shook his head. "I only wanted to protect my family. You un-derstand that, don't you, Avery? What happened wasn't Lilah's fault. I couldn't allow her to go to jail for my mistakes. My sins. Your father understood. Sallie's death was a crime of passion, not premeditated murder."

"Pat Greene didn't see the Pruitt boys leaving Sallie Waguespack's that night, did he?"

"No. I told him I did. Confessed to having an affair with her. Asked him to help me out. Because of how it looked."

"And he believed you?"

"He was my friend. He trusted me."

She made a sound of derision. "And the murder weapon in the ditch behind their trailer—"

"I planted it. The prints on the weapon and the blood on Donny's shoe as well. Pat didn't know."

She had looked up to him. Loved him. To know he had done this hurt. Her vision swam. "And Kevin Gallagher?"

"Kevin prepared Sallie for burial. All he knew was she was pregnant. I asked him to keep it quiet. Why exacerbate the situation? Why smear the poor woman's name any further?"

"And my dad?"

He drew a heavy breath. "Your daddy was hard to convince. In the end, he did it not just for me, but for Lilah and the kids."

"Those two boys," she whispered. "They were—"

"Trash. Delinquents. Only nineteen and twenty and had been busted a half-dozen times each. For drugs, attempted rape, drunk and disorderly conduct. They were never going to amount to anything. Never going to contribute anything to society but ills. To sacrifice them to save my family, it wasn't a difficult decision."

"You don't get to play God, Buddy. It's not your job."

His mouth twisted. "Your daddy said the same. I guess that old saying about the apple not falling far from the tree is true."

"What about Sal?" she asked. "Why include him, Buddy? You needed the *Gazette,* but for what? Swaying public opinion?"

"He wasn't included. He thought the crime went down exactly as officially reported. But I was able to use Sal and the *Gazette* as a way to focus the public's attention on the social context of the crime. Whip them into a state of outrage over the crime rate, the immorality of the young, the drug epidemic, and take their attention away from the crime itself."

"You bought into your own spin, didn't you?" Avery all but spat the words at him. "And The Seven was born. You and your buddies all got together to decide what was appropriate behavior and what wasn't. You took the law into your own hands, Buddy. You and your group became judge and jury. And things got out of hand."

"It wasn't like that. We loved this community, all of us did. We had—have—its good at heart. We only want to make life better, to keep things the way they had been. We keep watch on our friends and fellow citizens. Monitor the important things. If need be, we pay a friendly visit. Use a little muscle if necessary."

"Muscle? A palatable euphemism for what? A brick through the window? The threat of broken bones? Financial ruin through boycotts? Or just good old-fashioned cross burnings on the front lawn? What's the criteria for a death penalty in Cypress Springs?"

He looked shocked. "Good God, Avery, it's nothing like that. We're not terrorists. We're not killers. We offer help. Guidance. If that doesn't work, we suggest a change of residence." He lowered his voice. "If we didn't make things a little uncomfortable for them, what would their motivation for change be?"

She made a sound of disgust. "Motivation for change? You make me sick."

"You don't understand. It's all done in the spirit of caring and community concern. Nobody gets hurt."

"Actually, I think I understand too well." Avery glanced at Cherry. She was holding her mother, crying quietly. She returned her gaze to Buddy. "You're such a hypocrite. Making like you're Mr. Morality. Persecuting others for their sins, when all the while you're the biggest sinner of all."

Tears glistened in his eyes. "Do you think I haven't suffered for my sins? A day doesn't go by that I don't wish I could go back, do it all over. I had everything. A beautiful family. The love of a wonderful woman. The respect of my friends and the community. If I could make that choice again, I wouldn't go near Sallie Waguespack. None of this would have happened."

He held out a hand to her. "Don't look at me like that," he pleaded. "Like I'm some sort of monster. I'm still Buddy, you're still my baby girl."

"No." She took a step back. "Not anymore. Never again."

"You have to understand. I was afraid for my family. I did what I had to in order to protect them." He took another step toward her. "I had to do it, don't you see? A man protects his family."

"At all costs, Buddy?" she asked. "What lengths would you go? From covering up a murder to committing one?"

"No, never."

"Everybody involved in the cover-up is dead now, Buddy. Everyone but you. What am I supposed to think?"

"Daddy?" Cherry whispered. "What's she talking about?"

Buddy glanced nervously at his daughter. "It's not true, sweetheart. Don't listen to her. She's had a shock. She's confused."

"I'm not confused. You killed all your old friends. Why? Did they threaten to come clean? Go to the Feds because the guilt had become too much for them to live with? Is that why you killed your best friend, Buddy? Why you immobilized him, doused him in diesel fuel and—"

"No!" Lilah cried out. "No!"

Buddy darted his gaze between the women. "It's not true! I didn't have anything to do with that. I couldn't! I—"

"You went in the middle of the night. He opened the door because he trusted you. You immobilized him with a stun gun. Then you carried him out to the garage, doused him with fuel and set him on fire!"

"No!" His face went white.

"Hunter had nothing to do with any of this. You set up your own son."

"No. You have to believe me!"

"I can't believe anything you say. Not now. Not ever again."

It all made sense now—Lilah's depression and addiction. Hunter's break with the family. Cherry's dedication to keeping the family together, to making them look happy and normal.

"No one needs to know, Avery." Buddy lowered his voice, tone soothing. "We're a family. We're your family. We love you."

Tears choked her. She shook her head. She had believed that once. Had thought of this family as an extension of her own. "It's over, Buddy."

"We're all you have left, Avery." He took a step toward her, forcing her backward. "Cypress Springs is your home."

He took another step. He had her cornered, she realized. Had backed her into a wall, the only way out through him. She tamped down her rising panic.

"I'll need those journals." He held out a hand. "Laurie called me. Told me you'd been there. That you'd left Lancaster a note."

"One of your many spies."

"She was worried about you."

"Right. Worried about me."

"We love you, Avery," Lilah whispered. "You're one of us."

"Yes," Cherry piped in. "Give Dad the journals and everything will be okay."

Avery moved her gaze between the three, heart racing, struggling to stay calm. To assess her options. Three against one. One of them the size of a tree and packing a gun. Lilah looked on the verge of falling apart. Cherry seemed stunned, her reactions wooden. The little focus she possessed seemed directed toward supporting her mother.

Only Buddy posed a threat to her escape. Immobilize him and she could make it. But how?

Her pepper spray! She hadn't taken it out of her purse.

"Come on, baby girl." He stretched his hand out. "You know we only want the best for you. It's all in the past. We'll be one big, happy family."

"A family," she repeated, voice shaking. "You're right." She reached into her handbag. Her fingers closed around the cylinder of spray. She drew the can out and lunged forward, shooting the spray directly into Buddy's eyes, blinding him.

With a cry, he stumbled backward, clawing at his eyes. Avery darted past him. Out of the kitchen, into the front hall. She heard Lilah and Cherry calling her back.

The front door was locked. She fumbled with the dead bolt; after what seemed a century, it slid back and she raced out onto the porch. She paused there, realizing she didn't have a vehicle.

Behind her she heard the kitchen door fly open, heard the thunder of footfalls.

She leaped forward, hitting the stairs, racing down them. Into the yard. Avery glanced back. Buddy had gained on her, she saw. He called her name.

Headlights sliced across the dark road. Avery changed direction, running toward them, waving her arms wildly.

The white sedan pulled over. She grabbed the passenger door, yanked it open.

"Thank God! Can you giv—"

She bit the words back, a cry springing to her lips.

"Get in, Avery," Matt ordered. "Quickly, before it's too late."

She froze. Behind her, Buddy closed in.

She saw Matt had his gun. He motioned with it. "It wasn't Hunter," he said. "It was Dad. Come on, he's almost here."

She glanced back. Buddy was calling her name, going for his gun. She dived into the vehicle, yanking the door shut as she did.

Matt hit the autolock and floored the accelerator. The vehicle surged forward, fishtailing, tires squealing. Avery swiveled in her seat, craning her neck to see Buddy. He ran into the street, gave chase for a moment, then stopped.

She brought her shaking hands to her face, fighting hysteria. The urge to fall completely apart.

"Are you okay?"

She nodded, dropping her hands. "When did you...how did you find out—"

"About Dad?" He shook his head. "I love my dad. He's got a good heart, but he's weak. A total fuckup, Avery."

She didn't understand. "You're not making excuses for him, are you? He's a murderer, Matt."

Matt smiled. Oddly. Avery frowned, becoming suddenly aware of the closeness of the vehicle, that Matt kept one hand on his weapon, lying on the seat beside him.

The hair on the back of her neck prickled. "Aren't you going to put that away?"

He ignored her. "You were right to trust me, Avery. Dad's over-emotional. He means to do the right thing, but emotion gets in the way. It's what makes him weak."

*Matt was in cahoots with his dad. One of The Seven. An accomplice to murder.*

*And she had gotten into the car with him. He had a gun.*

She saw a stop sign ahead. She shifted slightly in her seat in an attempt to hide what she was about to do. As he slowed the sedan, she inched her hand toward the door handle, grasped it and yanked.

The door didn't budge. Matt laughed and eased through the intersection without stopping. "Childproof locks, Avery. How stupid do you think I am?"

"I don't know what you're talking about, Matt. I didn't—"

"Say good-night, Avery."

Before she realized his intention, he struck her in the temple with the butt of his gun. Pain jackknifed through her skull; in the next instant, she felt nothing at all.

## CHAPTER 52

Avery came to slowly. She ached all over; her head throbbed. Moaning, she opened her eyes.

She lay on a bed, she realized. A bare mattress. She tried to sit up but found she couldn't. Her arms had been anchored above her head, wrists bound tightly. Her legs were tied to opposite bedposts.

*Buddy, his confession. Matt picking her up. The gun.*

Fear exploded inside her. Blinding, white hot. It stole her ability to think. To reason. With it came panic. She fought her restraints, tugging and twisting, getting nowhere.

She stopped, wrists and ankles burning, breath coming in trembling gasps. Tears choked her. She fought them as well. She would not give in. She would not lie down and die.

*They would not get away with this. She wouldn't let them.*

In an attempt to center herself, Avery closed her eyes. She drew in as deep a breath as she could and expelled it slowly. Then repeated the process. She needed calm. Fear and panic bled her ability to think. To reason. She needed to be able to do both if she was going to escape.

She opened her eyes, a semblance of calm restored. The only light in the room came from the open doorway to the right of the bed. The air was damp, heavy. It stank, the smell familiar, though she couldn't place it. The single window stood open. From outside came the sounds of insects, more dense than she was accustomed to.

*He had taken her outside the city limits.* She traveled her gaze over the room, taking in what she could from her prone position. Spare. Rough-hewn. A hunting cabin, she thought. At the edge of woods. Or along the bayou.

The same one Gwen had been lured to? Avery searched her memory. Gwen had said the junction of Highway 421 and No Name Road.

That would put her south of Cypress Springs. Not far from the old canning factory.

The sour smell, she realized. Of course. The same smell that rolled into town when the wind shifted to a northerly direction.

The stench of the burned-out factory.

Matt appeared in the doorway, a dark silhouette against the rectangle of light. "Rise and shine, beautiful."

"Untie me and I will."

She all but spat the words at him and he laughed. "Somebody wake up on the wrong side of the bed?"

"Bastard."

He sauntered across the room, humming the tune from the children's nursery rhyme "The Itsy-Bitsy Spider." He reached the bed, bent and tiptoed his fingers up her thigh in time with the tune. She saw he had his gun tucked into the waistband of his jeans.

His fingers made the juncture of her thighs and stilled—the tune died on his lips. He cocked his head and gazed at her, expression curiously blank. "I'm sorry it's come to this, Avery. I really am."

"Then let me go, you psycho prick."

"Such language. I'm disappointed in you."

He climbed onto the bed and straddled her, placing a hand on either side of her head. The position brought his pelvis into contact with hers. The butt of the gun pressed into her abdomen.

"You betrayed me, Avery. You betrayed us."

"Don't talk to me about betrayal. You killed my father!"

He laughed softly and trailed a finger down the curve of her cheek, then lower, across her collarbone to her breast. "You always were too smart for your own good. Too opinionated."

He bent and kissed her. Lightly at first, then deeply, forcing his tongue into her mouth.

Avery fought the urge to fight and instead lay frozen beneath him. Her lack of response seemed to frustrate him and he broke the contact.

As he did, she spit in his face. He jerked away, face flooding with angry color. Rearing back, he slapped her. Her head snapped to the side; she tasted blood and saw stars.

But she didn't cry out. She wouldn't give him the satisfaction.

"You know what?" He curled his fingers around the neck of the T-shirt Cherry had lent her. "For a smart girl you do some really stupid things."

He yanked the fabric so hard she came off the bed. The T-shirt gave, ripping from neck to belly button, revealing her naked breasts. He covered them with his hands, squeezing tightly. "Like pissing off the guy who holds your life in his hands. And now, your breasts as well."

He tightened his grip, pinching the nipples, twisting. She swallowed the whimper of pain that flew to her lips. He bent forward so that his face hovered just above hers. His stale breath stirred against her cheek.

Avery shuddered. If the eyes were the windows to the soul, he had none.

"You were supposed to be mine. I chose you. Not once, but twice. And you broke my heart. The first time by leaving. The second by giving yourself to my brother."

He laughed. "You look so surprised. How stupid do you think I am? I was suspicious that day at Tiller's Pond. Like a fool, I gave you the benefit of the doubt. After I found you at his place that morning, I knew."

She whimpered, thinking of Hunter. Of what she had gotten him into.

And what she had suspected him of.

Matt's mouth twisted into a thin line. "Did you think of me, Avery? While you fucked my brother? While you betrayed—" He bit the words back, though he shook with a rage so potent the bed quaked with it.

*He could kill her now, this moment.*

*He wanted to.*

Avery shrank back against the mattress, losing her grip on her emotions. Fear became terror, rampaging through her.

For the first time, her own death became a stark reality. She pictured it. Matt's hands around her neck, squeezing and squeezing...being unable to fight him except with her frantic thoughts. Her silent screams for help.

Her fear seemed to calm him. He looked pleased. "I like you this way," he said softly, straightening. "Helpless."

He moved his hands over her breasts, his touch changing from punishing to coaxing. He brought his hands to her waist, then curved his fingers around the waistband of her drawstring pants.

"Remember how it used to be between us?" he asked, trailing his fingers across her abdomen, dipping them lower and dragging the fabric down. Revealing her belly button, then abdomen, the top of her panties and pubic mound.

He bent and pressed his face to the vee, breathing deeply, making a sound of pleasure. "When we were together this way?"

Bile rose in her throat. She fought gagging.

"It was so good. Nobody's ever come close to making me feel the way you did. We were meant to be together."

*Get smart, Avery. Play along. Give him what he wants.*

*There was always a chance. Always.*

"Yes," she whispered, voice quaking. "I remember."

"How did we come to this?" he whispered. "You left me. Why?"

"I was young. Stupid." She looked up at him in what she hoped he would take as adoration. "I didn't know how strong you were. I didn't see your power."

His mouth thinned in fury. "Don't bullshit me. You left. You fucked my brother. You—"

"I'm not!" she cried, cutting him off, trying another tack, using his own words against him. "I see it now, I understand why I left. I thought you were like...that you were going to be like your dad. I love him but he's not...not strong like you."

Matt stilled. His gaze bored into hers. She pressed on. "You were so brilliant. You sailed through school. Your SAT scores were perfect and yet...you chose to stay in Cypress Springs and go into law enforcement. Like your dad. You see why I thought that, Matt?"

He studied her a moment more, then inclined his head in agreement. "I needed to lead. I had a mission."

"I understand that now."

"Dad's weak. He's been a disappointment."

"Unwilling to do what's necessary," she said, making a guess.

"Exactly." He looked at her as if he was the proud parent, she his gifted child. "Too often, his emotions rule. His heart."

He shook his head sadly. "A leader can't be swayed by emotion. A leader must always keep his focus on the big picture."

"The cause. In this case, the good of the community."

"Yes." Matt searched her gaze. "Dad was the leader of the original Seven. Did you know that?"

She shook her head.

"He proved too weak to lead. He bowed to pressure from others in the group. Mostly your father."

"My dad?" She struggled to inject just the right amount of surprise and disappointment into her tone.

"Oh yeah, your dad. The great Dr. Phillip Chauvin." Dislike dripped from each word. "He threatened to go to the Feds. They had crossed the line, he'd claimed."

Matt leaned closer. "There is no line when it comes to war. Do you understand, Avery? Life and death. Black or white. Win or lose."

"No compromise."

"Exactly." He trailed a finger tenderly over the curve of her cheek. "Some are sacrificed for the good of the many. Individual rights lost...but quality of life maintained."

"My father wouldn't go along with that?"

"A do-gooder pussy. He nearly ruined it for everyone."

She bit down on her lip to keep from defending her father. From cheering him aloud.

"Tonight, did Buddy tell you everything? About that night, about Sallie Waguespack?" He answered his own question. "Of course he didn't. He wouldn't."

Matt laughed. "That night, Hunter and I had fought about that new kid, Mike Horn. Remember him? His dad was the plant manager over at the canning factory."

He didn't wait for her reply but went on. "I didn't like the way Mike was acting, like he owned the place. Like he was going to take *my* place. I figured we should give him a little lesson in humility, me, Hunter and a couple of the other guys. Hunter refused to back me up. Told me he liked Mike. And that what I wanted to do was wrong."

Matt's face twisted. "He'd been pulling that shit a lot that summer, refusing to go with the program. I called him on that. And on his feelings for you. He wanted to fuck you. I saw that, too. Everybody saw it. I accused him of doing it. We came to blows," he finished simply, "and he left the house. Went over to Karl's."

"Karl Wright's?"

"Yes. I couldn't sleep. I heard the front door. I thought Hunter had changed his mind, come home to apologize."

"But it wasn't Hunter?"

"No. It was Mother. She was sobbing, hysterical. Covered with blood. It was splattered on her hands and face. Her clothes."

"At first I panicked. I thought she was hurt. Then I realized what she was saying. She had killed someone. Dad's girlfriend. His lover. It was an accident, she didn't know what to do."

Avery pictured the scenario. Lilah covered with blood, hysterical. Matt sixteen and terrified. Reeling with all his mother was telling him.

"I didn't either. Dad was out. I didn't know for sure where. I couldn't call the department. So I went.

"It was just as Mom had said. With one exception—the woman wasn't dead. She must have lost consciousness. By the trail of blood, I saw that sometime between when Mom left and I arrived, she had tried to pull herself to the door. She didn't make it, she couldn't pull herself up to get it open.

"At first I meant to help her. To convince her to be quiet, not to tell anyone about the affair or about Mom.

"She laughed at us," Matt continued. "She laughed at me. How was I going to like seeing his father's bastard take his place in their home? Seeing all of them made a laughingstock. She called me stupid, Avery. *Me.* Can you imagine that? And the whole time she's bleeding all over the place. Struggling not to pass out." He made a sound of disgust. "Like she's the one in charge.

"She wouldn't shut up," he went on. "I begged her to. I was crying. She laughed at me...the things she said were so ugly. So...vile.

"So I shut her up. I put my hands over her nose and mouth and pressed and pressed until she didn't say anything anymore."

Avery shuddered, recalling her image of earlier, of Matt choking the life out of her.

"It felt good," he murmured, a small smile tipping the corners of his mouth. "I felt powerful. Unbeatable."

He leaned toward her. "Power, Avery. My hands. I always knew I was special. I saw things, understood things others didn't. Things regular people couldn't. As I watched her die, I knew that I was meant to lead. That I had the power over life and death."

Avery stared at him, mouth dry, heart hammering. Horrified. That summer...they had been together back then. They had seen each other every day—had been physically intimate. She had considered spending her life with him.

She would have sworn she knew everything about him.

*She hadn't known him at all.*

She found her voice. It shook. "So my dad knew you—"

"Killed her? No." He shook his head. "Dad found me there. He promised to protect me. To take care of everything. Told me to get out of there, to keep it to myself."

"He never told anyone, did he? Not even Lilah."

He grinned. She found something about the way his lips stretched over his teeth more terrifying than if he had growled. "He was going to save me. That's a hoot, isn't it? He was going to save *me?* But over the years he has served his purpose. In a limited way, he shared my vision."

In a lightning-quick change of mood, his eyes filled with tears. "We could have been a family," he said. "We could have had children together, grown old together."

The thought that she had imagined that very thing, not long ago, made her ill. She hid her true feelings as best she could. "It's not too late, Matt. Let me go. I won't make any trouble, we can be together."

He looked away, then back. "I'm really sorry, Avery. I didn't want this to happen. None of it. But in a conflict one must sacrifice individual wants and needs for the good of the many."

She caught her breath at his meaning. "It's not too late, I can change. I see now. I understand what you're fighting for."

He bent and pressed his mouth to hers in a hard kiss. One that smacked of finality. "It's not about me, Avery. Not about what I feel or what I want. The generals have called for action. They've voted."

"But you're their leader. They'll do what you—"

"I can't take my eyes off the big picture." He cradled her face in his palms. "No matter how much I want to."

"What are you going to do to me? Kill me? The way you killed Elaine St. Claire and Trudy Pruitt?" Her voice quivered. "The way you killed Gwen?"

He didn't deny it. "I don't enjoy the killing. I do it because it's a necessity. Because—"

From the doorway came the soft click of a gun's hammer falling into place. "Off the bed, son."

Matt twisted, hand going to his weapon.

"Try it and you're dead," the older man warned.

"You will be, too." Matt's hand hovered over his weapon. "And poor Avery will lie on this bed and rot."

Buddy's aim didn't waver. "Drop the fucking gun. To the floor. *Now!*"

Matt hesitated, then slid the weapon from his waistband and tossed it to the floor.

"Good boy. Now, off the bed. Hands up." He motioned with the gun. "To the wall."

Matt lifted his hands, climbed off the bed. "Think this through, Dad. Don't make a mistake."

Buddy moved into the room, gun trained on his son. "Hands on the wall." When Matt obeyed, Buddy bent, never talking his gaze from the other man, retrieved the gun and slid it into his waistband.

"It's okay, baby girl," he said, inching toward the bed. "Everything's going to be okay."

He freed Avery's hands, then feet. She saw that his cheeks were wet.

She pulled up her pants, then scrambled into a sitting position. After tying the pieces of T-shirt together, she scrambled off the bed and crossed to stand behind Buddy.

"You have to stop, Matt." Buddy took a step toward his son. "The killing has to stop."

Matt turned, held out a hand to his father, expression pleading. "We're in this together. Everything I've done, I've done for us. The family. The community."

Tears trickled down Buddy's cheeks. "You're ill, son. I should have faced it long ago but I didn't want to see. That night...Sallie Waguespack, I thought I was doing the right thing. But it wasn't right. I've been covering up and making excuses all these years. And these past months, pretending I didn't suspect something was wrong."

"It's not me, Dad. It's her. She won't keep quiet. We have to keep her quiet. To protect the family. She's just like Sallie."

"I didn't know, baby girl," Buddy said, voice heavy with pain. "Not about your daddy. Not about the others. I thought...let myself believe it wasn't happening. That all the deaths were just what they appeared to be."

Matt's expression went soft. "What would you have had me do? Phillip was going to the district attorney. The others were going to back him up. Tell everyone about Sallie and The Seven. I only meant to protect us."

"I know. I'm sorry." He removed his handcuffs from the pouch on his utility belt. "I've got to cuff you."

"Don't do it, Dad." His eyes filled with tears. "Please, don't cuff me."

Avery saw the emotional toll this was taking on the older man. She ached for him—the father having to face the consequences of his mistakes and the terrible truth about his own flesh and blood.

"I've got to son. I'm sorry."

Matt held out his arms. "I'll come quietly then. If you believe this is the right thing, I'll do whatever you say."

"I'll protect you as best I can, Matt. Within the law." Buddy lowered his weapon, crossed to his son.

Matt's gaze flicked to Avery's. In his she saw triumph.

"Buddy!" she cried, seeing the switchblade cupped in Matt's palm. "It's a trick!"

Matt lunged forward, catching his father by surprise. The blade popped out. He buried it in the side of Buddy's neck.

"No!" Avery screamed. A look of surprise crossed the older man's face; he reached up to grab the blade. Matt twisted it, then yanked it out. Blood sprayed.

Buddy looked at his son, mouth working. He took a step. Wobbled, then crashed to the floor.

Avery turned to run. Matt grabbed her around the middle, dragged her to his chest and brought the blade to her throat. She saw that his hand was splattered with blood. His father's blood.

"See, Avery? Weak. Stupid." He gazed down at his father's still-twitching form. "And a traitor as well."

She saw no remorse in his expression. No regret. "You're crazy. A psychotic, murdering son of a bitch!"

"I'm a soldier. I'm fighting for something bigger than you or I or an old man who'd forgotten what was important." He bent and retrieved his father's handcuffs. Wrenching an arm behind her back, Matt cuffed one wrist, then the next.

He turned his emotionless gaze on her. "You have been judged and found guilty, Avery Chauvin. Of crimes against this community. Of attempting to bring an end to a way of life that has existed for a century. The Seven will decide your fate."

# CHAPTER 53

Avery fought to keep hysteria at bay as Matt forced her deeper into the bowels of the charred canning factory. The odor, simply unpleasant from the outside, turned foul inside. Overpowering, like the stench of the grave.

Her throat and eyes burned. She saw that parts of the interior, though fire damaged, were still intact. Here and there a wall stood, oddly unmarred. A piece of untouched furniture sat beside a gaping hole in the flooring, as if the flames had been fickle, choosing one but not another.

Matt nudged her forward, gun between her shoulder blades. Obviously, he had spent a good bit of time here. Though the place was as dark as the devil's will, he guided her through the charred landscape without hesitation.

He pressed his mouth to her ear. "We're going up. But watch your step, you wouldn't want to miss your date with my generals."

"Go to hell."

He laughed, the sound delighted. "We're there, don't you think?"

She did, though she wouldn't give him the satisfaction of a response.

They made their way up the fire-ravaged stairs. As they did he
murmured directions in her ear, "Step left, skip the next stair, go
all the way right."

She stumbled and righted herself, a difficult feat without her
arms for balance. He didn't offer a hand and she sensed he enjoyed
watching her struggle. That her discomfort amused him.

Finally at the top landing, she could see. A portion of the roof
was gone and moonlight spilled through the opening, revealing a
rabbit's warren of doors, hallways and half walls.

They stopped in front of a closed door fixed with a padlock.
"We're here," he said.

He took his eyes off her as he unlocked the door. She glanced
back toward the stairs. She could take her chances, run. But how
far would she get before she stumbled, fell through the floor or he
shot her in the back? Two steps? A half-dozen?

"Go ahead," he murmured as if reading her thoughts. "Take
your chance. As you lay bleeding to death from internal injuries,
you'll beg me to finish you off with a bullet."

"Bastard."

"You think so, that's understandable, I suppose." He unfastened
the padlock, swung the door open. "But future generations will
hold me up as a hero. A visionary."

"Future generations?" she spat. "You'll be reviled, then forgotten as you rot in a cell at Angola. Or the Feliciana Forensic Facility for the Criminally Insane in Jackson."

"Poor Avery," he murmured. "Blind like the others. In you go."
He grabbed her arm and shoved her violently through the door.
Without her arms to break her fall, she landed on her knees, then
pitched forward. Her chin struck the concrete floor.

Matt chuckled as he slammed and locked the door behind her.
She managed to get to her feet, ran to the door. She threw herself
against it. "Bastard!" she shouted, kicking it. "You won't get away
with this!"

"Don't waste your energy, there's no way out."

The whispered advice came from behind her. Avery whirled around. "Gwen?"

"The one and only."

Avery searched the interior, eyes not yet accustomed to the darkness. "Where are you?"

"Here."

She saw her then, on the floor, pressed into the far corner. Avery hurried to her side and knelt beside her. "Thank God, I thought...I thought you—"

"Were dead. I did, too."

Avery saw that she was hurt. The right side of her head was crusted with dried blood, her blond hair matted with it.

Avery pictured the blood on Gwen's bathroom door. He must have knocked her out. "When did he do it?"

"The storm," Gwen whispered. "I awoke, he was there, in my room. I thought he was going to kill me. But he brought me here, instead." Gwen bent and rested her forehead against Avery's. "I prayed you'd come. But not this way."

*With the police.*

*But Matt was the police.*

"We're going to get out of this." Avery frowned. "He said The Seven would decide my fate. I think they're meeting here tonight."

"He's going to kill us, isn't he?"

*He or one of his generals.* "Let's not think about that now." Avery moved her gaze over the room's walls. Judging by its size and the shelving along one wall, the room had been a storage closet. "Have you looked for a way out?"

"There's none."

"You're sure?"

"Yes." Gwen's voice broke. "I don't want to die, Avery. Not now. Not like this."

"We will if we give up, that's for sure. Can you stand?"

She nodded and, using the wall for leverage, inched to her feet.

"Good," Avery murmured. "Our only shot may be trying to over-power him when he comes for us. One of us can rush him while the other goes for his gun. Or runs."

It sounded lame even to Avery's own ears. Overpower Matt? Her arms were secured behind her back and Gwen was almost too weak to stand. But she refused to give up. Refused to die without a fight.

"All right," Gwen said, though her voice quivered. "You tell me what to do and I'll do it."

A rapping sound caught her attention. Avery stilled, listening. It had come from behind the shelves.

The sound came again and Avery realized what it was. Matt, calling The Seven to order.

"Come on, Gwen. Let's see if we can move these shelves."

The shelves were metal and heavy, though not bolted in place. Together they eased one unit away from the wall, Gwen using her arms, Avery her body as a wedge.

They managed to create a space big enough to slip behind.

Once behind the shelves Avery found herself, absurdly, reassured by the small, tight space. It felt safe. Like a womb. Like a child's perfect hiding place. The one where nobody could ever find her.

As a kid she'd had several. She'd been good at hide-and-seek, had had the ability to slip into nooks and crannies and remain still and silent for long periods of time. Sometimes so long, the person who was "It" gave up.

Even as she wondered if Matt would give up if she was quiet enough, still enough, she acknowledged the stupidity of the thought.

Gwen followed her in. They both put an ear to the wall.

Matt was talking. He named her and Gwen as defendants, listing their crime as treason. He called for questions and comments from his generals.

Who were they? Avery wondered, straining to hear. Old friends of hers? Neighbors? Someone she had gone to school with? Would they feel any loyalty to her? Any regret?

Gwen met Avery's eyes and shook her head, indicating she couldn't hear what they were saying.

Avery couldn't either and pressed her ear closer, straining. Matt murmured a reply she couldn't make out, then paused as if listening to another question. She heard him mention his father, voice breaking.

Buddy had not been a part of this inner circle, that had become clear to her back at the cabin. That he had not been party to their extremist ideology had also become obvious. But still, she wondered, would they simply sit back and condone his murder?

If their silence was an indication, they accepted their leader's actions without question. Who were they? she wondered again, disbelieving. Who had he convinced to join his insane cause?

Avery jumped as Matt once again called for order. "A vote, then," he said loudly. "Guilty or not?"

Silence ensued. The seconds ticked past. Avery realized that she was sweating. Holding her breath though she had no real doubt what the outcome would be.

"It's unanimous then," Matt boomed. "The Seven find Gwen Lancaster and Avery Chauvin guilty of treason."

CHAPTER 54

Hunter paced the length of the windowless interrogation room.
Two CSPD uniforms had retrieved him from his home that morning. His father had requested they pick him up, they'd said. Bring
him in for questioning. Cooperation hadn't been an option.

They had dumped him here, told him Buddy would be in shortly
and left. That had been nearly twelve hours ago.

He stopped. Moved his gaze over the room. A single table made
out of wood. Three chairs, also made out of wood. They'd been
around a while and bore the evidence of each of those years in the
form of cigarette burns, chips, scratches and carvings. He continued his inspection. No fire alarm. No phone. Reinforced door,
locked from the outside.

*This was wrong. He had known it was wrong this morning. Had
sensed a setup.*

*The officers had said it was about Avery. She was in trouble.
Buddy had said to tell him that.*

So he had come. And left Avery on the outside. Alone.

He pivoted and crossed to the door. "This is bullshit!" he shouted and pounded on it. "Charge me or release me!"

He pressed his ear to the door, swearing at the silence on the other side. He had to get out of here. Avery was in trouble.

He pounded again. "Hey! I gotta take a piss. Unless you want a mess to clean up, you better get your asses to this doo—"

The door swung open. A pimply-faced officer with big ears stood on the other side, Cherry directly behind him.

"Cherry?" Hunter said, surprised. "What are you doing here?"

"Dad needs our help. Inside," she ordered the officer, nudging him forward.

With a gun, Hunter saw. A big gun. A .357 Magnum, long barrel. He returned his gaze to hers. "You really know how to use that?"

"I'm not dignifying *that* with an answer." She grabbed his arm with her free hand. "Come on, we need to get out of here."

She pulled him through the door, slamming and locking it behind him. She pocketed the key. The officer began pounding on the door.

"What the hell's going on?"

"We'll talk in the car." She hurried forward. "Sammy there was manning the station alone, but the patrol guys are going to be checking in soon."

"What time is it?"

"Eight-thirty."

"I've been locked in that room since early this morning, I need to use the john."

"Make it quick."

She was waiting for him when he emerged moments later. Wordlessly, they went to her car and climbed in. His mother sat in the back seat. She had been crying: her eyes were red and swollen, her skin blotchy.

She looked on the verge of falling apart.

He glanced over at Cherry. "Somebody better start talking, fast."

Cherry pulled away from the curb. "Dad said if we didn't hear from him by eight, to come and get you."

"Get me? What was I doing there?"

"He wanted you to be somewhere safe. He figured locked up at the CSPD was about as safe as he could find."

"What the hell are you talking about?"

"Matt's the one," she said. "And he's got Avery."

## CHAPTER 55

"The one?" Hunter moved his gaze between the two women. "What do you mean?"

"The one who killed Elaine St. Claire and Trudy Pruitt." Cherry's voice shook. "He killed Avery's dad as well. At least, we think so. Dad told us before he went after them."

"I didn't know," Lilah whispered. "I thought...all these years, I thought I killed Sallie Waguespack. And now—" her voice broke "—and now I wish I had."

"It's not your fault," Cherry murmured. "You didn't know what he had become, neither did I."

Hunter struggled to come to grips with what they were saying. Struggled not to give in to panic. "What's he become? I don't understand. What did you have to do with Sallie Waguespack's death?"

Lilah met his eyes. "I better start at the beginning."

She told him about his father's affair, Buddy's lover's pregnancy. About going there to plead for her husband.

And about what followed.

"Until tonight, I thought I'd killed her. Buddy...he kept that secret from everyone."

"When people began dying, he reasoned the deaths away," Cherry interjected. "He accepted them as accidents and suicides because...the other was unthinkable.

"Avery forced him to reevaluate," his sister continued. "Her questions. Her unshaking belief that her father hadn't killed himself. Then, when Trudy Pruitt was killed—"

"He was forced to admit what was happening," Hunter said. "That everybody involved in the cover-up had croaked. Except him."

"And Matt." She flexed her fingers on the steering wheel. "He knew for certain today, when he learned about Avery's mother's journals. That's why Matt set the house on fire."

"Slow down. Avery's mother journaled—"

"Every day since she was a teenager," Lilah said. "Avery called about them the other day, wondering if I had any idea what happened to her mother's journals. I mentioned the call to Matt."

Cherry took over. "Avery found the journals. Her mother wrote about The Seven. And Sallie Waguespack being pregnant. Somehow Matt found out and torched her house to destroy the evidence. And now, Gwen Lancaster's missing."

Lilah moaned. "That poor girl. I tried to warn her. I called...was going to meet her...try to convince her to go. Buddy overheard me...he kept me from..."

She dissolved into tears. Hunter looked at his sister, who continued. "Dad checked out Gwen's room, found evidence that indicated foul play. He figured Matt...that if he had her, had her cell phone. That he'd retrieved Avery's messages."

And now he had Avery. Hunter went cold with fear.

Silence fell between them. Cherry broke it. "There's one more thing, Hunter. Matt knew about you and Avery. That you had become...romantically involved. He told Dad. He was in a rage. A cold rage. Dad was afraid for your life."

"So he locked me up."

"Yes. Until he could figure out what to do about Matt. How to protect him."

"Protect Matt!" Hunter exploded. "He's a murderer! He should be behind—"

"He's his son!" she returned, cutting him off. "What was he supposed to do?"

"The right thing, dammit! People are dying!"

She fell silent. Lilah sobbed quietly. Hunter fought to get a grip on his emotions.

"What about Tom Lancaster?" he asked. "And McDougal? How do they fit in?"

"Dad didn't know for sure." She turned onto Highway 421. "Matt was obsessed with The Seven, which could explain Lancaster. But McDougal, he didn't see a connection. There might be none."

"What about Avery?" he demanded. "Where is she?"

"Dad thought the old hunting cabin. The one Grandpa used."

"You've called the authorities, right?" They didn't respond and he made a sound of disbelief. "The sheriff? State police?"

"Buddy said we should keep it to ourselves. Keep it in the family."

"Son of a bitch! Cell phone?" They shook their heads. "How many guns do we have?"

"Just the one."

"Shit. Fucking great."

"But Buddy's here," Lilah said. "He'll—"

"He's in trouble. Or he would have called long before now."

The women couldn't argue with that and they rode the rest of the way in silence. They turned onto No Name Road and moments later the access road that led to the cabin.

They reached it. Two cars sat out front—an unmarked sedan with a dome light on the dash and a CSPD cruiser.

"They're here," Cherry said, voice quivering. She looked at Hunter. "What now?"

He thought a moment. "One of us should stay here, stand watch. Keep the car running in case we need to get out fast. Honk if there's trouble."

Hunter and Cherry looked at their mother then at each other, silently acknowledging she was incapable of the responsibility.

"I'll do it," Cherry offered. "Mom can stay with me. You take the gun."

Lilah tried to argue; Hunter cut her off. "If there's gunfire, I don't want to be worrying about you instead of my own hide. Got that?"

"I agree," Cherry said quickly. "Absolutely."

She handed him the gun, butt out. "You know how to use one of these?"

He took it from her. Like his sister and brother, he had grown up handling a gun. It had been a while but some things you never forgot. He checked the chamber, saw that it carried a full round and snapped it shut. "Yeah," he answered. "Point and shoot."

He climbed out of the car. Weapon out, he crossed to the other vehicles and peered inside. They were empty.

He glanced back at Cherry and pointed toward the cabin. She nodded.

He made his way cautiously toward it. A traditional raised cabin, he climbed the three stairs to the front porch. Half-rotted, they creaked under his weight.

The cabin door was unlocked. He eased it open, then slipped through, pausing to listen.

It was silent. Too silent. The hair on his arms stood up. He inched across the main room, toward the kitchen. It proved empty. The small window above the sink stood open; flies buzzed around an overflowing garbage pail. He saw dirty dishes in the sink.

The cabin might be empty now, but it had been occupied recently. He swiveled, crossed to the bathroom. He found it as deserted as the other two rooms.

Only the bedroom remained. He made his way there, heart pounding. The first thing he saw was the bed, the nylon rope attached to the foot posts, the length coiled on the bare mattress.

*Someone had been tied to the bed.* The blood rushed from his head. He laid a hand on the doorjamb for support.

*Not someone. Avery.*

He shifted his gaze and froze. Peeking out from the far side of the bed was the toe of a boot. One he recognized—alligator hide, a deep green-hued black.

His father had worn those boots, made from the hide of a gator he'd caught, for twenty years.

Denial rose in him as he made his way into the room. Around the bed. His father lay facedown in a pool of blood, head twisted at an unnatural angle.

Hunter stumbled backward. Pivoting, he ran back through the cabin and onto the porch. His sister sat behind the wheel of the vehicle, door open. "Cherry," he shouted. "Use Dad's radio, get an ambulance. Tell them an officer's down."

She leaped out of the vehicle, alarmed. "An officer? Dad or—"

"Do it, Cherry. Now!"

Without waiting for her to comply, he returned to his father's side. He knelt beside him, felt for a pulse. Found none.

At a sound from behind him, Hunter turned. Lilah stood in the doorway, eyes on her husband. A cry spilled past her lips, high and terrible.

Cherry came up behind her and stopped dead. "Dad?" The color drained from her face. "No." She shook her head. "No!"

Lilah made a move to go to her husband's side. Hunter jumped to his feet, caught her in his arms, stopping her. She fought him, pummeling him with her fists, cursing him.

He held her until the fight drained out of her. He met his sister's eyes. "Help me get her outside."

Cherry blinked. Her mouth moved. He saw that she trembled. She looked a hairbreadth from falling apart herself.

"Cherry," he said softly, "it's a crime scene. The police—"

"We know who did it." Her voice shook. "Matt killed Dad."

*His brother. His twin. A murderer capable of killing his own father.*

And he had Avery.

"Where are they?" he demanded. "Where's Matt taken Avery?"

His sister looked startled by his question. Confused. "I don't... know. I don't—"

"Think, Cherry! They're on foot. Where could he have taken her?"

She shook her head, her gaze riveted to their father's still form. "There's nothing out here. Nothing. Just the—"

"Canning factory," he finished for her. "Cherry, help Mom to the car. Then call the sheriff's department and the state police. I'm going after them."

# CHAPTER 56

Avery and Gwen waited by the door. Nearly an hour had passed since The Seven had found them guilty. They had made their plan; feeble though it was, it was their only chance.

"What's he waiting for?" Gwen whispered. "Where did he go?"

Avery didn't know. She had expected him to come for them right away. Perhaps he was preparing, setting the rest of his plan in motion, putting the final pieces in place. She shook her head, indicating she didn't know.

"Do you really think this will work?"

Avery heard the note of panic in her friend's voice. The edge of hysteria. *Seven against two. What hope did they have?*

"What do we have to lose by fighting?" Avery countered softly, more, she realized, to convince herself than Gwen. "They're going to kill us anyway."

From the other side of the door came the sound of footsteps. Avery looked at Gwen. The other woman's face had gone white. Avery nodded and moved to the far right side of the door. She took her place directly in front of it, though far enough back not to get hit when it swung open.

They heard him at the door, unlocking the padlock. Avery tensed, readying herself. The door eased open. She held her breath, waiting for the right moment. Praying it would come.

It did. Avery lunged at him, using her body as a battering ram, aiming for his middle. As she had prayed she would, she caught him by surprise, nailing him square in the chest.

Matt stumbled. The gun flew from his hand. She heard it clatter to the floor.

"Run, Gwen!" she screamed. "Run!"

Her friend did, her feet pounding against flooring as she tried to race for the stairs. Avery expected to hear the others coming to Matt's aid, expected him to call for them; neither occurred. She wondered if they had left the building, had left the dirty work to him.

Avery regained her balance and threw herself at him again, this time knocking him down. He landed with a grunt of pain.

"Bitch!" he screamed, slamming his fist into her face. Her head snapped to the side, the explosion of pain unimaginable. She couldn't catch her breath, realized she was sobbing.

He straddled her, put his hands to her throat and squeezed. She fought as best she could, twisting, turning. Flailing her legs. Her lungs burned. Pinpricks of light danced in front of her eyes.

*Let Gwen make it, she prayed. Please, God, let her make it.*

From below came the sound of something crashing to the floor. Matt eased his grip, straightening. Twisting as if to listen.

"What's going on?" Matt shouted. "Blue? Hawk? Have you got her?"

Silence answered. He released her, jumped to his feet, listening. Air rushed into her lungs. Avery sucked it greedily in, gasping, coughing.

"Hawk!" he screamed. "Talk to me."

Avery rolled onto her side, caught sight of his gun. A half-dozen feet to her right, just behind where he stood. Tears stung her eyes. Cuffed, what could she do?

A whimper slipped past her lips. Matt turned. Looked down. He saw the weapon, saw her gaze upon it.

He looked at her and smiled. "Is that what you're wanting?" He bent and retrieved it. "It's just not fair, is it?"

She dragged herself to her feet, took a step, stumbled and went down. Still, she didn't give up. She inched herself along the floor like a worm. Unwilling to say die.

He laughed as he followed, taunting her. "Gutsy little Avery," he mocked. "I admire you. I do. Such a shame it didn't work out between us, with my brains and your determination we would have made awesome babies."

He stepped over her, then in front, blocking her path. She lifted her head, met his gaze defiantly.

His teeth gleamed bright white against the dark shadow of his face. He lifted the gun. "End of the road, sweetheart."

## CHAPTER 57

Avery came to and found herself bound to a chair. Her head throbbed. Something liquid rolled down her cheek, then splashed onto her collarbone. Blood, she realized as what had happened came rushing back—Matt, the butt of his gun.

She was still alive. Why?

Her eyelids flickered up. Her vision swam. She made out a table, figures grouped around it, sitting in silence.

Seven figures. Matt and his generals.

One of them turned and stood. Matt. He picked up the lantern at his feet. A camping lantern, turned down low.

He lifted the lantern, brought it close to her face. She squinted against the feeble light, right eye burning. Bloody. He smiled. "You've looked better, Avery."

A retort sprang to her lips, it came out a garbled croak.

His smile widened. "In case you're wondering, Gwen didn't make it."

A moan escaped her, one of grief and denial. Of hopelessness.

He turned toward the table. "Gentlemen," he said, holding the lantern high, "I have good news. Ms. Chauvin has returned to the world of the living. For how long is up to her."

The soft glow from the lantern fell across the men sitting closest to her. Avery blinked, vision going in and out of focus. *It couldn't be.* She traveled her gaze, straining to make out the figures at the far side of the table.

*Cadavers. In various stages of decomposition.*

A scream rose to her throat. She looked at Matt, waiting for the punch line.

It didn't come.

"Avery, I think you know Karl Wright." He indicated a badly decomposed body directly across from her. "General Hawk to us."

*Karl Wright. Matt's oldest friend. The man Cherry loved. The man she had planned to marry.*

But he'd moved to California. He'd up and left Cypress Springs without a word to anyone but Matt.

*Anyone but Matt.*

A sound of horror slipped past her lips. *Matt had killed his best friend.*

Avery shifted her gaze to the cadaver to the right of Karl. Less decayed than all but one of the others, the corpse appeared to be that of a young man. A Tulane University sweatshirt, logo partially obliterated by blood, hung on the decomposing form.

"Tom Lancaster," Matt offered, seeing the direction of her gaze.

*They found his car, abandoned. His body was never recovered.*

Avery moved her gaze again, this time to the other nearly intact corpse.

*Luke McDougal missing, his car found empty.*

That first day, she remembered, down at the CSPD, the missing persons flyers on the bulletin board. There'd been several.

Too many for such a small community.

Avery's teeth began to chatter. She fought falling apart. *Matt inducted members to The Seven through murder.*

She found her voice, though it trembled. "Tell me how it went down, Matt? Did you just happen upon Luke McDougal, broken down by the side of the road and offer him a ride? Is that when you decided to recruit him?"

Matt smiled. "Not on sight, of course, but soon after. One of the generals had recently defected, I needed a replacement. I offered him a lift and discovered we saw eye to eye, General Blue and I."

Defected? How did that happen? she wondered, hysteria rising up in her. When the bodies became so badly decayed, they could no longer stay propped up in a chair? When they disagreed too vocally with their leader?

Matt looked at the corpse that had been Luke McDougal and smiled. He paused as if listening to something the man said, then nodded and chuckled. "I completely agree, Blue."

Avery watched the exchange, the full realization of what was happening hitting her. Matt believed them to be alive. He heard them speak, vote for life or death, offer comment.

He returned his attention to her. "General Lancaster was more difficult to convince. At first, he didn't understand our cause. But I could see that he wanted to. And that he could be a wonderful addition to our number.

"In the end he believed wholeheartedly in our cause. When I explained the group's vision, there were actually tears in his eyes. He begged to be a member. He pledged his total allegiance to us. Gwen would be proud of him, he has become a tremendous asset."

Avery pictured Tom Lancaster begging. Willing to pledge and promise anything to save his own life.

Having no idea that becoming one of The Seven equaled a death sentence.

"And of course, you know Sal." Matt turned, smiled and nodded toward another corpse. "Our member of the old guard."

"Sal?" she repeated. "But he was...shot. Waked and buried—"

*In a closed-casket ceremony.*

*Matt switched the bodies. But with whose?*

"General Wings," Matt murmured. "He faked his own death, Avery. He decided to devote his life to our cause." He turned and smiled at the half-decapitated corpse. "I've been grateful for his dedication. His wisdom has proved invaluable to us."

Matt arched his eyebrows, then nodded and turned back to her.

"Just so you know, he has been your champion through this whole thing."

"Who's buried in Sal's casket, Matt? Just some poor slob you picked up?"

"A worthless, homeless drunk. A nobody whose life I gave purpose, Avery." He motioned to the final two figures at the table. "Generals Beauregarde and Starr, outsiders who were drawn to our cause."

"So this is it?" she said, voice shaking. "The infamous Seven. A group formed," she paused to rest, "to counter the crime wave in Cypress Springs resorts to murder. Seems to me, the cure is worse than the illness."

"You sound just like your bleeding-heart father. He ruined the original Seven, reduced them to a system of little more than tattletales and whiners. I wasn't about to allow him to ruin us."

"How did you do it?" she asked. "How did you kill him?"

"It was easy. Phillip wanted to believe me a malleable weakling who would bend to his wishes—the way Buddy and the other Seven had all those years ago. So he underestimated me."

"He trusted you. You knew that. You knew he would open the door to you in the middle of the night. Even though he was groggy from the sleep medication he'd taken before going to bed."

She narrowed her eyes, hate rising up in her, nearly choking her. "Medication you knew he was taking. How? He never locked the doors... Did you go through his medicine cabinet?"

Matt laughed, the sound pleased. "It didn't take even that much effort. Heard it from Earl over at Friendly Drugs."

*One of The Seven's network of eyes and ears.*

Matt glanced at his generals, then back at her, expression disgusted. "I see what you're thinking. That Earl had no right discussing your dad's private business. People like you never understand. Private business is a nice euphemism for immoral self-indulgence. Human weakness. Such self-indulgences corrupt. They spread from citizen to citizen like a disease, until a whole community is infected."

She fought to keep her tone controlled. It wavered slightly and she cursed the telltale show of vulnerability. "And as not only sher-

iff but son of Cypress Springs's chief of police, you heard everything, didn't you? It was easy. You knew every citizen's every
step? You made it your business to know."

He puffed up, proud. "Mail. Medications. Police calls. What they
ate and drank, when they had sex."

"And Elaine St. Claire's weakness?"

"Promiscuity."

*She died of internal injuries. An artificial phallus had been in-
serted into her, it had torn her to shreds.*

"What about Pete Trimble?"

"Poor old Pete. Chronic D.W.I. He refused to give up the bottle, refused our efforts to get him into a program."

*Drunk, he was crushed by his own tractor.*

She thought of the kids who had overdosed, the one into autoeroticism who had hung himself. Of Trudy Pruitt's tongue cut out
of her head. Avery understood. "Their mode of death mirrored
their crime."

He inclined his head. "They died as they lived, a fitting punishment, we believe."

Bile rose in her throat. She swallowed past it. "And my dad? The
others involved in the Waguespack cover-up? What were their
crimes? Knowing too much?"

"Treason," he said softly, regretfully. "They began to talk
amongst themselves. Began speculating about Sallie Waguespack's
death and the way their good friend Chief Stevens told them it went
down. They began speculating that someone had retooled The
Seven. Before they could be silenced, they went to Phillip."

"Retooled The Seven?"

"We are the elite, Avery. The best, operating in secret, willing
to do whatever necessary to protect what we hold dear. What the
original group was supposed to be."

"Cypress Springs's very own version of Delta Force?"

"I like that analogy."

"You would. And the group of seven men at Dad's wake and funeral, who were they?"

"Nobody. Nothing but an unfortunate number of men standing
together."

She processed that, then went on. "My dad figured out what was going on?"

"To a degree. But he made a mistake, he thought Dad was the one. Behind it all. He had decided to go to the D.A. about Sallie Waguespack. He went to Lilah first, to prepare her."

"And she told you."

"Yes." He smiled. "After his suicide, she assumed that he hadn't been able to do it and had killed himself instead. She understood guilt, you see. How it ate at a person."

Avery curled her hands into fists, cuffed behind her back. "So you woke him up in the middle of the night. He opened the door and you immobilized him with a stun gun."

A look of surprise, then respect, crossed his features.

"You had everything ready in the garage," she continued. "The diesel fuel, the syphoning hose."

He inclined his head. "It's not easy to get away with murder these days, forensic science being what it is. The tazer leaves no detectable mark but offered me the time I needed to carry out my plan. That he was groggy from the sleep medication helped."

Tears choked her. She struggled to force the image of her father from her mind, force out what she imagined were his last thoughts. The way he had suffered.

"How did you know?" he asked. "What made you so certain?"

"The slipper," she said. "It was wrong."

"It fell off when I carried him to the garage. A detail I shouldn't have ignored."

"Even without the slipper, I wouldn't have bought the story. My father valued life too much to take his own." She paused. "Unlike you, Matt. Someone disagrees with your politics and you kill them. You're no better than a terrorist."

Color flooded his face. She had angered him. His voice took on the tone of a teacher speaking to a rebellious student. "In a war, Avery, there are only two sides. The good guys and the bad guys. For a cause or against it. They were against us. So they were eliminated."

"And who's been watching you, Matt? Who's been keeping tabs

on your activities? Making certain your behavior doesn't veer outside the appropriate?"

She had caught him off guard, she saw by his momentary confusion. "My generals, of course," he answered. "I'm not all-powerful, Avery. I don't want to be. Absolute power corrupts absolutely."

"They're dead, Matt. Your generals are rotting corpses. No one is monitoring you, and if they do, you kill them in the name of the cause."

"You're not helping yourself, Avery. We reevaluated and were prepared to make you an offer. Of an opportunity. Join us. You're smart, courageous. Use those qualities to better the world."

The children's story *Peter Pan* popped into her head, the place in the tale when Captain Hook offers to spare Wendy's and the Lost Boys' lives—*if* they join him, become pirates. Avery had always admired Wendy's bravery. The courage of her convictions in the face of certain death.

Wendy hadn't died. Peter had saved her.

There would be no Peter Pan to save her, Avery acknowledged. Only the courage of her own convictions.

"You have three minutes to decide, Avery." He set his watch. "And the clock's ticking."

# CHAPTER 58

Hunter crouched behind the partially gutted wall, sweating, listening to Avery and his brother. *Three minutes. Shit.*

He squeezed his eyes shut in an attempt to force out what lay in the adjoining room. Cadavers. Murder victims.

*Ones his brother thought were alive.*

If he focused on that, he would be defeated. If he focused on what his brother had become, he would be defeated. If he allowed himself to dwell for even a minute on Avery strapped to that chair, he would lose it.

He needed a plan. Reasoning with Matt was out, that had become obvious. What was left? Charge in, guns blazing?

It sucked. It was all he had.

"Time's up, Avery. Are you with us or against us?"

Hunter tensed, waiting for the right moment, praying for it.

"Please, Matt," she begged, "listen to me. You're in the grip of some sort of paranoid delusion. There is no war. Your generals are

corpses, victims of murder. You need a doctor, Matt. A psychia-
tri—"

He cut her off. "So be it."

Hunter launched himself into the doorway, .357 out, aimed at
his brother's chest. "Drop the fucking gun, Matt! Now!"

Avery cried out his name. He didn't look at her, didn't take his
eyes off his brother.

"The cavalry arrives," Matt said, then laughed, moving neither
his gaze nor his aim from Avery. "In a last-ditch effort to save his
true love's life."

"Drop the gun."

"And why would I do that?"

"Because it's over, Matt. Because I'll kill you if you don't."

"And I'll kill her. So I guess it comes down to who's the better,
faster shot."

"I'll take my chances."

"That's your right, of course. But how are you going to feel
watching her die? Always wondering if maybe, just maybe, you
could have saved her."

*He was right, dammit. Every minute could be the difference be-
tween life and death. Avery's life or death.*

Hunter's gaze flicked to Avery, then back. Matt saw it and
laughed. "Reading you like a book, bro. Always could."

"Cherry and Mom are going for the police."

"Bullshit."

"They know you killed Dad."

"You're grasping at straws." His features tightened. "Let's stop
fucking around. Lay down your piece."

"You won't get away with this," Hunter warned. "Too many
people have died. After this, you won't be able to cover your
tracks."

"I already have, actually. You're crazy, Hunter. On a murder
spree. You hate Cypress Springs and your family. Everybody knows
that. Tom Lancaster's Tulane student ID will be found in your
apartment. As will Luke McDougal's class ring and Elaine St.
Claire's crucifix. You discovered Elaine St. Claire's body and Mc-
Dougal's vehicle. Your voice is on Trudy Pruitt's recorder...thank

you, Avery, for alerting me to that. And to the paper with Gwen Lancaster's name and room number on it."

Fury rose up in Hunter. "Everything nice and neat, just like Sallie Waguespack."

"Just like," he agreed.

Hunter tried another tack. "I just realized why you went into law enforcement, Matt. So you can hide behind your gun. The badge."

"If that helps, believe it."

Hunter laughed. "You never fought unless you knew you could win. And you can't win without the gun."

"I could always take you. I still can."

"Prove it, then. You throw yours, I'll throw mine. Just you and me, no hardware. Winner takes all."

Matt narrowed his eyes. "You think you can take me, bro? You think you're that tough?"

Hunter bent, laid his gun on the floor. He took a step toward his brother, hands up. "I'm willing to give it a try. How about you?" When his brother hesitated, Hunter clucked his tongue. "Or when it really counts, are you just a yellow-belly chicken?"

The tension crackled between the two men. Matt glanced at his silent generals as if for their okay, then nodded. "All right." He crossed to the table and laid his gun on top, then faced his brother, a smile tugging at the corners of his mouth. "Come on, let's dance."

They advanced, circled each other, both waiting for the right moment to throw the first punch.

"Don't chicken out now, Matt," Hunter taunted. "Hate to have the cops arrive and see you're both yellow *and* crazy."

Matt lunged. Only then did Hunter see the knife. Avery did, too, and screamed a warning. Hunter threw himself to the right. But not fast enough to avoid contact with the blade. Matt buried it in his shoulder, lost his grip on it and his footing.

A shot rang out. They both went down.

Cherry stood in the doorway, a shotgun to her shoulder. She had it aimed at them, though even at this distance Hunter saw how unsteady she was. That she was crying.

Hunter silently swore. She hadn't gone for the police. Secrets had won again.

Matt's expression went slack with surprise. "Cherry?" he said.

"You killed Dad, Matt." Her voice broke. "How could you do that? You shouldn't have done it."

"Dad turned on us, Cherry. He turned on the family. He sided with an outsider against us. He had to be eliminated."

She shook her head. "Family sticks together. They always stick together."

"That's right," Matt murmured, tone coaxing. "I taught you that." He got to his feet slowly. "You're my baby sister, but you always took care of us, of all of us."

He took a step toward her and she took a step back. "Don't come any closer."

"He's trying to trick you," Hunter said to Cherry, following Matt to his feet. He grabbed the knife and yanked it out of his shoulder. He went momentarily light-headed at the pain, at the whoosh of blood spurting from the wound. "He's out of his mind. Look around—"

"Don't listen to him." Matt's expression became pleading. "He's not one of us. He left us, remember? He broke our hearts."

"I remember," she whispered. "The two of you fought that night. Something about school. And Avery. It always scared me when you got like that, Matt. When you got like...this."

Her gaze flicked to Hunter. "Dad was working. Mom had been on edge all day, then had gone out. I went to bed but couldn't sleep. I was scared. It felt like...everything was falling apart."

She drew in a broken breath. "That's when I heard Mom. She was crying. I crept out of bed...I saw the blood. Heard everything. About Dad...his girlfriend...that Mom had...hurt her. Matt told her not to worry, that everything would be all right. I saw him get his car keys.

"I sneaked outside, climbed into the bed of his pickup. Pulled the tarp over me. There...I sneaked in after Matt. I saw what he did."

She'd only been ten at the time, Hunter thought. He imagined her terror. Her confusion. If only he had been home, she could have come to him.

It all made sense now. The way they had withdrawn from him, shut him out. They'd all been a part of the same secret club.

*It all made sense.*

"I kept quiet." She shifted her gaze from Matt to Hunter. "I wanted to tell you, but I was afraid. I didn't know what would happen if I did. They'd split us up. Send Mom and Matt away."

Hunter ached for his little sister, alone with her terrible secret. Frightened and vulnerable. No wonder she had been so angry with him.

"I'm so sorry, Cherry," he said. "I didn't know. I didn't know you needed me. If I had, I would have been there for you. I promise."

"But he wasn't," Matt said sharply. "He abandoned you. Abandoned us. While I stayed. What I did was for all of us."

Cherry turned the shotgun on Hunter. "It wasn't his fault, Hunter. Don't be angry with him. I was there, I saw. He was pushed into doing what he—" Her words cracked on a sob. "That woman was awful. A cheap whore who had stolen my daddy.

"When Avery came back, I was so happy. I thought, if she and Matt got back together, if she would just stay and love him, everything would be okay. The way it was before. But now...I wish she'd stayed away. I wish you had both stayed away. You've ruined everything!"

"It's not true," Hunter said quickly. "Nothing's been okay since that night. And nothing could be. You've been living a lie, all of—"

"It's all their fault," Matt cut him off. "They're outsiders. Traitors to the family. To Cypress Springs."

"Ask him about Karl," Avery called out, voice high, desperate-sounding. "He didn't go to California! He's here, in this room. Ask Matt if it's true."

Cherry looked at Matt. "What's she talking about?"

"I need you, sis. You take care of me. Of all of us. Don't abandon me now, not when I need you most."

"He killed him, Cherry!" Avery struggled against her restraints. "Like he's going to kill all of us. Ask him about Karl and the cause."

"Matt?" Cherry whispered, voice shaking.

"He put the cause before love, sis." Matt held a hand out. "You can't hold that against him. The cause is everything."

Matt glanced toward the table as if for verbal confirmation from the other man. Cherry followed his gaze to the circle of the silent, a look of horror crossing her face. She took a step back, her hold on the shotgun slipping.

"No." She shook her head; her voice rose. "No!"

Matt used the moment and leaped forward. Hunter shouted a warning and dived for his own gun. Avery screamed.

A blast shattered the quiet. Hunter turned in time to see the force of the shot propel his twin backward. Matt seemed to hang suspended a moment, standing yet weightless, before he went down.

The shotgun slipped to the floor. Sobbing, Cherry fell to her knees beside their brother.

# CHAPTER 59

In the next instant the room filled with the sound of police sirens. Minutes later, a contingent from both the state police and the West Feliciana Parish Sheriff's Department stormed the factory.

Avery had learned that Lilah and Cherry had called the state police; it had taken some convincing, but they had agreed to send a trooper to the cabin. While waiting, Cherry had remembered that her father carried a shotgun in the trunk of his cruiser. She had retrieved it and gone to back up Hunter.

If she hadn't, Avery knew, she and Hunter would be dead. Like Gwen. Buddy. Her father. And so many others.

Avery and Hunter had been transported by ambulance to West Feliciana Parish Hospital in St. Francisville. She'd required fifty stitches to her face and head. A CT scan had revealed neither blood nor swelling to her brain, but the doctor had decided to keep her overnight for observation anyway. Considering, she had come through relatively unscathed.

*Unscathed.* Tears flooded her eyes. She would never be the

same. She hurt deep down, in a way no amount of pain medication, no doctor's skill, could relieve.

"Hello, gorgeous."

Avery turned her head toward the doorway. The pillowcase crackled with the movement. Hunter stood there, fully dressed, smiling at her. "What are you doing up?" she asked.

"Been released."

"No fair." She winced, thinking of Matt's knife sinking into Hunter's shoulder. "Are you all right?"

"Just a flesh wound. Real ugly, lots of blood. No real damage."

"That's not what I meant."

"I know."

His gaze held hers. In his she saw reflected the horror of the past hours. Hers, she knew, reflected the same.

"The police talk to you, too?" he asked.

"Yes." She had been questioned by both the state police and sheriff's department. She had answered questions until her words had begun to slur from fatigue and pain medication. The doctor had stepped in then, firmly insisting that the rest of their questions would have to wait until morning.

"You want to go for a ride?"

"A ride? Are you busting me out of here?"

"That's an idea, but no." He disappeared; a moment later reappearing pushing a wheelchair. "I've got a surprise for you."

He rolled the chair to her bedside. After locking the chair's wheels, he lowered the bed rail and helped her into the seat.

"You know I don't need this thing."

"I know no such thing. And quit being so independent. It was hard enough getting the nurse to approve this trip."

She looked up at him, ready to argue. He stopped her by pressing a quick kiss to her mouth.

Hunter rolled her out of the room and down the hall, toward the nurses' station. The night nurse smiled as they went past. They moved by the empty lounge, with its drink and snack machines, then stopped at a patient's room. The door stood ajar.

Hunter nudged it the rest of the way open and wheeled her in.

A woman lay in the bed. Dangerously pale, hooked up to monitors and by IV to all manner of bags and drips.

But alive. She was alive.

"Gwen?" Avery said, her voice a husky croak.

The woman's eyelids fluttered up. She looked their way, staring blankly at Avery a moment, then her mouth curved into a weak smile. "Avery? Is that...really—"

"Yes, it is." Tears of joy flooding her eyes, Avery climbed out of the chair and moved slowly to the other woman's side. She caught her hand, curled her fingers tightly around Gwen's. "Matt told me you were dead."

"He thought...I was," she managed to say.

Her voice fading in and out, she recounted being shot, going down, then managing to get to her feet and making it to the road. There, she collapsed.

Gwen's eyes closed and Avery looked up at Hunter. "How did you know she was here?"

"I heard the emergency room nurses talking about the woman brought in with a gunshot wound. Apparently, a motorist found her unconscious by the side of Highway 421 and brought her to the emergency room. They rushed her into surgery."

"A motorist?" Avery questioned Hunter. "Out there, at that time of night?"

"A miracle," Hunter murmured. "The hand of God at work."

*Her thoughts exactly.* She turned back to the other woman and found Gwen looking at her, eyes wet. "Is Matt, is he—"

"Dead?" She nodded, bent and kissed her forehead. "I'm so glad you're alive."

"That's enough, you two," the nurse said quietly from the doorway behind them. "Ms. Lancaster needs her rest."

"Can't I stay?" Avery asked, not wanting to let go of Gwen's hand, afraid, irrationally, to leave her. "I promise to be quiet."

"You need your rest as well." The woman's expression softened with understanding. "She'll be here in the morning, Ms. Chauvin."

In the morning, Avery thought. No three words had ever sounded so sweet.

# EPILOGUE

*Monday, March 31, 2003*
*9:00 a.m.*

Avery watched as Hunter shut the U-Haul trailer's door and snapped the padlock. He gave the lock a yank to make certain it was secure and turned toward her. "Ready?"

She nodded and climbed into the Blazer. Gwen had headed back to New Orleans two days ago, anxious to leave Cypress Springs behind as quickly as possible. Avery missed her already. She and Hunter had promised to stop and visit on their way through the city.

They couldn't stay long, though. Her editor expected her at her desk, bright and early the following Monday morning. She had a story to write. A big one.

Sarah whined. She sat in the back; her pups crated in the cargo area. "It's okay, girl," Avery murmured, scratching her behind the ears. "No worries."

Avery turned forward in her seat. As she did she caught a glimpse of herself in the side mirror and cringed.

"I saw that," Hunter murmured, checking traffic and pulling away from the curb.

"I look like Frankenstein's bride. And my stitches itch."

"I think you look beautiful."

"Haven't you heard? Blind men aren't supposed to drive."

He laughed softly, reached across the console and squeezed her hand. "I'm really glad you're alive."

She curled her fingers around his, a sudden, surprising knot of tears in her throat.

They turned onto Main Street, easing past town square and its startlingly white gazebo. People stopped, looked their way. A few waved, others simply stared.

Everybody had heard the story. One bigger than the Waguespack murder. Reactions had ranged between shock, disbelief, anger. Many had expressed their sorrow, their confusion. How could this have happened? And here? Cypress Springs was such a nice place to live. A number of citizens had been brought in, questioned by the FBI about The Seven, past and present. No arrests had been made as yet.

Cypress Springs was in mourning. For its dead. For a way of life that had been built upon a lie. Change was coming.

Avery caught sight of Rauche's Dry Goods, at the corner of Main and First Streets. "Hunter, pull over."

He did, drawing the SUV to a stop in front of the store. As she had four weeks ago, she climbed out and gazed down Main Street, at the quaint buildings and lovely town square, the unchanged storefronts.

It looked wrong, she thought. An anachronism. Time marched on—life progressed, for better or worse. All else was unnatural. Like an elixir that promised eternal youth.

Hunter came to stand beside her. "You okay?"

She glanced up at him. "Going to be. How about you?"

"I keep waking up at night wondering why him and not me? We were brothers. Twins. It could have just as easily been me."

The police shrinks believed that Matt had suffered from delusional disorder, a psychotic disorder related to paranoid schizophrenia with a major difference: the afflicted person was able to function normally *except* when acting on their delusions.

Complete and accurate diagnosis was difficult, the psychiatrist had explained, because they could now only be privy to the after-math of Matt's delusions. The shrink had speculated that the incident with Sallie Waguespack had planted the seed that later provided a dramatic outlet for his illness. Ideology that had fed into his delusions had also been reinforced by his family, the community and his chosen profession.

Avery found Hunter's hand, curled her fingers around his. "No," she murmured, "it couldn't have been you."

He met her eyes, his filled with gratitude. "All those years, feeling abandoned by my family. Shut out. Nobody said anything, but I felt it. After that night, everything was changed. Now I know why."

She rubbed her cheek against his shoulder, hurting for him. "I'm so sorry, Hunter."

"Me, too. About everything but you." He met her eyes. "I'm going to help Cherry and Mom through this," he said, tone fierce. "I'm going to be there for them."

The district attorney had decided to waive charges against either of them. Because of Cherry's age at the time of the murder, because of the time that had passed, lack of evidence and the fact the real murderer was dead.

Even so, Cherry had acknowledged that she and Lilah couldn't stay in Cypress Springs. They'd already put the house up for sale, already seen a Realtor in Baton Rouge. Cherry had decided to open that catering business she and her mother had been talking about for so long.

The were going to emerge intact, Avery thought. Finally free of the secrets that had been slowly killing them.

"I know how my novel ends," Hunter murmured suddenly.

"You do?"

"Not the specifics. Just that my hero's going to be okay. And that's good enough."

She understood. She felt the same. She didn't know for certain what the future held, she only knew she was ready to face it. Starting now.

Standing on tiptoe, she kissed him. "What do you say we get the hell out of here?"

## Acknowledgments

I've become a bit of a fixture at a local coffeehouse, sitting in a quiet corner, feverishly tapping away at my laptop keyboard. I share this with you because many of the people who I intend to acknowledge here, I connected with while sitting in that corner. A friendlier bunch you won't find; I think of us as "Cheers" for the caffeine set.

I continue to be humbled and amazed by the enthusiasm and generosity shown me by the various professionals I approach for information, hat in hand. Thank you one and all. Without your generous contribution of time, personal insights and professional expertise, *In Silence* would have been much more difficult to bring to life. I hope you are pleased with the way I used the fruits of your labor.

I begin with my fellow coffee addicts: Renee Plauché and Linda Daley, who blew me away with their generosity toward me, a total stranger. Renee, a University of New Orleans graduate student in counseling, overheard me discussing avenues to research mental illness and offered help. She went so far as to lend me her textbooks, including the DSM IV, (that I now know to be), *the* clinician's guide to diagnosis. Likewise Linda, hearing that I was tackling the subject of suicide, offered to share the story of her own father's suicide. With a master's in psychology and couseling, she was able to give me both professional and personal insights into suicide and its emotional aftermath. Captains Ralph and Patrick Juneau, Jefferson Parish Fire Department, for the crash course on all things fire: from arson to turn-out gear. Stephanie Otto, nursing student, Charity School of Nursing, for on-the-spot medical terminology and procedure information.

From beyond the coffeehouse walls: Michael D. Defatta, chief deputy coroner, St. Tammany Parish Coroner's Office, for taking time out of his busy schedule to meet and answer my questions about the role of the coroner in criminal investigations and forensic pathology, particularly as it applies to burn victims. Frank Jordan, director of Emergency Medical Services, Mandeville Fire District #4, for his explanation of death by fire. Mrs. Barbara Gould, wife of West Feliciana Parish coroner Dr. Alfred Gould, for the long chat and great quote. Pat McLaughlin, friend, fellow author and journalist, for giving me a glimpse into the mind of the investigative reporter. Tom Mincher, owner of America Hunter Gun and Archery Shop, for information about hunting rifles and ammunition.

Thanks to my friends and colleagues who not only make the journey a smooth one, but a heck of a lot of fun as well. The amazing Dianne Moggy and the entire MIRA crew. My assistant, Rajean Schulze. My agent, Evan Marshall. My publicist, Lori Ames.

To my family, without whose love and support the days would be long, indeed.

And last but unquestionably first, thanks to my God, the one responsible for it all.